Scottish Business Law

Scottish Business Law

Moira MacMillan
LLB DPA LLM Solicitor
Assistant Head of Department of Law and Public Administration
Glasgow Caledonian University

Sally Lambie
LLB LLM
Lecturer in Law
Glasgow Caledonian University

Third Edition

London · Hong Kong · Johannesburg · Melbourne · Singapore · Washington DC

Pitman Publishing
128 Long Acre, London WC2E 9AN
Tel: +44(0)171 447 2000
Fax: +44(0)171 240 5771

A Division of Pearson Professional

First published in 1991
Second edition 1993
Third edition 1997

A CIP catalogue record for this book is available
from the British Library

ISBN 0 273 62035 5

10 9 8 7 6 5 4 3 2

Typeset by Avocet Typeset, Brill, Aylesbury, Bucks
Printed and bound in Great Britain by Clays Ltd, St Ives plc

The publisher's policy is to use paper manufactured from sustainable forests

This edition is dedicated to the
memory of Sally's husband
IAN CARRUTHERS LAMBIE

Contents

PART 6 BUSINESS ORGANISATIONS

PART 7 THE LAW OF DELICT

PART 8 EMPLOYMENT LAW

Preface

As with previous editions, this book is aimed primarily at those students who are studying law as part of a course where law is not the main discipline. We hope that it will prove to be particularly useful to SCOTVEC students studying law at national certificate, higher national certificate and higher national diploma level. We believe that it is also a suitable text for students on Accountancy, Business Studies and Commerce degree programmes in Scottish universities. Our aim has been to provide such students with a single textbook which satisfies their needs in a straightforward manner.

In this edition we have sought to update the text to include consideration of a raft of new legislation including the Requirements of Writing (Scotland) Act 1995 and, in the consumer area, the Sale and Supply of Goods Act 1994, the Unfair Terms in Consumer Contracts Regulations 1994, the Sale of Goods (Amendment) Act 1995 and the General Product Safety Regulations 1995. Employment law has seen the enactment of two new consolidation acts, the Employment Rights Act 1996 and the Industrial Tribunals Act 1996. Also in the area of employment we include the Disability Discrimination Act 1995, the Pensions Act 1995, the Collective Redundancies and Transfers of Undertakings (Protection of Employment) Regulations 1995 plus updates on the various health and safety regulations. There is also coverage of the Commercial Agents (Council Directive) Regulations 1993 and the Trade Marks Act 1994. Almost 100 new cases have been added.

We are grateful for the assistance and helpful comments of our colleagues at Glasgow Caledonian University and the staff at Pitman Publishing.

We have attempted to state the law as at 1 June 1996 but as always we remain responsible for any errors in the text.

M. MacMillan
S. Lambie

Preface

Table of cases

Table of statutes

TABLE OF STATUTORY INSTRUMENTS

Part 1
INTRODUCTION TO THE SCOTTISH LEGAL SYSTEM

1 The nature and sources of Scots law

THE NATURE OF LAW

The purpose of this text is to assist students in their study of business law as it applies in Scotland. As many students who use this text will be studying law for the first time it is necessary to begin with a brief introduction to the Scottish legal system.

One should start by considering the nature of law itself. The easiest approach is to regard the law as being made up of a collection of individual rules which govern society. Rules which form the law are compulsory and enforceable. Should a person be in breach of a rule of law, that breach shall carry with it a sanction. A breach of one of the rules which form part of the criminal law may lead to a fine or imprisonment. A breach of one of the rules which form part of the civil law may lead to a court order for the payment of monetary compensation.

In order that these rules which make up the law may be applied to society, it is necessary that each country has a legal system. A legal system requires bodies to make the law, courts to enforce the law and legal personnel to run the system and advise the public.

The Scottish legal system therefore comprises those legal rules which apply within the geographical territory of Scotland, drawn from a variety of sources, together with Scottish courts and legal personnel to enable their enforcement. A study of the Scottish legal system therefore requires a consideration of:

1 the historical development of Scots law;
2 the structure of the law;
3 the sources of the law;
4 the Scottish courts and tribunals;
5 arbitration as a means of resolving disputes;
6 the personnel of the law in Scotland.

THE HISTORICAL DEVELOPMENT OF SCOTS LAW

The title of this text is *Scottish Business Law*. This section of the text forms part of a study of the 'Scottish' legal system. Why is this; why 'Scots' law? The answer is that Scotland has its own legal system independent of that which operates in the rest of the United Kingdom. Nowadays many rules of law are the same north and south of the border. As far as possible, when the United Kingdom Parliament in Westminster makes new laws, these laws apply throughout the whole of the United Kingdom.

However, this is not always possible because in many respects Scots law differs greatly from English law. It is often impossible to draft a new law which will 'fit onto' both systems. Accordingly, some Acts of Parliament apply to the whole of the United Kingdom, some apply to England and Wales and Northern Ireland only, some apply to England and Wales only, some apply to Northern Ireland only and some only to Scotland.

In addition, many of our rules of law are not found in Acts of Parliament at all. Much of our law forms part of what is called the 'common law'. The common law is made up of those rules of law which evolved over generations, as customs practised by the people took on the force of law. The common law of Scotland developed quite separately from the common law of England.

Many areas of law differ markedly north and south of the border. The Scots law of property is very different and there are differences in the law of contract and delict and in family law. Scottish criminal law is also very different and there is no right of appeal to the House of Lords in Scottish criminal cases. There is a separate Scottish court structure which follows its own rules of evidence and procedure.

Surprise is often expressed that such a small land mass as Great Britain maintains two separate legal systems. How is it that this state of affairs came about in the first place? When Elizabeth I of England died without children, James VI of Scotland, the son of Mary Queen of Scots, became James I of England. Despite this Union of the Crowns in 1603 Scotland continued as a separate state and maintained its own parliament in Edinburgh. However, by the Act of Union in 1707 Scotland and England united as Great Britain under a single parliament at Westminster. Scotland was guaranteed the retention of its independent legal system, church and system of education.

In any event, it would have been very difficult to merge the two legal systems as they were so very different. Most legal systems of the world may be classified according to whether they belong to the **Continental** or **Civilian** class of legal systems based on Roman law, or to the **Anglo-American** class of legal systems based on English common law.

The countries of continental Western Europe such as France, Italy and Germany and their former colonies throughout the world fall into the former category. England and countries which were part of the British Empire and also the United States fall into the latter category with the exception of the state of Louisiana in the United States and Quebec in Canada.

Scotland is one of the few countries of the world which is said to have an independent or mixed legal system. Scotland does not fall neatly into either of the two main categories. Scots law is derived largely from Roman law but it has also been subject to common law influences. However, if Scots law had to be so classified, then it would fall more happily into the Continental or Civilian class of legal systems. The Scottish legal system is said to be deductive, whereby courts reach decisions by applying general principles of law to the facts of a particular case – ie the decision results from the principle. By contrast, the English legal system is inductive in character, whereby the decisions of the courts give rise to principles of law – ie the principle results from the decision.

This leads us to consider why it is that by 1707 Scotland and England had developed legal systems which were so different in character. One would have expected two countries which are so geographically proximate and which are both cut off from mainland Europe to have developed very similar legal systems. One would have expected an exchange of ideas between the two countries. However, the fact is that at crucial stages of development of the Scottish legal system influences from elsewhere than England have been predominant. There have been strong historical connections with the legal systems of the continent.

The Scottish legal system has to be considered in the context of the political and economic climate which prevailed in Scotland during the period of its development. Scottish legal history may be loosely divided into four main periods: The **Feudal Period** (1018–1286); the **Dark Age of Scottish legal history** (1286–1603); the **Roman Period** (1603–1837); the **Modern Period** (from 1837 to date).

The Feudal Period

In 1018 the victory of the Scots over the Northumbrians at the Battle of Carham established the boundaries of Scotland. The Feudal Period was largely a period of English influence. The Scottish King, Malcolm Canmore married the Anglo-Saxon Princess Margaret in 1070 and she brought Saxon influence to bear on both church and state. The process of Anglicisation increased during the reign of David I. David, who came to the throne in 1124, had trained as a knight at the court of the English king. David introduced much of what he had seen in England, including the feudal system of land tenure, which developed in later centuries and which still forms the basis of land ownership in Scotland today. David also sought to extend the influence of the crown by introducing the office of Sheriff. Appointed from among the Scotto-Norman barons, the Sheriffs were the military, financial and judicial representatives of the king. The Sheriffs held courts in their castles dealing with both civil and criminal matters. However, the more remote areas of Scotland remained untouched by these developments and in such areas local customary laws prevailed. In any event, by the end of the feudal period, increasing differences between Scots law and English law were appearing.

The Dark Age of Scottish legal history

In 1286 King Alexander III was killed. His granddaughter, the Maid of Norway, who was only a tiny child, was sent by ship to succeed him. She died before she reached Scotland leaving no single person with an outright claim to the Scottish throne. Edward I of England was called upon to choose between thirteen claimants and chose John Balliol who acknowledged Edward I as his feudal overlord. Balliol proved to be a weak king and his rivals among the Scottish nobility formed a council which entered into an alliance with France. In response to this Edward I of England invaded and quickly subjugated Scotland. Balliol was replaced by an English Governor in 1296. This was followed by the Wars of Independence against England which culminated in Robert the Bruce's defeat of the English at Bannockburn in 1314. In 1327 England gave up its claim to sovereignty over Scotland by the Treaty of Edinburgh (though the Treaty was later renounced by Edward III of England).

A peaceful and prosperous period did not follow. Following the death of King Robert the Bruce in 1329 the history of Scotland was marked by the breakdown of the authority of the monarchy and almost continuous warfare if not against the English then among the various factions of the Scottish nobility. This state of affairs persisted until the Union of the Crowns in 1603. This was not the climate in which one could expect a legal system to develop and it is not surprising that there were few legal developments during this period. However, the Court of Session was set up in 1532 by James V during one of the more settled spells. The Court of Session remains to this day the most senior civil court which sits in Scotland. As a consequence of the setting up of this court, legal writings in the form of Practicks were produced which provided notes of legal decisions.

The Roman Period

The period of the Renaissance led to the rediscovery of Roman culture throughout Europe. Roman law was taught in the universities of mainland Europe and was received into the legal systems of European countries. Quite literally thousands of Scots students studied principles of Roman law at French and Dutch universities. These students later used these principles in Scotland as practitioners and judges. Until about 1800 Roman law was the major influence on the development of Scots law. This period saw the development of the law through legal writing. Many of these writings have the status of 'institutional writings'. Such writings, in the absence of contrary authority in a statute or precedent, are taken to authoritatively state what the law of Scotland is on a particular point. The first institutional writing was Sir Thomas Craig's *Jus Feudale* published in 1655.

Viscount Stair's *Institutions of the Law of Scotland* published in 1681 forms the cornerstone of modern Scots law, drawing together Roman law, feudal law and native customary law and laying emphasis on the deduction of rules from first principles. Viscount Stair spent time at the University of Leyden in Holland from 1682 to 1688 before returning to Scotland where he once again became Lord President of the Court of Session, the Court's most senior judge. Events during this period include the setting up in 1617 of the General Register of Sasines in which, to this day, transactions relating to land are recorded.

The English executed Charles I in 1649 and from 1651 Cromwell made Scotland part of a Commonwealth with England. The Court of Session and the Scottish Parliament were suspended and neither sat again until the restoration of the monarchy in 1661. In 1672 the High Court of Justiciary, the supreme criminal court, was established. There had been a number of failed attempts since the Union of the Crowns to achieve full parliamentary union with England. England sought to put pressure on Scotland to agree to full union by passing the Aliens Act 1705 which declared that Scots were to be aliens in England and also prohibited trade between

Scotland and England. Representatives of each parliament met in London to agree the terms of union. Both parliaments approved the terms of the Treaty of Union and the first Parliament of Great Britain met at Westminster in October 1707.

The Modern Period

The Napoleonic Wars had put an end to study abroad. This period has seen English law replace Roman law as the major influence on developments in Scots law. This is in part due to the increase in statute as a source of new law and in part due to the fact that appeals in Scottish civil cases may be heard by the House of Lords. Another major aspect of English influence has been the increasing importance of judicial precedent or case law. Should a case have the status of a precedent it must be followed by lower courts in subsequent cases where the same point of law is at issue.

Another feature of the modern period which has had an impact on both the Scottish and the English legal systems has been the United Kingdom's membership of the European Union.

THE STRUCTURE OF THE LAW

As was stated previously, the law may be regarded as a collection of rules which govern society. These rules of law are categorised into various branches of the law. The main division is between those rules of law which make up **public law** and those rules of law which make up **private law**.

Public law encompasses the areas of **constitutional law**, **administrative law** and **criminal law**. Public law is generally concerned with the administration of government and the rights and duties of the organs of state.

Private law encompasses the areas of the **law of persons**, the **law of things** and the **law of actions**. Private law is generally concerned with the rights and duties of individual persons. The law of persons is made up of those rules which deal with the legal status of human beings and artificial persons such as registered companies. It includes the law relating to husband and wife and parent and child relationships.

The law of things deals with the law of obligations and property law. Accordingly those rules of law which make up the law of contract and the law of delict fall within the law of obligations, while property law includes the law of trusts, bankruptcy, succession and conveyancing.

The law of actions is concerned with matters of evidence and court procedure.

While students should be aware of the above classification of Scots law, it is vital that they understand that every rule of law is either a rule of **criminal law** or a rule of **civil law**.

The criminal law is made up of rules which forbid conduct which is considered sufficiently harmful to society as a whole so as to merit the label 'criminal'. Such conduct is punishable and enforcement of the criminal law is in the form of prosecutions brought by the state. A person accused of a crime is brought before the criminal courts which deal only with matters of criminal law. The court decides whether the accused is guilty or not and, if guilty, on the penalty to be imposed. A person found guilty of a breach of the criminal law may face a fine or imprisonment.

The civil law is made up of rules which govern the conduct of individuals in their dealings with other individuals. It is concerned with the rights and obligations of citizens of the state towards one another. It incorporates rules which may be used in the settlement of disputes. In civil matters the state does not take the initiative. Should an individual believe that his rights under civil law have been infringed, it is up to that individual to go to the appropriate civil court to seek a remedy. A common civil remedy is an order for the payment of damages – i.e. monetary compensation. Civil law encompasses all of private law plus those parts of public law other than criminal law.

Criminal law is made up of individual rules of law which declare certain conduct to be criminal. Examples of criminal conduct include murder, theft, assault, breach of the peace, careless or drunk driving, infringement of health and safety regulations, allowing one's child to truant from school, not having a TV licence.

Civil law matters include the law relating to contracts, actions for damages for negligence, the law governing wills and succession, divorce and house purchase.

It should be noted that a single incident may give rise to both criminal and civil consequences. For example, Bob may carelessly allow his car to mount the pavement and hit George, causing George severe injury. The likely criminal consequence of this incident is that Bob will be prosecuted for careless driving in one of the criminal courts. If found guilty he will be fined and either have his licence endorsed or he may even be disqualified from driving. In addition to the criminal prosecution by the state, the victim, George, may raise an action for damages against Bob in one of the civil courts. George's case will be that he has suffered loss as a consequence of Bob's negligence in breach of a duty of care owed by Bob as a road user to George as a pedestrian.

SOURCES OF LAW

In the previous section it was seen that the various rules which make up the law form part of either the criminal law or the civil law. Where do all these rules of law come from?

Each rule of law has either a **statutory source** or a **common law source**. A law which has a statutory source is made by a legislative body; that is a body with law-making powers. Within the United Kingdom, law in the form of statute is made by **Parliament** at Westminster or by individuals or bodies to whom Parliament has delegated some of its law-making powers. In addition, a law may have its source in the Articles of the Treaties which established the European Community or in legislation made by certain of the Institutions of the European Community.

Law made by the United Kingdom Parliament at Westminster takes the form of an **Act of Parliament**. Law made by those to whom Parliamentary authority has been delegated is known as **delegated legislation**. The majority of new law is statutory. European Community law takes the form of the **Articles** of the Treaties themselves or is found in **Regulations, Directives** or **Decisions** of the Commission or the Council of Ministers of the European Community.

Where a law has a statutory source, it will be found written down in an Act or in a piece of Delegated Legislation or in a European Regulation, etc.

However, not every rule of law has a statutory source; many laws form part of the common law. One is not able to find such laws written down in an Act of Parliament. A rule may have the force of law as a consequence of a court decision which has the status of a **judicial precedent**. Such a decision must be followed by lower courts. A rule may have the force of law as a consequence of being stated in one of the **institutional writings**. A rule may also have the force of law as a consequence of either **custom** or **equity**.

To summarise then the statutory sources of law are:

1 legislation in the form of an Act of Parliament;
2 delegated legislation;
3 European Community law.

The common law sources are:

(a) judicial precedent;
(b) institutional writings;
(c) custom;
(d) equity.

Legislation in the form of an Act of Parliament

Parliament is comprised of the House of Commons and the House of Lords and the Sovereign. Parliament at Westminster has, since 1707, produced Acts of Parliament which may apply in Scotland.

Earlier Acts of the pre-1707 Scottish Parliament may still be in force although such 'Scots Acts' are subject to the **doctrine** of **desuetude** which means that they are allowed to be regarded as having lapsed through lack of use. This doctrine does not apply to the provisions of Acts of the Westminster Parliament which cease to have effect only on being expressly amended or repealed by a later Act of Parliament.

As was previously stated, it is sometimes impossible to draft new Acts which can apply to the whole of the United Kingdom. This is because the existing law in Scotland differs from that applicable in England. Accordingly, some Acts are passed which apply throughout the United Kingdom, others may apply in England and Wales only, others may apply only in Scotland. Alternatively, it may be that an Act is passed with certain parts of it applicable to England and Wales and other parts applicable in Scotland such as the Unfair Contract Terms Act 1977.

Where an Act is passed which is to apply only in Scotland, the word 'Scotland' appears in brackets in the short title of the Act as in the Law Reform (Miscellaneous Provisions) (Scotland) Act 1990 or the Succession (Scotland) Act 1964. Otherwise the short title of the Act – i.e. the name by which the Act is known – gives no clue to the application of an Act. The presumption is that an Act applies throughout the United Kingdom but one must look within the Act where it may state that the Act does not apply to Scotland. For example, the Health and Safety at Work Act 1974 is applicable to the whole of the United Kingdom whereas the Theft Act 1968 applies only in England and Wales.

Proposed legislation takes the form of a **Bill**. There are various types of Bill:

1 Public Bills;
2 Private Bills;
3 Hybrid Bills.

Public Bills

These, if passed, become **General Acts**. They alter the general law of the land. They are introduced either by the Government or by an individual MP. Accordingly, they are known either as a **Government Bill** or as a **Private Member's Bill**.

Private Bills

These, if passed, become **Local** or **Personal Acts**. They affect a particular locality or body – e.g., an Act to give a local authority special powers to carry out a particular project. They may be introduced by **promoters** who are outsiders who petition Parliament to pass a Bill. Alternatively, the **Provisional Order Procedure** may be used to obtain the passage of a Local or Personal Act in terms of the Private Legislation Procedure (Scotland) Act 1936.

Hybrid Bills

These are Bills which are introduced as Public Bills and are found to affect private interests. Accordingly, a special procedure is then followed which enables individuals to lodge petitions against the passing of the Bill.

Procedure for the passage of a Public Bill through Parliament

Financial legislation must be introduced in the House of Commons. Otherwise, a Bill may start off in either the House of Commons or the House of Lords. Bills must pass through five stages in each House and must then obtain the Royal Assent in order to become an Act with the force of law.

The five stages are as follows:

First Reading – this is merely a formal reading of the title of the Bill and the Bill is ordered to be printed. Thereafter a date is fixed for the Second Reading;

Second Reading – the main points of the Bill are considered. Where the Bill relates only to Scotland, consideration is by the Scottish Grand Committee. The Scottish Grand Committee is made up of all the MPs for Scottish constituencies plus additional members so that the balance of power on the committee reflects that in the House of Commons as a whole. After consideration, the Bill is referred to Committee by being formally given a second reading before the whole House.

Committee Stage – the Bill is referred to a Committee for a line-by-line examination although it is possible that this stage might take place in the House of Commons itself. The Bill may be amended in Committee. Where the Bill relates only to

Scotland, the Bill is referred to the Scottish Standing Committee.

Report Stage – the state of the Bill is reported back to the full House. Amendments may be proposed at this stage but the Speaker does have the power to use the 'kangaroo' procedure whereby only certain amendments are discussed and others are put straight to a vote.

Third Reading – the motion that the Bill be read a third time is put to the House and if carried the Bill is sent to the House of Lords where it goes through a similar procedure.

Once the Bill has been passed by both Houses and has received the Royal Assent from the Queen it becomes an Act of Parliament. The Act's provisions may take effect as at the date of the Royal Assent. Alternatively, the Act may declare that its provisions shall take effect at a later date. The Act may enable a government Minister to bring provisions into effect over a period of time by the use of delegated legislation in the form of Commencement Orders.

An Act of Parliament may be amended or repealed by a subsequent Act of Parliament. It has also been established that the courts have the power to suspend the operation of a UK statute which is found to be in conflict with European Community Law (**R** *v* **Secretary of State for Transport, ex parte Factortame (No 2) [1991] 1 AC 603** – see p. 13).

Delegated legislation

Delegated legislation is in the form of regulations, orders and by-laws made by individuals or bodies to whom Parliament has delegated some law-making powers. Such delegated legislation – known also as secondary or subordinate legislation – has the same force of law as an Act of Parliament. Parliament empowers others to make law by passing an Act of Parliament which is an **enabling Act**, ie the provisions of the Act enable others to make laws.

Delegated legislation may take a variety of forms:

Statutory Instruments – these may take the form of **Orders in Council** or **Ministerial Regulations** or **Orders**. An Act of Parliament may authorise the Queen, advised by her Ministers in the Privy Council, to make Orders in Council. Such Acts may empower the Queen in Council to make regulations in times of emergency. The more common form of Statutory Instrument is an Order or Regulations made by a government Minister. The Secretary of State for Employment for example is empowered by the Health and Safety at Work Act 1974 to make detailed regulations on safety matters.

Local Authority By-laws – an enabling act such as the Local Government (Scotland) Act 1994 empowers local authorities to make by-laws which have the force of law in their own area. The City of Glasgow Council may for example make a by-law prohibiting the dumping of rubbish.

Regulations and By-laws of Nationalised Industries – bodies such as Scotrail are empowered by Act of Parliament to make by-laws. Passengers may be required to 'cross the line by the bridge only' or refrain from pulling the emergency handle without good cause.

Acts of Sederunt and Acts of Adjournal – the Court of Session, Scotland's senior civil court, is empowered to pass an Act of Sederunt which governs procedure in the civil courts. The High Court of Justiciary, Scotland's senior criminal court, is similarly empowered to pass Acts of Adjournal dealing with criminal procedure.

Any person or body to whom power to make law is delegated must exercise that power *intra vires*. This means that they must stay within the powers which they have been given. Should a government Minister stray beyond the powers which he has been given and produce Regulations which do not fall within the boundaries set by the enabling Act, he is said to be acting *ultra vires*. This means that the Regulations may be challenged in the courts where they may be declared to be invalid.

It has been argued that too much law is made in the form of delegated legislation and that this undermines democracy. Critics say that too much law is made by people who are not elected; that enabling Acts give wide and uncertain powers; that inadequate publicity is given to proposed Regulations which then become law without the opportunity for debate or challenge; that there are inadequate controls of delegated legislation.

Supporters of the use of delegated legislation counter with the argument that in a modern and complex society many new laws are required which Parliament does not have the time to pass in the form of an Act of Parliament. Moreover, it is argued that much delegated legislation is technical in nature and it would be a waste of MPs' time to debate it as they would not understand it. The use of enabling Acts allows Parliament to set the broad principles of the law and lets experts get on with working out the details. The use of delegated legislation allows flexibility and enables regulations to be amended speedily should unforeseen events occur.

It is also countered that there are adequate controls of the use of delegated legislation. Certain Statutory Instruments require only to be laid before Parliament before becoming law. However, some Statutory Instruments require positive parliamentary approval before becoming law. Others become law automatically unless within 40 days there is a resolution passed to annul them. Another safeguard is in the form of parliamentary scrutiny of delegated legislation by Select Committees of members of parliament and the lobbying of MPs by pressure groups who monitor government use of delegated legislation. In any event, as stated above, delegated legislation which is believed to be *ultra vires* may be challenged in the courts.

European Community law

The European Economic Community was established by the Treaty of Rome in 1957. Originally there were six members: Belgium, the Netherlands, Luxembourg, France, Germany and Italy. The same six states also established the European Coal and Steel Community in 1951 and the European Atomic Energy Community in 1957.

By the Treaty of Accession 1972, the United Kingdom joined the communities in 1973. Denmark and the Republic of Ireland also joined in 1973, Greece joined in 1981, Spain and Portugal joined in 1986 and Austria, Finland and Sweden joined in 1995. Accordingly there are at present fifteen member states.

The primary aim of the Treaty of Rome was to establish a single common market within Europe. However, the Treaty was amended by the Single European Act 1986 so that economic and monetary cooperation and greater cooperation in matters of foreign policy were added to the aims of the community. Subsequently, the Maastricht Treaty of 1992, which came into force on 1 November 1993, further amended the Treaty so as to establish the European Union. The European Union builds upon the existing communities and adds provisions on common foreign and security policy and co-operation on justice and home affairs. The Maastricht Treaty also added economic and monetary union to the list of community objectives and created the concept of citizenship of the European Union.

The United Kingdom Parliament passed the European Communities Act 1972 and the effect of this Act was to make European Community law part of the law of the United Kingdom. Where there is a conflict between European Community law and United Kingdom law, community law is to prevail. In the case of **R *v* Secretary of State for Transport ex parte Factortame [1990] 2 AC 85** the House of Lords reversed a decision of the Court of Appeal and reinstated an order of the Queen's Bench Divisional Court to suspend temporarily certain provisions of the Merchant Shipping Act 1988. The suspension was necessary to allow interim relief to Spanish fishermen who were caught by new provisions in the 1988 Act to prevent 'quota hopping' by Spanish fishing boats. The aim of the statute was to prevent Spanish vessels registering as British in order to gain access to the UK catch quota.

Sources of European Community law

European Community law comprises the provisions of the treaties which set up the three communities, secondary legislation made by the Institutions of the community and also UK law which implements European community provisions.

Primary community legislation takes the form of the **Articles of the Treaties** as amended by subsequent treaties, by the Single European Act 1986 and by the Maastricht Treaty on European Union 1992.

Secondary community legislation takes the form of Regulations, Directives and Decisions adopted by either the Council of Ministers or the Commission of the European Community.

Regulations are **directly applicable**, which means that they are automatically part of United Kingdom law as soon as they are made. The Westminster Parliament does not have to do anything to make them part of United Kingdom law. Regulations also have **direct effect**, which means that they confer rights on United Kingdom citizens which can be enforced in courts and tribunals within the United Kingdom.

Directives are not directly applicable. Directives which are addressed to the United Kingdom must be implemented by the United Kingdom within time limits specified in the Directive. However, the United Kingdom has discretion as to how the objectives of the Directive are to be achieved. The United Kingdom Parliament may pass an Act or the Directive may be implemented by the use of delegated legislation. Failure by a member state to implement a Directive may lead to the Commission taking enforcement proceedings against the member state before the European Court of Justice.

As a general rule, Directives do not have direct effect. An individual cannot claim to have been given rights by a Directive which he may seek to have enforced by his national courts. He must wait until the Directive has been implemented and then enforce rights given by the domestic legislation. However, the European Court of Justice has held that certain Directives may be capable of having direct effect. Where the time limit for implementation has elapsed and the provisions of the Directive are sufficiently clear, precise and unconditional so that the member state is left with no discretion as to how to achieve the required result, an individual citizen may be able to enforce the Directive in a dispute with a public body which is an organ of the member state. It has been held that the terms of a Directive cannot be enforced against a private individual.

However, in the case of **Colson *v* Land Nordrhein-Westfalen [1986] 2 CMLR 430** the European Court of Justice held that the law of a member state should be interpreted so as to give effect to the provisions of community law. However, the benefit of using the *Von Colson* principle was limited by the attitude that national courts had a duty to interpret domestic legislation in the light of a Directive only where that legislation had been specifically passed to implement the Directive. There was no such duty in respect of the interpretation of domestic legislation passed before the Directive was made.

However, a recent decision of the European Court of Justice in the **Marleasing Case (Case No 106/89 – Decision 13 November 1990)** has held that this attitude is incorrect and that all domestic legislation must be interpreted to give effect to a Directive whether or not that legislation was passed prior to the Directive being made.

Another milestone decision of the European Court of Justice is that of **Francovich *v* Italian Republic [1992] IRLR 84**. In this case it was held that an individual may sue a member state for damages for loss suffered as a result of the member state's failure to implement an EEC Directive. The case related to an employee's inability to recover wages owed by an employer who had become insolvent. The purpose of the Council Directive 80/987/EEC relating to the protection of employees in the event of the insolvency of their employer is to guarantee payment of employees' outstanding claims should their employer become insolvent. Member states should have brought into force laws to implement the Directive by 23 October 1983. However, on 2 February 1989 in the case of **Commission *v* Italy (Case No 22/87)** the European Court of Justice had held that Italy had failed to implement the Directive. Accordingly Mr Francovich and others brought actions in the Italian courts seeking compensation from the Italian Government. The Italian courts referred the matter to the European Court of Justice for a ruling. The European Court of Justice held that the Directive did not have direct effect against the state even although the time limit for implementation had passed. This was because the provisions of the Directive were not sufficiently unconditional and precise. However, the court went on to state that EC law lays down a general principle according to which a member state is liable to make good damage to individuals caused by a breach of Community law for which it is responsible. Failure by a member state to take all necessary steps to achieve the result required by a directive gives rise to a right to obtain damages where the following three conditions are met:

1 The directive confers rights for the benefit of individuals.
2 The content of these rights may be determined by reference to the provisions of the directive.

3 There is a causal link between the breach of the obligation by the member state and the damage suffered by the individuals affected.

In the Francovich case each of these conditions was met and it was held that the Italian courts had to ensure that he had the right to obtain compensation from the state for the loss he had suffered because of Italy's failure to implement the Directive. It should be noted that it is probably the case that a member state would be liable not only for failure to implement a Directive at all but also for **incorrect** implementation of a Directive. This decision opens the door to claims from employees in the private sector who cannot rely on the provisions of a Directive because of its lack of direct effect against private individuals. They now have an alternative cause of action against the government if they can establish that they have suffered loss as a consequence of being denied rights afforded to them by a Directive because of the government's failure to implement the directive properly. In the case of **Porter** *v* **Attorney-General for Northern Ireland** (settled, prior to hearing, on 26 June 1995) Mrs Porter brought a *Francovich* action based on the UK government's failure to implement correctly the Equal Treatment Directive 76/207. Mrs Porter was dismissed in 1987 aged 60 at a time when domestic law allowed different retiral ages for men and women. This was contrary to the Directive which should have been implemented by August 1978. Amending legislation outlawing different compulsory retiral ages for men and women did not apply in Northern Ireland until 26 January 1989. Mrs Porter lost an unfair dismissal claim because requiring a woman to retire at 60 had not been unlawful under domestic provisions when she was dismissed. Mrs Porter then raised an action suing the government in tort (delict) seeking five years' loss of earnings plus interest. In the event Mrs Porter accepted an offer of an out of court settlement in excess of £34,000 plus costs.

Decisions which are adopted by the Commission or by the Council of Ministers may be addressed to member states, to individuals and to corporations and are binding in their entirety upon those to whom they are addressed.

While Recommendations of the Commission do not have the force of law, ie they are not directly applicable and they do not have direct effect, it appears that as a consequence of a decision of the European Court of Justice they may have some indirect legal effect. In the case of **Grimaldi** *v* **Fonds des Maladies Professionelles [1990] IRLR 400 (ECJ)** the European Court of Justice stated that 'domestic courts are bound to take ... Recommendations into consideration in order to decide disputes submitted to them, in particular where they are capable of clarifying the interpretation of other provisions of national or Community law'. One example of this has been in respect of the 1991 Recommendation and Code of Practice on the protection of the dignity of women and men at work, which has been taken into account by UK tribunals dealing with sexual harassment cases (see below p. 440)

The Institutions of the European Community

The main Institutions established by Article 4 of the Treaty of Rome are a **European Parliament**, a **Council**, a **Commission**, a **Court of Justice** and a **Court of Auditors**. The Treaty also provides for the establishment of the European Investment Bank, a Committee of the Regions and an Economic and Social Committee, the latter's function being to act in an advisory capacity to the Council and the

Commission. A new Court of First Instance was set up as a consequence of the Single European Act 1986 to take some of the workload from the European Court of Justice.

The European Parliament

The European Parliament consists of 626 Members of the European Parliament (MEP) directly elected from the fifteen member states. Elections are held every five years. The United Kingdom elects 87 MEPs as do France and Italy; Germany elects 99 but other member states have fewer MEPs. The United Kingdom MEPs do not sit together in the parliamentary chamber but each MEP attaches himself to one of nine political groupings such as the Socialists or the European Democrats or the Rainbow Group.

Plenary sessions of the Parliament are held in Strasbourg in France although the Parliament also maintains staff and offices in both Brussels and Luxembourg.

It is the Council, not the Parliament, which has law-making powers and decides whether or not to adopt proposals for legislation drafted by the Commission. However, the role of the European Parliament, at one time limited to giving an opinion which could be ignored, has been increased, firstly by the Single European Act 1986 and more recently by the Maastricht Treaty on European Union which came into effect on 1 November 1993.

The precise procedure to be followed and the extent of the role of the European Parliament depends upon the Article of the EC Treaty from which the regulation is derived. Certain articles require only that the opinion of Parliament is sought prior to adoption of a regulation by the Council.

However, other articles require that the cooperation procedure, originally introduced by the Single European Act 1986 and now set out in Article 189c, is followed. Under the cooperation procedure, Commission proposals which require a qualified majority vote are passed to the Parliament for an opinion before being sent to the Council. The Council reaches a common position on the proposal after which the Parliament has an opportunity to give a second opinion. Should the Parliament reject the common position, the proposed regulation may be adopted by the Council only by a unanimous vote. Alternatively, the Parliament may propose amendments to the common position. These are examined by the Commission and should they be accepted, the Council can proceed to adopt the re-examined common position by a qualified majority vote or amend it by a unanimous vote. Any Parliamentary amendments which the Commission has not accepted require a unanimous vote of the Council in order to be adopted.

The Maastricht Treaty introduced a third possible procedure, set out in Article 189b and known as the co-decision procedure. It is under this procedure that the Parliament enjoys its greatest power, the power of veto. Where proposals are required to follow this procedure, the Council reaches a common position by qualified majority vote on Commission proposals after obtaining the opinion of Parliament. Should Parliament approve the common position the measure can be adopted by the Council. However, should Parliament reject the common position a conciliation committee comprising representatives of both the Council and the Parliament meets so that the Council can explain its position. Thereafter the Parliament either rejects the proposal or proposes amendments. A rejection means that the proposal is dead. Where Parliament proposes amendments, these are forwarded to the Council and Commission for consideration. These amendments can be adopted by the Council by a qualified majority vote unless the Commission refuses to accept them, in which case a unanimous vote is required. Should the Council reject Parliament's amendments, the conciliation committee is once again convened. Where the conciliation committee produces an agreed text this must be approved by the Parliament (by absolute majority) and by the Council (by qualified majority) in order to become law. Should either body fail to approve the text, the proposal is dead. Where the conciliation committee fails to produce an agreed text, the proposal also falls unless the Council backs down at this stage and agrees to adopt the former common position as amended. However, Parliament may still choose to reject this, in which case the proposal is finally dead.

Another function of the Parliament is to supervise the work of the Commission. The Parliament has power to resolve to dismiss the Commission but this has never been done. Parliament is also required to adopt the community budget. Since the Maastricht Treaty the Parliament is empowered to appoint an ombudsman to investigate allegations of maladministration by community institutions other than the European Court of Justice.

The Council

The Council, often referred to as the Council of Ministers, is made up of a single representative of the governments of each of the member states. The representative shall be the appropriate government minister depending upon the subject matter of the meeting; for example there may be a meeting of all the foreign ministers or of all the agriculture ministers. Member states take turns as President of the Council, each taking a six-month term.

It is the function of the Council to ensure that the objectives of the Treaty of Rome are achieved by ensuring the coordination of the economic policies of the member states. It is the Council which must take the final decision on secondary community legislation based upon proposals put forward by the Commission. As stated above, in respect of certain proposals, decisions may be taken only after the opinion of Parliament is sought. Certain decisions may be taken by simple majority vote, others by qualified majority vote and a few decisions require unanimity. Whether or not a proposal requires unanimity, or needs only a qualified majority to be adopted, depends on which Article of the Treaty the proposal is being brought under. For a qualified majority vote each member state is given a certain number of votes, eg Luxembourg two, the United Kingdom ten. The number of votes of all member states totals 87. In order to achieve a qualified majority, there must be 62 votes in favour of a proposal. Since Maastricht, 26 votes provide a blocking minority. Should the Council intend to amend a proposal by the Commission, such a decision requires a unanimous vote.

As the members of the Council are busy government ministers who spend most of their time in their own countries, much of the groundwork on proposed legislation is done by a committee called COREPER. COREPER is made up of permanent full-time representatives of each of the member states. These full-time representatives may be thought of as ambassadors to the European Community and they give consideration to proposals for legislation prior to a final decision being taken by the Council.

The Commission

There are 20 Commissioners. There must be at least one, and not more than two, Commissioners appointed from each of the member states. Commissioners are appointed for a five-year term which may be renewed. At present there are two British Commissioners. A Commissioner's first duty is to the Community not to the member state which nominated him.

The Commission, which is based in Brussels, has a number of functions. First, it initiates proposals for community legislation. In respect of certain areas of community law, the Commission itself has the power to make regulations. Second, the Commission fulfils its role as 'guardian of the treaties'. The Commission must ensure that community law is not being infringed by member states. The Commission may bring enforcement proceedings against member states. In addition, insofar as a breach of competition law is concerned, the Commission has the power to fine individuals and companies. Third, the Commission must implement policy decisions which are taken by the Council.

The European Court of Justice

The European Court of Justice sits in Luxembourg and its purpose is to ensure that in the interpretation and application of the Treaties the law is observed. The Court consists of 15 judges. A plenary session must sit together to hear cases brought before it by a member state or by one of the Institutions or a case which the rules of Court procedure say cannot be heard by a Chamber. Otherwise the Court is split into Chambers to hear cases, each Chamber consisting of three or five judges. The Court is assisted by nine Advocates-General (though this number will drop to eight when the term of office of the next Advocate-General to vacate office expires) whose task it is to provide an independent, reasoned legal opinion on a case to aid the judges. Judges and Advocates-General are appointed from the member states for a six-year renewable term.

Cases may take the form of direct actions or requests for a preliminary ruling. Direct actions may be brought by member states, by the Commission, by the Council, by individuals or by corporate bodies. The Court may consider allegations that a member state has failed to fulfil its Treaty obligations or that actions of the Council or Commission are unlawful. In terms of Article 177 of the Treaty of Rome, where a question concerning the interpretation of community law arises before a court or tribunal within a member state, that court or tribunal may refer the matter to the European Court of Justice for a ruling. Where there is no further appeal from the court or tribunal within the legal system of the member state, that court or tribunal **must** make an Article 177 reference.

In September 1989 a new court was set up to take some of the pressure of work off the European Court of Justice. Attached to the Court of Justice, the new **Court of First Instance of the European Communities** sits in Luxembourg and consists of 15 judges appointed for a renewable six-year term. The Court will as a rule sit in Chambers of three or five judges and one of the judges will fulfil the role of Advocate-General. The Court of First Instance originally had jurisdiction only in three types of cases: the 'staff cases' involving disputes between the community and its employees; cases concerning competition law; and applications for judicial review and possibly damages in relation to levies, quotas and prices set by the European Coal and Steel Community. Since 1993 the jurisdiction of the Court of First Instance has been extended so that it can now also hear any action brought by a natural or legal person against the act of a Community Institution. Article 177 references, however, remain outwith its jurisdiction. Appeal lies to the Court of Jurisdiction on a point of law only.

The Court of Auditors

The function of the Court of Auditors, which was established in 1975, is to audit the accounts of the Community to determine that there are no irregularities and that there has been sound financial management of the budget.

The Court of Auditors, which is based in Luxembourg, was given full Institution status by the Maastricht Treaty.

Judicial precedent

This forms part of the common law; it is a non-statutory source of law. Should a decision have the status of precedent it **must** be followed by lower courts in cases where the same point of law is involved. The operation of judicial precedent gives rise to a body of law known as 'case law'. This doctrine is also known as **stare decisis** – to stand by decisions. A decision which is a precedent is said to be **binding** on lower courts. Decisions which are not precedents are not binding but may be **persuasive**; they may be taken into account but they do not have to be followed.

A previous decision need be followed only if it has the status of precedent. In order to be a precedent that decision must have been:

1 a decision of a senior court whose decisions are binding; *and*
2 in point – i.e. the legal reasoning must deal with the same point of law as is now under consideration.

The decisions of only a few courts have the status of precedent.

In matters of interpretation of European Community law, decisions of the European Court of Justice must be followed by courts and tribunals within the United Kingdom.

Certain decisions of the House of Lords in London may be binding on the Scottish Civil Courts. House of Lords decisions on appeals from Scottish courts are precedents. House of Lords decisions relating to statute which is applicable throughout the whole of the United Kingdom are probably binding on the Scottish civil courts. House of Lords decisions on matters of purely English law are not binding on the Scottish courts. The most senior civil court which sits in Scotland is the Court of Session in Edinburgh. It is divided into the more senior Inner House and the less senior Outer House. The Inner House sits as two Divisions equal in status and each made up of three judges.

Decisions of the Inner House bind the Outer House and also the Sheriff Court which is still further down the court hierarchy. Each Division of the Inner House is bound by its own previous decisions and those of the other Division. However, the Inner House of the Court of Session may sit as a court of seven judges in order to overturn a decision of one of its Divisions. Decisions of the Outer House and Sheriff Court decisions never have the status of precedent.

The doctrine of judicial precedent is less strong in criminal matters. However, all Scottish criminal courts will follow law laid down by the High Court of Justiciary sitting as a Court of Criminal Appeal. The House of Lords has no part to play in Scottish criminal law.

The second requirement which must be fulfilled if a decision is to have the status of precedent is that the previous case must be 'in point' with the present one. The two cases must deal with the same point of law. Whether or not the facts of the two cases are similar is not necessarily important, what matters is that the same legal issue is at stake. Moreover, it is not the whole of a judgement which has the status of precedent. The only part of the decision which is binding is the part known as the *ratio decidendi* – the legal reason for the decision. The ratio of the case is distinguished from *obiter dicta* – other words, things said along the way.

Many decisions, particularly those of the higher courts, are reported in detail and the printed judgements often run to many pages. The whole judgement must be read in order to identify the *ratio decidendi* because it is only this part of the decision which is binding. One must attempt to isolate the point of law on which the court based its decision. However, in giving judgement a judge may embark upon an elaborate discussion of the legal background to the case. A decision may be full of judicial asides or *obiter dicta* where the judge may say 'now, had this been the case my decision would have been different ...'. Such *obiter dicta* are not binding but may be persuasive in later cases.

Judicial precedent is the most important source of law after statute. The advantages of applying the doctrine of judicial precedent are that it enables solicitors to advise their clients with some certainty as to the likely outcome of a case and whether a matter is worth pursuing. It allows for consistency of decisions throughout the country. Should two cases dealing with the same point of law be heard, one in Glasgow and one in Aberdeen, both courts are bound by the same precedent and the same decision should be reached in each court. Precedents also provide assistance for less experienced judges in the lower courts.

The main criticism of the doctrine of judicial precedent is that it makes the law rigid and a court may be forced to follow a very old decision which is out of step with the attitudes of modern society. In such cases, courts may try to avoid being bound to apply a precedent by drawing often artificial distinctions between the two cases.

A major drawback of the use of precedent is the practical difficulty that precedents are like policemen, you can never find one when you want one. Such problems may be eased by technological advances which have enabled the compilation of computerised databases containing reports of cases. The computer-literate lawyer is now able, in theory, to type in key words and phrases and be rewarded with a printout of cases in point.

Institutional Writings

Certain legal writings have the status of Institutional Writings. Where there is no statutory provision on a point and in the absence of a judicial precedent which states otherwise, such writings are taken to give an authoritative statement of the law of

Scotland. However, where there is a conflict between either statute or case law and a statement by an Institutional writer, statute and case law shall prevail. Those whose writings have the status of Institutional Writings are:

1 Sir Thomas Craig, whose *Jus Feudale* was published in 1655 and dealt with the development of civil, canon (church) and feudal laws.
2 Viscount Stair, whose *Institutions of the Law of Scotland* published in 1681 form the cornerstone of modern Scots law. He drew together Roman law, feudal law and native customary law and emphasised the deduction of rules from first principles.
3 Lord Bankton, whose *An Institute of the Laws of Scotland* was published in 1751.
4 Professor John Erskine, whose *Institute of the Law of Scotland* was published in 1773. A previous shorter work, *Principles of the Law of Scotland*, had been used as a textbook by his students at Edinburgh University and updated versions of this were so used into the 1900s. Erskine's work takes second place only to that of Stair.
5 Professor George Bell, whose *Commentaries on the Law of Scotland and on the Principles of Mercantile Jurisprudence* was published in 1810 and whose *Principles of the Law of Scotland* appeared in 1829.

Custom

Custom is now rarely a source of new law. Its main importance lies in the contribution which it has made to the common law of Scotland. The common law incorporated the customary responses of the community persistently practised over generations. A custom which took on the force of law was the right of a widow to succeed to her dead husband's estate.

It is still technically possible that a custom may be a source of new law but such a thing will be rare. A court may be asked to give effect to a custom when giving judgment. Before a court may do so:

1 the custom must add to existing law without running contrary to it;
2 the custom must be definite, certain and regularly practised;
3 the custom must be fair and reasonable;
4 the custom must have been practised for a sufficiently long time to justify its being accepted as binding.

Equity

As well as containing rules of strict law, the law of Scotland is also described as being based on principles of equity or equality or fairness. The Court of Session may exercise a special equitable power known as the *nobile officium* which allows the court to provide a remedy where the law otherwise provides none. The criminal court, the High Court of Justiciary, may also exercise such a *nobile officium*.

QUESTIONS

1 Define and distinguish between civil law and criminal law.

2 State whether the following are part of the civil law or of the criminal law:

(a) divorce;
(b) theft;
(c) breach of contract;
(d) delict;
(e) breach of the peace.

3 State whether the following would lead to criminal proceedings, civil proceedings or both:

(a) Jim fails to deliver goods ordered by John;
(b) Jean's husband leaves her and she wishes to divorce him;
(c) Stan fails to give way at a junction and he drives into and seriously injures a cyclist.

4 Define and distinguish between common law and statute.

5 The chief source of new law today is:

(a) custom;
(b) statute;
(c) judicial precedent.

6 Public Bills become:

(a) hybrid acts;
(b) general acts;
(c) local acts.

7 List the five stages which a Public Bill goes through in the House of Commons.

8 Is it true that a 'Scots Act' passed by the Scottish Parliament before 1707 only loses the force of law if it is expressly repealed by the Westminster Parliament?

9 Discuss delegated legislation as a source of law, giving the arguments for and against its use.

10 Indicate which of the following are examples of delegated legislation:

(a) the Divorce (Scotland) Act 1976;
(b) the Teachers Salaries (Scotland) Regulations;
(c) the General Development (Scotland) Order;
(d) the Sex Discrimination Bill.

11 Judicial precedent is also known as:

(a) *avizandum;*
(b) *obiter dicta;*
(c) *stare decisis.*

12 Which part of a precedent is the part which is binding?

13 In relation to judicial precedent, a Sheriff dealing with a civil matter is bound by the decisions of:

(a) only the Sheriff Principal;
(b) only a Lord Ordinary in the Outer House;
(c) the Outer House and the Inner House of the Court of Session;
(d) the Inner House and, sometimes, the House of Lords.

14 Which Treaty established the European Economic Community?

15 How many member states does the European Community have?

16 Which Act of the UK Parliament had the effect of making European Community law part of UK law?

17 If there is a conflict between UK law and European Community law, UK law prevails; true or false?

18 List the sources of European Community law.

19 What are the differences between an EC Regulation and an EC Directive?

20 List the five main Institutions of the European Community.

21 What is the function of COREPER?

22 What are the main functions of the Commission?

23 Where does the European Court of Justice sit?

24 What is the purpose of an Article 177 reference to the European Court of Justice?

2 The Scottish courts and arbitration

THE SCOTTISH COURT STRUCTURE

Civil law is applied in the civil courts using civil procedure and criminal law is applied in the criminal courts using criminal procedure.

Civil law provides rules of law regulating the rights and duties of individual citizens of the state in their dealings with one another. An individual wishing to enforce his rights under civil law must raise an action in the appropriate civil court. He must seek a civil remedy – e.g., monetary damages or an interdict or a decree of divorce.

Criminal law is concerned with conduct considered sufficiently harmful to society that it is declared to be criminal. Such conduct will be punished. Cases before the criminal courts are in the form of prosecutions initiated by the State. Where an accused is found guilty a penalty may be imposed perhaps in the form of a fine or imprisonment or a community service order.

THE CIVIL COURTS

The Scottish civil court structure comprises **the Sheriff Court** – including the Sheriff Summary Court, the Sheriff Ordinary Court and the Sheriff Principal, the latter exercising an appellate function; **the Court of Session** – made up of the Outer House of the Court of Session and the Inner House of the Court of Session. In turn the Inner House sits as two Divisions – the First Division and the Second Division; and **the House of Lords** sitting at Westminster.

The Sheriff Court

Scotland is divided into six **Sheriffdoms**: Grampian, Highland and Islands; Tayside,

Central and Fife; Lothian and Borders; South Strathclyde, Dumfries and Galloway; Glasgow and Stathkelvin; North Strathclyde.

Each Sheriffdom is divided into a varying number of **Sheriff Court Districts**. There are a total of 49 Sheriff Court Districts throughout Scotland. In each Sheriff Court District there is situated a Sheriff Court. Each Sheriff Court will have one or more **Sheriffs** to act as judge. The senior Sheriff in each Sheriffdom is known as the **Sheriff Principal**. Sheriffs will be either advocates or solicitors of at least ten years' standing. Existing sheriffs retire at 72 but those appointed after 31 March 1995 will retire at 70.

Jurisdiction of the Sheriff Court

A court's jurisdiction determines which cases it is legally competent to deal with. A court will have geographical jurisdiction; jurisdiction over certain persons; and jurisdiction over certain subject matter.

Jurisdiction over persons

In civil cases the person bringing the action – e.g., suing for compensation – is known as the **pursuer**. The person against whom the action is brought is known as the **defender**. The civil court which hears the case must have jurisdiction over the defender. In civil cases the Sheriff Court will have jurisdiction over the defender where:

1 The defender is resident within the geographical jurisdiction of the Sheriff Court – i.e., within the territory of the Sheriffdom. Conventionally, the action is raised at the Sheriff Court of the Sheriff Court District within which the defender resides. The Sheriff Court still has jurisdiction even if the defender is no longer resident there so long as he was there for at least 40 days and he has been away for less than 40 days and he has no other known address in Scotland.
2 The defender carries on business and has a place of business within the geographical jurisdiction of the Sheriff Court and is cited at his place of business or personally.
3 The defender owns or is the tenant of heritage – i.e., land and buildings – within the geographical jurisdiction of the Sheriff Court **and** the action is connected with that property.
4 The action is concerned with a contract to be performed within the geographical jurisdiction of the Sheriff Court.
5 If it is a delictual action – i.e., where the pursuer is suing for damages, for example for personal injury or damage to property caused by the defender's negligence – the delict, i.e., wrongful act, occurred within the area of the Sheriff Court's geographical jurisdiction.

Jurisdiction over subject matter (types of cases)

The Sheriff Court has a very wide jurisdiction in respect of the types of cases it is competent to deal with. Much of its jurisdiction overlaps with that of the Court of Session. However, certain cases are within the **privative jurisdiction** of the Sheriff Court – i.e., such cases can be heard only by the Sheriff Court. This includes cases not exceeding £1500 in value; actions for eviction from heritable property.

Similarly, certain cases fall within the privative jurisdiction of the Court of Session and include matters of status such as actions of declarator of marriage and petitions for the liquidation of a company with a paid up share capital exceeding £120 000.

Note, however, that actions of divorce which could previously only be heard by the Court of Session can now also be dealt with by the Sheriff Court. It is also the case that there is no upper limit on the value of cases which the Sheriff Court may deal with.

The Sheriff Court – small claims procedure

Since 30 November 1988 actions for payment of money not exceeding £750 may be pursued under the small claims procedure.

The procedure is meant to provide an inexpensive and straightforward means of allowing individuals to bring court action without requiring the services of a solicitor. Because the system should allow individuals to represent themselves, legal aid is not available for appearances by solicitors in small claims cases. However, a pursuer under this procedure may be represented by a friend if the Sheriff is satisfied that he is suitable. Of course if the pursuer can afford a solicitor, solicitors may also appear.

Many potential pursuers are discouraged from taking court action because of the fear that should they lose they face having to pay the other side's expenses as well as their own. An important feature of the scheme is that where the sum sued for is less than £200 no expenses are payable; where the sum sued for is between £200 and £750, expenses are limited to a maximum of £75.

There may be an appeal from the Sheriff to the Sheriff Principal only; there is no further appeal to the Inner House of the Court of Session.

The Sheriff Summary Court – Summary Cause Procedure

The Summary Cause Procedure is a streamlined procedure introduced into the Sheriff Court in 1976. Actions are raised by filling in a simple pre-printed form available from the Court. Once the form is complete it is forwarded to the Sheriff Court with a small fee and is returned to the pursuer bearing two dates – the Return Day and the Calling Day – and the Court's authority to serve a copy of the form on the defender. If the defender does not return his portion of the form to the Court by the Return Day the pursuer need only sign a book at the Court requesting a decree. If the defender returns the form stating his intention to defend the action both parties must appear at Court on the Calling Day when a Proof will be set at a later date. At the date of the Proof both parties must come to Court with their respective witnesses and evidence will be heard and the matter decided.

The Summary Cause Procedure is available for actions for the payment of sums of money over £750 and up to £1500 and also for claims for the recovery of heritable property, eg council house evictions.

Appeals in Summary Causes lie from the Sheriff to the Sheriff Principal on a point of law. The appellant asks the Sheriff to prepare a Stated Case setting out his findings in fact and law. There is the possibility of a further appeal to the Inner House of the Court of Session, again on a point of law, if the Sheriff Principal certifies that the case is suitable for such an appeal.

Sheriff Ordinary Court – Ordinary Procedure

Those cases which cannot be taken under the Summary Cause Procedure must follow Ordinary Procedure. As stated above, the jurisdiction of the Sheriff Court is very wide and will include actions for repayment of debt and actions for damages – in both instances where the sum sued for is over £1500 – succession cases, separation actions, divorce and actions for custody and aliment. Sheriffs also have a number of miscellaneous and administrative functions including applications for the adoption of children, bankruptcy matters, fatal accident inquiries and applications by Social Work Authorities.

There are two alternative routes of appeal from the Sheriff Ordinary Court. There may be an appeal direct to the Inner House of the Court of Session. Alternatively, there may be an appeal to the Sheriff Principal and if necessary there may be a further appeal from the Sheriff Principal to the Inner House of the Court of Session.

In most cases appellants elect to appeal, at least in the first place, to the Sheriff Principal. It is cheaper and quicker – the parties do not have to travel to Edinburgh nor do they have to employ Counsel which they would have to do if they appealed to the Court of Session. However, it should be noted that the Law Reform (Miscellaneous Provisions) (Scotland) Act 1990 proposed to give certain suitably qualified solicitors the right to appear before the Court of Session. The Admission as a Solicitor with Extended Rights (Scotland) Rules 1992 were approved by the Secretary of State for Scotland and the first solicitor appeared in the Court of Session during 1993. However, if a very complex point of law is involved and it is certain that whoever loses before the Sheriff Principal will appeal further it is possibly quicker in the long run to appeal direct to the Inner House.

There is the possibility of further appeal on a point of law to the House of Lords.

THE COURT OF SESSION

The Court of Session is the supreme civil court which sits in Scotland. It sits in Parliament House in Edinburgh. Judges are known as Senators of the College of Justice. There are now 27 full-time Senators of the College of Justice. In addition during 1991 and 1992 eight temporary judges were appointed. Those appointed were either senior Sheriffs or senior Queen's Counsel. Among those appointed as a temporary judge in 1992 was Sheriff Hazel Aronson who accordingly became the first woman to sit as a Court of Session judge. In 1996, as Lady Cosgrove, Hazel Aronson became the first woman to be installed as a full-time Senator of the College of Justice.

The Court of Session is divided into the **Outer House** and the **Inner House**.

The Outer House is a Court of First Instance. This means that cases start off here and are dealt with here. It is not a Court of Appeal. The Inner House is primarily a Court of Appeal although it can also be a Court of First Instance.

The Inner House, comprising of eight senators of the College of Justice, is split into two Divisions – the **First Division** and the **Second Division**. Each Division has a quorum of three. The rest of the Senators of the College of Justice sit individually as judges in the Outer House, with the exception of one who chairs the Scottish Law

Commission. Civil jury trials within Scotland are virtually non-existent.

The jurisdiction of the Court of Session is wide – in respect of subject matter basically all civil actions unless excluded by statute. It has privative jurisdiction in respect of actions of reduction whereby the court orders that an agreement or document or decree or will has no effect; actions of adjudication whereby title to heritable property is granted to the pursuer; actions for proving the tenor of lost documents; petitions for the liquidation of a limited company with a paid up share capital exceeding £120 000; and declarator of marriage.

Cases before the Court of Session at first instance may be in the form of an Action or a Petition. Both involve complex and fairly lengthy procedures. Whereas solicitors may appear in the Sheriff Court they generally have no right to be heard in the Court of Session and unless the parties represent themselves they will require the services of an advocate. However, as previously stated, in terms of the Admission as a Solicitor with Extended Rights (Scotland) Rules 1992 certain suitably experienced solicitors may obtain the right to appear in the Court of Session.

Although the Inner House may be a Court of First Instance its main task is to hear appeals from either the Sheriff Court or the Outer House of the Court of Session.

The Inner House consists of two Divisions equal in authority – each Division being manned by four judges of whom three sit at any one time. The First Division, when sitting, comprises the Lord President (Scotland's most senior judge) and two other judges. The Second Division comprises the Lord Justice Clerk and two other judges. In difficult cases the two Divisions may sit together to form a Court of seven judges. Exceptionally, judges from the Outer House have been called in to form a Court of fifteen.

Appeals are brought from the Outer House by means of a Reclaiming Motion. Fresh evidence is very rarely heard – it generally hears only legal argument. Decisions of the Divisions are either unanimous or by a majority – the presiding judge has no casting vote.

The jurisdiction of the Court of Session over persons is similar to that of the Sheriff Court except that the geographical jurisdiction of the Court of Session is the whole of Scotland. Accordingly, the Court of Session has jurisdiction: in respect of contracts to be performed in Scotland; delicts which occurred in Scotland; persons who are resident in Scotland; persons who own or are tenants of heritable property situated in Scotland (the property need not be the subject of the action).

THE HOUSE OF LORDS

This is a Court of Appeal in civil cases only. It has been argued that a right of appeal from the Inner House of the Court of Session to the House of Lords is not allowed for by the Act of Union 1707. However, such a right of appeal was established by the *Greenshields* case 1710/11.

The judges who sit in the House of Lords at Westminster are the Lord Chancellor and the Lords of Appeal in Ordinary. They will have held high judicial office for two years or have been advocates or barristers for at least 15 years. They may sit in the House of Lords for life but cease to hear cases at the age of 75. There are eleven law lords of whom two are by convention versed in Scots law. Usually, but not necessarily, one or both Scottish judges will be present at Scottish appeals. In addition, the present Lord Chancellor, Lord MacKay of Clashfern, is also a Scot thus bringing the present number of House of Lords judges trained in Scots Law to three. The quorum for House of Lords cases is three, but often five judges sit to hear appeals. Decision is by a majority. Appeal to the House of Lords is by way of a petition.

THE CRIMINAL COURTS

The criminal court structure in Scotland is made up of the **District Court**; the **Sheriff Court** – either the Sheriff Summary Court or the Sheriff Solemn Court; and the **High Court of Justiciary**, sitting either as a Trial Court or as a Court of Appeal. Note that the House of Lords is not a part of the Scottish criminal court structure – it hears only civil appeals.

The District Court

There is a District Court within the area of each District or Islands Council. Sitting as a judge there may be either a **Justice of the Peace** or a **Stipendiary Magistrate**. A Justice of the Peace (JP) need not be legally qualified, but when a JP sits as judge the Clerk of the Court, who is legally qualified, (generally a solicitor employed by the local authority which administers the District Court) must act as legal assessor. JPs are often local councillors. Their sentencing powers are limited.

A Stipendiary Magistrate must have been legally qualified for at least five years. Because he is legally qualified his sentencing powers are greater.

A JP may impose a fine of up to £2500 and imprisonment of up to 60 days for common law crimes. In respect of statutory offences, the Act of Parliament creating the offence may vary these sentencing powers.

A Stipendiary Magistrate may impose a fine of up to £5000 and imprisonment of up to three months (or up to six months if dealing with crimes of violence or dishonesty and the accused has previous convictions for such crimes). Again, when dealing with statutory offences sentencing powers may be limited by statute.

In general a criminal court has jurisdiction (ie is legally competent to deal with a case) where the crime took place within the area of its geographical jurisdiction. In addition, the crime must fall within the subject matter with which the court is authorised to deal.

The District Court is the lowest court within the criminal court structure. It deals only with the most minor crimes although its jurisdiction has been extended to relieve pressure on the Sheriff Court. It deals with such matters as breach of the peace, drunkenness, minor assaults, and minor statutory offences, although this has been extended to include certain endorseable road traffic offences. It can hear cases of theft, reset, fraud and embezzlement where the amount involved does not exceed £2500.

The representative of the State who prosecutes in the District Court is known as the **Procurator Fiscal**. The Fiscal is a solicitor in full-time employment as a civil servant in the employ of the Crown Office. The Crown Office is the department with responsibility for public prosecution in Scotland.

The accused may represent himself or be represented by a solicitor. Legal aid is available to an accused in the District Court provided he satisfies the means test.

Appeal from the District Court against conviction or sentence is by either Stated Case or Bill of Suspension direct to the High Court of Justiciary sitting as a Court of Appeal. The appeal will be heard on the Justiciary Roll.

The Sheriff Court as a Criminal Court

As previously stated, Scotland is divided into six Sheriffdoms and 49 Sheriff Court Districts. In each of these Sheriff Court Districts is a Sheriff Court manned by a number of Sheriffs who act as judge.

As well as having a civil jurisdiction the Sheriff Court also deals with criminal cases. The Sheriff Court is the busiest criminal court. It can deal with all crime which takes place within the area of its geographical jurisdiction **except** the crimes of murder, rape, treason and incest which can be dealt with only by the High Court of Justiciary.

Prosecuting in the Sheriff Court is the Procurator Fiscal. Administration of the Court is the responsibility of the **Sheriff Clerk** who is not legally qualified but is expert in matters of court procedure.

The accused may represent himself or be represented by a solicitor or sometimes by an advocate.

Proceedings in the Sheriff Court when dealing with criminal cases will be either **summary** or **solemn**.

Summary procedure

This is used for less serious cases. Under summary procedure there is no jury – the Sheriff sits alone deciding on both questions of guilt and, if guilty, on penalty. The document which is served on the accused setting out the alleged offence is known as the Summary Complaint. If the allegations involve a statutory offence there will be attached a Notice of Penalties which sets out the sentencing powers of the Sheriff for this particular offence. Also, where applicable, there will be attached a Schedule of Previous Convictions which will be brought to the attention of the Sheriff should the accused either plead or be found guilty. The Sheriff will take these into account when deciding on the sentence to be imposed.

The sentencing powers of the Sheriff under summary procedure are up to a £5000 fine and up to three months imprisonment (six months where the crime is one of violence or dishonesty and the accused has relevant previous convictions). Again, powers may be varied by statute.

Solemn procedure

This is used for more serious cases. Under solemn procedure the Sheriff sits with a jury of 15. The jury is the master of the fact – they decide on guilt. The Sheriff advises on law and decides the sentence. The document which is served on the accused under solemn procedure is known as the **indictment**.

The sentencing powers of the Sheriff under solemn procedure are an unlimited fine – and up to three years' imprisonment. Again, other sentencing powers may be set by statute in respect of statutory offences. If a Sheriff feels he does not have the powers to deal sufficiently severely with an accused he may remit the case to the High Court of Justiciary for sentence.

Under both summary and solemn procedure appeal is to the High Court of Justiciary. From summary procedure it is to the Justiciary Roll. From solemn procedure it is to the Scottish Court of Criminal Appeal.

The High Court of Justiciary

This is the supreme criminal court in Scotland. It is both a court of trial and a court of appeal.

As a court of trial

The most senior judge is the Lord Justice General. His deputy is the Lord Justice Clerk. The other judges are known as the Lords Commissioners of Justiciary. These are the same individuals who sit in the Court of Session as Senators of the College of Justice.

The High Court can hear cases on all crimes committed in the whole of Scotland *except* certain types of minor crime excluded by statute and reserved for the lower courts. Only the High Court can deal with murder, treason, rape and incest. Procedure in the High Court as a Court of Trial is always solemn. One or sometimes three judges sit with a jury of fifteen. Unlike the civil Court of Session which always sits in Edinburgh, the High Court of Justiciary as a Court of Trial may sit throughout the country. This is known as going out *on circuit*. The circuits are: Home (Edinburgh); West (Glasgow, Stirling and Oban); North (Inverness, Aberdeen, Dundee); South (Dumfries, Jedburgh, Ayr).

Prosecution in the High Court is conducted in important cases by either the **Lord Advocate** or the **Solicitor General** – the legal advisers to the Crown in Scotland. The Lord Advocate is the head of the Crown Office which has responsibility for public prosecution in Scotland. More frequently, prosecutions are conducted by one of the **Advocates Depute** – advocates who work full time for the Crown Office. Note that generally it is only advocates who have the right to appear in the High Court of Justiciary – most solicitors have no right to appear. However, in terms of the Admission as a Solicitor with Extended Rights (Scotland) Rules 1992 certain suitably experienced solicitors may obtain the right to be heard by the High Court of Justiciary.

There is no limit to the sentencing powers of the High Court of Justiciary.

Appeal against conviction or sentence is to the High Court of Justiciary sitting as the Scottish Court of Criminal Appeal.

As a court of appeal

Three or more Lords Commissioners of Justiciary hear appeals depending on the importance of the case. There is never a jury in appeal cases.

Appeals from summary courts are by way of either a Stated Case (available to both the accused and the prosecution) or a Bill of Suspension (available to the

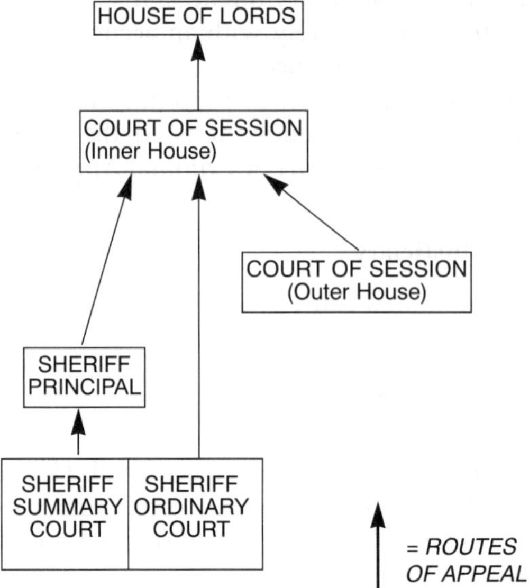

Figure 2.1 Routes of appeal in Scottish civil courts

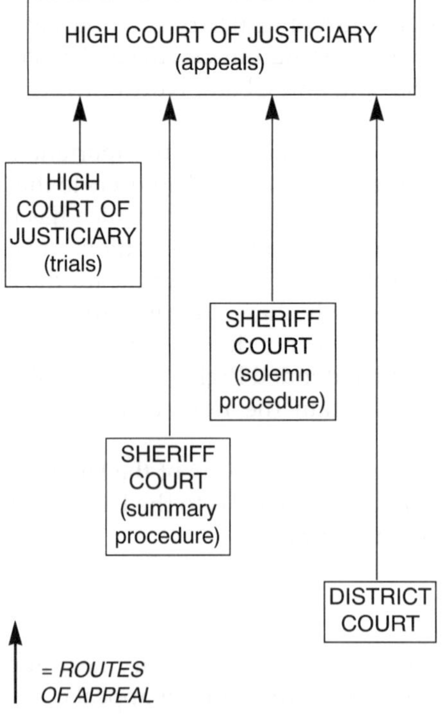

Figure 2.2 Routes of appeal in Scottish criminal courts

accused only) to the Justiciary Roll.

Appeals from solemn cases are to the Scottish Court of Criminal Appeal on the Criminal Appeal Roll.

The Court of Appeal may quash the conviction, refuse the appeal or modify the sentence.

Decisions of the High Court of Justiciary sitting as a High Court of Appeal are final and there is no further appeal to the House of Lords. The High Court of Justiciary when sitting as an Appeal Court always sits in Edinburgh – it does not go out on circuit as the Trial Court does.

Figures 2.1 and 2.2 summarise routes of appeal in Scottish civil and criminal courts.

ADMINISTRATIVE TRIBUNALS

As the amount of administrative law increases there is a greater potential for disputes arising between individual citizens and the state. Administrative tribunals provide an alternative forum to the ordinary courts for the resolution of such disputes.

There is no standard type of tribunal. Tribunals in the United Kingdom have developed in a somewhat haphazard manner, with different statutes establishing a variety of tribunals varying widely in constitution, function and procedure. Tribunals may hear appeals against decisions relating to entitlement to social security benefit, tax liability, VAT and national insurance contributions. Industrial Tribunals were originally set up to hear employers' appeals in respect of levies which they had to pay to industrial training boards. However, the jurisdiction of the Industrial Tribunal has increased greatly and most of its case load now relates to disputes between an individual employee and his employer. The Industrial Tribunal deals, among other things, with applications relating to unfair dismissal, redundancy, sex discrimination and equal pay.

The use of tribunals rather than the courts for the resolution of certain disputes is preferred for a number of reasons. It is often said that tribunals offer speed, cheapness and informality and allow for the determination of cases by experts. It is also said that the use of tribunals frees the courts from the burden of having to deal with literally hundreds of thousands of extra cases per annum.

Accordingly, tribunals offer a statutory machinery for the resolution of disputes, generally between an individual and the state but sometimes, as with the Industrial Tribunal, between two individuals. Statute does not always provide for the resolution of a dispute by setting up an administrative tribunal. Some statutes provide for a final decision by a government minister or for the setting up of a Public Inquiry to report to a government minister. Administrative tribunals differ from inquiries in that they are set up on a permanent basis, whereas inquiries are held as the need arises. Administrative tribunals function independently of government ministers whereas inquiries make recommendations to ministers which the minister need not follow. Tribunals are said to be judicial or 'court-like' in nature whereas inquiries are said to be administrative.

The composition and jurisdiction of administrative tribunals vary widely. Some tribunals, such as the Children's Hearings, need not have any legally qualified members. Some tribunals comprise only a single civil servant. Others, such as the Industrial Tribunal, are made up of a legally qualified chairman plus lay members who are not lawyers but who have relevant experience. Certain tribunals, such as the Immigration Appeal Tribunal, have jurisdiction throughout the United Kingdom. Some tribunals have jurisdiction only in Scotland such as the Crofters Commission and Children's Hearings.

Whether or not there is a right to appeal the decision of a tribunal depends upon the statute which set up the tribunal. The statute may provide that there is no right of appeal or it may allow an appeal to a higher tribunal or to a government minister or to the courts. However, even in the absence of a right of appeal, the courts maintain an over-riding jurisdiction to quash the decision of a tribunal on certain special grounds. This power of **judicial review** may be exercised should a tribunal act in an *ultra vires* fashion. The tribunal may have exceeded its statutory authority or failed to follow the proper procedure or failed to observe the rules of natural justice, so that an individual has not had a fair hearing.

The work of most administrative tribunals is supervised by the Council on Tribunals which was established by the Tribunals and Inquiries Act 1958. The Council now operates under the provisions of the Tribunals and Inquiries Act 1971 and its task is to keep under review the constitution and working of tribunals. The Council on Tribunals has a Scottish Committee which supervises tribunals in Scotland. The Council presents an annual report to the Lord Chancellor in England and to the Lord Advocate in Scotland. The Council on Tribunals is consulted on legislation dealing with tribunals and on proposed rules of procedure.

ARBITRATION

As an alternative to going to court, the parties to a dispute may agree to go instead to arbitration. The dispute is referred to a person known as an **arbiter** whose decision the parties agree to accept. The whole point of going to arbitration is to exclude the jurisdiction of the courts and accordingly there is no right of appeal should the arbiter 'get it wrong'. However, the courts are entitled to set an arbiter's decision aside in special circumstances, for example if the arbiter accepts a bribe.

The decision to go to arbitration may be taken before the dispute arises. Parties to a contract may include in that contract an **arbitration clause** which specifies that disputes arising under the contract shall be taken to arbitration. Alternatively, the decision to go to arbitration may be taken only once the dispute has arisen. The parties in dispute then prepare a **reference** or **submission** to arbitration which sets out the issue to be settled.

It is also possible that there may be a **judicial reference** to arbitration. A court as part of an ordinary court action may pass certain questions to an arbiter at the request of the parties. The arbiter's report will form part of the court's final decree. As well as private agreements to go to arbitration, a statute may provide that certain types of dispute are to be settled by arbitration. Unlike private arbitrations, some statutes may allow for an appeal from the decision of the arbiter to the court on a point of law.

Certain types of dispute cannot be settled by arbitration. Matters relating to status such as divorce cannot be the subject of arbitration. Criminal matters cannot be dealt with by arbitration.

There are a variety of reasons why people may prefer to go to arbitration rather than go to court:

1 Speed – the courts are very busy, it can take months if not years to obtain a court decree.
2 Informality – arbitration **may** be more informal and the parties themselves may agree on the procedure to be followed. However, the arbiter often sets out the procedure to be followed and in such instances it may be 'court-like'.
3 Cost – arbitration is possibly though not necessarily cheaper than going to court. The parties may pay lawyers to present their case to the arbiter in which event there is unlikely to be a saving. In addition, the arbiter has to be paid for his services and there is also the cost of hiring a venue.
4 Privacy – should the parties go to court the case is heard in public which will allow competitors access to sensitive information. Going to arbitration has the very real benefit of privacy.
5 Technical expertise – where a dispute centres around a very technical issue, for example a matter of building or engineering practice, a judge may not be the best person to determine the issue. By going to arbitration the parties can choose an arbiter who has the appropriate technical knowledge.

The parties to the dispute usually appoint a single arbiter. Alternatively, they may each appoint an arbiter. Where two arbiters are appointed it is common to appoint an oversman who makes the decision should the two arbiters fail to agree.

The arbiter may be a named individual or the holder of a particular office – for example the current President of the Royal Institute of Mining Engineers or a Court of Session Judge.

An individual should not act as arbiter where he has a personal interest in the outcome. For example, a person should not act as arbiter if he holds shares in a company which is one of the parties to the dispute unless his shareholding is disclosed and both parties are happy that he should nevertheless be appointed. Where the parties cannot even agree on who is to act as arbiter or where one of the parties fails to appoint his half of a pair of arbiters, the court may appoint an arbiter. The court may also appoint the oversman where there is a failure to agree on who should be appointed as such. Otherwise, a court does not have jurisdiction to deal with a dispute once the parties have agreed to arbitration. However, just as a judge in a court action can refer technical questions to an arbiter by judicial reference, an arbiter may ask the court to give a ruling on a point of law by means of a stated case.

Once the arbiter has delivered his decision, should the loser fail to abide by it, the winner may seek to enforce the decision by asking the court to award a **decree conform** – i.e., a decree in the same terms as the arbiter's decision.

As was stated above, the whole point of going to arbitration is to exclude the jurisdiction of the courts. The parties agree to accept the decision of the arbiter and, accordingly, in private arbitrations, there is no right of appeal to the courts should the loser disagree with the decision. However, the court does have an over-riding jurisdiction to set aside or reduce the decision of an arbiter on certain special grounds:

(a) The decision is tainted by corruption, bribery or falsehood.
(b) One of the parties discovers that the arbiter had an undisclosed interest in the dispute.
(c) The arbiter has gone beyond the terms of reference set by the parties – known as *ultra fines compromissi*.
(d) The arbiter has not gone far enough – he has not answered all the questions set by the parties.
(e) There has been a breach of natural justice – for example, the procedure was seriously flawed or the arbiter did not give each of the parties an equal chance to state their case.

PERSONNEL OF THE LAW IN SCOTLAND

The legal profession in Scotland

In Scotland, practising lawyers are either **solicitors** or **advocates**. A solicitor may become an advocate and an advocate may become a solicitor but no-one can be both at the same time.

Solicitors

Solicitors have their practices in towns and cities throughout Scotland. Solicitors practise as sole practitioners or in partnership with other solicitors. They give general legal advice on a wide variety of matters and draw up legal documents such as wills and documentation relating to house purchase. Solicitors may represent their clients in court in both civil and criminal matters. At present, solicitors may appear in the Sheriff Court in civil cases, and in the District Court and the Sheriff Court in criminal cases. Solicitors may defend their clients in jury trials in the Sheriff Court. Most solicitors have no right to be heard by the Court of Session, the High Court of Justiciary or the House of Lords. However, in terms of the Admission as a Solicitor with Extended Rights (Scotland) Rules 1992 certain suitably experienced solicitors may apply for the right to be heard in these courts.

Not all solicitors are in private practice. They may also work in central or local government or for large companies. A person cannot practise as a solicitor unless he has been admitted as a solicitor, his name is on the roll of solicitors and he has a current practising certificate issued annually by the Law Society of Scotland, the professional body to which all solicitors must belong.

In order to be admitted as a solicitor a person normally obtains a law degree from one of the five Scottish universities offering the LLB degree. There then follows a one-year course at university leading to a Diploma in Legal Practice. The final step is to complete a two-year training contract with a solicitor, although a restricted practising certificate is issued at the end of the first year of the training contract.

Advocates

Advocates have at present the sole right to appear in the higher courts: the Court of Session, the High Court of Justiciary and the House of Lords. In England, members of the roughly equivalent branch of the legal profession are known as barristers. Advocates in general are referred to as 'the Bar'. All advocates are members of the Faculty of Advocates which is headed by the Dean. Advocates are either senior or junior advocates or counsel, and the senior members of the Bar enjoy the title Queen's Counsel or QC. A QC is entitled to wear a silk gown and when a junior counsel becomes a QC this is referred to as 'taking silk'.

Advocates are self-employed, they do not form partnerships with other advocates. Persons who wish to become advocates obtain a law degree and the Diploma in Legal Practice. They must also pass an examination in evidence and procedure. They work for a year in a solicitor's office as a trainee and then spend nine months as a pupil of a practising advocate. It is up to the Faculty of Advocates whether or not to admit an individual to membership.

Advocates cannot accept instructions directly from members of the public but must take their instructions from a solicitor. Advocates are based in Edinburgh and do much of their work there. However, they are often instructed to appear in the Sheriff Court and they also appear at public inquiries. In addition, they have to travel to appear before the High Court of Justiciary when it is on circuit.

The judiciary in Scotland

There are 27 **Senators of the College of Justice** who sit as judges in the Court of Session and the High Court of Justiciary. Scotland's most senior judge is the **Lord President**. When the Lord President is sitting hearing criminal appeals in the High Court of Justiciary he is known as the **Lord Justice General**. The Lord President and his deputy, the **Lord Justice Clerk** are appointed by the Sovereign on the recommendation of the Prime Minister. The other judges who sit in the Court of Session or the High Court are appointed by the Sovereign on the recommendation of the Secretary of State for Scotland. The judges who sit in the High Court of Justiciary are also referred to as the Lords Commissioners of Justiciary. The judges in the superior courts are appointed from the ranks of the Faculty of Advocates and are usually Queen's Counsel. However, in terms of the Law Reform (Miscellaneous Provisions) (Scotland) Act 1990, persons who have been Sheriffs Principal and Sheriffs for a continuous period of not less than five years shall be eligible for appointment as judges of the Court of Session. Similarly eligible for such appointment shall be those solicitors who, under the provisions of the 1990 Act, have had a right of audience in both the Court of Session and the High Court of Justiciary for a continuous period of not less than five years.

The retirement age for judges in the superior courts appointed prior to 31 March 1995 is 75 but, under the Judicial Pensions and Retirement Act 1993, those appointed after that date will retire at 70.

Sheriffs, who sit as judges in the Sheriff Court, must have been legally qualified as an advocate or solicitor for at least ten years. Sheriffs are appointed by the

Sovereign on the recommendation of the Secretary of State for Scotland. Sheriffs appointed before 31 March 1995 retire at the age of 72, those appointed after that date at 70.

Justices of the Peace, who dispense justice in the District Court, are not legally qualified. They may be appointed on behalf of Her Majesty the Queen by the Secretary of State for Scotland. In addition, Scottish local authorities may nominate up to one-quarter of their councillors to serve as *ex officio* Justices. Justices of the Peace should be broadly representative of the community which they serve.

Stipendiary Magistrates may also be appointed to sit in the District Court. The local authority which administers the District Court has power to appoint as Stipendiary Magistrate a person who has been legally qualified for a period of five years. A Stipendiary Magistrate has wider sentencing powers than a Justice of the Peace; his powers are equivalent to those of the Sheriff in the Sheriff Summary Court. Only the City of Glasgow Council has appointed Stipendiary Magistrates.

The Law Officers and the system of public prosecution in Scotland

The Law Officers are the Sovereign's official legal advisers in Scotland and are known as the **Lord Advocate** and the **Solicitor General for Scotland**. They are appointed by the Prime Minister and change when the government changes. They may be Members of Parliament. Both the Lord Advocate and the Solicitor General shall be advocates and in important cases either may actually appear for the Crown in court.

The Lord Advocate is the head of the **Crown Office**, which is the government department responsible for the system of public prosecution in Scotland and is based in Edinburgh. The Lord Advocate and the Solicitor General for Scotland may represent the Crown in criminal cases before the High Court of Justiciary. However, it is generally Advocates Depute who prosecute in the High Court. Advocates Depute, who are often referred to as Crown Counsel, are appointed by the Lord Advocate.

Prosecutors in the Sheriff Court and the District Court are the Procurators Fiscal, who are full-time civil servants and report to the Crown Office. They are generally solicitors and they take the decision whether or not to prosecute individuals. More serious crime is reported to the Crown Office for instructions.

The permanent civil servant in charge of the administration of the Crown Office is a solicitor known as the **Crown Agent**.

QUESTIONS

1 List the courts which form part of the Scottish civil court structure.

2 Give three examples of cases which may be heard by the civil courts.

3 How many Sheriffdoms are there? Name them.

4 What is meant by the term 'jurisdiction'?

5 Describe the main features of the small claims procedure which operates in the Sheriff Court.

6 Give three examples of matters which might be dealt with by the Sheriff Ordinary.

7 An appeal from the Sheriff Ordinary lies to:

(a) the Outer House;
(b) the High Court of Justiciary;
(c) the Sheriff Principal;
(d) either the Sheriff Principal or the Inner House.

8 Under which types of procedure in the Sheriff Court would you bring an action for payment of:

(a) £400;
(b) £1200;
(c) £15 000?

9 Which court has jurisdiction to deal with a divorce action:

(a) the Sheriff Ordinary Court;
(b) the Outer House of the Court of Session;
(c) The High Court of Justiciary;
(d) either (a) or (b)?

10 The maximum award which can be made by the Sheriff Ordinary Court is:

(a) £10 000;
(b) £25 000;
(c) £90 000;
(d) none of these.

11 List the courts which form part of the Scottish criminal court structure.

12 Give three examples of cases which may be heard by the criminal courts.

13 When a person is served with a complaint he will appear:

(a) in the Outer House;
(b) in the District Court;
(c) in the Sheriff Summary Criminal Court;
(d) either (b) or (c).

14 A prosecution for rape must take place in which court?

15 An appeal from the Sheriff Solemn Court lies to:

(a) the Sheriff Principal;
(b) the Inner House;
(c) the Scottish Court of Criminal Appeal;
(d) the House of Lords.

16 The maximum custodial sentence which may be imposed by the Sheriff Solemn Court is:

(a) 6 months;
(b) 2 years;
(c) 3 years;
(d) 5 years.

17 How many persons serve on a criminal jury in Scotland?

18 Summary trials never involve a jury; true or false?

19 Solemn trials always involve a jury; true or false?

20 Trials before the High Court of Justiciary are always heard in Edinburgh; true or false?

21 Criminal appeals are always heard in Edinburgh; true or false?

22 The Procurator Fiscal is:

(a) a criminal prosecutor;
(b) a clerk in the High Court of Justiciary;
(c) a senior police officer;
(d) a judge in the District Court.

23 In which court would the following be found on the bench:

(a) a Stipendiary Magistrate;
(b) the Lord President;
(c) a single Lord Ordinary;
(d) a single Lord Commissioner of Justiciary;
(e) a Justice of the Peace?

24 State whether the following matters would be heard in the first instance by a court or by an administrative tribunal:

(a) A seeking a judicial separation from Mrs A;
(b) X claiming unfair dismissal by Y Ltd;
(c) D appealing a decision of the Inspector of Taxes;
(d) Mrs J seeking interim aliment from Mr J;
(e) Bert suing Bill for the repayment of a loan.

25 List the advantages of going to arbitration rather than going to court.

26 On what grounds may an arbiter's decision be set aside by a court?

27 Who is the person ultimately responsible for criminal prosecution in Scotland?

28 Who is Scotland's most senior judge and what qualifications are necessary to become a Senator of the College of Justice?

Part 2
THE SCOTS LAW OF CONTRACT

3 The nature and formation of a contract

THE NATURE OF CONTRACTUAL OBLIGATIONS

Introductory overview

When someone is asked whether they have entered a contract that day the answer is almost always 'no' They are generally surprised when assured that if they have bought a newspaper or something to eat, or have travelled by bus that day then they have indeed entered a contract. It is a common misconception that in order to have a contract there must be something in writing which is signed before witnesses. Admittedly, certain types of contract do require such formalities in order to be valid and binding, but the vast majority of contracts do not.

So – what is a contract? A contract might be described as a type of agreement but that is not specific enough. All contracts are agreements but not all agreements are contracts. What is the difference then between a mere agreement and a contract? *A contract is an agreement which the law will enforce.* A contract is an agreement which gives rise to obligations which the courts will enforce. If one of the parties to a contract does not perform his side of the bargain, then the courts will provide a remedy to the injured party. In such a 'breach of contract' situation this remedy may even extend to ordering the party in breach to do what he agreed to do. However, even if the courts do not order actual performance of a contractual obligation, the injured party generally will receive monetary compensation called 'damages'.

Thus a contract is a legally binding agreement. Central to the idea of contract are the notions of **agreement** and **obligation**. In fact, the law of contract forms part of the wider law of obligations which also includes the law of delict. In contract the obligations are undertaken voluntarily – it is up to individuals to decide whether they contract or not and on what terms. However, in delict the obligations are imposed by law – in certain situations we are under an obligation to take care not to do harm and if we fail in that duty, the law will impose a penalty; for example, all road users owe a duty to other road users to drive with due care. If a person drives negligently and as a result someone is injured, the victim may sue for damages under the law of delict.

If a student is to undertake a study of the law of contract, a more elaborate definition may prove helpful. Professor A. D. Gibb's definition is that 'a contract is an agreement between parties having the capacity to make it, in the form demanded by the law, to perform, on one side or both, acts which are not trifling, indeterminate, impossible or illegal, creating an obligation enforceable in a court of law.'

Certain essential features of a valid contract may be identified:

1 There must be full agreement on all material aspects – this is known as **consensus in idem**.
2 The parties to the contract must **consent** to contract – i.e., they have the intention to be legally bound.
3 The parties must have the **capacity** to enter contracts.
4 The contract must conform with any requirements as to **formality** – if such requirements apply.
5 The agreement must **not be prohibited by law** .

A study of the law of contract will therefore look at the following:

(a) Professor Gibb's definition and the above list of essential features in order to see how a contract is formed.
(b) The factors which might prevent a valid contract being formed at all, or which might allow a flawed contract to be set aside. For example, the presence of an **error** preventing true consent or consensus; or a lack of required formalities or a lack of capacity; or impossibility or illegality at the outset; or consent to contract being obtained by force or fear.
(c) The remedies for a breach of a valid contract.
(d) The ways in which contractual obligations are brought to an end – i.e., termination of contract.

However, before proceeding further it is helpful to present an initial overview of the essential features.

Consensus in idem

This is a concept which arises repeatedly in the study of contract. Literally it means agreement about the same thing. This state is essential to the creation of a valid contract and can be achieved only if the parties to the contract are in full agreement about all the important aspects of the contract.

When a contract is being formed there must be acceptance of an offer. There can be no *consensus in idem* until the offer and acceptance 'match'. For example, if A offers to sell his car to B for £500 and B agrees to buy A's car for £500, then there is *consensus in idem* and a contract. However, if A offers to sell B his car for £500 and B says that he wants to buy A's car but wants to pay only £450 for it, then there is no *consensus in idem* because the parties are not in full agreement – and there is no contract.

Also it might be that there is no *consensus in idem* because of some misunderstanding. For example, if A offers to sell B his car for £5000 and B accepts, there may appear to be a contract. However, A is intending to sell his four-year-old Mini and B, who does not know that A has a Mini, thinks that A is offering to sell A's other car – a one-year-old Jaguar. In such a situation, there is no true *consensus in idem* – the parties may think that they have agreed but the misunderstanding to this degree undermines *consensus in idem* and there is no contract.

Consent

The parties to a contract must consent to contract with one another. There must be the intention to **be legally bound**. Such consent must be full, free and voluntary. 'Gun to the head' consent will not count. In **Earl of Orkney *v* Vinfra (1606) Mor. 16,481** the Earl brought a court action for payment of money. Vinfra claimed that he had signed a document requiring him to make payment only because he was in fear of his life. The Earl with hand on dagger had threatened to stab Vinfra through the head if he did not sign. It was held that as Vinfra's signature had been obtained through force and fear there was no true consent and accordingly no valid contract.

This intention to be legally bound may be presumed to be either present or absent depending upon the type of transaction involved. Should you agree to go to a friend's house for dinner your friend may go to great trouble and expense to provide food for the meal. Should you fail to turn up all this expensive food may go to waste. Can your friend sue you for damages to compensate for his wasted time and money? The answer is 'no'. In order to be entitled to damages, your friend must show that you had a legal obligation to go to dinner. In such a situation as this there is no legal obligation; there is no contract because in accepting the invitation the necessary intention to be legally bound is not present.

Where persons are involved in business or commercial transactions it is presumed that they intend to create legally binding obligations whereas in social or domestic situations there is a presumption that no intention to enter a contract is present. However, in both cases there will be exceptions to the general rule.

Capacity to contract

If someone has capacity to contract, it means that the law recognises that person's ability to undertake legally binding obligations. Most human beings – known as *natural legal persons* – can make valid contracts. Some groups have limited capacity or no capacity at all; for example, children under 16 and the insane have no capacity to contract and special rules apply to young persons aged 16 and 17. There are also limitations placed on the contractual capacity of artificial legal persons such as local authorities or registered companies.

Formality

Most contracts do not have to be in writing nor do they require to be witnessed. However, some types of contract, such as a deed for the sale of land, do require to be constituted in a written document.

Not prohibited by law

An agreement which is illegal is not a contract. *Pacta illicita* are agreements prohibited by law, and as such will not be enforced by the courts. Where an agreement is already illegal when the parties attempt to form a contract, no contract comes into existence. Where a change in the law after the contract is formed renders a previously valid contract unlawful, the contract is brought to an end. The contract is said to be 'terminated by frustration'.

Not trifling, indeterminate or impossible

A contract is an agreement which the courts will enforce. In order that an agreement is enforceable as a contract, the agreement must not be trifling. The parties must have a 'patrimonial interest' – i.e., the parties must be able to show that they would suffer some material injury, measurable in monetary terms, as a consequence of a refusal to carry out the agreement.

Furthermore, an agreement cannot be a contract if its terms are too vague or 'indeterminate'. A court cannot enforce an agreement which is indefinite. In **McArthur** *v* **Lawson (1877) 4 R 1134** it was said that the test to decide whether an agreement was too indeterminate to be enforced was whether the court could, with certainty, give specific instructions as to what had to be done to perform the contract.

In this case the pursuer had entered into a contract of employment with the defender. The defender had sent the pursuer a letter specifying the nature of the pursuer's duties and the salary payable and stating that the period of employment would be two years. The letter then went on to say that at the end of two years, the pursuer would be given 'a substantial interest by way of partnership' in the defender's business. The letter stated that as a result, the pursuer's annual income would be 'considerably increased'.

When, at the end of two years, the pursuer was not made a partner, he brought an action for damages against the defender. His action failed. While the terms of the contract of employment were all completely specified, the rest of the letter was vague and indefinite and could not be enforced as a contract.

Where, at the time the contract is formed, it is already impossible to perform one's obligations under the contract, no valid contract comes into existence. Where performance of one's obligations becomes impossible, after formation but before performance is due, the contract may be brought to an end. Where impossibility of performance is caused by changed circumstances which are not the fault of either party, the contract is said to be terminated by frustration and both parties are freed from their obligations under the contract.

Flawed contracts

It may be that an attempt to form a valid and binding contract is undermined by some factor such as a misunderstanding or a lack of formality or capacity. As a result of such a flaw a contract may be **void** or **voidable**:

Void – although people do talk about 'void contracts', this is misleading because a void contract is no contract. If a contract is flawed to such a serious degree as to be void, no contract ever comes into existence. There is not and there has never been a contract. Neither party acquires any rights and neither party is under any obligation as a consequence.

Voidable – where a contract is formed which is flawed to a less serious degree, the result may be a 'voidable contract'. A voidable contract is one which is regarded as initially valid and binding and which gives rise to rights and obligations. However, a party to a voidable contract may rely upon the flaw as grounds for going to court and, by means of an action of reduction, asking the court to have the contract set aside. However, if neither party takes such action the contract persists as a valid contract.

A contract which is neither void nor voidable may nonetheless be **unenforceable**. For some reason the court cannot enforce the contract.

Sponsiones ludicrae, which include wagers and other gambling transactions, are regarded as unenforceable contracts. Such agreements are unenforceable because it is regarded as being beneath the dignity of the court to deal with them. Although it has been held that a stakeholder has a legal obligation to pay monies held to the winner of a bet, (**Calder *v* Stevens (1872) 9 M 1074**), there is authority, in **Kelly *v* Murphy 1940 SC 96**, to the effect that the promoter of a football pool is not a stakeholder. The *Kelly* case also held that an individual who claimed to have won a football pool was not entitled to the assistance of the court to enforce his claim against the promoter. This accepted view has been confirmed most recently by the Outer House in the case of **Ferguson *v* Littlewoods Pools Ltd 1996 GWD 21-1183**. In this case a syndicate sued Littlewoods for £2.5 million having completed a winning coupon which had not been forwarded to the company by a dishonest pools agent who had been stealing the stake money. Lord Coulsfield dismissed their action as a *sponsio ludicra*, the syndicate had been staking money on the chance accuracy of football forecasts. He took the view that in the light of the established case law, the matter would require examination by a larger court or by Parliament.

PROMISE – UNILATERAL OBLIGATIONS

In attempting to define a contract, we saw that central to the idea of a contract were the notions of agreement and obligation. It was stated that a contract is an agreement which creates legally binding obligations. The voluntary agreement between two or more parties produces obligations on both sides – i.e., bilateral obligations.

If we look at common instances of contracts such as a contract of employment or a contract for the purchase of a car, these may be identified as **bilateral contracts**; both parties to the contract have enforceable rights under the contract and each of the parties is under an obligation. For example, under a contract of employment the employer has the right to expect that the employee will work but he is under an obligation to pay wages for that work. Similarly, the employee has the right to be paid by the employer but is under an obligation to work for those wages. The buyer of a car expects that ownership of the car shall be transferred to him but he is under a corresponding obligation to pay the purchase price. The seller of the car has the right to expect payment but in order to be entitled to payment he must fulfil his obligation to transfer the ownership of the car to the buyer. It is clear then that both parties are subject to an obligation. Contract therefore involves a reciprocity of obligations created by the agreement of both parties to the contract and formed by the acceptance of an offer.

However, a feature of Scots law, unlike English law, is that it also recognises, as legally enforceable, **unilateral obligations** as well as binding bilateral obligations. A unilateral obligation involves one party undertaking to do something for a second party with no compensating obligation in return. X promises to do something for Y but Y need do nothing for X. Under Scots law that promise binds X, it being sufficient that X is judged as having consented to undertake an obligation. The person benefiting from the promise may sue to enforce the promise but the person making the promise cannot sue the beneficiary to force him to accept the kindness. A unilateral obligation is also known as a 'gratuitous promise'.

Examples of unilateral obligations include the promise of a gift or of a donation to charity; an undertaking to keep an offer open for a stated period of time; or the promise of a reward for information or for the return of lost property. Suppose Jim is wanting to sell his motorbike and Dave is interested in buying it. Jim may offer to sell the bike to Dave for £1800 which is at least £500 less than the usual second-hand price for such a bike. Dave cannot make up his mind and Jim says that he undertakes not to withdraw the offer to sell until noon on Tuesday in order to give Dave time to think about it. On Monday afternoon Dave returns to say that he is accepting Jim's offer and will buy the bike. Jim says that he sold the bike to someone else that morning. What is the legal position? Jim's statement that he would not withdraw the offer was a gratuitous promise. Jim was under an obligation not to withdraw the offer but Dave did not have to do anything in return. Jim's promise was binding under Scots law. Dave cannot demand that he be allowed to buy the motorbike but he is entitled to seek damages to compensate for any loss caused by Jim's failure to honour his obligation. In this case, if Dave cannot buy a comparable bike for £1800 he may be able to sue Jim for the difference between £1800 and the higher price he has to pay elsewhere. Authority for the binding nature of such undertakings is to be found in **Littlejohn *v* Hadwen (1882) 20 SLR 5 (OH)** and **A & G Paterson *v* Highland Railway Co. 1927 SC(HL) 32**. In the *A & G Paterson* case Viscount Dunedin stated at p. 38 that '... if I offer my property to a certain person at a certain price, and go on to say: "This offer is to be open up to a certain date," I cannot withdraw that offer before that date, if the person to whom I have made the offer chooses to accept it ...'.

A feature of such binding promises is that the promise does not have to be accepted to make it binding. Outright rejection of the promise removes the obligation but otherwise a promise once communicated cannot be withdrawn; it is said to be irrevocable.

The intention to be legally bound must be present for there to be an enforceable obligation, and a binding promise must be distinguished from statements of possible intention or hope or expectation. Similarly, to be effective the promise must be communicated to the intended beneficiary. Until it is so communicated the promise has no legal effect. A beneficiary cannot seek to enforce the terms of a promise which he found out about accidentally.

A gratuitous promise may be conditional; for example, the offer of a reward for the return of lost property. The payment of the reward is conditional upon the return of the missing item. In this situation the promise of a reward may be communicated to the general public by way of an advertisement. Anyone who sees the advertisement and returns the property is entitled to claim payment of the reward. However, if someone returns property in ignorance of the promise of the reward, they are not legally entitled to payment. This is because of the absence of communication of the promise.

A feature of a gratuitous promise is that only one person, the promisor, is under any legal obligation. The beneficiary of the promise can sue the promisor but the promisor cannot sue the promisee. However, it is technically possible to create a *gratuitous bilateral contract*. This occurs where the promise has been accepted and the product of the agreement of both parties is a contract. The consequence is that as well as the beneficiary of the promise being entitled to sue to enforce its terms, the promisor can also sue to force the promisee to accept his kindness.

At common law such a promise did not have to be made in writing – it could be validly constituted verbally. However should a dispute have arisen, the court would enforce the promise only if a special type of proof, 'proof by writ or oath' was available. Proof by writ required the production of something in writing by the person supposed to have made the promise. Proof by oath required the admission under oath of the alleged promisor that the promise had in fact been made.

However, now in terms of the Requirements of Writing (Scotland) Act 1995 s 1, a gratuitous unilateral obligation has to be in writing signed by the promisor in order to be validly constituted. One exception is that a gratuitous promise made in the course of a business can be consituted verbally. Proof by writ or oath has been abolished.

Nevertheless, a unilateral promise which should have been signed can still be enforced despite the lack of a signature, where 'significant actings' have followed. The promisee must show that he acted on the strength of the promise, that the promisor knew of his actions, that his actions were material (ie significant, not trivial) and that he will be prejudiced if the promise is not enforced because of the lack of the promisor's signature. Under the new law, **Smith *v* Oliver 1911 SC 103** would now be decided differently. Mrs Smith had promised verbally to pay for repairs to a Church but had died before they were complete. Her executors refused to pay. At common law the Church was unsuccessful because of the lack of proof by writ or oath (there was nothing written by Mrs Oliver and she could not admit to the promise because she was dead). However, under the 1995 Act the Church could claim that going ahead with the repairs on the strength of the verbal promise amounted to 'significant actings'. On this basis the Church would now be successful.

QUESTIONS

1 Tim wants to sell his car and Fred is interested in buying it. Tim's asking price 'for a quick sale' is £2000 which is at least £500 less than the usual second-hand price for such a car. Fred cannot make up his mind and Tim says that he undertakes not to sell the car to anyone else until noon on Tuesday to give Fred time to think about it. On Monday afternoon when Fred returns to say that he is going to buy the car, Tim tells Fred that he sold the car to someone else that morning. Advise Fred as to his legal position and discuss whether your advice would differ if Tim was a garage owner selling the car in the course of his business.

2 George, a wealthy local businessman, is concerned about the state of the scout hut. Its condition is so bad that it can no longer be used. George tells the Scoutmaster to have the repairs carried out and that he, George, shall meet the bill.

Later, as an afterthought, George writes to the Scoutmaster to say that he can order new camping equipment which George shall pay for.

The equipment has been delivered and the repairs are almost complete when George is killed in a car crash. His executors are refusing to meet the bills.

With full reference to authority, advise the Scoutmaster.

FORMATION OF A CONTRACT – OFFER AND ACCEPTANCE

Contract, unlike promise, involves bilateral obligations. Under a bilateral contract there are rights and obligations on both sides. There is a two-way flow of rights and obligations. An example of a bilateral contract is a contract of employment – the employer is under an obligation to pay wages but has the right to expect work in return and the employee is under an obligation to work but has the right to expect wages in return.

A contract is made up of an **offer** and an **acceptance** – without both there is no contract. Before there may be a contract the offer and acceptance must achieve the full agreement known as *consensus in idem*. Accordingly, a contract is formed when a definite offer is met by an unqualified acceptance, thus achieving consensus. Remember, OFFER + ACCEPTANCE = CONTRACT – and offer and acceptance must 'match'. For example, A offers to sell his car to B for £2000. B agrees to buy A's car for £2000. The offer and acceptance match – there is *consensus in idem* and a contract is formed. However, what if A offers to sell his car to B for £2000 and B says he wishes to buy the car but will pay only £1500 for it? The offer and acceptance do not match – there is no *consensus in idem* and no contract is formed. Neither A nor B are subject to any legally binding obligations.

In order to create a contract in the second situation, A would have to accept B's offer of only £1500 for the car. In the eyes of the law what happens is that the original offer by A disappears in the face of the qualified acceptance by B. B's statement is seen as a **counter-offer** – i.e., a new offer which A must in turn accept if there is to be a contract. Only if A agrees to accept £1500 will *consensus in idem* be achieved and a contract formed. It should be noted that if A rejects B's counter-offer to buy the car at £1500 that is an end to the matter. B cannot go back and attempt to 'accept' A's original offer to sell. A counter-offer kills off the original offer.

Before proceeding to look at offer and acceptance in more detail it should be pointed out that both offer and acceptance may be either **express** or **implied**. If an offer or acceptance is express this means that it is clearly set out either verbally or in writing. An offer or acceptance is said to be implied where either is assumed to exist from the way people act in certain circumstances. For example, when you go into a large department store to buy a shirt, you may select a shirt from a display counter and proceed to the cash desk where you place the shirt and the correct money on the counter. The cashier then rings the amount up on the till, takes your money, places the shirt and a receipt in a bag and hands it over to you. All this may take place without a single word being spoken. Nevertheless, a valid and binding contract is formed. The existence of an offer is implied by your actions and the existence of an acceptance is implied by the behaviour of the cashier. Similarly, at an auction sale offers to buy goods may be made by signalling bids to the auctioneer. The fall of the auctioneer's hammer constitutes acceptance. Again, a contract is formed though no words have been spoken; offer and acceptance are assumed to exist as a consequence of the actions of the parties in a given situation.

FEATURES OF OFFERS

An offer must be definite, capable of being accepted and the person making the offer must intend to be bound by the consequences of it being accepted. It should be pointed out that the intention of contracting parties when reaching agreement is judged by an objective standard – i.e., it is what the person appears to intend which counts rather than any secret intention. Intention is evidenced by outward appearances, not by innermost thoughts.

Sometimes it may be difficult to identify whether a communication is an offer or something else, such as an indication of a willingness to consider offers or a statement given in response to a request for information.

In **Philp & Co** *v* **Knoblauch 1907 SC 994** K wrote to P & Co in the following terms, 'I am offering today plate linseed for January/February shipment to Leith, and have pleasure in quoting you 100 tons at 41/3, usual plate terms. I shall be glad to hear if you are buyers, and await your esteemed reply.' The next day P & Co replied by telegram as follows: 'Accept hundred January/February plate 41/3 Leith, per steamer Leith'. The telegram was followed by P & Co's written confirmation of acceptance. P & Co argued that this amounted to offer and acceptance resulting in a binding contract. K tried to argue that his letter was not an offer but merely a quotation of prices.

The court held that K's letter was an offer and that the contract was concluded by the telegram from P & Co. Lord Ardwell stated (at p. 998) that K's letter was '... an absolutely definite offer of a specific quantity at a specific price.' His Lordship continued, '... "I shall be glad to hear if you are buyers" ... does not mean buyers in general, but buyers of the quantity specified at the price quoted, otherwise there would be no meaning in the phrase which follows, "and await your esteemed reply." This offer was accepted by telegram ... sent before the offer was recalled, and the letter and the telegram constitute, in my opinion, a concluded contract ...'.

In **Harvey** *v* **Facey [1893] AC 552** H sent a telegram to F which asked whether F would consider selling to H a property in Jamaica and further asked F to 'telegraph lowest cash price'. F replied 'Lowest cash price for Bumper Hall Pen £900'. H then sent a telegram which said 'We agree to buy Bumper Hall Pen for the sum of £900 asked by you'.

It was held by the Privy Council that this did not consitute a contract. The first telegram from H was a request for information. The reply from F was no more than an indication of the lowest price at which he would consider selling the property, it was not an offer to sell at that price. Accordingly, H's second telegram could not be an acceptance but was in fact itself an offer to buy the property at a price of £900.

The difference between an offer and an invitation to treat

It is important to make the distinction between an offer and an **invitation to treat**. An offer, if accepted, leads to the creation of a contract. An invitation to treat cannot be accepted so as to form a contract. It is an indication of willingness to trade or to enter into negotiations. An invitation to treat is really saying, 'make me an offer' or 'I am willing to consider offers'.

Examples of invitations to treat include the placing of goods in shop windows or on supermarket shelves. The shopkeeper does not offer to sell the goods on display, the customer must offer to buy. The shopkeeper may accept or reject that offer. Similarly, the sending out of catalogues and price lists will constitute invitations to treat. It is also a general rule that adverts are invitations to treat rather than offers. Accordingly, if when walking down Sauchiehall Street you see a shop with a colour TV in the window with a price tag stating that the TV costs £35 instead of £350, can you rush in, put down your money and demand that they hand over the television? Does the shopkeeper's action in putting the TV in the window with the wrong price tag constitute a legal offer to sell that television at that price? The answer is 'no' – it is merely an invitation to treat. You must go in and offer to buy the television and it is then up to the shopkeeper to decide whether or not to sell. It is unlikely that you will get the television for £35. It may well be that a complaint to the local trading standards officer might lead to the shopkeeper facing a criminal prosecution under legislation dealing with misleading price indications. However, that is a different matter altogether from the question of whether or not a contract exists to sell the TV at £35.

The following case established that placing goods on display in shops does not constitute an offer to sell those goods. In **Pharmaceutical Society of Great Britain** *v* **Boots Cash Chemists (Southern) Ltd [1952] 2 QB 795** problems arose when Boots went over to self-service shops. By law the sale of certain medicines had to be supervised by a registered pharmacist. If customers were serving themselves, did this mean that the sale was unsupervised? The sale of these medicines was a contract – thus the court had to decide at what point in time the contract was formed. To do this the court had to isolate the two component parts of the contract – i.e., offer and acceptance.

What constituted the offer? Was it placing the goods on the shelf? If so the customer's actions in picking up the medicine and putting it in her basket would be an acceptance and the contract would be formed there and then without any pharmacist being present. In such an event, Boots would be committing an offence. However, if placing the goods on the shelf merely constituted an invitation to treat, then the customer would be offering to buy the medicine at the checkout. The assistant would only then accept the offer and form a contract. Evidence was led that there was always a registered pharmacist in attendance at the checkout. On this analysis Boots would comply with the legislation.

The court took the view that the latter analysis was correct; goods placed on shop shelves constituted merely an invitation to treat – i.e., there was no contract until the customer's offer was accepted at the checkout.

Tenders

If you wish a wall or a garage built you may decide to seek various estimates or tenders from different builders before deciding to go ahead. In asking a builder to give you an estimate – known as a solicited tender – you are not offering to allow the builder to do the work at the tender price. You are merely inviting an offer which you will consider and which you may or may not accept. However, if you do accept the builder's tender, a contract is formed and the builder is legally bound to complete the specified work at the price quoted.

Special cases

There are some situations where it may be difficult to determine what constitutes the offer. In general, offers are addressed to a specific individual. However, an offer may be made to the general public and any individual's actions in response to the offer convert the general offer into an offer personal to him. The siting of vending machines would constitute an offer to provide a drink or cigarettes or a bar of chocolate to any individual who accepted the offer by putting money in the slot. Self-service petrol pumps in a petrol station constitute a general offer to sell petrol which is accepted by an individual filling his tank. Newsvendors displaying their newspapers on street corners are said to be making an offer to the general public which a particular individual may accept by putting down money and picking up a newspaper. In **Thornton** *v* **Shoe Lane Parking [1971] 2 QB 163** it was held that where entry to a car park is gained by taking a ticket from a machine which causes an automatic barrier to rise, the placing of the machine at the entrance constitutes the offer which is accepted by taking a ticket. The contract is formed at the moment the ticket is taken from the machine.

Adverts as offers

The general rule is that adverts are not offers but are invitations to treat. This makes sense. A shop may advertise suites of furniture for sale at 50 per cent off the normal price. The shop may have only five such suites available but if the advert constituted an offer the shop would be bound to provide such furniture to anyone who accepted. Imagine the chaos if one hundred people arrived at the shop claiming to accept the offer and demanding the furniture. As the advert is regarded as an invitation to treat, any prospective customer must offer to buy the furniture at the sale price and the shop is at liberty to refuse such offers.

Exceptionally, however, an advert may be held to constitute an offer depending on its terms. Where the wording of the advert displays an intention to be bound in contract to anyone who complies with any conditions set out in the advert, the advert will be regarded as an offer to contract. The concept can be best explained by reference to case law.

In **Hunter** *v* **General Accident Fire and Life Assurance Corporation Ltd 1909 SC 344, 1909 SC(HL) 30** an insurance company advertised in a diary that they would pay £1000 to the executor of any diary owner who had been registered at their head office and who was subsequently killed in a railway crash. Mr Hunter sent off the coupon from the diary to the insurance company and his registration was acknowledged. Some time later Mr Hunter was fatally injured in a railway crash. His wife's claim was rejected by the insurance company. The company argued that the advert was not an offer in law but merely an invitation to treat. It was held that the wording of the advert was such that Mr Hunter's actions in response to the advert had turned it into an offer to him as an individual. Mr Hunter's actions constituted an acceptance. Mrs Hunter was held entitled to the £1000. In the Court of Session Lord Kinnear stated that '[t]here may of course be a question whether a public announcement of this kind is in fact an offer, or whether it is a mere advertisement of a desire on the part of the advertiser to do business in a certain way. In the latter case it is not an offer; but if it contains a definite offer undertaking to pay money upon perfectly distinct specified conditions, then it is an offer, and when anyone into whose hands it has come, accepts the terms and performs the conditions, there is to my mind a perfectly valid contract.'

Of course under Scots law a contractual analysis in terms of offer and acceptance is not necessary in such a situation because, as we have already seen, Scots law recognises binding gratuitous promises. The insurance company's undertaking could have been enforced as a gratuitous promise. However, there is a tendency on the part of the Scottish courts to favour an offer and acceptance approach, partly because of the influence of English decisions such as the famous case of **Carlill** *v* **Carbolic Smokeball Company [1893] 1 QB 256**. Mrs Carlill saw an advert in a newspaper which stated that the manufacturers of the carbolic smokeball were so confident of its properties that they would pay £100 to anyone who bought a smokeball, used it according to instructions and who still got flu. In response to the advert Mrs Carlill bought a smokeball and used it to the letter of the instructions. Nevertheless, she caught flu. The company, however, refused to pay the £100 claiming that the advert was not an offer. It was held that the wording of the advert was such that it amounted to an offer which Mrs Carlill accepted by performing the actions demanded by the advert. Mrs Carlill was held entitled to the money.

The *Carlill* case also illustrates that there can be implied acceptance of an offer. In the *Hunter* case, the insurance company had known of Mr Hunter's acceptance because he had to register with the company. Mrs Carlill's acceptance was constituted by her actions in buying and using the smokeball. The manufacturers did not know of her acceptance until some time later when she lodged her claim.

The *Carlill* case further emphasises the necessity of communication of the offer. Had Mrs Carlill merely chanced to buy a smokeball without having seen the advert, she would not have been entitled to the £100. Her actions constituted implied acceptance of the offer only because they were in response to the offer.

To recap then, an offer is normally addressed to specific individuals and only those individuals are entitled to accept the offer. In addition, however, certain offers may be made to a particular category of persons, or to the world at large or to anyone satisfying conditions specified in the offer. This is made clear by Lord Kinnear's words in the *Hunter* case when he said, 'When a general offer addressed to the public is appropriated to himself by a distinct acceptance by one person, then it is read in exactly the same way as if it had been addressed to that individual originally.'

An offer can be accepted only by a person to whom the offer has been communicated. In **Thomson *v* James (1855) 18 D 1** at p.10 Lord President McNeill stated, 'An offer is nothing until it is communicated to the party to whom it is made.' An individual cannot attempt to accept an offer which he has found out about accidentally.

When does an offer lapse?

Once an offer is accepted a binding contract is formed. However, as a general rule an offer may be withdrawn by the offeror at any time until the offer is accepted. This right to withdraw an offer is known as *locus poenitentiae*. An exception to this is where the offeror has also promised not to withdraw his offer for a stated period of time. As was previously stated, such an undertaking is binding under Scots law.

Apart from this one exception the offeror is free to withdraw or revoke his offer at any time until acceptance. What if the offeror does not withdraw his offer but hears nothing from the offeree? If A today offers to sell his car to B for £800 and B does not respond right away, can B come back a year from now and purport to accept A's offer and demand delivery of the car? The answer is 'no'. An offer if not previously expressly withdrawn will eventually automatically lapse. Offers, if you like, have a limited shelf life.

Revocation of an offer

Revocation of an offer may be express or implied. Express revocation occurs when the offeror communicates to the offeree that the offer has been withdrawn. In certain circumstances there will be implied revocation – i.e., the offer automatically lapses without any need for communication of that fact to the offeree.

Implied revocation of the offer will occur:

1 if the offer is rejected;
2 if there is a counter-offer;
3 if either party dies or becomes insane *before* acceptance;
4 if a time limit for acceptance has been set and the time limit expires without acceptance;
5 if no time limit for acceptance has been set but the offer is not accepted within a reasonable time.

Certain of these require further explanation:

The effect of a counter-offer – A qualified acceptance which contains additional or contradictory conditions is regarded as a counter-offer. A counter-offer kills off the original offer. The effect is that the original offer disappears and is no longer capable of acceptance. In the comparatively recent Scottish case of **Wolf & Wolf *v* Forfar Potato Co Ltd 1984 SLT 100** a Scottish company sent a telex to a Dutch company offering for sale a quantity of potatoes. It was a condition of the offer that it had to be accepted by 5 pm the next day. The next morning the Dutch company sent a telex which purported to be an acceptance of the offer but which contained new conditions. The Scottish company advised by telephone that these conditions were unacceptable and the Dutch company sent another telex, still within the time limit, which 'accepted' the original offer. The Scottish company ignored the second telex and the Dutch company raised an action for damages for breach of contract. The court held that no contract had been formed. The first telex was a counter-offer which had the effect of causing the original offer to disappear. Accordingly, when the second 'acceptance' was sent there was nothing left to accept.

No acceptance within a reasonable time – An offer is presumed to lapse if it is not accepted within a reasonable time. What constitutes a reasonable time will be a matter of fact in each particular case. In respect of business offers, trade practice may be relevant. Where the offer is to sell goods which are perishable or which are known to have a fluctuating value, acceptance should be immediate otherwise the offer will be presumed to have lapsed. In **Wylie and Lochhead *v* McElroy and Sons (1873) 1 R 41** an offer to carry out iron work on a new building was not 'accepted' for five weeks during which time the price of iron increased. It was held that as there had been no acceptance within a reasonable time the offer had lapsed and no contract was formed. It was stated in the judgement that where such a fluctuating commodity as iron was concerned 'hours must suffice for a decision, not weeks or months'.

In **Glasgow Steam Shipping Company *v* Watson (1873) 1 R 189** there was an offer on 5 August to sell a year's supply of coal at 7 shillings per ton. The offer was purported to be accepted on 13 October by which time the price of coal had risen by 2 shillings per ton. It was held that there was no contract. In his judgement Lord Deas stated (at p. 195) that 'as regards such an offer as this, to supply an article which at all times fluctuates in price, it is altogether out of the question to hold it to have been a continuing offer for so long a period ...'.

Does a change in circumstances *before* acceptance cause implied revocation of an offer?

Should you offer to buy goods which are subsequently damaged, would the seller, in the knowledge that such damage has occurred, still be entitled to proceed to accept your offer? In the absence of specific authority, the law on this point is uncertain but it is arguable that it *is probably* the case that an offer will automatically lapse where such a material change in circumstances occurs. The Scottish Law Commission suggest in their 1992 Consultation Paper on Formation of Contract that the matter should be clarified by legislation to the effect that an offer is not to be terminated automatically by a change in circumstances but should be interpreted as being subject to an implied condition that it is to terminate in certain circumstances.

FEATURES OF ACCEPTANCE

A contract is formed when an offer is accepted. In order to create a contract the acceptance must 'meet' the offer; it must be unqualified, it must achieve *consensus in idem*. The acceptance must not contradict the terms of the offer nor should it introduce any new conditions. A qualified acceptance will not bind the offeror and form a contract.

As a general rule, the acceptance will take effect only when communicated to the offeror. However, there are exceptions to this. The terms of the offer may allow for implied acceptance through actions such as in the *Carlill* case. Where offer and acceptance are sent by post, the acceptance is deemed to be effective at the time it is posted rather than at the time it reaches the offeror.

Only the person to whom the offer is addressed may accept an offer, though as we have seen, an offer may be addressed to the world at large. The acceptance must comply with any requirements of the offer as to mode of acceptance; for example, the offer may specify that the acceptance should be in writing or sent by telex. Where no particular mode of acceptance is specified in the offer, as a general rule the acceptance should take the same form as the offer.

The offer cannot specify that silence shall be taken as acceptance. It is unacceptable that the offeree should have to go to the trouble of expressly refusing an offer. A cannot say to B that he offers to buy B's stereo for £100 and that if he does not hear from B by Saturday A will assume that there is a contract between them.

In terms of the Unsolicited Goods and Services Act 1971 as amended, where goods are sent which have not been ordered, such goods may be treated as a gift if they are not uplifted by the sender within a specified time. Moreover it is a criminal offence to demand payment for goods which are unsolicited.

It would seem that as an acceptance operates to form a contract, revocation of acceptance would be a practical impossibility. However, where a revocation of acceptance reaches the offeror before or at the same time as the acceptance, the revocation will prevent the acceptance becoming effective. For example, if the acceptance is being hand-delivered and the acceptor telephones the offeror to withdraw the acceptance before the messenger arrives, no contract will be formed.

CONTRACTS BY POST

Special rules apply to the formation of contracts by post.

General rule 1 – A contract is formed when the acceptance is *posted*, not when it arrives

Jacobsen, Sons & Co *v* **E Underwood and Son Ltd (1894) 21 R 654** illustrates rule

1. An offer to buy straw was subject to the condition that the offeree had to reply by Monday the 6th. The acceptance was posted on the 6th but did not reach the offeror, U, until the 7th. U took the view that the acceptance was late and that there was no contract. Accordingly, he refused to take delivery of the straw. J brought an action for damages for breach of contract.

It was held that a contract had been formed as the condition in the offer *had* been complied with. It was stated in the judgement that posting a letter of acceptance completes the contract and as the acceptance was posted on the 6th the contract was complete on the 6th as required by the offer. To avoid this, the offer should have said something like 'the acceptance to be in our hands by the 6th'. As it was, the general rule stood.

General rule 2 – Revocations must reach!

Thomson *v* **James 1855 18 D 1** illustrates rule 2. J offered by letter to buy land from T. T posted an acceptance on 1 December. Also on 1 December J posted a letter withdrawing his offer. The letters crossed in the post and each letter reached its destination on 2 December.

It was held that there was a contract. The acceptance was effective when it was posted; the revocation of offer could take effect only when it reached T. The revocation arrived after the acceptance was posted; one day too late.

Revocations

Revocation of offer

A revocation of an offer is effective only if it reaches the offeree *before* the acceptance is *posted*.

Revocation of acceptance

The only exception to general rule 1, a revocation of an acceptance is effective only if it reaches the offeror *before* or *at the same time* as the original letter of acceptance *reaches* the offeror.

Countess of Dunmore *v* **Alexander (1830) 9 S 190**. Although it is regarded as a controversial decision this case illustrates the rule that a revocation of acceptance is effective if it reaches the offeror before, or at the same time as, the original letter of acceptance. Lady Agnew's servant, Betty Alexander, was looking for a new job. The Countess heard about this and wrote to Lady Agnew asking for a reference and giving an indication of the wages offered. Lady Agnew replied recommending Betty and stating that Betty would work for those wages. This was viewed as an offer from Betty to the Countess. On 5 November the Countess posted an acceptance. She changed her mind, however, and on the following day posted another letter withdrawing her acceptance. Betty received the acceptance and the revocation of acceptance at the same moment. It was held that there was no contract.

Therefore in respect of revocation of acceptance only – it becomes a race between the original letter of acceptance and the letter withdrawing the acceptance. Otherwise the letter of acceptance is effective when posted and the contract is formed from that moment.

Examples of contracts by post

General rule 1

A posts offer	Monday
B receives offer	Tuesday
B posts acceptance	Wednesday → CONTRACT IS FORMED
A receives acceptance	Thursday

Revocation of offer

A posts offer	Monday
B receives offer	Tuesday
A posts revocation	Tuesday
B posts acceptance	Wednesday → CONTRACT IS FORMED
B receives revocation	Thursday
A receives acceptance	Thursday

The revocation of A's offer did not reach B until after B's acceptance had been posted. In the event that A's revocation of offer had reached B on Wednesday morning before B had posted his acceptance, no contract would have been formed.

Revocation of acceptance

A posts offer	Monday	
B receives offer	Tuesday	
B posts acceptance (2nd-class mail)	Tuesday	
B posts revocation (1st-class mail)	Wednesday	
A receives revocation	Thursday	
A receives acceptance	Friday	→ NO CONTRACT IS FORMED

The revocation of acceptance reached A before the original letter of acceptance reached A. Had both reached A at the same time, there would have been no contract. Had A received the acceptance on Thursday and the revocation of acceptance on Friday, a contract would have been formed.

Proposals to abolish the postal rule

In their Consultation Paper on Formation of Contract in September 1992, the Scottish Law Commission sought views on their proposed recommendation that Scots law should adopt, as part of its general law on the formation of contract, certain of the provisions contained in the United Nations Convention on Contracts for the International Sale of Goods (the Vienna Convention 1980). Such a step would lead to the abolition of the rule that a contract by post is formed when the letter of acceptance is posted. It is proposed that for all contracts, an acceptance of an offer should become effective at the moment the acceptance is communicated to the offerer. At the time of writing it remains to be seen whether the above will represent the final view of the Commission and if it does, whether the

Government will enact legislation to put the proposal into effect.

THE 'BATTLE OF THE FORMS'

It may be difficult to determine whether a contract has been formed where the parties each use their own pre-printed forms of standard conditions. Many businesses send orders on a standard form, on the back of which are printed their terms of business. Matters are complicated where the other party 'accepts' this order by using their own standard form of acceptance which contains contradictory conditions. It may even be that both standard forms contain a declaration that their terms are to prevail.

Notwithstanding this apparent conflict, the parties then proceed to perform the contract. The courts face a problem, should a dispute arise between the parties. Was there ever a valid contract in the first place? If there was a contract whose terms are to apply? It is arguable that when dealing with such problems the courts have stretched the offer and acceptance analysis of contract formation to the limit in order to achieve a satisfactory result – i.e., one which finds that a contract was formed. Usually the contract is governed by the terms of the party who 'fired the last shot' in the battle of the forms.

In the English case of **Butler Machine Tool Co *v* Ex-Cell-O Corpn [1979] 1 All ER 965** sellers of a machine sent their offer on a standard form containing conditions which included a clause allowing them to increase the price if costs rose before delivery. The buyers sent an acceptance using their own standard form which contained a different set of conditions. The buyers' form also incorporated a tear-off slip which declared that the sellers accepted the buyers' standard terms. The sellers signed and returned the tear-off slip together with a letter stating that delivery would be according to their original quotation. Problems arose when the sellers tried to increase the price in accordance with their price variation clause. It was held that a contract had been formed but on the buyers' terms. The buyers' standard form acceptance was to be regarded as a counter-offer. By returning the tear-off slip, the sellers were held to have accepted the terms contained in the counter-offer. The price variation clause did not form part of the contract.

In the Scottish case of **Uniroyal Ltd *v* Miller & Co Ltd 1985 SLT 101** a similar offer, counter-offer, acceptance approach was adopted. The buyers' offer was on a purchase order containing standard conditions. The sellers' acknowledgement using their own standard form was regarded as a counter-offer. The buyers' acceptance was implied as a consequence of taking delivery of the goods and the contract was held to be formed on the sellers' conditions.

QUESTIONS

1 In each of the following situations give your reasoned opinion as to whether there is a contract. Refer to case law in your answer.

(a) Tom sees a portable colour TV with a £50 price tag in the window of an electrical goods shop. He goes in and says that he will have it. The assistant states that the TV has been wrongly priced and that, if Tom wants it, he must pay £150.
(b) Jane writes to Sarah offering to sell her a car for £2000. Sarah writes back saying she wishes to buy the car but can afford only £1750. Jane replies that this is unacceptable. Sarah writes back to say that she will accept Jane's original offer and pay £2000. Jane says that she has decided to keep the car.
(c) The Bank of Falkirk has advertised that any student opening an account with them during the month of October will be given a free personal stereo. Dennis, a student, opens an account on 15 October but is told that the bank has run out of stereos and that these were being given away only while stocks lasted.

2 Angus would like to mark his 25th wedding anniversary by giving his wife a special gift. He asks a jeweller to give him a quote for making up a specially-designed gold and diamond ring. At the end of March the jeweller replies that the cost will be £500 and that the ring will take four weeks to make up. As his anniversary is still some time away, Angus does not reply accepting the quote and instructing the jeweller to proceed until mid-May. The jeweller tells Angus that if he wants the ring the price will now be £600 as the price of gold has gone up. Angus thinks that the jeweller must do the work at the original price. Advise Angus. Would your advice differ had Angus replied promptly?

3 Fred offered by letter to buy a consignment of eggs from Sam at a price of £1000. Sam posted his acceptance on 1 March. Also on 1 March Fred posted a letter withdrawing his offer. These letters crossed in the post and both arrived on 2 March. Fred refused to take delivery of the eggs claiming there was no contract. Sam has managed to sell the eggs elsewhere but for only £750. Advise Sam.

4 George advertises his Jaguar car for sale for £7000. Jean sees the advert and posts off a letter offering to buy the car for £6500. George gets Jean's letter on Monday and as there have been no other offers, he posts his acceptance by second-class mail on the same day. On his way back from the post office, George meets Eric who says he will pay George £7000 for the Jaguar. On Tuesday morning George posts another letter, this time by first-class mail, revoking his earlier acceptance. Jean receives both George's letters at the same time on Wednesday morning. Jean maintains that there is a contract and is demanding the Jaguar. What is the legal position?

CONTRACTUAL CAPACITY

An essential feature of a valid contract is that the parties to the contract have the necessary contractual capacity. An individual has contractual capacity if he is recognised by law as being capable of assuming legally binding obligations. Most natural legal persons – i.e., human beings – have full contractual capacity. Certain groups, however, have no capacity or have limitations placed upon their ability to make contracts (see below). Artificial legal persons – i.e., corporate bodies such as registered companies or local authorities – also have limitations placed upon the extent of their contractual capacity.

A study of contractual capacity is best approached by looking at those who cannot enter contracts at all and at those whose ability to enter contracts is limited.

Young persons under the age of majority

The age of majority in Scotland is 18. The law relating to the legal capacity of young persons under 18 has been radically altered by the Age of Legal Capacity (Scotland) Act 1991 which came into force on 25 September, 1991.

Prior to the coming into force of the 1991 Act, the capacity of those under 18 was determined according to whether they were pupils or minors. Pupils are girls under 12 and boys under 14 and they had no contractual capacity whatsoever. Any contract that a pupil attempted to make was void. Contracts were made on behalf of pupils by tutors who were generally the pupil's parents.

Minors are girls aged 12 and over but under 18 and boys aged 14 and over but under 18. At common law fairly complex rules applied in respect of their contractual capacity. However, the basic rule was that minors could contract but had to have the consent of their curator if they had one. Curators were generally the parents of the minor.

The 1991 Act replaces the previous two-tier system of capacity which distinguished between pupils and minors with a new system which distinguishes between children under 16 years of age and those aged 16 and over. It should be noted, however, that for purposes unconnected with the Act, the concepts of pupilarity and minority are retained. However, the terms tutor and curator have disappeared and have been replaced by the term 'guardian'.

Children under 16

The general rule, contained in s 1 of the 1991 Act, is that a child under 16 has no capacity to enter into any legal transaction. The words 'entering into a transaction' have a wider meaning than 'entering into a contract'. Section 9 of the Act defines a 'transaction' as also including making a will, bringing or defending a civil action, or making a gratuitous promise. Any transaction entered into by a child under 16 will be **void**. However, s 2 sets out certain exceptions to this general rule. A child under 16 may enter into a transaction so long as it satisfies each of two tests set out in the Act. The transaction must be:

1 of a kind commonly entered into by persons of his age and circumstances, and
2 on terms which are not unreasonable.

The wording of the section makes provision for 'everyday transactions' and also allows a child to enter into more sophisticated transactions as he grows older. An 8-year-old will commonly buy comics and sweets, a 10-year-old will commonly pay bus fares, a 15-year-old will commonly buy more expensive items such as concert tickets, clothes or stereo systems or may take a Saturday job. However, if there is any question of doubt as to the child's ability to enter into a transaction, a person should contract instead with the child's guardian.

Section 2 also provides that a child aged 12 or over may make a will and that children aged 12 or over must consent to their own adoption.

In addition the Act clarifies the law relating to a child's capacity to consent to medical treatment and other similar procedures including the donation of organs and blood. Basically anyone under 16 shall have legal capacity to consent on his own behalf to any such treatment when in the opinion of a qualified medical practitioner he is capable of understanding the nature and consequence of the procedure involved. The final decision on the level of the child's understanding rests with the doctor.

Young persons aged 16 and 17

In terms of s 1 of the 1991 Act, a person aged 16 or over shall have full legal capacity to enter into any transaction. However, in order to provide some protection for 16 and 17-year-olds, s 3 allows an application to be made to either the Court of Session or the Sheriff Court for a transaction to be set aside. The applicant must establish that it was a 'prejudicial transaction', i.e., a transaction which:

1 an adult, exercising reasonable prudence, would not have entered into had he been in the same situation as the young person at the time the transaction was entered into; and
2 has caused or is likely to cause substantial prejudice to the applicant.

Only the young person can be an applicant. The other party to the transaction cannot use this provision to terminate the transaction. An application must be made before the young person reaches the age of 21 and in addition certain transactions cannot be set aside at all. A young person cannot attempt to set aside a contract he has entered into in the course of his own business or which he ratified after reaching the age of 18. The court will not set aside a transaction which the other party entered into because of some misrepresentation by the young person, for example he may have pretended to be 18.

Businessmen may be unwilling to transact with 16 and 17-year-olds if they believe there is the possibility of the young person later challenging the transaction as prejudicial. Accordingly the parties to a **proposed** transaction may ask the Sheriff to ratify the transaction so rendering it unchallengeable at a later date. The Sheriff's decision on this is final.

The insane

As a general rule, those who are of unsound mind have no contractual capacity though it has been said that an insane person may contract during 'a lucid interval'. An insane person is incapable of giving the consent which is an essential feature of any valid contract. A contract entered into by an insane person is void – i.e., it has no legal effect. However, a person who has supplied necessaries to an insane person is entitled to be paid a reasonable price. In addition, a person – known as a *curator bonis* – may be appointed by the court to contract on behalf of a person who is insane.

A contract which is formed by a person who is already insane is void. In the case of **Loudon *v* Elder's Curator Bonis 1923 SLT 226**, the pursuers sought damages for breach of contract. Loudon & Co. were meat importers in Liverpool who had contracted to supply frozen meat to Elder who was a wholesale meat merchant in Dundee. Elder had entered into two such contracts with Loudon & Co. towards the end of March 1921. However, on 31 March 1921 Elder was certified insane and the contracts were cancelled. Thomas Hunter, who had been appointed as *curator bonis* to manage Elder's affairs, argued that as Elder had been insane at the time he ordered the meat and thus incapable of contracting, the contracts were null and void from the start. As such, no damages were payable. The court agreed. However, if a party to a contract becomes insane *after* formation of the contract, his insanity need not bring the contract to an end. It will depend upon whether *delectus personae* applies – i.e., if the personal involvement of the insane person is an essential requirement, the contract will be terminated as a consequence of his insanity. If the personal involvement of the insane party is not required, the contract may proceed.

Intoxicated persons

A person may attempt to contract while under the influence of drink or drugs or medication. The mere fact of intoxication does not render a contract automatically void or voidable. An individual must be so intoxicated that he no longer knows what he is doing and so cannot give the consent which is essential to the formation of a valid contract.

There are differing views on the effect of intoxication on the validity of a contract. One view is that even though, for example, a person is drunk to the degree of being unable to consent, the contract is not void (ie no contract ever comes into existence); but merely voidable (i.e., a contract is formed which may later be set aside by the court). There is also authority for the view that in respect of such voidable contracts, the right to have the contract set aside is lost unless the drunk takes immediate steps to get out of the contract, delay being fatal to a claim – **Pollok *v* Burns (1875) 2 R 497**.

An alternative, and preferable, view is that contracts by persons who are intoxicated are either valid or void depending upon the degree of intoxication. If someone is so drunk that they are incapable of consenting to the contract, then an essential pre-requisite is missing and the contract is void. If the person is drunk to a lesser degree, then the contract is valid. As was stated by Lord Benholme in the case of **Taylor *v* Provan (1864) 2 M 1226** (at p. 1233), a contract cannot be set aside merely because it is 'an after dinner bargain, when the buyer is in a more than usually liberal humour.' In this case P had offered to buy some cattle from T at a price which T refused. Later P offered to buy the cattle at the price of £15 per head asked by T. T accepted. P later tried to have the contract set aside on the ground that he had been intoxicated when he made the offer. It was found that P *had* been drunk but that he had not been sufficiently drunk to render him incapable of giving true consent. The contract stood.

Corporate bodies

Corporate bodies such as registered companies and local authorities are artificial legal persons. Such bodies are treated as legal persons in their own right independent of the human beings who are their members. The contractual capacity of such bodies is not unrestricted but may be limited by statute or by their own constitution. Contracts entered into by such bodies are valid only if within the powers which the body has been given. Contracts entered into which fall outwith a body's powers are said to be *ultra vires* and void.

Local authorities

Scottish unitary councils, established in terms of the Local Government (Scotland) Act 1994, may be described as 'creatures of statute'. They enjoy the powers given to them by the 1994 Act and other Acts of Parliament. Local authorities must operate within their statutory powers, otherwise their actions will be *ultra vires* and void.

Registered companies

Such companies are formed as a consequence of incorporation under the Companies Act 1985 or earlier companies legislation. Incorporation is by a registration procedure which requires that certain documentation be lodged with the Registrar of Companies (in Edinburgh for Scottish companies). If the documentation is in order the Registrar of Companies issues a Certificate of Incorporation which is the company's 'birth certificate'. Among the documents which must be lodged is the company's Memorandum of Association which governs the company's dealings with the outside world. One of the clauses of the memorandum is the objects clause which sets out the purposes for which the company has been set up.

Prior to the coming into force of the European Communities Act 1972 s 9, a contract which was not covered by the objects clause and was therefore *ultra vires* and void could not be enforced against a company by the person contracting with the company. For example, a company may state its objects to be the manufacture and sale by wholesale and retail of butter, cheese and yoghurt. The company enters into contracts for the purchase of milk, of cheese-making equipment, of a delivery van and of office equipment all in pursuit of its business as a manufacturer of dairy produce. All these contracts are *intra vires* (within the powers of the company) and valid. Such contracts may be enforced by and against the company.

However, should the dairy trade go into recession, the company might decide to diversify into pig breeding. It may enter into contracts for the erection of pig pens, for the supply of pig food and for the supply of straw. These contracts would not be covered by the objects clause and would as such be *ultra vires* and unable to be enforced by or against the company. The parties dealing with the company would be treated as knowing what the objects clause said, even if they had not checked, and would be left with no legal remedy against the company.

In an attempt to implement the EC First Directive on Company Law, s 9 of the 1972 Act sought to protect such persons contracting with companies by providing that any contract entered into by a person in good faith which has been decided on by the directors will be deemed to be within the contractual capacity of the company. In the above example, so long as they did not actually know that the contracts were *ultra vires* , the suppliers of the pig pens, the pig food and the straw would be able to enforce the contracts against the company, provided the contracts had been decided upon by the directors. It should be noted that the company could not enforce an *ultra vires* contract against an outsider.

The provisions of s 9 became s 35 of the consolidation act, the Companies Act 1985. However, the law relating to the capacity of companies and to the protection given to persons contracting with companies was changed yet again by the Companies Act 1989. Section 3A of the 1985 Act allows the object of a company to be to carry on business as a general commercial company in any trade or business whatsoever. As far as the protection of persons contracting with companies is concerned, the Companies Act 1985 s 35 was replaced. The effect is virtually to do away with the *ultra vires* rule altogether. The new s 35(1) provides that no act by a company may be questioned on the basis that it was beyond its legal capacity as stated in its memorandum. Furthermore, there is no duty on a person dealing with a company to investigate whether there is any limitation on the company's capacity. In practical terms, all contracts will be enforceable against the company.

QUESTIONS

1 Jean, aged 17, runs a market stall selling jewellery, which she makes. She has ordered a stone polisher for use in her jewellery-making. However, sales on her stall have fallen and she wants out of the contract. Someone has told her that this is possible because she is under 18. Advise Jean.

2 James, aged 15, seeks your advice. His mother gave him money to buy a duffle coat to wear to school during the winter. In a moment of weakness he bought a leather jacket which was reduced in a sale. Fearful of his mother's wrath he tried to return the jacket but the shop refused to refund his money. What is the legal position?

3 Joe has been negotiating with Sid to buy Sid's old tractor. Joe had always argued that Sid's price of £2000 was too high and had said that £1500 was his top offer. On Hogmanay somewhat the worse for drink, Joe offered to buy Sid's tractor for £2000 and Sid accepted. On January 2nd Joe contacted Sid to say that the deal was off because he was drunk when he made the offer. What is the legal position?

FORMALITIES

As was stated previously, it is a common misconception that contracts have to be formed in writing and require the signature of witnesses in order to be valid and binding. Under Scots law most contracts require no such formalities. Most contracts may be formed verbally or implied from the actions of the parties. Furthermore, the existence of most contracts may be proved if necessary by any type of evidence including the testimony of the parties and other witnesses.

However, some contracts do require to be formed in writing in order to be valid and enforceable.

The Requirements of Writing (Scotland) Act 1995 changes the law in relation to the constitution and proof of gratuitous promises and of bilateral contracts. The Act came into force on 1 August 1995. The purpose of the Act was to reform Scots law in relation to the requirement of writing for the formal validity of contractual and other documents. However, the general rule that writing is not normally required for the creation of a contract or unilateral obligation is restated.

At common law there were certain types of obligations, *the obligationes literis*, which had to be constituted in formal writing to be valid. The 1995 Act has done away with the *obligationes literis* and formal writing. The 1995 Act has substituted a different list of obligations which require writing and has simplified the type of writing which is needed.

The 1995 Act identifies those obligations which now require to be constituted in a written document. In terms of Section 1 these include the constitution of:

(a) a contract or unilateral obligation for the creation, transfer, variation or extinction of an interest in land;
(b) a gratuitous unilateral obligation except an obligation undertaken in the course of business;
(c) a trust whereby a person declares himself to be the sole trustee of his own property or any property which he may acquire.

However, to satisfy the requirements of the Act as to formal validity, all that is required is that the document is signed by the granter (s 2). The previous common law categories of 'formal writing' namely 'attested', 'holograph' and 'adopted as holograph' have all been abolished by the 1995 Act.

While the signature of the granter is all that is required in order that obligations covered by the Act are 'formally constituted', that of itself is not enough to make the document 'self evidencing' – i.e., presumed to be valid without additional evidence having to be presented to the court to show that this indeed is the granter's signature. Under the old common law, in order that a document was 'probative' in this way the signatures of two witnesses were required. Now, under the 1995 Act, only one witness has to sign in order to make the document 'self evidencing' (s 3). Alternatively the Act provides a procedure (s 4) whereby a court can grant a certificate to the effect that it is satisfied that the document was validly executed.

It is important not to become confused by the difference between the provisions of s 2 and s 3. Section 2 sets out what is required to *constitute* or *create* a valid and binding contract. If an obligation required by s 1 to be in writing is set out in a document signed by the granter, then the obligation is validly constituted. Section 3 deals with *proof* that the signature on the document is genuine. If the granter's signature has been witnessed by one witness then a court will presume the document is genuine without having to look any further. However, should there be no witness, the court will want evidence, probably in the form of sworn affidavits (statements) that the signature on the document is recognised as being that of the granter, before enforcing the obligations set out in the document.

The common law provisions relating to personal bar by *rei interventus* and homologation have been replaced by a new, statutory form of *rei interventus* (s 1(3) and 1(4)). A contract or unilateral promise which should have been signed can be enforced despite the lack of a signature, where 'significant actings' have followed. One party cannot get out of an informal contract or promise:

1 where the other party has acted in reliance on the contract or promise; and
2 where the first party knew of their actions and acquiesced; and
3 where these actions were material so that the second party would be prejudiced should the first party withdraw.

Wills also require to be constituted in writing, although particular rules apply to wills which will not be dealt with here.

QUESTIONS

1 George wants to buy Bill's newsagent's shop. George offers Bill £60 000 which Bill agrees to accept. Afraid that Bill might change his mind, George decides to draw up a formal contract there and then. George writes out an offer and signs it. George also writes out an acceptance which Bill signs. Two days later, Bill contacts George to say that he has changed his mind and is not selling. George argues that Bill is legally bound. With reference to statute discuss whether George is correct.

2 Mary has decided to lease an office from John and turn it into a coffee shop. Mary wrote out the offer of lease offering to lease the premises from John for 10 years at a rent of £5000 per annum and signed it. John did not reply in writing but accepted Mary's offer verbally and handed over the keys. Mary sent John her cheque for the first year's rent. Mary encountered difficulties obtaining planning permission for change of use of the premises and John assisted her in obtaining this. Mary spent considerable sums fitting out the premises as a coffee shop and has been trading for about six months. John has now been offered a much higher rent for the premises and wants to terminate Mary's lease. What will John be arguing and will he succeed?

4 Illegality and error

PACTA ILLICITA

If an agreement is illegal, it is a *pactum illicitum* – i.e., an unlawful agreement and as such is unenforceable. Certain contracts may be unlawful at common law or perhaps prohibited by statute. As a general rule, the courts will not enforce an unlawful agreement. The general principle is summed up in the maxim *ex turpi causa non oritur actio* (no action arises out of an immoral situation). Damages will not be awarded for the breach of such a contract and no order will be made for the return of property which has passed under the agreement. In other words, the loss lies where it falls, the law favouring the party in possession of property.

It is, however, accepted that a strict application of this principle might lead to injustice where an innocent party has been duped into entering an unlawful agreement. Where the parties to an unlawful agreement are not equally to blame the courts may grant an equitable remedy such as recompense. In **Cuthbertson *v* Lowes (1870) 8M 1073** the Weights and Measures Acts had declared that any contract which used Scots measure as opposed to imperial measure was void. C had sold to L two fields of potatoes at £24 per Scots acre. The potatoes were delivered but L did not pay for them. C brought an action for the price. As the contract was declared void by statute it could not be enforced. However, to allow L to keep the potatoes without paying for them would amount to unjust enrichment; L would unjustly benefit at C's expense. The court held that C was entitled to the value of the potatoes at the time of delivery.

However, where the pursuer has been a willing party to an illegal agreement and both parties are equally to blame – i.e., *in pari delicto* – the courts will not grant a remedy. In **Jamieson *v* Watt's Trustee 1950 SC 265** the Defence Regulations 1939 required that a licence had to be obtained before building work could go ahead. J, a joiner, obtained a licence authorising expenditure amounting to £40 in respect of work which J was to carry out for W. J sent W a bill for just over £114. W refused to pay any more than was authorised by the licence. J sought payment relying upon the decision in *Cuthbertson* v *Lowes*. The court held that the decision in *Cuthbertson* rested on its own facts. They distinguished between a contract declared by statute to be merely void and a contract which is declared to be illegal. In *Jamieson*'s case as the contract involved illegality, the equitable doctrine of recompense was inapplicable and Jamieson was held not to be entitled to payment.

A similar decision was reached in **Barr *v* Crawford 1983 SLT 481**. In this case, a woman alleged that she had paid the sum of £8000 to two individuals in order to obtain their assistance in influencing the decision of the Licensing Board. Her husband had been ill and she feared that his public house licence would not be renewed. Her court action to recover the money failed. The payment was a bribe and as such the agreement was illegal. Furthermore, the court found there was insufficient evidence to indicate that Mrs Barr was not *in pari delicto*.

As was stated above, an agreement may be unlawful at common law or may be declared unlawful by statute. A contract will be unlawful at common law if its purpose is the commission of a crime or the perpetration of a fraud. Contracts which promote sexual immorality are similarly unlawful. Also unlawful at common law are contracts which are contrary to public policy. Contracts with enemy aliens, agreements involving bribery and corruption of public officials or the judiciary, and contracts which are in restraint of trade are all viewed as being contrary to public policy.

In **Laughland *v* Millar (1904) 6 F 413 L**, the director of a company, reached an agreement with the managers of the company. The agreement was that the director would ensure that the shareholders agreed to pay a terminal bonus to the managers when the company was sold. The managers would then pay a share of the bonus to the director. The managers received a bonus of £700 but failed to pay L his share of £200. L brought an action for the payment of the £200. Lord McLaren stated (at p. 417) '… there is no point in the law of contract which is more firmly established than that when a contract … is a dishonest attempt to defraud a third person, then the one party cannot sue the other, but the property or fund in question must remain in its existing position.' It was held that the contract, being illegal, could not be enforced.

A case which illustrates the principle that an agreement promoting sexual immorality is an illegal contract which the law will not enforce is **Hamilton *v* Main (1823) 2 S 356**. A hotelier sought payment of a drinks bill amounting to £60. During a seven-day stay, the guest, Hamilton, had drunk 113 bottles of Port and Madeira plus other spirits while in the company of a prostitute. The court refused to enforce payment.

Restrictive covenants

Particular interest should be paid to the law's response to contracts in restraint of trade. Restrictive covenants may be found in contracts of employment, in contracts for the sale of a business and in partnership agreements. A restrictive covenant is a provision in a contract which limits one party's freedom to work where he pleases or for whom he pleases or in the line of business he pleases. For example, employers may insert into a contract of employment a condition which seeks to prevent an employee working for a rival employer for a certain period of time. As a general rule, contracts in restraint of trade are void but restrictive covenants are enforceable

if they can be shown to be **reasonable** in the interests of the parties and in the public interest. Slightly different considerations apply depending upon whether the restriction appears in a contract of employment or in a contract for the sale of a business: in the former, the courts are concerned that the employee is not prevented from earning his living; in the latter, where the buyer of a business has paid a sum for the goodwill, the court may be more inclined to find that a restriction is reasonable.

Employers are entitled to attempt to protect legitimate business interests so long as the restrictions imposed are no wider than is necessary to achieve such protection. However, as Lord President Clyde pointed out in **Scottish Farmers' Dairy Co. (Glasgow) Ltd** *v* **McGhee 1933 SC 148** (at p.152), 'The mere exclusion of competition never can be in itself a legitimate interest.' What are the legitimate business interests which an employer is entitled to take steps to protect? An employer is entitled to protect his trade secrets and other confidential information relating to his business practices, knowledge of which would be of advantage to his rivals. An employer may also attempt to prevent his existing customers being enticed away. In England, the High Court and the Court of Appeal have held that an employer's legitimate business interests include seeking to maintain a stable workforce. Accordingly, an employer can restrain a former employee from 'poaching' staff (**Alliance Paper Group plc** *v* **Prestwich [1996] IRLR 25** and **Ingham** *v* **ABC Contract Services Ltd** – unreported decision of Court of Appeal 12.11.93).

As stated above, the restrictive covenant will be upheld so long as its terms are no wider than is necessary to protect legitimate business interests. The court will take into account whether the employee is a legitimate target for a restrictive covenant – i.e., did he have access to trade secrets, was he in a position to solicit clients? It must also be determined whether the restriction is reasonable in terms of **area** and **time**. If the terms of the restriction are upheld as reasonable, the employer may ask the court to grant an **interdict**; for example, ordering the employee to stop working for a competitor. In addition, the employer may also seek damages for breach of contract.

When determining whether a restriction is reasonable, factors to be considered include the type of business involved and its radius of probable custom – from how far afield are its customers likely to come? Also relevant will be whether the business is in a rural or urban location as this will affect the density of population. A corner shop in a suburb may expect its customers to come from the immediate locality; a dentist in a town may expect his patients to come from further afield; an undertaker in a rural area may take all the custom within a 20-mile radius.

It must also be shown that the employee is a threat to the employer's legitimate business interests. The owner of a hairdressing salon may seek to place a restriction on the future employment of a stylist because customers are likely to follow a good hairdresser to another salon. Clients are unlikely to follow the junior who merely washes their hair. The stylist who leaves poses a threat to the employer's business, the junior does not. Other types of employees who might attract client loyalty include solicitors, dentists and accountants. In the same way, if the employer argues that the restriction is necessary to protect confidential information, it must be shown that the employee had access to such information. It must also be shown that the information could properly be described as a 'trade secret' and is not merely information which could be obtained from other sources. A scientist in a research and development department would be a legitimate target for a restrictive covenant.

The restriction must be no wider than is necessary in terms of both area and time. What is judged necessary will depend upon the facts of each case. In **Nordenfelt** *v* **Maxim Nordenfelt Guns and Ammunition Co Ltd [1894] AC 535** the seller of an armaments business agreed that he would not engage in the trade or business of an arms manufacturer for a 25-year period. This amounted to a worldwide restriction. In upholding the restrictive covenant as reasonable, the House of Lords took into account the fact that the nature of the business was such that the seller's former customers were the governments of nations the world over.

In **The Scottish Farmers' Dairy Co (Glasgow) Ltd** *v* **McGhee 1933 SC 148** a milkman was obliged not to carry on the trade of milkseller within one mile of his former employer's place of business. On leaving employment, he started working for a rival dairy company and sold their milk within the prohibited area to the customers of his former employer. McGhee's former employer sought interdict and damages against him. McGhee argued that the clause was illegal because it was in restraint of trade and wider than was necessary. The Inner House of the Court of Session held that the restriction in the agreement was not wider than was necessary in the circumstances for the protection of the employer's trading interests and was accordingly valid. The court found that the preservation of his business connection was a legitimate interest of every trader. In this case, it was particularly relevant that the only contact which the employer had with his customers was through the milkmen. The court found that if a popular milkman left and joined a rival employer, the goodwill for that area automatically transferred to the rival because customers would continue to buy milk from their usual milkman. In these circumstances Lord President Clyde stated (at p. 153) '… there seems to be nothing for it but to prohibit the [employee] from selling milk within the area for a time sufficient to allow a new roundsman to establish relations with the [employer's] customers within it.'

In **SOS Bureau Ltd** *v* **Payne 1982 SLT (Sheriff Court) 33** an employment agency sought an interdict against a former employee who had taken up employment with a rival agency. Ms Payne's contract of employment disallowed her for a period of one year from working for a competitor within a quarter of a mile of any of her employer's branches at which she had worked within six months prior to leaving. She was also forbidden to communicate with any client of the employer for the purpose of offering to provide services similar to those offered by the employer. Interdict was granted to the employer. The restriction was enforceable because in quality and in extent it was what was reasonably required to protect legitimate rights of the employers. The employers were concerned to protect their trade secrets. The Sheriff found that the employment agency business was highly competitive and therefore to know the trading policy, scales of fees and commissions, and the discount policy of rival agencies is of considerable benefit. Given that a legitimate interest was being protected, the Sheriff proceeded to consider whether the restriction was wider than was necessary to achieve such protection. The restriction was reasonable in respect of time being limited to one year, and of area there being a strict geographical limitation of only a quarter of a mile.

Similarly, in **Rentokil Ltd** *v* **Kramer 1986 SLT 114** Kramer's contract of employment prohibited him, for a two-year period, from canvassing anyone who had been a Rentokil customer during the period of two years immediately preceding the termination of Kramer's employment. Kramer took up employment with a rival firm and, it was alleged, canvassed at least four of Rentokil's former customers. Rentokil raised an action for interdict and damages against their former employee. Kramer argued the restriction was wider than was necessary but the court disagreed. Kramer had enjoyed full access to the pursuers' customer lists. The pursuers were entitled to protect their business connections and prevent Kramer using such information to their prejudice and to the advantage of his new employers. The protection sought was reasonable and interim interdict was granted.

In **A & D Bedrooms Ltd** *v* **Michael 1984 SLT 297** a UK-wide restriction was upheld as reasonable. Ms Michael was a qualified interior designer. Her contract of employment with the pursuers provided that she was not to work for a trade competitor of her employers anywhere in the UK for a one-year period after the termination of her contract. Contrary to this provision, Ms Michael took up employment with a rival company. It was argued for Ms Michael that the terms of the restriction were too wide and were purely designed to prevent competition. However, the Lord Ordinary found that as both the pursuers and Ms Michael's new employers carried on business throughout the UK it was not unreasonable that the restriction should cover that area. The evidence supported the view that the restriction was not to prevent competition only, but also to protect the employers from the disclosure of confidential information by an ex-employee to a business rival. Ms Michael did have access to such information and interim interdict was granted so as to prevent the defender working for the rival company.

It is settled law that where an employee has been wrongfully dismissed, his former employer cannot seek to enforce a restrictive covenant. In addition it has also been held in the case of **Living Design (Home Improvements) Ltd** *v* **Davidson (OH 28 May 1993)** that if a restrictive covenant is worded so as to apply after the employment is terminated 'however that comes about and *whether lawful or not*', it is unreasonable and unenforceable for that reason alone . The employer cannot be allowed to seek to rely on a contract which he may wrongfully bring to an end and a restrictive covenant which is so worded will fall even if the employee's contract is properly terminated. However, in **PR Consultants Scotland Ltd** *v* **Mann (OH 15 August 1995)** where the wording used was that the restrictions were to apply for 12 months following termination 'howsoever caused', the court refused to infer that this was intended to extend to unlawful termination of the contract. Lord Caplan held that it could be interpreted as covering the variety of ways in which a contract of employment may lawfully be terminated.

Similar considerations apply in respect of restrictive covenants in contracts for the sale of a business and in partnership agreements. In **Anthony** *v* **Rennie 1981 SLT (Notes) 11** a doctor sought an interdict against his former partner who had left the practice but now intended to return to join another local practice. The partnership agreement had provided that the outgoing partner would not engage in medical practice for a period of five years within a six-mile radius of Galashiels. This restriction was upheld as reasonable. However, in the case of **Dallas McMillan & Sinclair** *v* **Simpson 1989 SLT 454** a restrictive covenant which prohibited any partner in a firm of solicitors from practising within twenty miles of Glasgow Cross for five years was held to be too wide; in terms of its area and scope, the restriction went far beyond what was necessary to protect the firm's legitimate interests.

Similarly, in the case of **Randev** *v* **Pattar 1985 SLT 270** interim interdict was refused. The seller of a hotel business agreed not to carry on a hotel or restaurant business within a one-mile radius for a period of five years. He then went on to purchase another hotel within one mile. The purchaser sought an interdict. Lord Wylie found that the area of the restriction was reasonable. However, in respect of the time period, His Lordship stated that while a period of one, or perhaps two years might be regarded as a reasonable provision, he had serious doubts if a restriction for a period of five years was reasonably necessary to protect the purchaser's legitimate interests. Given these doubts as to the validity of the covenant, interim interdict was refused.

In respect of restrictive covenants two further points remain to be made. Firstly, where a restriction cannot be upheld because its terms are too wide, the court has no discretion to substitute a reasonable restriction for the unreasonable one. Accordingly, if an employer is too greedy and the restriction falls, he loses all protection and the former employee can work how and where and when he pleases. This was shown in **Empire Meat Co** *v* **Patrick [1939] 2 All ER 85**. An employer sought to place a five-mile restriction on the manager of his butcher's shop. It was found that the likely radius of custom was only two miles. The manager set up in competition almost next door. As the area of five miles was too wide, the restriction failed and the manager could stay where he was. Similarly in **Dumbarton Steamboat Co** *v* **MacFarlane (1899) 1 F 993** the seller of a carriers business agreed not to carry on business as a carrier anywhere in the UK for a period of ten years. The carriers business had been confined to the Dumbarton area. Three years later, the seller started a new carriers business between Glasgow and Dumbarton. The buyers sought an interdict. The area covered by the restriction was excessive and therefore unreasonable. It was also held that the court had no power to remodel the restriction and confine it to a more limited area.

Secondly, where there are a number of restrictions imposed and some are found to be reasonable and others are not, the court may uphold the reasonable parts of the covenant and discard the unreasonable parts – if the reasonable parts can stand alone and still make sense. This is known as **severability** and can be illustrated by reference to the case of **Mulvein** *v* **Murray 1908 SC 528**. A commercial traveller had agreed that he would not sell to or canvass any of his former employer's customers. He had also agreed not to sell in any of the towns or districts already traded in by Mulvein. The first restriction was reasonable, the second restriction was not. The court separated the two and allowed the first restriction to stand while discarding the second as being too wide and vague.

'Solus' agreements

An agreement whereby X agrees to sell only the goods of Y may be set aside by the court as being in restraint of trade. In the case of **Esso Petroleum Co. Ltd** *v* **Harpers Garages (Stourport) Ltd (1968) AC 269**, Esso entered into agreements whereby garages agreed to buy all their petrol from Esso. Such an agreement with one garage for a duration of four years and five months was found to be reasonable. However, a second agreement which required a garage to buy only Esso's petrol for a period of 21 years was unreasonable and held to be unenforceable.

Restrictive trade agreements between manufacturers

Manufacturers may agree among themselves to fix the price to be charged for certain types of goods or to limit the supply of goods. Alternatively, a manufacturer may attempt to impose in an agreement with a retailer, a minimum price at which goods may be resold. Such practices are now subject to statutory controls set out in the Restrictive Trade Practices Act 1976. Agreements between manufacturers have to be registered and, if they are found to be contrary to the public interest, such agreements shall be prohibited and they may be referred to the Restrictive Practices Court. The Resale Prices Act 1976 prohibits agreements which set a minimum price for the resale of goods unless it can be shown to be in the public interest.

The Restrictive Trade Practices Act 1976 applies also to restrictive agreements as to services. In the case of **Aberdeen Solicitors' Property Centre *v* Director General of Fair Trading 1996 SLT 523** the Office of Fair Trading demanded details of the practices of the Aberdeen Solicitors' Property Centre and also of the Edinburgh Solicitors' Property Centre whereby only solicitors could market properties through the centres and there was a prohibition on joint agencies with non-solicitor estate agents. These arrangements were regarded by the Office of Fair Trading as agreements falling to be registered under the Restrictive Trade Practices Act 1976. The two property centres successfully applied to the Restrictive Practices Court for the removal of these agreements from the register. The court held that while the centres' arrangements did amount to an agreement as defined by s 11 of the 1976 Act, they were covered by provisions in Schedule 1 exempting 'legal services'. Lord Marnoch found that the advertising and estate agency services provided by the centres formed part of the package of legal services provided by solicitors. As such the agreements were exempt and were ordered to be removed from the register. However, following this decision the Director General of Fair Trading referred the matter to the Monopolies and Mergers Commission to investigate whether the practices of the centres amount to a monopoly and restrict fair trade contrary to the Fair Trading Act 1973. At the time of writing the matter remains to be resolved.

QUESTIONS

1 Sid, a garage owner, wants to expand his car showroom. Unfortunately, his premises are in a conservation area and it seems unlikely that he will obtain planning permission for the extension. However, he is approached by the Director of Planning for Dunedin District Council. It is agreed that if Sid gives both the Director and the Chairman of the Planning Committee a substantial discount on new cars, planning permission will be granted. Sid gives each of the men £2500 off a new car. However, two months later Sid's planning application is refused. Sid intends to raise an action for the return of the discount. Will Sid's action succeed?

2 Tina and Dawn are sisters. Tina has worked as a research chemist for five years with Worldwide Pharmaceuticals plc. She has now been offered a similar post at a much higher salary with Global Pharmaceuticals plc. Tina is concerned that her contract of employment prohibits her from working for a trade competitor for two years should she leave Worldwide Pharmaceuticals.

Dawn is an accountant employed by Old, Mean & Nasty, Chartered Accountants in Stirling. Mr Old is semi-retired, Mr Mean has been ill and Mr Nasty spends most of his day on the golf course with the result that Dawn deals with most of the clients. Dawn now intends to set up her own practice in Stirling but is dismayed when reminded that her contract of employment prohibits her from either practising on her own account anywhere in Stirlingshire or canvassing her former employers' clients both for a period of two years.

With full reference to the law on restrictive covenants, advise Tina and Dawn.

ERROR AND MISREPRESENTATION AS FACTORS AFFECTING THE VALIDITY OF CONTRACTS

The validity of a contract may be impaired if there is some defect affecting the contract. Some defects are regarded by the law as so minor that the contract will be unaffected and remain valid. More serious defects will render the contract voidable. The most serious defects will render the contract void.

It has already been seen that defects such as a lack of capacity, or absence of formal writing when such is required will affect the validity of a contract. Where the parties to a contract enter into a contract under some mistaken belief – or error – then that too may affect a contract's validity. Whether as a result of the presence of an error a contract will nevertheless remain valid, or be rendered void or voidable, depends upon the seriousness of the error and also upon how the error came about – i.e., was the mistaken belief caused by something the other party said or did?

USEFUL TERMS

Students often find error complex because of the variety of terminology used. Accordingly, before proceeding further, it is intended to give a simple explanation of all the relevant terms.

Bilateral error – this time the error is two-sided – i.e., both parties enter the contract holding some mistaken belief.

Common error – this is a type of bilateral error – i.e., both parties to the contract hold a mistaken belief. Where there is common error both parties have made the *same* mistake. Both parties share the same mistaken belief. They both think the same thing and they are both wrong.

Error concomitans – any error which is not one of the errors in the substantials and which cannot be said to be essential error. This is viewed as a less serious error and will only affect a contract's validity if such an error has been *induced* (caused) by the other party to the contract. Even then, the presence of *error concomitans* will merely render the contract voidable, not void. Where *error concomitans* is uninduced the contract remains valid.

Error in the substantials – derived from Roman law. The Scottish institutional writer, Stair, said, 'Those who err in the substantials, ... contract not.' Where there is error in the substantials this is regarded as excluding true consent which is essential to a valid contract. Another institutional writer, Bell, classified such error and his classification may be summarised as follows.

There will be an error in the substantials if there is an error as to: (a) the **subject matter** of the contract, e.g., where one commodity is mistaken for another; (b) the **identity** of the parties to the contract, whenever the identity of the person is *material* to the contract; (c) the **price** or **consideration** given; (d) the **quality**, **quantity** or **extent of the subject matter** where the quality, quantity or extent is *material* to the contract; (e) the very **nature** of the contract – i.e., the mistake is about the type of obligation which is being undertaken, e.g., X thinks that he is hiring his car out to Y, when in fact he is signing a document of sale. What is meant by '**MATERIAL**' here? A belief is material to a contract if such a belief was what made a person decide to enter the contract in the first place – i.e., he entered the contract only because he believed 'X' to be the case.

Essential error – the effect which the presence of error has on a contract's validity depends very much on the seriousness of the error. The definition of essential error is to be found in **Menzies *v* Menzies (1893) 20R (HL) 108** – per Lord Watson – 'Error becomes essential whenever shown that *but for it* one of the parties would have declined to contract ...' The presence of such error will generally affect a contract's validity where such essential error is common, or mutual, or has been induced. Essential error will include but is wider than the older, classical concept of error in the substantials.

Induced error – one party enters into a contract subject to some mistaken belief but this time they hold such a belief because of something the other party has said or done (i.e., the error has been induced (caused) by the actions of the other party). This may be accidental (innocent misrepresentation) or deliberate (fraudulent misrepresentation) on the part of the other party to the contract.

Mutual error – this is also a type of bilateral error. Again both parties have contracted subject to some error. However, this time they have *misunderstood* one another. X and Y think that they have reached agreement but each has a different idea of what they have agreed. An example of mutual error would be the sale of a car where X thinks Y has agreed to buy X's Mini whereas Y thinks Y has agreed to buy X's Jaguar.

Unilateral error – only one of the parties to the contract has entered the contract subject to an error – i.e., holding some mistaken belief.

Uninduced error – a party to a contract may enter the contract subject to an error – i.e., mistaken belief. Where they have arrived at that mistaken belief as a result of their own misconception – and not because of anything the other party to the contract has said or done – then that is said to be an uninduced error.

Void – we talk about void contracts but this is actually misleading because a void contract is *no* contract. A void contract is a legal nullity. The defect affecting the contract is regarded as so serious that no contract ever comes into existence. As a result, neither party is ever under any legally binding obligation and neither party has any rights which the courts will enforce. Examples of void contracts include attempts by children under 16 to contract and contracts induced by force and fear. Strictly speaking, if a contract is void there should be no need to go to court. However, if one party is arguing that there **is** a valid contract and the other party is arguing that there is **no** contract because it is void, then inevitably the parties will end up in court. In such circumstances the appropriate court action is an *action of declarator of nullity*. The court merely declares what one of the parties had said all along – there is not and never was a contract for whatever reason.

Voidable – certain defects are not regarded as so serious as to render a contract void; certain less serious defects make the contract voidable. If a contract is flawed so as to be voidable the defect may be relied upon as a justification for going to court to ask the court to set the contract aside. However, unless and until such steps are taken the contract is regarded as valid and binding. Legal rights and obligations are created and remain until the voidable contract is reduced (set aside) by the court. Examples of voidable contracts are contracts subject to facility and circumvention and contracts entered into by intoxicated persons. The parties to a voidable contract may choose to ignore the defect and the contract will continue as valid and binding. However, if one of the parties wishes to rely upon the defect in order to have the contract set aside, he must go to court and raise an *action for reduction* of the voidable contract.

These are the main terms which will be encountered in a study of error and misrepresentation. In determining the effect of the presence of an error (or mistaken belief) on a contract's validity, **three main questions** should be considered:

1 How many people have contracted subject to error? Just one of the parties (unilateral error) or both (bilateral error)?
2 How serious is the error (or mistaken belief)? Is it an error in the substantials or merely non-essential error – i.e., *error concomitans*?
3 How was the error caused? Is it uninduced – i.e., the fault of the person holding the mistaken belief; or is it induced – i.e., caused by something the other party has said or done?

Before looking at each of the main types of error in more detail students may find it helpful to refer to the following.

Checklist on error and its effects on the validity of contracts

- Uninduced errors as to factual matters:

unilateral errors	–			contract valid
bilateral common errors	–	in substantials	–	contract void
	–	in *concomitans*	–	contract valid
bilateral mutual errors	–	in substantials	–	contract void
	–	in *concomitans*	–	contract valid

- Induced errors as to factual matters induced by either innocent or fraudulent misrepresentation:

if causes – error in substantials	–	contract void
if causes – *error concomitans*	–	contract voidable

An alternative approach to remembering

- Uninduced error:

if error in substantials	–	contract void
if *error concomitans*	–	contract valid
if unilateral	–	contract valid

- Induced error:

if error in substantials	–		contract void
if *error concomitans*	–		contract voidable
	–	uninduced unilateral	contract valid
	–	unilateral bilateral	contract void
	–	induced	contract void

• Error in substantials	–	uninduced	–	contract void
	–	induced	–	contract void
• *Error concomitans*	–	uninduced	–	contract valid
	–	induced	–	contract voidable

A contract may be in the proper form and made by persons with contractual capacity and yet may still be void or voidable. This may be because some error has occurred which affects the validity of a contract. The reason why an error affects the validity of a contract is because it may undermine the consent which is essential to a valid contract. This may arise because consent has been improperly obtained or because it has been given as a result of an error.

There are various ways in which an error may arise and different types of error have different effects on the validity of a contract. The law distinguishes between errors which are not induced by the other party to the contract and those which are induced by the other party either innocently or deliberately. The law also makes a distinction between errors which affect both parties and mistaken belief held by only one of the parties. It is now proposed to look at each of the various types of error in more detail.

ERROR AS TO THE LEGAL EFFECTS OF THE CONTRACT

Where a person misunderstands the legal effects of a transaction, the general rule was that it did not affect the validity of the contract. The Latin maxim – *ignorantia legis neminem excusat* – applied ('ignorance of the law excuses no one').

This meant that a person could not recover money paid under a mistaken belief as to a matter of law. Traditionally it had been held that an action of repetition under the *condictio indebiti* (a claim for the repayment of money which has been paid in the mistaken belief that payment was due) was not available when payment had been made under an error of law as opposed to an error of fact.

However, this position was overruled in the case of **Morgan Guaranty Trust Co of New York *v* Lothian Regional Council 1995 SLT 299**. The facts were that a merchant bank and a regional council had entered into a 'swap agreement' which involved each party making payments of money to the other on specified dates. The bank had paid a net sum in excess of £300 000 to the council when an English court held that such agreements were unlawful as they were *ultra vires* local authorities. The bank sought repayment but the Lord Ordinary held that the precedents stated that an error based on ignorance of the general law undermined the pursuer's right to a remedy. The sums paid in error as to the council's contractual capacity were not recoverable. On appeal a court of five judges overruled previous precedents and held that a payment made in error might be recovered by an action of repetition under the *condictio indebiti* irrespective of whether the mistake under which it was paid was one of fact or law and the error of law rule had no sound foundation in principle. To establish entitlement to the remedy the pursuer had to show that the sum which he had paid was not due and that the payment had been made in error.

UNINDUCED UNILATERAL ERROR

Unilateral error occurs where only one party to the contract enters the contract subject to some mistaken belief. The legal position appears to be that even if the error is so serious that had the true position been known the person making the error would not have entered that contract – if the error is their own and is not caused by (induced by) anything the other party has said or done, then the contract will remain valid and binding.

For example, X offers to buy Y's vase – X thinks it is a valuable antique worth at least £500. X does not let Y know of his belief because he hopes to resell for a great profit. In actual fact, it is worth only about £75. X pays £90 for the vase. Had X known the true value of the vase he would not have bought it. X's belief as to the value of the vase was not caused by anything Y said or did. It was purely X's own mistake. The contract is valid. In **Bennies Trustees *v* Couper (1890) 17 R 782** the Lord Justice Clerk said (at p. 785), 'This error was entirely his own error. It was not an error which anyone had done anything to induce. He is not in these circumstances entitled to an issue of essential error in order to prove that he made this error, and so to set aside his obligation.' And Lord Fullerton said in **Forth Marine Insurance Co *v* Burnes (1848) 10 D 689** , 'the notion that a party ... is entitled to get free on the ground that he was in error – i.e., that he found that he had made a bad bargain where he intended to make a good one – is so utterly preposterous as to be undeserving of any attention' (see also the case of **The Royal Bank of Scotland plc *v* Purvis** – discussed below).

There is one exception to the general rule that unilateral essential error does not invalidate a contract unless such error has been induced by the other party to the contract. This exception applies to *gratuitous contracts*. Where gratuitous obligations are involved, uninduced unilateral essential error may invalidate the contract.

UNINDUCED BILATERAL ERROR – COMMON ERROR

Common error occurs where both parties make the same mistake; they think the same thing and they are both wrong – i.e., both parties share the same mistaken belief. What effect does this type of error have on the validity of a contract?

It may be argued that if both parties contract under a common essential error the contract will be void as a result. Where the shared mistaken belief relates to a factual matter such as the very existence or non-existence of the subject matter of the contract – if their belief turns out to be incorrect the contract will be void. In **Couturier *v* Hastie (1856) 5 HL Cas 673** a contract was formed for the sale of a cargo of grain. At the time the contract was formed both parties believed the cargo to be in existence. Both were wrong – the grain was going bad so some had been dumped overboard and the rest had been sold before it went off completely. The contract for the sale of the grain was void.

However, in certain circumstances, it has been held that common error will not invalidate a contract:

1 Where it was suspected that the existence of something might be in doubt and it was implied that the parties were prepared to 'take a chance' – **Morton *v* Smith 1877 5 R 83**.
2 Where the common error was as to a matter of opinion. In **Leaf *v* International Galleries (1950) 2KB 86** both parties formed the incorrect opinion that a painting was by a famous artist; the contract stood.
3 Where the goods turn out to have unexpected qualities or value, the parties may be treated as having accepted that their bargain might turn out better/worse than expected. In **Dawson *v* Muir (1851) 13 D 843**, in a sale of vats for £2 for scrap, both parties thought the vats were worthless. They were found to contain lead worth £300. The seller wanted out the contract but it was held to be binding.

UNINDUCED BILATERAL ERROR – MUTUAL ERROR

Where there is a mutual error, again both parties contract subject to a mistaken belief. However – unlike common error where both parties think the same thing and they are both wrong – where there is mutual error, the parties misunderstand one another, they are at cross purposes. They think that they have reached agreement but each has a different idea as to what has been agreed.

An example of mutual error is the Jaguar and the Mini situation. A offers to sell his car to B for £2000. A has two cars – a Jaguar and a Mini. B does not know A has two cars – he thinks that he is being offered the Jaguar for £2000. B accepts A's offer. A thinks that B has agreed to buy the Mini for £2000. The contract is void as a result of this mutual error. This means neither A nor B has any legal rights or is under any obligation. A cannot insist that B takes the Mini. B cannot insist that A hands over the Jaguar.

Where the mutual error is sufficiently serious to be regarded as essential error, the contract will be void. The presence of essential error precludes full agreement and undermines consent. The definition of essential error was said to have been widened by Lord Watson in the 1890 case of *Menzies* v *Menzies* – error is essential where, but for the error, one of the parties would have declined to contract. Previously, essential error was thought to be limited to the five categories of error in the substantials – the 'but for' test would now allow other errors to invalidiate a contract. However, for the purposes of this text it is proposed to confine discussion to the effect on a contract of errors in the substantials.

Errors in the substantials

Error as to the subject matter of the contract

The parties are not thinking of the same subject matter when they make the contract. In **Raffles *v* Wichelhaus 1864 2 H&C 906** two ships both called 'Peerless' sailed the Indian cotton route. The contract was for the sale of 'the cargo of the Peerless'. One party was thinking of one of the ships and its cargo; the other party was thinking of the other ship and its cargo. The contract was void.

In **Scriven *v* Hindley 1913 3 KB 564** an auctioneer was taking bids for bales of tow. A bidder bid a very high price for the tow because he thought that the bales contained the more valuable commodity, hemp. Despite the very high bid the auctioneer did not realise the bidder's mistake. The contract was void.

Error as to identity but only if identity is material to the contract

A thinks that he is contracting with B but in fact he is contracting with C. This will be regarded as an error in the substantials and will render the contract void – only if A's belief that he was contracting with B was material to the contract. That is, A only entered the contract because he thought he was dealing with B. The fact that he was dealing with B as opposed to anyone else was a deciding factor in A deciding to go ahead with the contract.

Most cases on error as to identity relate to situations where the error was induced rather than uninduced and, accordingly, such cases will be dealt with in the section dealing with misrepresentation. (See *Morrisson* v *Robertson* 1908 SC 332 (identity material) and *MacLeod* v *Kerr* 1965 SC 253 (identity not material) which are considered below).

Error as to price

This arises when the parties to a contract think that they have agreed a price or a means of calculating a price, but one of the parties thinks they have agreed price X while the other party thinks that they have agreed price Y.

In **Stuart & Co *v* Kennedy (1885) 13 R 221** one of the parties thought that the price of stone was per superficial foot whereas the other party thought that the price was per lineal foot. The contract was void.

In **Wilson *v* Marquis of Breadalbane (1859) 21 D 957** W sold cattle to the Marquis thinking that the price was to be according to the quality of the cattle. The Marquis thought that the price had been agreed at £13 per head. The contract was void. *Note*: this would normally mean that W would keep his cattle and the Marquis would not have to take nor pay for them. In this case, by the time the dispute arose and was decided in court, W had already delivered the cattle to the Marquis and they had been eaten. Thus *restitutio in integrum* was impossible. This just means things could not be put back the way they were before the attempt to contract. Since W couldn't get his cattle back, the court as a matter of equity had to order that the Marquis pay for them. The Marquis was ordered to pay the market price of £15 per head.

Error as to the nature of the contract

A party may sign a document without intending to undertake any contractual obligation at all – eg he signs thinking he is signing as a witness whereas his signature binds him as a party to a contract. Alternatively, his mistaken belief may be that he is entering one type of contract when in fact he is binding himself to a different type of contractual obligation altogether.

In **McLaurin *v* Stafford (1875) 3 R 265** a man thought he was signing a will which of course would only take effect on his death. In fact, he signed a disposition which had the effect to giving away his property right away. This was void.

In **Ellis *v* Lochgelly Iron and Coal Co Ltd 1909 SC 1278** (at p. 1282) – it was stated that a situation where **uninduced** essential error will invalidate a contract includes '... a case where there is actual error as to the *corpus* [body] of the document which is being signed at the time. A case is put by Professor Bell where a person is thinking that he is signing one thing while he is in fact signing another.' However, the decision in Ellis has been put in doubt by the case of **The Royal Bank of Scotland plc *v* Purvis 1990 SLT 262** where a wife who signed a guarantee as guarantor for money lent to her husband's business sought to reduce the guarantee on the grounds that she had signed it under essential error as to the corpus of the document and its nature. The couple had been in the course of moving house and when her husband asked her to come to the bank to sign papers she thought she was signing a 'mortgage' document to do with the house purchase. She argued that had she known the document was a guarantee she would not have signed it. She had not asked what the document was and merely signed it without reading it when it was passed to her. She argued that neither the bank nor her husband had explained what it was, or had asked her to read it, or advised her to take independent legal advice. These arguments failed. Lord McCluskey held that when the wife went to the bank she knew that she was signing a document which gave rise to obligations of some sort. This was an uninduced unilateral error and she was not entitled to any remedy. His Lordship was of the opinion that once the parties have signed a formal written contract they will be held to have consented to the obligations set out in the document. There will be no inquiry into the state of mind of the signatories unless the possibility is raised of their signature having been induced by misrepresentation.

No relief is given to the person who is mistaken about the legal effects of a contract which he signs; nor to a person who signs the right type of contract but signs carelessly without bothering to read its terms.

Error as to quality, quantity or extent of the subject matter, where such quality, quantity or extent is material to the contract

A agrees to buy B's car thinking it has a 2-litre engine when in fact it has only a 1.5-litre engine; or A agrees to buy some land from B thinking it extends to 1.75 acres whereas it extends to only 1.72 acres. These mistaken beliefs as to quality and extent will be regarded as errors in the substantials only if it was material to the contract that the car had a 2-litre engine or that the land extended to 1.75 acres. This will be so only if the main reason A agreed to buy the car was because he thought he was buying a car with a 2-litre engine and, but for that mistaken belief, he would not have bought the car.

INDUCED ERROR – MISREPRESENTATION

Where there is induced error, one party enters into a contract subject to some mistaken belief and they hold this belief because of something the other party has said or done. The error has been induced by the actions of the other party. This may be accidental or deliberate on the part of the other party to the contract. As far as the effect on a contract's validity is concerned, it does not matter whether an error is caused by innocent as opposed to deliberate misrepresentation. The key question is: how serious was the error which was caused by the misrepresentation? Where an error in the substantials is induced, the contract will be void; where *error concomitans* is induced, the resulting contract is voidable.

A misrepresentation is a materially inaccurate statement of fact made prior to the contract being formed; statements of honest opinion, statements of intention and exaggerative language used in advertising are not generally regarded as misrepresentation. In **Flynn** *v* **Scott 1949 SC 442** S, when selling a second-hand van to F, stated that the van was in good running order. When, seven days later, the van broke down, F tried to reject the van. F alleged that S's statement about the van was a material misrepresentation which had induced him to enter the contract. It was held that S's statement had been simply an expression of opinion and not a misrepresentation entitling F to repudiate the contract.

Similarly, in **Hamilton** *v* **Duke of Montrose (1906) 8 F 1026** a statement made regarding the capability of an area of land to maintain a certain number of livestock was held not to be a misrepresentation of fact but a mere statement of opinion.

INNOCENT MISREPRESENTATION

This occurs where an error has been induced by an inaccurate statement of fact made by the other party. If the person making the statement honestly believed it to be true, then this amounts to innocent misrepresentation and not to fraud. In order to render a contract void or voidable it is not enough merely that a misleading statement has been made. The statement must have been materially inaccurate; it must have been relied upon; it must have induced an error in the mind of the party to whom it was made; it must have led to a contract being formed.

A contract induced by innocent misrepresentation shall, at the very least, be voidable. Where the error induced by innocent misrepresentation is an error in the substantials, the contract is void. Because innocent misrepresentation, unlike fraud, is not a civil wrong, it does not give rise to an action for damages. Where a contract is set aside because of innocent misrepresentation, property which has been handed over must be returned as must any deposits or other monies already paid. However, any additional losses sustained as a consequence of entering into a contract induced by innocent misrepresentation cannot be recovered.

The inability to sue for damages in respect of innocent misrepresentation may leave a pursuer with no effective remedy if the contract cannot be set aside. A court will not reduce a contract unless *restitutio in integrum* is possible; the parties must be able to be returned to their original position. If the contract has proceeded to a point where this is a physical impossibility, no remedy is able to be offered. This was shown in the case of **Boyd & Forrest** *v* **The Glasgow and South-Western Railway Co 1912 SC (HL) 93** where a builder contracted to construct a railway at a price agreed on the strength of inaccurate information innocently provided by the railway company. The actual cost of building the railway was £100 000 more than the contract price. The builders raised an action to recover this extra cost. Their action failed. As the court found that there had been innocent rather than deliberate misrepresentation, no damages were payable and the builders' remedy was limited to seeking reduction of the contract. However, by the time the action was raised, the railway had already been built. This meant that *restitutio in integrum* was a physical impossibility and the contract could not be set aside. The builders had to bear the loss.

DELIBERATE OR FRAUDULENT MISREPRESENTATION

The case of **Derry *v* Peek (1889) 14 App Case 337** produced the following definition of fraudulent misrepresentation. There is fraudulent misrepresentation where a person makes a false statement of fact either:

1 knowing it to be untrue; *or*
2 without belief in its truth; *or*
3 recklessly, not caring whether it is true or false.

It does not matter that there was no intention to cheat or injure the person to whom the statement was made; there will be fraud if a statement is made without any honest belief in its truth.

As with innocent misrepresentation, the fraudulent statement must have been relied upon by the other party and must have been a deciding factor in his decision to proceed to enter a contract. Where the error induced by fraud is an error in the substantials, the contract is void; where the error is *error concomitans*, the contract is voidable. Unlike innocent misrepresentation, fraud is a civil wrong and, accordingly, a pursuer may seek damages in addition to having the contract reduced. There is also authority to the effect that damages may be awarded even if the contract is not reduced. In **Smith *v* Sim 1954 SC 357** Smith bought a public house from Sim for £21 600 as the turnover was represented as being very high. Sim had stated the turnover as twice its true figure. Smith was held entitled to choose not to resile from the contract but to keep the pub and sue for damages of £10 000.

As with innocent misrepresentation, *restitutio in integrum* should be possible before a contract induced by fraud may be set aside. However, there is authority to suggest that this will be less rigorously applied in cases of fraudulent misrepresentation – **Spence *v* Crawford 1939 SC (HL) 52.**

SILENCE AS MISREPRESENTATION

The parties to a contract are said to contract 'at arm's length'; it is up to each of the parties to look after his own interests and to discover any material facts for himself. Accordingly, silence will not – as a general rule – constitute a misrepresentation. However, there are exceptional situations where silence will be regarded as equivalent to misrepresentation:

1 Where the appearance of an article is deceptive to the extent that the article appears to be what it is not. The very appearance of the goods is a misrepresentation and even though the seller does not positively represent that the articles are genuine, there will be misrepresentation unless the false impression is corrected. Accordingly, in **Patterson *v* Landsberg (1905) 7 F 675** offering for sale chairs which had an antique appearance but which had been faked

amounted to a misrepresentation. Similarly, in **Gibson** *v* **The National Cash Register Co Ltd 1925 SC 500** G had sought to buy new cash registers but the defenders had sold him second-hand cash registers which by reason of re-conditioning appeared to be new. This amounted to fraudulent concealment and although G decided to keep the machines he was held entitled to damages.

2 If a misleading incomplete statement is not completed; a half truth amounts to misrepresentation. In **Couston** *v* **Miller (1862) 24 D 607** C signed a deed which M had read over to him, but M had read out only part of the document leaving out an essential part. This was misrepresentation.

3 Where a true representation of fact is made but there is a change in circumstances before a contract is complete. The person who made the original statement must take steps to correct the false impression, otherwise there will be misrepresentation. In **Shankland** *v* **Robinson 1920 SC (HL) 103** it was held that where the seller of a machine had said that it was not going to be requisitioned by the government, he would be required to advise the prospective buyer should he discover that there were now plans to requisition the machine.

FAILURE TO DISCLOSE MATERIAL FACTS

A material fact is one which, if known, would be a deciding factor in a person's decision whether or not to contract. As was stated above, parties to a contract are said to contract at arm's length and each must take steps to discover material facts for himself. The general rule is that there is no requirement to disclose a material fact to the other party. Subject to what was said above in respect of silence as a misrepresentation, if X wants to know something it is up to him to ask – Y need not volunteer information. The operation of this general rule may be seen in **Gillespie** *v* **Russel (1856) 18 D 677** . In this case, the prospective tenant of a coal mine did not tell the owner that he had discovered that the mine contained a particularly valuable seam of coal. When the owner discovered this he tried to get out of the lease. He failed; the court held that the lease was valid and the concealment of such information by the tenant was not fraud. The general rule was confirmed recently by the First Division of the Inner House in **Mumford** *v* **Bank of Scotland; Smith** *v* **Bank of Scotland 1996 SLT 392.** In this case two wives whose husbands were in business together had signed deeds in favour of the bank giving the bank security over their homes so that an overdraft could be obtained for the business. In effect the wives were acting as cautioners (guarantors) in respect of their husbands' borrowings. The wives subsequently sought to have these deeds reduced, claiming that they had been induced to sign by misrepresentation by their respective husbands. They did not claim that the bank had actual knowledge of this misrepresentation but argued that the bank knew that the transactions were not to the wives' advantage and should have been put on enquiry as to whether there had been misrepresentation by the husbands. Accordingly the wives argued that the bank had a duty to disclose to them the nature of the documentation and the risk that they were taking in signing it. Their arguments were rejected. Under Scots law there is no general duty of inquiry or of disclosure by a bank to a cautioner. Furthermore, a bank is not liable for misrepresentations by a borrower to induce a person to act as cautioner unless it can be established that the bank knew of the misrepresentation. There is no duty on a bank to make any disclosure to a cautioner as to the borrower's indebtedness to the bank or to explain the nature and effect of documentation the cautioner is asked to sign. It should be noted that in finding against the wives, the Inner House refused to follow the House of Lords decision in the English case of **Barclay's Bank plc *v* O'Brien [1994] 1 AC 180** where in similar circumstances the wife was successful.

However, there are exceptions to this general rule. In respect of two categories of contract there must be full disclosure of material facts and a failure to make such disclosure will give grounds for reduction of the contract:

1 **Contracts *uberrimae fidei*** – these are contracts where the parties must act in the utmost good faith. They include contracts of insurance and invitations to take shares in a company. The parties must declare all material facts which are known to them and failure to do so will give grounds for reduction. In the case of **The Spathari 1925 SC (HL) 6** Demetriades, a Greek living in Glasgow, bought a ship with the intention of sailing it to Greek waters to be resold. He arranged for the ship to be transferred into the name of a Glaswegian named Borthwick so that Borthwick could arrange for the insurance of the ship. Borthwick insured the *Spathari* without disclosing the Greek's interest in the ship. When the ship sank *en route* to Greece the insurance company refused to make payment. It was held that the insurance company was entitled to refuse payment because of Borthwick's failure to disclose a material fact – i.e., the Greek connection. This was material because, as was stated by the Lord Chancellor, '... Greek vessels were taboo in the marine insurance world. They were sinking in alarming numbers, and underwriters fought shy of insuring them.' It was found that if the true facts regarding the vessel had been fully disclosed, she would not have been insured at all. The court dismissed arguments that if the insurers had wanted such information it was their duty to ask for it. The contract of insurance was a contract *uberrimae fidei* and the insured had a duty to make full disclosure.
2 **Contracts involving fiduciary relationships** – these include contracts between parent and child, principal and agent, trustees and beneficiaries and agreements between partners. Parties to such contracts must make full disclosure of material facts.

NEGLIGENT MISREPRESENTATION

The concept of negligent misrepresentation properly falls within the law of delict. Delict concerns liability in respect of conduct in breach of a duty of care. There is liability for damage caused through negligence. There may be liability where financial loss is caused by a negligent misstatement. One party is under a legal duty not to make misleading statements to another party and fails to take reasonable care in exercising this duty. As a result, someone is induced to enter into a contract on the strength of the negligent misrepresentation.

Negligent misrepresentation does not involve deliberate dishonesty but occurs where there has not been reasonable care in checking the accuracy of information given. However, before there can be liability for breach of a duty of care, a duty of care must have been owed in the first place. A duty of care arises when a person of some skill giving information knows – or ought to know – that this information will be relied upon.

What is the potential effect upon the validity of a contract where A enters the contract because of incorrect information *negligently* supplied by B and as a consequence A suffers loss? Where B is the other party to the contract, the effect of B's negligent misrepresentation may be to allow A:

1 to seek to have the contract reduced; *or*
2 to seek damages from B; *or*
3 to seek both reduction of the contract and damages.

Where B is not the other party to a contract but is merely a third party who has supplied information to A, this does not affect the validity of the contract which A has entered into. However, where A has suffered loss as a consequence of B's negligent misrepresentation, A may sue B for damages under the law of delict.

Delictual liability for negligent misrepresentation in the absence of a contractual relationship between the parties was established by the House of Lords' decision in the English case of **Hedley Byrne & Co** *v* **Heller and Partners [1964] AC 465**. In this case a bank was potentially liable for loss suffered by the pursuers as a consequence of the pursuers' reliance upon an inaccurate credit reference supplied by the bank. The bank was only saved because of an effective disclaimer attached to the reference. It had been unclear whether the decision in *Hedley Byrn* could be taken as also reflecting the position under Scots law. For the avoidance of doubt, the Law Reform (Miscellaneous Provisions) (Scotland) Act 1985 s 10(1) declared that notwithstanding the absence of fraud, damages are recoverable in respect of negligent misrepresentation.

THE EFFECT OF VOID AND VOIDABLE CONTRACTS ON THE RIGHTS OF INNOCENT THIRD PARTIES

What happens if A sells goods to B and B resells those goods to C and the original contract between A and B was for some reason void or voidable? What is the effect of such a situation on C's legal rights of ownership of the goods?

If the original contract between A and B was void –

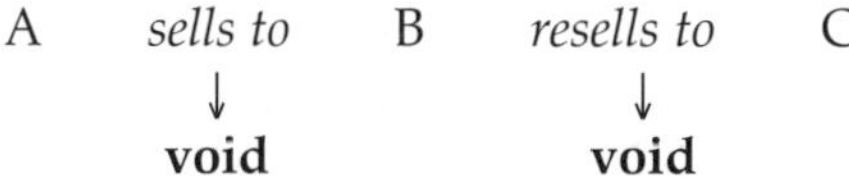

If A's original contract with B is void for whatever reason, then that means there never was any contract between A and B. Neither A nor B had any legal rights nor were they under any legal obligations.

The purpose of a contract of sale of goods is to transfer legal rights of ownership from one person to another. If a sale of goods contract is void, no rights of ownership ever transfer. If the contract between A and B was void, then A never lost his ownership rights and B never gained any ownership rights in the goods. This means that when B attempts to resell the goods to C he has no legal rights in the goods to transfer to C. The second contract must also be void. In a dispute between A and C as to who should have possession of the goods, A must win. C's only remedy is to sue B for the return of the price paid for the goods. (See **Morrisson** *v* **Robertson 1908 SC 332** below.)

If the original contract between A and B was voidable –

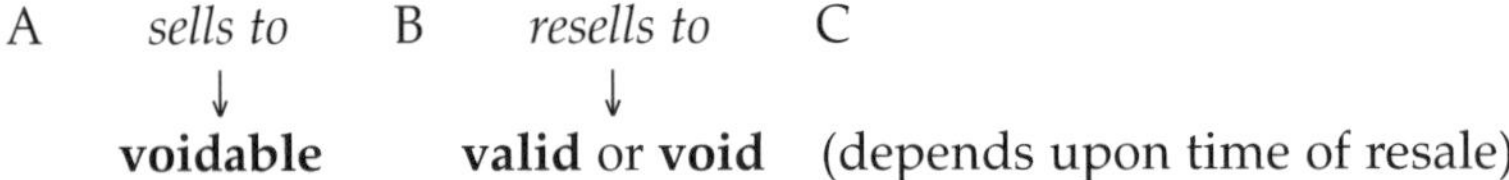

If A's original contract with B was voidable for whatever reason, then that means that until steps are taken to reduce the contract, a valid contract is in existence which gives rise to rights and obligations. Such rights and obligations persist until the contract is reduced. This means that under the original contract of sale of goods between A and B, A's legal rights of ownership transfer to B until A takes steps to have the contract reduced. If, before A takes such steps, B resells to C, B *does* have legal rights of ownership to pass on to C. The second contract will be valid. In such a situation in a dispute between A and C, C will win; A must sue B.

If B resells after A has acted, he will have no legal rights to pass to C and, accordingly, the second contract will be void. Thus in a dispute between A and C, C must return the goods to A. C's only remedy is to sue B for the return of the price. (See **MacLeod** *v* **Kerr 1965 SLT 358** below.)

In **Morrisson** *v* **Robertson 1908 SC 332** M was on his way to market to sell cattle when he met T, a con man, who pretended to be the son of Wilson, a well-known farmer. T said that it would save time if he just bought M's cattle for his 'father'. He also asked M to let him have the cattle on credit and asked him to send the bill to his 'father', Wilson of Bonnyrigg. Because he thought he was contracting with this well-known farmer, M agreed to part with the cattle. When he contacted Wilson, Wilson knew nothing about it. M tracked the cattle down to R, an innocent third party, who had bought the cattle in good faith from T, the con man. M brought an action against R for the return of the cattle. M won. Why did he win?

M contracted subject to an error. The error was an error as to identity – he thought he was contracting with Wilson when he was not. How serious was this error? It was an error in the substantials. An error as to identity is only an error in the substantials if identity is *material* to the contract. The question then becomes – did M only sell the cattle to T because he thought he was contracting with Wilson, or would he have parted with his cattle without cash payment to just anyone he happened to meet on the road? It was found that identity *was* material. M only sold the cattle as he did because he thought he was dealing with Wilson. The error in the substantials renders the contract void. In this case the error happened to be induced by fraud – T misrepresented his identity to induce M to contract. As the first contract between M and T was void, the second contract between T and R must also be void. T never obtained any ownership rights from M which he could pass on to R. M was entitled to the return of his cattle. R's only remedy would be to sue T if he could find him.

In **MacLeod** *v* **Kerr 1965 SLT 358** K sold his car to a con man who paid by stolen cheque. The con man then resold the car to a garage owner, G. However, in this case, unlike *Morrisson v Robertson*, the identity of the purchaser was not material to the contract. K did not agree to accept a cheque only because he thought he was dealing with the person whose name was on the cheque – he would have taken anyone's cheque. K was happy to sell the car to the man standing there before him. Accordingly the con man's fraud in paying for the car with a worthless cheque made the first contract voidable, not void. The con man resold the car before K acted to have the first contract reduced, the resale was valid, and G kept the car.

ERRORS OF EXPRESSION AND TRANSMISSION

Where the contract as expressed does not reflect the agreements reached by the parties what effect does that have on the validity of a contract? What is the effect on a contract's validity if there is a breakdown in transmission of either the offer or acceptance so that the message as received is not the message as sent?

Clerical error in a contractual document

If there is a clerical or arithmetical error in the document so that the document does not accurately set out what the parties have agreed, in such cases the court may be prepared to intervene to rectify the document and to enforce the contract as actually agreed. In **Krupp** *v* **John Menzies Ltd 1907 SC 903** it was agreed that a hotel manageress would be paid 1/20 of profits as salary. The written contract said that salary was to be 1/5 of profits. It was alleged that this was due to an arithmetical error by the clerk drawing up the written document. The manageress tried to claim the higher salary. The employers were held entitled to have the written contract varied '... to give expression to the true contract as agreed by the parties.' The Law Reform (Miscellaneous Provisions) (Scotland) Act 1985 ss 8 and 9 provide that either the Court of Session or the Sheriff Court can order a document to be rectified where the document fails to express accurately the agreement reached by the parties.

Faulty transmission of telegram or telephone call

If the message received is not the message as sent; or where the line goes dead half-way through a telephone call; or where a message is in code and when decoded is given a different meaning, there is no valid contract. In **Verdin Brothers** *v* **Robertson (1871) 10 M 35** the defenders had sent a telegram to the pursuers requesting delivery of a consignment of salt. Because of the fault of telegraph officials, a totally scrambled message was received by the pursuers. As a result of this, the pursuers sent the salt to the wrong address. By the time the mistake was realised the salt was too late for the defenders' purposes and they refused to take delivery. The pursuers sued for the price. Their action failed. The defenders could not be in breach of contract because there was no valid contract in the first place. Because the order which was delivered was not the order which was sent there was no *consensus in idem* and accordingly no contract of sale.

Misstatement of terms by offeror – 'slip of the pen' cases

What if a person offering to sell a fairly new car intends to write £10 000 and by a slip of the pen writes £1000? If the offer is accepted, is the offeror legally bound to hand over the car for £1000? Much depends upon the state of knowledge of the person receiving the offer. If the offeree actually knew that the offeror intended to ask £10 000, then he would be acting in bad faith if he tried to hold the offeror to £1000. There would not be an enforceable contract.

If the offeree does not have actual knowledge of what the offeror was intending to write, the court will decide if a reasonable person receiving such an offer would have realised that a mistake had been made. If it was obvious that this was a mistake, the offeror will not be bound.

In the case of **Steel's Tr *v* Bradley Homes 1972 SC 48** X had offered payment of money with interest of 10 per cent from 16 March 1971. Y accepted this in writing but later realised he had made a mistake and had meant to ask for interest from 16 March 1969. Y tried to have the contract set aside because of his mistake in writing 1971 when he had meant to write 1969. However, the court held that Y was not entitled to have the contract reduced because Y's true intention was unknown to X, and could not reasonably have been known to him.

Another case dealing with an error of expression was that of **Angus *v* Bryden 1992 SCLR 626**. In this case A sought to rectify a dispostion of fishing rights. He had meant to sell only river fishings but the disposition (the formal document implementing the bargain) also included sea fishings at the mouth of the river. A approached the case on two fronts. His first argument was that on a proper interpretation of the missives (ie the offer, counter offer and acceptance) the sea fishings were not included in the sale and all that was needed was a rectification of the disposition – either at common law or under the Law Reform (Miscellaneous Provisions) (Scotland) Act 1985 s 8 – so that it reflected properly the agreement which had been reached. A's alternative argument was that if the missives did include the sea fishings in the sale, that bargain should be reduced on the grounds of the uninduced unilateral error contained in A's qualified acceptance. Lord Cameron upheld A's first argument that the missives had not included the sea fishings. However, he proceeded to discuss A's alternative argument that if the sea fishings *were* included in the missives, it was as a result of an unintentional but material error on A's part that this error was known to B and that B's acceptance had not been in good faith.

Lord Cameron was of the opinion that in such circumstances the court could go behind the disposition and consider the circumstances in which the missives came to be concluded. He also thought that the earlier case of **Steuart's Trs *v* Hart (1875) 3 R 192** was still good law and was binding; its ratio being that an unintentional error being an error of expression by one party is a wrong for which our law provides a remedy, the error being of the nature of essential error, that is, one but for which the party making the error would not have contracted. The remedy is based on the bad faith of the defenders in taking advantage of what they knew to be an unintentional error.

His lordship followed the decision in *Steel's Tr* v *Bradley Homes* but did not follow the decision in the case of **Spook Erection (Northern) Ltd** *v* **Kaye 1990 SLT 676**. In the Spook Erection case, Lord Marnoch stated that he did not consider himself bound by *Steuart's Trs* v *Hart* and did not follow the decision in *Steel's Trustee*. However, the issue in *Spook Erection* related to the uninduced unilateral error of the seller of property as to its true value. Such an uninduced error does not give grounds for reduction of the contract; whether the buyer knew the true value and realised that the seller did not makes no difference. Such an error of intention is distinct from an error of expression.

FACILITY AND CIRCUMVENTION

This consists of two elements – both of which must be present in order to render a contract voidable. One party must be facile – i.e., suffering from a weakness of resolve, a weakness of the normal adult will. It does not amount to insanity and thus the person does have contractual capacity. Facility is generally associated with the elderly or those recovering from serious illness. A person may also be regarded as facile as a consequence of intoxication. To establish circumvention, the other party must be shown to have taken advantage of the weakness so as to benefit from it.

In the case of **MacGilvray** *v* **Gilmartin 1986 SLT 89** the pursuer, who was the executor of his dead mother's estate, asked the court to set aside a deed, signed by his mother, which transferred heritable property to his sister. The pursuer alleged that there had been facility and circumvention. At the time the deed was signed, the mother had been suffering from severe depression due to the death of her husband. The pursuer alleged that his sister had taken advantage of her mother's facility so as to persuade her to transfer the property. The court sustained the pursuer's arguments and the deed was set aside.

UNDUE INFLUENCE

This will render a contract voidable. There must exist a relationship of trust which has been abused by the person in the position of trust. Where there is such a relationship and the stronger person gains advantage, the court will pay particular interest as to whether the weaker party has had the benefit of independent advice. Relationships where undue influence might arise are those between parent and child, doctor and patient, solicitor and client, etc.

In **Gray** *v* **Binny (1879) 7R 332** a father left an estate to his son. The mother persuaded the son to transfer the estate to her. This was reduced on the ground that the mother and the family solicitor, who was the mother's creditor, had taken advantage of the son's ignorance of his rights and of his confidence in them.

In **Forbes** *v* **Forbes' Trustees 1957 SC 325** a wife entered into an ante-nuptial contract on the advice of her father. Seven years later she tried to have the contract reduced claiming that when she entered the contract she had been subject to unduly exercised parental control considering that the contract prevented any release of capital. She did not succeed, it being held that the father had acted in the interests of the daughter and had not abused her confidence in him.

FORCE AND FEAR

Where consent to a contract has been obtained by physical violence or threats of such violence or other unjustified threats sufficient to overcome the will of a reasonable person, having a mind of ordinary firmness, the contract will be void through lack of true consent, as in **Earl of Orkney** *v* **Vinfra (1606) Mor 16481**.

It should be noted, however, that lawful threats such as the threat to sue for a debt do not constitute inducement through force and fear – **Lamson & Co** *v* **McPhail 1914 SC 73**.

QUESTIONS

1 What is meant by the terms 'void' and 'voidable'?

2 Define and distinguish between 'uninduced error' and 'induced error'.

3 Define and distinguish between 'common error' and 'mutual error'.

4 Discuss what would constitute an error in the substantials and describe the effect of such an error on the validity of a contract.

5 What is meant by identity being 'material' to the contract?

6 Define and distinguish between 'innocent misrepresentation' and 'fraudulent misrepresentation'.

7 Freda has advertised for sale a valuable antique silver teapot. A well-dressed gentleman in a smart car arrives at her home early one evening, introduces himself as Mr RT Swindell, senior partner in a local firm of solicitors and shows Freda his business card. It is his wife's birthday and the teapot is just the thing. They agree a price and Freda has already packaged the teapot when Mr Swindell discovers that he has left his chequebook at the office. He asks if he may take the teapot and send a messenger with the cheque the next day. Reassured by the fact that he is a well-known local businessman, Freda parts

with the teapot. Two days pass and no cheque arrives. Freda decides to call at Mr Swindell's office. She is aghast to discover that Mr Swindell is not the gentleman who bought the teapot. She then discovers that the local antique shop had bought the teapot from the impostor the previous day.

What is the effect of the above on the validity of Freda's contract? Can Freda get the teapot back from the antique shop? Give detailed reasoning and support your answer with case law.

8 Bob took out a life insurance policy. He responded to all the questions and answered truthfully that he did not participate in scuba diving, rock climbing or parachuting. He did not volunteer the information that his favourite hobby was hang-gliding. Bob has now been killed while hang-gliding and the insurance company are refusing to pay. What is the legal position?

9 Jean has entered into a contract of employment with Dave. They have agreed that in addition to her salary, Jean shall be paid a bonus equivalent to two per cent of the sales which she makes. In her written contract the bonus is defectively expressed as 20 per cent of sales. Can Jean hold Dave to this?

5 The construction of the contract

INTERPRETATION

Should a dispute arise between the parties to a contract, the court is required to determine the terms of the contract. Having determined the contract's terms, the court must then proceed to interpret them. In so doing the court attempts to give effect to the apparent intention of the parties as expressed in the contract. The intention of the parties is determined by what they said, not by what they meant to say. As a general rule, the court will prefer an interpretation which allows a contract to be given effect to. However, this may not always be possible if, for example, the language used is too vague in which case the contract shall fall.

The terms of the contract

Express terms – these are terms clearly set out and agreed upon by the parties either verbally or in writing.

Terms incorporated by reference – these are terms which are imported into the contract by reference to provisions set out in full elsewhere. For example, the parties to a contract may declare that their contract is to be subject to model terms approved and published by a professional body.

Implied terms – these are terms which the law may hold to be included in a contract even though the parties have not expressly included them. Terms may be implied generally into contracts by statute, or by judicial precedent, or by custom. In addition, a court may find it necessary to imply a term into a particular contract in order to achieve business efficacy for that contract. For example, the Sale of Goods Act 1979 provides that it shall be an implied term of any sale of goods contract that goods sold in the course of a business shall be of satisfactory quality.

As a general rule a term cannot be implied if it contradicts an express term in the contract. However, certain terms implied by statute cannot be 'got rid of' by an express term in the contract.

Rules of interpretation

Intervention – as stated above, the court must interpret the contract so as to give effect to the intention of the parties as expressed in the contract. In so doing, words should generally be given their ordinary, everyday meaning. The court must interpret the contract as formed by the parties; the court is not to rewrite the contract for the parties unless there is statutory authority for intervention, such as under the Consumer Credit Act 1974 provisions on extortionate credit bargains.

Extrinsic evidence – this is evidence from outwith the contract itself and the use of such evidence as an aid to interpretation may be curtailed. In terms of the **parole evidence rule**, where the contract is in writing, any verbal evidence is inadmissible. Under the present law, when a document appears to contain the terms of a contract, the general rule is that extrinsic evidence cannot be led to prove an additional term. Parties may have agreed to an additional term which is not in the document. However, if one of the parties denies having so agreed, he can found on the document and extrinsic evidence is inadmissible.

The Scottish Law Commission, in its **Report on Three Bad Rules in Contract Law (Scot Law Com No 152)** published on 11 January 1996, recommended that the rule which disallows extrinsic evidence to prove an additional term of a contract or unilateral voluntary obligation should be replaced by a presumption that a document which appears to contain all the express terms of a contract does contain all those terms. However, this presumption should be capable of rebuttal and extrinsic evidence should be admissible for that purpose.

However, evidence may be admitted of the meaning of foreign words or technical terms. In addition where there is a latent defect in the contract, i.e., an error which is not obvious on the face of the deed, extrinsic evidence may be allowed to show that an agreement was reached which differs from that which is defectively expressed in the deed.

The *contra proferentem* rule – ambiguous words and phrases must be interpreted contrary to the interests of the party who is now relying upon them.

The *ejusdem generis* rule – where the contract refers to a list of things which are of the same type or which share common characteristics followed by general words (e.g., 'and other things'), these 'other things' are interpreted as being restricted to items of the same type or having the same characteristics as those actually listed.

EXCLUSION CLAUSES

One party to a contract may seek to include a term which excludes or limits his civil liability for the consequences of a breach of contract or negligence on his part. Such a term is known as an '**exclusion clause**' and may be included as an express term of the contract. Alternatively, one party may seek to incorporate such an exclusion clause into the contract by reference to conditions found in another document or on a notice or on a ticket.

For example, should you leave your coat in a cloakroom, there may be a notice which states, 'The management accepts no liability whatsoever for loss of or damage to items deposited in this cloakroom, whether such damage is caused by the negligence of our employees or otherwise.' Similarly, should you park your car you may receive a ticket on which it is stated, 'Cars are parked entirely at the owner's risk.' To what extent are such exclusion clauses effective? Limitations on the use of such clauses exist both at common law and under statute, the relevant statutory provision being the Unfair Contract Terms Act 1977.

Limitations on the use of exclusion clauses at common law

At common law an exclusion clause will be given effect to only if its terms are incorporated in the contract. Where an exclusion clause is an express term of the contract, then at common law it shall be upheld. However, a term which would be upheld at common law may be rendered ineffective by the provisions of the Unfair Contract Terms Act 1977.

Where the defender seeks to rely upon an exclusion clause contained in a notice or on a ticket, he must establish that the terms of the exclusion clause have been incorporated into the contract. In a series of cases known as '**ticket cases**', the courts have had to decide the circumstances in which clauses on tickets are effectively incorporated into the contract. The two key points are the nature of the ticket upon which the clause appears and the knowledge of the person receiving the ticket. Before a clause on a ticket will have effect at common law:

1 the ticket should be of a type which a reasonable person might expect to form part of the contractual documentation; *and*
2 reasonable steps must have been taken to bring the condition to the notice of the person receiving the ticket.

An exclusion clause contained in or referred to on a ticket is unlikely to be incorporated into the contract should the person receiving the ticket reasonably regard it merely as a voucher which entitles him to a service or as a receipt which proves payment. In **Taylor *v* Glasgow Corporation 1952 SC 440** Mrs Taylor visited Woodside Public Baths in Glasgow for the purpose of taking a bath. On paying sixpence she received a ticket which she was to give to the bath attendant. On the front of the ticket it said, 'For conditions see other side' and on the back there was a clause which said that Glasgow Corporation was not liable should users of the baths be injured. Mrs Taylor fell down a stair in the baths and was injured. She alleged that her injury was due to the negligence of the Corporation's employees. The Corporation argued she was barred from raising an action for damages because of the exclusion clause in the contract. Mrs Taylor knew that there was printing on the ticket but did not read the condition. It was held that the ticket was not of a type which a person could reasonably be expected to study for conditions. Mrs Taylor was entitled to regard the ticket she received as a voucher which she had to hand over in order to obtain use of a bath. The exclusion clause was ineffective and she could proceed with her action.

However, in the same case it was stated that certain types of tickets, such as railway tickets and cloakroom tickets, are ones upon which a reference to conditions is sufficient notice of those conditions – so long as the reference is legibly printed on the front of the ticket.

Where there is nothing on the front of the ticket but an exclusion clause is printed on the back, the exclusion clause is ineffective if the person receiving the ticket was unaware of the condition. This was the case in **Henderson & Others *v* Stevenson (1875) 2 R (HL) 71** where a condition on the back of a steamer ticket excluded liability for loss of luggage. There was nothing on the front of the ticket and Stevenson's attention was not specifically drawn to the condition on the back. The steamer sank and Stevenson raised an action for damages for lost luggage. It was held that the exclusion clause had not been incorporated into Stevenson's contract with the steamer company.

Even where a clause is on the front of the ticket it may be ineffective as in the case of **Williamson *v* The North of Scotland Navigation Co 1916 SC 554**, where the clause was printed in the smallest type known so that it was almost impossible to read. In this case the company had not done what was reasonably sufficient to give the customer notice of the condition. In **Hood *v* The Anchor Line 1918 SC (HL) 143** sufficient notice was given of the conditions by printing on the envelope which contained the ticket a conspicuous notice asking passengers to read the conditions of the enclosed contract. The ticket itself also had on the front, in large type, a statement that the contract was subject to conditions and a further request to passengers to read the contract carefully.

What is clear is that notice of the exclusion clause must be given to the other party to the contract *before* the contract is formed. Terms cannot be incorporated into a contract after the contract is complete. For example, a hotel puts up notices on the doors of the bedrooms to the effect that the hotel owners are not liable for loss of or damage to guests' property. Such a notice is ineffective should a guest's property be damaged because of the negligence of hotel staff. The guest would see the notice only after checking into the hotel – i.e., after the contract with the hotel was formed; by then it is too late to incorporate new conditions into the contract.

This point was emphasised in the English case of **Thornton *v* Shoe Lane Parking Ltd [1971] 2 QB 163**. Operators of a car park sought to exclude liability for damage to cars and personal injury via exclusion clauses printed on the parking tickets and on notices within the car park itself. Users of the car park obtained the tickets from an automatic machine at the entrance to the car park. As taking the ticket constituted an acceptance of a standing offer made by the machine, the conditions would not come to the notice of car park users until after the contract had been formed. Similarly the notice would be seen only after contract formation. Accordingly the exclusion clause was ineffective.

Statutory limitation on the use of exclusion clauses: Unfair Contract Terms Act 1977

At common law an exclusion clause which was either an express term or effectively incorporated into the contract would be upheld. However, exclusion clauses are now also subject to controls imposed by the Unfair Contract Terms Act 1977 which is an act which limits the extent to which civil liability can be avoided by means of contract terms or by the use of non-contractual notices. Part I of the Act applies only in England and Wales and Northern Ireland, Part II of the Act applies only in Scotland and Part III of the Act applies to the whole of the UK. The Act as originally enacted did not apply in Scotland to non-contractual notices, although Part I of the Act did apply to such notices in England and Wales. However, the Law Reform

(Miscellaneous Provisions) (Scotland) Act 1990 s 68 amended the 1977 Act so that, as from 1 April 1991, non-contractual notices in Scotland are also subject to the Act's provisions.

Accordingly, the Act previously controlled provisions in notices only where those provisions were imported into a contract. The Act now also controls the use of notices which attempt to exclude liability where there is no contract between the person who is relying on the notice and the person who is injured. For example, the 1977 Act now applies in Scotland to exclusion clauses in survey reports prepared by surveyors whose contract is with a building society and not with the house purchaser. Prior to 1 April 1991, should a surveyor negligently have failed to notice rising damp in a house, his liability to the purchaser could be excluded by an exclusion of liability clause in the survey report. Now such clauses will be effective only if the surveyor can persuade the court that it was fair and reasonable for him to rely on the clause.

The 1977 Act controls the use of exclusion clauses by persons who are in business. Business in this context includes a profession and the activities of central and local government. Where a business person includes an exclusion clause in a contract of a type to which the Act applies, or in a non-contractual notice, certain clauses may be void and others upheld only if it is fair and reasonable in the circumstances to do so.

The 1977 Act s 15 sets out the types of contract to which the Act applies:

(a) contracts which transfer the ownership or possession of goods from one person to another – e.g., contracts of sale of goods or contracts of hire;
(b) contracts of employment or apprenticeship;
(c) contracts relating to services – e.g., contracts of carriage of goods, left luggage and cloakroom sevices, car parking and garage repairs, other forms of repair services, laundry and dry-cleaning services, loan services;
(d) contracts relating to the liability of an occupier of land to persons entering upon or using that land – e.g., contracts relating to the use of cinemas, discos, theatres and fairgrounds;
(e) contracts relating to a grant of any right or permission to enter upon or use land not amounting to an interest in land – e.g., contracts whereby a person enters onto land to carry out repairs or other work, *not* contracts for the sale of land.

The 1977 Act does *not* apply to contracts of insurance or to contracts relating to the formation, constitution or dissolution of companies or partnerships.

The 1977 Act s 16 contains controls in respect of a term of a contract or a provision in a notice which attempts to exclude liability for either a breach of contract or for negligence. Where a contractual term or a provision in a notice attempts to exclude liability for death or personal injury, that term or provision shall be **void**; where a contractual term or a provision in a notice attempts to exclude other liability (eg liability for damage to property) that term or provision shall be upheld only if it was **fair and reasonable either to incorporate that term in the contract or to allow reliance on the provision in the notice**.

The 1977 Act s 17 also applies the 'fair and reasonable' test to certain terms in **consumer contracts** and **standard form contracts**. A consumer contract is a contract in which:

(a) one party is dealing in the course of a business;
(b) the other party is not dealing in the course of a business *and*
(c) *if* it is a contract for the sale or hire of goods, the goods are of a type ordinarily supplied for private use or consumption.

There is no statutory definition of a standard form contract but it may be described as one where the customer is required to deal on the basis of written standard terms prepared and invariably used by the other party in the course of his business. Note that the 'customer' under a standard form contract may also deal in the course of a business – i.e., a standard form contract may be between two businesses. In terms of s 17, any term in either a consumer contract or a standard form contract which:

(a) excludes or restricts liability for breach of contract, or enables a party not to perform his contractual obligations at all, *or*
(b) enables a party to render performance which is substantially different from that which the consumer or customer reasonably expected,

shall be ineffective unless it was fair and reasonable to incorporate the term in the contract.

In the case of **Elliot *v* Sunshine Coast International Ltd 1989 GWD 28-1252** a lady with a weak bladder had booked a coach holiday to Spain only after she had checked with the tour operator that the coach would have a toilet as stated in the brochure. Unfortunately her coach did not have a toilet and she refused to board. In the subsequent action for repayment of her money the tour operator sought to rely on a term in the booking form which allowed them to alter the form of transport used. The Sheriff Principal was of the opinion that to provide a coach without a toilet was to 'render a performance substantially different from that which the consumer reasonably expected from the contract'.

The 1977 Act s 18 provides that a term in a consumer contract is ineffective if it requires the consumer to indemnify another person, if it was not fair and reasonable to incorporate that indemnity clause. For example, Sarah hires caterers for a party she is holding. The caterers include an indemnity clause in the contract to the effect that should one of their waiters negligently pour soup over one of Sarah's guests, Sarah shall reimburse the caterers for the amount of any compensation which the caterers have to pay to Sarah's guest. Because this is a consumer contract, the court will uphold the indemnity clause only if it considers the clause to be fair and reasonable.

The 1977 Act s 20 controls the extent to which the implied terms in a sale of goods contract or a hire-purchase contract may be excluded. This will be discussed more fully in the chapters on sale of goods and consumer credit, but, basically, where the contract is a consumer contract the terms implied by statute cannot be excluded by an express term in the contract. Where the contract is a contract between two businesses, the test is whether the exclusion of the implied term was *fair and reasonable*. The exception to this latter point is the implied term as to the seller's right to sell the goods; any attempt to get rid of this implied term is *always* void irrespective of whether the buyer is a consumer or another business.

What is meant by 'fair and reasonable'?

The 1977 Act s 24 provides guidelines on how to determine whether it was fair and reasonable either to incorporate a term in a contract or to allow reliance on a provision in a notice. In respect of contractual terms, a court must take into account only those circumstances which were known, or ought to have been known, to the parties at the time the contract was made. In respect of provisions on notices, regard shall be had to all the circumstances at the time liability arose, or would have arisen but for the notice.

In determining whether an exclusion clause was fair and reasonable as between two businesses for the purposes of s 20 of the 1977 Act, the court must have regard to the guidelines set out in Schedule 2 to the 1977 Act. The court should have regard to such matters as the relative strength of the bargaining positions of the parties; whether the customer could have obtained the goods elsewhere; whether the customer agreed to the exclusion clause in exchange for a discount; whether the customer had accepted such clauses in the past; and whether the goods were made to the special order of the customer.

Section 24 further provides that the onus of proving that a contractual term or a provision in a notice is fair and reasonable lies on the party who is trying to rely on that term or provision.

The provisions of ss 20 and 24 and Schedule 2 were considered in the case of **Denholm Fishselling Ltd *v* Anderson 1991 SLT (Sh. Ct.) 24**. In this case A bought a consignment of fish from D in the fish market in Peterhead. Some time later eleven of the boxes of cod were found to be unfit for human consumption. A refused to pay for them and D raised an action for payment. A argued that the fish were not of merchantable quality in breach of the warranty implied by the Sale of Goods Act 1979 s 14. D countered that the implied term as to quality was effectively excluded by a term of the contract between the parties.The 1977 Act s 20 controls the extent to which such implied terms may be excluded and provides that where the contract is between two businesses, the test is whether it was fair and reasonable to include the exclusion clause in the contract. In terms of s 24 and Schedule 2, in determining whether an exclusion clause was fair and reasonable as between two businesses, the court should have regard to factors such as the relative strength of the bargaining position of the parties, whether the customer could have obtained the goods elsewhere and whether the customer knew of the terms as a result of having dealt with the seller in the past. In this case A argued that the exclusion clause was not fair and reasonable because the parties' bargaining positions were not of equal strength. A pointed to the fact that all the fish sellers in Peterhead and elsewhere in Scotland used the same standard conditions set out in a printed document and argued that this put buyers at a disadvantage because they dealt with what was effectively a monopoly. The clause in question provided that 'Buyers shall be afforded a reasonable opportunity to examine all fish exposed for sale and shall be held to have satisfied themselves, before completion of the transaction, as to their condition, weight and quantity, and in every other respect.' The effect of the clause was that risk passed to the buyer at the time of sale and he was not entitled to withhold payment if the goods were subsequently found to be defective. A also argued that it was impracticable to make an exhaustive examination of the fish before the sale and it was unfair to deprive him of a remedy in respect of defects which he could not discover until it was too late.

The Sheriff nevertheless found that the exclusion clause was fair and reasonable and ordered A to pay for the fish. A appealed but the Sheriff Principal agreed with the Sheriff and refused the appeal. The Sheriff Principal rejected the monopoly argument. He held that the fact that all the sellers used the same terms did not create a monopoly and that A could buy fish from any one of many sellers. It was stated that the use of standard conditions did not of itself mean that there was an inequality of bargaining power. This may be so where a customer has the option of giving his custom to another seller who does not impose such conditions but it fails to take account of the fact that A could not have obtained his fish elsewhere on less onerous terms. The Sheriff Principal was also of the opinion that the clause was fair and reasonable in the context of the commercial realities of the fish market where it might be difficult to prove either that the defect existed at the time of the sale or even that a particular box of fish was bought from a particular seller. The use of the clause would therefore in his view eliminate the possibility of difficult and costly disputes.

Finally, in terms of the 1977 Act s 25, the Act not only strikes at clauses which purport to exclude or restrict liability, but also at those clauses which seek to curtail one party's rights to pursue a claim. Such clauses might include a requirement to complain within a certain number of days or might attempt to restrict the range of remedies available.

The Unfair Terms in Consumer Contracts Regulations 1994

These regulations, which came into force on 1 July 1995, seek to implement the EC Directive on Unfair Terms in Consumer Contracts 93/13 EEC. While there is a degree of overlap between the Unfair Contract Terms Act 1977 and the new regulations, there are also differences, in that while the Act primarily controls terms seeking to limit or exclude liability, the regulations go further in declaring that 'an unfair term in a contract concluded with a consumer by a seller or supplier shall not be binding on the consumer'. There is provision for the severance of the unfair term, where that is possible, to allow the rest of the contract to stand.

The regulations provide that an unfair term is 'any term which contrary to the requirement of good faith causes a significant imbalance in the parties' rights and obligations under the contract to the detriment of the consumer'. In determining whether the term is fair, the following should be taken into account:

1 the nature of the goods or services in question;
2 the circumstances attending the conclusion of the contract;
3 all other terms of the contract.

Schedule 2 to the regulations gives guidance on what is relevant when determining whether the requirement of good faith has been met. Relevant factors include:

(a) the strength of the parties' bargaining positions;
(b) whether the consumer received an inducement to agree to the term;
(c) whether the goods or services were made or supplied to the special order of the consumer;

(d) the extent to which the seller or supplier has dealt fairly with the consumer.

The regulations apply only to contract terms which have not been 'individually negotiated'. The burden of proving that a term has been individually negotiated is on the seller or supplier. A term will not have been individually negotiated where it has been drafted in advance and the consumer has been unable to influence its substance. Accordingly, standard form consumer contracts will be subject to the regulations.

The regulations define a 'seller' and a 'supplier' as a person who for purposes related to his business sells or supplies goods or services. A 'consumer' is a natural person who contracts for purposes which are outside his business.

Contracts to which the regulations apply must also be expressed in 'plain, intelligible language'. Where there is any doubt as to the meaning of a term, it must be interpreted in the consumer's favour.

It should be noted that unlike the 1977 Act, the regulations do apply to insurance contracts. However, the regulations do not apply to:

(i) employment contracts;
(ii) contracts relating to succession rights;
(iii) contracts relating to rights under family law;
(iv) contracts relating to the incorporation and organisation of companies or partnerships.

Also excluded from the scope of the regulations are terms which define the subject matter of the contract or concern the adequacy of the price or remuneration, as against the goods or services sold or supplied.

As a final point, the Director General of Fair Trading is empowered to seek an interdict in the Court of Session to prevent the use of a particular unfair term.

TITLE TO SUE

A contract is an agreement which creates rights and obligations which are legally enforceable. Should one of the parties fail to perform their obligations under a contract, the other party may take steps to enforce the contract. A party with the right to raise a court action to enforce a contract is said to have a **title to sue**. As a general rule, only those persons who are parties to the contract enjoy a title to sue on the contract. Third parties do not as a general rule acquire any rights or obligations under a contract entered into by others. It may be in C's interests that a contract between A and B should go ahead. This does not of itself give C the right to take enforcement action should A be in breach of contract.

There are, however, exceptions to the general rule that third parties have no title to sue. A third party may obtain a title to sue as a consequence of an **assignation** (transfer) of contractual rights or obligations. Alternatively, a third party may enjoy a title to sue as a consequence of the parties to the contract creating a ***jus*** *quaesitum tertio*. In addition, rights to sue may be transmitted on **death** or **bankruptcy**.

Assignation of contractual rights and obligations

It may be possible for one party to a contract to transfer his rights or obligations under that contract to a third party. The person who makes the transfer is known as the **assignor** or ***cedent***. The third party to whom rights or obligations are transferred is known as the **assignee**. No special form of words is required in order to make the transfer; however, the fact of the assignation should be intimated to the other party to the contract.

Whether or not a particular right or obligation may be assigned depends upon whether ***delectus personae*** is present. There is *delectus personae* where X enters into a contract with Y only because of the personal skills which Y has. X has deliberately chosen Y and will not be prepared to accept a substitute. The oft-quoted example is of a contract to have one's portrait painted; the painter cannot insist that someone else will paint the portrait instead. Where there is an element of *delectus personae* the contract may not be assigned.

In determining which rights are transferable the law also distinguishes between contracts which are **executed** and those which are **executory**. Executed contracts are able to be completed simply by making payment of money or by making delivery of a particular item of property. Rights to receive such payments or take delivery of such property may be transferred – without the consent of the person who is obliged to make payment or delivery – provided there is no express term in the contract which prohibits assignation. In respect of executory contracts, more is required for the performance of contractual obligations than mere payment or delivery of a particular item. Where there is *delectus personae*, then neither rights nor obligations under an executory contract may be assigned without the consent of the other party.

Where assignation has taken place, the assignee 'steps into the shoes' of the assignor. The assignee's position in law is only as good as that of the assignor. This was illustrated in **The Scottish Widows' Fund *v* Buist (1876) 3 R 1078** where the benefits under an insurance policy were assigned to Buist. However, the assignor had made false statements as to his state of health and as such the policy was void. It was held that the assignee had no right to payment under the policy on the assignor's death.

Jus quaesitum tertio

A third party may obtain a title to sue as a consequence of the parties to the contract creating a *jus quaesitum tertio*. Where a contract has as one of its objects the creation of a benefit in favour of a third party, this may give rise to a *jus quaesitum tertio* which gives the third party the right to bring a court action to enforce his rights under the contract. The parties to the contract must have intended to benefit the third party. Such intention may be expressed by naming the third party or otherwise identifying him, for example by referring to a distinct class of persons to which the third party belongs. It is possible that such intention may be implied but only if the third party is the sole person to benefit. There must be evidence that the intention was to create an irrevocable right in favour of the third party. Accordingly there should be either delivery to the third party of the document which created the right or something equivalent to delivery such as intimation to the third party of the creation of the right in his favour.

In the case of **Aberdeen Harbour Board *v* Heating Enterprises (Aberdeen) Ltd 1990 SLT 416**, the defenders H were plumbing subcontractors who were alleged to have caused a fire which damaged premises owned by A. H had been engaged by the main contractors C who were employed by F, a tenant in the premises. H denied responsibility for the fire but argued that should they be found liable they were entitled to be indemnified by C. H claimed they were entitled to rely on a clause in the main contract between the tenant (F) and the main contractor (C) which provided that the tenant as employer accepted sole responsibility for fire damage and undertook to take out fire insurance. On the question of whether the main contract between C and F created a *jus quaesitum tertio* on H, Lord Dunpark expressed the opinion that it did not. The relevant clause in the main contract made no reference to the subcontractor and it was not possible to read into the contract any implied term which would give H any right under the clause. There was absolutely no indication that C and F intended to confer upon the subcontractors any benefit under the clause and accordingly there was no *jus quaesitum tertio*. The fact that the subcontractors knew about the fire insurance clause in the main contract was irrelevant.

Where it just so happens that a third party will benefit should a contract between A and B go ahead, no *jus quaesitum tertio* is created. This was clearly illustrated in **Finnie *v* Glasgow & South Western Railway Co (1857) 3 Macq 75** where two railway companies agreed rates to be charged for the carriage of coal along a particular railway line. When the charges were increased, a customer who used the route sought to enforce the original price-fixing agreement. It was held that he had no title to sue. Although he had benefited as a consequence of the contract, the original contracting parties had not had as their purpose the intention of conferring such a benefit. Accordingly, no *jus quaesitum tertio* was created.

Where a *jus quaesitum tertio* is created, the third party may raise an action either along with or independently of one of the original contracting partie's. In **Lamont *v* Burnett (1901) 3 F 797** B contracted to purchase L's hotel for £7000. In addition, B sent a covering letter along with his offer in which he stated he would pay £100 to L's wife because of her kindness during his visits to view the hotel. L accepted the offer 'as supplemented' by the covering letter. B paid the purchase price but refused to pay the £100 to L's wife. Mrs L raised an action against B for payment of the £100. It was held that the contract between L and B had created a *jus quaesitum tertio* and that Mrs L was therefore entitled to payment.

Transmission on death or bankruptcy

On death, rights and obligations under contracts entered into by the deceased pass to the executors of the deceased – unless there is *delectus personae* present in which case the contract is terminated.

When a person becomes insolvent and is sequestrated, a permanent trustee is appointed whose task it is to ingather the debtor's property and distribute it among the creditors. The permanent trustee has a title to sue on those contracts entered into by the debtor before sequestration. The permanent trustee elects whether or not to adopt such contracts. The permanent trustee cannot adopt a contract should *delectus personae* be present. Failure to adopt contracts amounts to a breach of contract which will force the other original contracting party to lodge a claim in the sequestration.

QUESTIONS

1 Joe arrives at the Hotel Splendide and books a room at the reception desk. On the reception desk there is a large notice which states that the hotel shall not be responsible for injuries to the guests nor for loss of or damage to their property however caused. Two days later, Joe discovers that the maid has left the door of his room unlocked and that some money, his watch and his camera have been stolen. On his way downstairs to report the theft, Joe's foot catches on a frayed piece of carpeting and Joe falls breaking his ankle and tearing his brand-new leather jacket. Joe raises a court action against the hotel but the hotel claim that he is barred from doing so in terms of the notice at reception. With full reference to both common law and statute, discuss whether or not the hotel is correct.

2 Sue takes her small daughter Jane to the local park. At the entrance to the children's play area there is a notice which states that persons using the play area do so at their own risk and that Dunedin District Council take no responsibility for personal injury or damage to property arising from the use of park facilities. While Sue is pushing Jane on the roundabout, the sleeve of Sue's expensive leather jacket catches on a jagged piece of metal on the underside of the roundabout. The jacket is ruined but Sue is worried that the effect of the notice is that she has no claim against the Council. Advise Sue.

3 Dave owes Paul £50 and is refusing to pay claiming that he does not have the money. Paul knows that Pete owes Dave £50 but Dave is refusing to raise an action against Pete for payment. Dave says that Pete will pay eventually and when he does, Dave will pay Paul. Paul thinks it would be a good idea if he, Paul, sued Pete direct for the £50. Discuss whether Paul is entitled to do this.

4 Steve is buying a new house. As part of the financial arrangements, he is to assign the benefits of an insurance policy on his life to the building society which is giving him a mortgage. When he is completing the proposal form for the life insurance, Steve neglects to mention that he has a serious heart condition. Steve dies of a heart attack and the insurance company are refusing to pay the building society. Advise the building society of their position in law.

6 Breach of contract and termination

WHAT IS A BREACH OF CONTRACT?

If either party to a valid contract fails, without just cause, to perform their obligations under the contract, then that is a breach of contract.

WHAT FORMS MAY A BREACH OF CONTRACT TAKE?

Anticipatory breach

This may occur where there is a time lag between the date of formation of the contract and the date upon which it is due to be performed. After formation but before performance, X gives notice to Y that X no longer intends to perform his obligations under the contract. Where this happens Y has a number of options:

1 He can do nothing and wait until the due date for performance in the hope that X will change his mind. If X fails to perform his obligations, Y may then either seek a court order requiring performance by X or resile (withdraw) from the contract and sue for damages (monetary compensation).
2 Y does not have to wait until the due date for performance before taking action. When X gives notice that he is not going to perform his part of the bargain, Y can immediately either seek a court order requiring performance on the due date or resile and sue for damages.
3 Y's third option has caused legal controversy. Despite X giving notice that he will not be performing **his** side of the bargain and in effect attempting to 'cancel' the contract, can Y merely ignore this and carry on and proceed to perform his own (Y's) side of the bargain? Can Y perform his part of the contract and sue for payment? The House of Lords, by a very narrow majority, said 'yes, he could'

in **White & Carter Ltd** *v* **McGregor 1962 SC (HL) 1**. Although the dissenting judges said it was absurd to allow such unwanted performance, the majority said it was open to the innocent party to perform the contract and claim contractual payment as a debt.

Failing to perform the contract

Without giving prior notice, X either refuses or for some reason fails to carry out his contractual obligations. This is said to amount to a **repudiation** of the contract by X. A repudiation is a **material breach of the contract** in response to which the innocent party can choose to resile altogether from the contract without having to perform his own obligations. Contract rests on the concept of mutuality – i.e., X cannot insist that Y performs Y's obligations unless X himself has performed his own (X's) obligations.

Delayed performance

The contractual obligations are not performed on the due date. For example, a shop fails to deliver furniture on the day promised, or a builder says he will complete a new garage in ten days and after three weeks it still is not finished. The options open to the innocent party in this situation are said to depend upon whether or not 'time was of the essence' – i.e., was the delay in performance a material breach, a very serious breach which goes to the very root of the contract? If the delay amounts to a material breach, the innocent party has the right to resile. However, if the delay is not material then the only remedy will be a claim for damages.

Unsatisfactory/defective performance

Again the options available to the innocent party will depend upon how serious a breach this is. It must be determined whether the performance conforms to the requirements of the contract or not, and if it does not conform, does it amount to a material or merely a trivial breach of contract? Remember – only a material breach entitles an innocent party to resile; if the breach is not material, the only remedy is damages and the innocent party will still have to perform their side of the bargain.

WHAT REMEDIES ARE AVAILABLE TO THE INNOCENT PARTY?

The innocent party may wish to withdraw from the contract altogether without having to perform his own obligations. This is known as **rescission**. This remedy is available only as a response to the other party's material breach of contract; it is unavailable in the case of a less serious breach of contract.

As an alternative to rescission, the innocent party may wish to force the party in breach to do what he has promised to do. In certain cases the innocent party may be entitled to ask the court for a decree *ad factum praestandum* ordering the contract breaker to perform his obligations. A court order saying 'do something' is known as an **order for specific implement**. Where the obligation is of a negative character, the appropriate order is an **interdict** – a court order saying 'don't do that' or 'stop doing that'.

In certain situations these court orders will not be granted and in such cases the appropriate remedy is **damages** – i.e., monetary compensation. Other possible remedies include **retention** and **lien**.

It is intended to consider each of these remedies in turn.

RESCISSION AS A REMEDY FOR BREACH OF CONTRACT

As indicated above, the choice of remedy available to the innocent party depends upon the seriousness of the breach. Only if the breach can be said to be a material breach will the remedy of rescission be available. In the face of a material breach the innocent party may resile – i.e., declare the contract to be at an end and withdraw altogether. As well as resiling the innocent party may claim damages in addition.

If X fails to perform one of his contractual obligations – and such an obligation goes to the very heart of the contract – then that is said to be a material breach of contract. In committing a material breach, X is said to have **repudiated** the contract. Repudiation, by itself, does not bring the contract to an end. Faced with repudiation by X, Y may, at his option, accept the repudiation and treat the contract as being at an end – i.e., may resile.

What will amount to a material breach?

It was said in **Wade *v* Waldon 1909 SC 571** at p. 576 that '... in any contract which contains multifarious stipulations there are some which go so to the root of the contract that a breach of **those** stipulations entitles the party pleading the breach to declare that the contract is at an end. There are others which do not go to the root of the contract, but which are part of the contract and which would give rise, if broken, to an action for damages.'

The facts of this case were that a comedian had been booked, a year in advance, to appear for a week at the Pavilion Theatre in Glasgow. The contract required him to send, 14 days before he was due to appear, confirmation of his appearance, together with details of his act, to be used for publicity purposes. When the comedian failed to give confirmation of his appearance or to send publicity material 14 days in advance of the show, the theatre management cancelled the booking.

Wade v *Waldon* illustrates the dangers of treating as material a breach which the courts later hold not to be material. The theatre had resiled following the comedian's breach of contract which the theatre had regarded as material. The comedian did not agree that his breach was material and sued for damages to compensate for the loss he suffered as a result of the theatre withdrawing from the contract. The court held that the comedian had been in breach but that his breach was not material. In fact, in resiling without justification it was the theatre management who committed a material breach of contract, thus entitling the comedian to damages. Therefore, to resile without justification is in itself a material breach.

Also as indicated above, refusal or failure to perform the contract will prima facie be a material breach of contract.

Failure to perform on time and defective performance may or may not be material depending upon the circumstances of a particular contract. For the avoidance of doubt, the parties may include an express term in their contract declaring which matters are to be considered material and which are not. Such an express term will be conclusive and will be given effect to by the courts. It is allowable to declare what might otherwise be regarded as quite trivial terms to be material to the contract. Therefore, if you wish to be within your rights to tell a shop that they can keep their goods if they fail to meet their promised delivery date, then you should declare it to be a material condition of the contract that the goods be delivered by a certain date.

A material breach remains a material breach even if the party in breach honestly but mistakenly believes that he is not acting in breach of contract. In **Blyth** *v* **Scottish Liberal Club 1983 SLT 260** an employee was in dispute with his employers as to the extent of his employment duties. He refused to carry out certain tasks because he firmly believed that he was in the right and that such tasks did not form part of his contractual duties. He was wrong. His employers regarded his actions as a material breach of the contract of employment and terminated the contract. The court held that the employers had been entitled to resile.

A DECREE *AD FACTUM PRAESTANDUM* AS A REMEDY FOR BREACH OF CONTRACT

The innocent party may wish to force the contract breaker to perform his contractual obligations. Accordingly, he may seek a court order requiring the party in breach to do something or not to do something. If such orders are ignored, this amounts to **contempt of court** which could lead to fines or even imprisonment. As an alternative, the innocent party may ask the court to authorise him to implement the contract himself and then recover the cost from the contract breaker. An order from the court requiring positive action from the contract breaker is known as an **order for specific implement**. Such an order requires the defender to do something.

An order from the court requiring the contract breaker *not* to do something or to stop doing something is known as an **interdict**. Interdicts are commonly used as a means of enforcing restrictive covenants – whereby employees agree not to set up in competition with their employer should they leave. If a covenant is found to be reasonable in its terms, the court may order a former employee to close down his new business if it contravenes the terms of the covenant.

Situations in which the court will not grant an order for specific implement

1 Where the obligation is to pay **money**; the court takes the view that the appropriate remedy is an action for payment; to grant an order could lead to someone in contempt being imprisoned for civil debt which is no longer competent in Scots law.

2 Where the contract involves a **personal** or **intimate relationship**; forced compliance would be worse than non compliance; includes partnership and employment.
3 Where it would mean ordering someone to do the **impossible**.
4 Where the **court cannot enforce the decree** – e.g., the defender is outside Scotland.
5 Where there is **no good reason for preferring this remedy** – i.e., there is said to be **no *pretium affectionis***; there is no special quality affecting the goods (eg they are unique) which would make this remedy necessary; the contract goods could be obtained from another supplier and then the innocent party could sue for any extra cost; the court will not grant the order merely to satisfy the innocent party's determination to 'make X deliver those goods if it's the last thing I do'. For example, this remedy would be appropriate if you were buying the Mona Lisa – if the other party fails to deliver, you cannot get another elsewhere. However, if the contract is for 20 dozen eggs, then the court says: 'Don't ask for specific implement, but get the goods from someone else and if they cost you more, sue for the difference.'
6 The court believes it would cause **exceptional hardship** if it granted the order, or it would be **inconvenient** , or **unjust**.
7 The court believes that **damages are sufficient and appropriate** in the circumstances.

DAMAGES AS A REMEDY FOR BREACH OF CONTRACT

Every breach of contract entitles the innocent party to damages even if they are only nominal ones. Damages take the form of monetary compensation, the purpose of which is to put the party not in breach into the position he would have been in had the contract been performed. The purpose of damages, therefore, is to compensate the party not in breach. The purpose of damages is not to punish the person who breaks the contract. The motive of the party in breach is totally irrelevant in the question of damages. Also, the amount of damages is measured by the amount of the innocent party's loss – not by reference to what the party in breach has gained as a result of not going through with the contract.

Measure of damages – i.e., how much is payable?

The party not in breach may not receive the full amount of damages which he is claiming. Firstly, before anything is payable it must be established that the breach did in fact cause the loss claimed for. In addition, there are two factors which may limit the amount of damages payable. These are the principles of **minimisation of loss** and **remoteness of damage**.

Minimisation of loss

The party claiming damages must take reasonable steps to keep his losses down.

For example, if a market gardener contracts to purchase oil for the heating system serving his greenhouses and the supplier fails to deliver, the market gardener cannot just sit back, allow himself to run out of oil, watch as all his plants die and then hope to sue for all the losses suffered by his business. The court will take the view that any reasonable person would have ordered the oil from an alternative supplier and then sued for any difference in price.

The law requires the party not in breach to take all 'reasonable steps' to minimise his loss; he is not expected to go to extraordinary lengths. **In Gunter & Co *v* Lauritzen (1894) 1 SLT 435 (OH)** G & Co contracted to buy from Danish merchants a consignment of Danish hay. G & Co intended to resell the hay at a profit. When the hay arrived in Aberdeen, it was found not to conform to the contract and was rejected. G & Co brought an action for breach of contract against L claiming the lost profit on the resale. L tried to argue that G & Co had failed to minimise their loss. It was established that such Danish hay was not available on the open market in Aberdeen. However, L argued that it could have been obtained in three separate lots from suppliers throughout Scotland. The Lord Ordinary found that if a purchaser could readily supply himself with goods which were of the same quality and currently available in the open market at the time and place of delivery, then he would have to supply himself or be barred from recovering damages. However, in the present case His Lordship found that the goods in question were of a very special kind, unavailable in Aberdeen and obtainable only by 'hunting all over the country'. In these circumstances, it was held that 'there was no duty on the purchaser to make extraordinary exertions to supply himself with the goods elsewhere' and G & Co were entitled to recover the whole amount of their lost profit.

Remoteness of damage

The party in breach is not always liable to compensate the party not in breach for the whole amount of the latter's losses. If a stone is dropped into a pond, the ripples spread out across the pond; in the same way, our actions may have untold consequences. However, the law does not hold us responsible for *all* the consequences of our actions. The law will impose a cut-off point beyond which we are not legally responsible.

As far as damages for breach of contract are concerned the party not in breach can only recover if the loss which did result was **reasonably foreseeable as liable to result** if there was a breach of contract. Moreover, whether or not something was reasonably foreseeable is determined on the basis of what was known by the party in breach **at the time the contract was made**. So, at the time the contract was made did the party in breach have actual knowledge, or should he be treated as having knowledge, sufficient to allow him to reasonably foresee that, if he breached the contract, the loss which did result was liable to result?

The law distinguishes between loss which would arise in the normal course of things and loss which arises only in special circumstances – i.e., **normal loss** and **abnormal loss**. Everyone is treated as knowing what the 'normal course of things' involves; however, people must be actually told of any special circumstances which might give rise to abnormal losses should there be a breach of contract. In normal circumstances, of which people are held to have implied knowledge, if there is a breach of contract which leads to normal loss, and if such normal loss would have been a reasonably foreseeable consequence of the breach on the basis of such knowledge at the time the contract was made, then **general** or **ordinary damages** will be payable to compensate for the normal loss. If special circumstances apply, then the party in breach must have had actual knowledge of such circumstances before it can be judged whether on the basis of such knowledge he could have reasonably foreseen, at the time the contract was formed, that his breach would cause an abnormal level of loss. If his knowledge was sufficient to make abnormal loss a reasonably foreseeable consequence of a breach of contract, then **special damages** will be payable to compensate for the abnormal loss.

The following table may help:

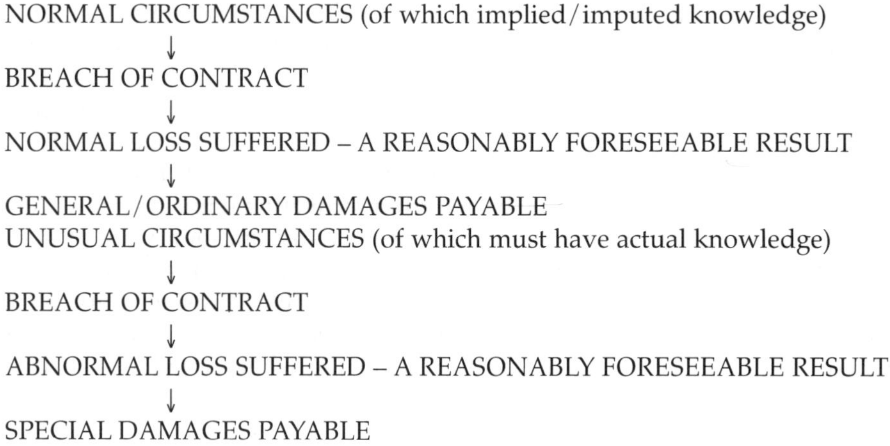

NORMAL CIRCUMSTANCES (of which implied/imputed knowledge)
↓
BREACH OF CONTRACT
↓
NORMAL LOSS SUFFERED – A REASONABLY FORESEEABLE RESULT
↓
GENERAL/ORDINARY DAMAGES PAYABLE
UNUSUAL CIRCUMSTANCES (of which must have actual knowledge)
↓
BREACH OF CONTRACT
↓
ABNORMAL LOSS SUFFERED – A REASONABLY FORESEEABLE RESULT
↓
SPECIAL DAMAGES PAYABLE

Case law on remoteness of damage

The most famous case is the English case of **Hadley *v* Baxendale 1854 9 Exch. 341**. The plaintiff's flour mill was at a standstill because of a broken crankshaft. A carrier contracted to take the crankshaft to be used as a pattern for a replacement. The carrier said he would deliver the crankshaft in two days but he delayed and, as a result, the mill was out of action longer than was anticipated. The mill owner sought damages to compensate for the loss of profit caused by the delay. He lost. Why did he lose?

In normal circumstances – the crankshaft being a vital piece of equipment – mills would generally carry a spare. In normal circumstances, what loss would the carrier be able to foresee as arising as a consequence of his delay? The answer is 'none'. The carrier would assume that the mill would be operating on the spare crankshaft which all mills had. Therefore his delay would cause no loss. However, in this case special circumstances applied – this must have been the only mill in England that did not have a spare crankshaft. During any delay the mill would sit idle and lose more profit. Had the carrier had actual knowledge of this unusual circumstance, he would have been able to foresee that any delay would cause loss. But he was not told – he did not have actual knowledge of the special circumstances – so he was not in a position to reasonably foresee that his breach would give rise to lost profit. As the loss was not reasonably foreseeable as liable to result, it was found to be too remote from the breach for the carrier to be liable. No damages whatsoever were payable in this case.

Victoria Laundry *v* **Newman [1949] 2 KB 528** also illustrates the difference between General and Special Damages. The laundry ordered a boiler which was 20 weeks late. They sued for additional profits lost because they were deprived of the new boiler. The defendants knew the use the boiler would be put to and knew it was required as soon as possible. However, they had not had specific notice of the profits in respect of which damages were claimed. These came under two heads: (*a*) there was a very high demand for laundry services and it was argued that with the new boiler extra business worth £16 per week could have been taken on; and (*b*) they had lost very valuable government contracts which would bring in £262 per week.

It was held that the laundry could recover in respect of the lost profit of £16 per week for additional general laundry business, as such an increase in business was reasonably foreseeable in the normal course of things. However, the defendants could not have reasonably foreseen the loss of £262 per week in respect of lost government contracts unless they had had actual knowledge of them at the time the contract was formed – i.e., they would have to have been told about them. Damages were not payable in respect of this loss.

In **'Den of Ogil' Co Ltd** *v* **Caledonian Railway Co (1902) 5 F 99** the owners of the steamship *Den of Ogil* brought an action for damages in the sum of £300 in respect of lost profit and other outlays caused by the ship being delayed at Plymouth. The ship had a broken piston and a replacement had to be sent from Port Glasgow. McGregor, the stationmaster at Port Glasgow, had been told that the carriage was urgent and that the senders were willing to pay for the item to be sent at high cost by passenger train. However, the railway company did not know that the item was a piston, nor did they know that the ship was a large one with a crew of 57. There was a delay of three to four days in delivering the piston. The defenders admitted breach of contract but disputed the amount claimed. The question to be determined was whether the railway company had been given sufficient notice of the special circumstances to enable them to foresee the level of loss claimed for. It was held that they had not been given sufficient notice of the special circumstances and the shipowners were not entitled to claim for loss of profit caused by the delayed sailing. The damages awarded were limited to £50.

The question of remoteness of loss in contract was considered recently by the House of Lords in **Balfour Beatty Construction (Scotland) Ltd** *v* **Scottish Power plc 1994 SLT 807**. Balfour Beatty were building a roadway and as part of the works had to construct an aqueduct to channel a canal over the new road. This operation required a continuous pour of concrete and accordingly Balfour Beatty set up a concrete batching plant and contracted with the electricity board (Scottish Power's predecessors) for the supply of electricity to the plant. At a critical point in the construction of the aqueduct, the electricity supply failed. Because of various technical reasons remedial work on the aqueduct was not possible; the construction company had to demolish the whole structure and start again. Accordingly, Balfour Beatty raised an action for damages for breach of contract against Scottish Power in the sum of £229 102.53. The Lord Ordinary dismissed their claim holding that while there had been a breach of contract, the loss suffered was too remote. The electricity board had not been informed of the highly technical nature of the operation, of the need for continuous pour and of the drastic consequences of a failure in the electricity supply.

Balfour Beatty appealed to the Inner House and won. The Second Division were prepared to infer sufficient technical knowledge on the part of the electricity board to allow them to reasonably foresee that some form of remedial works would be necessary even though they could not appreciate the full extent of the work which would be have to be done.

However, Scottish Power appealed and the House of Lords held that the Inner House had been wrong. In the leading judgement Lord Jauncey stated (at p. 810) that '[i]t must always be a question of circumstances what one contracting party is presumed to know about the business activities of the other. No doubt the simpler the activity of the one, the more readily can it be inferred that the other would have reasonable knowledge thereof. However, when the activity of A involves complicated construction or manufacturing techniques, I see no reason why B who supplies a commodity that A intends to use in the course of those techniques should be assumed, merely because of the order for the commodity, to be aware of the details of all the techniques undertaken by A and the effect thereupon of any failure or deficiency in that commodity'. Lord Jauncey went on to find that the Lord Ordinary had been correct to find that the demolition and reconstruction of the aqueduct was not within the reasonable contemplation of the electricity board. The House of Lords restored the original judgement of the Lord Ordinary and awarded expenses against Balfour Beatty.

Damages for non-pecuniary loss

Substantial damages, as opposed to nominal damages, are generally payable only where loss can be measured in money terms. Accordingly, damages would not generally be payable solely in respect of disappointment etc. However, where it can be shown that the major part of the contract raises expectations of a non-pecuniary nature, then it has been held that substantial damages may be awarded. In **Diesen *v* Samson 1971 SLT (Sh Ct) 49** damages were awarded in respect of disappointment suffered when a wedding photographer failed to turn up. In this case, many of the guests had travelled from Norway and had attended the wedding in national costume. It was not possible to recreate such scenes for a photograher at a later date.

In **Jarvis *v* Swan Tours [1973] 1 All ER 71** damages were payable for disappointment when a skiing holiday did not live up to expectations raised by the brochure. The holiday was a chalet holiday said to have a house party atmosphere, and plenty of activities were to be laid on for the single traveller. The plaintiff found himself in the chalet all alone and almost all the activities were cancelled.

RETENTION AND LIEN AS REMEDIES FOR BREACH OF CONTRACT

Retention involves the party not in breach withholding the performance of his own obligations (including withholding payment of money). This can be done where both claims arise under the same contract – e.g., a customer withholding payment for carriage of goods against his claim for damages for damage caused to the goods.

Lien involves the party not in breach retaining or refusing to deliver the other party's goods. Such a right might be exercised by a repairer who refuses to hand over the goods which he has repaired until he has been paid for the repair.

REMEDIES FOR BREACH STIPULATED IN THE CONTRACT

Rather than wait until a breach occurs and then have to go to court to obtain a remedy and allow the court to determine the amount of damages payable, the parties to a contract may agree at the outset the damages payable in the event of a breach of contract. Such clauses in contracts are known as **conventional** or **liquidate damages clauses**. The courts will uphold such contractually-stipulated remedies *provided* that they are satisfied that the clause in the contract represents a genuine effort to estimate in advance the loss which various types of breach will cause. This is known as a *genuine pre-estimate of loss*.

Where the court is satisfied that a clause in a contract stipulating an amount to be paid in the event of breach of contract represents a genuine pre-estimate of loss – i.e., is a proper conventional/liquidate damages clause – the court will order payment according to the terms of the clause. Note, though, that the court will become involved only in the event that the party in breach refuses to pay the contractually stipulated amount. However, if the court believes that the contractual clause is an attempt to bully, or punish, or penalise the party in breach – i.e., is in effect a **penalty clause** – then they will not uphold the clause but will proceed to determine the amount of damages according to the normal principles of minimisation of loss, remoteness, etc.

In determining whether a contractual clause represents a genuine pre-estimate of loss or is a penalty clause, the court is not persuaded by the name of the clause alone. It is the effect of the clause which the court is interested in. So, a clause may be called a 'penalty clause' and be upheld; or be called a 'liquidate damages clause' and be set aside – the name in itself is not conclusive.

Courts are likely to be interested in whether different levels of damages are paid according to the seriousness of the breach. If this is so, the clause is more likely to be upheld and enforced. If, however, a single lump sum is payable for **all** breaches – serious or otherwise – then the clause is likely to be thrown out as a penalty clause. Liquidate damages clauses often take the form of **delay clauses** where so much per day or per week is payable for each day or week the party in breach is late in completing the performance of his obligations. If a liquidate damages clause is upheld, the parties must take the amount of damages provided for by the clause. If their actual loss is higher or lower that makes no difference – it is just hard luck for one or other of the parties.

Cases on conventional damages

Elphinstone *v* **Monkland Iron & Coal Co Ltd 1886 13 R (HL) 98**. Tenants under a mineral lease were required to reinstate the land once mining had ceased. They failed to do so. The lease contained a Penalty Clause which said that £100 per acre was to be paid for every acre not reinstated by the due date. The court held that, although it was called a penalty clause, its effect was that it was a liquidate damages clause in that it linked the amount of damages payable to the extent of the breach – i.e., the more land not reinstated, the higher the damages. The clause was upheld.

Dingwall *v* **Burnett 1912 SC 1097**. A lease of a hotel contained several obligations of varying importance but £50 in liquidate damages was to be paid for breach of any one of them. The tenant was in breach of one of the obligations. The court held that (*a*) the £50 clause was an unenforceable penalty and not a valid liquidate damages clause. This was because the amount of the damages was not in any way linked to the seriousness of the breach; (*b*) since the contractual clause was unenforceable, the court would assess damages payable according to normal principles. The court awarded £300! The law may award damages in respect of an actual loss which is greater than an amount provided for in an unenforceable penalty clause.

The court may accept that it is sometimes impossible to estimate in advance the consequences of a breach of contract. In such circumstances the court may be willing to uphold a clause which might otherwise appear arbitrary. This was so in the case of **Clydebank Engineering & Shipbuilding Co** *v* **Castaneda (1904) 7 F (HL) 77**. The Spanish Government ordered four torpedo boats from the Scottish company. The contract contained a hefty delay clause for late delivery. The boats were months late and the penalty amounted to £75,000 which the yard refused to pay. The Scottish company argued that it was a penalty and not a valid liquidate damages clause. In the meantime, the rest of the Spanish fleet had been sunk by the Americans off Cuba. The House of Lords decided to uphold the clause – the sums payable *were* liquidate damages because in the circumstances it would have been impossible to make an accurate pre-estimate of loss.

QUESTIONS

1 Define breach of contract and discuss the forms which a breach of contract may take.

2 List the various remedies which may be available for breach of contract.

3 Discuss rescission as a remedy for breach of contract. When is it not available?

4 What is the most common remedy for breach of contract?

5 Define and distinguish between general damages and special damages.

6 Explain what is meant by 'being required to minimise your loss'.

7 George owns a small supermarket. He has contracted to purchase a consignment of tinned peas from Dunedin Wholesale Ltd. The delivery date comes and goes and George looks set to run out of peas. George declares that he will force

Dunedin Wholesale Ltd to make the delivery if it is the last thing he does! He has decided to seek an order for specific implement of the contract. Will George succeed?

8 Sandy runs a small business manufacturing garden gnomes. He orders some machinery from Makeit Ltd which will enable him to increase his production to meet an already insatiable demand from garden centres for garden gnomes. Sandy calculates that his profits will increase by £250 per month as a result. In addition, ordering this new machinery has enabled Sandy to accept a 'rush order' for 500 gnomes to be used in a display at the National Garden Festival. A much higher than usual price per gnome is being paid by the Festival organisers and Sandy expects to make £750 profit on this order alone. However, Makeit Ltd are four weeks late in delivering the machinery and Sandy loses the Festival order. Advise Sandy.

9 Bob has been tempted by the claims of a holiday brochure relating to a chalet holiday in a ski resort. It describes the house party atmosphere as being particularly suitable for persons travelling alone, and outlines the programme of various entertainments and activities which will be available. Once there, he finds that he is the only person in the chalet and as a consequence, most of the events are cancelled. His enjoyment of the holiday is very much spoiled and, disappointed, he wonders whether he can sue for damages. Advise Bob.

10 Sue McBjorg, a world class tennis player, has entered into a sponsorship deal with a company which manufactures tasteful tartan tennis wear. She is paid £20 000 per annum to advertise their clothing. A condition of the contract is that she must wear their dresses at all tournaments. The contract further states that any breach of this condition shall render Sue liable to pay £10 000 in liquidate damages. At the Scottish Open Tennis Championships she is shown on television in the final wearing a dress manufactured by her sponsor's major rival. Is Sue liable to pay the £10 000?

'TERMINATION OF CONTRACTUAL OBLIGATIONS

A contract is an agreement which gives rise to legally binding obligations. When a contract comes to an end, these obligations are extinguished. Contractual obligations may be extinguished in a number of ways: Performance; Payment; Prescription; Acceptilation; Confusion; Compensation; Delegation; Novation; Frustration. An easy way to remember this list is to use the following phrase – **P**arrots **P**retty **P**olly **A**nd **C**hirpy **C**harlie **D**o **N**ot **F**ly!

Performance

As stated above, a contract is an agreement which gives rise to obligations. A contract is terminated by performance when both parties to the contract have fully performed their respective obligations. The majority of contractual obligations are terminated by performance.

Payment

An obligation may be to pay money rather than to perform an act. Such an obligation is discharged when the debtor makes payment in the manner demanded by the contract.

Prescription

This concerns the lapse or creation of rights once a certain length of time has passed. The law of prescription was overhauled by the Prescription and Limitation (Scotland) Act 1973 which took effect in 1976. Positive prescription allows certain rights to be created after a period of time has passed and become unchallengeable. Certain rights are created after a period of ten years; others after a period of 20 years, such as the creation of a public right of way.

In so far as the termination of obligations is concerned, we are more interested in **Negative Prescription**, which allows certain rights which have not been exercised for a certain length of time to lapse. Rights which have prescribed can no longer be exercised. In terms of the 1973 Act, there is the **Short Negative Prescription** – whereby certain obligations are extinguished after five years have elapsed – and the **Long Negative Prescription** – whereby certain other obligations are extinguished after 20 years have elapsed. Also the 1973 Act has been amended so that obligations arising from defective products prescribe after 10 years (see p. 315).

Most contractual obligations lapse after five years, including the obligation to pay rent or interest and also obligations arising from breach of contract. It should be noted that certain rights and obligations never lapse, such as the right to recover stolen property. Accordingly, certain obligations lapse after either five, ten or 20 years *unless* these periods have been interrupted either by a *relevant claim* or by a *relevant acknowledgement*. A relevant claim means that the prescriptive period has stopped running because the person to whom the obligation is owed has raised a court action. A relevant acknowledgement means that the prescriptive period has stopped running because the person who should perform the obligation has taken some steps towards performance or has admitted in writing that the obligation still exists.

Acceptilation

The parties to a contract may agree to end the contract before performance or before full performance. It may be that each of the parties agrees to waive performance by the other, or that one party having performed his part of the bargain agrees to discharge the other party from performance of his contractual obligations.

Confusion

This occurs where a person becomes both the creditor and the debtor under a contract. As a person cannot owe money to himself, the obligation to make payment is extinguished. This could happen where, for example, an uncle lends money to his nephew, an impoverished student. Prior to the loan being repaid the uncle dies and leaves his entire estate to his nephew. The effect is that as the nephew would now owe money to himself, the debt is extinguished by confusion.

Compensation

This may occur where X and Y owe each other money. The two debts may be set off against one another so as to extinguish the obligation of one of the parties. For example, if X owes Y £200 and Y owes X £50, compensation will result in X owing Y £150 and Y's obligation to X being at an end. In order that compensation may occur, both debts must be 'liquid' – i.e., the amount is clearly ascertainable. Also both debts must be due for payment; a present debt cannot be set off against a future one.

Delegation

Should a new debtor be substituted for an existing debtor, the existing debtor's obligation is extinguished. Such an arrangement requires the consent of the creditor. It is important to provide that the new obligant X is undertaking the obligation instead of the original obligant Y and it is not merely the case that it has been agreed that Y's obligation to perform the contract is to be carried out by X, but that Y's obligation is not extinguished: **W.J. Harte Construction Ltd *v* Scottish Homes 1992 GWD 226**.

Novation

Novation occurs when a new obligation is substituted for a prior obligation. The effect is to extinguish all liability for the prior obligation. Again, it must be expressly provided that the new obligation is in substitution for the prior one. Failure to so provide will result in the presumption that the new obligation is additional to the prior one and not instead of it. Again, see **W.J. Harte Construction Ltd *v* Scottish Homes 1992 GWD 226**.

Frustration

Where performance of the contract is already either impossible or illegal at the time the contract is formed, then the contract is ***void ab initio*** (void from the start). However, where the contract becomes either impossible or illegal at a later date, after formation but before performance is due, then this is known as **supervening impossibility** and **supervening illegality** and the contract is said to be **frustrated** as a result. Frustration may also occur where performance of the contractual obligations is still possible and legal, but due to a change in circumstances, performance will be so **radically altered** that it can no longer be said to represent the contract which the parties consented to at the outset.

Frustration brings the contract to an end. For there to be frustration the supervening circumstances which cause the contract to become impossible or illegal must not be the fault of either party. Accordingly, where there is frustration, no damages are payable. However, any monies already paid over under a contract which has been frustrated must be repaid subject to any deductions for part performance. In addition, there shall not be frustration of a contract where the contract provides for how such events are to be dealt with.

Frustration is not a breach of contract. A breach of contract involves a failure without just cause to perform one's obligations under a contract. In a breach of contract situation damages are payable. When a contract is frustrated, both parties are the victims of an unforeseen event which is not the fault of either party. It is also crucial to understand that frustration does *not* make a contract void. Should a contract be void, it has *always* been void; no valid contract has ever existed. Frustration is something which happens to valid contracts. The effect of frustration is that the law regards the contract as being brought to an end. The following diagram illustrates this.

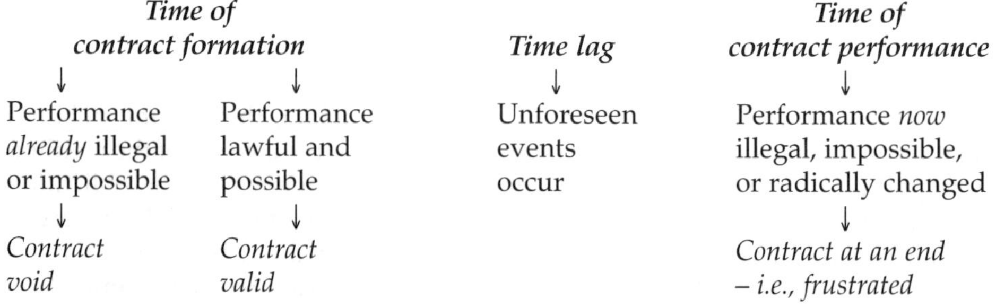

CIRCUMSTANCES WHICH MAKE A CONTRACT IMPOSSIBLE OR ILLEGAL

Supervening impossibility

A change in circumstances may make a contract impossible to perform. This may be due to a change in external circumstances of which there are two types: *rei interitus* and constructive total destruction. Supervening impossibility may also arise as a consequence of a change in personal circumstances.

Rei interitus

This occurs where something essential to the contract is destroyed. The destruction must not be the fault of either party. In **Taylor** *v* **Caldwell(1863) 3 B) S 826** a music hall which had been booked for a series of concerts burned down before the first concert. The fire was not the fault of the hall owner. It was held that the contract was brought to an end by frustration.

Constructive total destruction

A contract may be impossible to perform where something essential to the contract is not totally destroyed but is badly enough damaged as to be unfit for the purposes of the contract. Less than total destruction is sufficient to frustrate the contract. In **London and Edinburgh Shipping Company** *v* **The Admiralty 1920 SC 309** a ship was not sunk but was so damaged as to be totally unfit for the charter. The contract was ended by frustration.

There may also be constructive total destruction where something essential to the contract becomes unavailable as in **Mackeson** *v* **Boyd 1942 SC 56** where the existing lease between owner and tenant of a house was terminated by frustration as a consequence of government requisition of the house during wartime.

A change in personal circumstances

Where a contract depends upon the personal skills of an individual, a change in personal circumstances due to death, illness, bankruptcy or insanity may frustrate the contract. An element of *delectus personae* must be present before frustration can result. For example, if the owner of a painting and decorating business becomes seriously ill, then this is unlikely to affect contracts which he has entered; his staff will continue to decorate people's houses. However, should a well-known portrait painter contract to paint your portrait and then develop an illness which causes him to lose the power of his hands, the contract will be terminated by frustration. In the latter situation, the necessary element of *delectus personae* is present: you have chosen him to paint your portrait. You would not be willing to have someone else turn up to fulfil the contract. In **Robinson** *v* **Davison (1871) LR 6 Exch 269** a contract to perform a concert was terminated by frustration when the pianist became ill.

Supervening illegality

A contract may be brought to an end by frustration due to a change in the law which makes the contract illegal. Government regulations may prohibit imports or exports. If a change in the law merely makes a contract more difficult or less profitable to perform, then the contract shall not be frustrated – performance must actually be forbidden by law. In **James B Fraser & Co Ltd** *v* **Denny, Mott & Dickson Ltd 1944 SC (HL) 35** F Ltd contracted to purchase imported pine timber from D Ltd. By emergency wartime legislation the import of timber became illegal. It was held that further performance of the contract had been frustrated by supervening illegality. Similarly, in **Cantiere San Rocco SA** *v* **Clyde Shipbuilding and Engineering Co Ltd 1923 SC (HL) 105** a contract between an Austrian company and a Scottish company was terminated by frustration due to the outbreak of the First World War. It would be illegal to do business with an enemy alien. However, at the outbreak of war, the Austrian company had already paid the first instalment of the purchase price to the Scottish company. It was held that at the end of the war, the Austrian company was entitled to be repaid the amount of the instalment.

Supervening circumstances which radically alter the nature of the contract

A contract may not be fully impossible or illegal as a consequence of a change in circumstances. However, it may have turned into something different which was not contemplated by the parties at the outset. To hold the parties to such a contract would be holding them to something which they had not consented to. In **Jackson** *v* **Union Marine Insurance Co (1874) LR 10 CP 125** a contract provided that the transport by ship of iron rails was to proceed 'with all possible speed unless prevented by the perils of the sea'. The ship ran aground in January, was refloated in February but was not repaired until August. In the meantime, the rails were sent on by another ship. The delay *had* been caused by the perils of the sea as allowed by the contract. However, it was held that the shipowner could not enforce the contract after such a long delay, because to postpone performance for so long would impose a condition on the other party which had not been originally agreed to.

Under this heading may be considered what has come to be known as **commercial impossibility**. However, it should be stressed that the fact that the changed circumstances make the contract less profitable is not enough to frustrate the contract – **Davis Contractors** *v* **Fareham UDC (1956) AC 696**.

There may be extinction of contractual obligations as a consequence of what has been described as **frustration of purpose**. This may be illustrated by two English cases which have come to be known as the 'Coronation cases'. In **Krell** *v* **Henry [1903] 2KB 740** rooms were hired overlooking the route of the King's coronation procession. The King took ill and the coronation was postponed. It was held that the contract was terminated by frustration – people had not paid for rooms just to look at a street – the whole basis of the contract (i.e., the event) had disappeared. It has, however, been suggested that the Scottish courts would have taken a different view.

By contrast, the case of **Herne Bay Steamboat Co** *v* **Hutton [1903] 2KB 683** had a different outcome. The King was due to review the fleet off Spithead. The contract was for the hire of a pleasure boat to go out to view the spectacle. When the King took ill, his visit was cancelled. However, the contract for the boat hire was *not* frustrated. Plenty of people hired the boat merely for an outing; others would be happy to go out to see the assembled fleet. There were plenty of other reasons why the boat might have been hired, apart from seeing the King.

QUESTIONS

1 Mary is organising her 21st birthday party. She has booked the local hall and has paid a £40 deposit. She has also paid £20 for invitations to be printed. Two days before the party, she is telephoned by the owner of the hall who tells her that there has been a fire at the hall and that it is so severely damaged that it will be out of use for months. Mary has to cancel the party. What is her legal position?

2 Jim and his wife Hilda intend to celebrate Jim's retirement by taking a world cruise. This is to be the holiday of a lifetime. Jim has bought a video-camera to record the experience and Hilda has spent large sums on tropical clothing to wear on the voyage. A week before they are due to sail, they are informed that the cruise has been cancelled. The ship has been requisitioned by the Government to sail as part of a fleet which is going to the aid of a British colony which has been invaded by a foreign power. What are Jim and Hilda's rights, if any, against the cruise line?

3 Fred, an importer of foreign cheeses, contracted to purchase a regular supply of French soft cheeses with a delivery each month for six months. After the second delivery, due to a health scare, the Government introduced regulations banning the import of such cheeses. Fred's suppliers are threatening to sue for breach of contract. Advise Fred.

4 James is very excited at the prospect of a visit to Glasgow by the Queen. He agrees to pay Bill £200 for the use of one of Bill's offices overlooking George Square where the Queen will attend an open-air concert. Due to illness the Queen's visit to Glasgow is cancelled but Bill demands the £200. What is the legal position?

Part 3
SALE OF GOODS

7 The contract of sale of goods

THE SALE OF GOODS ACT 1979

Most people enter into contracts of sale of goods everyday. A person may buy a newspaper on the way to work and then buy a packet of sandwiches and a can of lemonade for lunch. These purchases constitute contracts of sale of goods. Most people shop for food at least weekly thus entering into a contract of sale of goods. Purchases of clothes, records, electrical goods, furniture and cars are all contracts of sale of goods.

Special rules, over and above the common law of contract, apply to such contracts. These rules of law are to be found in the Sale of Goods Act 1979 (hereafter referred to as 'the Act'). However, the rules of the common law of contract continue to apply to contracts of sale of goods, except in so far as they are inconsistent with any of the Act's provisions. It should be noted that the Sale of Goods Act 1979 was amended by the Sale and Supply of Goods Act 1994. The 1979 Act in its amended form applies to contracts for sale of goods entered into on or after 3 January 1995. References in the text are to the Act as amended.

Definition of a contract of sale of goods

The Act's provisions apply to contracts where the seller transfers or agrees to transfer the property (ownership) in the goods to the buyer for a money consideration called the price (s 2(1)).

Types of contract – sales and agreements to sell

Where the ownership of the goods transfers to the buyer at the time the contract is made – i.e., at the time of acceptance of an offer – the contract is known as a **sale**. Where the transfer of ownership from seller to buyer is to occur some time after the formation of the contract – e.g., after a specified period of time has passed or once conditions are fulfilled – the contract is known as an **agreement to sell**. An agreement to sell becomes a sale once the time has elapsed or the conditions are satisfied.

Types of conditions

A contract may be subject to two types of conditions, **suspensive conditions** and **resolutive conditions**.

A suspensive condition is one which must be fulfilled before a sale is able to proceed. The presence of a suspensive condition means that a contract is an agreement to sell and not a sale. An example would be the condition that a sale will go through only if the buyer obtains a bank loan.

A resolutive condition is one which will have the effect of dissolving the contract should it be fulfilled. An example of this in a context other than sale of goods would be a condition that insurance cover shall lapse if an insured car is not kept overnight in a garage.

Real rights and personal rights

Where there is a sale the buyer acquires **real rights** in the goods. This means that the buyer has a right of ownership which may be exercised against the whole world. Where there is an agreement to sell, the buyer merely acquires **personal rights** which may be exercised only against the seller. This means that the buyer may not consider the goods as his own and his remedies are limited to bringing an action for breach of contract against the seller should the seller fail to implement the contract.

What are 'goods'?

The Act's provisions apply only to contracts of sale of 'goods'. What are 'goods' for the purposes of the Act? Section 61(1) of the Act defines 'goods' as all corporeal moveables except money. The section also provides that growing crops and things attached to, or forming part of, the land and which must be severed from the land before sale are also to be regarded as goods. Accordingly, a farmer's agreement to sell his potato crop or a landowner's agreement to sell a forest for timber would be contracts of sale of goods to which the Act would apply.

What is meant by 'corporeal moveables'?

All property in Scotland is classified as either heritable or moveable. Heritable property consists of land and buildings. Moveable property consists of things which are not heritable – i.e., property other than land and buildings. Moveable property may be either corporeal moveable property or incorporeal moveable property. Corporeal may be thought of as meaning tangible or having physical substance. Corporeal moveable property is property you can see and feel. It includes cars, clothing, food, furniture, jewellery, books, boats, caravans – in fact any property which has a physical presence and which is not land and buildings.

Incorporeal moveable property is property which has value, which can be bought and sold but which does not have physical substance. It is perhaps easier to think of it as a right rather than a thing – e.g., ownership of copyright in a book or of the patent of the everlasting lightbulb or the goodwill of a business.

Joe may buy Tom's grocery business at a price of £35 000. The price of the business may be broken down as amounting to £20 000 for the premises (heritable property), £5000 for the stock (corporeal moveable property) and £10 000 for the goodwill of the business which Tom has built up over the years (incorporeal moveable property).

The rules of law contained in the Sale of Goods Act 1979 apply only where the contract is for the sale of corporeal moveable property. The Act does not apply to contracts for the purchase of a house or the transfer of copyright.

Classification of goods

'Goods' are further classified for the purposes of the Act. In terms of s 5 of the Act goods may be either **existing goods** or **future goods**. Existing goods are goods which the seller owns or has in his possession at the time the contract is made. Future goods are goods which the seller will have to manufacture or acquire from a third party after the contract is made. A contract for the sale of future goods shall be an agreement to sell.

It is also necessary to distinguish between **specific goods** and **unascertained goods**. Specific goods are defined by s 61 of the Act as being goods which are identified and agreed on at the time the contract of sale is made. At the time of offer and acceptance, the buyer knows the very item which he is going to own. A contract for the sale of specific goods would be the sale of a second-hand car, a red Mini, registration number ABC 123. The buyer knows he is buying that car and no other. A sale of a brand-new car may or may not be a contract of sale of specific goods. Should the buyer pick out a brand-new car on the showroom floor, it will be a sale of specific goods only if the car on the showroom floor is the very car which the buyer will end up owning. If the buyer is to receive a car just like the one on display, the contract does not relate to specific goods but to unascertained goods – i.e., goods which are not identified and agreed on at the time the contract is made.

There are two types of unascertained goods:

1 Unascertained goods which are **an unsevered portion of a particular quantity of goods**. In this case, the buyer knows the bulk from which his goods will come – e.g., 100 tonnes of wheat from the 1000 tonnes being transported aboard the ship HMS *Glasgow*. The 100 tonnes of wheat are not specific goods because at the time of contract formation the buyer could not know which of the grains of wheat in the ship's hold would come together to form his 100 tonnes. The buyer can identify *his* wheat only when it is separated from the other 900 tonnes; for example, when it is loaded onto his trucks on the quayside.
2 Unascertained goods which are purely **generic goods**. Generic goods comprise of a quantity of a commodity from any source whatsoever – e.g., 100 tonnes of wheat or 10 tonnes of coal. The buyer neither knows nor cares where the seller is obtaining his supplies from.

Whether goods are specific or unascertained, is important in determining the particular point in time at which ownership transfers from seller to buyer.

Perishing of specific goods

In addition, where goods are specific goods, special rules apply as to the effect on the contract of the perishing of the goods. In terms of s 6, where there is a contract for the sale of specific goods and the goods without the knowledge of the seller have already perished by the time the contract is made, the contract is void.

In terms of s 7, where there is an agreement to sell specific goods and subsequently the goods, without fault on either side, perish before the agreement to sell becomes a sale and the risk of anything happening to the goods passes to the buyer, the agreement is terminated.

Goods 'perish' when they are physically destroyed but the term has also been held to cover goods which are stolen.

Perishing of generic goods

Generic goods are a quantity of a commodity, such as 10 tonnes of coal, from an unspecified source. Where there is an agreement to sell generic goods, the contract is not terminated by frustration should the seller's supply of the goods be destroyed. The loss falls on the seller who must obtain such goods elsewhere or face an action for breach of contract.

Capacity to enter a contract of sale of goods

The common law of contract regulating contractual capacity applies equally to contracts of sale of goods. Section 3 of the Act does provide that where a person supplies necessaries to a person who is insane or to a person who lacks capacity through intoxication, the supplier of those necessaries is entitled to be paid a reasonable price for them. Note that the statute provides for the payment of a *reasonable* price rather than the contract price which may be judged to be too high.

Formalities of a contract of sale of goods

A contract of sale of goods requires no special formalities. Section 4 of the Act provides that the contract may be made in writing, or verbally, or it may be implied from the conduct of the parties.

The price

The definition of a contract of sale of goods states that 'the seller transfers or agrees to transfer ownership of goods to the buyer in exchange for a money consideration called the price'. Money must change hands, otherwise the Act's provisions do not apply to the contract. The Act does not cover barter – i.e., a straight exchange of goods. However, part-exchange is covered by the Act so long as some money changes hands. Accordingly, the Sale of Goods Act 1979 applies where, for example, Sid buys a new car from a garage and meets the purchase price of £8000 by trading in his present car for £3000 and paying £5000 in cash.

Section 8 of the Act provides that the price may be fixed by the contract, or left to be calculated in a manner set out in the contract, or determined by the course of dealing between the parties. Where the contract does not fix a price, the buyer must pay a reasonable price. What constitutes a reasonable price will depend upon the circumstances of each case, but it is generally held to be the market price of the goods at the time of delivery.

Section 9 provides that where there is an agreement to sell and the parties have agreed that the price is to be fixed by a third party who is to value the goods, failure by the third party to make the valuation shall cause the agreement to be terminated. However, should the goods have been delivered to and used by the buyer, a reasonable price has to be paid for them. Where the valuer is prevented from making the valuation by one of the parties, the innocent party is entitled to bring an action for damages against the party preventing the valuation.

THE IMPLIED TERMS

Sections 12–15 of the Act operate to incorporate by implication into a contract of sale of goods certain terms which protect the buyer. These implied terms are automatically part of a contract of sale of goods. The parties do not have to include these provisions as express terms in their contract.

The consumer in a large department store does not say to the assistant at the cash desk, 'I offer to buy this shirt and it is a material condition of the contract that Bloggs plc own the shirt and have the right to sell it; that the shirt is as described on the packet; and that the shirt is of satisfactory quality and reasonably fit for my purpose of wearing it.' The buyer does not have to make this statement. These terms are automatically part of his contract with Bloggs plc. They are incorporated into the contract as implied terms by the Sale of Goods Act 1979.

What are the implied terms?

Title

Section 12 deals with implied terms about title. In terms of this section there are incorporated into a contract of sale of goods the following implied terms:

(a) in a sale, that the seller has a right to sell the goods;
(b) in an agreement to sell, that the seller will have the right to sell the goods at the time when ownership transfers to the buyer;
(c) that the goods are free from any charge or encumbrance in favour of a third party which was not disclosed to the buyer before the contract was made;
(d) that the buyer will enjoy quiet possession of the goods undisturbed by the claims of any third party.

The seller may not have the right to sell goods; for example, because they have been stolen or remain subject to a hire-purchase agreement. Should the police take possession of goods because they are stolen property, the buyer may bring an action for damages against the seller for breach of the term as to title implied by s 12 of the Act.

A buyer of second-hand furniture, which the seller has stored in a warehouse, may go along to pick up the furniture only to be told that it is not being released until outstanding storage fees are paid. Again, in such circumstances the seller of the furniture is in breach of the term implied by s 12 to the effect that the goods are free from any charge or encumbrance in favour of a third party (in this case the warehouse owner).

A third party may raise a court action claiming that the buyer's use of the goods infringes some right enjoyed by the third party; for example, the goods infringe the third party's copyright. In such a situation, the seller is once again in breach of his contract with the buyer. The seller is in breach of the implied term that the buyer will enjoy quiet possession of the goods.

A number of cases have illustrated the operation of the Sale of Goods Act 1979 s 12.

In **Rowland *v* Divall [1923] 2 QB 500** a stolen car had to be returned to its true owner. The buyer brought an action against the seller of the car based on breach of the term, that the seller had the right to sell the car, implied by s 12. It was held that the buyer was entitled to the return of the whole purchase price even though he had enjoyed three months' use of the car.

In **Niblett Ltd *v* Confectioners Materials Co [1921] All ER 459** there was a breach of the implied term that the buyer will enjoy quiet possession of the goods. The buyer of tins of condensed milk discovered that the labels on the tins which were marked 'Nissly Brand' infringed the trademark of the Nestlé Company. The Nestle Company could have obtained a court order preventing the resale of the milk. In order to re-sell the tinned milk, the buyers had to remove the offending labels thus reducing the value of the goods. The buyers of the milk successfully sued the sellers for damages for breach of the warranty implied by s 12.

In **McDonald *v* Provan (of Scotland Street) Ltd 1960 SLT 231** the front half of a stolen Ford car was welded to the rear half of another Ford. This composite vehicle was then sold to Provan Ltd who bought it in good faith and resold it to McDonald. Three months later, the police took the car from McDonald on the ground that at least part of it was stolen property. McDonald sought damages from Provan Ltd, alleging breach of the terms implied by s 12. It was held that if the alleged facts, which were hotly disputed, could be proved by the pursuer, they would amount to a breach of the terms that the seller had a right to sell the goods; that the goods were free from any charge or encumbrance; and that the buyer would enjoy quiet possession of the goods.

The protection afforded to the buyer by s 12 may be limited where it is made clear that the seller's title might be defective and the buyer goes through with the sale anyway. In such cases, the seller must disclose all *known* charges or encumbrances to the buyer and warrant that he shall not disturb the buyer's quiet possession of the goods.

Description

Section 13 deals with description. In terms of this section, there is implied into any contract of sale of goods which is a sale of goods by description the requirement that the goods will correspond with the description.

What is a sale by description? It is evident that if goods are bought by mail order, then the sale is a sale by description. Similarly, if there is an agreement to sell future goods – i.e., goods which still have to be manufactured or acquired by the seller – then that too will be a sale by description. The Act also makes it clear that a sale of goods which have been personally selected by the buyer may be a sale by description. Section 13(3) provides that a sale of goods is not prevented from being a sale by description just because the goods are exposed for sale and are selected by the buyer. The seller may describe the goods verbally or on a written notice and the buyer, in selecting those goods, may rely upon that description. The goods may be contained in packaging on which the goods are described. The seller may select goods because of what is said on the packet, in which case it is a sale by description.

For example, sheets may be wrapped in cellophane on which there is a label which states that the sheets are for a double bed. If, on unwrapping the sheets, they are found to be for a single bed, the seller is in breach of the term in the contract implied by s 13 to the effect that the sheets would conform to the description on the packet.

In **Grant** *v* **Australian Knitting Mills [1936] AC 85** the buyer of underpants, which still contained traces of a chemical, contracted a skin condition which spread over his entire body and was so severe that he almost died as a result. On appeal from the Australian courts to the Privy Council in London it was stated that ' there is a sale by description even though the buyer is buying something displayed before him on the counter; a thing is sold by description, though it is specific, so long as it is sold not merely as the specific thing but as a thing corresponding to a description'.

There has been some difficulty over which types of complaint might be sustained as claims that there has been a breach of the implied term as to description. A distinction must be drawn between the description of goods and the quality of goods. It has been suggested that description is concerned with words which identify the goods. There is a breach of the implied term as to description if the words used do not accurately identify the goods. Where a buyer's complaint is related to the quality of the goods this falls to be dealt with as a breach of the terms implied by s.14 of the Act dealing with satisfactory quality and fitness for purpose.

In **Border Harvesters Ltd** *v* **Edwards Engineering (Perth) Ltd 1985 SLT 128** there was a sale of certain equipment to be used for drying grain. The equipment was described as being capable of certain levels of performance. The buyers were dissatisfied with the performance of the drying equipment and raised an action for damages against the sellers. As part of the buyer's case, it was claimed that the sale was a sale by description. Lord Kincraig held that it was not a sale by description stating, 'what was contracted for in this case was a Kamas dryer; what was supplied was a Kamas dryer. What the dryer was capable of doing was in my judgement not part of the description of the goods supplied.'

A contract may expressly or impliedly provide that a sale is a sale by sample. The buyer orders goods having been shown a sample of them. Where a sale of goods is a sale by description, as well as by sample, the goods – when they arrive – must correspond not only with the sample but also with the description given.

Satisfactory quality and reasonable fitness for purpose

Section 14 deals with satisfactory quality and reasonable fitness for purpose. As a general rule, there is no implied term about the quality of goods or their fitness for any particular purpose. Two exceptions to this are to be found in ss 14(2) and 14(3).

Section 14(2) – satisfactory quality. Where the seller sells goods in the course of a business, there is an implied term that the goods supplied under the contract are of satisfactory quality – except that this implied term does not extend to any matter making the quality of goods unsatisfactory:

(a) which is specifically drawn to the buyer's attention before the contract is made; or
(b) where the buyer examines the goods before the contract is made, which that examination ought to reveal; or
(c) in the case of a contract for sale by sample, which would have been apparent on a reasonable examination of the sample.

What is meant by 'satisfactory quality'?

Section 14(2A) provides that 'goods are of satisfactory quality if they meet the standard that a reasonable person would regard as satisfactory, taking account of any description of the goods, the price (if relevant) and all other relevant circumstances'.

Section 14(2B) gives further guidance by stating that the quality of goods includes their state and condition and – *in appropriate cases* – their:

(a) fitness for all the purposes for which goods of that kind are commonly supplied;
(b) appearance and finish;
(c) freedom from minor defects;
(d) safety; and
(e) durability.

Thus it can be seen that the general test of satisfactory quality is set out in s 14(2A), but when applying that basic test, such factors as are appropriate from the list in s (2B) can be taken into account. Accordingly, a new fridge may be delivered with a slight scratch on one side affecting the product's 'appearance and finish'. Although this is a factor which contributes to the quality of goods, the fact that the scratch affects the appearance of the fridge will not of itself mean that the fridge is not of satisfactory quality. For that to be the case, the appearance of the fridge must be such that a reasonable person would not regard it as satisfactory.

It is worthy of note that the provisions on satisfactory quality replace the former provisions relating to 'merchantable quality'. The Scottish Law Commission had considered 'merchantable quality' in its report No 104 on 'Sale and Supply of Goods' 1987 Cmnd 137. The report criticised the implied term as to 'merchantable quality' because of the emphasis which its definition placed on 'usability' rather than on 'acceptability' to the consumer. It was felt that quality should not be determined merely by reference to whether an item is technically fit for its purpose but should encompass considerations of the sort now contained in the new s 14(2B) set out above. The amendments put into effect by the Sale and Supply of Goods Act 1994 sought to give effect to the recommendations contained in the report.

Section 14(3) – reasonable fitness for purpose. Where the seller sells goods *in the course of a business* and the buyer, *expressly or by implication*, makes known to the seller any particular purpose for which the goods are being bought, there is an implied term that the goods supplied under the contract are reasonably fit for *that* purpose, whether or not that is a purpose for which such goods are commonly supplied – except (a) where circumstances show that the buyer does not rely on the skill or judgement of the seller; *or* (b) where circumstances show that it is unreasonable for the buyer to rely on the seller's skill and judgement.

Where the goods have only one obvious use the buyer is not required to actually (i.e., expressly) tell the seller the use which he intends to put the goods to. In such circumstances, the seller will be treated as knowing the purpose for which the goods are being bought (ie the seller has implied knowledge). For example, in **Priest** *v* **Last [903] 2 KB 148** a hot-water bottle burst causing severe scalding. It was held that the buyer had, by implication, made his purpose known. How many purposes can a hot-water bottle be put to? However, should goods have several possible uses, in order to obtain the protection of s 14(3), the buyer must tell the seller what he intends to use the goods for.

In **McCallum** *v* **Mason 1956 SC 50** McCallum, a nurseryman, thought that his tomato plants were looking yellow and so he consulted Mason who dealt in fertilisers. Mason said that he would add some extra magnesium sulphate to his own brand of fertiliser and that this mixture, if applied to the plants, should do the trick. McCallum bought two bags of the mixture and applied the contents of one bag to his tomato plants which all died. The following season, McCallum used the second bag to treat tomato plants and chrysanthemum plants. These plants also died and McCallum had the mixture analysed. A weedkiller, sodium chlorate, had been added instead of magnesium sulphate. McCallum sought compensation for the loss of *all* the plants which died over the two seasons alleging that the mixture supplied by Mason was not reasonably fit for its purpose. It was held that McCallum was entitled to be compensated only in respect of the first crop of tomato plants. This was because McCallum had only disclosed to Mason his intention to use the mixture on the first crop of tomato plants.

Section 14(3) shall not apply 'where the circumstances show that the buyer does not rely, or that it is unreasonable for [the buyer] to rely, on the skill or judgement of the seller ...'. Reliance on the seller's skill or judgement does not normally have to be proved by the buyer. In **Grant** *v* **Australian Knitting Mills [1936] AC 35** it was stated that '... the reliance will in general be inferred from the fact that a buyer goes to the shop in confidence that the tradesman has selected his stock with skill and judgment.' Partial reliance upon the seller will allow the buyer to found upon s 14(3) in respect of defects relating to those matters where reliance *was* placed.

There is held to be no reliance where the buyer is more expert than the seller or where the seller provides goods in accordance with a detailed specification provided by the buyer. In **Teheran-Europe** *v* **St Belton [1968] 2 QB 545** there was held to be no reliance upon the seller in respect of Persian regulations on tractors which were bought for export to that country. The tractors did not comply with Persian law. The buyer failed in an action against the seller because it was found that the buyer was far more expert on Persia and its requirements than the seller.

The requirement that the sale is 'in the course of a business'

The undertakings that the goods shall be of satisfactory quality, or reasonably fit for a particular purpose, apply only when the seller is selling goods in the course of a business. Section 61(1) of the Act provides that 'business' includes a profession and the activities of any government department, or local or public authority. However, if a business sells goods which are not the normal type of goods it deals in, the sale is still regarded as a sale in the course of a business. In these circumstances, the buyer enjoys the benefit of the provisions implied by s 14. For example, a firm of solicitors decides to buy a new word-processor and to sell their old typewriter. The sale of the typewriter would be a sale in the course of a business even though the sale of typewriters is not the solicitors' normal line of business.

Private sales between two individuals neither of whom is dealing in the course of a business are not covered by s 14. However, s 14(5) provides that a sale by a private individual will be regarded as a sale in the course of a business where that individual uses an agent who then sells the goods in the course of a business. For example, if a private individual places a painting with an auctioneer for sale, the sale will be regarded as a sale in the course of a business and s 14 will apply – unless (a) the buyer knows that the seller/principal is a private individual not selling in the course of a business; *or* (b) reasonable steps are taken to bring this fact to the buyer's notice before the contract is made.

The relationship between satisfactory quality and reasonable fitness or purpose

If goods are not of satisfactory quality, then it follows that they are not reasonably fit for their purpose. However, goods may not be reasonably fit for a particular purpose and yet still be held to be of satisfactory quality. A buyer may purchase goods intending to use them for a particular purpose. Should the goods be unable to be used for the buyer's *particular* purpose, they will not be reasonably fit for the purpose for which they were bought. However, the seller is liable for a breach of the term as to reasonable fitness for purpose implied by s 14(3) *only* if the buyer has made his particular purpose known to the seller, expressly or by implication.

For example, John goes into a hardware store to buy a tube of glue suitable for mending a glass ornament. John is sold a tube of wood glue which is not suitable for sticking glass to glass. The tube of glue is obviously not fit for John's particular purpose. However, the glue is of satisfactory quality because it will stick wood together. John, therefore, has no remedy under s 14(2) dealing with satisfactory quality. He has a remedy under s 14(3) – i.e., for breach of an implied term that the glue was fit for John's particular purpose – *only* if John told the shop assistant that he required a glue which was suitable for mending glass. If John did not expressly say why he wanted the glue, he will have no remedy.

A case which illustrates this is **Griffiths *v* Peter Conway Ltd [1939] 1 All ER 685**. A lady purchased a tweed coat. She had exceptionally sensitive skin and the coarse tweed material caused her to contract dermatitis. A person with normal skin would have suffered no ill effects as a consequence of wearing the coat. Therefore it was held that the coat *was* of general merchantable quality (the term which preceded 'satisfactory quality'). The seller was not in breach of the term implied into the contract of sale by s 14(2) of the 1979 Act as it then stood. However, the coat was not fit for this lady's particular needs. She required a coat of a fabric which would not irritate her skin. Nevertheless, the seller would be in breach of the term implied by s.14(3) of the Act – i.e., that the coat would be reasonably fit for the lady's purposes – *only* if she had made her skin condition and her resultant requirements known to the shop. As she had not done so, she had no remedy under either s 14(2) or s 14(3) of the Act.

A similar situation arose in the case of **BS Brown & Son Ltd** *v* **Craiks Ltd 1970 SC (HL) 51** in which textile merchants placed an order for the manufacture of a quantity of rayon cloth. The textile merchants wanted cloth which was fit for making dresses but, due to a misunderstanding, this was not made clear to the manufacturers. The manufacturers thought the cloth was for industrial use and produced cloth which was fit for such use but could not be used to make dresses. The textile merchants failed in their action against the manufacturers. Although the cloth was not fit for their particular purpose, they had not made their purpose known and because the cloth could be sold for other purposes such as making bags, the cloth was of general merchantable quality (as the term then was).

Goods supplied under the contract

The provisions of s 14 apply to goods 'supplied' under the contract. Accordingly, the requirements of merchantable quality and reasonable fitness for a particular purpose extend not only to the goods themselves but also to the packaging they come in. For example, the seller of a bottle of lemonade will be liable to the buyer if the buyer is injured when a defective glass bottle which contains the lemonade shatters.

The seller's liability is 'strict'

Another point to stress is that where a seller is in breach of a term implied by s.14, his liability is said to be 'strict'. This means that the buyer is not required to prove that the seller is at fault – i.e., has been negligent. The seller of a defective toaster cannot try to escape liability to the buyer by blaming the manufacturer. This is because s 14 operates by putting the requirement that the goods are of satisfactory quality and reasonably fit for the buyer's purpose into the *contract* between seller and buyer. Thus, if the goods sold are not of satisfactory quality, the seller is in *breach of contract* – fault just does not come into it. Should the seller of a defective toaster be required to compensate the buyer, the seller will then have to sue the manufacturer. Sections 12, 13 and 15 operate in the same way.

The seller's liability is not limited to returning the purchase price. Should defective goods cause damage to other property belonging to the buyer, or injure the buyer, then the seller is required to compensate the buyer in respect of these losses also. For example, Fiona buys a brand-new iron for £24 from Smith's Household Supplies Ltd. It has a defective thermostat and the first time Fiona uses it, the iron burns a hole in a brand-new silk blouse which cost £35. As well as seeking to reject the iron and obtain the return of the purchase price of £24, Fiona will also be entitled to claim £35 to compensate for the ruined blouse. It should be noted that presuming the iron was made by a reputable manufacturer, there is no way that Smith's could be regarded as being 'at fault'. The shop could not have known about the defect in the iron. However, the statute operates so as to place upon the retailer primary liability to the buyer in respect of defective goods.

It must be stressed that the Sale of Goods Act 1979 deals only with the seller's liability to the **buyer** of defective goods. Under the Act's provisions, the seller has liability only to those persons with whom he contracts. The seller's potential liability to persons who are injured while using defective goods, but who did not themselves buy the goods, must be considered under either the common law of delict or the provisions of Part I of the Consumer Protection Act 1987. The law relating to liability for defective products will be considered separately in the chapter dealing with Product Liability.

'Sale goods'

The fact that goods are bought in a sale does not of itself diminish the buyer's rights *unless* the reason for the reduction in price is a defect – e.g., 'slight seconds' – *and* this defect was drawn to the buyer's attention *before* the contract was made. Notices which proclaim 'no money refunded on sale goods' or for that matter 'no refunds given' would be unlawful under the Consumer Transactions (Restrictions on Statements) Order 1976, as amended. Such notices have no effect and their display is also a criminal offence.

Problem areas associated with section 14

The first problem is to determine what is enough to satisfy the requirement that goods are of satisfactory quality or reasonably fit for a particular purpose. The second problem is to determine when the buyer has the right to reject the goods and to demand the return of the whole purchase price. In certain circumstances, the buyer must keep the goods and his remedy is limited to claiming damages.

When are goods of 'satisfactory quality' or 'reasonably fit for their purpose'?

Traditionally, the courts allowed a depressingly low standard of quality of goods to be regarded as satisfying the requirements of s.14. One example of the traditional judicial approach is to be found in **Millars of Falkirk Ltd *v* Turpie 1976 SLT (Notes) 66**. The buyer sought to reject a brand-new car because of an oil leak from the power- assisted steering unit. The court stated that one small, easily remediable and not particularly dangerous fault did not make the car unfit for its purpose and unmerchantable (as the term then was). The amended s 14(2) dealing with satisfactory quality was intended to address this problem.

However, even before the introduction of the concept of satisfactory quality, the courts had begun to take on board the notion of **consumer acceptability** as a measure of merchantability (as the term then was) and reasonable fitness for purpose.

In **Bernstein *v* Pamsons Motors [1987] 2 All ER 220** a brand-new Nissan Laurel car costing £8000 came to a dead halt after only three weeks and 140 miles. The engine had seized up due to some latent manufacturing fault. Justice Rougier held that the car was not merchantable (as then required) under s 14, although the car could be repaired so as to be 'as good as new'. It should be noted, however, that in this case the buyer's remedy was restricted to damages. He was not allowed to reject the car because, in the view of the court, his use of the car, albeit limited, amounted to 'acceptance' of the goods under s 35 of the Act. (The concept of acceptance and its consequences are discussed below.)

In **Rogers** *v* **Parish (Scarborough) Ltd [1987] QB 933** a new Range Rover costing £16 000 developed, within the first six months, substantial defects affecting the engine, gearbox and the bodywork. During that time, attempts were made to remedy the defects and the vehicle was driven 5500 miles although 'in a manner which gave [the buyer] no satisfaction'. The buyer eventually sought to reject the vehicle and get his money back. The dealers refused to take the Range Rover back.

At first instance, the judge backed the dealers. He took a traditional approach, finding that none of 'the defects ... were such as to render the vehicle unroadworthy, unusable or unfit for any of the normal purposes for which a Ranger Rover might be used ... [The defects] were capable of repair and the defendants attempted to repair them at no cost to the plaintiffs ... Some of the defects did recur ... but the fact that these defects had been satisfactorily dealt with on one occasion can only mean that they were susceptible to further repair ... the very fact that during the first six months of its life the plaintiffs were able to use the vehicle for a distance in excess of 5000 miles demonstrates that it had plenty of use. Accordingly, the plaintiffs must fail in their allegations that the vehicle was not of merchantable quality (as it then was) and unfit for the purposes for which it was required'.

The buyer appealed to the English Court of Appeal and won. It was no longer acceptable to take the old fashioned view that it is enough that a car can be driven in safety from A to B; rather a vehicle would require to be capable of being driven 'with the appropriate degree of comfort, ease of handling and reliability and ... with pride in the vehicle's outward and interior appearance'. The buyer was entitled to have high expectations of a luxury brand-new vehicle costing £16 000. Another Court of Appeal judge agreed adding that '... the quality [of a vehicle] is not determined merely by asking if it will go'.

Despite the fairly extensive use of the Range Rover, the buyer was held entitled to reject it. It should be noted that the court in this case did not consider whether the buyer was barred from rejecting the car by his 'acceptance' of it because the dealers failed to include this argument in their case.

When does the buyer have the right to reject the goods and to demand the return of the whole purchase price?

A new s 15B(1) states that where the seller is in breach of any terms of a contract, whether express or implied, the buyer shall be entitled:

(a) to claim damages, and
(b) if the breach is *material* – to treat the contract as repudiated and reject the goods.

In terms of s 15B(2) where the contract is a *consumer contract*, a breach of the terms implied by ss 13, 14 and 15 will be regarded as a material breach. Accordingly, where goods are not as described, where they do not correspond with a sample, where they are not of satisfactory quality or fit for their purpose, a consumer has an automatic right to reject the goods and demand a refund.

A consumer contract is defined as a contract in which:

1 one party deals in the course of a business;
2 the other party (the consumer) does not deal in the course of a business; and
3 in a sale of goods contract, the goods are of a type ordinarily supplied for private use or consumption.

Should the buyer intend to reject the goods he must intimate this fact to the seller. However the right to reject the goods is lost and the buyer's remedy is limited to keeping the goods and claiming some compensation where the buyer is found to have *accepted* the goods.

Section 53A(1) provides that the damages generally payable will be such as to compensate for the estimated loss directly and naturally arising from the breach.

When the seller makes delivery, the buyer must be given a reasonable opportunity to examine the goods to check that they conform to the contract. In terms of s 35, where goods are delivered to the buyer and he has not previously examined them, the buyer is not treated as having accepted the goods until he has had a reasonable opportunity of examining them to ascertain that they are in conformity with the contract. Where a consumer signs a delivery note without having examined the goods, this cannot be regarded as acceptance of the goods.

Section 35 also provides that the buyer is deemed to have **accepted** the goods:

(a) when he intimates to the seller that he has accepted them; *or*
(b) when the goods have been delivered to him and he does anything with the goods which is inconsistent with the seller still being the owner; *or*
(c) when a reasonable length of time has passed without the buyer having intimated to the seller that he is rejecting the goods.

What will amount to 'a reasonable time' for retention of the goods without rejection is still not altogether clear but in many cases it will be measured in days rather than in months. However, the reasonable time within which goods must be rejected will start to run only once the buyer has had an opportunity to examine the goods. It is arguable that in Scots law, as far as hidden, latent defects are concerned, a buyer can use the goods for some time without being barred by acceptance from rejecting them so long as he rejects the goods quickly once the faults come to light.

It should be noted that allowing a seller to attempt a repair is not to be treated as constituting 'acceptance' of the goods by the buyer.

In the situation where goods are delivered in instalments, the fact that earlier instalments have been accepted does not prevent the buyer exercising his right to reject a later instalment. Section 35A provides that where the buyer has the right to reject goods, he has the option to reject all of the goods or to accept some and reject the others. However, where the goods are regarded as a commercial unit, i.e., where the value of the goods as a collection is greater than the total value of the goods would be if they were sold individually, there is no right of 'partial rejection' and the buyer must reject the whole commercial unit.

Sale by sample

Section 15 deals with sale by sample. A contract of sale is a sale by sample where there is an express or implied term to that effect in the contract. The mere fact that the buyer has been shown a sample is not enough to make the contract a sale by sample to which s 15 applies. The provisions of s 15 incorporate into a contract of sale by sample the following implied terms:

(a) that the bulk will correspond with the sample in quality;
(b) that the buyer will have a reasonable opportunity of comparing the bulk with the sample;
(c) that the goods will be free from any defect, rendering them of unsatisfactory quality, which would not be apparent on reasonable examination of the sample.

In **Ruben** *v* **Faire Bros [1949] 1 KB 254** the buyers had been shown a sample of Linatex fabric. The sample was soft. The bulk, when it arrived, was crinkly. The sellers said that if the buyers warmed the fabric it would go soft. It was held that the sellers were in breach of the term implied by s 15. The bulk should correspond to the sample in quality *without* the buyer having to do anything to it to make it correspond.

EXCLUSION OF THE IMPLIED TERMS

The extent to which a seller may attempt to exclude or restrict liability for a breach of the terms implied by ss 12–15 of the Sale of Goods Act 1979 is governed by the Unfair Contract Terms Act 1977 s 20. Section 20 of the 1977 Act provides as follows:

(a) Any attempt to exclude or restrict the seller's liability for breach of the terms as to title implied by s 12 shall be void.

In respect of an attempt to exclude or restrict liability for breach of the terms implied by ss 13, 14 and 15, a distinction is drawn between **consumer contracts** and **non-consumer contracts**:

(a) Any attempt to exclude or restrict the effect of these sections in respect of a consumer contract is void.
(b) Any attempt to exclude or restrict the effect of these sections in respect of a non-consumer contract shall have no effect if it was not fair and reasonable to incorporate the exclusion or limitation clause in the contract.

What is a consumer contract?

A consumer contract is one in which: (a) one party deals in the course of a business; *and* (b) the other party, the consumer, does not deal in the course of a business; *and* (c) the goods are of a type ordinarily supplied for private use and consumption. If these conditions are not satisfied, the contract is a non-consumer contract. A contract between two businesses is a non-consumer contract.

With regard to a clause which attempts to exclude or restrict the effect of ss 13, 14 and 15 in respect of a non-consumer contract, it is for the person who seeks to rely on the exclusion clause to prove that it *was* fair and reasonable to incorporate it in the contract. In determining whether it was fair and reasonable to incorporate a term in a contract, the court shall take into account only those circumstances which were known or ought reasonably to have been known to the parties at the time the contract was made. The court shall also take into account the guidelines for the application of the reasonableness test set out in Schedule 2 to the Unfair Contract Terms Act 1977 – i.e.,

(a) the relative strength of the bargaining positions of the parties and whether the customer could have gone elsewhere;
(b) whether the customer received an inducement, such as a discount, to agree to the exclusion clause, and whether the customer could have got similar terms elsewhere without having to agree to an exclusion clause;
(c) whether the customer knew, or should have known, about the exclusion clause having regard to any custom of the trade and whether the customer had accepted similar exclusion clauses in previous dealings with the seller;
(d) where the term excludes or restricts liability if some condition is not complied with, whether it was reasonable to expect that compliance with that condition would be practicable;
(e) whether the goods were manufactured, processed or adapted to the special order of the customer.

It would appear that where the customer has no choice but to accept an exclusion clause because the seller enjoys a monopoly position in the market place, the court is less likely to find that an exclusion clause is reasonable. Where the customer accepts a discount in exchange for agreeing to an exclusion clause or where such exclusions are accepted as normal trade practice, the court may be inclined to find that the exclusion clause is reasonable. It will be unreasonable to declare that the seller will not be liable for defective goods unless the buyer complains within 24 hours of taking delivery of the goods. Compliance with such a requirement would not be practicable. It is probably reasonable for a seller to declare that he does not guarantee that goods are fit for a particular purpose where he is manufacturing them to a specification drawn up by the customer.

QUESTIONS

1 (a) Define a contract of sale of goods.
(b) What is the difference between a sale and an agreement to sell?
(c) Define 'goods'.
(d) What is meant by 'future goods', 'existing goods', 'specific goods', 'unascertained goods' and 'generic goods'. Give examples of each type.

2 What are the implied terms in a contract of sale of goods? What does 'implied' mean in this context?

3 What is meant by 'satisfactory quality' and what is the difference between satisfactory quality and 'reasonable fitness for a particular purpose'? Illustrate your answer with examples.

4 What is meant by the buyer having 'accepted' the goods and what effect does such acceptance have on his ability to reject faulty goods?

5 In what circumstances may the implied terms be excluded from a contract of sale of goods?

6 Helen has bought from a local department store, a pair of sheets described on the box as 100 per cent cotton. On unpacking them she discovers that they are nylon. She returns to the store to find that there are no suitable sheets in stock. Helen demands the return of her money but the store is prepared only to give her a credit note. Advise Helen.

7 Andrew has bought a new toaster from a local electrical goods shop. On the first morning he uses it, the toaster goes on fire. The toaster is destroyed and Andrew's wallpaper is badly scorched. When Andrew complains to the shop manager, he is told that it is nothing to do with them and that Andrew must complain to the manufacturer as the toaster is still under guarantee. Advise Andrew.

8 James has bought a house with a large garden. He is an inexperienced gardener and he visits his local garden centre in order to buy weedkiller. He needs a weedkiller which will kill weeds which are spoiling a rockery. The product which he is sold not only kills the weeds, but all the plants in the rockery as well. Has James any remedy against the garden centre?

9 Jane buys a new typewriter from a firm of office suppliers. She is a student and needs the typewriter to type essays. When she uses the machine, she discovers

that it is faulty. When Jane tries to return the typewriter, the seller points out a clause on the invoice which states that the statutory implied terms are excluded from the contract of sale. The seller offers to try to repair the typewriter but says that Jane must meet the cost of the repair. Advise Jane.

Would your advice differ if Jane had bought the typewriter for use in the course of a business?

8 The transfer of property, performance and breach

TRANSFER OF PROPERTY (OWNERSHIP) AS BETWEEN SELLER AND BUYER

When the law refers to a person having property in goods, it means that the person has rights of ownership in the goods. He enjoys real rights in those goods which he can exercise against the world at large; the goods are his, he is the owner. A person who has possession of goods is not necessarily the owner of those goods. Jim may lend to John a copy of a textbook. Jim does not have the book in his possession but the book still belongs to Jim. Jim remains the owner of the book. John may have possession of the book but that does not give him rights of ownership in the book.

Similarly, a point which must be stressed is that in a contract of sale of goods, possession of the goods is not conclusive as to their ownership. Delivery is *not* conclusive as to who owns the goods. Transfer of ownership may occur before, or even after, delivery of the goods has taken place.

The rules governing transfer of ownership of the goods from seller to buyer are to be found in the Sale of Goods Act 1979 ss 16, 17, 18 and 19.

In certain situations it is important to be able to determine precisely when ownership transfers from seller to buyer. Unless the parties agree in the contract that payment is to be made on an earlier date, the seller cannot sue the buyer for payment until ownership has passed to the buyer. If the seller goes bankrupt after he has been paid for the goods but before he has delivered them, whether or not ownership has passed makes all the difference to the buyer's position. If ownership has passed, the buyer can claim the goods. If ownership has not passed, the buyer is merely an unsecured creditor in the bankruptcy and is likely to lose his money. If it is the buyer who goes bankrupt after delivery of the goods but before he had paid for them, the same principle applies. If the seller is still the legal owner of the goods, he is entitled to have them returned. If ownership has already passed to the buyer, the seller is an unsecured creditor. Unless otherwise agreed, subject to two exceptions, s 20 of the 1979 Act provides that it is the owner of the goods who bears the risk of anything happening to them, irrespective of whether or not delivery has taken place.

The statutory provisions governing transfer of ownership of goods rely heavily on the distinction between specific goods and unascertained goods. Before proceeding further it is therefore necessary to recap on the meaning of these terms. Specific goods are goods which are identified and agreed upon at the time the contract is made. At the time of acceptance of the offer, the buyer knows exactly which item will be his. A sale of a second-hand car is a contract for the sale of specific goods. The buyer knows he will be getting a particular car and no other.

If a buyer buys a chair which a shop has on display *and* the buyer knows that the chair which he shall receive is the actual chair on display and not just one like it, the contract for the sale of the chair is a contract for the sale of specific goods. Where the buyer orders furniture which the shop must obtain from the manufacturers, the contract between the buyer and the shop is a contract for the sale of unascertained goods. Unascertained goods are goods which form an unsevered portion of a particular quantity of goods such as ten jars of coffee from the seller's stock of thirty jars of coffee. Generic goods are a form of unascertained goods and are a quantity of a commodity from an unspecified source – e.g., ten tons of coal.

Remember also that existing goods are goods which the seller already has in his possession at the time the contract is made. Future goods are goods which, at the time the contract is made, the seller still has to manufacture or obtain from a third party.

Transfer of ownership of unascertained goods

Prior to 19 September 1995, s 16 provided that where there is a contract for the sale of unascertained goods, ownership does not transfer to the buyer *unless and until* the goods are ascertained. Ownership in goods will be able to pass only once the parties know which particular items are going to be appropriated to the contract.

The effects of this provision may be seen in **Hayman & Son** *v* **McLintock 1907 SC 936**. A flour merchant sold and was paid for some sacks of flour. His stock of flour was stored in a warehouse owned by a third party called Hayman. The sale of a certain number of sacks of flour was intimated to Hayman and he acknowledged to the purchasers that he was holding the contract number of sacks of flour on their behalf. Hayman kept records of the number of sacks to which each of the purchasers was entitled, but he did not separate that number of sacks from the rest of the sacks belonging to the flour merchant, nor did he label any sacks with the names of the purchasers.

The flour merchant went bankrupt and a trustee in bankruptcy was appointed to take possession of all the merchant's property so that it could be sold in order to repay the merchant's creditors. The trustee in bankruptcy claimed *all* the sacks of flour held by Hayman. It was argued that some of the sacks belonged to the purchasers. It was held that the trustee in bankruptcy was entitled to all the flour. Section 16 specifically provided that where there is a sale of unascertained goods, the property shall not pass until the goods have been ascertained. In this case nothing had been done to ascertain the goods. If the buyers had got Hayman to label their sacks or to put them into another room, ownership would have passed. However, this had not been done and it was not enough to get a general acknowledgement that a certain number of sacks out of a larger number were held for the buyers. Ownership of the sacks of flour had not passed to the purchasers.

The *Hayman* case illustrates the harsh effect s.16 had on buyers of unascertained goods forming part of an identified bulk who, having paid for the goods, lost out when the seller became insolvent. However, following a joint report by the English and Scottish Law Commissions in July 1993 'Sale of Goods forming part of a bulk' (Law Com. No. 215; Scot. Law Com. No. 145), the Sale of Goods (Amendment) Act 1995 was passed. The purpose of the Act is to amend the law relating to the sale of unascertained goods forming part of an identified bulk and undivided shares in goods and it applies to contracts entered into on or after 19 September 1995. It operates by amending s 16 so that its provisions operate subject to a new s 20A. It also adds to rule 5 in s 18.

Section 20A provides that where there is a contract for the sale of a specified quantity of unascertained goods which form part of an identified bulk then, unless the parties agree otherwise, on payment of either some or all of the price, property in an undivided share in the bulk immediately passes to the buyer and the buyer becomes an owner in common of the bulk.

For example, A agrees to buy 100 tonnes of grain which is part of a cargo of 1000 tonnes of grain on board the ship *The Caledonian*. Once A pays all or part of the price he acquires property in an undivided share in the bulk and his claim would be preferred to that of a receiver or trustee in bankruptcy.

Transfer of ownership of specific goods

Section 17 provides that where there is a contract for the sale of specific goods, ownership of the goods passes when the parties to the contract intend that it should. The parties' intention may be determined by reference to the terms of the contract, the conduct of the parties and the circumstances of the case.

A case in which the intention of the parties was ascertained from their conduct was **Woodburn *v* Andrew Motherwell Ltd 1917 SC 533**. Farmer W sold to M Ltd six haystacks at an agreed price per ton. It was agreed that the hay was to be placed at M Ltd's disposal so that M Ltd could put it into bales. Farmer W agreed that he would then take the bales to the railway station so that they could be weighed to ascertain the freight cost. It was agreed that this would also allow the total price for the six stacks of hay to be calculated. Some of the hay which had been put into bales by the buyers was destroyed by fire before it left the seller's yard. A dispute arose as to who should bear the loss. The general rule is that the owner of the goods bears the risk of their destruction. It fell to the court to determine who had owned the goods at the time of the fire. It was held that the actions of the seller in placing the hay at the disposal of the buyers and the actions of the buyers in putting the hay into bales, indicated that the parties clearly intended that ownership should pass when the goods were placed at the disposal of the buyer in order that the hay could be converted into bales. Accordingly, at the time of their destruction, the bales were held to have belonged to M Ltd and M Ltd had to bear the loss.

Ascertaining intention

Section 18 provides five rules for ascertaining intention when this cannot be ascertained either from the terms of the contract or from the conduct of the parties. Rules 1 to 3 apply to specific goods, Rule 4 applies to goods delivered on approval and Rule 5 applies to unascertained goods.

Rule 1

Where there is an unconditional contract for the sale of specific goods in a *deliverable state*, ownership passes to the buyer at the time the contract is made. The buyer becomes the owner when the contract is formed, even though at that time the goods may not have been delivered or paid for. Goods are said to be in a 'deliverable state' when they are in such a state that the buyer would, under the contract, be bound to take delivery of them.

In **Tarling** *v* **Baxter (1827) 6 B) C 360** there was a contract for a sale of a haystack. It was a contract for the sale of specific goods because the buyer knew the precise stack of hay which he was getting. The hay was in a deliverable state at the time the contract was formed. Under Rule 1, ownership of the hay transferred to the buyer as soon as the contract was made. However, the hay was not to be delivered until some time afterwards. In the period between formation of the contract and delivery, the haystack was destroyed by fire. It was held that it was the buyer's hay at the time of the fire and, accordingly, the buyer's loss.

Rule 2

Where there is a contract for the sale of specific goods and the *seller* is bound to do something to the goods to put them into a deliverable state, ownership passes to the buyer only once this has been done and the buyer has been notified.

In **Gowans (Cockburn's Trustee)** *v* **Bowe) Sons 1910 2 SLT 17** a firm of potato merchants agreed to buy a farmer's whole potato crop. It was agreed that when they were ready, the potatoes would be lifted from the ground by the farmer and put into a pit on the farm. The buyers were then to put the potatoes into bags and remove them. The farmer went bankrupt after the potatoes had been lifted and pitted but before the buyers had removed them. The potatoes were claimed by the seller's trustee in bankruptcy but it was held that the potatoes belonged to the buyers. The growing potato crop constituted specific goods which had to be put into a deliverable state by the seller. Under Rule 2, ownership of the goods passed to the buyers once the potatoes had been lifted and pitted, and the buyers notified that this had been done.

Rule 3

Where there is a contract for the sale of specific goods and the *seller* is to weigh, measure or otherwise test the goods in order to calculate the price, ownership passes to the buyer only once this has been done and the buyer has been notified that it has been done.

In **Nanka-Bruce** *v* **Commonwealth Trust Ltd [1926] AC 77** X agreed to sell a consignment of cocoa to Y at an agreed price for a certain weight. The total weight of the consignment was uncertain. Y was going to resell the cocoa to a third party and it was agreed that the third party would weigh the consignment and that would allow a calculation of the price which was to be paid by Y to X. The Privy Council held that because it was not the seller who was to do the weighing, Rule 3 did not apply and ownership would pass to the buyer beforehand according to Rule 1 or 2.

Rule 4

When goods are sold to the buyer on approval or on a sale-or-return basis, the buyer becomes the owner when: (a) he notifies the seller that he is accepting the goods; *or* (b) he acts in a way which indicates he is adopting the transaction; *or* (c) he retains the goods without rejecting them after a time-limit set for their return has expired; *or* (d) there is no set time-limit for the return of the goods, but the buyer retains the goods without rejecting them beyond a reasonable time.

In **Poole *v* Smith's Car Sales (Balham) Ltd [1962] 1 WLR 774** P, a car dealer, had left a car with another dealer, S Ltd, in August 1960, on the understanding that S Ltd would try to sell the car. P was to receive £325 and S Ltd would keep any sum over that amount. By November 1960, P had received neither the money nor the return of the car. P wrote to S Ltd demanding either the price or the car by 10 November. The car was returned in a damaged condition at the end of November. Under Rule 4, ownership in goods supplied on a sale-or-return basis will transfer to the buyer, in the absence of a fixed time limit for the rejection of the goods, after a reasonable period of time has elapsed. It was held that, as a 'reasonable time' had elapsed by November, ownership of the car had passed to S Ltd and they were bound to pay the price to P.

The case of **Bryce *v* Ehrmann (1904) 7 F 5** is authority for the proposition that the act of pawning goods which are held on a sale-or-return basis constitutes an 'adoption' of the transaction which has the effect of transferring ownership of the goods to the buyer and renders him liable to pay the price.

Rule 5

Where there is a contract for the sale of unascertained or future goods by description, ownership transfers to the buyer when such goods, complying with the contract description, are *unconditionally appropriated* to the contract in a deliverable state. Appropriation of the goods may be either by the seller with the buyer's consent, or by the buyer with the seller's consent. Such consent may be express or implied, and may be given either before or after appropriation.

For example, there is unconditional appropriation by the buyer with the seller's consent where the buyer fills up his tank with petrol in a self-service garage. By setting up in this fashion, the seller gives implied consent in advance to the buyer putting petrol into his own tank. The bulk of petrol is stored in tanks under the garage forecourt. If the buyer intends to buy ten gallons of petrol, that ten gallons of petrol becomes ascertained only as the required number of gallons is appropriated by transfer into the buyer's car tank. Also, there is unconditional appropriation by the seller with the buyer's consent when a coalman delivers coal into an outside bunker which the buyer has left unlocked ready for the delivery. Leaving the bunker unlocked implies the buyer's consent to the coal being appropriated to the contract.

Rule 5 also provides that delivery of goods to a carrier for onward transmission to the buyer counts as unconditional appropriation if the seller does not retain his rights in the goods until some condition has been satisfied such as payment of the price.

In **Pignatoro** *v* **Gilroy [1919] 1 KB 459** 140 bags of rice were sold. Only 125 were delivered and the seller asked that the remaining 15 bags be uplifted by the buyer from the seller's warehouse. No reply was made and the bags were not uplifted. One month later, the 15 bags were stolen. It was held that as notice of appropriation had been given to the buyer in respect of these bags of rice, ownership had passed to the buyer and it was the buyer's rice which had been stolen.

In **Wardars** *v* **Norwood [1968] 2 QB 663** the sale of 600 frozen kidneys was a contract for the sale of unascertained goods. This was because at the time the contract was made the buyers did not know which 600 kidneys they would get from the sellers' stock of thousands of kidneys. The sellers gave the buyers a delivery note for 600 kidneys and the buyers sent carriers with the delivery note to pick up the goods. The carriers got the kidneys and a receipt, but forgot to switch on the refrigeration in the truck and the kidneys went off. Whose kidneys went off? Who bore the loss? It was held that under Rule 5, ownership passed when the sellers handed a receipt to the carriers. The kidneys belonged to the buyers. The buyers would still have to pay the sellers for the ruined kidneys. It would be up to the buyers to sue the carriers for compensation in respect of their negligence in forgetting to switch on the refrigeration.

Rule 5 has been added to by the Sale of Goods (Amendment) Act 1995. The addition puts into statutory form what has come to be known as 'ascertainment by exhaustion'. What is meant by this can be explained by the following example. There is a contract for the purchase of 100 bottles of claret which form part of the seller's stock of 500 bottles. Once other purchasers have taken delivery of their wine, so that only the contract amount of 100 bottles is left, it is possible to identify the buyer's goods, and therefore property in the wine will pass.

Transfer of risk

Section 20 deals with the passing of risk and provides that, unless the parties agree otherwise, the risk of damage to or destruction of the goods lies with the owner. Accordingly, the seller bears the risk until ownership transfers to the buyer. Once ownership has transferred, the buyer bears the risk. This is the case even though the goods have not been delivered.

One exception to this rule occurs where delivery has been delayed because of the fault of one of the parties. The party responsible for the delay must bear the risk of loss which would not have occurred had delivery gone ahead as planned. In addition, buyer and seller owe each other a common law duty to take reasonable care of the other's goods while holding them as custodian. A claim for breach of this duty would be based on delict.

Retention of ownership

Section 19 deals with retention of ownership by the seller. The seller may include a clause in the contract which provides that, notwithstanding delivery of the goods, ownership of the goods shall not pass to the buyer until some condition is fulfilled. Such clauses are often called **Romalpa Clauses** after an English case in which the legal effect of such clauses was considered. The most usual provision is that ownership shall not pass to the buyer until the seller has been paid. This is the simplest form of 'retention of title' clause and is referred to as a 'price-only' retention clause.

Other clauses, known as 'all-sums' retention clauses, are more ambitious and provide that ownership in the goods shall not pass to the buyer until *all sums* owing to the seller are paid. This would include monies owing in respect of other, unconnected transactions.

Are such clauses valid and binding? Until November 1990 a distinction was made in Scots law between price-only retention clauses and all-sums retention clauses. It was generally agreed that a simple price-only retention clause was valid and effective. However, in two decisions of the Outer House of the Court of Session, it was held that all-sums retention clauses were invalid and ineffective, and did not prevent ownership of goods passing to the buyer. These two decisions were **Emerald Stainless Steel Ltd** *v* **South Side Distribution Ltd 1982 SC 61** and **Deutz Engines Ltd** *v* **Terex Ltd 1984 SLT 273**. In these two cases, Lord Ross took exception to the all-sums clauses because in his opinion they were attempting to create a right in security over corporeal moveable property without transfer of possession of the property to the creditor. What does this mean?

If X wants to borrow £5 from Y, Y may want some 'security' in case X does not repay the money. X may say to Y that he will give him a letter which says that if X does not repay the £5, Y shall be entitled to X's watch. In Scots law, this letter is meaningless and does not give Y an effective 'right in security' over X's watch. In order to create a valid right in security over the watch, X would have to physically hand it over to Y.

There is an exception to the rule that in order to create a security over corporeal moveable property, the property must be handed over to the creditor. A registered company may create a security in favour of a creditor over company assets, including both heritable property and corporeal moveables, by means of a document known as a 'floating charge'. Also, generally, in order to create a security over heritable property (land and buildings), the debtor signs a formal document known as a 'standard security' which must be registered in either the General Register of Sasines or the Land Register in Edinburgh.

What Lord Ross was saying in the two Outer House decisions considered above was that the sellers were trying to use a retention of title clause to create a security over corporeal moveables by the back door. Accordingly, the clauses were held to be ineffective. However, the *Emerald Stainless Steel* and the *Deutz Engines* decisions have been overruled by the House of Lords in **Armour and Another** *v* **Thyssen Edelstahlwerke AG 1990 SLT 891**. Thyssen, a West German steel manufacturing company, sold a quantity of steel to Carron Company in Falkirk. There was a clause in the contract which provided that all goods delivered by the sellers were to remain the seller's property until all debts owed by the buyers to the sellers were settled. Carron Company went into receivership and Armour and Mycroft were appointed as joint receivers on behalf of two banks which were owed money by Carron Company. Steel supplied by Thyssen, worth £71 769 was lying at Carron Works. A dispute arose between the receivers and Thyssen as to the ownership of the steel. The receivers argued that ownership had passed to Carron Company and that the steel formed part of Carron's assets which could be distributed to creditors other than Thyssen. Thyssen argued that they were protected by the retention of title clause and demanded payment of £71 769.

The receivers won both at first instance in the Outer House of the Court of Session and on appeal to the Inner House. Judges in both the Inner and Outer Houses approved the decisions in *Emerald Stainless Steel* and *Deutz Engines*. However, Thyssen appealed to the House of Lords and won. The House of Lords held that the clause in the contract between Thyssen and Carron was not a right in security in disguise but was 'simply one of the conditions of what [was] a genuine contract of sale'. Carron Company never became the owners of the steel and Thyssen were held entitled to decree for payment of the price.

The reasoning of the House of Lords was that in order to create a right in security, the property which is offered as security, X's watch in the above example, must belong to the debtor. Something cannot be offered as security by X if X does not own it. In the *Armour* v *Thyssen* case, the retention of title clause could not be an attempt to create a right in security over Carron's steel in favour of Thyssen, because the very point of the clause was to prevent Carron ever becoming the owner of the steel. Carron could not, in law, offer a right in security over property which they did not own. The 'all sums' retention of title clause was an effective retention of title clause as allowed for by the Sale of Goods Act 1979 s 19.

TRANSFER OF TITLE

It is a general rule of law that only the owner of goods can transfer the property in them to someone and give that person real rights of ownership. This general rule is summed up in the maxim ***nemo dat quod non habet*** – i.e., no-one can give that which he does not have. Stolen goods will almost always be returned to their true owner. This may not always be possible, for example, where there is ***specificatio*** which occurs where the goods have been irretrievably converted into something else. Grapes may be converted into wine or olives into oil. The end product becomes the property of the manufacturer so long as he has acted in good faith. The manufacturer can sell the end product and give a good title to the buyer. However, the manufacturer would still have to pay the value of the stolen ingredient to its true owner.

Section 21 of the 1979 Act restates the general rule. It provides that where someone who does not own goods, sells them without the authority or consent of the true owner, the buyer does not acquire a good title. The true owner may recover the goods even from an innocent buyer who has bought them in good faith. However, there are a number of exceptions to the general rule both at common law and under statute. In such circumstances, a third party may acquire rights to the goods which will allow him to retain the goods in a dispute with their original owner:

1 The owner may be **personally barred**, by his own conduct, from denying the seller's authority to sell the goods. This may arise as a consequence of allowing the seller to have possession of the goods in circumstances which would give

rise to a presumption that he had the owner's consent to the sale (s 21(1)).

2 A buyer may obtain a good title when he buys goods from a **mercantile agent,** such as an auctioneer or a warehouseman. The mercantile agent must have possession of the goods with the owner's consent, the sale must take place in the ordinary course of the agent's business and the buyer must not have been aware of the agent's lack of authority to make the sale.

3 **Pawnbrokers** give a good title when selling items which have not been redeemed.

4 Where **the seller of goods has a voidable title** but his title has not been avoided at the time of the resale, the third party buyer acquires a good title *if* he has acted in good faith and did not know about the defect in the seller's title (s 23).

5 Where **the seller, who is still in possession** of goods after selling them to X, then sells the goods again to Y, Y obtains a good title to the goods. Y must have bought the goods in good faith and have known nothing about the previous sale. X in this situation cannot demand the return of the goods from Y and X's remedies are restricted to claiming damages from the seller for breach of contract (s 24). For example, Lucy goes along to her local garden centre and buys and pays for an ornamental sundial, the only one of its kind in stock. The garden centre owner agrees to deliver the sundial the following day. The sundial does not arrive and when Lucy makes inquiries she is told that an assistant sold the sundial by mistake to Mr Brown who took the sundial with him. What is Lucy's position in law? Lucy's contract with the garden centre was a contract for the sale of specific goods. Lucy knew exactly which sundial she was getting because it was the only one the garden centre had. Under Rule 1 of s 18 of the Act, the sundial – being in a deliverable state – became Lucy's property immediately the contract was made, even though delivery was not to take place until the following day. What has happened is that the garden centre has sold a sundial which did not belong to them. Under the general rule stated in s 21 of the Act, Mr Brown, in such circumstances, would not obtain ownership rights in the sundial. However, Mr Brown is protected by the exception stated in s 24 so long as he did not know about the previous sale to Lucy. Lucy cannot demand the return of the sundial from Mr Brown. Lucy's only remedy would be to sue the owner of the garden centre for damages for breach of contract. The amount of damages would be the return of the purchase price plus any extra Lucy has to pay to obtain the same sundial elsewhere.

6 Where **the buyer is in possession of goods** which still belong to the seller and the buyer resells them to an innocent third party who acts in good faith and has no knowledge of the rights of the original seller, the third party acquires a good title to the goods (s 25).

In **Archivent Sales & Development Ltd** *v* **Strathclyde Regional Council 1985 SLT 154** A Ltd had sold goods to R Ltd who were building contractors. In the contract between A Ltd and R Ltd there was an effective price-only retention of title clause which provided that A Ltd would remain the owners of the goods until the price had been paid notwithstanding delivery of the goods to R Ltd. R Ltd had entered into a building contract with the Regional Council and, in terms of the building contract, the Council were to become owners of materials once they were on site. A Ltd delivered the goods into R Ltd's possession on the Council's building site. When R Ltd went into liquidation, a dispute arose between A Ltd and the Council as to who had the right to the goods. A Ltd argued that the goods belonged to them by virtue of the retention of title clause. The Council sought the protection of the Sale of Goods Act 1979 s 25 and argued that R Ltd, as a buyer in possession of the goods, had delivered them to the Council in terms of the building contract. The Council argued that s 25 applied and that R Ltd had been able to give the Council a good title to the goods. The court held that the requirements of s 25 had been satisfied and found in favour of the Regional Council.

THE DUTIES OF THE PARTIES – DELIVERY, ACCEPTANCE AND PAYMENT

The Sale of Goods Act 1979 s 27 provides that it is the duty of the seller to deliver the goods, and it is the buyer's duty to accept the goods and pay for them, in accordance with the terms of the contract.

Section 28 provides that unless otherwise agreed, for example if the sale is on credit, the seller need not deliver the goods unless the buyer is ready to pay for them. Similarly, the buyer does not need to pay for the goods until the seller is willing to deliver them.

Section 29 sets out some general rules about delivery:

(a) The contract may provide whether the seller is to send the goods to the buyer or whether the buyer is to pick them up. If the contract is silent on the matter, the place of delivery is taken to be the seller's place of business if he has one, and if not, the seller's residence. However, if the contract is a contract for the sale of specific goods and both parties know that the goods are elsewhere, then the place of delivery is the place where the goods are located. Where the goods are in the possession of a third party, there is held to be no delivery until the third party acknowledges to the buyer that he is holding the goods on the buyer's behalf.
(b) Where the contract provides that the seller is to deliver the goods by sending them to the buyer but no specific date for delivery is fixed, the seller must deliver the goods within a reasonable time. Delivery must also take place at a reasonable hour of the day.
(c) Unless otherwise agreed, the cost of putting the goods into a deliverable state must be borne by the seller.

Section 30 deals with the delivery of the wrong quantity of goods. Where *too few* goods are delivered, the buyer may reject the goods only if the shortfall is material. Where he chooses to accept the goods he must pay for that smaller amount at the contract rate. Where *too many* goods are delivered the buyer may accept and pay for the contract amount and reject the rest. Alternatively, he may accept the whole delivery and pay for the extra goods as well. However he has the right to reject the whole consignment only if the surplus is material.

Section 35A applies where the buyer has the right to reject goods because of a breach on the seller's part which affects some or all of the goods. In such circumstances the buyer has the right of partial rejection and may accept some of the goods, including all those goods unaffected by the breach, and reject the rest.

Section 31 provides that, unless otherwise agreed, the buyer is not required to accept delivery of the goods by instalments.

Section 32 deals with delivery to a carrier. Where, in terms of the contract, the seller is to send the goods to the buyer, delivery to a carrier is deemed to be delivery to the buyer. However, the seller is required to contract with the carrier on terms which are reasonable having regard to the nature of the goods and other circumstances. If the terms of carriage are not reasonable and the goods are lost or damaged in transit, the buyer is entitled to refuse to treat delivery to the carrier as delivery to himself. Alternatively, the buyer may accept the goods but bring an action for damages against the seller. **In Young *v* Hobson & Partner (1949) 65 TLR 365 CA** the seller arranged for the carriage of goods at the 'owner's risk'. The seller could have contracted with the carrier for delivery of the goods at the carrier's risk at no extra cost. The goods were damaged in transit. It was held that the buyer could reject the goods because the seller was in breach of his duty under s 32 to make the best possible contract with the carrier. Where the seller is to send goods to the buyer by a route involving sea transit, the seller must give the buyer sufficient notice to enable the buyer to arrange for the insurance of the goods while they are at sea. If the seller fails to give notice, the goods remain at the seller's risk during such sea transit.

Section 33 deals with delivery of goods at a distant place. Where the seller agrees to deliver the goods *at his own risk*, the risk of damage to or destruction of the goods remains with the seller until delivery is effected, even though ownership has passed to the buyer. However, even in these circumstances, s 33 provides that, unless otherwise agreed, the buyer must still take any risk of deterioration of the goods which commonly occurs in the course of transit. For example, it may be the case that when tomatoes are being carried in transit one per cent of the load is always ruined because tomatoes are fragile. This is the sort of normal deterioration which the buyer is supposed to accept as his loss even when the seller is delivering 'at the seller's risk'. The seller would continue to bear the risk of the tomatoes being stolen or being destroyed in a motorway pile-up.

Section 34 deals with the buyer's right to examine the goods. The buyer has a duty to accept goods which are delivered and which conform to the contract. The act of acceptance is distinct from taking delivery of the goods. In terms of s 34, if the buyer takes delivery of goods without having previously examined them, he is not deemed to have accepted them until he has had a reasonable opportunity of examining them in order to determine whether they conform to the contract. Also, unless otherwise agreed, when the seller delivers the goods, the buyer is entitled, on request, to have a reasonable opportunity of examining the goods in order to determine whether they conform to the contract.

Section 35 deals with acceptance of the goods by the buyer. The buyer is deemed to have accepted the goods: (a) when he intimates his acceptance to the seller; *or* (b) when he does anything in relation to the goods which is inconsistent with the seller still being the owner; *or* (c) when he has retained the goods and has not intimated rejection of the goods to the seller within a reasonable time. The significance of the buyer having accepted the goods is that he loses the right to reject the goods and demand the return of the whole purchase price; he no longer has the right to resile from the contract. Once the buyer is deemed to have accepted the goods, his remedy, should the seller be in breach of contract, is limited to claiming damages.

Section 36 provides that, unless otherwise agreed, where the buyer rightfully refuses to accept goods which have been delivered, he is under no obligation to return them to the seller. All the buyer is required to do is to notify the seller of his refusal to accept the goods.

Section 37 deals with the buyer's liability for failure to take delivery of the goods. Where the buyer wrongfully neglects or refuses to take delivery, he is liable in damages to the seller. The seller's claim for damages may include a reasonable charge for care and storage of the goods.

REMEDIES FOR BREACH OF A SALE OF GOODS CONTRACT

The seller's remedies

Where the nature of the buyer's breach of contract is a refusal to accept and pay for the goods, the seller may bring an action for damages for non-acceptance against the buyer. Where the nature of the buyer's breach of contract is non-payment of the price, the seller may bring an action for payment of the price against the buyer. In addition to these personal remedies against the buyer, the unpaid seller also enjoys certain rights against the goods themselves.

The rights of the unpaid seller against the goods

For the purposes of the Sale of Goods Act 1979, the seller is an 'unpaid seller' either: (a) when the whole of the price has not been paid; *or* (b) when payment was by a negotiable instrument (a document equivalent to money) which has been dishonoured – e.g., the buyer's cheque has bounced.

The unpaid seller's lien – sections 1–43

The unpaid seller who is still in possession of the goods has the right to retain possession of them until he is paid. The seller enjoys this right, even though ownership in the goods may have passed to the buyer. The seller has this right: (a) where he has not agreed to give credit; *or* (b) where the goods were sold on credit but the period of credit has expired; *or* (c) where the buyer becomes insolvent. (The buyer is insolvent, for the purposes of the 1979 Act, if he has either ceased to pay his debts in the ordinary course of business or he cannot pay his debts as they fall due.)

Where an unpaid seller has already delivered some of the goods, he is entitled to retain the remainder, so long as the part-delivery is not to be regarded as an indication that the seller was giving up or waiving his lien.

The seller's lien on the goods comes to an end: (a) when he delivers the goods to a carrier for onward transmission to the buyer and he does not reserve the right of disposal of the goods; *or* (b) when the buyer lawfully obtains possession of the goods; *or* (c) when the seller gives up the right by waiver.

Stoppage in transit – sections 44–46

This is the right of the unpaid seller to resume possession of the goods while they are still in transit and to retain them until he is paid. Again, this right may be exercised once the ownership of the goods has passed to the buyer. An unpaid seller may exercise this right only when the buyer becomes insolvent and the right is exercisable only while the goods are in transit.

Goods are in transit from the time they are delivered to a carrier until the buyer or the buyer's agent takes delivery of them from the carrier. The transit ends if the buyer obtains possession of the goods before they reach their appointed destination. The transit also ends once the goods have reached their appointed destination and the carrier has informed the buyer that he is holding the goods on the buyer's behalf. After such notification to the buyer, the seller cannot resume possession of the goods. In **Muir *v* Rankin (1905) 13 SLT 60** the seller sent goods to the buyer by rail and tried to exercise stoppage in transit when he heard that the buyer was insolvent. The buyer had already been to the station, had been given an 'advice note' and had signed the delivery book. Although the goods were still at the station, transit was at an end because the carrier's actions indicated that they were holding the goods for the buyer. The seller could not exercise the right of stoppage in transit.

Transit is not at an end while the goods remain in the carrier's possession after being rejected by the buyer. In these circumstances the seller may resume possession of the goods. Difficulties arise when goods are delivered to a ship which has been chartered by the buyer. Everything depends on the terms of the charter. If the ship's captain is regarded as a carrier, the transit continues and the goods may be stopped. If the ship's captain is regarded as the buyer's employee or agent, the transit is at an end and the seller loses the right to repossess the goods. The transit is at an end and the seller's right of stoppage in transit is lost, where the goods remain in the carrier's possession only because he wrongfully refuses to deliver the goods to the buyer. Where part delivery of the goods has been made to the buyer, the remainder of the goods may be stopped in transit so long as there is nothing to indicate an agreement to give up possession of all of the goods.

The seller exercises his right of stoppage in transit either by actual repossession of the goods or by serving notice on the carrier. When notice is given to the carrier, the carrier must redeliver the goods to the seller. The seller must bear the expenses of redelivery.

Resale – section 48

An unpaid seller who has exercised his right of lien or stoppage in transit may resell the goods either: (a) if the goods are perishable; *or* (b) if he gives notice to the buyer of his intention to resell and the buyer does not pay the price within a reasonable time. In addition, there may be an express term in the contract which gives the seller the right to resell the goods should the buyer default. The seller may recover from the original buyer damages for any loss which the seller suffers on the resale. The buyer on the resale acquires a good title from the seller as against the original buyer.

The seller's remedies against the buyer

An action for the price – section 49

The general rule is that *where ownership of the goods has passed to the buyer* and he wrongfully neglects or refuses to pay the price, the seller may raise an action against the buyer for payment of the price. However, where the contract provides for payment on a specified date, then once that date has passed without payment, the seller may raise an action for the price irrespective of whether or not ownership has passed to the buyer.

An action for damages for non-acceptance – section 50

Where the buyer wrongfully neglects or refuses to accept and pay for the goods, the seller may bring an action against him for damages. The amount of damages payable is the estimated loss arising ordinarily from the buyer's breach of contract. Where there is an available market for such goods, the damages shall amount to the difference between the contract price and the market price either (a) at the time when the goods ought to have been accepted, where the contract fixed a date for acceptance; *or* (b) at the time of the buyer's refusal to accept, where no date was fixed for acceptance.

It should be borne in mind that s 37 of the 1979 Act also allows the seller to bring an action for damages for refusal to take delivery and to include in his claim a reasonable charge for the care and storage of the goods.

The buyer's remedies against the seller for breach of contract

Damages for non-delivery – section 51

Where the seller wrongfully neglects or refuses to deliver the goods, the buyer may bring an action against him for damages. The amount of damages payable is the estimated loss naturally arising from the seller's breach of contract. Where there is an available market for such goods, the damages shall amount to the difference in price between the contract price and the market price either (a) at the time when the goods ought to have been delivered, where the contract fixed a date for delivery; *or* (b) at the time of the seller's refusal to deliver, where no date was fixed for delivery.

Specific implement of the contract – section 52

The buyer may ask for an order for the specific implement of the contract from the court. This means that the buyer asks the court to order the seller to perform his contractual obligation to deliver the goods. The use of this remedy is curtailed in that it is available only in respect of specific goods and, even then, the buyer must persuade the court that he has a sound reason for preferring this remedy. The buyer must show that he cannot obtain goods of the same kind elsewhere. Accordingly, the court will not grant an order for specific implement of a contract to sell, say, a one-year-old Ford Escort car because such cars are readily available. However, the court would be disposed to order specific implement of a contract to sell the Mona Lisa because such an item is unique.

Rejection of the goods and damages – sections 15B and 53A

Section 15B(1) states that where the seller is in breach of any terms of a contract, whether express or implied, the buyer shall be entitled to claim damages and, if the breach is material, to treat the contract as repudiated and reject the goods. In terms of s 15B(2), where the contract is a *consumer contract*, a breach of the terms implied by ss 13, 14 and 15 automatically will be regarded as a material breach.

Section 53A(1) provides that the damages generally payable will be such as to compensate for the estimated loss directly and naturally arising from the breach.

It will be recalled that once the buyer has accepted the goods, the right to reject the goods is lost. The buyer's remedy is then limited to retaining the goods and claiming damages. Where the breach is that the goods are not of the contractual quality, s 53A(2) provides that the damages shall be an amount equal to the difference between the actual value of the goods and the value which the goods would have had had they been in conformity with the contract.

The Supply of Goods and Services Act 1982

Contracts for the transfer of property in goods and for the hire of goods

The Sale and Supply of Goods Act 1994 added new provisions, which apply in Scotland from 3 January 1995, to the Supply of Goods and Services Act 1982. The purpose of these new provisions was to make statutory provision for terms, such as are implied into sale of goods contracts under the Sale of Goods Act 1979 ss 12–15, to be implied into contracts for the transfer of property in goods (new ss 11A–E of the 1982 Act) and into contracts for the hire of goods (new ss 11G–K of the 1982 Act). Contracts for the transfer of property in goods to which the 1982 Act applies include barter and the exchange of tokens for goods.

QUESTIONS

1 Why may it be important to know *when* ownership of goods passes from seller to buyer?

2 What particular rules regarding the passing of property are contained in the Sale of Goods Act 1979 ss 16, 17 and 18?

3 Do goods *always* remain at the risk of the owner?

4 What is meant by the maxim *nemo dat quod non habet* and what are the exceptions to the general rule expressed in the maxim?

5 Describe the nature of the seller's duty to deliver the goods.

6 What are the seller's remedies should the buyer refuse to take delivery of the goods?

7 What personal remedies may the unpaid seller exercise against the buyer?

8 What are the rights of the unpaid seller against the goods?

9 What are the rights of the buyer when the seller is in breach of contract?

10 Sally spots an antique table in a local antique shop. The table is just what she wants but is badly scratched. Sally says she will buy the table if the shop owner will have it french-polished to disguise the scratches. Gerald, the shop-owner, agrees and says that the table should be ready in about two weeks. Ten days later, Gerald phones Sally to say that the table is ready. Sally tells him that she will send a van to pick up the table the following day. Overnight, the antique shop is burgled and the table is among the items stolen. Gerald is demanding payment for the table. Advise Sally.

11 Peter, an accountancy student, sends away for a textbook costing £40 on 30 days' approval. When the book arrives, Peter underlines some key passages in pen and folds down page corners to mark his place. Peter decides that he cannot afford to keep the book and, after photocopying one of the chapters, he returns it to the publishers within the 30-day period. What is the legal position?

12 Sam, a local builder, visited the premises of Builders Merchants Ltd and selected a new cement-mixer, the last one the sellers had in stock. Sam also ordered 30 bags of cement and 20 bags of sand. The cement-mixer plus the bags of cement and sand were to be delivered by the seller the following day. Overnight, a fire engulfed Builders Merchants Ltd's premises and the cement-mixer and all other stock items were destroyed. Nevertheless, Builders Merchants Ltd are now demanding payment for the cement mixer and for the bags of cement and sand. Advise Sam.

13 Alf, an antiques dealer, sells some furniture to Harry. Harry pays for the furniture but does not want it delivered until he returns from holiday a fortnight later. While Harry is on holiday, Alf's assistant sells the furniture by mistake to Jim who takes delivery on the spot. When Harry returns, Alf explains the situation and offers a full cash refund. However, this does not satisfy Harry who wishes to claim the return of the furniture from Jim. Advise Alf.

14 George has sold a consignment of ball bearings to Dave and has yet to receive payment for the goods. George has sent off the consignment to Dave using Acme Carriers. The next day, George hears that Dave has gone bankrupt. What are George's options?

Part 4
CONSUMER PROTECTION

9 False trade descriptions and consumer credit

INTRODUCTION

We have already seen that, apart from common law remedies, the consumer has statutory protection under civil law if he has a complaint against a manufacturer or the retailer who sold him the goods. His remedy is provided under either the Sale of Goods Act 1979 (as amended by the Sale and Supply of Goods Act 1994), the Unfair Contract Terms Act 1977, the Unfair Terms in Consumer Contracts Regulations 1994, or the Consumer Protection Act 1987 Part 1. The disadvantage of bringing a civil claim for damages is the trouble and the expense. The small claims procedure introduced in 1988 in the Sheriff Court was designed to help the consumer in this respect, when his claim was for no more than £750. However, since the 1970s, in the area of consumer protection, an important development has been the extension of criminal law as a means to assist the consumer. Under criminal law, it is the State, and not the consumer, which has the trouble and expense of initiating court proceedings. The main purpose of a prosecution is, of course, to impose criminal sanctions. However, a criminal court has the power to make a compensation order, and any retailer or trader, convicted of an offence, can be ordered by the court to pay compensation to any person who has suffered loss because of the offence. Another advantage of having this consumer protection legislation, which imposes criminal sanctions, is that the mere threat of prosecution can persuade a trader or retailer to offer compensation, in order to avoid facing a prosecution and possible bad publicity. The consumer will receive advice and help from his Local Trading Standards Office and, very often, the Trading Standards Officer will settle the individual consumer's dispute with the trader, without any further action being necessary.

Thus, a retailer can be guilty of an offence under the Consumer Protection Act Part 2, and the General Product Safety Regulations 1994 if he supplies, or offers to supply, or exposes for supply, goods which fail to comply with the general safety standard which is explained in the Act and the Regulations. A prosecution is also possible for various offences under the Consumer Credit Act 1974, the Trade Descriptions Act 1968 and the Consumer Protection Act 1987 Part 3.

UNSAFE GOODS

The Consumer Protection Act 1987 Part 1 (see p. 312) provides consumers and others with a civil remedy against producers of unsafe products. The provisions of Part 1 allow consumers to sue the producer of the unsafe goods for damages for death, personal injury or damage to private property.

The Consumer Protection Act (CPA) Part 2 imposes **a general safety requirement** on consumer goods and makes breach of this requirement a criminal offence. Part 2 of the Act replaces the earlier Consumer Protection Acts and Consumer Safety Acts which applied to certain goods. The CPA Part 2 applies to all consumer goods which are defined as those intended for private use or consumption. However, there are a number of exceptions where some products are covered by other legislation like the Food Safety Act 1990. Thus Part 2 does not apply to growing crops, food, water, feeding stuffs, fertilisers, gas, aircraft, motor vehicles, drugs, tobacco, goods that are not new and goods which are for export.

Section 10(1) of the CPA states that a person will be guilty of a criminal offence if he:

(a) supplies any consumer goods which fail to comply with the general safety requirement;
(b) offers or agrees to supply such goods; or
(c) exposes or possesses any such goods for supply.

Thus manufacturers and retailers could be prosecuted under the Act.

Section 10(2) explains the **general safety requirement**: consumer goods must be reasonably safe, which means that the risk of death or personal injury must be reduced to a minimum, having regard to all the circumstances.

The circumstances which a court would have to consider include the following:

(a) How the goods are marketed. This will include the way the goods are advertised, any warnings and instructions supplied with the goods, the group of people targeted, like children or the elderly, and also the intended use of the goods.
(b) Any relevant published safety standards. It is a rebuttable presumption and not an absolute defence that the general safety requirement has been met if the goods comply with statutory standards drawn up by various national and European Community bodies. Goods meeting these standards could be those that carry the CE mark, the BSI Safety mark, the BSI Kitemark or the BEAB mark for electrical goods.
(c) Whether there were any reasonable ways in which the goods could have been made safer.

Enforcement of the CPA Part 2

The local trading standards officer can issue **suspension notices** to stop suppliers selling goods when he reasonably suspects that there has been a breach of the general safety requirement. The Act provides a right of appeal against the imposition of a suspension notice and a right for a supplier to claim compensation should the trading standards officer issue such a notice without justification.

Alternatively, the trading standards officer can apply to the procurator fiscal for a **forfeiture order** which gives him the right to seize the goods.

The Secretary of State for Trade and Industry has powers under the Act to issue **a prohibition notice** to stop suppliers selling unsafe goods without his consent. The Secretary can also issue **a warning notice** requiring a trader at his own expense to publish a warning about goods the Secretary of State considers unsafe.

Finally, a manufacturer or retailer could face **prosecution in the criminal courts** for breach of the general safety requirement or for failing to comply with a notice.

The defences available to a manufacturer or retailer

1 That the manufacturer or retailer took all reasonable precautions and exercised all due diligence to avoid the commission of an offence.
2 That the offence was due to the fault of another person or due to reliance on information supplied by the other person. If relying on this defence the person charged must identify the other person. Thus an employee could be charged with an offence where his actions have caused the commission of an offence by his employer.
3 It is a defence for a retailer (not the manufacturer) to show that he did not know or had no reason for suspecting that the goods failed to comply with the general safety requirement.

The General Product Safety Regulations 1994 came into force in October 1994. These Regulations implement the EC General Product Safety Directive. They revoke the Approval of Safety Standards Regulations 1987 and the CPA s 10(3)(b)(ii) but do not repeal the rest of the CPA Part 2. The Regulations complement/supplement the provisions of the CPA Part 2 regarding product safety and the Food Act 1990 which covers the safety of food. The result is very confusing. The Regulations do not have the same exceptions and cover some goods not covered by Part 2 of the CPA. For example food, motor vehicles, drugs, growing crops, second-hand goods and tobacco are covered by the Regulations but not by the CPA Part 2. So second-hand car dealers beware! However, the new Regulations adopt the enforcement provisions in the Act and both must be read together. Where both apply, the general safety requirement in Regulation 7 takes precedence over the general safety requirement in the CPA s 10. The 1994 Regulations impose requirements concerning the safety of products intended for consumers or likely to be used by consumers if such products are to be placed on the market by producers or supplied by distributors. The Regulations apply to second-hand products (but not to antiques). They do not apply to products supplied for repair or reconditioning before use provided the supplier clearly informs the person to whom he supplies the product that it could be unsafe. Also not covered is any product which is already covered by specific

Community law rules regarding safety of that product. However, there is a presumption (unless the contrary is proved) that a product is a safe product if it complies with the specific rules of the law of the UK laying down the health and safety requirements which the product must satisfy in order to be marketed.

Producers and to a lesser extent distributors have duties under the Regulations. A producer is defined as a manufacturer of the product or an own-brander. When the manufacturer is outwith the Community and he does not have a representative in the Community then the producer will be the importer into the European Economic Area. Producers can also be other professionals in the supply chain insofar as their activities may effect the safety of the product. A distributor means any professional in the supply chain whose activity does not effect the safety properties of a product.

Regulation 7 (the general safety requirement) states that 'no producer shall place a product on the market unless the product is a safe product'. A safe product is defined as any product which under normal or reasonably foreseeable conditions of use, including duration, does not present any risk or only the minimum risks compatible with the product's use, considered as acceptable and consistent with a high level of protection for the safety and health of persons , taking into account in particular:

(a) the characteristics of the product, including its composition, packing and instructions for assembly and maintenance;
(b) the effect on other products where it is reasonably foreseeable that it will be used with other products;
(c) the presentation of the product, the labelling, any instructions for its use and disposal and any other information provided by the producer; and
(d) the categories of consumers at serious risk when using the product, in particular children.

Regulation 8 requires producers to supply consumers with the relevant information to enable them to assess risks inherent in a product throughout the normal or reasonably foreseeable period of its use and to take precautions against these risks. The producer must also adopt measures commensurate with the characteristics of the products which he supplies to enable him to be informed of the risks which these products might present and take appropriate action, including if necessary withdrawing the product from the market.

Regulation 9 requires a distributor to act with due care in order to help ensure compliance with the requirements of Regulation 7 and in particular he shall not supply products to any person which he knows or should have presumed on the basis of his information to know are dangerous products and he shall participate in monitoring the safety of products placed on the market and pass on information on the product risks.

Any person who contravenes Regulations 7 or 9 commits a criminal offence. In addition it is a criminal offence for a producer or distributor to offer or agree to place on the market any dangerous product or expose any such product for placing on the market or to offer or agree to supply any dangerous product or expose or possess any such product for supply. This is subject to the due diligence defence – that the person charged took all reasonable steps and exercised all due diligence to avoid committing the offence and if the person alleges that the offence was due to the act or default of another or to reliance on information given by another, he must identify the other person.

MISLEADING DESCRIPTIONS

It is inevitable that almost every sale of goods will involve a description of these goods. For example, a jumper described as 'pure wool' must be made of wool and a tin with a label marked 'baked beans' must contain beans, and not peas. A description can be applied verbally, or it could be on the packaging of the goods, or in an advert. We have previously explained the civil remedies available to a purchaser should the goods he purchases not conform to their description. These remedies were found under the law of contract (error, misrepresentation and breach of contract) and also under the Sale of Goods Act 1979 s 13 (the implied term regarding description). Alternatively, if the consumer is paying for services, rather than for goods, again, inevitably the business performing the service will either verbally or in writing state what they will undertake to do. Should these services turn out to be misdescribed or not performed satisfactorily, then under the law of contract the consumer has a civil remedy (error, misrepresentation or breach of contract). We now turn to examine the criminal law covering misleading descriptions of goods or services.

The Trade Descriptions Act 1968

This Act prohibits:

(a) false trade descriptions as to goods (s 1);
(b) false or misleading statements about services (s 14).

The Trade Descriptions Act (hereafter referred to as the TDA) is designed to protect the public and does not control purely private transactions, nor statements by a private consumer to a dealer, but it does control statements made by one dealer to another in the course of business.

The offence

The Trade Descriptions Act 1968 s 1 provides that any person who in the course of a business:

(a) applies a false trade description to any goods; *or*
(b) supplies, or offers to supply, any goods to which a false trade description is applied;

is guilty of a criminal offence.

Note that under s 1 only traders can be prosecuted. The trader can be a manufacturer or retailer, and in a recent case, an auctioneer was found guilty of an offence. The trader could also be the buyer. In **Fletcher *v* Budgen [1974] 2 All ER 1234** a car dealer told a private seller that there was no possibility of repairing his car and that it was only fit for scrap. The dealer then bought the car for £2, repairing it at a cost of £56, and then he advertised it for sale at £135. It was held that an offence could be committed by a buyer, who applies a false trade description to goods when purchasing them in the course of trade or business.

Definition of trade description (s 2)

First, the section explains that a trade description is an indication, direct or indirect, and by whatever means given, of any of the following matters with respect to any goods:

1 Quantity, size or gauge. For example, 'enough to treat 60 m^2' or a size 12 dress.
2 Composition. For example, 'leather handbag', 'made with butter'.
3 Method of manufacture, production, processing or reconditioning. For example, 'handmade chocolates', 're-sprung chair'.
4 Fitness for purpose, strength, performance, behaviour or accuracy. For example, 'will not break or chip', 'removes oil stains', and the description 'good condition' being applied to a second-hand car. In **Robertson *v* Dicicco [1972] RTR 431, DC** a car was advertised as a 'beautiful car'. It was held that 'beautiful' and other similar adjectives, when applied to a car were likely to be taken as an indication of running quality as well as a description of its appearance and so if, as in this case, that is inaccurate, and the car is unfit for use, then this is a misleading indication regarding the car's performance.
5 Any other physical characteristics. For example, 'Harder than tungsten'.
6 Testing by any person and the results thereof. For example, 'as tested by doctors'.
7 Approval by any person. For example, approval by a consumer body or institution.
8 Date or place of manufacture, production, processing or reconditioning. For example, 'Sheffield Steel' or 'Scotch Whisky'.
9 Other history including previous ownership or use. For example, this could be important to a consumer buying antiques or paintings and would also include a mileometer reading on a car.

From the above list, it can be seen that the scope of the term 'trade description' is very wide. The first five categories deal with the physical characteristics of the goods, while the rest mainly deal with its history. They are all matters of fact, the truth or falsity of which can be established by evidence and it has been held that the label of 'extra value' is not a trade description within the definition of s 2. (As we shall see, claims regarding value are now subject to the Consumer Protection Act 1987 Part 3.)

Under s 2 the indication can be 'indirect'. An example could be a bottle of whisky with a tartan label. This could be taken as an indirect indication that the whisky is Scotch. If it turns out to be Japanese, this could be a false trade description for the purposes of the Act.

The TDA s 3 explains what is the meaning of 'false' as applied to trade descriptions. The Act prohibits those trade descriptions which are obviously deceptive, ie those which are 'false to a material degree', but it also covers that which 'though not false, is misleading to a material degree' and further, 'anything which though not a trade description, is likely to be taken for one, is deemed to be a false trade description if false to a material degree'.

Many offences, committed under the TDA, concern descriptions of cars, as we have already seen in the *Fletcher* and the *Robertson* cases. Particular problems have arisen with the number of miles shown on the mileometer and with the other problem, 'How new is a new car?'

In **Regina** *v* **Ford Motor Co [1974] 3 All ER 489** a consumer bought a 'new Ford Cortina' from a dealer. Unknown to either party, the car supplied under the contract had been damaged before delivery to the dealer. It was repaired by Ford's agents, at a cost of £50. Ford were charged with supplying a car to which a false trade description ('new') had been applied. Held that they had not committed an offence because:

(a) the repairs were not intended to conceal significant defects but to restore the car to a sound condition and so did not amount to a false trade description; *and*
(b) the car was not falsely described as new simply because although slightly damaged (as here), the damage could be repaired and, after the repairs, it would be as good as new.

The court, however, did accept that a point must be reached when the damage is so serious that a car could no longer be capable of being repaired and still qualify for the description 'new'. For example, damage which involves distortion of the vehicle frame or chassis. The court also made it clear that a car was not 'new' if it had been previously sold by a retailer, or if it had been driven for a mileage greatly in excess of the distance from the manufacturer to the retailer.

Mileage readings

Car dealers have to be careful of the TDA s 1 in relation to the odometer of second-hand cars, which might show a different mileage from that which the car has actually done. If an honest dealer has any doubts about the mileage reading, he should either cover it up or display a notice disclaiming the accuracy of the reading, but making sure that the notice is bold and precise. If he fails to do so, and is prosecuted under the Act, he will not be able to rely on the defence of due diligence in s 24 which we will discuss later.

FALSE AND MISLEADING STATEMENTS AS TO SERVICES

The TDA s 14 provides that it shall be an offence for any person in the course of a trade or business:

(a) to make any statement which he knows to be false; *or*
(b) recklessly to make a statement which is false (recklessly does not imply dishonesty) as to any of the following matters:
   (i) The nature or provision of any services, accommodation or facilities provided in the course of any trade or business, or the time or manner of their provision, or their evaluation by any person.
   (ii) The location or amenities of any accommodation provided in the course of any trade or business.

It can be seen that, under this section, an offence could be committed by a contractor/tradesman, or a hotel, or tour operator. It could also cover misdescriptions of professional services, as in one case where an architectural student falsely represented himself as being fully qualified and was employed to draw up plans. This was held to be an offence under s 14.

Often s 14 will apply to false statements made by contractors about the work they have completed. For example, a plumber could assure the householder that his new bathroom was fully plumbed in. If the plumber knows that the work has not been completed properly then an offence has been committed under s 14. The false statements must refer to something that the trader knew as a matter of fact. Section 14 does not apply to such statements which amount to a promise to do something in the future which does not happen. (In this plumber example, if he agrees to carry out the job of replumbing the bathroom, and does not do so then no offence has been committed.) The party making the statement could intend to carry out his promise – this is not covered by s 14. But, the party when he made the statement, might never have intended to carry out the promise – this would be an offence under s 14, although it would be very difficult to prove.

In **Wings Ltd** *v* **Ellis [1985] AC 272**, Wings Ltd, tour operators, produced and distributed to travel agents a brochure which incorrectly stated that a hotel in Sri Lanka had air-conditioning. Later, Wings Ltd discoverd their mistake and advised all their staff, agents and clients who had already booked that holiday. Eight months later, Mr Wade read the brochure and the mistake was not drawn to his attention. Wings Ltd were found guilty of an offence under s 14 because, although when the brochure was originally published Wings were not aware of the mistake, at the time when Mr Wade read the brochure they knew that the information was false. Moreover, an offence was committed by Wings Ltd every time the uncorrected brochure was read and relied upon by clients.

In **British Airways Board** *v* **Taylor [1976] 1 All ER 65** we see that a statement about future conduct did come within s 14. A passenger, who had a return ticket from London to Bermuda, received from BOAC a written confirmation that he had a booking on a particular flight. When he arrived at the airport, he was informed that the flight was full and he was not allowed on board. In court, it was established that BOAC, in common with other airlines, had a practice of booking more travellers on a flight than they had seats for. Thus, their assertion and confirmation that the passenger had a seat on that flight was, when made, false. This practice also gives rise to civil liability under the EC Regulations on Denied Boarding Compensation on Scheduled Flights 1991, which provide minimum rules for compensation in these circumstances.

Note that regarding package holidays, s 14 must be read in conjunction with the

Package travel, Package holidays and Package tours Regulations 1992 which were enacted to implement the EC Package Travel Directive 90/314. These Regulations are very detailed and breach of the duties can give rise to both civil and criminal liability. The main civil obligations are to provide consumers with information that is not misleading and certain basic information specified in Schedule 2 must be included in the contract. It is also a criminal offence not to provide this information.

DEFENCES AVAILABLE UNDER THE ACT TO A PERSON CHARGED WITH A BREACH OF SECTIONS 1 OR 14

Under the TDA s 24 it is a defence for any person charged with an offence under the Act to prove:

(a) that the commission of the offence was due to a mistake, or due to reliance on information supplied to him, or to the act or default of another person, or to an accident, or due to some other cause beyond his control; and
(b) that he took all reasonable precautions and exercised all due diligence to avoid the commission of such an offence by himself or any person under his control.

The onus is on the accused to show that he fulfils (a) and (b) and, moreover, if he alleges that it is the fault of another person, he must, within seven days of the hearing, give written notice to the prosecution, identifying that other person, who will often be an employee of the accused.

In **Ford** *v* **Guild 1990 SLT 502** the accused, a motor trader, was charged with supplying a motor vehicle to which a false trade description had been applied contrary to the TDA s 1. The mileage reading on the vehicle was 32 257 miles, whereas the vehicle had travelled no less than 72 300 miles. It was not disputed that the mileage was supplied by the previous owner, a man called Dalrymple. Dalrymple told the accused that the mileage was correct and gave him the name and address of the person from whom he had purchased the vehicle. The accused did not check this and if he had, he would have discovered that the name was fictitious. The High Court found that the accused could not rely on the defences of s 24. The accused had relied on information given to him by another person but he had not taken all reasonable steps and exercised all due diligence to avoid committing an offence. He did not know Dalrymple, he had no service documents relating to the car and he failed to take further steps to check what Dalrymple had told him.

In **Costello** *v* **Lowe 1990 SLT 760** Costello was the sales manager of a garage. He was charged with supplying a motor vehicle to which a false mileage reading had been applied contrary to the TDA s 1. When Costello bought the vehicle, he noticed that it had been used as a taxi and that it had a surprisingly low mileage reading of 35 000 miles. The truth was that the car had travelled 135 000 miles. There was no documentation supplied with the vehicle to support the reading. Costello knew that the police maintained a record of the mileage of taxis but he did not attempt to obtain this information from them. The court held that the accused could not rely on the defences of s 24. He had relied on information given to him by another person but he had not taken all reasonable precautions nor exercised all due diligence. The fact that the accused did not believe that the police would give such information was not sufficient in the circumstances to preclude the court from deciding that he had not taken all reasonable steps to avoid committing an offence.

The main defence under the Trade Descriptions Act is therefore provided by s 24. Section 25 provides a second defence which relates particularly to the innocent publication of an advertisement. Where, for example, a newspaper published an advertisement which contravenes the Act, the newspaper may avoid conviction by putting forward the defence that in taking the advert, they did not know or suspect that its publication would constitute an offence.

As an alternative to the two defences provided by the Act, an individual may avoid prosecution by showing that the offence was the fault of another person. In terms of s 23 of the 1968 Act, if X commits an offence but can show that this was due to the actions of Y, it may be that both X and Y are prosecuted. However, it is possible that X may escape prosecution while Y alone is prosecuted.

MISLEADING PRICE INDICATIONS

In the past, the control of misleading price indications was regulated by the TDA s 11 and the Price Marking (Bargain Offers) Order 1979. This early legislation prohibited certain specific practices and has now been repealed. The TDA only applied to the price of goods. The Consumer Protection Act 1987 s 20 applies to the price of goods, services, accommodation or facilities. Thus hotels, restaurants, retailers and any professional person or tradesman must take note of the new provisions. The law is now found in The Consumer Protection Act 1987 Part 3, ss 20–26, which came into force in March 1989. The law is complemented and extended by a Code of Practice.

The CPA s 20 states that it is an offence for any one in the course of a business to give a misleading statement to any consumer as to the price at which any goods, services, accommodation or facilities are available.

The terms 'services' and 'facilities' are to include:

(a) the provision of credit, banking or insurance services;
(b) the purchase and sale of foreign currency;
(c) the supply of electricity;
(d) the provision of off-road parking facilities;
(e) the provision of facilities for parking caravans;
(f) the provision of services.

The list given is only a sample and could include the provision of other services. The Act specifically excludes those services provided by an employee under a contract of service and those services provided by authorised persons as defined by the Financial Services Act 1986.

An offence is committed in three possible situations:

1 The price indication was misleading when it was originally given.
2 The price indication may have become misleading as a result of subsequent events.
3 Where no fixed price is involved, the method of determining the price may be stated in a misleading way.

In all three cases, the test of whether a price indication is misleading is based upon what the consumers to whom it was addressed might reasonably infer from the indication:

Example 1: A simple statement that a business or professional charges £x for goods or services is an offence, if untrue. This means that even if this was a simple mistake an offence is committed.

Example 2: A retailer advertises a price in a monthly magazine, but the manufacturer changes the recommended price during the month and consequently the retailer raises his price. This is an offence because the consumer's expectation is that the price will last the period of the publication.

Examples of presently misleading price indications

1 A false indication that the price is less than it actually is. For example, quoting a reduced price which only applies to a limited range of goods, or only applies to cash sales.
2 The price depends on a set of circumstances and this is not made clear. For example, it only applies to cash customers or it does not apply to part-exchange deals.
3 Cases where the indication suggests that the price includes matters for which an additional charge is in fact being made. For example, 'free' when in fact a charge is being made for postage or administration costs.
4 An indication which falsely suggests that the person giving the indication expects the price to be maintained, increased or decreased. For example, 'the permanent sale' or 'buy now – prices shortly to increase'.
5 Comparing the price of something with that of another model without stating that the price for the other model has since been reduced.
6 Comparing the price of goods or services with a claimed value. For example comparisons with a bogus RRP or MRP (Recommended Retail Price or Manufacturer's Recommended Price).

The Code of Practice on Pricing

The Code gives practical guidance on what could be regarded as a misleading price indication. Failure to comply with the Code does not by itself give rise to any criminal or civil liability, but it could be used as evidence either by the Procurator Fiscal to establish that the accused committed the offence or it could be used by the accused to establish that he did not commit an offence.

The defences

A number of defences are available to a charge of either giving a misleading price indication or to the charge of giving a price indication which has become misleading. The first defence is a general defence, the rest are more specific. In all cases the Code of Practice may be taken into account:

1 The accused has a defence if he can show that he took all reasonable steps and exercised all due diligence to avoid committing the offence.
2 The trader had to comply with a statutory regulation.
3 Where the misleading price indication is in a book, magazine, film or broadcast it is a defence to show that the material was published editorially rather than as advertising material.
4 A person whose business is publishing or arranging the publication of advertisements and who publishes a misleading price based on information that he was given, has a defence, provided that he can show that he received the advertisement in the ordinary course of business and had no reason to believe that the publication of the advertisement would be unlawful.
5 There is a specific defence for a supplier (whether a producer or wholesaler) who recommends a reselling price to his customers and who advertises this price to consumers in the belief that it was being adopted by his customers.

The Property Misdescriptions Act 1991

This Act makes it a criminal offence for any person in the course of an estate agency business or a property development business (excluding conveyancing services) to make false or misleading statements about heritable property. The statement can be made verbally or by pictures or any other method of signifying meaning.

The misdescription must be a statement; it must be about a prescribed matter; it must be made in the course of estate agency or land development business and it must be false and misleading. The 'prescribed matters' are listed in the Property Misdescriptions (Specified Matters) Regulations 1992 and include almost any detail of a property such as location, aspect, facilities, fixtures, etc.

The liability is strict and disclaimer notices cannot be issued along with property details in an attempt to limit liability. One defence is available to the accused – that he/she took all reasonable steps and exercised all due diligence to avoid committing the offence. However, if the making of the statement is due to the act or fault of an employee, the employee shall be guilty of an offence and the employee may be prosecuted and punished whether or not criminal proceedings are also taken against the employer.

QUESTIONS

1 With reference to the Trade Descriptions Act 1968, explain fully what is 'a false trade description'.

2 Fred owns a 1975 Morris Minor, which has been giving him a 'lot of trouble'. He takes it to Harry, a second-hand car trader, who assures him that the car is 'only fit for scrap' and offers him £100. Fred, reluctantly, accepts this sum for his car. One month later, Fred spots his car, in Harry's showroom window, reconditioned, polished, and priced at £600. Advise Fred.

3 Catherine is attracted by a very pretty embroidered blouse, described as 'hand-sewn', which she sees displayed in a shop window. The assistant tells her that every blouse is unique and the shop purchases these blouses directly from a tiny island in the West Indies. Catherine buys one, only to learn later, that they are mass produced in Bradford. Advise Catherine on the relevant criminal and civil law.

4 Susan purchased a four-year-old Ford Escort from Donald, a motor trader. The mileage reading on the car was 25 040 miles. Susan asked Donald if he knew the previous owner. Donald assured her that the car had only one previous owner, an elderly lady. The registration documents did verify that the vehicle had only had one lady owner. Subsequently, Susan discovered that the true mileage reading was about 90 000 miles and that the car had been sold to Donald by a lady taxi driver. Advise Donald as to whether he has committed an offence and if he is charged are there any defences open to him?

5 Mr and Mrs Smith booked a holiday in Spain with Sea and Sand Tours. The agents assured the Smiths that all the rooms in their hotel had sea views and that the hotel had a wonderful sports complex and olympic-sized swimming pool. In fact, when the Smiths went on holiday to Spain, they found that they had no sea view from their room and the complex and pool were in the process of being built. When the Smiths returned and complained, the tour operators said that they were not at fault as they had relied on the information, which they received from the hotel. Have the tour operators committed a criminal offence?

6 Brentwood Stores have advertised that they are having a closing down sale. Displayed in their shop window is a notice 'Fantastic reductions on all stock'. In fact many of their goods have not been reduced at all. Has the store committed an offence?

CONSUMER CREDIT

Nowadays many people are unable to, or choose not to, pay cash for all their purchases. Most people buy large items, such as cars, on credit. The use of credit cards has become increasingly common. At some time or another a person may require a loan or an overdraft facility from their bank. Prior to the enactment of the Consumer Credit Act 1974, there were a number of different Acts of Parliament each dealing with different forms of credit. The aim of the Consumer Credit Act was to establish, for the protection of consumers, a new system which applied uniform controls to all types of credit. In so doing it repealed previous legislation regulating credit including the Moneylenders Act 1900 and the Hire Purchase (Scotland) Act 1965.

The 1974 Act requires the Director General of Fair Trading to license those who provide credit. Anyone who seeks to be licensed to carry on a consumer credit business must satisfy the Director that he is a fit person to engage in such activities. In particular, he must not have committed any offence involving fraud, dishonesty or violence and he must not have engaged in unfair business practices. It is a criminal offence to engage in consumer credit business without a licence.

The Act also seeks to control the ways in which those offering credit seek business. There is statutory regulation of the form and content of advertisements which indicate a willingness to provide credit. If such an advertisement is false or misleading, the advertiser commits a criminal offence. The Act also controls the extent of canvassing off trade premises. For example, it is a criminal offence to turn up at a private house uninvited in order to try to persuade the householder to take out a loan with a finance company. It is also a criminal offence to send a document to a person under 18 inviting him to borrow money, or to obtain goods or services on credit, or even to apply for more information about obtaining credit. It is also an offence to send someone a credit card if he has not asked for it. There is also statutory regulation of the form and content of quotations given to prospective customers.

REGULATED AGREEMENTS UNDER THE CONSUMER CREDIT ACT 1974

A personal credit agreement is an agreement by which one person known as 'the creditor' provides another person, 'the debtor', with credit of any amount. Protected debtors under the 1974 Act include individuals and partnerships but not corporate bodies such as registered companies.

A **consumer credit agreement** is a personal credit agreement where the creditor supplies the debtor with credit not exceeding £15 000. 'Credit' includes a cash loan and any other form of financial accommodation. Accordingly, the Act would apply to hire purchase agreements, bank loans and overdrafts, the issue of credit cards and budget accounts with shops – so long as the amount of credit provided does not exceed £15 000. This figure of £15 000 does not take into account any interest payable, so the Act would apply to a person borrowing £13 000 and repaying £16 000. Similarly the Act would apply where a person buying a car at a price of £18 000 paid a deposit of £5000 and borrowed £13 000 to finance the balance.

The provisions of the Consumer Credit Act 1974 protect debtors who enter into agreements which are **regulated** by the Act. There are various types of consumer credit agreements which are covered by the 1974 Act. Collectively these are known as **regulated agreements** and they include the agreements listed below.

Running account credit and fixed-sum credit

Running account credit is a facility which allows the debtor to receive credit on demand up to an agreed credit limit. Running account credit will include bank overdraft agreements, the use of certain credit cards and budget accounts with shops.

Fixed-sum credit is a facility whereby the debtor receives credit of a fixed amount either in a single sum or in instalments. Examples of fixed-sum credit include hire purchase agreements, credit sale agreements, conditional sale agreements and bank loans.

A hire purchase agreement is a contract where one person hires goods from another person in exchange for periodic payments with the option to buy the goods at the end of the hire period. If the option to purchase is exercised, the price is taken to be the hire payments which have been made. Ownership of the goods does not pass until the last payment has been made.

A conditional sale agreement is an agreement for the sale of goods under which the purchase price, or part of it, is payable by instalments. The ownership of the goods remains with the seller until all payments have been made.

A credit sale agreement is an agreement for the sale of goods under which the purchase price is payable in five or more instalments but which is not a conditional sale agreement. Ownership of the goods passes to the buyer at once.

Restricted-use credit and unrestricted-use credit

A restricted-use credit agreement involves credit being given only for a specified purpose. The credit may be given to finance a transaction between the creditor and the debtor, such as where an electrical goods shop offers credit terms to customers to enable them to buy one of their cookers. Alternatively, the credit may be given to enable the debtor to buy the goods of a third party, such as where the debtor obtains a bank loan for the sole purpose of buying a car and the bank insists on paying the money direct to the supplier. Another example of restricted use credit would be where a debtor owes money to a variety of creditors and decides to refinance his borrowing. He may do this by entering into a fresh consumer credit agreement with a person known as a debt-adjuster. The debtor takes out a fresh loan with the debt-adjuster and the debt-adjuster pays off all the debtor's existing creditors. This is a form of restricted-use credit.

An unrestricted-use credit agreement is one which leaves the debtor free to use the credit in any way and for whatever purpose he chooses. Where the debtor takes out a loan from a finance company with no indication of the purpose of the loan, this is an example of unrestricted-use credit.

Credit cards – restricted-use or unrestricted-use credit?

The use of credit cards involves three parties: the debtor, the creditor (the credit card company) and the supplier of goods or services paid for with the credit card. Once the debtor uses his credit card, the supplier is paid by the creditor and the creditor sends a periodic statement to the debtor. The debtor may then choose to pay off his indebtedness in monthly instalments. Certain cards may be used by the debtor to obtain cash from banks. When the card is used in this way it is regarded as unrestricted-use credit because the cash can then be spent anywhere. The debtor may spend the cash in places where the card may not be used. However, where the debtor uses the card to obtain goods or services from suppliers who have an arrangement with the credit card company, that is regarded as restricted-use credit. Accordingly, depending upon how it is used, the use of a credit card may fall within two categories of consumer credit agreement. Where an agreement falls into more than one category it is known as a multiple agreement. An agreement between a debtor and a creditor who supplies the debtor with some form of credit card, or token or voucher, is known as a credit token agreement.

Debtor-creditor-supplier agreements and debtor-creditor agreements

All regulated agreements, whether for fixed sum or running account credit, and whether for restricted-use or unrestricted-use credit, fall into one of two main categories of credit transaction. A consumer credit agreement will be either a debtor-creditor–supplier agreement or a debtor–creditor agreement.

A debtor–creditor–supplier agreement occurs where the creditor is also the supplier of the goods, such as where the electrical goods shop offers credit terms to customers who buy a cooker from them. Another example of a debtor–creditor–supplier agreement is where there is a pre-existing arrangement between the supplier and the creditor that the creditor will give credit to the supplier's customers. For example, Sparky Electrical Shop in the High Street may have an arrangement with Acme Trust Finance plc whereby Acme agrees to give credit to Sparky's customers. Should a customer wish to buy goods from Sparky on credit, one of Sparky's assistants will be able to produce an Acme application form for credit. The Acme form is filled in by the customer on Sparky's premises and sent off by Sparky to Acme.

A debtor–creditor agreement is one where credit is given to finance a transaction between the debtor and a supplier and there is no pre-existing arrangement between the creditor and the supplier. For example, John decides to buy a new TV set. He obtains a loan of £400 from his bank or from a finance company. He can then use this money to buy a TV from whichever supplier he pleases. The supplier need not even know that John has borrowed to finance the purchase.

Whether or not a transaction is a debtor–creditor–supplier agreement may be of great significance to the debtor. Section 75 of the Consumer Credit Act 1974 provides that, where there is a debtor–creditor–supplier agreement, if the debtor has any claim against the supplier in respect of a misrepresentation or breach of contract, he shall have a like claim against the creditor. The creditor and the supplier shall be liable jointly and severally. This means that the debtor can pursue the creditor for the full amount of any claim. The creditor must then look to the supplier for repayment. The section applies only to claims where the goods or services supplied cost more than £100 and less than £30 000.

For example, John books a holiday to Spain with Sunflight Holidays and pays the £500 cost of the holiday using his credit card. Sunflight Holidays become insolvent and John's holiday is cancelled. Because of the pre-existing arrangement between Sunflight and the credit card company, John's payment for the holiday by credit card is an example of a debtor–creditor–supplier agreement. Sunflight's failure to supply John with his holiday is a breach of contract. John is entitled under s 75 of the Consumer Credit Act 1974 to seek repayment of the cost of the holiday from the credit card company. Section 75 would also apply to situations where the supplier supplied faulty goods to the debtor.

Consumer hire agreements

All of the above are examples of consumer credit agreements. The Consumer Credit

Act 1974 also applies to consumer hire agreements.

A consumer hire agreement is an agreement made by the owner of goods for the hiring of those goods to an individual known as 'the hirer'. In order to be a consumer hire agreement, the agreement:

1 must not be a hire purchase agreement;
2 must be capable of lasting for more than three months;
3 must not require the hirer to pay more than £15 000.

An example of a consumer hire agreement would be an agreement by a sole trader who is a builder to hire a cement mixer for a period of six months at a cost of £200 per month. Note that the hiring of goods to a registered company cannot be a consumer hire agreement.

Exempt agreements

Certain consumer credit agreements are not regulated by the provisions of the Consumer Credit Act 1974. The only provisions of the 1974 Act which do apply to exempt as well as to regulated agreements are provisions dealing with extortionate credit bargains. An extortionate credit bargain is one which requires the debtor to make payments which are grossly exorbitant or which otherwise grossly contravenes ordinary principles of fair trading. The Sheriff Court has the power to re-open an extortionate credit bargain and make an order for the purpose of relieving the debtor from payment of any sum in excess of that which is fairly due and reasonable.

Those agreements which are exempt include:

1 agreements where land is offered as security and the creditor is a local authority or a body, such as a building society, friendly society, trade union or charity, specified in an order made by the Secretary of State;
2 agreements where the number of payments required to be made does not exceed four;
3 credit card agreements where the debtor is required to clear off in one payment the whole amount shown in each statement;
4 agreements where the rate of interest payable does not exceed a specified rate;
5 certain agreements which have a connection with a country outside the United Kingdom.

Small agreements

These are consumer credit agreements, except hire purchase and conditional sale agreements, where the amount of credit provided does not exceed £50. Small agreements are exempt from certain of the provisions of the Consumer Credit Act 1974.

Non-commercial agreements

Such agreements, where the creditor does not provide credit in the course of a business, are exempt from certain of the provisions of the Consumer Credit Act 1974. For example, should a mother lend some money to her daughter, the loan would be a non-commercial agreement.

ENTERING INTO A REGULATED AGREEMENT AND RIGHTS OF CANCELLATION

Formation of the contract – withdrawal of an application for credit

A consumer credit agreement is a type of contract and is therefore formed when there is acceptance of an offer. Until there is acceptance, no binding contract exists. Accordingly, the offer may be withdrawn at any time before acceptance. Where the debtor has filled in an application for credit, the application constitutes the offer. That offer may be revoked at any time until the creditor's acceptance is effective. Under the common law of contract, where the contract is being formed by post, the prospective debtor's revocation must reach the creditor before the creditor's acceptance is posted. Section 57 of the Consumer Credit Act 1974 provides that notice of intention by the debtor to withdraw from a prospective credit agreement may be given, in writing or verbally, to the supplier as well as to the creditor. Notice to the supplier is as effective as notice to the creditor. Where the prospective debtor effectively gives notice that he is not going ahead with the credit agreement, any linked transaction with a supplier of goods and services is cancelled. A contract with a supplier is a linked transaction if the credit agreement is a debtor–creditor–supplier agreement and the credit is being taken out to finance the transaction with the supplier.

For example, Angus sees a car in Honest Eddie's car showroom. Angus agrees to buy the car but he requires credit. Honest Eddie can arrange finance for Angus through Acme Trust Finance plc. Angus fills in an Acme application form in the car showroom. Honest Eddie states that he will send the form to Acme and Angus can expect Acme's acceptance within three or four days. In the meantime, in exchange for a deposit of £200, Honest Eddie allows Angus to take the car away. That night, Angus decides that he has been too hasty and that he cannot really afford the car. The next morning, prior to his finance application being accepted by Acme, Angus returns the car to the showroom and tells Honest Eddie that he is not going ahead with the credit agreement or the car purchase. In terms of s 57 of the 1974 Act, this verbal intimation to Eddie has the effect of revoking his offer to enter into a credit agreement with Acme. Because Angus has effectively prevented the credit agreement being formed, his contract with Eddie to buy the car is cancelled. Angus must return the car but is entitled to his deposit back. If Eddie is unwilling to return the deposit, Angus can keep the car until he gets the £200 back.

Form and content of a regulated agreement

Section 60 of the Consumer Credit Act 1974 provides for regulations to be made which govern the form and content of regulated agreements. The appropriate regulations are the Consumer Credit (Agreements) Regulations 1983 and their purpose is to ensure that the debtor is made aware of his rights and duties under the agreement and of the cost of the credit. The regulations provide that there must be a heading on the first page of the document which declares which type of regulated agreement it is; for example, Hire Purchase Agreement Regulated by the Consumer Credit Act 1974. In addition, the document must contain the following information:

1 The names and addresses of the parties.
2 The cash prices where it is a restricted-use, debtor–creditor–supplier agreement.
3 The amount of any deposit.
4 The amount and timing of each payment.
5 The amount of the total charge for credit.
6 The APR, which is the annual percentage rate of the total charge for credit.
7 The total amount payable.
8 Details of any security to be provided by the debtor.
9 Details of any charges payable by the debtor if in default.

The regulations require that the agreement must also provide information about the protection and remedies available to the debtor under the 1974 Act. Such information might include details of the debtor's right to cancel certain types of agreement or his right to settle the debt earlier than agreed.

The 'credit', the 'total charge for credit' and the 'total amount payable'

The meaning of these terms is best explained by reference to an example. John enters into a consumer credit agreement whereby he buys a car priced at £12 000. He pays a deposit of £2000 and borrows £10 000 from a finance company. The interest payable on the loan is £3000. Accordingly, the 'credit' is £10 000. The 'total charge for credit', ie what the credit costs the debtor, is £3000. The 'total amount payable' is £13 000, ie the amount of the credit plus the amount of the total charge for credit.

Signing the agreement

Section 61 sets out the statutory requirements on how a regulated agreement must be executed (signed). The agreement which is presented to the debtor for signature must be readily legible and must include all the terms of the agreement other than implied terms. The agreement must contain all the information required by the Consumer Credit (Agreements) Regulations 1983. The agreement must be completely ready for signature; the debtor should not be asked to sign an agreement where blanks still have to be filled in.

The agreement must be signed by the debtor and also by or on behalf of the creditor. The document must contain a 'signature box' in which the debtor must sign. No-one else must sign in this box. A regulated agreement which does not comply with the requirements of s 61 is said to be improperly executed. An improperly executed regulated agreement cannot be enforced against a debtor without a court order.

The debtor's right to copies of the agreement

A regulated agreement becomes executed only once it has been signed by both parties. Until both parties have signed, it is said to be unexecuted. Sections 62 and 63 of the Act provide that the debtor must receive at least one and sometimes two copies of the agreement. Whether the debtor has the right to one or two copies depends upon whether the agreement is fully executed or not when he signs it. If, when the debtor signs the agreement, it has already been signed by the creditor, or if both parties sign the agreement at the same time, the agreement is fully executed and the debtor is given a copy of the agreement at once. In this situation the debtor only has the right to this one copy. If, when the agreement is presented or posted to the debtor for signature, it has still to be signed by the creditor, the debtor is given a copy of the unexecuted agreement. Within seven days of the creditor adding his signature, a second copy of the agreement must be given to the debtor. If the agreement is of a type which the debtor has the right to cancel, the second copy must be sent by post.

In the case of credit token agreements, the second copy of the agreement may be sent along with the credit card, etc. As well as receiving a copy of the agreement, the debtor must receive copies of all documents referred to in the agreement. Where the agreement is one which the debtor has the right to cancel, every copy of the agreement must include notice of the debtor's cancellation rights. Should the creditor fail to supply the debtor with copies of the agreement as required by the Act, the agreement cannot be enforced against the debtor without a court order.

The debtor's right to cancel certain agreements within a cooling-off period

As was stated above, an application for credit may be withdrawn at any time before it is accepted by the creditor. An effective withdrawal prevents the formation of a binding consumer credit agreement. However, in addition, s 67 of the Act enables the debtor to cancel certain types of regulated agreement even after a contract has been formed. Certain types of consumer credit agreement are subject to a cooling-off period which enables the debtor to have second thoughts about going ahead despite the application having been accepted by the creditor. Only certain regulated agreements are cancellable. In order that a debtor has the right to cancel a concluded agreement, certain key requirements must be satisfied:

1. During negotiations prior to the contract being formed, **verbal representations** must have been made, **in the presence of the debtor**, by either the creditor, or – if it is a debtor–creditor–supplier agreement – by the supplier; and
2. The agreement must have been signed by the debtor **off trade premises**. The debtor has no right to cancel a regulated agreement if he signs the agreement at the premises of either the creditor or the supplier. The debtor has the right to cancel if he signs the agreement in his own home or at his own place of work.

These provisions were originally enacted to protect consumers from high-pressure doorstep salesmen who turned up uninvited and talked a householder into buying something on credit. Cancellable agreements therefore involve the elements of verbal hard sell, face to face with the consumer, plus the signing of the agreement away from the premises of the creditor or supplier. It should be noted that an agreement is cancellable even where the verbal hard sell takes place at the premises of the creditor or supplier, so long as the agreement is signed elsewhere. Accordingly, a consumer who is talked into buying a car on credit at the car showroom, may still cancel the credit agreement so long as he signed the agreement at home or at his own workplace.

Exercising the right to cancel

If a regulated agreement is cancellable, every copy of the agreement which is given to the debtor must include a notice telling the debtor of his right to cancel and indicating how and when this may be done. The notice must include the name and address of a person to whom notice of cancellation may be given. Where the debtor is to receive two copies of the agreement, the second copy contains the notice of the debtor's right to cancel. Where the debtor receives only one copy of the agreement, a separate notice of the debtor's right to cancel must be sent to him within seven days of the agreement being made.

The debtor must exercise his right to cancel by serving a notice of cancellation within the cooling-off period of five days. The cooling-off period of five days starts to run from when the debtor receives either the notice of his right to cancel or his second copy of the agreement. Day one of the five-day cooling-off period is the day after receipt of either the notice or the second copy of the agreement. The notice of cancellation must be in writing and may be delivered in person or sent by post. Where the debtor sends the notice of cancellation by post, the notice effectively cancels the agreement so long as it is posted within the five-day period. If posted within the cooling-off period, the notice is effective even if it reaches the creditor after the five days are up. The notice is effective in such circumstances even if it fails to arrive at all. However, it is wise to send the notice of cancellation by recorded delivery post so that there is a record of it having been posted.

The effect of the notice of cancellation is to cancel the consumer credit agreement with the creditor and any linked transaction, for example with the supplier in a debtor–creditor–supplier agreement.

Consequences of cancellation

Section 71 provides that any sums already paid by the debtor, such as a deposit, must be returned to him.

Section 72 provides that if goods have already been supplied to the debtor, these must be returned. The debtor is under no duty to deliver the goods to the creditor or supplier. His duty is to take reasonable care of the goods and hand them over when asked for them. However if, 21 days after cancellation, the goods have still not been picked up, the debtor is freed from his duty to take reasonable care of them. Special categories of goods such as perishable goods, or goods which have already been consumed, or spare parts which have been fitted so that their return is not practicable, need not be returned by the debtor. In respect of such goods the supplier loses out. In addition, the debtor has the right to retain goods until he receives the return of any deposit or of goods which he gave in part-exchange.

Section 73 provides that where the debtor traded-in goods in part-exchange, he must receive, within ten days of the date of cancellation, either the return of his goods or a sum equal to the part-exchange allowance. It is up to the supplier whether he returns the goods or their part-exchange value.

The effect of cancellation on a linked transaction

A consumer credit agreement may be linked to another transaction. One type of linked transaction is defined as a transaction entered into by the debtor as a condition of the credit agreement. In addition, where a consumer credit agreement is a debtor–creditor–supplier agreement and the purpose of the credit agreement is to finance a transaction between the debtor and the supplier, the transaction between the debtor and the supplier is a linked transaction. A transaction is also a linked transaction where the debtor entered into it so as to induce the creditor to enter the principal credit agreement.

Where the debtor effectively cancels a regulated agreement, any linked transaction is also cancelled. If at the time of cancellation of the credit agreement, the linked transaction is not yet concluded, the effect of the cancellation of the credit agreement is to prevent the formation of the linked transaction.

The practical effects of cancellation of a credit agreement are best illustrated by use of an example.

Mr and Mrs Smith have decided that they would like to have a conservatory added to the rear of their house. They contact a number of companies who sell conservatories. The sales representative of Sunny Porches Ltd agrees to call at their home. Mr Gordon of Sunny Porches Ltd arrives at the Smiths' home one Sunday and persuades them of the advantages of buying his company's product. Mr Gordon also advises the Smiths that his company has negotiated a special preferential credit package with Acme Trust Finance plc. The Smiths agree to order a Sunny Porches Ltd conservatory at a price of £10 000. Seven thousand pounds of the price is to be financed by the Acme credit package. Mr Gordon fills in an Acme application form which the Smiths sign. The Smiths also complete an order form for the conservatory to be supplied by Sunny Porches Ltd. The Smiths pay a £250 deposit by cheque payable to Sunny Porches Ltd.

In the days which follow certain events occur which make the Smiths unhappy. They are advised that their site is unsuitable for certain of the features which Mr Gordon had said were possible. In addition, the completion date suggested by Mr Gordon turns out to be unrealistic. Sunny Porches Ltd have still to formally accept their order when the Smiths receive a formal acceptance of their credit application from Acme Trust Finance plc. The Smiths are alarmed. They now have grave doubts about proceeding with the conservatory but they appear to be contractually bound to the credit transaction with Acme. What is their legal position?

The Smiths need not worry. Their agreement with Acme is a debtor–creditor–supplier agreement. This is because there is a pre-existing arrangement between Sunny Porches Ltd and Acme. In addition, their agreement with Acme is cancellable. This is because of the verbal representations made by Mr Gordon, the salesman, prior to the agreement being made and also because the Smiths signed the agreement in their own home. The copy of the completed agreement which the Smiths have received from Acme will include notice of their right to cancel the agreement. The Smiths must send a written notice of cancellation to Acme within five days of receiving the completed agreement. If they do so their agreement with Acme is cancelled. In addition, the effect of cancelling the credit agreement with Acme is that their conservatory order is also automatically withdrawn. The purchase of the conservatory is a linked transaction because the credit agreement with Acme was entered into as a debtor–creditor–supplier agreement to finance the conservatory purchase. The Smiths are entitled to the return of their £250 deposit. It should be noted that the result would have been the same even if their order had already been accepted by Sunny Porches Ltd.

PROVISIONS ON DEFAULT AND TERMINATION

Default notices

If the debtor is in breach of a regulated agreement, s 87 provides that a default notice must be served on the debtor before the creditor can take certain types of enforcement action. A default notice must be served before the creditor can become entitled to:

1 terminate the agreement;
2 demand earlier payment of any sum;
3 recover possession of any goods or land;
4 treat any right conferred on the debtor by the agreement as terminated, restricted or deferred;
5 enforce any security.

It should be noted that none of the above steps can ever be taken unless the terms of the agreement entitle the creditor to take such action. Section 87 does not operate so as to authorise such action. What s 87 means is that even if the agreement allows for such enforcement action, it cannot be taken without first of all serving a default notice. The creditor does remain entitled to take immediate steps to prevent the debtor drawing on further credit. For example, the debtor may be prevented from making further use of a credit card.

Section 88 provides that the default notice must specify the nature of the alleged breach of the agreement. In addition, if the breach is capable of being remedied, the notice must state what action is required to remedy it. If the breach cannot be remedied, the notice must state the amount of any sum required to be paid as compensation for the breach. The notice must also state the date by which action must be taken or compensation paid. The debtor must be given not less than seven days to take the required action or pay the compensation. The notice must also spell out the consequences of non-compliance with the default notice.

Section 89 provides that if before the specified date, the debtor takes the necessary steps as required by the notice, the breach must be treated as never having happened.

Should the debtor fail to remedy the breach, the creditor may pursue such remedies as are provided for in the regulated agreement.

Protected goods under a hire purchase or a conditional sale agreement

It will be recalled that where a regulated agreement is a hire-purchase or a conditional sale agreement, the ownership of the goods remains with the creditor until the debtor makes the last payment. The terms of the agreement may entitle the creditor to seize possession of the goods should the debtor be in breach of the agreement. It must be noted that the creditor never has the right to enter the debtor's premises in order to seize possession of goods unless the debtor gives consent at the time. Any term of the agreement which purports to give the debtor's consent in advance to the creditor's entering premises has no effect.

However, the provisions of s 90 of the Act operate so as to restrict the right of the creditor to recover possession of goods under a hire-purchase agreement or a conditional sale agreement. In terms of s 90, if the goods have become 'protected goods', the creditor is not entitled to recover possession of the goods without a court order.

Goods are said to be protected goods when:

1 the debtor is in breach of the agreement;
2 one-third of the total price of the goods has been paid by the debtor;
3 the creditor remains the legal owner of the goods.

Should the creditor seize protected goods without a court order, the regulated agreement will be terminated as a result. In addition, the debtor will be freed from all liability under the agreement and shall be entitled to the return of all payments made under the agreement.

It should be noted that the creditor does not require a court order for the return of protected goods if the agreement is terminated by the debtor, or if the debtor gives informed consent to the repossession, or if the goods are in the possession of a third party.

Even if the creditor does go to court to seek an order for the return of protected goods, it is not necessarily the case that the court will grant such a 'return order'. In terms of s 129 of the Act, the Sheriff Court may make a 'time order' which may reschedule the debtor's payments so as to take into account the debtor's ability to pay. It must be pointed out, however, that the Scottish courts do not utilise their power to make time orders.

In addition, in respect of hire-purchase and conditional sale agreements, s 133 empowers the Sheriff to make a 'transfer order'. The effect of the order is to transfer the creditor's title to certain goods to the debtor. This option is open to the Sheriff only where the amount already paid is greater than the sum of the unpaid balance plus one-third of the unpaid balance. For example:

amount already paid = £90;
unpaid balance = £60;
one-third of the unpaid balance = £20;
£60 + £20 = £80;

£90 is greater than £80, therefore the Sheriff has the option of making a transfer order.

Termination of a regulated agreement where the debtor can afford to make early payment

Section 94 provides that a debtor under any type of regulated consumer credit agreement has the right to make complete payment ahead of time. This may occur if the debtor comes into some money and decides to pay off some of his borrowing. He can do this at any time on giving written notice to the creditor. Where the regulated agreement is a hire-purchase or conditional sale agreement, the debtor becomes the owner of the goods when early settlement is made. Section 95 provides that a debtor who makes early settlement under s 94 is entitled to a rebate. The amount required to pay off the debt is to be reduced by the rebate. The amount of the rebate shall be either an amount specified in the agreement or an amount calculated according to the Consumer Credit (Rebate on Early Settlement) Regulations 1983. The debtor gets the benefit of whichever amount is the greater.

Termination of a hire-purchase or a conditional sale agreement where the debtor cannot afford to keep on paying

It will be recalled that under a hire-purchase or a conditional sale agreement, the creditor remains the owner of the goods until the last payment is made. A debtor under a regulated hire-purchase or conditional sale agreement may suffer financial difficulties and be unable to keep up the payments due under the agreement. He may therefore consider exercising his right under s 99 of the Act to terminate such an agreement before the last payment is made. This means that the debtor will be required to return the goods. In addition to returning the goods, the debtor may have to pay a certain amount of money to the creditor. The amount payable by a debtor who terminates an agreement under s 99, is calculated by reference to s 100 of the Act. The debtor must pay off any arrears due as at the date of termination. In addition, where the debtor has not already paid one-half of the total price payable under the agreement, he must pay a sum equal to the difference between what he has paid and one-half of the total price. He may be ordered by the court to pay more where he has not taken reasonable care of the goods.

QUESTIONS

1 Define and distinguish between fixed-sum credit and running-account credit giving examples of each type.

2 Define and distinguish between restricted-use and unrestricted-use credit giving examples of each type.

3 Describe a hire-purchase agreement, a conditional sale agreement and a credit sale agreement. At what point does the debtor become the owner under each of these agreements?

4 What is the difference between a debtor–creditor–supplier agreement and a debtor–creditor agreement?

5 John buys a washing machine on credit. He signs the application form for credit and it is signed at the same time by the shop manager who is authorised to sign on behalf of the creditor. How many copies of the agreement is John entitled to and when is he entitled to them?

Would your answer differ if the form had to be sent away to be signed by the creditor?

6 Sandy buys a cooker from a high street electrical store. The shop has an arrangement with Acme Trust Finance plc whereby Acme provides the store's customers with credit if required. Sandy fills in an Acme application form in the shop and it is sent off to Acme by the store manager. The cooker, when it arrives, is faulty and does not work at all. The store sends a van to collect the cooker and the manager promises to provide a replacement. A week later Sandy, who still has not received a replacement cooker, hears that the store has become insolvent. Advise Sandy.

7 Mary is persuaded by Sharp, a door-to-door salesman, to buy a colour television set. She signs an agreement at her home under which she agrees to pay a £100 deposit, which she gives to Sharp, and the balance of the price by ten monthly instalments of £40. She has now changed her mind and wonders if she can get out of the agreement. Advise Mary.

8 Sam is buying a car on hire purchase. He has recently been made redundant and has failed to make the last three hire purchase payments. He has received a default notice from the creditor stating that they intend to recover possession of the car. Sam seeks your advice. He has already paid £900 and there is only £600 left to pay. He does not want to lose the car but he cannot afford the present level of payments. He also wants to know whether the creditor is entitled just to come and take the car away. Advise Sam.

9 Describe the right of the debtor to discharge his debt earlier than agreed.

Part 5
THE LAW OF AGENCY

10 Agency

THE AGENCY RELATIONSHIP

It is hard to envisage any kind of business organisation that could function without either employees or agents. The distinction is that an employee performs certain services for his employer in return for a wage or salary, while an agent, representing his principal, again usually in return for payment, enters into transactions with third parties. If the agent is acting with the authority of his principal, this will result in the principal being in a legally binding contract with a third party. When the task has been properly completed, the agent incurs no obligations or rights under that contract with the third party. An agent can be an employee of his principal or he can be performing services for him in the capacity of an independent contractor, or the agent could even be a partnership or company representing another organisation.

For example, if you go into a large store like Marks & Spencer to purchase a shirt, you will negotiate the contract of sale with a shop assistant. This assistant is both an employee and an agent of Marks & Spencer. She is an agent because she is authorised by her employer to sell goods to the general public. She will have no authority to reduce the price of anything that she is selling. Provided she acts within the authority given by her employer/principal, your contract will be with the principal, Marks & Spencer, and the assistant incurs no liability under the contract. It follows that the relationship of agency involves two contracts. The primary contract is between the agent and the principal and, under this contract, the agent is given authority to represent the principal in transactions with other parties. Provided the agent carries out these instructions properly a second contract is formed between the principal and the third party. This relationship is illustrated below:

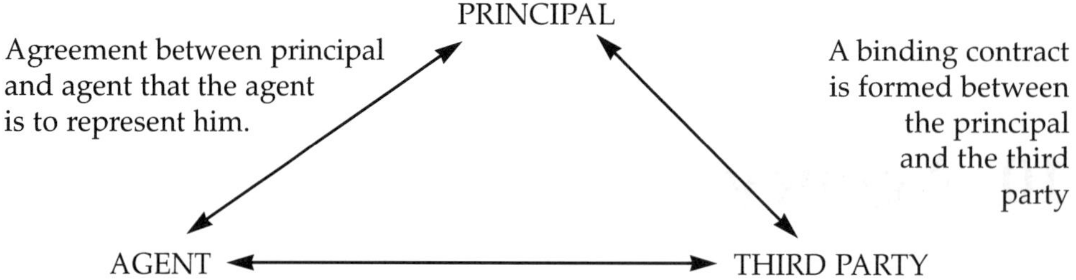

CONTRACTUAL CAPACITY

The agent and the principal must have contractual capacity to enter into the agency agreement. Regarding the validity of the second contract, which is between the principal and the third party, it is the contractual capacity of the principal that is important and not that of the agent. For example, if the agent is a child under 16-years old, he may still bind a principal in the contract with the third party. On the other hand, if the principal is under 16, he cannot extend his contractual capacity by using an agent, with full contractual capacity, to enter into contracts with third parties. The child's contract with the third party remains void.

CONSTITUTION OF AGENCY

It is important to recognise the different ways in which agency may be constituted. Proof that the relationship was agency can be vital to the liability of the principal/employer if there is a dispute as to whether someone was carrying out orders and transactions, in the capacity of agent, or as an independent contractor.

Agency may be constituted in five ways.

1 By an express contract

This contract between the principal and the agent can be agreed verbally or in writing. Obviously, a written agreement is desirable as it will define the agent's powers and duties clearly. A formal deed of factory and commission, or power of attorney, may be drawn up.

2 Implied by law or by the actions and conduct of the parties

Under the Partnership Act 1890 s 5, every partner is to be regarded as an agent of the firm, and of the other partners, in carrying on the firm's business. Also, a director of an incorporated company is impliedly an agent for the company in all matters usually entrusted to directors.

Agency can be implied from the employment of a person to a particular job, for example a manager. If that position normally involves entering into transactions with customers or the general public, then it is implied that he is an agent with the usual authority customarily conferred on such employees in order to carry out that job.

3 By holding out

Where a course of conduct has indicated that one party has been acting intentionally for the other with the latter's consent, the latter is said to have held out the person as his agent and is barred from denying that the relationship of agency exists. This can happen quite easily in business where an employer has limited, or has withdrawn, his authority from an agent. If the third party (the customer or supplier) has not been informed, by the principal, about this change then the agency relationship continues and the principal will be bound by the actions of his employee.

4 Ratification

The relationship of agency can be constituted by the principal subsequently ratifying, or endorsing, the unauthorised actions of the agent. It is not necessary for a relationship to have existed at the time of the agent's action but, usually, there is some kind of existing relationship. The agent in these circumstances is often an employee who has entered into a contract without any authority at all or possibly he may have exceeded the limited authority which had been conferred on him. The ratification may be express or inferred from the conduct of the principal. Certain conditions are necessary for ratification:

(a) The agent must have been acting as an agent with an identifiable principal in mind. He must not have entered the contract taking a chance that later he would find someone interested in adopting the transaction.
(b) When ratifying, the principal must have full knowledge of the actions of the agent. The principal can only subsequently ratify what he himself had legal power, and capacity, to do at the date of the agent's contract. It follows that if the principal is a company, the company must have been registered, and have existed, at the date of the contract. Therefore, a company cannot ratify contracts made by its promoters prior to its incorporation, although, in those circumstances, it can enter into a new contract on the same terms as the old.

5 By necessity

In certain circumstances where an emergency arises, a person is deemed by law to have the authority to act as agent for another party. For this to happen, it must be impossible for the person acting as agent to contact the principal. For example, in an emergency, the master of a ship has power to put into harbour and order repairs to his ship, or sell the cargo, if it is in danger of perishing or being spoilt. He can take these steps if he cannot contact the owners to ask for authority to proceed and the law recognises that he has not personally entered these contracts but has acted as an agent of necessity. Such a way of constituting agency is justified in Scotland on the principle of *negotiorum gestio*. This is the management of the affairs of a person who is absent, or not capable of taking care of his own affairs, and in an emergency they are undertaken for him, without his knowledge, by another party acting from altruistic motives. The *negotiorum gestor* must have acted for the benefit of the absent party and not for himself and he must take reasonable care of the other's property. He is not entitled to be paid for what he does but he is entitled to be reimbursed for all reasonable expenses even if it turns out that his actions have not benefited the absent party.

AUTHORITY OF AN AGENT

It has already been explained that a principal can find himself contractually bound to a third party as a result of his agent's actions. Whether the principal is bound depends on what the agent has done and what 'authority' he had at the time. In this context, authority can be actual or ostensible and the distinction between the two is explained below.

If the agent acts within his actual authority, his principal is bound by the contract with the third party and the agent incurs no liability under that contract.

If the agent acts outwith his actual authority but within his ostensible authority, the principal is bound by the contract with the third party. However, as he has acted beyond his actual authority and disobeyed his principal, he will be in breach of their agency agreement and, consequently, the principal could sue him or terminate the agreement.

If the agent acts outwith his actual **and** his ostensible authority, the principal will not be bound by the contract with the third party (although, as we mentioned before, he might choose to ratify the contract). The agent will be personally liable to the third party who could sue him for breach of warranty of authority if the contract is not carried out.

An agent may be a general agent, that is an agent acting for his principal in all his affairs, or acting for him in all of his affairs of a particular kind. A solicitor is a general agent. A general agent may have actual and ostensible authority. A special agent has only the powers actually given to him to carry out one particular task and he can never have ostensible authority.

The distinction between actual and ostensible authority

Actual authority is the authority which the principal has expressly or impliedly conferred on the agent. The agent can be given express instructions as to the kind of transactions and tasks which he can perform for his principal. These instructions can be given verbally or in writing. The agent can also have actual authority conferred impliedly. This implied authority will be to do anything necessary for, and incidental to, what is usual in his business, trade or profession, for the purpose of carrying out his function. The exercise of the usual or customary authority in these circumstances will be regarded as actual authority and the principal will be bound unless he has expressly limited the agent's authority.

Ostensible authority is authority which has not been actually conferred on the agent by the principal but which the third party dealing with the agent is entitled to believe existed. The third party is thus entitled to rely on the agent's authority because, in the past, the principal, by words or conduct, has represented, or held out, the agent as having authority to act for him. Consequently, the principal is barred from denying that the agent has authority and will be bound by the contract with the third party.

Examples of ostensible authority are as follows:

1 In the past, the agent had no authority from the principal or he only had limited authority. Since then, the agent has exceeded this authority in his transactions with a third party and the principal has permitted it to happen without protest.
2 In the past, the agent did have actual authority to carry out transactions with third parties. Since then, the principal has removed, or limited, his agent's authority without notifying the change to these third parties. In these circumstances, the third parties are entitled to assume that the agent still has his principal's full authority.
3 In the past, the agent had carried out transactions acting within his implied authority, the usual authority of agents in his business, trade or profession. Since then the principal has instructed the agent and has either removed or limited the agent's authority without notifying the changes to third parties. As the third parties do not know, they are entitled to assume that agent can still act within his implied authority.

In **International Sponge Importers *v* Watt 1911 SC (HL) 57** International Sponge Importers had a traveller called Cohen. Cohen called on the customers and took orders, but also carried with him bags of sponges which he could sell 'on the spot'. He was authorised by his employers only to accept payment by cheque payable to the company. In the past, Watt & Sons had given Cohen cheques, made out to him personally, in spite of the fact that the company sent out invoices with directions for payment on them. The company, in the past, had accepted payment this way and had not contacted Watt & Sons to object. One day, Watt & Sons paid Cohen in cash which he embezzled. He then disappeared. The principals sued Watt & Sons for the missing payment. The court held that they were not entitled to be paid again by Watt & Sons as the customer was entitled to assume from their prior dealings with the agent, Cohen, that he had authority to receive payments in any way.

In **Watteau *v* Fenwick [1893] 1 QB 346** the manager of a pub was forbidden to buy cigars on credit. In spite of this limitation on his actual authority, he did so and the principal, the owner of the pub, was held bound by this contract, as it was within the usual authority conferred on managers.

In all cases, if a principal wants to protect himself, and effectively limit the authority of his agent, he should always notify third parties of these new limits. If an agent has left his employment and has no authority to act for the principal then all third parties who dealt with that agent in the past should also be notified of this fact. If the third party has been notified, then the principal will not be bound and the agent will be personally liable. However, if, in any circumstances, the third party should have suspected that the agent was acting outwith his actual authority, the principal again will not be bound.

In **Reckitt** *v* **Barnett and Company [1929] AC 176** an agent, who had authority to write cheques for his principal, paid a private debt of his own, drawn on his principal's account. The principal was held entitled to recover this money from the third party, as the latter should have suspected that an agent would have no authority to pay private debts in this way.

THE PERSONAL LIABILITY OF AN AGENT

An agent will be personally liable if he exceeds his actual and ostensible authority, because there will be no contract between the third party and the principal. This personal liability arises because an agent is held to impliedly warrant to the third party that he has authority to bind his principal. The third party can sue him for damages for breach of warranty of authority.

In **Anderson** *v* **Croall & Sons (1903) 6 F 153** at a horserace meeting, there was one race where the winning horse had to be put up for sale to the highest bidder. The horse which came second in the race was standing outside the auction ring with the stable boy. The auctioneer presumed the horse was to be sold and indicated to the boy to bring it into the ring. The auctioneers, Croall & Sons, auctioned the horse and sold it to the highest bidder, Anderson. It turned out that the owner had no intention of selling the horse. The auctioneer had sold it without authority and there was no contract of sale between the owner and Anderson. Anderson successfully sued the auctioneers for breach of warranty of authority.

LIABILITY OF THE AGENT

This depends on how the agent represents himself to the third party. So far, we have seen that the agent's liability depends on whether he has authority to transact. Normally, the contract entered into with the third party is within the agent's actual authority and he incurs no liability for defective performance of that contract. However, an agent can be liable to his principal if he acts beyond his actual authority, but still within his ostensible authority, and he will be liable personally to the third party, if he acts beyond his actual and ostensible authority.

Apart from the question of authority, the agent's possible liability also depends on **how** he contracts with the third party. He could tell the third party that he is an agent of a particular principal, or he could say that he is an agent, but not disclose who he represents, or he may not mention that he is an agent at all. The agent's liability will vary depending on which of the three ways he decides to contract.

Agent contracting for a named principal

In this situation, the agent will incur no personal liability on the contract provided he acts within his authority. The exceptions to this are where the agent accepts personal liability or where it is implied by trade or custom.

Where an agent is signing a letter on behalf of his principal, he must take great care to make it clear that he does so in his capacity as an agent or he could incur personal liability. The usual way to do this is to put after his signature words like 'for and on behalf of' followed by his principal's name, or '*per pro*' or 'P.P.' followed by the principal's name.

In **Stewart** *v* **Shannessy 1900 SLT 162** Shannessy was an agent for two bicycle companies. He employed Stewart as a representative and sent him a letter confirming his appointment and detailing his pay and conditions of service. This letter was written on the notepaper of one of the companies and signed by Shannessy without any indication that he was signing as an agent for that company. Stewart took his instructions from, was always paid by Shannessy, and was ultimately dismissed by him. Stewart sued for arrears of pay and the court held that Shannessy was personally liable as he had signed the letter of appointment personally, without indicating his status as agent.

Agent contracting for an undisclosed principal

In this situation, the third party knows that he is dealing with an agent but, at the time, he does not know the identity of the principal. In this situation the agent remains personally liable even if the identity of the principal is later revealed. If the agent is buying goods, he must pay for them and, if he is selling them, he must deliver the goods or he could be sued for breach of contract. The only qualification to this rule is if the identity of the principal is disclosed to the third party who then elects to treat the principal as the debtor, then the agent is no longer liable on the contract.

Agent contracting ostensibly as a principal

When the agent contracts in his own name without mentioning that he is an agent, he makes himself personally responsible for the contract. Again, if the third party discovers the existence, and identity, of the principal, he may elect who to hold liable on the contract. Once the third party has made this election, he cannot change his mind.

THE RELATIONSHIP BETWEEN AN AGENT AND HIS PRINCIPAL

This special relationship gives the agent certain rights against his principal but also imposes on him certain duties which he owes that principal.

The rights of an agent

Remuneration

An agent is entitled to be paid for carrying out his duties. His remuneration might be in the form of a salary or he could be paid a percentage commission on all contracts which he secures. Occasionally, he is paid a basic salary plus commission. If there is no express agreement as to how much he is to be paid, then he should receive the customary rate for the job, or for his services. If there is no customary rate, he will be paid on the basis of *quantum meruit*, ie a reasonable amount for the work which he has done. An agent who has carried out his duties in accordance with the terms of his agreement with his principal will become entitled to payment. He is entitled to be paid even if the contract causes the principal a loss or if it is not carried out through the fault of either the principal or the third party.

In **Dudley** *v* **Barnet 1937 SC 632** the court held that commission was due to be paid to estate agents who had found a suitable tenant for the premises of the defender who had thereafter accepted an offer from another interested party.

It is possible to have a gratuitous agency – this is called a mandate. It remains of practical importance only in the context of powers of attorney and proxies to vote at company meetings. Thus, a mandate is a gratuitous contract whereby one party (the mandant) authorises another (the mandatary) to act on his behalf. In general, the mandatary has the same rights and duties as other agents, the only difference being that he is not entitled to be paid.

Reimbursement of expenses and relief

An agent is entitled to recover from his principal all expenses properly incurred in carrying out his duties. The principal must also relieve his agent of any liability which he incurs, again while properly carrying out his duties.

In **Stevenson & Sons** *v* **Duncan (1842) 5 D 167** the principal refused to implement the contract which the agent had completed with the third party. The third party sued the agent for damages for breach of warranty of authority. The agent sued the principal and was held entitled to be indemnified by the principal.

Lien

An agent has a right of lien (a right in security) over his principal's goods properly in his possession. This lien is in security for every claim an agent might have against his principal, arising from the agency relationship. The extent of the lien does not infer a right to sell the principal's goods and it depends on the type of agency.

The duties of the agent owed to his principal

To carry out his principal's instructions personally

If the Agent fails to carry out his principal's instructions and causes him loss, he will be personally liable and can be sued for damages. In the absence of precise instructions, he must act in the best interests of his principal or according to trade usage. He should carry out his duties personally. This obligation is expressed in the Latin maxim *delegatus non potest delegare* and certainly applies where there is any element of *delectus personae* in the choice of the agent. This means that the principal chose that agent because he possessed some special skill or expertise. However, there are exceptions to this rule and authority to delegate the task to a competent assistant, or sub-agent, may be expressly given to the agent or implied by usage.

To exercise skill and care

An agent must exercise due skill and care in performing his tasks. If the agent is a professional person, he must demonstrate the degree of care and skill to be expected of a reasonably careful and competent member of his profession. A gratuitous agent must take reasonable care. If the agent fails to take care and his principal suffers loss, he could be sued for damages for negligence.

To keep proper accounts

An agent must keep proper accounts when he is buying or selling for his principal and he must keep separate accounts for all his principals, if he represents more than one. The circumstances, the nature of the business and the custom of that trade will usually dictate what is required. If he fails to keep proper accounts, he will be liable for any loss which the principal suffers even if the agent has not been dishonest.

To act in good faith and always in the best interests of the principal

Agency is a fiduciary relationship, and the agent in this position of trust must never allow his own intersts to conflict with those of his principal, nor must he use any confidential information that he acquires for his own advantage, nor can he make any secret profit or gain any financial advantage from his position as agent, without permission.

Conflict of interests

The agent should not allow his personal interests to conflict with those of his principal. Thus, if he is selling goods for his principal, he should not buy them for himself without the permission of his principal. The same would apply if he is buying for his principal; he should not sell him goods that he owns without telling the principal. In these circumstances, the principal can have the contract set aside and can claim any profit for himself.

In **McPherson's Trustees** *v* **Watt (1877) 5R (HL) 9** Watt, a law agent for the pursuers, had to sell four houses for them. He arranged to sell them to his brother, on the understanding that the brother would then sell two of the houses to Watt for half the purchase price. The court held that the contract for the sale of the houses was invalid. A solicitor, as a law agent, has a duty to act in good faith and there must be no conflict of duty and interest.

Secret profits

An agent's only reward for acting is his remuneration and any secret profits, commission or benefit which the agent makes may be recovered by the principal unless he knew what the agent was doing and did not object.
If the agent does make a secret profit, there are certain possible civil consequences:

1 the agency contract may be terminated by the principal and the agent dismissed;
2 the agent is not entitled to be paid for that transaction;
3 the principal is entitled to recover the secret commission from the agent;
4 regarding the contract with the third party, the principal may choose not to implement it;
5 the principal may sue the third party for damages if any inducement has been offered by him, as bribing an agent is a delict, a civil wrong;
6 the arrangement between the agent and the third party is a *pactum illicitum* and so not legally enforceable. The agent cannot sue the third party if he fails to pay him the secret commission.

In **Solicitors Estate Agency *v* MacIver (Sh Ct) 1990 SCLR 595** the estate agents failed to disclose to their client that they had received a discount of 18 per cent on their newspaper advertising and they did not pass on the discount to their client. The discount was remuneration which the agents were under a duty to disclose. The contract of agency was held to be unenforceable. The estate agents have appealed to the Court of Session.

In **Morrison *v* Thomson [1874] LR 9 QB 480** a broker, employed to buy a ship, dealt with the broker of the party who was selling the ship. It was agreed by them that, if the contract was completed, the seller's broker would give the other broker part of his commission which would depend on the price of the ship. The broker who accepted the secret commission was found to be in breach of his fiduciary duty and ordered by the court to give it to his principal.

We can see from this decision that, for the agent to be in breach of his fiduciary duty, the principal does not have to suffer any loss. All that is necessary is for the agent to have gained and made a profit beyond his agreed remuneration.

The final point to note is that the third party and the agent could be prosecuted because, under the Prevention of Corruption Acts 1906 and 1916, it is a criminal offence to both offer and accept any gift or consideration as an inducement.

Liability of the principal for the actions of his agent

Usually, an agent acts with the authority of his principal in any transactions with third parties and, when the contract is completed, he has no right to enforce this contract, nor is he liable for any defective performance of it. However, he cannot avoid being personally liable to a third party for his negligence or fraud, whether he was authorised by the principal or not. But, the third party may have a choice as to whether to sue the agent or the principal in some circumstances, as the principal is vicariously liable to a third party for harm caused to him by the agent, provided the agent is acting within his actual, or ostensible authority at the time of the negligent act.

In **Lloyd *v* Grace Smith & Co [1912] AC 716** a solicitor's clerk was an agent for his firm and had authority to carry out conveyancing transactions for clients. The firm was found liable in damages to a client who had been fraudulently induced by the clerk to assign to him some properties. The clerk had told the client that the properties would be sold and the proceeds re-invested for the client.

TERMINATION OF AGENCY

As agency is a contractual relationship it may be terminated in any of the ways in which a contract may be terminated, as discussed in Chapter 6.

Agency may be terminated by:

1 Mutual agreement – where both parties agree to end the relationship on a certain date.
2 The principal – who may withdraw his authority at any time. However, if the agency was created for a fixed period of time, the principal could be liable for damages for breach of contract if he terminates the relationship early without justification. The agent is entitled to be paid any expenses, salary or commission due to him. If the agent is paid by commission, he must be allowed to complete any transaction in which he is involved.
3 The agent – who may withdraw from the agency at any time but not in the middle of a transaction if this might cause loss to his principal. If the agency was created for a fixed period of time, the agent could possibly be liable for breach of contract if he terminates the relationship early, without justification.
4 The business of the principal coming to an end, or if the principal goes into liquidation, or if he is made bankrupt. However, the agent's bankruptcy need not terminate the agency.
5 The death of either party; but it is doubtful whether insanity will have the same effect unless it is permanent.
6 On the expiry of a fixed period of time; or when the object of the agency relationship has been completed; or when the object becomes impossible, due to circumstances changing through no fault of either party.

The Commercial Agents (Council Directive) Regulations 1993

The student will have noticed that the law of agency is based on common law. However, a small number of agents will benefit from the recent Commercial Agents (Council Directive) Regulations 1993 which implement the EC Commercial Agents Directive 86/653 and came into force on 1 January 1994.

What kind of agents and activities are covered by the Regulations?

The new Regulations are designed to protect commercial agents – self-employed agents – and not employee-agents like sales managers or purchasing representatives. Only self-employed agents who buy and sell goods for their principal are covered. The Regulations exclude directors who are officers of a company, partners acting for the partnership, insolvency practitioners, commercial agents who are acting gratuitously or commercial agents operating in the commodity market.

The Schedule to the Regulations gives the following guidelines as to which activities of the commercial agent will be primary activities and therefore within the scope of the Regulations. The commercial agent must be buying or selling goods and these transactions are normally concluded on a commercial basis and are likely to lead to further transactions with other customers in the same geographical area or among the same group of customers. The schedule lists a number of indications that will show that the above relationship exists:

1 the principal is the manufacturer, importer or distributor of the goods;
2 the goods are specifically identified with the principal in the market in question;
3 the agent devotes a substantial amount of his time buying or selling these goods either for his principal or a number of principal dealing in the same goods;
4 the goods are not normally available in the market in question unless bought or sold by an agent; and
5 the arrangement is described as a commercial agency.

(Note that if one of these indications is missing the presumption is that the agency is not covered by the Regulations. Also mail order agents and consumer credit agents are not covered by the Regulations).

Duties of the agent and principal – Regulations 3 and 4

The statutory duties are very similar to the common law duties and both the principal and the commercial agent 'must act dutifully and in good faith.' In particular, the commercial agent must make proper efforts to negotiate and conclude his transactions, comply with the principal's instructions and communicate to his principal all the necessary information available to the agent. Also the principal's particular duties are to provide his commercial agent with the necessary documentation concerning the goods and to obtain for his agent the necessary information for carrying out the transaction. In addition he must notify the commercial agent within a reasonable time if (a) he anticipates the volume of transactions will be significantly lower than the agent could normally have expected or (b) he has accepted or refused or not carried out any transaction which the commercial agent procured for him.

The parties may not derogate from these duties and breach of any of these duties by either party will give the other the right to sue for damages (lost income) for breach of contract.

The rights to commission and payment – Regulations 6–12

In the absence of any agreement the commercial agent is entitled to be paid the customary and usual remuneration for agents of his kind or if there is no customary practice he is entitled to a reasonable amount. Where the agent is not properly paid he has two basic rights – the first arises during the agency agreement, the second after the agreement is terminated. The rights are:

1 The right to commission where the transaction has been concluded by him or where the transaction is concluded with a third party who he acquired as a

customer for transactions of the same kind. This right extends to all transactions concluded where the commercial agent had an exclusive right to a specific geographical area or to a specific group of customers.

2 The right to commission on transactions concluded within a reasonable period after the agency contract was terminated provided the transaction resulted from his efforts when he was an agent or provided he or the principal had received the customer's order before the agency contract came to an end. Because of this right, new agents will not be entitled to the commission which is due to a predecessor unless it is fair and equitable that the commission be shared between the two agents.

Commission has to be paid once the principal has or should have executed (carried out) the transaction or the third party has executed the transaction. Principals can no longer postpone paying a commercial agent until the principal has been paid. The Regulations require the commission to be paid not later than the last day of the month following the quarter in which it became due. Any attempt to change this rule will be void if it is to the agent's detriment. The right to be paid commission is only to be denied if it is clear that the transaction with the third party is not going ahead and this is not due to the fault of the principal.

The agency contract and notice requirements – Regulations 13–16

The principal and the commercial agent have the right to receive on request a written statement of the terms of the agency contract. If a fixed term agency contract continues to be performed by both parties after the termination date it will be deemed to be converted into an agency contract for an indefinite period. Any agency contract for an indefinite period may be terminated by either party giving notice. There are new statutory minimum periods of notice required and the parties cannot agree on shorter periods of notice. The minimum period of notice is one month for the first year, two months for the second year commenced and three months for the third year commenced and for subsequent years. If the parties agree on longer periods of notice, the principal's period of notice must not be shorter than the commercial agent's. The notice requirements do not apply if one party is entitled to immediately terminate the contract because a repudiatory breach by the other party or where exceptional circumstances arise.

The commercial agent's right to indemnity or compensation – Regulations 17 and 18

This right is an entirely new concept in the law of agency. It arises after the agency agreement has been terminated and the parties may not agree to derogate from Regulations 17 and 18 before the agreement ends.

A commercial agent is entitled to be indemnified or compensated for damages provided he notifies his principal of his claim within one year. He only has a right to an indemnity if the agency agreement provides for this but there is no such condition for the right to compensation.

The commercial agent has the right to an indemnity if he has brought the principal new customers or has significantly increased the volume of business with existing customers and the principal is still benefiting from this new or increased business. The amount of the indemnity paid to the agent must be fair and equitable in all the circumstances which will include the commission the commercial agent has now lost in relation to these customers but this amount is subject to a maximum of one year's commission (based on the average over the past three years)

The commercial agent is entitled to be compensated (and this can be in addition to being indemnified) when the termination of the agency contract has either deprived the agent of the commission which he would have received for carrying out the transactions which have substantially benefited the principal or the termination has not enabled the agent to recoup the costs and expenses he incurred carrying out his duties.

The indemnity or compensation will not be paid to the commercial agent if, because of his conduct the principal was justified in terminating the agency contract or if the commercial agent has terminated it. However the agent can still claim payment if his termination was justified by circumstances attributable to the principal or if the agent cannot continue because of age, infirmity or illness or if with the agreement of the principal he has assigned his rights and duties under the agency contract to another.

Finally, Regulation 20 provides that a restraint of trade clause is only valid and enforceable by the principal if it is in writing, only covers the geographical area, the group of customers and the goods covered by that commercial agent, and lasts no longer than two years after the termination of the agency contract.

QUESTIONS

1 Describe the various ways in which agency may be constituted.

2 What is the difference between the actual and ostensible authority of an agent?

3 The promoters of a company, which was being formed to run a new restaurant, entered into a contract with Delightful Kitchens Ltd to completely refit the kitchen of the new restaurant. Once the new company was registered, it ratified this contract with Delightful Kitchens Ltd. Unfortunately, the restaurant has failed and the company is in liquidation. Delightful Kitchens Ltd have not been paid. Advise them.

4 Jack is the Chief Vegetable Produce Buyer of Presco Stores. Prescos have authorised him to enter into contracts with farmers to supply their stores with vegetables. However, Jack is not to purchase potatoes, because Prescos have a special contract with a grower in Cyprus.

Jack contracts with Sid to purchase Sid's cabbage crop. He enters into a contract with Joe to buy Joe's potato crop. He makes a contract with Jim to buy Jim's carrot crop and also completes a contract whereby Jim will supply eggs to

Presco's Glasgow Store. He had previously made such a contract for eggs with Jim, in respect of Presco's Edinburgh Store.

What is Presco's legal position in respect of these contracts with Sid, Joe and Jim?

5 Walter is the Purchasing Agent for a large construction company, Buildit Ltd. The company have recently won a contract to build a shopping complex and have costed the sum available for the cement and bricks at £700 000. Walter is instructed to purchase these materials for the job within this figure. What is the legal liability of the parties in the following situations:

(a) Walter concludes a contract with Black & Sons to supply the necessary materials at £750 000.
(b) Walter concludes a contract with White & Sons to supply the necessary materials at a cost of £700 000. However, subsequently, it comes to the notice of the managing director of Buildit Ltd that Walter received a present of 'a weekend for two in Paris' from White & Sons.
(c) Walter concludes a contract with Green & Sons to supply the necessary materials at £700 000. Subsequently, it comes to light that Green is Walter's brother-in-law.

6 George has his own business selling computer equipment. He has a commercial agency agreement with Bloggs & Co who manufacturer an excellent PC which retails at a competitive price. His contract allows him to sell Bloggs & Co's computers to all retail outlets in Scotland. Bloggs & Co have now terminated his agency contract giving him one month's notice. They have decided to employ their own sales manager. George is upset as the commission from representing Bloggs & Co was his main source of income. He represents other manufacturers of computer equipment but for the last seven years he has devoted most of his time into expanding and developing Bloggs & Co's sales. Recently he has been working on deals with two new retailers. The final contracts have not been completed as yet and he is worried that he will not manage to close the deals within a month. Advise George.

Part 6
BUSINESS ORGANISATIONS

11 Sole trader, partnership and company formation

CHOICE OF BUSINESS ORGANISATION – SOLE TRADER, PARTNERSHIP OR REGISTERED COMPANY?

If a person is thinking of starting a business, he must consider what legal form it should take. He may opt to carry on business as a sole trader or he may take advantage of new provisions which allow the formation of a single member private limited company. However, if he is proposing to go into business with other persons, he must decide whether to form a partnership or a registered company. He must consider the main features of each type of business organisation and weigh up their relative advantages and disadvantages.

Carrying on business as a sole trader

The person who carries on business as a sole trader retains the right to manage and control his business. He enjoys all the profits of the business. However, the business remains his legal responsibility and he is personally liable for the debts of the business. Should the business become insolvent, the sole trader may be declared 'bankrupt' and sequestrated so that all his property may be taken to satisfy his creditors. The individual sole trader is indistinguishable in law from his business; the individual is the business and the business is the individual.

The sole trader does not operate under any special legal rules. No formalities are involved in setting up or running the business. No information relating to the business need be made public and no returns are required to any government department other than the Inland Revenue for tax purposes. The disclosure requirements of the Business Names Act 1985 do apply to the sole trader if he is carrying on business under a name other than his own. If, for example, John Smith runs a florists called 'Blooms', his own name as the true owner of the business must be displayed on the premises and on business stationery. The main advantages of carrying on business as a sole trader are the degree of control and privacy enjoyed.

One disadvantage is restricted access to sources of capital for expansion. The main disadvantage is the sole trader's unlimited personal liability for business debts.

General features of a partnership

A partnership is a voluntary association of two or more persons who carry on business together with the purpose of making a profit. Each partner contributes something in the way of skill, work or financial investment. Each partner has the right to participate in the running of the business. Each partner is regarded as an agent of the firm and so has the power to bind the firm to business contracts which he makes. Both at common law and in terms of s 4(2) of the Partnership Act 1890, a partnership firm in Scotland is a legal person distinct from the partners of whom it is composed. As a consequence of having a separate personality, a firm may enter contracts and sue and be sued in the firm's name. A partnership may own its own property. However, the title deeds to heritable property must be in the name of the partners in trust for the firm.

General features of a registered company

Companies are corporate bodies formed by registration under the Companies Act 1985. As a consequence of incorporation under the 1985 Act, a company enjoys separate legal personality distinct from that of its members and directors. As a consequence of this separate corporate personality, companies may also enter contracts and sue and be sued in their own name. Company property belongs to the company and the title to heritable property may be in the company's name.

Partnerships and companies contrasted

Liability for business debts

Because of the separate legal personality of the firm, creditors of a partnership must first of all look to the firm for payment. However, if the firm's assets cannot meet business debts, the partners remain jointly and severally liable for the debts of the firm. This means that any one of the partners may have to pay all the business debts and then seek repayment of their share from the other partners. This means that the potential liability of individual partners for the debts of the firm is unlimited.

By contrast, the members of a limited company, for example its shareholders, are said to enjoy **limited liability**. The liability of an individual member to contribute to paying off the debts of a company is limited to the amount, if any, still required to fully pay up his shares. In companies where the liability of members is limited by guarantee, all a member is required to contribute to pay off the debts of the company is the amount which he has guaranteed to contribute.

The limited liability enjoyed by members of companies is regarded as the major advantage of forming a company rather than entering into a partnership. However, in respect of small private companies, the benefit of limited liability may be more illusory than real because creditors such as banks may require individuals to guarantee loans which are given to the company.

Formalities in formation

No special formalities are required to establish a partnership. A partnership may be constituted verbally or its existence may be implied from the actions of the parties. However, it is advisable to draw up a written contract of co-partnery. Accordingly, setting up a partnership need involve little expense.

A company is formed by registration under the Companies Act 1985. This entails the delivery of documentation, including a Memorandum of Association and Articles of Association, to the Registrar of Companies in Edinburgh. Forming a company involves greater expense and publicity than entering into a partnership.

Formalities in carrying on the business

Partnerships are not subject to any special requirements in relation to the running of the firm's business. There is no need for any public disclosure of information and no returns need be made to any government department other than to the Inland Revenue for tax purposes. A major advantage of a partnership is privacy.

Companies must comply with many more formalities. Company accounts are open to public inspection and must be audited annually. An annual return and copies of other documentation must be filed with the Registrar of Companies. Companies lack privacy and face higher administrative expenses.

Both partnerships and companies may be subject to the disclosure requirements of the Business Names Act 1985.

Number of members

A partnership must have a minimum of two partners. In general, a partnership must have no more than twenty partners. However, there are exceptions to the general rule and firms of solicitors, accountants, stockbrokers and certain other professionals may have more than twenty partners.

A public limited company must have at least two members but there is no upper limit on the number of members. From 15 July 1992, private companies limited by shares or by guarantee may have one member. There is no upper limit on the number of members a private company may have.

Transferability of shares

Section 24(7) of the Partnership Act 1890 provides that, unless otherwise agreed, no person may be introduced as a partner without the consent of all existing partners. This is because of the element of *delectus personae* which is present in the partnership relationship.

A shareholder in a public company must always be able to freely transfer his shares without the consent of the company. A private company may retain a right of pre-emption which means that the company must have first refusal if a member wants to sell his shares.

Changes in membership

Section 33 of the Partnership Act 1890 provides that, unless the contract of co-partnery states otherwise, a partnership is automatically dissolved by the death or bankruptcy of any partner.

By contrast, companies are said to enjoy **perpetual succession**. A company's continued existence and operation is unaffected by changes in membership or by the death, bankruptcy or insanity of members.

Management of the business

Section 24(5) of the Partnership Act 1890 provides that, unless otherwise agreed, every partner may take part in the management of the partnership business. Section 5 of the Act also provides that every partner is an agent of the firm, with ostensible authority to bind the firm and his partners.

By contrast, members of the company are not agents of the company and they have no right to take part in its day to day management. Management of the company is in the hands of directors who may or may not be shareholders.

The granting of security when borrowing

A creditor may be unwilling to lend unless some security is offered. The idea of such security is that, should the debtor fail to repay a loan, the creditor has a right to some part of the debtor's property. For example, when an individual borrows money from a building society to finance the purchase of a house, the house is offered as security to the building society. The borrower signs a document known as a standard security which is then registered. If the borrower fails to keep up his loan repayments, the building society may take possession of the house and sell it to recover their money.

Partnerships may grant a standard security over heritable property but if they wish to offer moveable property as security, it must be physically handed over to the creditor. This is often impractical. For example, if a partnership carries on business as a haulage contractor, a major asset would be its fleet of lorries. Under Scots law the lorries cannot be offered as security unless they are handed over to the creditor. If they are handed over to the creditor the firm cannot run its business.

A company finds it easier to borrow. A company may grant a standard security over its heritable property. However, there is also a special type of security, known as a floating charge, which is available only to companies. A company can sign a document which creates a floating charge and the document is registered with the Registrar of Companies. In terms of the floating charge, a company may offer as security any heritable or moveable property owned by the company at the time the security is triggered. The operation of the floating charge may be thought of as having a dustbin lid floating over the assets of the company. It hovers harmlessly while things go well and allows the company to use and buy and sell property. Should, however, an event occur which causes the security to be triggered, such as non-payment of the loan or the company becoming insolvent, the charge attaches. This may be thought of as the dustbin lid crashing down and trapping underneath all the property which the company owns at that particular moment in time. The creditor then sends in an individual known as a receiver who can sell off as much of the property as is necessary to repay the creditor. The ability to grant a floating charge is of great benefit to companies.

The advantages of forming a company

In summary, the advantages of entering into a partnership are that there are fewer formalities and administrative expenses, both at the time of formation and subsequently. A partnership also enjoys greater privacy.

However, on balance, the advantages offered by incorporation, namely limited liability, free transferability of shares, perpetual succession and easier access to borrowing, are generally regarded as outweighing the advantages of a partnership.

THE PROVISIONS OF THE BUSINESS NAMES ACT 1985

The Business Names Act 1985 contains provisions relating to the names under which persons may carry on business in Great Britain. The 1985 Act deals with the business names of sole traders, partnerships and registered companies. Additional controls relating to the names of registered companies are found in the Companies Act 1985. The main purpose of the Business Names Act 1985 is to ensure the disclosure of the true identity of the persons who run a business. A person who wishes to pursue a legal claim against a business must know who is behind the business if he is to be able to raise a court action.

A sole trader or a partnership or a registered company may carry on business under a name which does not consist of their own surnames or the name of the company. The provisions of the Business Names Act apply where persons trade under a business name which does not consist merely of their own name or their name plus permitted additions. For example, Paula Smith and Jean Jones may carry on a business as hairdressers under the business name of 'A Cut Above the Rest'. If they traded as Smith and Jones, the provisions of the 1985 Act would not apply. However, if they use the business name, 'A Cut Above the Rest', the provisions of the Act do apply.

The 1985 Act operates by imposing disclosure requirements on the businesses to which it applies. Failure to comply with the disclosure requirements is a criminal offence. In addition, a business which has not complied with the statutory disclosure requirements may be barred from enforcing a civil claim against a customer.

When does the Business Names Act apply?

Section 1 provides that the 1985 Act applies in the following cases:

(a) *Sole traders* – the Act's provisions apply if an individual carries on a business under a name which does not consist just of his surname, or of his surname plus permitted additions.

(b) *Partnerships* – the Act's provisions apply if a partnership carries on a business under a name which is not made up just of the surnames of the partners, or of their surnames plus permitted additions.
(c) *Registered companies* – the Act's provisions apply if a company carries on business under a name which is not the name under which it is incorporated, or its corporate name plus permitted additions.

'Permitted additions'

Sole traders can add their forename or its initial. Initials include any recognised abbreviation such as 'Wm' for William. Therefore the Act would not apply if John Smith carried on business under the name of 'Smith', or 'John Smith', or 'J Smith'.

Partnerships can add the forenames or initials of individual partners. Where two or more partners have the same surname, they may add an 's', for example, the partnership of James Grant and David Grant may trade under the name of 'Grants'. In this case the Act would not apply.

Where a sole trader or a partnership or a registered company buys a business they may choose to indicate that they are trading as successors to the former owner. The Act does not apply if they trade under their own name with some addition such as 'formerly Jones & Co'.

Prohibition of the use of certain business names

Section 2 of the Act provides that certain names are prohibited unless prior written consent is obtained from the Secretary of State. These are names which suggest a link with a government department or a local authority or names which include any word or expression which may be specified in regulations made under s 3. Failure to comply with s 2 is a criminal offence and a person convicted under the Act may be fined. Should the breach continue, on a second or subsequent conviction, a person may be fined again or the court may impose a daily penalty for each day the contravention continues.

The disclosure requirements

Section 4 provides that persons covered by the Act must state on all business letters, orders for goods, invoices, receipts and written demands for payment of debts:

(a) in the case of a sole trader – the individual's name;
(b) in the case of a partnership – the name of each partner;
(c) in the case of a registered company – the name under which the company is incorporated.

In addition, in respect of each person named, there must be stated an address in Great Britain where service of documents will be effective. Section 4 also requires such names and addresses to be displayed in premises where the business is carried on. Such information must be contained in a notice displayed in a prominent position so as to be easily read. A written note of such names and addresses must also be given immediately to any customer or supplier who requests it.

In respect of the requirements relating to disclosure on documents such as business letters etc, partnerships of more than 20 partners are exempt so long as the document does not contain the name of any of the partners other than the one who signs the document. In addition, the document must give an address at which a full list of partners may be inspected during business hours.

Contravention of s 4 is a criminal offence. In respect of a first offence a person may be fined. In respect of a second or subsequent conviction, a person may be fined or a daily penalty imposed. Where an offence is committed by a company, a director, the company secretary or some other officer may be criminally liable as well as the company.

Civil remedies for breach of section 4

If a person brings court proceedings to enforce a contract made while he was in breach of the s 4 disclosure requirements, the action shall be dismissed if the defender shows:

(a) that he has been unable to pursue a claim arising out of the same contract because of the pursuer's breach; *or*
(b) that he has suffered some financial loss in relation to the contract because of the pursuer's breach;

unless the court is satisfied that it is equitable to allow the proceedings to continue.

THE LAW OF PARTNERSHIP

Having examined the different kinds of business organisations, we now take a detailed look at one particular kind of organisation – a partnership.

The common law was codified by the **Partnership Act 1890** and, where the Act is silent on a particular matter, the common law rules will still apply. The Act is mainly a guide and many of the provisions may be modified by the express agreement of the parties.

Definition of partnership

Bell, one of the Institutional Writers, described 'partnership' as:

> a voluntary association of two or more persons for the acquisition of gain or profit, with a contribution for that end of stipulated shares of goods, money, skill and industry; accompanied by an unlimited mandate or power to each partner to bind the [firm] in the line of its trade, and a guarantee to third parties of all the engagements undertaken in the social name.

The Partnership Act 1890 s 1 states that a partnership is the relationship which exists between persons carrying on a business in common, with a view to profit.

There are a few points that must be noted regarding this definition:

1 The minimum number of partners is two. Under the Companies Act 1985 s 716, the maximum number is twenty. However, the section then gives some exceptions: partnerships formed for carrying on a business as solicitors, accountants and as members of recognised stock exchanges may have more than twenty partners. The section also provides that the Secretary of State may, by statutory instrument, allow other partnerships to exceed the maximum of twenty and orders have been made excepting valuers, estate agents, land agents, actuaries, consultant engineers, building designers and loss adjusters.
2 The purpose of the relationship must be to make a profit and the Partnership Act s 45 defines the word 'business' as 'including every trade, occupation or profession'. Thus, groups and associations like charities, clubs and church organisations cannot be partnerships.
3 Partnerships are usually formed to exist for an indefinite time but there is nothing in the definition that excludes joint ventures which are partnerships, with no firm name, formed to carry out one particular transaction. Once the transaction is completed the joint venture ends automatically.
4 A company incorporated under the Companies Acts, and therefore having a separate legal personality, can become a partner.

The separate legal personality of the firm

The Partnership Act 1890 s 4 states that, in Scotland, a firm is a legal person distinct from the partners of whom it is composed, but an individual partner may be charged on a decree or diligence against the firm, and on payment of the debts is entitled to relief, pro rata, from the firm and its other members.
A few points should be noted regarding s 4:

1 In Scotland, a firm has a separate legal personality which is distinct, and separate from, the legal personality of the individual partners. This distinguishes partnerships from unincorporated associations but the section immediately qualifies that statement and, so, distinguishes a partnership from incorporated bodies.
2 The partners are liable, jointly and severally, for the debts of the firm. The liability of each partner is normally unlimited and he is liable 'to his last penny' to the creditors of the firm. The firm is the primary debtor and the partners can be regarded as cautioners or guarantors for the firm's debts. In a sequestration, the creditors must sue the firm first, so the liability of the partners is secondary to the liability of the firm.
3 A partner who has paid a debt of the firm is entitled to pro rata relief from the other partners. Thus, in 1995, KPMG, a large firm of accountants, decided to incorporate the part of their firm which audits public limited companies in order to protect the personal assets of their partners in the event of claims of negligence against the organisation.
4 In Scotland, a partnership can, in its own name, own moveable property. However, heritable property must be held by a specified individual or group of individuals. This differs from a company, which can own heritable property in its own name. In practice, heritable property is held in the name of the partners as trustees for the firm.

Does a partnership exist?

The answer to this question can be very important to a creditor who is looking for payment of a debt owed. If a person denies being a partner, then the intention of the associated parties, and all the circumstances, will have to be examined. A written partnership agreement is not always available. The definition, in s 1 of the Act, refers to an association of persons working together with a view to profit. This idea of persons sharing profits is essential for the existence of a partnership but, as we shall see, it is not conclusive evidence.

The Partnership Act 1890 s 2 states that, although receipt of a share of the profits is prima facie evidence that a partnership exists, it is not conclusive. The section gives a number of examples where a person will not be regarded as a partner without further evidence. These include the following:

1 The receipt by a person of a debt paid by instalments out of the profits of a business.
2 The wages of an employee paid by a share of the profits of the business.
3 A person being the widow or child of a deceased partner and receiving, by way of an annuity, a portion of the profits made in the business.
4 A loan to a person engaged, or about to be engaged, in any business with the agreement that the lender shall receive a rate of interest varying with the profits.
5 A person receiving by way of an annuity, or otherwise, a portion of the profits of a business in consideration of the sale by him of the goodwill of the business.

Formation of a partnership

There are no formal legal requirements for setting up a partnership. What is required is the agreement of the parties, and this may be found in express terms or implied by the actions of the parties. Express agreement can be found in a written partnership agreement. Alternatively, the agreement can be verbal or even implied from the actions of the parties. The parties can decide on any terms that will suit them and, provided all the partners agree, these terms can be changed at any time. The usual express terms will cover such matters as the name of the firm, what kind of business they are planning to run, the amount of capital each partner will contribute, how the profits will be distributed and what will happen if a partner wishes to leave the firm.

It is only where the agreement does not cover certain matters that reference will be made to the rules in s 24, which says that, unless the partnership agreement states otherwise, the rights of every partner are as follows:

1 To share equally in the capital and profits of the business and to contribute equally to any losses.
2 To be indemnified by the firm for any personal liabilities incurred, or payments made, in the course of the firm's business.
3 To receive interest at the rate of 5 per cent on any payments made on behalf of the firm, or advanced to the firm beyond his agreed capital contribution. No interest is payable on capital, unless the partnership agreement so provides.
4 To take part in the management of the business. A partner is not entitled to be

paid for acting in the partnership business unless this is expressly stated in the partnership agreement. A partner's reward is his share of the profits.

5 To have access to the firm's books, which are to be kept at the firm's principal place of business.

6 To object to the admission of a new partner, or to any change in the nature of the business. Such changes specifically require the consent of all the partners. Other differences can be decided by a majority vote. (Note that s 25 provides that no majority of partners can expel any partner unless such a power is contained in the partnership agreement. Even where there is such a power, it must be exercised in good faith.)

The fiduciary duty of a partner

The first point to note is that under common law a partnership is a contract *uberrimae fidei* – a contract of utmost good faith. It means that every partner must deal honestly with his fellow partners. He must disclose to the others all material facts, not only at the time the partnership is formed but throughout its existence. A partner must not make any secret profit out of his position, nor use information he acquires for his own benefit.

The Partnership Act clarifies this fiduciary duty.

Section 28 states that it is the duty of every partner to render true accounts and full information of all things affecting the partnership.

Section 29 states that it is the duty of every partner to account to the firm for any benefit derived by him without the consent of the other partners from any transaction concerning the partnership, or from any use by him of the partnership property, name or business connection. This section applies also to transactions undertaken after the partnership has been dissolved by the death of a partner and before the partnership has been completely wound up.

Section 30 states that, if a partner, without the consent of the other partners, carries on any similar business which competes with the firm, he must account for, and pay to the firm, all profits made by him in the other business.

In **Pillans Bros *v* Pillans (1908) 16 SLT 611 (OH)** three brothers set up a partnership as rivet, bolt and nut manufacturers in Motherwell and elsewhere. The following year, one of the brothers, Richard, bought a similar business four miles from Motherwell. The firm and his brothers brought an action against him. The court held that one partner cannot acquire a benefit for himself, to the exclusion of his partners, in relation to any matter connected with the business in which they are all interested. In this case, the new business belonged to the firm and Richard was bound to account to the firm, and to his brothers, for the profits of the new firm, from the date on which it was acquired.

The authority of a partner

Under s 5 of the Act, 'every partner is an agent of the firm and of his other partners for the purposes of the business of the partnership; and the acts of every partner who does any act, carrying on in the usual way, business of the kind carried on by the firm of which he is a member, bind the firm and his partners, unless the partner so acting has in fact no authority to act for the firm in the particular matter, and the person with whom he is dealing either knows that he has no authority, or does not know or believe him to be a partner'.

A partner's authority as an agent for the firm and the other partners can be express and implied. The partnership agreement can expressly define, or limit, the power of any of the partners. Under s 5, the partner's implied authority is the power to enter into transactions which are connected with the usual business of the firm.

If a partner acts within his express authority and enters into a contract with a third party, the firm is bound by his actions. If he exceeds his express authority, his actions could still bind the firm if the contract was one which is within the ordinary course of that business. Another possibility is that, if a partner exceeds his express authority, the other partners might agree to adopt, or ratify, the transaction and thus the firm will be bound. However, if the third party knew that the partner was exceeding his express authority, or should have suspected that he was exceeding it, then the firm is not bound, and the partner will be personally liable.

In **Paterson Brothers *v* Gladstone (1891) 18 R 403** Paterson Brothers, a firm of builders and joiners, had three partners: Robert, William and John. The partnership agreement stated that William alone should take full charge of the financial transactions of the firm. Robert signed the firm's name on some promissory notes payable to Gladstone, a money-lender. Gladstone advanced Robert money on them, the rate of interest being 40 per cent. Robert used this money for his own private purposes. The court held that the firm was not liable to pay the amount due on the promissory notes.

Robert was acting beyond his express authority. The court had to decide whether the transaction was within his implied authority. Was it within the ordinary course of that business? This was a reputable firm of builders and so Gladstone's suspicions must have been alerted that this transaction was unusual, particularly as the rate of interest was so high. Gladstone could have quite easily checked with the other partners that the action was authorised by the firm. Accordingly, the firm was not bound by Robert's act.

The liability of a partner

Liability for the firm's debts

As was discussed earlier, every partner is jointly and severally liable for the debts of the firm. Any creditor has to sue the firm first. If a partner pays a debt of the firm, he has a right of relief against the other partners and may call on them to contribute a share, according to the terms of the partnership agreement.

Liability of any incoming or outgoing partners

Under s 17 of the Act, a new partner is not liable for anything done, or for debts incurred, before he became a partner. An outgoing, or retiring, partner remains liable for all wrongful acts and debts incurred before he departed, but he could remain liable for obligations incurred after his retirement if he fails to give adequate notice to those dealing with the firm about his retirement. Notice should be put in the *Edinburgh Gazette*. Sometimes, the other partners will agree to indemnify a retiring partner against any subsequent claims but this does not affect his continuing liability to creditors for the debts incurred while he was a partner. However, the new partnership can take on this liability with the agreement of the creditors. This is an example of **novation**, as the creditors effectively agree to give up their claims against the old firm and enter into a fresh agreement with the new firm.

Liability for delicts

Under ss 10, 11, and 12, the firm is vicariously liable for the delicts and negligent acts of a partner if they are committed in the ordinary course of the firm's business, or with the express agreement of his co-partners. This liability is limited to cases where the loss or injury had been caused to a person who was not a partner of the firm. The firm is also liable when one partner acting with apparent authority receives the money or property of a third party and misapplies it. Each partner is liable, jointly and severally, after the firm. However, the firm is not liable to one partner who has been injured by another partner acting in the ordinary course of the business. In such a case the injured partner would have to sue the other partner personally.

In **Mair *v* Woods 1948 SC 83** several men entered into a joint adventure which was a fishing trip. At the end of the trip the catch was to be sold and the profits distributed. During the trip, Mair was injured with a boat hook by one of the others and he brought an action for damages against the other members. The court held that a partnership, or joint adventure, was not vicariously liable to a partner injured by the negligence of another partner, acting within the scope of his authority.

Liability by 'holding out'

Under s 14, any person who represents himself (by words or by conduct), or knowingly permits himself to be represented or held out as a partner in a particular firm, is liable to any person who gives the firm credit, on the basis of that representation. This applies whether the representation has, or has not, been made, or communicated to the person giving credit by, or with the knowledge of, the apparent partner.

Such a person does not actually become a partner, although he can be treated as if he were liable as a partner by third parties who relied on the representation. If the third party knows that he is not really a partner, then there is no liability. A firm which holds someone out as being a partner will be liable for the debts incurred by that apparent partner. If a person has held himself out as a partner and has had to pay a business debt, then he may seek relief from the firm.

In **Hosie *v* Waddell (1886) 3 SLT 16** Hosie brought an action for non-payment of a debt against Waddell, who maintained that he had paid the money to Cameron, who he thought was Hosie's partner. Hosie said that Cameron had never been his partner and was only the manager of his business. The court held that, in the circumstances, Hosie had held out Cameron as his partner. It was common knowledge that Hosie had in the past planned to make him his partner and he had taken no steps to notify his change of plans to Waddell. Therefore, the payment to Cameron satisfied Waddell's debt to Hosie.

The Limited Partnerships Act 1907

This Act allows the formation of a limited partnership, consisting of one or more general partners and one or more limited partners. A limited partner is often called 'a sleeping partner' or 'a dormant partner'. The liability of the limited partner for the debts and obligations of the firm is limited to the amount which he contributed to the capital of the firm, and to protect his limited liability, he must not take part in the management of the firm. If he does, he becomes liable with the other partners for debts incurred while he is involved. There must always be at least one general partner who conducts the business and remains liable for the firm's debts and obligations. A limited partnership must be registered with the Registrar of Companies in Edinburgh. Such partnerships are not common, as a private limited company will provide the same advantages for all the participants. A limited partner cannot withdraw his contribution while the firm continues in business and, if he does, he remains liable for the amount of his contribution. A limited partner cannot dissolve the partnership without the consent of the general partners but he can assign his interest in the firm with the consent of the general partners, provided notice is given in the *Edinburgh Gazette.*

Dissolution of a partnership

Under s 32, subject to any provisions in the partnership agreement, a partnership is dissolved under the following conditions:

(a) If entered into for a fixed term, by the expiry of that term. If, however, the business just carries on without further express agreement, the partnership will be deemed to be continuing on the same terms as before by virtue of 'tacit relocation'. In the Act, such a partnership is referred to as a 'partnership at will'.
(b) If entered into for a single adventure or undertaking, by the completion and termination of that adventure or undertaking.
(c) If entered into for an indefinite period of time, by any partner giving notice to the others of his intention to dissolve the partnership.
(d) By mutual consent.
(e) By the death or bankruptcy of any partner (s 33).
(f) By changing circumstances which make the continuance of the partnership illegal (s 34). For example, if one of the partners was an enemy alien in wartime.
(g) Like other contracts, a partnership may be rescinded on the grounds that it was induced by fraud or misrepresentation. Also, as it is a contract *uberrimae fidei*, proof that a material fact was concealed from the other partners will justify rescission.

In addition, under s 35, on the application of one of the partners, the court may order the dissolution of the partnership in the following cases:

(a) A partner suffers from some mental disorder or insanity.
(b) A partner suffers from some permanent incapacity.
(c) A partner conducts himself in a way that is prejudicial to the carrying on of the business.

(d) A partner persistently commits a breach of the partnership agreement or conducts himself in a way that it would be unreasonable to expect the other partners to continue working with him.
(e) Where the business can only be carried on at a loss.
(f) Whenever circumstances have arisen which, in the opinion of the court, render it just and equitable that the partnership be dissolved.

Note that, after dissolution, the authority of each partner to bind the firm continues, so far as is necessary to complete transactions already started at the time of dissolution and also to wind up the affairs of the partnership. However, the partners cannot enter into new contracts.

The winding-up

This is usually completed by the partners themselves but there is provision in s 39 for this to be done by the court if any partner, or his representative, applies for it.

On dissolution, the value of the partnership property is realised and, if the partnership agreement is silent on the question, the proceeds are used to satisfy the following debts in the order in which they appear below:

(a) The debts and liabilities of the firm to outsiders.
(b) Paying any advance made by a partner beyond his agreed contribution to the capital.
(c) Repaying to each partner his contribution to the capital.
(d) The residue is divided between the partners in the same proportion as they shared the profits.

If the assets are insufficient to pay these debts, then the deficiency has to be made up from, first, the profits; next from the partnership capital and, lastly, if still necessary, from the partners contributing in the proportion in which they received their share of the profits.

FORMATION OF REGISTERED COMPANIES

Types of companies

A registered company is a corporate body created by registration under the Companies Act 1985. Companies may also be incorporated by the grant of a charter by the Crown or formed by a private Act of Parliament. Chartered companies include bodies such as the BBC and Oxford University, or professional bodies such as the Institute of Chartered Accountants. Only a handful of trading companies now operate under charter.

In the past, statutory companies were formed by a special Act of Parliament where it was necessary for them to have powers to compulsorily purchase land and monopolistic rights. Such companies included railway companies, canal companies, water companies and gas companies. As a consequence of nationalisation, most statutory companies were taken over by public boards. More recently, many nationalised industries have been privatised and the public corporations replaced by registered companies such as British Gas plc. The remainder of this chapter is concerned with the nature of registered companies and their formation under the provisions of the Companies Act 1985.

The nature of a registered company

A registered company is a corporate body which has been incorporated by registration either under the Companies Act 1985 or under previous companies legislation. As a consequence of incorporation, the company acquires separate corporate personality. It becomes an independent legal person in its own right, distinct from its members and officers. A legal person is someone with status in the eyes of the law; a person having rights and duties under the law. The law recognises natural legal persons who are human beings and also artificial legal persons such as registered companies.

It is the key element of separate corporate personality which gives rise to the features which make a company so attractive as a vehicle for carrying on business: the company may sue and be sued in its own name; only the company has rights and duties under the contracts which it enters; the company has title to its own property; it enjoys the benefits of perpetual succession; and its members may enjoy limited liability.

The leading case on the concept of separate corporate personality and its effects is that of **Salomon *v* Salomon & Co Ltd [1897] AC 22**. Salomon formed a company. The seven members of the company were Salomon plus six members of his family. The six family members held one share each and Salomon held 20 000 shares. Salomon, as an individual, sold his boot business to the new company, Salomon & Co Ltd. The contract price was £30 000. In payment, Salomon received 20 000 £1 shares in the new company. Salomon became a secured creditor in respect of the remaining £10 000. The company failed and was wound up with assets amounting to only £6000; £7000 was owed to unsecured creditors. In addition, the £10 000 balance of the purchase price of the business was still owed to Salomon. Salomon, as the only creditor with security, claimed he should be paid first. This would leave nothing for the rest of the creditors. The unsecured creditors claimed that Salomon and the company were really one and the same person and, since a person cannot owe money to himself, they should be paid first. The House of Lords held that the company was a separate person entirely from Salomon as an individual. One person, the company, owed money to another person, Salomon. Salomon was held entitled to the £6000 and the unsecured creditors got nothing.

Subsequent decisions have upheld the rule in *Salomon*'s case. In **McAura *v* Northern Assurance Co Ltd [1925] AC 619** the majority shareholder in a company transferred the ownership of a forest to the company. The shareholder had taken out an insurance policy on the forest but the company did not insure the forest after the transfer of ownership. When the forest burnt down, the insurance company refused to make payment to the individual shareholder. The insurers argued that he had no insurable interest in property belonging to someone else, namely the company. The court agreed with the insurance company.

In **Lee *v* Lee's Air Farming Ltd [1961] AC 12** Mr Lee formed a company in which he held 2999 of the 3000 shares. The business of the company was aerial crop spraying and Mr Lee, as director, appointed himself as chief pilot. Mr Lee was killed when his plane crashed. Legislation provided that widows of employees killed at work could claim compensation from the employer who could then claim repayment from a government fund. Mrs Lee sought payment of such compensation. It was held that, following the rule in Salomon's case, Mr Lee as an individual was employed by the company and Mrs Lee was entitled to the compensation.

As a consequence of the concept of separate corporate personality, there exists what has come to be known as the 'veil of incorporation'. As a general rule the courts will not look behind the separate personality of the company to the reality beyond. Only in certain circumstances will the courts disregard the rule in Salomon's case and 'lift the veil of incorporation'.

In the following situations, the court will ignore the concept of separate corporate personality:

1 Where the number of members of a *public* company falls below the statutory minimum of two. Where this continues for more than six months, the remaining member becomes personally liable for the debts of the company.
2 Where an officer of the company, for example the company secretary, signs a cheque or similar document on behalf of the company without stating the company name or wrongly stating the company name, the officer is personally liable if the company fails to pay.
3 Where the company is a mere 'sham' formed by an individual to do something which the individual himself is legally barred from doing. In such cases the court will not permit this misuse of separate corporate personality.
4 Where, in time of war, the company is thought to be under the control of enemy aliens. Normally, the nationality of a company depends upon the situation of its registered office and the nationality of its members is irrelevant. However, during the First World War, it was held that to trade with a company registered in England would amount to unlawful trading with the enemy because all the members of the company bar one were German.
5 An English decision, **DHN Food Distributors** *v* **Tower Hamlets LBC [1976] 3 All ER 462** suggested that individual companies should not be regarded as separate entities where they formed part of a group of companies and in reality the group traded as a single commercial enterprise. However, in the Scottish case of **Woolfson** *v* **Strathclyde Regional Council 1978 SC (HL) 90**, where the facts were very similar, the opposite view was taken. In the Woolfson case, two companies owned premises and a third company carried on business in them. The Woolfson family were majority shareholders in all three companies. The premises were compulsorily purchased by the Regional Council. Compensation was payable under a variety of headings. Simply put, the total compensation would be greater if the three companies were regarded as being in reality one person. Less would be paid if the companies were regarded as being three separate legal persons. It was held there was no basis for disregarding the rule in Salomon's case and each of the three companies was a separate legal person.

Classification of registered companies

Registered companies may be classified according to whether they are public companies or private companies. In addition, companies may be classified by reference to whether or not the members of the company enjoy limited liability. There are three types of registered company:

1 companies where the liability of the members is limited by shares;
2 companies where the liability of members is limited by guarantee;
3 companies where the liability of the members is unlimited.

Liability of the members limited by shares

The liability of the company to pay its debts is not limited. However, the liability of the members to contribute towards paying off the debts of the company is limited to the amount, if any, which remains unpaid on the shares which they hold. If a member's shares are fully paid up then he has no further liability to contribute to the assets of the company. Companies where liability is limited by shares may be either public or private companies.

Liability of the members limited by guarantee

The liability of a member of a company limited by guarantee is limited to an amount specified in the memorandum of association. The specified amount represents the amount which he has agreed to pay towards the assets of the company if it is wound up. At one time a guarantee company could also be registered with a share capital which meant that members had to pay any amount outstanding on their shares plus the amount of the guarantee. Such dual liability companies are no longer able to be registered. Any new guarantee companies must be registered as private companies.

Liability of the members is unlimited

The liability of members to contribute to the assets of the company is unlimited. Members may be called upon to pay any amount. Such a company can only be registered as a private company.

Public companies and private companies

A public company must be registered as a public company and it must state in its memorandum of association that it is a public company.

A private company is a company which is not a public company.

The differences between public and private companies

Number of members – a public company must have a minimum of two members. There is no upper limit on the number of members a public company may have. Until 14 July 1992 a private company also had to have a minimum of two members. However, in terms of the Companies (Single Member Private Limited

Companies) Regulations 1992, from 15 July 1992 private companies limited by shares or by guarantee may be formed by one person or may have one member. There is no upper limit on the number of members a private company may have.

Company name – the name of a public company must end in 'public limited company' or 'plc'. The name of a private company must end in the word 'limited' or 'ltd'.

Free transfer of shares – members of a public company must be free to transfer their shares as they please. The articles of a private company may provide for a right of pre-emption so that when a member wishes to transfer his shares, they must be offered first to existing members.

Share capital – a public company must have a minimum issued share capital with a nominal value of £50 000. Private companies are subject to no minimum capital requirement.

Dealings in shares – the shares of a public company may be listed on the stock exchange. Those of private companies may not. A public company can offer shares and debentures to the public. A private company may not do so.

Directors and company secretary – a public company must have a minimum of two directors. A private company needs only one director. A director of a public company must retire at 70 whereas there is no upper age limit on the directors of private companies, unless the company is a subsidiary of a public company. The company secretary of a public company must now have minimum qualifications.

Accounts – a public company must produce audited accounts within seven months after the end of the accounting period. A private company must produce accounts within ten months and may be able to obtain partial exemption from publishing accounts.

Commencement of business – a private company can start trading as soon as it obtains its certificate of incorporation from the Registrar of Companies. A public company, once incorporated, is not allowed to commence business until it obtains a further certificate from the Registrar of Companies, known as a 'trading certificate'. In terms of the Companies Act 1985 s 177 the Registrar will not issue the trading certificate unless he is satisfied that the nominal value of the allotted share capital is not less than £50 000 and that not less than one-quarter of the nominal value of the issued shares plus the whole amount of any premium has been received. This requires further explanation.

A company will state in its memorandum of association, its nominal or authorised share capital and its division into shares of a fixed amount. This represents the number of shares which a company is entitled to issue. For example, £100 000 divided into 100 000 £1 shares. Although the nominal value of each share is £1, the shares may be issued at a price higher than their face value. If £1 shares are issued at a price of £1.50, the extra 50 pence is known as the premium.

The issued capital represents the nominal value of the shares which have been allotted to members. For example, if 50 000 shares have been issued, the issued capital is £50 000. However, the company may not receive full payment for the shares at once. The amount which they have actually received towards payment for the shares which they have issued is known as the paid up share capital. The amount still to be received is referred to as the 'balance on call'.

In order to obtain a trading certificate, a public company must have an issued share capital of at least £50 000. Of that £50 000, the company must have received payment of at least one-quarter of the nominal value of the shares issued. If £50 000 worth of shares have been issued, the company must have received at least £12 500 in payment. If the shares were issued at a premium of 50 pence, the company must have received payment of the whole premium for every share issued. Accordingly, if 50 000 £1 shares have been issued at a price of £1.50, the company must have received payment of £25 000 in respect of the premium payable. In order to obtain their trading certificate the company must show that they have received a total of £37 500.

If a public company which has been incorporated does business without a s 117 certificate, third parties may enforce contracts against the company. If the company fails to honour such contracts, the third party may bring an action against the company's directors who shall be jointly and severally liable.

Promoters and pre-incorporation contracts

Promoters

A company is formed by incorporation under the Companies Act 1985 by the issue of a certificate of incorporation by the Registrar of Companies. Incorporation is achieved by the promoters of a company. A promoter has been defined as 'one who undertakes to form a company with reference to a given project, and to set it going, and who takes the necessary steps to accomplish that purpose'. This definition does not include persons who act in a professional capacity on behalf of the promoter, such as solicitors or accountants.

The relationship between a promoter and the company which he is forming is a fiduciary one. As a consequence of this, a promoter is not allowed to make a secret profit. He is under an obligation to disclose to the company any advantage gained from acting as promoter. A promoter *is* allowed to make a profit for himself so long as the company is fully aware of it. There must be disclosure to an independent board of directors or to potential members of the company. In the event of non-disclosure of a secret profit there are a number of remedies which the company may exercise against the promoter. The company may bring an action for the recovery of the amount of the secret profit. If the secret profit was made as a result of the sale of property by the promoter to the company, the company may resile from the contract and recover the purchase price.

A promoter has no legal entitlement to be paid for his services. However, the articles of the company usually give the first directors discretionary powers to pay all the expenses incurred in promoting and registering the company. In practice such powers are generally exercised.

Pre-incorporation contracts

Prior to incorporation, a company has no legal personality and therefore cannot have contractual capacity. However, the promoter may enter into contracts for the purchase or lease of premises, or for the purchase of machinery, raw materials, office equipment or stock, in anticipation of the company being formed. Contracts made ostensibly on behalf of a company yet to be registered are known as pre-incorporation contracts. When the promoter enters into such contracts he is not regarded as the agent of the company. This is because an agent must have a principal who is a legal person with contractual capacity.

The result is that the company, once formed, has no rights or liabilities under contracts entered into by the promoter prior to incorporation. The company cannot sue to enforce such a contract and cannot be sued by the third party. If the company, once formed, does not honour the transaction, the third party may bring an action for breach of contract against the promoter. The liability of the promoter in respect of pre-incorporation contracts is clearly laid down in s 36(4) of the Companies Act 1985.

Such liability may be avoided by inserting a clause in the contract which expressly frees the promoter from liability. Alternatively, the promoter may choose to prepare contracts in draft form, to be entered into by the company after incorporation.

Registration procedure

A company is formed when the Registrar of Companies (in Edinburgh for Scottish companies) issues a **certificate of incorporation**. The certificate of incorporation proves conclusively that the statutory requirements in respect of registration have been complied with. If the company is a public company, the certificate must contain a statement to that effect. As at the date given on the certificate, the company is created as a corporate body with legal personality. On that date, a private company may commence business but a public company must wait until it obtains its trading certificate under s 117 of the 1985 Act.

In order to obtain the certificate of incorporation, the following documents must be delivered to the Registrar of Companies together with the registration fee:

1 The memorandum of association.
2 The articles of association – these may be drawn up specially for the company, or standard statutory Table A articles may be adopted.
3 A statement signed by the subscribers to the memorandum containing details of the first directors and company secretary including the signed consent of these persons to act; and the address of the registered office.
4 A Statutory Declaration of Compliance, made by a solicitor or by one of the first directors or company secretary, to the effect that all statutory registration requirements have been complied with.

If the Registrar of Companies considers everything to be in order and that the name and objects of the company are lawful, he issues a certificate of incorporation and publishes a notice in the *Edinburgh Gazette* that it has been issued.

The memorandum of association

The memorandum of association may be thought of as the company's constitution or charter. It defines the company's activities and powers and contains information of interest to outsiders dealing with the company. It is one of the documents which must be delivered to the Registrar of Companies in order to achieve incorporation. The Companies (Tables A–F) Regulations 1985 provide model forms of memorandum. Table F gives the model form of a memorandum for a public company limited by shares and Table B provides the model for a private company limited by shares.

The memorandum of association must state:

1 the name of the company;
2 whether the registered office is to be in England and Wales, or in Wales, or in Scotland;
3 the objects of the company;
4 if the liability of the members is limited by shares or by guarantee;
5 where the company has a share capital, its amount and its division into shares of a fixed amount.

In addition, if the company is a public company, the memorandum must contain the statement, 'The company is to be a public company'.

The final clause of the memorandum of association is the association clause. This contains a statement that the subscribers to the memorandum wish to be formed into a company. The memorandum must be signed, if it is a public company, by at least two subscribers who state how many shares they wish to take. The signatures must be witnessed.

The name clause

If a company is a public company, its name must end in the words 'public limited company' or 'plc'. If a company is a private company its name must end with the word 'limited' or 'ltd'. Certain private companies limited by guarantee may apply to be allowed to dispense with the use of the word 'limited' in their name. Such exemption is restricted to non-profit making companies with charitable, religious or educational objects.

The Registrar of Companies keeps an index of the names of all registered companies. The Registrar has powers to control the choice of a company name. No company may have the same name as an existing company. No company may choose a name which, in the opinion of the Registrar, would suggest a link with the government or with a local authority. A company name must not include words or expressions which are prohibited by regulations made under the 1985 Act or words which are considered offensive.

A company may change its name voluntarily by passing a special resolution. A change of name may be compulsory where the Registrar believes that the name is too similar to that of another company or is misleading the public. If the Registrar fails to act, another company may bring a court action for 'passing off' to stop the use of a name which it alleges is causing confusion between the two companies (see pp. 245–7). In the event of a change of name, the Registrar makes the necessary change in the register and issues an altered certificate of incorporation.

The registered office clause

The clause does not give the address of the registered office but merely states whether it is to be situated in England and Wales, or in Scotland, or in Wales. A separate statement of the address of the registered office is given to the Registrar when application for registration is being made. The registered office is the place where contact may be made with the company. It is the place where documents and writs may be effectively served. Certain of the company's registers must also be kept here. While a company may change the address of its registered office within the country in which it is registered, it is not allowed to move its registered office across borders. A company which states that its registered office is to be situated in Scotland can move its registered office from Edinburgh to Aberdeen, but it cannot move it to Manchester. The registered office clause cannot be altered.

The objects clause

This clause sets out the purposes for which the company has been set up. The traditional position was that the company had to act within the confines of the objects clause at all times. Any act which was not covered by the objects clause was said to be *ultra vires*, ie outwith the powers of the company, and void. If the company entered into a contract which was *ultra vires*, the contract could not be enforced by or against the company. Outsiders dealing with the company were placed in a dangerous position because of the doctrine of constructive notice. Under this doctrine they were treated as knowing what the objects clause said, even if they had not read it.

The position of outsiders contracting with companies was improved by the passing of the European Communities Act 1972. Section 9 of the 1972 Act, which later became s 35 of the Companies Act 1985, provided that any contract entered into by a person in good faith and which had been decided upon by the directors was deemed to be within the contractual capacity of the company and was enforceable against the company. However, further changes were made by the Companies Act 1989.

First, s 3A in the Companies Act 1985 allows a company to state that its object is to carry on business as a general commercial company in any trade or business whatsoever. Where such an objects clause is adopted, the *ultra vires* rule ceases to have any relevance whatsoever.

Second, as far as the protection of persons contracting with companies is concerned, s 35(1) provides that no act by a company may be questioned on the basis that it was beyond its legal capacity as stated in the memorandum. In practice, all contracts entered into by a company shall be enforceable by and against the company.

In terms of s 4 of the Companies Act (inserted by s 110 of the Companies Act 1989), a company is free to amend its objects clause by passing a special resolution.

The limitation of liability clause

Where the liability of members of a company is limited either by shares or by guarantee, the memorandum must state that the liability of the members is limited.

The capital clause

Where the company is one where the liability of members is limited by shares, this clause states the amount of the nominal or authorised share capital of the company and its division into shares of a fixed amount. For example, the clause might state that, 'The share capital of the company is £100 000 divided into 100 000 shares of £1 each'.

The authorised share capital represents the number of shares which the company may issue. In this example, the nominal or 'par' value of each share is £1. As was stated above, the shares may be issued at a price higher than their nominal value. The difference between the nominal value of the share and the higher price at which it is issued is called the premium.

A public company must have a minimum authorised share capital of £50 000.

The articles of association

The articles of association deal with the internal affairs of the company and govern such matters as the issue and transfer of shares, the appointment and powers of directors, the conduct of company meetings and the payment of dividends. A company may draw up its own articles. If a company does not register its own articles, the model form of articles contained in Table A of the Companies (Tables A–F) Regulations 1985 shall automatically apply.

Articles are required to be printed rather than typed, divided into numbered paragraphs and signed by each subscriber to the memorandum. The signatures must be witnessed. The articles may be altered by a special resolution in general meeting. In addition, new provisions, introduced by the Companies Act 1989, allow the articles of a **private** company to be altered, without the need for a meeting, if all the shareholders agree in writing.

The company's power to alter its articles cannot be excluded. However, any alteration of the articles is void if it conflicts with the memorandum of association and no member of the company may be compelled by an alteration of the articles to accept increased liability unless he has consented in writing. Furthermore, it has been held that the power to alter the articles must be exercised in good faith and for the benefit of the company as a whole.

The legal effect of the memorandum and articles

The effect of the provisions of the Companies Act 1985 s 14(1) is that the memorandum and articles are regarded as forming a contract between the company and each member. Section 14 has been interpreted so that the result is that:

1 Individual members can enforce the provisions of the articles against the company **if** the member is enforcing a right which he enjoys in his capacity as a member. In **Wood *v* Odessa Waterworks Co (1889) 2 ChD. 636** the articles of a company required the company, if it declared a dividend, to pay it in cash. The company passed a resolution to pay a dividend by issuing debentures rather than paying cash. The shareholders were held entitled to a court order preventing this resolution being put into effect.

2 The provisions of the articles are enforceable by the company against each of the members. In **Hickman *v* Kent or Romney Marsh Sheep Breeders Association [1915] 1 Ch 881** the articles of association provided that disputes between the association and its members had to be referred to arbitration. A dispute arose when the association refused to register some of Hickman's sheep and he was threatened with expulsion. Hickman sought an injunction from the court to prevent this. It was held that the association was entitled to have the court action suspended until arbitration took place.

3 Individual members of the company can enforce the provisions of the articles against one another. In **Rayfield *v* Hands [1960] Ch 1** the articles provided that if a member wished to transfer his shares, he had to inform the directors, 'who will take the said shares equally between them at fair value'. The directors refused to purchase the plaintiff's shares. It was held that the articles created a contract between the plaintiff and the directors in their capacity as members. The directors were contractually bound to purchase the shares.

4 The provisions of the articles cannot be enforced against the company by outsiders or by members who are pursuing rights in another capacity. In **Eley *v* Positive Life Assurance Co Ltd (1876) 1 Ex D 88** the articles provided for Eley's appointment as company solicitor. He acted as solicitor for some time and also acquired some shares in the company. The company dismissed Eley and he brought an action for breach of contract based upon the provision in the articles. His action failed because the articles did not constitute a contract between the company and Eley in his capacity as solicitor. The company's action did not infringe any rights under the articles, such as the right to vote at meetings, which Eley enjoyed in his capacity as a member of the company.

QUESTIONS

1 Sam and David are thinking of setting up in business as joiners. They intend to lease premises and the cost of buying a van and equipment would amount to something in the region of £12 000. Sam has £10 000 to invest and David £5000. They seek your advice on whether they should enter into a partnership or form a private company. Advise them.

2 State, with reasons, whether the provisions of the Business Names Act 1985 would apply in the following situations:

(a) George Brown and Fred Smith carry on business under the name of Brown and Smith.
(b) Dunedin Haulage Ltd carry on business under the name of Dunedin Haulage Ltd (formerly Fairley & Co).
(c) Duncan Brown carries on a restaurant business under the name 'The Pizza Pantry'.

3 Give the definition of a partnership. How is a partnership constituted?

4 What is a partner's liability for the debts of the firm?

5 In which circumstances may a partnership be terminated?

6 John, Paul and George carry on business in partnership in Glasgow. The firm has a retail business where musical instruments and amplifiers are sold. Discuss the legal implications of the following events:

(a) John informs Paul and George that he wishes to introduce his best friend Ringo as a partner.
(b) Paul has been convicted of embezzling funds from his local golf club of which he was treasurer.
(c) George has ordered a guitar and some hi-fi equipment ostensibly for the firm.
(d) It transpires that George, without the consent of his two partners, has for the past year been conducting for his personal benefit and profit, a business competing with the partnership.

7 Discuss the principle of separate corporate personality as enunciated in the case of *Salomon* v *Salomon & Co Ltd* [1897] *AC* 22 and describe the circumstances in which the rule in the *Salomon* case may be disregarded by the courts.

8 Describe the main differences between a public and a private company.

9 List the documents which must be lodged with the Registrar of Companies when applying for registration of a company.

10 Describe the purpose and contents of a company's memorandum of association and discuss the legal effects of the articles of association.

12 Business property and rights in security

NATURE OF OWNERSHIP

When we speak of property we may mean one of two things. We may be referring to a person's ownership of an item, or we may be referring to the item itself.

Property as the right of ownership is said to bring with it the right of exclusive possession, and the right to use, enjoy and dispose of a thing, except insofar as the rights of ownership are restricted by the law or by agreement. For example, an owner's right to do what he wants with land and buildings may be restircted by statutory provisions such as the Town and Country Planning (Scotland) Act 1972 or by the common law of nuisance.

An individual may be the sole owner of property. However, there are other forms of property ownership whereby a single piece of property is owned by two or more persons. Property may be owned either jointly or in common.

Joint property

Where property is owned by two or more persons jointly, the rights of ownership vest in the group as a whole, ownership is said to be *pro indiviso*. No-one has an independent right in the property. An individual cannot transfer his right in joint property separately to anyone either during his lifetime or on his death, eg by a provision in his will. On the death of one joint owner, his right passes to the surviving joint owners. Members of a club are joint owners of 'club property'. Similarly partnership property is held jointly.

Common property

Where property is owned by two or more persons in common, each owner enjoys a separate title to his own share of the property. Each owner has the right to dispose of his share as he pleases, either during his lifetime or on his death. Accordingly, on death, the share of one common owner does not pass to the surviving common owners.

Each common owner has a right of veto in respect of proposals regarding the management of the property unless they relate to essential repairs which must go ahead.

For as long as property is held in common, no single owner may lay claim to a particular part of the property as his share. However, any of the common owners may demand that the property is divided up. Where the owners cannot reach agreement on how this is to be done, or where the nature of the property is such that physical division is impracticable, the court may be asked to order the sale of the property and a division of the profits.

Common interest

There is another type of right which is known as common interest. It arises where several owners, each with their own individual rights in separate properties, are united by some form of common interest. The right of an individual owner to do as he pleases with his property is restricted by the common interest of the others. The most common example of a situation where common interest arises is found in the case of tenement property. As well as owning their own flat within the tenement, each of the owners has an interest in the whole building. The rights and obligations of the owners normally will be regulated by the title deeds to the property. However, in the absence of such provision, the common law of tenement will apply.

Possession

Ownership brings with it the right of exclusive possession. The institutional writer Stair defined possession as the holding or detaining of any thing by ourselves, or others for our use. Possession requires both an act of the body and an act of the mind. The act of the body involves the physical detention and holding of the property. The act of the mind involves the intention to make use of the property for one's own benefit. This intention is known as the *animus possidendi* and without it there can be no possession but merely custody, as for example when an employee has custody of his employer's property. There may be either natural possession or civil possession. There is natural possession if the act of detention is done by the owner himself; for example, jewellery is worn or a house is occupied. Civil possession occurs where the property is held by others on the owner's behalf; for example, a landlord has civil possession of his house through a tenant or an employer has civil possession of property through an employee.

There is a general presumption that the person in possession of corporeal moveable property (ie tangible property other than land and buildings, e.g., cars and jewellery) is the owner of such property. Such a presumption must be overcome by providing evidence to the contrary.

In addition possession of heritable property (i.e., land and buildings) brings with it certain benefits. A person who has openly and peacefully possessed heritage for at least seven years, and whose possession is based on an apparently valid title, is entitled to exercise certain possessory remedies should his ownership be challenged. He may seek an interdict preventing his removal from the property, or an order allowing him to regain possession if he has been removed, until the question of who is the true owner is finally determined.

The *bona fide* possessor who genuinely but mistakenly believes he is the owner of heritage acquires the right to retain the 'fruits' of the property in the form of crops or rents and is also entitled to payment from the true owner for any improvements carried out. There is no liabiliby for 'violent profits', which are penal damages that would have to be paid to the true owner only by a person occupying the property in bad faith.

Finally, in terms of the Prescription and Limitation (Scotland) Act 1973, where a person has openly and peacefully possessed heritage for a continuous period of ten years and his possession is based on an apparently valid title deed recorded in the General Register of Sasines or the Land Register, his ownership of the land cannot be challenged.

Landownership

In Scotland this is based on a feudal system of landownership which dates back to the twelfth century. Every landowner should be able to trace the ownership of their property back to an original grant of the land by the Crown. The feudal chain began with the king granting land to noblemen in exchange for their loyalty. These noblemen would in turn grant part of that land to others, also in exchange for service or other homage. Each person granting a portion of land to another would become the grantee's superior. The grantee is known as the feuar. In more recent times land was sold in return for a purchase price plus the payment of an annual feu duty. However, since 1974 no new feu duties have been able to be imposed and whenever heritable property is sold the obligation to pay feu duty is extinguished by a once-and-for-all lump sum payment to the superior. Despite the removal of the annual payment of money, the feudal relationship between superior and feuar persists and the superior is entitled to impose and enforce feuing conditions – for example, forbidding the keeping of pigeons in the garden.

When a contract is formed for the purchase of heritable property, that is when missives are concluded by the acceptance of an offer, the purchaser obtains only a personal right – a *jus ad rem* – to sue the seller for damages should the sale not go through because of the seller's failure to implement the transaction.

A purchaser obtains a real right – a *jus in re* – i.e., a right of ownership which can be defended against the whole world, only when a disposition granted by the seller is registered in either the General Register of Sasines or the new Land Register.

CLASSIFICATION OF PROPERTY

Property, in the sense of items of property, may be classified according to whether it is:

1 heritable or moveable;
2 corporeal or incorporeal;

3 fungible or non-fungible.

Heritable or moveable property

The most important division is the division of property into either heritable or moveable property.

Heritable property – or heritage – consists of land; things permanently attached to the land such as buildings; things which are part of the land such as trees and grass and minerals; and rights connected with the land such as a servitude right of access.

Moveable property is property which is capable of motion. All property other than heritable property is moveable property.

Corporeal or incorporeal property

Property may also be classified according to whether it is corporeal or incorporeal. Corporeal property is tangible, it has a physical presence. You can see and touch corporeal property, e.g., a car. Incorporeal property is intangible, it has no physical presence. Incorporeal property consists of rights, e.g., copyright.

Accordingly the interaction between heritable and moveable property on the one hand, and between corporeal and incorporeal property on the other, means that any item of property will fall into one of four groups:

1 **Corporeal heritable property** – such as land or buildings.
2 **Incorporeal heritable property** – such as leases and servitudes.
3 **Corporeal moveable property** – such as cars, furniture and jewellery.
4 **Incorporeal moveable property** – such as patents, trade marks and copyright.

Patents, trade marks and copyright are also forms of what has come to be known as intellectual property. Intellectual property and its protection will be discussed later in the chapter.

The **goodwill** of a business is a special case. Goodwill is always incorporeal. However, depending on the circumstances it may be either heritable or moveable. Where the goodwill of a business arises mainly from the favourable location of the business premises, it will be incorporeal heritable property. Where the goodwill stems from the personal reputation of the seller of the business, it will be incorporeal moveable property.

Fungibles or non-fungibles

Property may also be classified as either fungible or non-fungible. Fungible property is property which can be weighed out or measured and is destroyed through being used, such as grain or coal. By its nature, fungible property may be replaced by equal quantities of the same quality. By contrast, non-fungible property is something with an individual value, such as an antique vase or a pedigree bull, which cannot be replaced by something similar. For example, should you lend a five-pound note (fungible) to a friend you would be quite happy to be repaid by being given five one-pound coins or a different five-pound note. However, should you lend a painting (non-fungible) for display in a charity exhibition you would not be happy to have a different painting returned to you, even if it was one of a similar value.

Fixtures

Anything annexed to heritable property, that is fastened to or connected with it and not merely set alongside it, is a fixture. On becoming a fixture, what was previously moveable becomes heritable and belongs to the owner of the heritage. Also, as a general rule, once something has become a fixture it cannot be removed except by the owner of the heritage. Whether or not something is a fixture may be important when heritable property, business premises or a house, for example, is being purchased. The seller must include in the contract a provision that it is his intention to remove a fixture. In the absence of any such provision in the contract, the purchaser may argue that a particular article is a fixture and as such is included in the purchase price and must be left. The seller may disagree and contend that the article is not a fixture and may be removed by him. Certain factors which assist in determining whether or not an article is a fixture were set out by a court of seven judges in the case of **Scottish Discount Co Ltd** *v* **Blin 1986 SLT 123**:

1 The degree and extent of physical attachment to the heritage.
2 Whether the article can be removed without damage to either the article or the land or building to which it is attached.
3 Whether the attachment was of a permanent or quasi-permanent nature.
4 Whether the building was specially adapted to accommodate the article.
5 The extent to which the use or enjoyment of the land or building would be affected by the removal of the article.
6 The intention of the person attaching it as evidenced by the nature of the article and the building and the manner in which it is attached.

The greater the degree of physical attachment of the article to the heritage, the more likely it is that an article is a fixture. However, very heavy items which are attached to the ground merely by their own weight have been held to be fixtures. In addition certain moveables which are regarded as accessory to heritage are known as constructive fixtures, for example the key to a house.

The fact that an article is physically attached to the land or building is not of itself conclusive evidence that the article is a fixture. Also relevant to the question of whether or not an article is a fixture is the purpose of the attachment. If the purpose was to improve the heritage, then the article is likely to be considered a fixture. However, if the article was attached so that it could be better enjoyed for itself, e.g., a painting hung on a wall, then it is probably not a fixture. Similarly, notwithstanding a degree of physical attachment to the heritage, carpets nailed to the floor would not be regarded as fixtures.

Who has the right to remove fixtures?

In certain exceptional cases, a person other than the owner of the heritage may have the right to remove a fixture. For example, a tenant may be able to remove trade fixtures which have been attached by him for the purposes of his trade and also ornamental fixtures which have been attached for his better enjoyment of them. However, this right of removal is subject to the requirement that neither the heritage nor the fixture are damaged in the process.

INTELLECTUAL PROPERTY AND ITS PROTECTION

This sort of property is an important business resource. It consists of patents, trade marks, service marks, designs and copyright.

Patents

An inventor of a new product or process may apply to the Patent Office in London for the grant of a patent which will give him a monopoly right in the invention for a period of 20 years. Prior to a patent being granted, the invention must satisfy three conditions:

1 It must be new – it must not form part of the existing state of the art, i.e., it must not have been available to the public in any form or manner prior to the application being made.
2 It must involve an inventive step – i.e., an expert in the field would not regard it as merely an obvious development of existing technology.
3 It must be capable of industrial or agricultural use.

In terms of the Patents Act 1977, a patent is incorporeal moveable property. Its value may be exploited by 'selling' the patent or by granting a licence to allow someone to make the product or use the process. It may be offered as security for a loan. A patent prevents others making or selling or using a product or making use of a process without the inventor's consent. Should the inventor's rights under the patent be infringed, he may obtain an interdict and possibly also damages or an accounting and payment of profits. He may also seek delivery or destruction of any products which infringe the patent.

Trade marks and service marks

Trade marks are found on goods and indicate a trade connection between the goods and the person entitled to use the mark either as its proprietor or as a registered user or licensee. An example would be 'Kodak'. A service mark is used in connection with services and indicates that a particular person is connected in the course of a business with the provision of those services. Examples of these would include 'TSB' or 'McDonald's'. Essentially the purpose of such marks is to enable consumers to distinguish the goods or services offered by one business from those offered by another.

The relevant law is now to be found in the Trade Marks Act 1994 which came into force on 31 October 1994. The 1994 Act replaced the Trade Marks Act 1938 and sought to implement the EC Directive to Approximate the Laws of Member States Relating to Trade Marks (89/104/EEC).

In terms of the Trade Marks Act 1994, a person who wishes to obtain a property right in a trade or service mark (as incorporeal moveable property) may seek to register the mark in the Register of Trade Marks. The proprietor of a mark can transfer his ownership of the mark to someone else. In addition he may, by means of a licensing agreement, allow others to use the mark; details of such licences must be registered. In addition registration gives the proprietor the rights and remedies afforded by the Act. Registration is for an initial period of ten years and may be renewed for successive periods of ten years thereafter.

Registration of a mark can be sought only in respect of a particular class of goods or services. An applicant for registration must state the goods or services for which the mark is to be registered and state that the mark is being used by him in relation to such goods or services, or that he has a *bona fide* intention to make such use of the mark. In addition a representation of the mark must be inserted in a box on the application form.

Section 1(1) of the 1994 Act defines a 'trade mark' as being 'any sign capable of being represented graphically which is capable of distinguishing goods and services of one undertaking from those of other undertakings' and 'may, in particular consist of words (including personal names), designs, letters, numerals, or the shape of the goods or their packaging'.

Registration of a trade mark may be refused on either 'absolute grounds' or 'relative grounds'. Absolute grounds for refusal are linked to the nature of the mark itself, for example the mark is devoid of any distinctive character or it consists exclusively of indications of characteristics of goods and services such as kind, quality, quantity, purpose, value, origin or time of production. A trade mark will not be registered if it is contrary to public policy or accepted morality, if the public are likely to be deceived or if the application is made in bad faith. Relative grounds are concerned with the trade mark being identical with or similar to an earlier trade mark. Registration of a trade mark in respect of a particular class of goods or services gives the proprietor the exclusive right to use the mark in relation to goods and services of that particular class. That right will be infringed if another person uses in the course of trade an identical sign in relation to identical goods or services. There will also be an infringement where another person uses an identical sign in relation to similar goods and services *or* a similar sign in relation to identical or similar goods and services *and* the public are likely to be confused. Even where an identical or similar sign is used in relation to goods which are not similar to those for which the trade mark is registered, there will be an infringement if the registered trade mark has a reputation in the UK which will be damaged or unfairly exploited by the use of the sign.

In the event of such infringement, various remedies are available to the proprietor of the trade mark. The proprietor may seek an interdict forbidding further misuse of the mark and may seek to have the offending mark removed from the defender's goods. In the event that the mark is unable to be removed, the goods themselves may be ordered to be destroyed. An order may also be sought for the delivery to the proprietor of the trade mark of any infringing goods. In addition, the proprietor may seek damages or an accounting and payment of profits made by the defender through his misuse of the mark.

However, the Act provides that a registered mark is not infringed by 'the use of indications concerning the kind, quality, quantity, intended purpose, value, geographical origin, the time of production of goods or of rendering of services, or other characteristics of goods or services' or 'the use of the trade mark to indicate the intended purpose of a product or service'. This defence was considered in **Bravado Merchandising Services Ltd** *v* **Mainstream Publishing (Edinburgh) Ltd 1996 SLT 597**. In this case the owner of a trade mark 'Wet Wet Wet', the name of a pop group, sought an interdict against the publishers of a book about the group entitled 'A Sweet Little Mystery – Wet Wet Wet – The Inside Story'. It was claimed that the appearance of the name of the group on the cover of the book was an infringement of the trade mark. Lord McCluskey held, in the Outer House, that the publishers were using a mark identical to that registered by the proprietor in relation to books, which were goods for which it was registered. However, interdict was refused because the publisher's use of the mark was as an indication of the main characteristic of the book – the protected name could be used in the title of a book about the group as its use was to indicate what the book was about.

The Trade Marks Act 1994 creates certain criminal offences in relation to the unauthorised use of a trade mark. It is an offence, without the consent of the proprietor, to apply to goods or their packaging a sign identical to, or likely to be mistaken for a registered trade mark. It is also an offence to sell or expose for sale goods where the goods or their packaging bears such a sign. It is also an offence to apply such signs to material to be used for labelling or packaging goods or for advertising goods. A person found guilty of an offence faces on summary conviction up to six months' imprisonment and/or a fine of up to £5000 and on indictment up to ten years' imprisonment and an unlimited fine.

In addition to seeking to harmonise trade mark law throughout the European Community by means of the above Directive, the EC adopted on 20 December 1993 the Community Trade Mark Regulation which seeks to create a unitary or single trade mark which has effect throughout the whole of the Community. A Community Trade Mark Office has been established in Alicante in Spain and has been accepting applications for the registration of Community Trade Marks since January 1996.

Protection of unregistered marks: the law of passing off

Many businesses fail to register their trade or service marks and such unregistered marks lack the protection afforded by statute. In addition, certain aspects of a product's 'get-up', e.g., a distinctively shaped container, are ineligible for registration as a trade mark and so its producer must look to the common law for protection. At common law there is no right of property in a trade name or mark. However, a business may prevent the use by others of a name or mark by means of **a common law action for passing off**. The pursuer in a successful passing off action will obtain an interdict and possibly damages.

It is a delict for one business to pass off its own goods or services as those of another business. This is because a business enjoys a right of property in the *goodwill* or reputation which has been established in respect of its goods or services or in respect of its trade name or mark. A business is entitled to take action to prevent misrepresentation by the defender causing either harm to or the misappropriation of this goodwill. It is not a defence to a passing-off action that the defender's misleading use of a name or mark or packaging was not deliberate. Similarly it is not a defence to argue that no-one was actually misled; it is enough that the public was likely to be misled.

In order to be successful in an action for passing off, the pursuer must establish that the defender's activities are likely to cause harm to the pursuer's goodwill. The pursuer's goodwill is likely to be harmed only if the defender's activities cause confusion in the minds of the public. Obviously, before this is possible, the pursuer's name or logo must be firmly established in the minds of the public as being associated with the type of goods or services he makes or provides. If there is no likelihood of confusion, an action for passing off will fail. Accordingly the pursuer must persuade the court that there would be such confusion; e.g., the public will believe that they are buying the pursuer's goods or that the pursuer has control over or responsibility for the defender's goods or services. A pursuer may lose sales should the public buy the defender's goods believing them to be the pursuer's. In addition, the defender's goods, while looking the same as the pursuer's or bearing the pursuer's name or logo, may be of inferior quality, thus also causing damage to the pursuer's reputation and a further loss of sales in the future.

A recent successful passing-off action where likelihood of confusion was established was that of **Reckitt & Colman Products Ltd *v* Borden Inc. [1990] 1 All ER 873**. The plaintiffs in this case were the manufacturers of a well-known and long-established product, the Jif lemon, which was a lemon-shaped container containing lemon juice. The defendant's product, which, while not identical, was of a similar lemon shape and contained lemon juice, was held likely to confuse the public because of its deceptively similar 'get-up'. A product's 'get-up' includes its design and packaging. Similarly, in the case of **Haig & Co *v* Forth Blending Co 1954 SC 35**, the pursuers obtained an interdict to prevent the defenders selling whisky in an unusually shaped bottle which was sufficiently similar to the pursuer's own well-known Dimple brand bottle to cause confusion to customers and bar staff alike.

It will be easier for a business to establish that the public associate a particular name with its goods or services when the name is an invented or 'fancy' word. As a general rule a business cannot claim a monopoly in a descriptive word which is applicable to a class of goods rather than the goods of one particular business. For example, in the case of **McCain International Ltd *v* Country Fair Foods Ltd [1981] RPC 167**, the plaintiffs had been the first company to introduce 'oven chips' into the United Kingdom. It was held that the words 'oven chips' were descriptive of the product and that McCain could not claim a monopoly in that name. So long as other companies distinguished their product from that of McCain, they could use the words 'oven chips' in the name of their product. People buying 'Country Fair Oven Chips' would not think they were buying 'McCain Oven Chips'.

However, it is possible that a descriptive word may become so linked in the minds of the public with the goods or services of one business that the word acquires a secondary meaning associated with that business and other businesses may be prevented from using it. In addition a combination of descriptive words used together may enjoy protection. In the case of **Orkney Seafoods Ltd, Petitioners 1991 SLT 891**, Orkney Seafoods Ltd presented a petition asking the court to grant an interim interdict against a group of traders who had formed a group called Orkney Seafood Specialists to prevent the passing off of the latter's products as those of the petitioners. The petitioners had used the name for 15 years and had spent considerable sums promoting the name which, they argued, had become associated in the minds of the public with their products. They argued that they had acquired substantial goodwill and business reputation in that name and that the close similarity in names would confuse their customers and potential customers. The respondents argued that, as this was a descriptive name, the petitioners could claim no monopoly in it. Lord Wylie conceded that the words 'Orkney' and 'Seafood' or 'Seafoods' were words of description in respect of which the petitioners could not claim a monopoly. However, he stated that the question arose as to whether the use of these words in combination was calculated to lead to confusion. His lordship also took into account that the respondents' brochure was very similar to that of the petitioners. It was held that a prima facie case had been established that the similarity in name would cause confusion and lead to passing off the new group's products as those of the existing company. Interim interdict was granted.

There will be no likelihood of confusion where the pursuer and the defender are 'not engaged in a common field of activity'; i.e., they are not in the same or a related line of business. In the case of **Granada Group Ltd *v* Ford Motor Company Ltd [1973] RPC 49** Granada Televison failed to prevent Ford calling one of its models the Ford Granada because no-one would think that the television company had anything to do with the car. Similarly in **Scottish Milk Marketing Board *v* Drybrough & Co Ltd 1985 SLT 253** the pursuers failed to persuade the court that the public would confuse Scottish Pride Butter with Scottish Pride Lager

It is also worth noting that several manufacturers of a particular product are able to share in the goodwill which that product enjoys. Any one of those manufacturers may bring a passing-off action against anyone who seeks to cash in on the product's popularity by marketing an inferior imitation. Such cases have included the case of **Erven Warnink Besloten Vennootschap *v* J Townend & Sons (Hull) Ltd [1979] AC 731** in which a manufacturer of advocaat, a high-quality liqueur whose ingredients included brandy and fresh eggs, obtained an injunction (an English form of interdict) against the manufacturer of an inferior and cheaper product called 'Keeling's Old English Advocaat' which was made from Cyprus sherry and dried eggs. It could not be said that the public would confuse Keeling's Old English Advocaat with Warnink's Advocaat; they would not buy Keeling's in the mistaken belief that they were buying Warnink's. However, it was held that the reputation of genuine advocaat could suffer as a consequence of the deceptive use of the name by an inferior product.

Similarly, in the case of **Lang Brothers Ltd *v* Goldwell Ltd 1982 SLT 309**, the petitioners established that as blenders of Scotch whisky they had an interest in the reputation and goodwill enjoyed by the product. They took exception to a beverage known as 'Wee McGlen', which consisted of English ginger wine mixed with Scottish malt whisky. They argued that the 'get-up' of the product in a bottle with a tartan label and an advertisement featuring a be-tartaned Scotsman amounted to a passing off by the respondents of their product as a wholly Scottish product and was calculated to take advantage of the reputation and goodwill which attach to Scotch whisky. The petitioners feared that damage would be done to that reputation and goodwill as a consequence of the respondent's alleged misrepresentation.

As a final point it should be noted that activities which give rise to a civil action for passing off may also amount to a criminal offence in terms of the Trade Descriptions Act 1968 (see pp. 171–6).

Copyright

The rights of the owner of the copyright in certain creative works are protected by the Copyright, Designs and Patents Act 1988. Copyright in a work exists automatically without the need for any registration of the right. The types of works in which copyright may subsist are listed in s 1(1) of the Act as follows:

(a) Original literary, dramatic, musical or artistic works.
(b) Sound recordings, films, broadcasts or cable programmes.
(c) The typographical arrangement of published editions.

However, there is no copyright in original literary, dramatic and musical works unless and until the work is recorded in writing or otherwise; it is not enough that the idea for a book or a tune is in your head. Such works must be original in the sense that they are not copies of someone else's work. The idea need not be new but the way it is expressed should be. Literary works include any work, other than a dramatic or musical work, that is written, spoken or sung. The definition includes tables, compilations and computer programs. A dramatic work includes a work of dance or mime while a musical work is defined by the Act as a work consisting of music excluding any words or action intended to be sung, spoken or performed with the music. An artistic work is defined as a graphic work, photograph, sculpture or collage, irrespective of artistic quality; a work of architecture; or a work of artistic craftsmanship. A 'graphic work' includes such things as paintings, diagrams, maps, charts, engravings or etchings. A work of artistic craftsmanship might include a piece of fine furniture or an item of designer jewellery.

The duration of copyright depends upon the type of work involved. In respect of literary, dramatic, musical or artistic works, copyright exists during the lifetime of the author and then for a further 70-year period running from the end of the calendar year in which the author dies. Copyright in sound recordings and films exists for a period of 50 years from the end of the calendar year in which it is released (i.e., broadcast or shown in public) and, if it is never released, for 50 years from the end of the calendar year in which it is made. In respect of broadcasts and cable programmes, copyright lasts for 50 years from the end of the calendar year in which the broadcast was made or included in a cable programme service. The copyright in a typographical arrangement of a published edition exists for a period of 25 years from the end of the calendar year in which the edition was first published. This latter right protects the way a publisher has set out a book, e.g., in terms of the layout and the typeface used; it protects the 'look' of the book. This is a separate right from the author's right in the literary work itself and it can exist when copyright in the literary work has expired. For example, a publisher may produce a new edition of Shakespeare's sonnets; the sonnets themselves are not copyright but the publisher enjoys copyright in the appearance of the book.

The author, that is the creator of the work, may not always be the owner of the copyright. The general rule, that the creator is always the first owner of the copyright, does not always apply. For example, where the author is an employee who has created the work in the course of his employment, then, unless there is a provision to the contrary in the contract of employment, the copyright belongs to the employer. Copyright in a work may be assigned (i.e., transferred) to someone else; the assignation must be in writing and signed by the owner. For example, an author may transfer copyright in a book to his publisher. In addition copyright passes on death either in terms of a will or under the rules of intestate succession where there is no will. The copyright owner may, while retaining ownership, grant licences permitting licensees to (say) perform a play or broadcast a musical work. In terms of the 1988 Act, even although the author has transferred ownership of the copyright to someone else, he retains what are known as moral rights. These moral rights apply only in respect of literacy, dramatic, musical and artistic works and films. They include the right to be identified as the author of the work or the director of a film and the right to object to derogatory treatment of a work.

Section 16 of the 1988 Act sets out the rights of copyright owners. The copyright owner has the exclusive right to:

(a) copy the work;
(b) issue copies of the work to the public;
(c) perform, show or play the work in public;
(d) broadcast the work or include it in a cable programme service;
(e) make an adaptation of the work or do any of the above in relation to an adaptation.

The above are acts restricted by copyright and anyone who does any of these acts without the permission of the owner is said to have infringed the copyright. Remedies which may be available to the owner of the copyright and to any exclusive licensee include damages, interdict and an accounting and payment of profits. However, if it can be shown that at the time of the infringement the defender did not know and had no reason to suspect that copyright existed, there is no entitlement to damages and the pursuer's remedies will be limited to seeking an interdict and an accounting and payment of profits. On the other hand, the Act does make provision for the payment of additional, exemplary damages where there has been a particularly flagrant breach of copyright, and where the profit made as a consequence of the infringement would exceed the amount of damages which would normally have to be paid. In addition, the copyright owner may ask the court to order that infringing copies of the work are delivered to him.

The Act sets out certain actions known as the 'permitted acts' and these provide a defence to an infringement action. Permitted acts fall under a number of headings including 'fair dealing' in relation to a copyright work for the purposes of research and private study or for the purpose of criticism, review and the reporting of current events. Other permitted acts may be carried out by educational establishments, libraries and archives and in the course of public administration. Examples of these include making use of copyright work in an examination question or the performance of a copyright work before an audience consisting solely of teachers and fellow pupils; a librarian making a copy of an article for a person who requires the copy for his own private research or study; and making use of copyright material in the course of a statutory inquiry.

Designs

The law relating to rights in a design is complex. Certain designs are eligible for protection as a *Registered Design* in terms of the Registered Designs Act 1949, as amended. In respect of other designs there may be a *Design Right* in terms of the Copyright, Designs and Patents Act 1988. Some designs may qualify for dual protection. Matters are further complicated by the possibility of an overlap with the law of copyright in that a design in the form of a drawing may be protected as an artistic work.

In order to be a Registered Design, a design *must* have aesthetic qualities, i.e., it must be pleasing to the eye as a thing of beauty. In broad terms the aesthetic quality of a registered design is what distinguishes it from a Design Right which generally exists in respect of more functional designs. A person must buy the object made to the design because of what it looks like, not because of what it does. In terms of the Registered Designs Act 1949, a 'design' means features of shape, configuration, pattern or ornament applied to any article by an industrial process, being features which in the finished article appeal to and are judged by the eye. There can for example be a registered design in respect of patterned fabric or wallpaper; these could not be the subject of a design right because they relate to the surface decoration of an article. However, that is not to say that there cannot be articles which can be registered under the 1949 Act and in respect of which there can also be a design right under the 1988 Act. In order to be protected, a new and registrable design must be registered in the Register of Designs. Once registered, protection lasts for up to 25 years.

The creator of a registered design is known as the author and as a general rule the author is the first owner or proprietor of the registered design. However, where the design is created in the course of employment, or where the design is commissioned by someone who has paid for the design, the first proprietor of the registered design will be the employer or the commissioner. Rights in a registered design may be assigned and licensing agreements may be entered into. The registered proprietor enjoys the exclusive right to make, import, sell or hire articles made to the design and he may bring enforcement proceedings against anyone who infringes these rights. Remedies include interdict and damages although the latter are unavailable in respect of an innocent infringement.

A 'design right' is a property right which automatically subsists in an *original* design without the need for registration. A 'design' is defined in the 1988 Act as the design of any aspect of the shape or configuration of the whole or part of an article. Whereas there may be a registered design in respect of a two-dimensional article, a design right must be in respect of a three-dimensional article. Designs in respect of which a design right subsists are those which have been recorded in a design document or which have been made up into an article since 1 August 1989 when the relevant provisions of the Act came into force. Protection lasts either for 15 years from the end of the year in which the design for the article was created or for 10 years from the end of the year in which it was first marketed – according to whichever period expires first.

However, in terms of the 1988 Act certain aspects of a design are excluded from the protection afforded by a design right. There can be no design right over methods of construction. Furthermore, there cannot be a monopoly right over that part of an article's shape which enables it to fit on to another article so as to enable either article to function. This is known as the 'must fit' exclusion and would for example prevent a car manufacturer claiming a design right over the design of that part of an exhaust pipe which fits on to the car. To allow such a right would give car manufacturers a monopoly over spare parts for their vehicles. There is a similar exclusion known as the 'must match' exclusion which prohibits an exclusive design right over any feature of shape which an article must have in order to match the appearance of another article of which it is to form an integral part. Again the example of car parts may be used to illustrate this exclusion: the exterior appearance of a door panel cannot be the subject of a design right because its appearance is necessary if it is to match the rest of the car when fitted.

The first owner of a design right is usually the creator of the design. However, where the design is created in the course of employment or as a result of a commission, the first owner will be the employer or the commissioner. Alternatively, in certain limited circumstances, the person who first markets articles made to the design will be the owner of the design right. Design rights can be transferred and they pass on death either in terms of a will or under the rules of intestate succession where no will is made. Licences may be granted; during the last five years of the design right they must be granted if requested. The owner of the design right has the exclusive right to reproduce the design by making articles for sale or hire and action may be taken against anyone infringing this right. The owner or an exclusive licensee may seek an interdict, damages or an accounting and payment of profits, although damages are unavailable in respect of an innocent infringement. As with a breach of copyright, an award of additional, exemplary damages is possible in respect of a particularly flagrant breach and orders for the delivery or destruction of the goods may be sought.

RIGHTS IN SECURITY

A creditor may be unwilling to lend or advance credit unless some security is offered. The idea of such security is that, should the debtor fail to pay, the secured creditor has a real right to some part of the debtor's property and this right is preferred to the claims of any other creditors.

It is a general principle that an effective right in security cannot be created merely by agreement. At common law delivery of the property being offered as security, or some act deemed to be equivalent to delivery, is required. Those rights in security which conform to the general principle and are founded on possession may be classified according to whether they are created by contract or are implied by law. In addition there is a class of rights in security which represent an exception to the general principle and do not require the creditor to have possession of the property offered as security.

Exceptions to the general principle requiring possession

Hypothecs

Certain securities, known as **hypothecs** are exceptions to the general rule that delivery of property is required to create a security. Hypothecs allow a creditor to enjoy a real right in security over property which remains in the debtor's possession. Certain hypothecs may be created by contract (i.e., conventional hypothecs), others are implied by law (i.e., legal hypothecs).

There are only two types of hypothec which may be created by contract: bonds of bottomry and bonds of respondentia. These are very rare but allow a ship or its cargo to be offered as security to enable the voyage to continue.

The legal hypothecs include the landlord's hypothec for rent which gives a landlord security over certain corporeal moveable property, such as the tenant's business equipment or stock, for 12 months' rent. The landlord can obtain the court's authority to sell the property. A superior has a similar hypothec for feu-duty. Solicitors also have a hypothec for expenses incurred in a court action over both the expenses awarded to the client and over any property recovered as a consequence of the court action. Finally there are the maritime hypothecs giving a right in security over a ship, which right may be enforced by a court order for the sale of the ship. Seamen have a right in security over their ship for the payment of their wages. In addition the master of a ship has an additional hypothec for all expenses properly incurred. Those who salvage a ship or who repair or provision a ship in a foreign port also enjoy this right in security. Finally, the owner of a ship which has been damaged in a collision with another ship has a hypothec over that other ship for damages.

Securities founded on possession and created by express contract

Securities over heritable property

As it is impossible to deliver heritable property to the creditor, the recording of the security document is regarded as the equivalent of delivery. A document known as a Standard Security drawn up in the statutory form and signed by the debtor must be recorded in either the General Register of Sasines or the Land Register in Edinburgh. This is the type of security document which must be signed by a house purchaser when borrowing money from a building society to buy the house. Should the borrower fail to maintain mortgage payments, the terms of the Standard Security would allow the building society to repossess and sell the house.

Securities over corporeal moveables

Special statutory provisions apply to mortgages of ships and aircraft, otherwise securities created by contract over corporeal moveables are in the form of a contract of pledge. A contract of pledge involves delivery to the creditor of the property offered as security, to be retained until repayment of the debt. The creditor has no right to use the property while it is in his possession. It should be noted that the security lasts only while the creditor has possession of the property.

Actual delivery of the goods has been held to include the situation where the goods are put into a lockfast place and the key given to the creditor. In addition to actual delivery there may also be symbolical or constructive delivery. Symbolical delivery involves delivery of a bill of lading to the creditor. A bill of lading is a document which is signed by a ship's captain and is a receipt for goods which have been shipped. However, it is also regarded as a symbol of the goods themselves and so delivery of the bill of lading is regarded as equivalent to delivery of the goods. Constructive delivery occurs where the goods are in storage and the debtor addresses a delivery order to the storekeeper requiring the goods to be delivered to the creditor. This must be intimated to the storekeeper who thereafter holds the goods on the creditor's behalf.

Securities over incorporeal moveables

These are created by assignation and intimation. If a house purchaser wishes to offer an insurance policy as security in respect of a loan from a building society, this is achieved by signing an assignation or transfer of the policy in favour of the building society and then intimating the fact of the assignation to the insurance company.

Securities founded on possession and implied by law: liens

A lien is a right to retain moveable property until a debt is paid. The creditor must have possession of the property in order to exercise the right and the lien persists only for as long as the creditor remains in possession. There are both special and general liens. Special liens allow the retention of property until a specific debt is paid whereas general liens allow retention of property until all debts arising out of a course of dealing have been paid. An employee in possession of his employer's property may exercise a special lien enabling him to retain the property until he is paid. A banker has a general lien over all bills, notes and negotiable securities which he holds in his capacity as monetary agent. A solicitor has a general lien over all papers, including wills and title deeds, which have been lodged with him by his client. Hoteliers have certain rights at common law and under statute over a guest's luggage in respect of an unpaid bill.

FLOATING CHARGES AND RECEIVERSHIP

Nature of a floating charge and its creation

A floating charge is a type of security which may be offered by a registered company over all or any part of its property. Such a security does not exist at common law in Scotland and was introduced by statute in 1961. The present law is to be found in the Companies Act 1985, which deals with floating charges, and in the Insolvency Act 1986, which contains the provisions on receivers. A company signs a document which creates a floating charge and details of the charge together with a certified copy of the document creating it must be sent to the Registrar of Companies within 21 days. Failure to register will render the floating charge ineffective as a right in security. It should also be noted that a further consequence of a failure to register is that the debt becomes immediately due for payment on demand. A floating charge must also be registered in the register of charges maintained by the company at its registered office.

A company may offer as security all or any part of the heritable or moveable property owned by the company at the time the security is triggered. Once a floating charge has been granted, company property can be bought and sold as normal without the creditor's consent. The operation of a floating charge may be thought of as having a dustbin lid floating over the assets of the company. It hovers harmlessly while things go well but should an event occur which causes the security to be triggered, the charge attaches. The dustbin lid comes crashing down, trapping underneath either all or part of the property the company owns at that particular moment in time depending on the terms of the floating charge. The creditor then sends in an individual known as a receiver who sells off as much of the attached property as is necessary to repay the creditor. Events which trigger the security are the company going into liquidation or the appointment of a receiver.

Appointment of a receiver

A receiver may be appointed by the holder of the floating charge or by the court. Where the floating charge attaches the whole of, or substantially the whole of, the company's property the receiver is known as an administrative receiver. The holder of the floating charge may appoint a receiver on the occurrence of any event specified in the floating charge as entitling him to make the appointment. In addition a receiver may be appointed should any of the following events occur:

1 There has been a demand for payment of the whole or any part of the principal sum secured by the charge and 21 days have expired without payment being made.
2 Two months have passed and during the whole of that time, interest due and payable under the charge has been in arrears.
3 The making of an order or the passing of a resolution to wind up the company.
4 A receiver has been appointed under another floating charge created by the company.

It is also open to the holder of the floating charge to petition the Outer House of the Court of Session to appoint a receiver. The court may make such an appointment on the occurrence of any event specified in the charge as entitling the holder to appoint a receiver. In addition the court may appoint a receiver where it is satisfied that the position of the holder of the floating charge is likely to be prejudiced if no such appointment is made. Finally the court may appoint a receiver should any of the events set out at 1–3 above have occurred. It should be noted that appointment by the court is rare.

The fact of the appointment of a receiver must be notified within seven days to the Registrar of Companies, who will enter details of the appointment in the Register of Charges. The receiver himself has a duty to notify the company and other creditors of the company of his appointment and public notice of his appointment must also be given.

The company is then required to provide the receiver with a statement of affairs giving details of matters such as the company's assets, debts and liabilities, the names and addresses of its creditors and the securities held by them. Within three months of his appointment, or later with the court's permission, the receiver provides a report to the Registrar of Companies, to the holder of the floating charge under which he was appointed, to the trustee for any secured creditors and to the secured creditors themselves. This report should cover the events leading up to his appointment, the actual or proposed disposal of attached property, the actual or proposed carrying on of the company's business, the amounts likely to be payable to the holder of the floating charge and to other creditors and a summary of the company's statement of affairs and his comments on it. The report must also be made available to the unsecured creditors, generally at a meeting of such creditors unless the court directs that a meeting need not be held. If a meeting of unsecured creditors is held, they may appoint a small committee of creditors to represent their views to the receiver.

Functions and powers of a receiver

As stated above, the function of the receiver is to enforce repayment of the sums due to the creditor who holds the floating charge. He does this by selling off those company assets which are attached by the floating charge and then distributing the money according to a statutory pecking order. The receiver may choose, if possible, to keep the company's business running as a going concern until he decides on how the assets are to be sold off.

In performing his functions, the receiver is regarded as the agent of the company. The receiver is personally liable on contracts which he enters into unless he expressly excludes such liability in the contract. It should be noted that the receiver cannot exclude his personal liability on employment contracts adopted by him. Where there is no exclusion of liability clause in the contract the receiver has a statutory right to be indemnified out of the attached property. The appointment of a receiver does not automatically bring to an end contracts which have been entered into previously by the company. It is up to the receiver whether or not to implement any pre-existing contracts. Should the receiver refuse to implement such a contract, the only remedy open to the other contracting party is to bring an action for damages for breach of contract against the company.

In carrying out his functions, the receiver enjoys any powers set out in the document which created the floating charge. He also has additional statutory powers which are set out in full in Schedule 2 of the Insolvency Act 1986 but which include powers to:

(a) take possession of any attached property and to sell or otherwise dispose of it;
(b) borrow money, grant securities and appoint professional advisers;
(c) bring or defend legal proceedings and to go to arbitration;
(d) use the company seal and to sign documents;
(e) carry on the business or any part of it and to employ and dismiss employees;
(f) make an arrangement or compromise on behalf of the company;
(g) call up any capital which remains 'on call';
(h) establish subsidiaries and to transfer to them the whole or any part of the business; and

(i) present or defend a petition for the winding-up of the company.

The receiver owes a duty to the company to exercise these powers without negligence and to obtain a reasonable price when selling attached property.

Ranking

The powers of the receiver are however subject to the rights of any person who:

1 has 'effectually executed diligence' on the property of the company prior to the appointment of the receiver; or
2 holds over all or any part of the property of the company a fixed security or a floating charge ranking prior to or *pari passu* (equally) with the floating charge under which the receiver was appointed.

What does this mean? There may be several creditors each with different types of security over company property. In addition the company may have granted more than one floating charge and as a consequence there may be more than one receiver. In determining the competing claims of the secured creditors it has to be decided who has the 'best' security, i.e., who has the right to be paid first. The document creating the floating charge may include an express provision forbidding the creation of any future fixed securities or floating charges which rank prior to or *pari passu* with it. The floating charge may also seek to make provision on how it is to rank in relation to any existing fixed securities or floating charges; however, any such provision would require the consent of the holders of such existing securities. In the absence of any express provision, it is the case that a fixed security, such as a standard security over heritage which has been recorded before the floating charge has attached, has priority over the floating charge. Similarly, a landlord's hypothec for rent would take priority over the floating charge. Where the company has granted more than one floating charge, they rank in relation to one another according to when they were registered. In such circumstances the receivers may be thought of as forming a queue; the receiver appointed under the floating charge with priority goes in first and only when he has finished does the next receiver go in. Where the Registrar of Companies has received more than one floating charge for registration in the same post, they rank equally and any receivers appointed must act as joint receivers.

Furthermore a creditor may have gone to court and obtained a decree for payment of a debt owed by the company. However, a decree is not a cheque payable to the pursuer; should the company still not pay, the judgment must be enforced by the pursuer by means of the procedure known as diligence. Where the process of diligence has reached a certain stage before the receiver is appointed, the person doing diligence has better rights than the holder of the floating charge under which the receiver was appointed.

There are different forms of diligence depending upon the type of property the creditor seeks to attach. In respect of moveable property belonging to the debtor, but which is in the possession of a third party, the appropriate form of diligence is Arrestment, which prevents the third party handing over the property to anyone. In order to gain possession of the arrested property, the creditor must then bring an

Action of Furthcoming to obtain a court order requiring the third party to deliver the property to the creditor. Where moveable property is in the possession of the debtor or the creditor, the appropriate form of diligence is Poinding, which prevents the property being removed. Again, poinding on its own does not give the creditor a real right in the property and to complete the diligence the poinding must be followed by a Warrant Sale with the proceeds going to the creditor.

In respect of heritable property, a creditor who has obtained a decree may obtain Letters of Inhibition, which are served on the debtor and registered in the Register of Inhibitions and Adjudications. The effect of inhibition is that the debtor cannot voluntarily sell the property or grant a standard security over it.

In so far as the powers of the receiver are subject to the rights of those who have 'effectually executed diligence', the effect of the various forms of diligence may be summed up as follows:

1 Where an arrestment has occurred *after* the creation of the floating charge but there has been no action of furthcoming *before* the appointment of the receiver, there is no effectually executed diligence. However, it is the case that a mere arrestment will have priority over the floating charge where the arrestment pre-dates the creation of the floating charge.
2 Where there has been a poinding *after* the creation of the floating charge but there has been no warrant sale *before* the appointment of the receiver, there is no effectually executed diligence. However, as with arrestments, a mere poinding will have priority over a floating charge where the poinding pre-dates the creation of the floating charge.
3 An inhibition is not effectually executed diligence but nonetheless where it pre-dates the creation of the floating charge it ranks above the floating charge and if the receiver wished to sell the heritable property, the inhibitor would have to be paid before the holder of the floating charge. Where the inhibition post-dates the creation of the floating charge but pre-dates the appointment of the receiver, the inhibitor will be paid after the holder of the floating charge but before the ordinary creditors. An inhibition which post-dates the appointment of the receiver has no effect at all on the powers of the receiver.

As a final point, it should be noted that in **Sharp *v* Thomson 1995 SLT 837** the Inner House held that a floating charge which had attached took priority over a disposition of heritable property which had been delivered to but had not been registered by the buyers at the point when the floating charge was triggered. As the transfer of ownership took effect only on registration, the heritage still formed part of the company's property and was caught by the floating charge.

Distribution of money by the receiver

Section 60(1) of the Insolvency Act 1986 sets out the order in which the receiver must distribute any money realised from the sale of attached property. Certain persons have to be paid before the holder of the floating charge under which the receiver was appointed. The order of distribution is as follows:

1 The holder of any fixed security which is over attached property and which

ranks prior to or *pari passu* (equally) with the floating charge.

2 All persons who have 'effectually executed diligence' on any part of the attached property.
3 Creditors in respect of all liabilities, charges and expenses incurred by the receiver.
4 The receiver himself in respect of his own expenses and remuneration and any indemnity to which he is entitled out of attached property.
5 The preferential creditors entitled to payment under s 59 of the Insolvency Act 1986, the preferential debts being:
   (a) Certain debts due to the Inland Revenue including up to 12 months' PAYE deductions.
   (b) Certain debts due to Customs and Excise including up to 6 months' VAT, 12 months' car tax and 12 months' betting and gaming duties.
   (c) Certain social security contributions.
   (d) Sums owed in respect of contributions to occupational pension schemes and state pension scheme premiums.
   (e) Up to 4 months' remuneration due to employees up to a maximum of £800 per employee, plus accrued holiday pay and including any monies borrowed, perhaps from a bank, to pay such remuneration.

Only once all persons in categories 1–5 above have been paid, is the receiver entitled to make payment to the holder of the floating charge under which he was appointed.

Termination of receivership

The holder of the floating charge may apply to the court to have the receiver removed on cause shown and in addition the receiver must vacate office during the receivership if he ceases to be a qualified insolvency practitioner. However, generally the receiver resigns office on completion of the receivership after paying over any surplus funds to the person entitled to them, such as a receiver acting under another floating charge or a liquidator. Notice must be given to:

1 the holder of the floating charge under which he was appointed;
2 the holder of any other floating charge and any receiver appointed by him;
3 the members of any committee of creditors;
4 the company, or if it is in liquidation, its liquidator.

Notice must also be given to the Registrar of Companies.

QUESTIONS

1 Define and distinguish between (a) heritable and moveable property; (b) corporeal and incorporeal property; and (c) fungibles and non-fungibles – giving examples of each type of property.

2 How would the following items of property be classified?

(a) a watch;
(b) a tree;
(c) a servitude right of access over a neighbouring piece of land;
(d) 1 cwt of sugar;
(e) the goodwill of a business.

3 Edinburgh Machine Tools Ltd have spent several years and considerable sums of money developing a revolutionary new type of cutting tool. The company's Research and Development Manager gave an interview in a trade magazine describing the concept behind the new tool and discussing how certain teething problems had been overcome. The company also put a prototype of the new tool on display at a trade fair in Glasgow at which they also distributed literature describing the new features which the tool incorporated. The company is looking forward to reaping the rewards of marketing the new tool. However, International Tools plc, a leading multinational manufacturer of machine tools, have brought out a virtually identical tool at a price which undercuts the Edinburgh company's. Edinburgh Machine Tools Ltd believe that the larger firm have made use of the information available in the magazine and at the trade fair to produce the rival product. What is the legal position?

4 Define and distinguish between trade marks and service marks, giving examples of each.

5 George MacLeod owns a chain of 15 restaurants throughout Scotland, each known as 'Granny MacLeod's Family Restaurant'. The restaurants have a reputation for cleanliness and for good quality food at reasonable prices. He has received a letter about one of his restaurants in Dundee complaining that the food was cold, the service poor and the restaurant grubby. George is surprised because he does not have a restaurant in Dundee. On investigation, it appears that someone has opened a restaurant in Dundee called 'Granny McLeod's Restaurant', using a similar style of interior decoration as George's. The menu is also similar but is more expensive and on the day George visited, the restaurant was grubby. George has never bothered to register the name of his restaurants as a service mark. He seeks your advice as to whether there is anything he can do to protect the reputation of his business.

6 An amateur dramatic society intend to stage a production to raise money for charity. They are on a shoe-string budget and are trying to decide whether to stage a production written by Shakespeare, or by Noel Coward, or by Andrew Lloyd Webber. Taking into account purely legal considerations what would you advise?

7 Tiptop Teapots plc have paid considerable sums to obtain the exclusive rights to manufacture a very unusual style of teapot designed by a well-known designer whose work is very fashionable and whose designs fetch high prices in trendy shops. Tiptop are appalled to discover that a far cheaper version of the teapot is flooding the market and is widely available in chain stores. Advise Tiptop.

8 Explain briefly what you understand by the phrase 'a right in security'.

9 John is buying a flat and is having to borrow £30 000 from the Auchenshuggle Building Society to finance the purchase. In addition, John's solicitor has suggested that he may wish an endowment mortgage which involves John taking out a policy with an insurance company as part of the financial arrangements so that on maturity of the policy the capital borrowed from the society is paid off. Advise John as to the types of right in security which he will have to grant and how these will be created.

10 What is a major advantage of a floating charge when a debtor wishes to offer corporeal moveable property as a security? Can either an individual or a partnership grant a floating charge as security to a creditor?

11 Which events cause a floating charge to attach to the property offered as security?

12 Which events justify the appointment of a receiver and what are the receiver's functions once appointed?

13 Acme Ltd have granted several floating charges to different creditors. Which creditor will have the best security?

14 John has been appointed as receiver to Beta Ltd. He discovers that prior to his appointment, Brown, a creditor of Beta Ltd, had obtained a court decree for payment of the sum of £5000. In an attempt to enforce the decree, Brown had arrested goods belonging to Beta Ltd which were in a carrier's warehouse. As at the date of John's appointment, no further steps have been taken by Brown. Who will have the right to be paid first, Brown or the holder of the floating charge?

Part 7
THE LAW OF DELICT

13 Introduction to the general principles of delict

Delict is part of the Law of Obligations. When studying delict, we find that the Law imposes an obligation on each one of us not to cause unjustifiable harm to other persons or their protected interests. The main function of this area of civil law is to define the circumstances in which an individual or a corporate body, on finding that his interests are, or have been, harmed by another's wrongful act, may seek a remedy. The wrongful act is described as a **civil wrong** or a **delict** and the remedies available are either an interdict to stop the wrong recurring or compensation, sometimes called 'reparation'.

Legally protected interests

The law recognises and gives protection to certain interests of the individual or groups of individuals. The main interests are usually described as freedoms or rights. For example, the freedom from personal injury; the right to life and liberty; the right to enjoy a good reputation; the right to enjoy the company, the affection and perhaps financial support of one's family; the freedom to work, to enter into contracts and to freely associate with other persons.

The difference between Scots law and the English law of torts

The English Law of torts developed differently from Scots law. It is often regarded as being a series of separate torts and not, as in Scotland, as arising always from the same general principles of delictual liability. In some areas, there are marked differences between the two systems but in the important area of negligence, the modern law is quite similar and English precedents can be relied upon.

THE DIFFERENCE BETWEEN DELICTS AND CRIMES

A delict is sometimes referred to as a civil wrong. However, delicts are not the only wrongs recognised by the law. There are also criminal wrongs called 'crimes' or 'offences', the consequences of which are deemed harmful to the community. These criminal wrongs result in the wrongdoer being prosecuted by the State in a criminal court and, if found guilty, punished. The punishment can be a fine – ie a sum of money paid by the wrongdoer to the State and, note, not to the victim. On the other hand, delicts or civil wrongs do not lead to the criminal prosecution of the wrongdoer, but to civil proceedings in the form of an action for damages against the wrongdoer in a civil court. If the action is successful, a sum of money, which this time is called 'damages' or 'compensation' or 'reparation', will be paid to the injured party.

The distinction between crimes and delicts does not depend on the kind of wrongful act itself. The conduct will be regarded as a crime if it is not only harmful to the victim but to the public at large. Such conduct must be suppressed and discouraged by the State. Therefore, the State takes action and the wrongdoer is prosecuted by public action. If the conduct is regarded as a wrong to only the individual, then the State does not interfere, and the wronged individual's remedy is to bring an action in a civil court for damages.

The distinction between crimes and delicts is rendered slightly difficult because there is sometimes an area of 'overlap'. For example, assault is a crime for which the wrongdoer will be prosecuted in a criminal court and perhaps punished by way of imprisonment or fine. However, assault is also a delict and the injured victim, can sue his attacker for damages in a separate action in a civil court. To make matters more confusing, it is possible for a compensation order to be made by the criminal court. However, in practice, this is only done where the injuries are minor. Finally, if the injured victim of a crime cannot find the wrongdoer or if the wrongdoer has no assets and is not worth suing, a claim may be made under the Criminal Injuries Compensation Scheme.

DELICTUAL LIABILITY AND CONTRACTUAL LIABILITY

The main differences between the two are as follows:

1 In delict, the primary obligation, which is usually referred to as a duty, is not to harm others unjustifiably, and the secondary obligation is to compensate a person injured by such unjustifiable harm. Both obligations are imposed on everyone of us by the law (*ex lege*), which is quite independent of the will of the parties involved. To explain this another way, there need be no relationship between the parties. In fact, they might never have met until they were brought together by chance or accident. In contract, the obligation to perform the terms of the contract and the obligation to accept performance arise from the voluntary consent and agreement of the parties to the contract;

2 A delictual duty, arising *ex lege*, not to cause unjustifiable harm is owed to all persons who may foreseeably be harmed by breach of this duty, while a contractual obligation or duty is only owed to the other party to the contract;

3 Under the law of delict, an action for damages is to compensate the pursuer for the loss of what he already had and to restore him (as far as money can do so)

to the position he was in before. Under the law of contract, an action for damages is to compensate the party loyal to the contract (ie the party not in breach of the contract) for the loss of what he could reasonably have expected to gain if the contract had been properly carried out. This is best explained by a very simple example.

Suppose Angus sells Bert a painting for £10 000, fraudulently representing that it is the work of a famous artist, while in fact Angus knows that it is a forgery and worth only £100. In these circumstances, Bert could sue Angus for damages because fraud is a delict, a civil wrong. His damages would be £9900, the amount necessary to put him in the same position which he was in before (he can also return the painting and get his £100 back). On the other hand, suppose Bert can prove that Angus guaranteed as a term of the contract that the painting was genuine and that the value of such a painting on the open market is £12 000. Then Bert could have sued Angus for breach of contract and the damages would be £11 900 – i.e., the sum necessary to put Bert in the position he would have been if the contract had been properly carried out according to its terms.

THE GENERAL PRINCIPLES OF DELICTUAL LIABILITY

The law does not provide a remedy and compensation for all those who suffer some misfortune or loss. The rule is that for delictual liability (ie for the defender to be obliged to pay compensation) there must be a harm caused by a legal wrong and the legal wrong must be caused by *culpa* (fault) on the part of the wrongdoer. *Culpa* means that the person liable is responsible because in a legal sense he is to blame for what happened, and he directly or indirectly caused or permitted the harm complained of. *Culpa* generally indicates the presence of morally reprehensible conduct. To explain this another way, some delicts can be committed intentionally (for example, a deliberate fraud) but most are committed unintentionally or negligently (for example, negligent driving where someone is injured because the driver has failed to take reasonable care in driving his vehicle). In both situations, there will be fault or *culpa* on the part of the wrongdoer.

This is one of the general principles of delict – there can be no delictual liability without fault. However, we will see later that there are some exceptions to this rule in cases of vicarious liability where the defender is liable for the actions of another person and in cases of strict liability where the defender's liability can arise again without fault on his part. In fact, he could have tried his best to prevent the wrong happening at all.

Damnum injuria datum

This is the main principle for delictual liability in that there must be a harm caused by a legal wrong. This is expressed neatly in the above Latin maxim. All three elements of this maxim must be present before an action can be brought. There must be:

1 wrongful conduct (intentionally or negligently done);
2 there must be loss or injury suffered by the pursuer;
3 there must be causation – i.e., a link between 1 and 2.

Note what happens when there is no legal wrong or no loss or injury; these situations are covered by another two Latin maxims.

Injuria sine damno

This covers cases where there is a legal wrong or infringement of a legally-protected interest but no proof of actual loss. For example, driving a car recklessly or negligently could be a criminal offence and it could potentially be a delict; however, if no-one is injured, such conduct will not give rise to delictual liability.

Damnum absque injuria

Loss by itself does not give rise to delictual liability. The clearest example of this is competition in trade. Suppose someone in the same line of business as X opens up next door, advertises, cuts his prices and even sets out to deliberately ruin X. X definitely suffers loss but he cannot sue his neighbour. The reason is that the neighbour's conduct is justified in law and the neighbour owes X no duty of care or duty to refrain from such conduct.

The wrongful conduct

To give rise to delictual liability, the defender's conduct must have been voluntary. For example, if a sleepwalker broke a valuable vase, he could not be sued as there is no delictual liability. Similarly, if a driver died at the wheel and his vehicle mounted the pavement and injured a pedestrian, his conduct again is involuntary and his estate would incur no liability.

The conduct of the defender can either be a positive act or an omission – i.e., a failure to act. For example, a failure to fence a hole or light an obstruction on the road or provide a safe system of working for employees. However, there is only delictual liability for an omission if, in the circumstances, the person concerned was under a legal obligation to do something. So if you are standing by a loch and someone is drowning and you make no attempt to save them, you cannot be delictually liable and be sued for damages if you did not owe that person a duty of care.

DEFINITION OF A DELICT

A delict is voluntary conduct, by act or omission, by a person in breach of a duty, imposed on him by law, not to cause unjustifiable harm to other persons or their legally-protected interests. This conduct may be intentional or unintentional.

Who is liable for committing the delict?

Under Scots law the general principle is *Culpa tenet suos auctores*, which simply means he who does the wrong is responsible and liable for it. Another interpretation could be, no-one is responsible for the delict of another person. For example, a husband or wife is not liable for the wrongs of their spouse.

Joint and several liability

Where two or more persons have contributed, either equally or in varying proportions, to the commission of a delict, they are liable jointly and severally. This means that the injured party can sue them together in the one action or just sue one of the wrongdoers and recover full damages from that party. If one of the wrongdoers has paid the full amount, then he in turn can recover a contribution from the others in proportions to what the court considers just – **Law Reform (Miscellaneous Provisions) (Scotland) Act 1940.**

In **Drew** *v* **Western SMT 1947 SC 222** a bread van's rear lights were on but obscured. A bus ran into the back of the van and killed the van boy. The boy's father brought two actions – against the owners of the bus and the owners of the van. The court held the parties were jointly and severally liable. The wrongdoers had contributed to one common harmful result, the death of the boy, even though their acts or omissions were quite separate and distinct.

The Law Reform (Contributory Negligence) Act 1945 also allows the court to apportion fault in the same way as the 1940 Act, but between the pursuer and the defender in the case where the defender successfully pleads the defence of contributory negligence. This defence will be discussed later, but at this point the following case demonstrates the court apportioning liability between defenders sued jointly and severally and then deducting an amount for the pursuer's contributory negligence.

Davies *v* **Swan Motor Co [1949] 2 KB 291** Davies, a dustbin man, was standing on the running board of the dustcart while it was moving. He had been warned not to do so. Davies was killed when the dustcart collided with a bus when turning a corner. The court apportioned liability for the accident in the proportions, two-thirds to the bus company and one-third to the dustcart employers. The court then decided that, although Davies had not caused the accident, he had contributed to his own injury to the extent of one-fifth. So the total amount of damages payable to his widow was reduced by one-fifth.

Vicarious liability

As stated previously, the general rule for liability is *culpa tenet suos auctores*. However, in certain circumstances, the commission of a delict by one person may impose liability on another person who is not at fault. Vicarious liability is an exception to the '*culpa tenet*' maxim and it can arise in partnership, agency and, more frequently, in the field of employment. As the student will be aware, 'vicarious' means 'in place of another'. The judges have sought to justify vicarious liability by referring to two maxims:

1 *Respondeat superior* – let the master (the employer) be responsible.
2 *Qui facit per alium facit per se* – a person who does something through the actions of another is liable as if he had done it himself.

Thus liability is transferred to the person benefiting or gaining in some way by the actions of the wrongdoer. In practical terms, the person benefiting is more likely to be able to pay or will be covered by insurance.

Vicarious liability of the employer for his employees' actions

An employer is liable for the wrongful acts or omissions of an employee provided the act is done within the scope of employment. Vicarious liability is an example of joint and several liability in that the injured party can sue the employee, personally, and/or the employer who is vicariously liable. If the employer is found vicariously liable, then it is open to him to sue the employee for the amount he has paid in damages. However, in practice, this rarely happens and the employer is insured against such risks.

In **Lister *v* Romford Ice and Cold Storage Co [1957] AC 555** both Lister and his father were employed by the company. While working, the son, who was a lorry-driver, reversed and knocked down his father, who recovered damages from the company. The company's insurers paid the amount of damages and then brought an action against Lister to recover the sum which they had paid to the injured third party (who just happened to be Lister's father). The House of Lords held that they were entitled to that amount.

Bringing an action against the employer

The pursuer, the person injured by an employee, in order to bring an action against the employer (the defender), must prove that the wrongdoer has been negligent. Then he must prove:

1 that the wrongdoer was an employee of the defender; *and*
2 that the delict (the wrongful act) was committed within the scope or course of his employment.

The first essential

The first essential is to establish that the relationship between the employer and the person working for him is that of employer/employee (under a contract of service) and not employer/independent contractor (working under a contract for services). Later in the section on Employment Law, we will examine the various tests that the courts have devised to ascertain whether a person is working under a contract of service or a contract for services. These tests are: the control test; the integration test; the multiple test; and other variations of the multiple test. It is important to establish the relationship because the general rule is that an employer is not vicariously liable for the negligent acts of independent contractors working for him, the theory being that an independent contractor is not under the control of his employer and so remains responsible for his own negligent acts.

However, there are certain situations where an employer will be personally liable for the actions of a contractor, usually because in some way he is controlling or is responsible for the operation:

1 Where the contractor is authorised or instructed to commit a delict by the employer. For example, if a passenger orders his taxi-driver to drive fast and an accident happens, then both the passenger and the driver are at fault. In **Stewart** *v* **Adams 1920 SC 129** a man was held liable when he employed a contractor to repair his boat and instructed him to throw the paint scrapings over a hedge where a neighbour's cow ate them and died.
2 Where the employer instructs an incompetent contractor to do a job for him. An employer is always under a duty to take care in picking a qualified, experienced and apparently capable contractor or tradesman. If the incompetent tradesman negligently causes injury to a third party or to his property, then the employer will be personally liable.
3 Where the employer instructs the contractor to carry out an inherently dangerous operation, in certain circumstances, the employer will be personally liable for injury to third parties. For example, rock blasting, working on gas pipes, digging holes in the public highway.
4 Where the employer is under a statutory duty to take care, he cannot escape liability for an accident by delegating it or employing an independent contractor to do it for him.
5 Where the employer is controlling and directing an operation and the contractor is obeying instructions, then the employer will be personally liable for any injury or damage caused to third parties.

The second essential

The second essential for the employer to be vicariously liable is for the pursuer to show that the employee was acting within the scope or course of his employment. This is usually quite clear; the employee will be doing his job as instructed by his employer and an accident happens affecting a third party. Equally, if an employee has finished work or if he is using the employer's tools and equipment for his own purposes, then the employer is not vicariously liable. However, there have been situations where it has not been clear as to whether the employee was acting within his scope of employment or not, and the courts have had to settle the matter. In **Kirby** *v* **NCB 1958 SC 514** some miners took a break and went to smoke in an unauthorised area. This resulted in an explosion which injured Kirby. The NCB were not held vicariously liable. Smoking was expressly forbidden by statute. Lord President Clyde said that whether an employee was acting within the scope of his employment depended on the facts of each case. He gave four guidelines:

1 If the employer actually authorised the act he is vicariously liable for it.
2 Where the employee does some work which he is appointed to do, but he does it in a way that his employer has not authorised and would not have authorised had he known of it, the employer is nevertheless still liable.
3 If the employee uses his employer's time or his employer's tools (vehicle?) for his own purposes the employer is not liable.

4 If the employee is employed only to do a particular job or a particular class of work and he does something outside the scope of that work, the employer is not liable.

We will look at some more cases to clarify these points.

(a) Usually the delict must be committed during working hours; therefore, accidents happening while the employee is commuting are 'not within the scope of employment'. However, it all depends on the facts.

In **Smith** *v* **Stages [1989] AC 928** two men were employed to install insulation in power stations. They were sent on a job for a week in Wales – and were paid their hourly rate for the journeys to Wales and back to the Midlands plus travelling expenses. How they were to travel was not mentioned by their employer. They decided to go in Stages's car. At the end of the job, after working 24 hours without a break they drove home. Stages drove into a wall and Machin, the other employee, was injured. Machin sued Stages for negligence (he turned out to be uninsured) so the employer was joined as a defendant on the grounds that he was vicariously liable for the negligence of the driver. Machin died in the middle of the proceedings. The House of Lords found the employer vicariously liable. The fact that the employees were paid wages for the time travelled was an important factor. Lord Lowry gave six rules as guidance:

(i) commuting to work even in transport provided by the employer is not within the course of employment unless the employee's contract requires him to use the employer's transport – that would be within the course of employment;
(ii) travelling between sites during the course of a day is within the course of employment;
(iii) being paid wages for travelling time indicates that the employee is 'on duty' while travelling – but being paid travel expenses does not;
(iv) travelling in the employer's time from home to a place of work different from the employee's usual place of work is within the course of employment;
(v) a deviation from or interruption of a journey undertaken in the course of work (unless it is merely incidental to the journey) will for the time being (which could include an overnight interruption) take the employee out of the course of his employment;
(vi) return journeys have the same status as the outward journey.

(b) Problems have arisen where an employee is doing what he was employed to do, but he is doing it in an unauthorised or in a negligent way. It is clear from a number of decisions that in these circumstances the employee is within the scope of employment and his employer vicariously liable.

In **Century Insurance** *v* **Northern Ireland Transport Board [1942] AC 509** an employee was delivering petrol. Contrary to instructions, he lit a cigarette, threw the match away and caused a fire in the garage. It was argued that smoking was outside the scope of his employment and it was a totally unauthorised act. The court held that the employee was still within the scope of employment, he was still doing his job – although in an unauthorised and negligent way – and the employers were vicariously liable for the damage he had caused.

In **Williams *v* Hemphill 1966 SC (HL) 31** a lorry and a driver were hired to pick up some BB boys and their equipment from summer camp. The driver's employer instructed him to take the boys from Benderloch to Glasgow by the usual route. The boys persuaded the driver to deviate from his route (they wanted to see some girl guides) and, while deviating, an accident happened and some boys were injured. The case was brought by the father of a boy who had not asked the driver to deviate. The employers argued that they were not vicariously liable for the driver's negligent driving and that the deviation had taken the driver outwith the scope of his employment. The court decided that the driver's job was to take the boys to Glasgow. At the time of the accident, he was still doing that, although in an unauthorised way; the deviation was not for his own purposes and so he was still within the scope of employment.

(c) In cases where the employee has committed a delict while doing something that he was not authorised to do, the court will take into consideration the purpose of his actions. If they decide that the employee's actions were entirely for his own purposes or that he was off on 'an independent frolic of his own' as one judge described it, then the decision will be that he was outwith the scope of employment. However, if it can be argued that the purpose of the unauthorised act was to further his employer's interests or protect his employer's property, then that will be within the scope of employment.

In **Rose *v* Plenty [1976] 1 All ER 97** a milk-float driver knew that children must not under any circumstances be employed to help on his milk round. There was a notice to that effect displayed in the dairy. Rose, a 13-year-old boy was injured helping the driver on his round. The employers protested that it was expressly forbidden to have anyone on the milk-float and so, when the accident happened, the driver was outwith the scope of employment. The court held that the boy was there on the float to help the driver do his job, further the employer's interests and so it was within the scope of employment.

In **Poland *v* John Parr & Sons [1927] 1KB 236** a van driver thought that a boy was stealing from the back of his employer's van. He hit him and the boy fell under a wheel and was injured. Obviously, the driver was not employed to assault boys; that was not part of his job. However, it was held that he had acted in that way to protect his employer's property and so this brought the act within the scope of his employment.

In **Neville *v* C&A Modes 1945 SC 175** the employers were held vicariously liable for the actions of the manager and staff wrongfully detaining and accusing a customer of shop-lifting. Again, although not employed to do this, they were acting for their employer's benefit in an attempt to protect his property, and this brought the act within the scope of employment.

However, note the different facts and decision in **Warren *v* Henlys Ltd 1958 2 All ER 935**. An employee in a garage thought that a customer, Warren, was going to drive away without paying for his petrol. There was an argument, Warren paid for his petrol and then the employee hit Warren and knocked him to the ground. It was held that in these circumstances, assault was not within the scope of employment. The act was beyond what was necessary in the circumstances and dictated by personal malice.

(d) When the employee acts in breach of an express prohibition by the employer, this may appear to be outwith the scope of employment. However, it is not always the case, as was seen in *Rose* v *Plenty*. There are orders given by the employer to the employee which amount to some restriction as to what he can actually do as part of his job, or on how to do the job. Breach of the former will mean that the employee has gone beyond the limits of his job – i.e., outwith the scope of employment; breach of the latter will mean that the employee was doing his job in a way, unauthorised, perhaps totally prohibited by his employer, but he was still doing the job – so he remains within the scope of employment. There have been problems where employees give others a prohibited lift in a vehicle.

In **Conway *v* George Wimpey & Co 1951 2 KB 266** a driver employed by Wimpey was under strict orders not to carry passengers and a notice to this effect was clearly displayed in the cab of the lorry. The driver gave a lift to Conway, who was injured as a result of the driver's negligence. Conway was not a fellow employee, in fact had no connection with the employer's business and this is what distinguishes Conway's case from Rose, the milk boy. The Court held that George Wimpey were not vicariously liable, as the act of giving a lift was outwith the scope of employment and at the time of the accident Conway knew it was prohibited.

In **Young *v* Edward Box & Co 1951 1 TLR 789** Box Ltd's foreman gave his consent to the giving of a lift to Young in one of the company's lorries, although it was forbidden. Owing to the negligence of the driver, Young was injured and the employers were held vicariously liable as granting permission for the giving of a lift was within a foreman's usual authority.

QUESTIONS

1 Bill is employed by Hedgehog Trucking Ltd as a lorry driver. One day, he caught a youth spraying grafitti on the cabin of his truck. Beside himself with rage, he punched the youth and seriously injured him. The youth's companion just stood nearby laughing and jeering. Panic-stricken, Bill rushed the injured boy to hospital. While he was at the hospital, he phoned Hedgehog Trucking to tell them what had happened and was instructed to report back to the office immediately. A nurse was coming off duty and asked him for a lift. Giving lifts is against company rules but on this occasion, Bill obliged. While he diverted to take the nurse home, Bill drove negligently and the nurse was injured. Finally, he got back to the office and had just parked his damaged lorry, when he met the injured youth's friend, who unwisely made a cheeky remark about the damage to his vehicle. Bill pursued the boy down the street and kicked and punched him. The boy had to be taken to hospital to join his friend. Advise the youth, his friend and the nurse as to whether they can sue for damages for their injuries.

2 Miranda owns a self-service filling station which has, at the back, a workshop where car repairs are carried out. Miranda employs Bert to look after the filling station and his sole task is to collect payment from the customers for their petrol. Last Friday was an eventful day at the garage. Advise Miranda on her rights and liabilities in the following situations:

(a) On Friday morning, Bert mistakenly believed that Mr Smith, a customer, was not going to pay for his petrol as he had got back into his car after filling up his tank. In fact, Mr Smith had just got into his car to find his wallet. Bert rushed out of the office, dragged Mr Smith from his car, punched him and knocked him to the ground. Mr Smith has a fractured arm and is planning to sue Miranda.

(b) Later Bert, who is not employed to do any repair work, took it upon himself to move a customer's car which was blocking the entrance to the workshop. He reversed into a wall and the owner of the car, Mr Brown, is saying that Miranda is liable.

(c) Fred, a petrol tanker driver for Fuelo Petroleum Ltd, arrived to fill the tanks of the petrol pumps in the forecourt. Fred lit a cigarette, even though this is strictly against his company's rules and threw away his match. There was an explosion and Miranda's garage has been burnt to the ground.

14 Negligence

As noted previously, delict is concerned with intentional wrongful acts and also instances where liability is incurred unintentionally. The latter is the commonest kind of delictual case and is called **negligence**. Negligence is not the same as carelessness. For negligence, as we shall see, the defender must owe a duty of care.

One of the problems with negligence is that it is difficult to prove. The burden of proof rests with the pursuer – i.e., the injured party – and although the same general principle applies (*damnum injuria datum*), an action for negligence, as the student will see, is a little more complex.

The pursuer bringing an action for negligence must prove the following:

1 The defender is under a legally-recognised duty of care to guard against a foreseeable kind of harm and this duty of care is owed, by the defender, in the circumstances to the pursuer.
2 There was a breach of this duty of care; a failure by the defender to attain the standard of care required in the circumstances.
3 The breach was the effective cause of some legally-recognised harm to the pursuer.
4 Once liability for harm is established, then damages will extend to cover all the natural and direct consequences, or foreseeable consequences, of the defender's conduct and will not extend to those losses which are too remote.

THE DUTY OF CARE

The duty of care must be established before any question of the potential liability of the defender can be considered. Regarding negligence, under common law there is only one standard of care and that is to take reasonable care in the circumstances (cases where the duty is to take exceptional care are dealt with later under 'Strict Liability'). In many cases, it has been well settled by precedent that a duty of care is owed in certain circumstances. For example, employers owe their employees a duty to take reasonable care for their safety at work. Drivers owe a duty to take reasonable care not to cause unjustifiable harm to other road-users and pedestrians.

Sometimes it is not clear in a particular situation whether a duty of care exists or not. In order to decide, the court will apply the general principle laid down in **Donoghue** *v* **Stevenson 1932 AC 562**. The alleged facts of the case were that Mrs Donoghue and her friend had gone to a cafe in Paisley for a ginger beer ice-cream soda. Mrs Donoghue's friend bought the two drinks. After having drunk some of this concoction, Mrs Donoghue topped up her glass with ginger beer from an opaque bottle when a decomposed snail slid into her glass. As a result, she suffered shock and gastro-enteritis and was off work for some time. Mrs Donoghue could not sue the owner of the cafe because she had no contract of sale with him. Her only possible remedy was in delict against the manufacturer on the basis of his fault in not taking care in the production of the ginger beer. The House of Lords held that the manufacturer of a product did owe a duty of care because of the relationship between himself and the ultimate consumer. At the end of the day, Mrs Donoghue did not have to prove the facts because the manufacturer settled out of court after the legal point was clarified.

Lord Atkin's speech sets out a neighbour principle – a principle that can be used to decide if a duty of care exists and if so to whom.

> The rule that you are to love your neighbour becomes, in law, you must not injure your neighbour; and the lawyer's question, 'who is my neighbour?' receives a restricted reply. You must take reasonable care to avoid acts or omissions which you can reasonably foresee would be likely to injure your neighbour. Who, then, in law, is my neighbour? The answer seems to be – persons who are so closely and directly affected by my act that I ought reasonably to have them in contemplation as being so affected when I am directing my mind to the acts or omissions which are called into question.

So in a case where there has been an unintentional wrong done, and in the absence of a precedent in point, then the court uses the principle of liability as in *Donoghue v Stevenson* to decide whether a duty of care exists or not. A duty of care exists if it was reasonably foreseeable that a person's acts or omissions were likely to cause harm to another in the pursuer's position. So, reasonable foresight determines the existence of the duty of care. This test is not subjective in that we do not ask, 'Did this defender actually foresee the harm?'. A more objective approach is taken and the appropriate question is, 'Would a reasonable person in the position of the defender have been able to contemplate or foresee the harm?'. If the court decides that a reasonable person would have foreseen the harm, then a duty of care exists. If the court decides that no duty of care exists, the pursuer's case fails immediately. This will happen even though loss has occurred.

The principle of 'reasonable foreseeability' was applied in **Muir** *v* **Glasgow Corporation 1943 SC (HL) 3**. The manageress of a tearoom in a park permitted a picnic party, caught in the rain, to have their picnic in the tearoom. Two men carried a large tea-urn along a passage, behind some children who were buying sweets. One man let go of his handle (he could not explain what happened and the cause of the accident remained unexplained) and six children, including the pursuer, were scalded. The House of Lords held the defenders not liable. A reasonable person in the manageress's position could not reasonably have foreseen that her granting of permission for the tea-urn to be brought in would result in children being scalded and, consequently, there was no duty of care owed by her to take precautions against the occurrence of such an event. There was no duty, so there was no liability.

It is not always necessary when applying the test to foresee the precise injury which happened. In **Hughes** *v* **Lord Advocate 1963 SC (HL) 31** the facts were that a manhole was uncovered in the road. A canvas shelter was put over the hole and lit paraffin lamps placed around the shelter. The men went for tea and while they were away, two boys opened the canvas. It was held that while it could be argued that an explosion in a manhole in a road (caused by a paraffin lamp being knocked into the hole) was unforeseeable, that kind of explosion was no different from the danger of fire in some form. The danger of fire in those circumstances was reasonably foreseeable. It was established that there was a duty of care to guard against physical injury by fire of some kind. It was irrelevant whether a meddling child upset a lamp over himself and was burnt or as happened in this case the meddling child knocked the lamp into the hole where it exploded and the child fell in and was badly burnt.

The reasonable foreseeability test is usually confined to cases where the injury to the pursuer was caused by the defender's own negligent act. The exception to this general rule would be situations where the wrongdoer is the employee or agent of the defender and thus the defender is vicariously liable for the third parties' negligent acts. In most other cases which involve the actions of third party, the question to be decided is whether or not the third party's actions amount to a *novus actus interveniens* which breaks the chain of causation and becomes the real cause of the accident. However, in the next case the actions of the boys did not amount to a *novus actus interveniens* because it was argued the officers were guarding and supervising the boys and their escape was reasonably foreseeable – just what one expects to happen if the officers are negligent in their supervision of the boys under their control.

In **Home Office** *v* **Dorset Yacht Co Ltd [1970] 2 All ER 294** there were some borstal boys encamped on Brownsea Island under the supervision of prison officers. The boys escaped in the night while the officers were asleep and boarded a yacht moored nearby with the intention of sailing it to the mainland. However, they had an accident and damaged a yacht belonging to the Dorset Yacht Company. The court had to decide in these circumstances whether the prison officers owed a duty of care to the owners of the yacht. It was held that they did because a special relationship existed on the one hand between the officers and the boys in their custody and on the other hand between the prison officers and the owners of yachts moored nearby. The court made it clear that the officers' duty of care was limited and only owed to a particular class of person – in other words – only owed to those persons who they could reasonably foresee had property situated in the vicinity of that place where the boys were detained and it was very likely that the boys would steal or damage that property.

In **Smith & Others** *v* **Littlewoods Organisation [1987] 1 All ER 710** Littlewoods had bought a cinema in Dunfermline with a view to demolishing it and building a supermarket. For a number of months the cinema remained empty and unattended. It was regularly entered by trespassers and on two occasions fires were started inside by vandals, but no-one informed Littlewoods. Finally a fire was started which seriously damaged two adjoining properties. The owners of the properties brought actions for damages against Littlewoods. Were they liable for the actions of the unknown third parties? The House of Lords held that Littlewoods were under a general duty to exercise reasonable care to ensure that the condition of their premises was not a source of danger to neighbouring property. However, this did not extend to the actions of the vandals as they had not known about the vandalism and the previous attempts to start fires. Lord Mackay said for a duty of care to arise in a case involving third party intervention, the resulting damage would not only have to be reasonably foreseeable but very likely or highly probable.

Lord Goff, in his judgement, gave some guidelines: liability for harm caused by third parties could only be claimed in special circumstances. These are:

1 Where a special relationship existed between the third party and the defender by virtue of which the defender is responsible for controlling the third party.
2 Where a source of danger was negligently created by the defender and it was reasonably foreseeable and highly probable that third parties might interfere and cause damage.
3 Where the defender had knowledge or means of knowledge that a third party had created or was creating a risk of danger on his property and he had failed to take reasonable steps to abate it.

On the facts of this case there were no special circumstances and so Littlewoods owed no duty of care to the owners of the adjoining properties.

Between 1969 and 1980 a series of thirteen murders and eight attempted murders were committed by Peter Sutcliffe, known as 'the Yorkshire Ripper'. The mother of his last victim brought an action for damages for negligence against the Chief Constable (**Hill *v* Chief Constable of West Yorkshire [1988] 2 All ER 238**). It was argued that the police owed a duty of care because it was reasonably foreseeable that harm would come to future potential victims if Sutcliffe was not quickly apprehended. This was an attempt to establish that the police are liable for the criminal acts of an unknown third party. However, the House of Lords held that reasonable foreseeability by itself is not sufficient to establish a duty of care. There must also be 'proximity of relationship' between the pursuer and the defender. This was lacking in this case because Miss Hill was only one of a large group of members of the public at risk. She was not an individual at special risk and so no duty of care was owed to her as an individual. The House of Lords also stated that there should be no duty of care owed in these circumstances on the grounds of public policy. To impose such liability could lead to the police carrying out their function 'in a detrimentally defensive frame of mind'.

The duty must have been owed by the defender to the pursuer

Once the pursuer has established that the defender owed a duty of care, he must further show that he, the pursuer, was within the ambit of the duty or within the area of risk. A duty of care is not owed to the whole world but only to those persons within the ambit of the defender's duty to take reasonable care to avoid causing harm to others. The law sets a limit on the number of persons who are owed the duty of care for practical reasons. If the number of possible claims was not limited, one small accident could possibly have a 'knock on' effect and give rise to hundreds of claims. The test is 'was the pursuer one of those within the area of foreseeable risk of injury?' or to say it another way 'should the occurrence of some harm to a person placed where the pursuer was have been reasonably contemplated or foreseen by the defender?'.

In **Bourhill** *v* **Young 1943 SC (HL) 78** Mrs Bourhill was unsuccessful in her claim for damages against the representatives of a motor cyclist, Young, who was killed when he carelessly overtook a tram and hit another car. Mrs B was getting off the tram on the other side, out of sight of the motor cyclist. She did not even see the accident but she heard it. She maintained that because of the noise and then the sight of blood on the road, she suffered nervous shock and miscarried. To succeed in her case, she had to show that Young was in breach of a duty of care which was owed amongst others to her. The court held that Young owed a duty to drive with reasonable care to other road users, including the passengers of the other car involved in the accident but held that Young could not possibly have foreseen that his failure to take care would cause injury to Mrs B in her position behind the tram. She was outwith the ambit or area of potential danger.

There was a breach of the duty of care

The breach is a failure to attain the standard of care required in the circumstances. For negligence the standard is always to take reasonable care. This standard is fixed by what we should expect in a similar case from the hypothetical reasonable man – i.e., a man of ordinary sense, knowledge, skill and prudence.

There is only one standard and it applies whether the defender is an employer, a driver, a tradesman or a professional person. Although the standard is always the same, the degree of care required to reach that standard will vary according to what was required in those particular circumstances. So, in dangerous circumstances, a reasonable man will take greater precautions. For example, he would take more care if he was handling petrol rather than water, or handling a loaded gun rather than a walking stick, or if he was driving on a busy road rather than all alone on a moor.

The degree of care required in the circumstances depends on the hypothetical reasonable man, weighing up, on one hand, the probability of injury and how serious the injury *could be* against how easy it *would be* in the circumstances to avoid the risk, and how expensive. This approach to assessing risk is noticeable in some cases.

In **Bolton** *v* **Stone [1951] AC 850** a batsman in a cricket match hit a ball over a fence 7 feet high and 17 feet above the pitch, 78 yards from the crease. The ball hit a person who was walking another 22 yards on the other side of the fence. There was evidence that no-one had previously been injured while walking past and that the ball had only gone over the fence six times in the last 30 years. The passerby's claim for negligence failed because while an accident of that kind was reasonably foreseeable, the chance of it happening was very small and so a reasonable man considering the safety aspect would have thought it right not to take any more steps to prevent the danger.

But then consider **Paris** *v* **Stepney Borough Council [1951] AC 367**. The standard of care owed to all Stepney Borough Council's employees was the same – i.e., reasonable care for their safety – but a greater degree of care should have been taken for Paris's safety in the circumstances where it was known by the employer that he was blind in one eye. The kind of job Paris was doing was not particularly dangerous; there was no duty to supply goggles to the other employees doing the same job. A freak accident caused a piece of metal to go into Paris's good eye which rendered him blind. The court decided that in the circumstances there was a duty to supply Paris with goggles. As he had only one good eye, any injury could potentially have serious consequences. The employer failed in his duty of care in that he should have provided goggles for this handicapped employee.

So, one would expect a reasonable man to take greater care when he is dealing with young children and disabled or elderly persons. A blind man suddenly stepping on to the road, would have no claim against a careful driver, if the driver could not be expected to know that the pedestrian was blind. However, if the Electricity Board dig up a pavement near a home for the blind, in those circumstances, they would be expected to take greater precautions than normal to prevent pedestrians falling into the hole.

The standard of care expected of a professional person or a tradesman is the same skill and knowledge that a careful and competent member of his profession or trade would exercise in the same circumstances. For example, if we were considering a case of medical negligence and it is established that the doctor deviated from the normal practice, that in itself would not amount to negligence. It would be negligence if such a deviation is a course of action which no other doctor of ordinary skill would have taken in those circumstances if he had been acting with ordinary care.

Some developments regarding the duty of care

The famous dictum by Lord Atkin in *Donoghue* v *Stevenson* led to the general principle for liability being established and this principle is referred to as the **foreseeability test**. There have been some restrictions placed on the application of this test which we will now examine. These developments have particularly affected (a) pure economic loss and (b) nervous shock (post-traumatic stress disorder).

Pure economic loss

The law has always protected the economic interests of the pursuer where there is intentional wrongdoing. For example, a person could sue for damages if another businessman 'passed off' goods under his name or trademark and they were not his (see p. 245). In the past, regarding unintentional wrongs (negligent acts), the court would only award damages as long as the loss came from a physical injury, either to the pursuer or to his property. For example, if the court had had to calculate Mrs Donoghue's damages, she would have recovered pecuniary loss for being off work plus her medical bills – this is financial loss flowing from the original injury, her upset stomach

When we talk about 'pure' economic loss, we are referring to a loss that can be measured in money – i.e., pecuniary loss – but which arises from the negligent act without personal injury to the pursuer or damage to his property. The law has always been cautious in this area and in fact until quite recently the decisions suggested that there was a presumption that no liability for pure economic loss existed under the law of delict.

The justification for restricting claims for pure economic loss is the 'floodgates argument' – that one minor breach of duty could give rise to hundreds of claims for enormous sums of damages. For example, consider an accident caused by the negligence of one driver which blocks a busy bridge like the Kingston Bridge in Glasgow in the morning rush hour. Persons who are physically injured or whose vehicles are damaged will have a claim against the driver. But consider how many drivers and passengers have been held up – say for one hour – and consequently are late for work, miss important meetings or miss planes or trains. These people could have financial losses and also their employers could suffer the loss of their services for an hour. However, these 'victims' of the accident cannot claim because these losses are purely economic. Some authorities refer to this kind of loss as secondary economic loss.

Look at the early case of **Allan** *v* **Barclay (1864) 2M 873** where the pursuer claimed damages because he had lost the services of an employee who had been injured in a road accident due to the defender's negligence. The pursuer was unsuccessful – this is pure economic loss. There had been no actual personal injury to the pursuer or his property. The only person who could sue for damages in these circumstances was the injured employee. The same principle applies in **Reavis** *v* **Clan Line Steamers 1925 SC 725**. The proprietor of an orchestra was unsuccessful when she tried to claim damages for her financial loss because half her orchestra had been drowned or badly injured when there was an accident on a steamer. The injured members could have sued but not the employer.

In **Dynamco** *v* **Holland Hannen & Cubitts (Scotland) Ltd 1972 SLT 38** Dynamco brought an action for damages against some contractors working near their factory, claiming that they had negligently interrupted Dynamco's supply of electricity. One of the excavators of Holland, Hannen & Cubitts had damaged the cable belonging to the Electricity Board. The contractors had not taken proper steps to find out where the cables lay. Dynamco argued in court that the contractor owed a duty of care not to damage such cables and so cause damage to the businesses of the surrounding occupiers of premises. As a result of a power failure for 15 hours, Dynamco suffered considerable financial loss. The court held that this loss was not recoverable as it did not arise directly from damage to the pursuer's own property.

In a decision of the Inner House of the Court of Session, a pursuer again was found unable to recover damages for this kind of pure economic loss. In **Nacap Ltd** *v* **Moffat Plant Hire Ltd 1987 SLT 221** the pursuer was a contractor who had been carrying out work on a pipe. Under the contract with the owner of the pipe, the pursuer had to compensate or indemnify the owner for any damage to the pipe. The pipe was damaged by the defenders and the pursuers had to make good the pipe under contract. The pursuers sought to recover their loss from the defenders. The Court found the defenders not liable as they owed no duty of care to the pursuers. The reason was because of the nature of the harm suffered by the pursuers. It was pure economic loss, that is loss arising from damage to property which did not belong to the pursuer and as such was not recoverable.

However, the principle of no liability for pure economic loss has been qualified by the decisions of some recent cases. Liability can arise in two situations: (a) where there is financial loss caused by negligent misstatement and (b) in limited circumstances where financial loss is caused by careless acts.

Negligent misstatement

The original position of Scots law was that there could only be liability for negligent misstatement which caused financial loss, if the parties were in a contractual relationship. For example, an accountant preparing accounts for his client would be liable. Alternatively, there could be liability if the parties were in a fiduciary relationship, that is where one party is depending on the other and the other party is in a position of trust. In all other situations and relationships, there is a duty to be honest but no duty to be careful and it was thought that the general principle of liability laid down by *Donoghue* v *Stevenson* could not be applied if only financial loss resulted.

However, note the important case of **Hedley Byrne & Co *v* Heller & Partners [1964] AC 465**. A firm of advertising agents asked a bank whether one of its clients, Easipower, with whom they intended to do business, was creditworthy. The reply, which was stated to be 'without responsibility on our part', was that the client was creditworthy. Relying on this information, the agents placed adverts for their client on credit. The advertisers lost money when the client company went into liquidation. They sought to recoup their losses from the bankers who, they maintained, had been negligent. Until that point in time, negligent misstatement did not give rise to liability where there was no contract between the parties. The decision of the House of Lords that a duty could arise in these circumstances was a complete U-turn. The basis of the duty was said to be 'reliance'. However, reliance on the information by the pursuer is not enough in itself to create a duty: the party supplying the information must also know or should have realised that his skill and judgement are being relied upon by the other party. This reliance created a special relationship between the parties on which a duty of care could be founded – although in this case the defendants' disclaimer protected them from liability.

This was a very important case as it opened the door for claims to be made for pure economic loss. This has important implications for businesses – particularly professional firms when one considers how often information and reports drawn up by them for a client are then read and acted upon by third parties. In each case the third party who has suffered pure economic loss (the pursuer) will have to establish that a duty of care is owed to him using the principles established by *Hedley Byrne* of reasonable foreseeability plus proximity plus reliance.

In general, a reasonable person, knowing that his skill and judgement were being relied upon by someone (with whom he has no contractual relationship), has three options open to him:

1 he does not give his opinion nor advice, or
2 he gives an answer with a clear qualification that he accepts no responsibility for it but he has to remember that such a disclaimer will possibly be subject to the Unfair Contract Terms Act 1977, or
3 he gives an answer without qualification and then must remember that following the principles of *Hedley Byrne* he has accepted responsibility for it and

owes the party who receives this advice and relies on it a duty to take reasonable care in giving an accurate answer.

In the past twenty years the *Hedley Byrne* (HB) principles have been followed in many cases where the pursuer cannot base his claim on breach of contract. We will look at some of these under four main headings:

1. The HB principles can be used to establish that a surveyor owes a duty of care to the purchaser of property regarding the contents of report requested by a building society.
2. The HB principles with limitations on the scope of the duty of care (see *Caparo Industries*) can apply to reports of accountants acting as auditors.
3. The HB principles can be used to establish a duty of care owed by a solicitor to intended beneficiaries under a will.
4. The HB principle can be used to establish that a duty of care is owed by an employer to a former employee regarding the contents of a reference.

1 Negligent reports of surveyors

The duty of care arises because the surveyor knows or should know that his report will be relied upon by the building society *and* the purchaser of the property. However, the surveyor's liability is limited. His duty of care is owed to the first purchaser who is named by the building society when the request for the survey is made. It does not extend to subsequent purchasers of that particular property.

In **Martin *v* Bell Ingram 1986 SLT 575** Martin, wishing to buy a house, approached a building society for a loan. The building society requested Bell Ingram, a firm of surveyors to carry out a survey and issue a report to them. The report drew attention to some minor faults but failed to mention serious problems with the roof. The problems with the roof did not come to M's attention until he tried to sell the house. Because of the defects the value of the house was greatly reduced. Martin successfully sued Bell Ingram for negligent misstatement which had caused him pure economic loss. Although the surveyor had attached a disclaimer to the original report it was not seen by Martin until after the purchase of the house. The building society had given a verbal report to Martin without mentioning the disclaimer so, unlike the *Hedley Byrne* case, the disclaimer was not effective.

Subsequent cases have reached the same conclusions regarding the liability of surveyors and even in cases where the disclaimer is seen by the prospective buyer before he puts in an offer for property. Such a disclaimer is subject to the 'fair and reasonable' test laid down in the Unfair Contract Terms Act 1977 which now applies in Scotland to non-contractual notices. In **Smith *v* Eric Bush [1989] 2 WLR 790** the House of Lords held that such disclaimers could not exclude the liability of surveyors for negligent reports as under the UCTA 1977 it would not be fair or reasonable for a building society or a surveyor to impose on a purchaser the risk of losses resulting from the incompetence of the surveyor.

2 Duty of care owed by accountants/auditors to shareholders is subject to a number of clear limitations.

There have been a number of cases where this issue has been considered. However the leading case is **Caparo Industries** *v* **Dickman [1990] 2 WLR 358**. In this case, Caparo Industries owned shares in Fidelity plc. Caparo planned a takeover, and after seeing the audited accounts bought more shares and later made a successful takeover bid for Fidelity. They relied on the set of accounts drawn up for Fidelity by Dickman which showed a substantial pre-tax profit. These accounts were later discovered to be inaccurate, they should have shown a substantial loss. Caparo Industries suffered financial loss and sued the auditors. The House of Lords found the auditors not liable for Caparo's financial loss. The auditors of a public company owed a duty of care to their client (Fidelity plc), and to the body of shareholders of the company as a whole. They did not owe a duty of care to the individual shareholders of Fidelity nor a duty of care to the public at large and/or prospective shareholders who might have bought shares relying on the accounts because there was no proximity (closeness) between them. Furthermore, the auditor did not owe a duty of care to the individual shareholders of the company who relied on the accounts and bought more shares. It was held that the three criteria for the imposition of a duty of care to avoid causing injury in the form of pure economic loss were foreseeability of damage, proximity between the parties and, finally, the reasonableness of imposing a duty in the circumstances. When a statement is put into general circulation it is reasonably foreseeable that it might be relied upon by every person who reads it. There can be no proximity between the maker of the statement and the party who relies on it unless it is shown that the maker knew that the statement would be communicated to that party either as an individual or as a member of an identifiable class and that this would be specifically in connection with a particular transaction and that the party would be very likely to rely on it for the purpose of deciding whether to enter that transaction.

3 Duty of care owed by a solicitor to the intended beneficiary under a will

In **White** *v* **Jones [1995] 2 WLR 187** a father fell out with his two daughters and he subsequently revised his will, leaving them nothing. Three months later they were reconciled and he wrote to his solicitors instructing them to draw up a new will including legacies of £9000 for each daughter. The solicitors delayed in carrying out his instructions and he reminded them again. The father died without signing the new will. The daughters sued the solicitors. The House of Lords decided 4:1 that solicitors did owe a duty of care to the intended beneficiaries in these circumstances. Lord Goff said there should be a remedy based on the *Hedley Byrne* principle because of the assumption of responsibility by the solicitors to rewrite the will.

4 A duty of care is owed by an employer to his former employee to take reasonable care regarding the content of a reference

In **Spring** *v* **Guardian Assurance PLC [1994] 3 WLR 354** an employee successfully sued his former employers. All insurance salesmen have to be registered with LAUTRO, the insurance industry's self-regulatory body established under the

Financial Services Act 1986. Guardian Assurance was concerned about the conduct of their salesman, Spring, in connection with one transaction and when they heard that he was planning to leave and join a competitor, they dismissed him summarily. They gave the prospective employer an unfavourable reference. This made it impossible for the employee to re-register with LAUTRO or to obtain other employment in the industry, thus causing him financial loss. The reference accused Spring of fraudulent selling practices. This was incorrect. Although he had been incompetent he had not acted fraudulently. Spring claimed damages for negligent misstatement. Three of the Law Lords held that a duty of care arose under the three part test laid down in the *Caparo Industries* case because (1) it was foreseeable that the harm would occur (2) the parties were in sufficient proximity and (3) it was fair, just and reasonable to impose a duty of care. (See also page 346.)

LIABILITY FOR CARELESS ACTS WHICH CAUSE PURE ECONOMIC LOSS

A duty of care can be owed by a contractor to the owner of building with a defect where there is no contract between the owner and the contractor.

This was the decision of the House of Lords in **Junior Books *v* Veitchi & Co 1982 SLT 492**. Veitchi & Co were specialist flooring subcontractors. They had a contract with the main contractor to lay a floor but had no contract with Junior Books (JB) who had employed the main contractor. Two years after it had been laid, the floor developed cracks and had to be relaid. It was defective but not dangerous. JB sued Veitchi for negligence and for damages for the financial loss which they had suffered i.e., cost of a new floor, cost of moving the machinery out while this was being done and the cost of wages paid to employees unable to work while the floor was relaid. This damage was financial loss – purely economic. The House of Lords stated that the *Hedley Byrne* principles could be used in this case, where a negligent act had caused pure economic loss and that a duty of care could arise where there was a sufficient relationship of proximity between the wrongdoer and the person who suffered the damage. In fact their Lordships found it difficult to imagine a greater degree of proximity in the absence of a direct contractual relationship (ie the relationship between JB and Veitchi was a unique relationship nearly equal to a contractual relationship) . In deciding that there was sufficient proximity they listed the following facts: Veitchi were nominated subcontractors; they were specialist floor contractors; they knew what products were required by JB and they were entirely responsible for the composition and construction of the floor. Veitchi must have known that JB were relying on their skill and experience (in fact JB did rely on Veitchi's skill and experience) and must have known that if they did the work negligently then at some time JB would have to have the floor relaid.

Since the *Junior Books* case there have been many statements made about this decision. These *dicta* have really restricted the effect of the decision. Although the decision has not been overturned it has never been followed and it appears to be a special one decided on its own facts.

Before leaving this topic, the student must note that the decision in the case of **Anns** *v* **Merton London Borough Council [1978] AC 728** has now been overturned. Very simply, the case decided that the local authority owed a duty of care in carrying out its building control functions to occupiers of buildings for the cost of remedying a dangerous defect in a building. In this case the defect to the building had resulted from the negligent failure by the authority to ensure the building had adequate foundation. If the defect in the building becomes apparent before injury or damage occurs, then the loss is purely economic. However, the House of Lords held that this was material physical damage. The test for such liability established in the *Anns* case was a two-stage test: first, reasonable foreseeability of harm creates a prima facie duty of care and, second, if the first part of the test is satisfied, are there any factors, like public policy considerations, which might reduce or limit the scope of the duty, the class of person to whom it is owed, or the damages to which breach may give rise?

The case which clearly overturns the above decision is **Murphy** *v* **Brentwood District Council [1990] 2 All ER 908**. Murphy purchased a newly-built house, which had been constructed on an in-filled site on a concrete raft foundation. The plans regarding the foundation were submitted to the Local Authority. The Authority referred the plans to consulting engineers for checking and, on their recommendation, approval was granted. It was not until 11 years later that it came to light that the foundations were defective. Murphy sold the house, subject to the defect, and obtained £35 000 less than its market value would have been, had it been in perfect condition. At this point it is important to note that the kind of loss complained of was firmly recognised as pure economic loss, because the damage suffered by the owner of the building, in such circumstances, was neither material nor physical damage. The defect was a defect in quality; the value of the building had been reduced. Such an economic loss is recoverable under contract but not, in the absence of a special relationship of proximity, recoverable in tort or delict. (To explain this in another way, if the defective foundations had caused the house to fall down and the residents were fatally injured then the loss would have been damage to property and physical injury – this would be recoverable.) Seven Lords of Appeal (three of them Scottish law Lords) of the House of Lords heard this case. They held that the Council had owed no duty of care to the plaintiff when it had approved the plans to avoid causing pure economic loss. This decision overturned the decision in *Anns* and all the subsequent decisions based on *Anns*.

Thus, it can be seen that the *Murphy* decision is very important regarding the area of pure economic loss. The case emphasises that pure economic loss is generally irrecoverable. Exceptionally, it will be recoverable, if it is negligent misstatement or where the relationship is akin to contract as in *Junior Books*, but there was no 'special relationship' between Murphy and the Local Authority.

LIABILITY FROM NERVOUS SHOCK OR PHYCHIATRIC INJURY

In Scotland a claim for damages can be brought for nervous shock sustained through what was seen or heard by the pursuer without direct physical contact or injury. However, the student must note that there is no liability if the pursuer only suffers a 'wee fright' or grief, distress or emotion (**Simpson** *v* **ICI 1983 SLT 601**) . The term 'nervous shock' has been criticised by judges as being out of date and as 'a misleading and inaccurate' description. Whatever term is used, for liability to arise the shock must have induced a recognised medical condition. For example, clinical depression, acute anxiety problems, psychotic disorders. Another form of nervous shock is post-traumatic stress disorder (PTSD), which is caused by being involved in or witnessing a single catastrophic event or accident.

Psychiatric injury can develop from long term subjection of the body to mental stress, overwork or worry. If this has been caused by the employer's breach of his duty of care, the employee might be successful in suing for damages. The employer was held liable for this in **Walker** *v* **Northumberland County Council [1995] IRLR 35** which is discussed on page 349. See also **Johnstone** *v* **Bloomsbury Health Authority [1992] QB 333** on page 339.

Psychiatric injury or nervous shock caused by a single event, accident or catastrophe can affect two kinds of victim, the primary victim, and the secondary victim. Different rules apply depending on the kind of victim.

(a) the primary victim is a person who is physically injured in an accident and who suffers either physical or psychiatric injury or who is involved in an accident but is not actually physically injured but reasonably fears for his safety at the time and this brings on psychiatric injury. In **Bourhill** *v* **Young 1942 SC (HL) 78** it was established that there could be liability for injury in the form of nervous shock. The test is whether the defender could have reasonably foreseen injury to the pursuer in the form of nervous shock. In **Page** *v* **Smith [1995] 2 All ER 736** Page was the driver of a car who was directly involved in a collision with Smith's car. Page was a 'primary victim' who suffered no physical injury but claimed that the accident had brought on a shock induced psychiatric illness – a fresh attack of ME. This was a complaint he had suffered from on and off for years but before the accident had been in remission. A majority of the judges held that the rule 'you have to take your victim as you find him' applied. Once liability for negligence is established the victim has to be taken as he is whether he has an 'egg-shell skull' or an 'egg-shell personality'. Their Lordships held that a negligent driver was liable for damages for nervous shock suffered by a primary victim if personal injury of some kind was reasonably foreseeable as a result of the accident and it made no difference whether the personal injury was physical or psychiatric. The case was referred back to the Court of Appeal to decide the issue of causation.

(b) the secondary victim is a person who suffers shock or psychiatric injury because of seeing injury to another person or fearing for the safety of another. The student will have noticed the cautious approach of the courts to allowing liability for pure economic loss. This is justified on the basis of the 'floodgates' argument. This argument is also applied to claims for damages for psychiatric injury suffered by secondary victims and restrictions are put on such claims. The justification being that without some sort of restriction one catastrophe could give rise to thousands of claims from persons who viewed it. Thousands of claims would clog up the court system and the cost of compensation would be unacceptable.

The law has been developing in this area and now it is possible for a secondary victim to successfully sue for damages for nervous shock but he can only claim if he can establish that his shock-induced injury was reasonably foreseeable and that he had the required degree of proximity. To ascertain proximity there are three basic factors/conditions/limitations which have to be examined:

1 the pursuer has to be in a class of persons whose claims should be recognised;
2 the proximity of the pursuer to the accident in terms of time and space; and
3 the means by which the shock was caused.

The first important case where a secondary victim was successful was in **McLoughlin *v* O'Brian [1983] AC 410.** Mrs McLoughlin was at home when her husband and three children were involved in a serious accident two miles away. One daughter died immediately and two hours later Mrs M saw the rest of the family undergoing treatment in casualty (still in much the same condition as they had been at the accident with all the blood and gore). As a result of being informed about the accident and seeing her family at the hospital she suffered severe and persistent shock. The House of Lords held that she was entitled to claim damages for nervous shock which was a reasonable and probable consequence of O'Brian's negligent driving. The limitations to a nervous shock claim were satisfied. Mrs M was the wife and mother of the victims. Although she was not present at the accident, Lord Wilberforce said that to insist on direct aural and visual perception would be impracticable or unjust and under the 'immediate aftermath doctrine' one who came very soon on the scene should not be excluded from claiming. He added that as regards communication, the law should not compensate for shock brought on solely by communication by a third party.

In the leading case of **Alcock & Others *v* Chief Constable of South Yorkshire Police [1991] 4 All ER 907** All five of the judges endorsed the approach of Lord Wilberforce in *McLoughlin* that in addition to the test of reasonable foreseeability, the right to claim must be decided by reference to the three tests of proximity. In this case, before the start of a major football match at Hillsborough football stadium, the police responsible for crowd control allowed an excessively large number of spectators into some of the sections or pens which were already full. The result was that 95 spectators were crushed to death and over 400 injured. Scenes from the grounds were broadcast live on television during the course of the disaster and shown later on the news. However, in accordance with television broadcasting guidelines none of the scenes depicted the suffering or dying of recognisable victims. Sixteen persons brought actions for damages for injury by shock against the Chief Constable. It was admitted that the deaths and injuries of the primary victims had been caused by the negligence of the police. The problem in this appeal was whether these secondary victims could claim damages for nervous shock. Some had viewed the disaster from other parts of the ground, some were outside the stadium and some had viewed the scenes on television. The House of Lords held that persons (secondary victims) could only recover damages if first the reasonable foreseeability test was satisfied and then the three possible limitations on the duty of care would have to be examined. Taking these in turn:

1 The class of persons whose claims should be recognised will be those with ties of love and affection to the primary victim. The House of Lords made it clear that the quality of the relationship was important rather than reference to a particular marital or blood bond. The closeness of tie must be proved by the

pursuer and although this could be presumed in the case of parents, children and spouses it could extend to other relationships involving intimate association like engaged couples and even friends if it could be proved that the tie of love and affection was real and not a fleeting or distant one. They were divided as to whether a bystander could ever claim. Only Lord Ackner thought it possible 'if in the circumstances a reasonably strong-nerved person would have been so shocked' but the circumstances would have to be particularly horrific. He gave as an example a bystander viewing a petrol tanker careering out of control into a school and bursting into flames.

2 The proximity of the claimant to the accident must be sufficiently close in time and space. This requirement will be satisfied if the claimant is present and witnesses the accident or it can be extended to include the case where the pursuer sees the 'immediate aftermath' as in the *McLoughlin* case. In the *Alcock* case a narrower view of what constitutes the 'immediate aftermath' was taken. Although Mr Alcock had been in the grounds and had searched for his brother-in-law for hours before he found him in the mortuary some eight hours after the disaster the House of Lords held that even if this identification could be described as part of the aftermath, it was not part of the immediate aftermath and his claim was not allowed .

3 The means by which the shock was caused. The shock must come through sight or sound of the event or its immediate aftermath. It was accepted in *Alcock* that there can be no liability where the shock results from being told about the accident by a third party nor viewing the event on television or hearing it on the radio. This could not be equated with being within sight or hearing of the disaster. Although it was reasonably foreseeable that scenes of the disaster would go out live on television the television authorities had observed the code of ethics which prevents live transmission of scenes where recognisable people are suffering and dying. However, Lord Ackner said that there may be cases where viewing simultaneous television pictures of a disaster may be treated as equivalent to sight and sound of an accident. He gave as an example parents watching on television a live broadcast of their children in a hot-air balloon and then the balloon bursting into flames. Clearly the impact of such pictures would be as great as, if not greater than, the actual sight of the accident.

Note that we return to the point that those secondary victims who have no bond of love and affection with the primary victim, i.e., bystanders, cannot claim. In **McFarlane *v* EE Caledonia Ltd [1994] 2 All ER 1** McFarlane was a painter who was working on the Piper Alpha rig. His accommodation was on the rig's standby vessel the Tharos. At the time of the fire on the oil rig he was on the Tharus which moved close to the rig to attempt firefighting and rescue operations. Although he offered to assist he did not carry out any rescue activities and he choose to stand on deck and watch. He claimed damages for PTSD. The Court of Appeal took into account the *Alcock* decision and found that McFarlane was not a participant or rescuer but a mere bystander. Lord Justice Stuart-Smith said that both as a matter of principle and policy the court should not extend the duty of care to those who are mere bystanders or witnesses of horrific events unless there is a significant degree of proximity which requires both nearness in time and space and a close tie of love and affection between the pursuer and the actual victim. He continued that it had not been shown that it was reasonably foreseeable that a man of ordinary fortitude and phlegm in McFarlane's position would be so affected by what he saw that he would suffer psychiatric injury.

In **Robertson and Rough** *v* **Forth Road Bridge Joint Board [1995] IRLR 251** the pursuers were working with Smith on the bridge when gale force winds lifted a sheet of metal from the back of a pickup truck and swept Smith who sitting on the sheet of metal over the side of the bridge. He landed on a girder below the level of the bridge and was found dead by the pursuers a few minutes later. As a result of witnessing the accident Robertson and Rough suffered nervous shock and PTSD. Their claims did not succeed on the grounds that neither pursuer could claim a sufficiently close tie of love and affection to the deceased nor could the claim be justified on the basis that the accident witnessed by the two men was so horrific that an ordinary bystander would foreseeably suffer nervous shock.

Rescuers are a special case – the rules applying to bystanders do not apply to rescuers

When a rescuer suffers psychiatric injury as a result of participating in a rescue operation after an accident or catastrophe the three conditions regarding proximity are relaxed. The justification is that as a matter of public policy rescuers should not be discouraged. In **Chadwick** *v* **BTC [1967] 2 All ER 945** Chadwick was a 44 year old window cleaner. When he was 28 he had suffered some psychoneurotic symptoms but he had not had them for 16 years and was not, so the court decided, someone who would be likely to relapse under the ordinary stresses of life. There was a terrible train disaster. Mr C heard about it on the news and went to the scene, which was close by, to help. As a result of the horror of his experiences he suffered a psychoneurotic condition; he never recovered and died. His wife successfully claimed damages. It was held that a duty of care is owed to rescuers as it is reasonably foreseeable that people will attempt to rescue others and could suffer nervous shock as a result of the scenes arising from the railway's negligence.

Thus in the cases of *McFarlane* and *Robertson and Rough* if the pursuers had produced evidence that they were assisting to rescue the primary victims they might have succeeded with their claims. Regarding professional rescuers like the emergency services, in the past they were usually denied compensation by the courts if they suffered physical injuries. This view was held because it was felt that it was within the normal risk of their job. However, in **Ogwo** *v* **Taylor [1988] 1 AC 431** a fireman successfully claimed damages for physical injuries from the housholder whose negligence caused the fire, and then damages were allowed for psychiatric injuries in **Hale** *v* **London Underground**. Hale was a fireman at the fire at the Kings Cross Underground Station. He suffered no significant injury at the time apart from exhaustion but did later suffer symptoms of PTSD which led to his retirement on the grounds of ill health. He was awarded £144 390. In June 1996 it was reported in the *Glasgow Herald* that £1.2 million was awarded in 'out of court' settlements to 14 police officers who were on duty at Hillsborough and suffered PTSD as a result of helping remove the dead and injured fans from the pens. In 1995 six other police officers failed in their claims for PTSD – they had helped with the injured and dying fans on the pitch. Their appeal against this decision has still to be heard.

As a final point there are two interesting cases to consider. In **Attia** *v* **British Gas Plc [1987] 3 All ER 455** Mrs A successfully sued for damages for nervous shock brought on when she returned home to discover that the Gas Board had negligently set her house on fire. Also, in **Clark *v* Scottish Power plc 1994 SLT 924** Mrs Clark successfully sued for damages for psychiatric illness which was brought on after she returned to find an unjustified forced entry had been made to her house to switch off her electricity supply.

BURDEN OF PROOF

Having discussed what amounts in law to a duty of care, we must now return to examine what the pursuer must establish in order to succeed in bringing an action for damages for negligence. The onus of proof is on the pursuer; he must show that 'on the balance of probabilities', the defender has been in breach of a duty of care owed to the pursuer and this breach has caused his injury. This burden of proof can sometimes be very difficult. The accident has happened but the pursuer cannot produce evidence which will show fault on the part of the defender. There is a rule of evidence expressed in the maxim *'res ipsa loquitur'* ('the facts speak for themselves') which can assist the pursuer in certain circumstances.

The fact that the accident happened in those circumstances raises a prima facie case of fault on the part of the defender. If *res ipsa loquitur* applies, the burden of proof shifts to the defender – he has to rebut the inference that he has been negligent. For example, the defender parked his car at the top of a hill, the car slips its brakes and runs down the hill causing damage to the pursuer's wall. *Res ipsa loquitur* applies – the inference is that the owner of the car was at fault.

Three conditions are necessary before *res ipsa loquit*ur applies:

1 The offending 'thing' must have been under the control or management of the defender or his employees.
2 Such accidents do not usually happen when due care is exercised by those in control. For example, bags of sugar do not fall out a warehouse window if they have been stacked carefully.
3 There must be an absence of an explanation for this accident.

In **Scott *v* London and St Katherine Dock Co [1861] All ER 246** Scott, a custom house officer, was walking past a warehouse when he was hit by six bags of sugar. The bags were being lowered to the ground by a crane from the upper part of the warehouse. There was no warning and the area had not been fenced off. The rule of *res ipsa loquitur* operated to assist Scott as the sugar was in the control of the dock company or their servants. An accident like the above does not happen if those in control use proper care. In the absence of an explanation, the presumption is that the accident arose from lack of care by the defendants.

In **Ward *v* Tesco Stores [1976] 1 WLR 810** Ward claimed damages for the injuries she received when she slipped on some yoghurt, spilt on the floor of the supermarket. Contractors were employed to clean the floor every night and the floor was also swept about five or six times a day. All Mrs Ward could prove was that she had slipped on the yoghurt. Applying the principle of *res ipsa loquitur*, the court held that Mrs Ward had a prima facie case of negligence. The floor was under Tesco's control and management; had the floor been kept 'yoghurt-free' the accident would not, in the normal course of events, have happened. Tesco's evidence of how often the floor was cleaned did not rebut the presumption of negligence.

In **Cassidy** *v* **Minister of Health [1951] 2 KB 343** Cassidy went into hospital to have two fingers operated on. He came out of hospital with four useless fingers. The trial judge dismissed the action as Cassidy had failed to prove negligence by the hospital. However, the Court of Appeal held that the principle of *res ipsa loquitur* applied. The onus lay on the hospital to prove that they had not been negligent and they failed to do so.

When the principle applies, the burden of proof shifts to the defender but he can still rebut the inference that he has been negligent by:

(a) proving positively that there has been no lack of care on his part and showing exactly what did happen; *or*
(b) by providing a reasonable explanation of how the accident could have happened and that explanation is consistent with his not being negligent.

In **Devine** *v* **Colvilles 1969 SC (HL) 67** there was an explosion at Colvilles. Devine, a workman, was 15 feet above the ground on a platform. When the explosion occurred he jumped off and hurt himself. The explosion occurred in a hose and the probable cause was that rust had got into the hose and this should have been excluded by a filter. The defenders argued that they were not at fault. The principle of *res ipsa loquitur* was applied. The 'thing', the exploding hose, was under the control and management of the defender. Such explosions do not occur if due care is exercised. No-one knew the exact cause of the explosion. However, the defender's explanation of what happened did not clearly establish that they were not negligent. Colvilles were found liable.

In **O'Hara** *v* **Central SMT 1941 SC 363** a bus was about to stop when it suddenly swerved and a passenger, standing waiting to get off, fell on to the road and was injured. The court accepted the plea of *res ipsa loquitur*; there was prima facie evidence of negligence by the driver. The bus was the 'thing' under the control of SMT's driver, and buses don't usually swerve if due care is being exercised. However, the driver said that a pedestrian had run in front of the bus. The court held that if he could prove this then the presumption that he had been negligent would be rebutted.

If a defender rebuts the presumption of negligence then the onus of proof returns to the pursuer.

QUESTIONS

1 Tom was walking along a one-way street on his way to an interview for a new job with better salary and prospects than he had with his present employer. Before he crossed this street, he checked to ensure that there was no traffic coming in the usual direction. He was half-way across the road when he was

knocked down by Susan, who was driving too fast and in the wrong direction. Tom suffered terrible injuries and an ambulance had to be called. As a result of his injuries, Tom was off work for several months and, of course, did not get the new job as he had hoped. George, a shopkeeper, witnessed the accident and comforted Tom until the ambulance arrived. As a result, George was very upset and was unable to go to work for the rest of that week. A neighbour told Tom's widowed mother about the accident and she rushed to the hospital to see him. When she arrived, Tom was still in casualty, waiting to be attended by a doctor. She was very shocked when she saw his injuries and since that day, a year ago, she has suffered from clinical depression.

Discuss the extent of Susan's liability in these circumstances.

2 Colin, Sid and Jack set out one morning to walk the West Highland Way. On the way to the start of their walk, they saw a bus, with no driver at the wheel, rushing down a hill towards them. They all tried to get out of the way but unfortunately Colin's arm was crushed against a wall and later, in hospital, had to be amputated. An investigation revealed that the bus had been parked with the handbrake on, at the top of the hill outside the bus depot while the drivers changed shifts. No-one knows how the bus was put into action.

Shocked, but determined to continue, the remaining three walked on past a golf course. Unfortunately, Sid was hit by a golf ball which had been sliced out of bounds by Bill, a club member. Sid lost five teeth. First aid was administered to him in a nearby pub, called The Bull and Cow. While the two friends were there, they decided to have a drink. Unfortunately, when Jack took a gulp of his beer, he found the remains of a decomposed mouse at the bottom of his mug. He was very ill with gastro-enteritis and was off work for a fortnight.

Advise Colin, Sid and Jack as to whether they can sue for damages for their injuries and if they can, who is liable?

3 Fastjob Ltd hired a digger from Planthire Ltd to carry out an important construction contract for Wholesales Ltd. The digger was accidently destroyed when a lorry owned by Deliverit Ltd and driven by Bob, their employee, careered off the road on to the site. The construction contract for Wholesales Ltd was delayed and Fastjob had to pay liquidate damages to Wholesale Ltd. Advise Fastjob as to whether they can sue Deliverit for this loss.

4 Mrs Smith placed a window box on the outside window sill of her tenement flat (three floors up). She meant to ask a joiner to attach it securely to the sill but she then forgot.

Three weeks later during a gale the window box fell into the street below. John was injured. He was the only employee of Financial Services Ltd who could work the computer in their office. Financial Services had to employ a replacement computer expert to cover for the six weeks when John was absent from work.

Advise John and Financial Services Ltd.

CAUSATION

It is essential for the pursuer to prove that the defender's wrongful act, his negligence, has caused the harm or injury to the pursuer. Causal connection must be proved from the facts. The courts distinguish between two kinds of cause:

1 The ***causa sine qua non*** is a factor, possibly but not necessarily, a breach of duty, which was only a prerequisite of the harm which has occurred, part of the background of events leading to the harm. A *causa sine qua non* may be essential in that, but for it, the harm would not have happened but it is not the effective cause of the harm and does not imply liability.
2 The ***causa causans*** is the real, predominant or effective cause of the pursuer's loss or injury. Using one's commonsense is the way to choose the real or dominant cause from a number of causal factors. The *causa causans* is not necessarily the nearest in time or space to the harm. It is the one that the man in the street would say had materially caused the harm.

Sometimes there is only one possible cause (*causa causans*) which clearly caused the injuries. Causation is not an issue. For example, driver A reverses his car without looking behind him and hits another vehicle belonging to B. A is in breach of the duty of care which he owes to other road users including B. A's breach is the *causa causans* of the damage to B's vehicle.

Alternatively, the court might decide that the pursuer has proved that there were two effective causes which together contributed to the one harmful result. In such a case the two defenders will be held jointly and severally liable. Under the Law Reform (Miscellaneous Provisions) (Scotland) Act 1940 the court can apportion blame. (See **Drew** *v* **Western SMT 1947 SC 222** p. 267.)

When several factors (happening in sequence or concurrently) have possibly caused the harm, then the court will have to decide which of these factors was the real and effective cause (or causes) of the harm. They will have to pick the *causa causans* out of perhaps the many factors that were present and came together to produce the harm – *but for* these other factors the damage would not have happened.

In simple terms, the defender's negligent act must be identified as causing the harm suffered by the pursuer or adding materially to the risk.

In **McGhee** *v* **NCB 1973 SLT 14 (HL)** McGhee worked in a brickworks in hot dusty conditions. He contracted dermatitis and sued his employers on the grounds that they were in breach of their duty to take reasonable care for his safety. His skin was covered with brickdust at work. His employers failed to provide showers and McGhee had to cycle home with brickdust on his skin. The House of Lords decided to take a broader view of causation in this case. The employers admitted that they had been in breach of their duty of care but maintained that it had not been proved that their failure to provide showers had caused McGhee's dermatitis. Medical witnesses could not explain the process by which dermatitis developed but they did say that the failure to provide showers added materially to the risk of dermatitis. That was enough for the House of Lords – it was held that on the balance of probabilities the employer's breach of duty caused or materially contributed to McGhee's injury.

In **Kay's Tutor** *v* **Ayrshire and Arran Health Board 1987 SLT 577** a two-year-old boy was admitted to hospital suffering from suspected meningitis and was mistakenly given a massive overdose of penicillin. As a result, the child went into convulsions and developed paralysis on one side of his body. The child recovered from the effects of the penicillin and from the meningitis but was later discovered to be deaf. The Health Board admitted liability for the negligence of the doctor and the resulting convulsions but denied responsibility for the deafness. The House of Lords had to decide which of the two competing factors (the overdose or the meningitis) had caused the deafness. There was no medical evidence that an overdose of penicillin had ever caused deafness but there were many cases where meningitis had. The pursuers failed to establish causation – i.e., there was no proven link between the negligence of the doctor and the deafness. It could not even be argued that the overdose had materially contributed to the child's injury.

Novus actus interveniens

Sometimes the connection or link between the initial wrongful conduct and the ultimate injury or damage may be broken by a fresh intervening factor called a *novus actus* (a new act). This intervening factor can sometimes replace the initial wrong and it becomes the effective cause of the injury. There is a presumption against a *novus actus* breaking the chain of causation and so it is up to the defender to persuade the court that the new event or intervening factor has superseded his negligent act and become the dominant cause of the harm.

To break the so-called chain of causation, the *novus actus* must be something unexpected and extraneous (outwith the sequence of events) and not something that one would expect to happen naturally or inevitably. In short, the intervention of a *novus actus* will not break the chain of causation if it is the very kind of thing that could be expected to happen and something which the defender was supposed to take reasonable care to prevent. A *novus actus* can be an action by the pursuer himself, or by a third party or even a natural event like a hurricane

In **Knightly** *v* **Johns [1982] 1 All ER 851** Johns negligently overturned his car at the exit of a one-way tunnel. S, the police inspector in charge, who had forgotten to close the tunnel, ordered Knightly to ride on his motorcycle the wrong way along the tunnel to close the entrance. While doing so, Knightly was involved in an accident with a car, driven by C. Neither Knightly nor the driver were negligent. The Court of Appeal held that the police inspector had been negligent by forgetting to close the tunnel and, secondly, by ordering Knightly to close it in a dangerous way. The police inspector's actions amounted to a *novus actus*, breaking the chain of causation between John's negligence and Knightly's accident. So the police inspector (and his chief constable) were liable for Knightly's injuries.

In **McKew** *v* **Holland, Hannen & Cubitts 1970 SLT 68** McKew's leg was injured at work. This made him stiff and weakened his left leg. A few days later, he was coming down some stairs when his injured leg 'gave way' beneath him. In order to save himself, he jumped the rest of the stairs, landing on his 'good' leg, breaking his right ankle and a bone in his leg. The court had to decide whether McKew could sue his employers for the injuries to both legs or not. The House of Lords held that the employers were only liable for the first injury and that

McKew's action of jumping down the stairs was not a natural thing to do in these circumstances. It was unreasonable, and as a *novus actus interveniens* broke the chain of causation.

When considering whether the pursuer's own actions amount to a *novus actus*, note that actions which are instinctive – like seeking to rescue people or their property, or taking action in an emergency – do not normally break the chain of causation as it is foreseeable that people will try to help. There is also a possibility that if the pursuer's actions do not break the chain of causation and so liability still remains with the defender, the pursuer's actions may show sufficient lack of care for his own safety that they amount to contributory negligence.

Actions by third parties which arise naturally and are foreseeable again will not break the chain of causation.

An example could be where the injured pursuer requires medical treatment and the treatment goes wrong. The actions of the doctor do not usually amount to a *novus actus* breaking the chain of causation, since treatment is foreseeable as the likely outcome of a negligent act and doctors can never guarantee that a patient will recover. However, if the treatment goes wrong and it can be regarded as medical negligence, that would be unexpected and unwarranted and could break the chain of causation. Finally, the criminal act of a third party, even reasonably foreseeable, will usually amount to a *novus actus interveniens* unless there are special circumstances as described by Lord Goff in **Smith** *v* **Littlewood** – see p. 276.

REMOTENESS OF DAMAGE

Once it has been established that the defender has been negligent, there is still the problem to resolve as to the extent of the damages. Some of the resulting injuries will be too remote from the original negligent act and so the defender will not be liable. There is unfortunately no straightforward test that can be applied to determine the extent of liability of the defender for damages.

In **Allan** *v* **Barclay (1864) 2M 873** Lord Kinloch said 'the grand rule on the subject of damages is that none can be claimed except such as naturally and directly arise out of the wrong done; and such therefore, as may reasonably be supposed to have been in the view of the wrongdoer'.

Lord Kinloch's statement does not give a clear test. The first part states that damages can only be claimed for the natural and direct consequences of the wrongful act; the second part states that the consequences must be reasonably foreseeable. The position has not yet been settled in Scotland as to which test is correct and the debate continues. In approaching the question, it is helpful to note that the following cases consider two kinds of situation. First, where the damage is not remote in time or space from the defender's negligent act but it happens in a quite unexpected or unforeseeable way and, second, where the damage is remote in time or space from the original negligent act.

There are two schools of thought:

(a) *The Polemis school* – once liability for negligence is established, then the defender is liable for all the direct consequences of the negligent act, *even though they could not be reasonably anticipated*. In ***Re* Polemis [1921] 3 KB 560** a ship had on board some petrol. Arab stevedores, employed by the charterers of the ship, dropped a plank into the hold of the ship. The plank struck something, which made a spark which ignited the petrol vapour in the hold. The resulting fire destroyed the ship. The court held that although it was foreseeable that the negligent act of dropping the plank could cause *some* damage to the ship, its cargo or to a crew member, it was not really foreseeable that the whole ship would be destroyed. Nevertheless, the employers were liable for the total destruction of the ship because it was held that a defender is liable for all the direct consequences of his negligent act.
(b) The *Wagon Mound school* – once liability for negligence is established, then the defender is liable for all consequences *which are reasonably foreseeable* . In ***Re* The Wagon Mound [1961] AC 388** an accident happened again in a dock, this time in Sydney. The ship was being loaded with oil and due to negligence by the employees of Overseas Tankship some of the oil spilt into the sea and floated over to where some workmen were welding. Work was suspended for a while but then continued. A spark from the welding equipment ignited a rag which was floating on the oily sea; the oil went on fire and the whole wharf was engulfed in flames, resulting in considerable losses. The Privy Council held that Overseas Tankship, the owners of the ship, could not have reasonably foreseen that this would happen as a result of spilling oil. Also, it was not reasonable to expect oil to go on fire this way and Overseas Tankship were not liable.

Having two tests is very confusing for the student. The only note of comfort is that in practice the result is usually the same. Foreseeable consequences are usually direct and direct consequences are usually foreseeable. This takes us back to Lord Kinloch's test in **Allan** *v* **Barclay**.

The egg-shell skull rule

The test of remoteness of damage must be qualified by the rule that once a wrongdoer has been found negligent – i.e., his liability has been established, then the wrongdoer must take his victim as he finds him and he is liable for all the consequences of the victim's injury. It would appear that this rule only applies to personal injuries and not to damage to property. For example, if the victim has a weak heart or a thin skull and dies from injuries which would not have killed an ordinary man, the wrongdoer is liable for his death.

In **Smith** *v* **Leech Brain and Co Ltd 1961 3 All ER 1159** Smith's husband was burnt by a splash of molten metal on his lip while working. The accident happened because of his employer's negligence in not providing adequate protection for their employee. The burn promoted cancer in tissues which already had a premalignant condition. He had six operations but eventually died. The employers were held liable for his death.

In **Page** *v* **Smith [1995] 2 All ER 736** which is discussed on page 286. Page, a victim of a road accident, claimed the accident had brought on an attack of ME, an illness from which he had suffered for many years. The House of Lords applied the egg-shell rule.

QUESTIONS

1 With reference to the law of negligence, explain and distinguish between a *'causa sine qua non'* and a *'causa causans'*.

2 Donald is a children's entertainer. One day, after his show on the beach at Largs, a number of children had followed him to his van to watch him pack his equipment into his car. He shouted 'goodbye' and drove off without checking that all the children were standing clear of his car. Unfortunately, he ran over eight-year-old Alan's right foot. June, a passing first-aider, applied a tourniquet to Alan's crushed foot and offered to drive him to the local hospital. Due to delays caused by road works and an anti-poll tax demonstration, the journey took an hour longer than it normally took. Again unfortunately, June forgot to slacken the tourniquet. As a result, Alan's right foot had to be amputated. Mr Dim, the surgeon assigned to carry out the operation, misread the instructions given to him and he amputated Alan's left foot.

Discuss the legal liability of the various parties.

3 Bob, a driver for Hedgehog Trucking, was driving his lorry far too fast through Ayr. He rounded a corner, to discover a newly-installed pedestrian-crossing with the lights at red against him. Mrs Sweet was pushing Baby Sweet over the crossing. As Bob was driving in excess of the speed limit, he could not stop his vehicle in time and he badly injured Mrs Sweet. Mrs Sweet had no chance of getting out of the way but she did manage to push the pram across the road. The pram rolled into the path of Clarence, who was slowing down for the crossing. Clarence managed to swerve and avoided hitting the pram but he damaged his car when he hit a lamppost. The lamppost fell and injured Dick, a pedestrian. Dick's injuries were not serious but he suffered from a heart condition and the next day he died in hospital from a heart attack.

Advise Mrs Sweet, Clarence and Dick's widow as to whether they have any legal remedy.

STRICT LIABILITY

So far our discussion of the law of delict has concerned the area covering the common law of negligence where the standard of care required is 'reasonable care in the circumstances'. There are other forms of liability, namely strict liability and absolute liability. In strict liability cases, the defender will be liable despite the absence of 'fault' in the ordinary sense – the duty is to take effectual precautions to prevent harm happening. However, even in strict liability cases, there are certain defences open to the defender; the liability is strict but not absolute. There are very few forms of strict liability under common law. Most instances arise under statute. We now deal with breach of a statutory duty.

BREACH OF STATUTORY DUTY

Sometimes Parliament will impose what is called a 'statutory duty' on certain persons (i.e., the duty is laid down in an Act of Parliament or statutory instrument). Very often that person owes a similar duty under common law, and an injured party can bring a claim based on breach of both duties.

When bringing an action for breach of statutory duty, the pursuer must first show that the Act does allow a civil action for damages. In some Acts the intention of Parliament is clearly stated. For example, the Health and Safety at Work Act states that a civil action cannot be brought. However, in the past, frequently, the legislation did not make this intention clear and the courts were then left to interpret the legislation and ascertain whether civil liability was intended or not.

To ascertain the intention of Parliament, the courts will consider the construction and wording of the Act and reach a decision by taking into account the following factors:

1 If the Act imposes a duty but no sanction or remedy is mentioned, then there is a presumption that a civil action may be brought.
2 Again where the Act is not clear, the courts will look at the existing law prior to the Act and if, for example, the existing common law remedies are adequate, they will decide that parliament did not intend a civil remedy for breach of statutory duty.
3 If the Act provides a criminal sanction, then the presumption is that there is no civil remedy. However, if it is clear that the Act was passed for the benefit of a specific class of persons, a group of people rather than as a means of protecting the general public, the courts have held that a civil remedy is available (e.g., the Factories Act, which was passed to protect persons working on the factory premises).

CONDITIONS FOR BRINGING AN ACTION FOR BREACH OF STATUTORY DUTY

If the pursuer can show that the Act does provide a civil remedy and has therefore grounds for bringing an action, he must then prove the following:

1 The duty imposed on the defender by the Act must be owed to the pursuer.
2 The defender was in breach of this duty.
3 On the balance of probabilities that the breach caused the damage or injury suffered by the pursuer.
4 When establishing whether there has been a breach of the duty, it is important to find the standard required by the Act. The standard of the duty of care under common law is that 'of reasonable care in the circumstances'.

However, the standard of statutory duties vary – there is not one single standard. Sometimes the Act will impose a **qualified duty** (which is very often similar to the common law standard). For example, 'so far as is reasonably practicable' or 'reasonable care in the circumstances' (e.g., the Occupier's Liability (Scotland) Act 1960). Sometimes the Act will impose a **strict duty** (e.g., the Consumer Protection Act (1987 Part 1)). Sometimes it will be an **absolute duty**. For example, the Factories Act 1961 s 14 – 'every dangerous part of any machinery shall be securely fenced'. So, if a duty is in absolute terms, then mere non-observance is the statutory equivalent of negligence proved. This point is illustrated in the case of **John Summers *v* Frost [1955] AC 740**. Frost's thumb was injured in a factory when it came into contact with a grinding wheel which was not completely fenced. John Summers argued as their defence that to fence this machine securely would make it unusable. This was rejected by the court because it is no defence to argue that an absolute duty is unreasonable.

15 Defences

There are many defences to an action based on delict. The defender may make **a defence based on a point of law**. For example, he could argue that he owed no duty of care to the pursuer in the circumstances; or that he did take reasonable care; or that his actions were not the effective cause of the injury sustained by the pursuer. The defender could also make **a defence based on a point of fact** and prove that the pursuer's case is factually incorrect.

In addition there are some particular named defences. These do not deny that the defender has been negligent but if they are successful, they may either absolve the defender completely or, if it is a partial defence, they may reduce the amount of damages that the defender has to pay.

CONTRIBUTORY NEGLIGENCE

This defence is used where it is established that the defender has been negligent *but* the pursuer's own actions, in failing to take care for his own safety, have in part contributed to the injuries which he has suffered – ie he is partly to blame for his own loss or injury. Contributory negligence need not amount to breach of a legal duty of care. It need only be lack of care for one's own safety. Formerly, if established, it was a complete defence. However, since the **Law Reform (Contributory Negligence) Act 1945** it is available as a partial defence. Section 1 of the Act provides that where a person suffers damage as a result partly of his own fault and partly of the fault of another, his claim shall not be defeated but his damages will be reduced to such an extent as the court thinks just and equitable having regard to the pursuer's share in the responsibility for the damage. (Note there is nothing to prevent a court in extreme cases holding the pursuer 99 per cent at fault.

The defence is available in both common law cases of negligence and in cases of breach of statutory duty. In all cases the onus is on the defender to establish the defence.

Typical examples of contributory negligence are: a passenger putting his head out a railway carriage window; a pedestrian stepping on to the road without looking; driving too fast; failing to wear a seat belt; taking a lift with a drunk driver; riding a motor cycle without a crash helmet.

In **Davies** *v* **Swan Motor Co [1949] 2 KB 291** cited earlier, Davies, a dustbin man, was standing on the side steps of his dust cart when it went round a corner and a bus ran into it. Davies was injured and later died. The court decided that both drivers had been negligent and that Davies had contributed to his death to the extent of one-fifth – i.e., he was one-fifth to blame and so the damages awarded to his widow were reduced by one-fifth.

In **Sayers** *v* **Harlow Urban Council 1958 2 All ER 342** Sayers found herself locked in the cubicle of a public toilet. This was due to a fault in the lock. Eventually, having tried in vain to attract attention, she tried to climb over the door. The Court of Appeal held that her attempted escape did not amount to *novus actus interveniens*. The local authority was held liable for the injury she sustained when she fell trying to climb out. However, her damages were reduced by 25 per cent because she had put her weight on a fragile fitting – the toilet-roll holder and had thus contributed to her injuries.

Some special cases where there are limitations on the defence

It will always depend on the circumstances and there is no definite age limit but usually young children and the elderly or infirm will be less readily held to have contributed to their own injury. The same view applies in rescue cases, bearing in mind that in the face of imminent danger, a rescuer's actions are usually instinctive even though he is not always successful in his attempt.

Situations where the defence cannot be pleaded

The agony rule – if due to the defender's fault, the pursuer finds himself in a position of danger, it will not amount to contributory negligence if he makes a mistake and suffers injury which he could have avoided.

The dilemma rule – where again in a situation created by the defender, the pursuer picks the wrong course of two options open to him. In **Wallace** *v* **Bergius 1915 SC 205** a driver of a car saw another car coming towards him on the wrong side of the road. He held his course until an accident was inevitable, then he crossed to the other side of the road – so did the other driver – crash! It was held that the first driver had been put in a position of danger by the other driver's conduct and the defender could not plead contributory negligence.

CONSENT

A person has no right of action if he has expressly or impliedly consented to something being done to him and that act would normally be regarded as a delict. To be effective as a complete defence, the consent must be freely given and it must be wide enough to cover the kind of conduct being complained about. For example, express consent to an operation or to medical treatment or to an examination; or the implied consent of a sportsman playing a game under normal rules. He could not sue a fellow player if, for example, he broke his leg. However, this could not be used as a defence if he was injured as a result of a deliberate and vicious foul.

In an emergency, perhaps to save life or property, the defence of necessity may be used to justify some delictual action done without consent.

VOLENTI NON FIT INJURIA

This means, basically, 'to a person who is willing no injury is done'. In other words, the pursuer has voluntarily assumed the risk of the harm that befell him. It appears to be similar to the defence of consent. However, the basis of this defence is that in the circumstances the pursuer has consented to waive the duty of care owed to him by the defender, whereas the basis of the defence of consent is that the pursuer has consented to absolve the defender from liability for doing something to him which would amount to a breach of the duty of care owed to the pursuer by the defender.

Before the defence of *volenti non fit injuria* can be used it must be shown that the pursuer freely and voluntarily with full knowledge of the risk agreed to take that risk. So it is important to establish that the pursuer had a free choice. If he accepts a risk out of duty or because he is afraid that he will lose his job, then it is not a free choice.

In **Smith** *v* **Baker [1891] AC 325** Smith was employed by Baker to drill holes in rocks and he was aware that a crane regularly swung loads of stones over his head. A stone fell and injured him. Baker tried to rely on the defence of *volenti non fit injuria*. He was unsuccessful. It was held that Smith had continued working knowing the risks but that he had not voluntarily accepted the risk as there had been many complaints to management about the danger.

Rescue cases

The defence cannot be used by the defender in cases where someone has unsuccessfully attempted a rescue. The rescuer is not held to have freely and voluntarily assumed risk of injury if he is acting under a social or moral duty particularly when saving lives.

In **Baker** *v* **Hopkins [1959] 3 All ER 225** a doctor died in attempting to rescue two men who were overcome by fumes down a well. He had been warned not to go down the well but, in an effort to try to save the lives of the two men, he tied a rope round himself and went down. The rope got caught and unfortunately he died. The defence of *volenti non fit injuria* was not allowed. Nor was he found to have contributed to his own death as he did use a rope. Nor did his actions in these circumstances amount to a *novus actus interveniens*. Hopkins & Son were held liable for his death.

Cases of spectators at dangerous sports

In several cases, it has been held that persons who voluntarily attend various kinds of games and sports take the risk of being injured. The knowledge of the risk is there because an accident is always a possibility which any reasonable spectator can foresee. For example, being hit by a cricket ball or a golf ball or a car leaving the racetrack. So a spectator takes the risk of any injury arising from the normal course of the game even if the sportsman shows lack of skill or judgement. But the spectator does not voluntarily undertake risk of injury if the sportsman's conduct shows a reckless disregard for the safety of spectators. This is the difference between a tennis ball or racquet accidentally landing in the crowd and a bad-tempered player deliberately throwing the ball or racquet into the crowd in anger.

DAMNUM FATALE

This means an 'act of God'. The defence is that the cause of the accident was due to natural forces which could not have been reasonably foreseen nor could they be reasonably guarded against. These natural forces would have to arise without human intervention. For example, an earthquake in Scotland could be regarded as *damnum fatale* but not in some other countries. It has been held that an extraordinary fall of rain cannot be regarded in Scotland as *damnum fatale*! This is a complete defence and is one of the few defences available to a defender subject to strict liability.

IMMUNITY

In certain circumstances, individuals have a general exemption or immunity from delictual liability. In such cases, if immunity exists, it is incompetent to bring an action against them.

1 The Queen, as an individual, is wholly immune but not other members of the Royal family.
2 The State or the Crown is not immune from being vicariously liable for the actions of its servants since the passing of the Crown Proceedings Act 1947. However, the Crown is immune and so not liable for an action of state in its dealings with other states and the subjects of other states.
3 Foreign sovereigns, heads of foreign states, foreign governments, ambassadors, their family and embassy staff (but only for acts within the scope of their duties) are immune from delictual liability.
4 Judges of the Court of Session and High Court and the Sheriff Court are completely immune from liability for their judicial acts.
5 Members of Parliament are not liable for defamation in connection with any statement made in the House of Commons and they also have qualified

privilege over statements made outside the House, provided they are made in the course of their duty.

6 In certain circumstances, trade unions have immunity from certain delictual actions. Under the Trade Union and Labour Relations (Consolidation) Act 1992, as amended, trade unions have a general immunity in respect of acts done in contemplation or furtherance of a trade dispute. These delictual acts are usually referred to in English law as the 'economic torts'. They are: conspiracy; inducing breach of a contract which can be extended to unlawful interference in contract; and intimidation. The immunity is only available if the delict was done 'in contemplation and furtherance of a trade dispute' and the members of the union have supported the action in a properly conducted ballot. The restrictions on the immunities are explained in the Act.

PRESCRIPTION AND LIMITATION OF ACTIONS

This is not really a defence as such and a claim, being brought, may be perfectly valid but because of the passage of time, the right to bring the action or the obligation to pay damages has been lost or extinguished. The law is codified by the Prescription and Limitation (Scotland) Act 1973 as amended. There is a different length of time depending on the type of harm suffered.

Personal injuries and death

An action for damages for physical injuries or death must be commenced within three years from the date of death or from when the injuries were sustained. The Act provides for this time to be extended in certain cases or at the discretion of the court. The running of the limitation period is stopped by the commencement of a court action.

Damage to property or economic loss

With claims for damage caused to property or for pure economic loss, there is no time limit by which the action must be started, but the actual obligation to make reparation is extinguished after five years. One exception to this is that under the Consumer Protection Act 1987 Part 1: obligations to make reparation for damage caused by dangerous products prescribe after ten years.

QUESTIONS

1 Clearly explain the defences of 'contributory negligence and '*volenti non fit injuria*'.

2 Peter was cleaning the windows of his shop in the High Street. For a short

period of time he blocked the pavement with his step-ladder. This caused Donald, a pedestrian, to step off the pavement on to the road. He did this without checking that the road was clear. Unfortunately, Susan, a van driver, who was delivering goods to Peter's shop, pulled into the kerb rather quickly and knocked down Donald. Donald was taken to hospital with a broken leg. Advise the parties as to their legal position.

3 John was employed by the Edinburgh Bus Co. One day he parked an empty minibus with the key in the ignition, unlocked and unattended outside a public house while he went inside to attend to a call of nature. When he came out, the minibus had disappeared. The minibus, driven by an unidentified third party was involved in an accident several hours later. The minibus had skidded into Mr Smith's car which was badly damaged. Mr Smith's wife had been sitting in the back seat without a seatbelt on. She was injured in the accident. Mr & Mrs Smith are planning to sue the Edinburgh Bus Co. Advise them.

16 Particular forms of business liability

In the earlier chapters we examined the general principles of negligence, breach of statutory duty and defences. We now consider some particular forms of business liability, namely liability arising from the use of business property, the liability of occupiers for dangerous premises, the liability of producers of dangerous products, the liability of professional persons and the liability of employers for the safety of their employees at work.

LIABILITY ARISING FROM THE USE OF BUSINESS PROPERTY

Liability for nuisance

A business organisation will have to have premises or land on which to carry out their business operation. In this respect they could either own the property or rent it. The term 'nuisance' is used rather loosely to cover any use of business property (or private property) which causes a continuing serious disturbance or inconvenience to one's neighbour. The nuisance must be a 'continuing wrong' or repeated occurrences. One or more isolated incidents will not amount to nuisance affecting the neighbour's peaceful enjoyment of his property. It does not matter if the nuisance was happening before the pursuer 'arrived on the scene'. An interdict is the usual remedy, although damages may be awarded for resulting harm. In **Webster *v* Lord Advocate 1985 SLT 361** Webster bought a flat near Edinburgh Castle. Every year a military tattoo takes place at the castle. Webster sought an interdict on the grounds that the noise from the erection of the stands for the audience constituted a nuisance. It was argued that the noise had affected the neighbourhood for years and that on the grounds of public policy her action should not succeed. The court held that it was not relevant that this nuisance had happened before Webster had bought the flat.

In the past it was thought that liability for nuisance was strict and so the pursuer did not have to establish that his neighbour had failed reasonably to prevent the disturbance or harm. However, because of the decision of the House of Lords in the following case it would appear that for the defender to be found liable he must have been at fault.

In **RHM Bakeries *v* Strathclyde Regional Council 1958 SLT 214** the bakery was flooded not only by rainwater but also by sewage from a blocked sewer under the control of the local authority. When bringing their claim, the pursuers did not aver or establish that the damage to their bakery was caused by fault on the part of the council. It could have been argued that the council were at fault because they had failed either to maintain or repair the sewage pipe. The pursuers presumed that the liability for nuisance was strict. RHM Bakeries failed in their action as the House of Lords stated that Strathclyde Regional Council would be liable only if they were at fault to some extent.

However, in most cases of nuisance the pursuer will not have a problem establishing fault. The plea of *res ipsa loquitur* will assist the pursuer and the defender's fault will be inferred.

Examples of possible nuisances are noise, vibration, offensive smells, pollution of the air or water, music played loudly and excessively, water flooding, balls being continually hit out of sports grounds and accumulations of offensive rubbish.

Liability for the escape of a dangerous thing from one's land

An individual or a business organisation could be liable if something potentially dangerous is kept or accumulated on their land and through their fault is allowed to escape and this causes harm to their neighbours. This kind of liability differs from liability for nuisance in that the 'thing' accumulated on the defender's land is not there naturally, is clearly potentially dangerous and the escape is a single event rather than a continuing disturbance. Possible examples could be water accumulated unnaturally, ie water held on the land because a dam had been built; combustible materials which go on fire and the fire spreads; or stored explosives detonating and rocks and rubble being thrown into the neighbourhood.

The Scottish authority is **Kerr *v* Earl of Orkney (1857) 20D 298** where the Earl built, half a mile upstream from Kerr's mill, a dam which burst and the water swept away his neighbour Kerr's houses, mill and machinery. Liability was held to be strict.

However, in *RHM Bakeries* v *Strathclyde Regional Council*, which was a case concerning a claim for nuisance, their Lordships referred to this liability for the escape of a dangerous thing and said that in such cases the defender's fault would have to be established. Lord Cullen endorsed this view in **McQueen *v* The Glasgow Garden Festival 1995 SLT 211.** McQueen, a spectator at a fireworks display was injured by a rocket which exploded before take-off because of a manufacturing defect. Lord Cullen said there was no strict liability in such cases against the organiser which must be decided in terms of nuisance law.

LIABILITY FOR DANGEROUS PREMISES

The law is now found in the **Occupiers' Liability (Scotland) Act 1960 s 2.** This Act is concerned with liability for dangerous premises. It states that the occupiers of land, buildings or other private premises must take such care in the circumstances of the case as is reasonable to see that any person coming on to these premises will not suffer injury or damage to themselves or to their property, in respect of dangers which are due to the state of the premises or to anything done or omitted to be done on them.

Who are 'occupiers'?

The term includes any person or corporate body in actual possession, physical control and occupation of the premises, whether they are the owner, the tenant, the licensee or any other person with the right of possession and control. Contractors who have taken possession of premises while working there may be regarded as occupiers, and the term has also included a person in charge of a fairground on another person's land.

The premises

Primarily, this covers land or buildings but also mentioned in the Act is 'any fixed or moveable structure including any vessel, vehicle or aircraft'. This has been held to include moveable property which a visitor may end up on, for example, a ladder, a gangway or scaffolding.

Visitors to the premises

The duty of care is extended to persons entering the premises. Regarding trespassers, although the standard of care owed to them is the same, the circumstances of the trespass are relevant and will be taken into account in deciding whether or not the standard of care exercised was reasonable. Examples of 'visitors' will include guests, clients, customers, contractors, firemen, a patient in a hospital, a hospital visitor, a customer in a restaurant or pub, children in a playground or spectators at a sporting event.

The standard of care required of the occupier

The standard is one of reasonable care in the circumstances. This overturns the law prior to the Act where a different standard of care was owed to visitors depending on whether they were classed as invitees, licensees or trespassers. Now each case is to be decided on its own facts, and whether a visitor was invited or not is just another factor to take into account in deciding whether or not the occupier took reasonable care.

Determining whether reasonable care has been taken will involve examining the facts and taking into account the nature of the danger, the purpose of the visit and the knowledge of the parties. Reasonable care will probably be shown to have been taken if the occupier has inspected the premises regularly; if there are no traps, hidden dangers or allurements; warnings should be given of known dangers or they should be fenced off; goods should be carefully stacked; lifts should be properly maintained; stairs and handrails kept in good repair; dark passages and stairs properly lighted; and vicious dogs kept under control.

Children, the elderly and the infirm

The standard of care is always the same – ie such care as is reasonable in the circumstances. However, if the occupier knows or should have foreseen that young children or the elderly will be on his premises, he would, in taking reasonable care, probably have to take greater precautions to provide for the safety of these categories of visitors. For example, children are inquisitive, are attracted to dangerous things like fires, water, dangerous machines, pylons, scaffolding and anything else that could be classed as an allurement.

In **Glasgow Corporation** *v* **Taylor [1922] 1 AC 44** a seven-year-old child picked and ate some poisonous berries in a Glasgow park and subsequently died. The berries looked like cherries and would be tempting to any child. The court held that the berries constituted an allurement to young children. The Parks Department had knowledge of the poisonous nature of the berries and had displayed no warnings nor had they fenced the bush off. The court held that as occupiers Glasgow Corporation had failed in their duty to take reasonable care.

In **McGlone** *v* **British Railways Board 1966 SC (HL) 1** a 12-year-old boy climbed up a transformer belonging to the Board and received a shock and severe burns. The Board had surrounded the transformer on three sides with a high fence and on the other side was the railway; there was also a sign warning of the danger. In this case, the court held the Board had implemented their duty of care: they looked at all the circumstances – ie the high fence, the warning notice, the age of the boy and the fact that, at his age, he knew he should not be in that place.

Excluding liability under the Act

The Act expressly states that the occupier's duty to persons entering his premises 'may be extended, modified or excluded by agreement'. This obviously allows the occupier to put on tickets or on a notice a clause excluding his liability for injury to a visitor provided that he has a contractual relationship with that person. Under common law, a clause on a notice would have to be incorporated into the contract. If the occupier is acting 'in the course of a business', then the clause would also be subject to the Unfair Contract Terms Act 1977. Under this Act, the occupier cannot exclude liability for breach of his duty of care if the exclusion is in respect of personal injury or death. Also, in respect of damage to property, he cannot exclude liability unless it is fair and reasonable to put such a term in the contract.

Defences

The defence of contributory negligence can be used by an occupier faced with a claim. The Act also states that it does not impose on an occupier any obligation to a person entering the premises 'in respect of risks which that person has willingly accepted as his'. This means that the occupier also has available the defence *volenti non fit injuria.*

In **Titchiner** *v* **British Railways Board 1984 SLT 192** Titchiner (who was 15) and her boyfriend were struck by a train. She was seriously injured and the boy was killed. She sued BRB on the grounds that they were in breach of their duty as occupiers under the 1960 Act. The couple had been in the habit of crossing the line

– there were several gaps in the fence that ran along beside the line. Titchiner admitted that she was aware of the danger of crossing the line. The Court of Session found that in relation to this 15-year-old girl they had discharged their duty of care. They also accepted BRB's defence of *volenti non fit injuria* – Titchiner was aware that trains ran on this line and that it would be dangerous to cross the line.

QUESTION

1 Mr and Mrs Smith took their seven-year-old twins, Molly and Peter, for the day to Rutlans Holiday Camp. They parked their car in the official car park for day-visitors and paid the man at the gate. The car park was situated below a steep cliff. In the past, rocks had fallen from the cliff and had caused damage to cars. Mr Smith was unaware of the danger and there was no warning on the parking ticket about the risk. While the Smiths were enjoying their picnic in the picnic area of the holiday camp, Molly wandered a short distance away from her parents. She ate some berries which she found on a bush. The berries looked like cherries but, in fact, they were poisonous and half an hour later she became very ill and an ambulance was summoned to take her to hospital. Peter had to go to hospital in the same ambulance as he had received a very deep cut to the back of his leg. His injury was caused by a piece of metal which was loose and sticking out at the bottom of the children's slide. When Mr Smith got back to the car park, he found that a five-ton rock had fallen on top of his car, totally destroying it.

   Advise the Smith family as to whether Rutlans are liable in these circumstances.

2 John bought a country house. He obtained planning permission to convert it into a residential home for the elderly, retaining a private flat for his family. Dick, a neighbouring farmer, was annoyed that John managed to buy the property and he frequently fired guns day and night on his own land. He claimed that this was necessary to keep down the rabbit population on his land. When John complained, Dick said, 'too bad, I have been shooting rabbits for years'. A few weeks after the first residents moved into the house Dick allowed the 'Young Farmers' to hold a barbecue. It was a very wild night and many of the new residents were unable to sleep. Five of them moved to another residential home fearing that this could be a regular event. This caused loss of income to John.

   Advise John and Dick.

STRICT LIABILITY FOR DEFECTIVE PRODUCTS

The law is to be found in the Consumer Protection Act 1987 Part 1, hereafter referred to as the CPA. To assist in understanding this area of the law, the student should be aware of the main chain of supply of goods. There are different routes, but a common example could be:

In the above example there will be contracts between:

1 the farmer/manufacturer,
2 the manufacturer/wholesaler,
3 the wholesaler/retailer, and
4 the retailer/purchaser,

but no contract between the purchaser and his family and friends and no contract between the purchaser and the manufacturer.

Goods supplied like this may, in some circumstances, cause injury or harm to other persons. Depending on the relationship between the person responsible for the defect in the foods and the injured party, liability can arise contractually, delictually or under statute. The CPA supplements and does not replace this law. We find that, sometimes, an injured party will have a choice as to which method he will use to sue for damages. On some occasions, there will be only one remedy open to him and on others, the law will provide no remedy. We now proceed to see how the law of contract, the law of delict and the CPA interact in this area.

Liability in contract

The safety and suitability of the product is not often specifically mentioned as an express term of a contract of sale. Therefore, the law has implied terms into the contract to protect the buyer. The Sale of Goods Act 1979 s 14 as amended by the Sale and Supply of Goods Act 1994 provides that 'where the seller sells goods in the course of a business, there is an implied term that the goods under the contract are of satisfactory quality (unsafe goods will not be satisfactory). Except (a) regarding defects specifically drawn to the buyer's attention before the contract is made; *or* (b) if the buyer examines the goods before the contract is made, as regards defects which that examination ought to reveal.

So, a buyer of a defective product, having a contract with the seller, has a remedy. He can bring an action against the seller for breach of contract – that is breach of the implied term in s 14 of the 1979 Act. This term imposes strict liability on the seller in that it is not necessary for the buyer to prove fault on the part of the seller. The seller's liability depends solely on whether there was a breach of the implied term. However, only the immediate buyer has the remedy under the Act.

Delictual liability

Prior to the passing of the Consumer Protection Act 1987 (CPA), if the user, but not the buyer, suffered harm as a consequence of using, or consuming, the defective product, he could not use the Sale of Goods Act, as he had no contract with the seller. Therefore, he had to rely on the law of delict. The person who had suffered harm had to prove that someone in the chain of supply, usually the manufacturer, had been negligent. The student will remember the case of **Donoghue *v* Stevenson [1932] AC 562** established that a manufacturer owes a duty of care to avoid acts or omissions which he can reasonably foresee as likely to injure the ultimate consumer of his goods. The main problem for the injured user, or consumer, is the difficulty of proving that the manufacturer has been negligent and, even if he succeeds, the manufacturer might be able to rely on a number of defences.

Liability under the CPA

Reform of the law

In the '70s and '80s, there was a growing public concern at the problems experienced by claimants, such as the thalidomide victims, in trying to recover damages under the existing law of contract and negligence. At the same time, the policy of the European Community was to make manufacturers strictly liable for damage caused by defects in their products. Eventually in 1985, the Council of Ministers adopted the Directive on Product Liability. The result was the passage, by the UK Parliament, of the Consumer Protection Act 1987 Part 1 which implements that directive.

The Act extends the concept of strict liability to cover defective goods and a claimant no longer has to establish that he has a contract with a seller of the goods. Any injured person may sue even if he was not using the product but was merely a bystander. Nor does the injured party have to prove that someone in the chain of supply has been negligent. Under the CPA, the claimant only has to show that: (a) there has been injury or damage; (b) that there is a dangerous defect in the product; *and* (c) the defect caused the injury or harm.

THE PROVISIONS OF THE CONSUMER PROTECTION ACT 1987 Part 1

Section 1 – What is a product?

The Act describes a product as being any goods (including components and raw materials) as well as gas, water and electricity. Thus, all standard consumer goods are products.

Land and buildings are not products but items used in their construction like bricks, wood and cement are. There is also an exception concerning agricultural produce which is defined as 'any produce of the soil, of stockfarming or of fisheries'. So, produce which has been grown and harvested, or fresh fish or meat which has not undergone any processing like canning or preserving, will not be considered a product for the purposes of the Act.

Section 2 – Who is liable under the Act?

The Act states that, in the first place, the producer is liable. The Act gives a number of definitions of the producer. He can be any of the following:

(a) The manufacturer.
(b) The abstracter of the product; for example a miner or quarryman.
(c) The processor of the product. To qualify, the processor must have altered the essential characteristics of the product; for example a bean canner, or petroleum refiner.
(d) An own brander, which would cover those who represent themselves as producers, by putting their own name on a product. Many of the large supermarkets do this.
(e) The person who imported the product into the European Community.

Finally, any supplier in the chain of supply **but he will only be liable if** (1) the claimant requests the supplier to identify the producer (anyone from (a) to (e) as described above) or to identify his own supplier; *and* (2) the request is made within a reasonable time and the complainant himself cannot reasonably identify the producer; *and* (3) the supplier fails to comply with the request within a reasonable time.

A supplier is a person who supplies goods. The CPA s 45 defines supplying goods as selling, hiring, lending or supplying them under a hire purchase contract. It also covers providing goods in exchange for any consideration other than money (e.g., trading stamps or giving goods as a prize or gift).

Section 3 – What is a defect in a product?

The fact that a product does not work or function is not enough. For the purposes of the Act, there is a defect in a product if its safety is not what persons are generally entitled to expect. This level of safety does not depend on what the consumer expected. It is objective in that it depends on what persons 'generally are entitled to expect', taking into account such factors as the product's design, the purpose for which it was marketed, the use of any warnings or instructions and the time when the product was supplied.

The producer will have to try and anticipate misuse, as safety will be considered against what might reasonably be expected to be done with the product, and care will have to be taken with advertising and promotional material to avoid increasing the public expectations of that product.

Section 5 – The kind of damage that gives rise to liability

The act defines this damage as covering death, personal injury or any loss or damage to any property. There is no liability for pure economic loss. The following points apply to damage to property:

(a) The loss or damage must be to private property and damage to commercial property is not covered by the Act. For example, damage to a private car is covered but damage to a company car is not.
(b) No claim can be made under the Act if the loss or damage to property does not exceed £275.
(c) The producer is not liable under the Act for loss or damage to the defective product itself. For example: (i) if a toaster 'self-destructs' due to an electrical fault, causing no damage to its surroundings, then there is no liability under the Act; (ii) if a toaster explodes due to an electrical fault causing injury to Mrs X and damaging the kitchen, Mrs X may recover damages under the Act for her injuries and damage to her property – i.e., the kitchen – but there is still no liability under the Act for the loss of the toaster itself. (Consequently, claims for damage to the actual product must continue to be brought under the Sale of Goods Act or under the law of delict.)

The rule applies not only to the actual defective product, but also there is no liability for damage caused by any component or product *supplied with the main product*. For example, if someone bought a car with a defective battery which leaked acid and seriously damaged the car, the owner of the car could neither sue the producer of the battery for the damage to the car nor for the loss of the battery. However, this rule only applies when the component has been supplied as part of the main product. If the owner of a car has had to replace the battery and this second battery turns out to be defective and causes damage to the car, again the owner could not claim under the Act for the damage to the second battery, but he could claim for the damage done to his car.

Section 4 – The producer's defences

The CPA lists a number of defences available to the producer if the injured party has established a prima facie claim. Regarding the claim, we must remember that the injured person's claim will fail immediately if he cannot establish that:

(a) the product is of the kind covered by s 1 of the CPA;
(b) his chosen defender is a producer or supplier who fits the description given under s 2 of the CPA;
(c) the defect in the goods is covered by s 3;
(d) the damage is covered by s 5;
(e) the defect in the product caused the damage.

The particular defences available to the producer under the Act

(a) The defect is attributable to compliance with a statutory provision.
(b) The defender did not at any time supply the product to another. This would cover stolen products or products which were intended solely for the producer's own use.
(c) The supply of the product to another was not done during the course of a business or for profit. This could be a housewife donating a home-made cake for the church sale.

(d) The defect did not exist in the product at the relevant time. The 'relevant time' means when the goods were supplied not when they were produced. Under this defence, the producer could argue that the defect has been caused by 'wear and tear'. Alternatively, he could argue that the goods have been deliberately tampered with, as happened in some supermarkets, where poison was put into yoghurt and slivers of glass into disposable nappies.

(e) The development risks defence is that the state of scientific, or technical knowledge at the relevant time was not such that a producer of products of a similar kind might be expected to have discovered the defect, had it existed in his products while they were under his control. This has been a controversial defence and it is to be reviewed. At present, there will be no liability if no other producer of the same product could have discovered the defect. This defence is wider than what was intended under the Community Directive which refers to the general state of scientific and technical knowledge and not just that in the industry in which the producer was operating. The defence appears to be 'at odds' with the strict liability of the producer, and innocent victims will still be denied a remedy under the CPA if the producer can show that he was not at fault, because there was no way he could have been aware of the defect due to lack of scientific knowledge in his industry.

(f) The CPA retains the plea of **contributory negligence**. The producer could plead this defence if the injury or damage is caused partly by a defect but also partly by the fault of the injured person. The amount of damages awarded will be reduced in the proportion as the court thinks just and equitable having regard to the injured party's share in the responsibility for the damage or injury. The defence could be pleaded, if, for example, the pursuer failed to follow instructions or warnings or had put the product to a totally unreasonable use. Or if he had stored the product badly or failed to maintain or service it or continued using it after the defect became apparent.

(g) The producer could use the defence of *volenti non fit injuria*. This is a complete defence and, if established, the victim recovers no damages. For example, this defence could be used by the manufacturers of cigarettes.

Final points to note

(1) There is no liability under the CPA for any particular product supplied before 1 March 1988. Nor is a producer liable for a defective product after ten years from the relevant time of supply of the product. In addition to this ten-year prescriptive period, the CPA provides a primary three-year limitation period for actions for personal injury or death.

(2) **Section 7 – Disclaimers and exclusion clauses**. Under the CPA, the liability of a producer to consumers cannot be limited or excluded by any contract term or notice for damage caused by a defect in a product. Section 7 makes no distinction between personal injury or damage to property. Note that it is still possible for businesses to allocate liability amongst themselves by means of contract terms and exclusion clauses. The Unfair Contract Terms Act 1977 will still apply to such terms.

(3) The European Commission is taking the UK to the ECJ maintaining that the UK has failed to implement properly the 1985 Product Liability Directive. The

problem is the development risks defence. According to the Commission, the Directive requires the defence to be objective and the defence in the CPA s 4(1)(e) is subjective. The Commission considers that the UK has changed the strict liability imposed by the Act into liability for negligence.

QUESTIONS

1 Explain the main difficulties which an injured consumer faces in bringing an action for negligence against a manufacturer under common law. Then, explain how the consumer's position has improved since the passing of the Consumer Protection Act 1987 Part 1.

2 With reference to the Consumer Protection Act 1987 explain the following:

(a) 'The Act places liability on the producer.' Who is a 'producer' for the purposes of the Act?
(b) What is 'a product' for the purposes of the Act?
(c) What constitutes a defect in the product?
(d) What defences are available to a producer under the Act?

3 Mr Eggbert, a poultry farmer, supplies fresh chickens to Freezo Chickens Ltd, who process the chickens into handy catering packs. Fred Brown, a customer of Freezo, served such a chicken in his restaurant to Mr and Mrs MacDuff, who were celebrating their wedding anniversary. As a result of eating the chicken, the MacDuffs contracted salmonella-poisoning and were seriously ill. Advise them on any claim they might have under the Consumer Protection Act and/or the Sale of Goods Act 1979 and/or the law of negligence.

4 Mrs Smith bought a microwave oven from Tartan Electrics. The microwave was supplied to them by McNab Wholesalers Ltd, who had imported it from the manufacturers, Magic Microwaves in Hong Kong. Two days after Mrs Smith had purchased the microwave, it went on fire. Advise Mrs Smith as to whether she has a remedy under the Sale of Goods Act and/or the Consumer Protection Act *if*:

(a) the microwave is totally ruined but there is no other damage; *or*
(b) the microwave is totally ruined and it set fire to her kitchen causing damage, valued at £240. Also she, personally, received burns to her hands and arms when she attempted to extinguish the fire.

LIABILITY FOR PROFESSIONAL NEGLIGENCE

The number of cases of professional negligence has increased dramatically in the last 20 years because of the growth of the consumer society with increased demand for services and greater public expectations of quality. A professional person implicitly holds himself out as possessing the degree of skill and knowledge reasonably to be expected of a normally careful and competent member of his profession.

The standard of care

This is measured against the skill and competence expected from reasonably competent members of the relevant profession. The same standard of competence is expected from the professional in the first year that he qualifies as one would expect from an older and more experienced member of that profession. Having said that, the standard of care will also depend on the rank of the professional. If the professional professes to be a specialist, consultant or an expert in his field, this must be taken into account and greater skill may be expected from such a person than from a general practitioner. In deciding whether the standard has been achieved, reference can be made to professional knowledge, methods and practice possessed at the date of the alleged misconduct. A departure from normal and accepted practice is not necessarily evidence of negligence. However, if in similar circumstances no other reasonable member of his profession would have taken such a course of action, then this will be a strong indication of malpractice.

Duty of care owed to the client

Professional liability arises from the contract between the professional and his client but that does not exclude delictual liability. Unless the contract states otherwise, the standard of care is the same.

Duty of care owed to others

The professional person owes a duty of care to all persons who might reasonably foreseeably be harmed by lack of care on his part. If his negligence causes physical damage to another person or his property, he will be liable. The professional also has a duty of care to any person who he knows, or should know, is likely to rely on his advice whether it was that person who asked for the advice or not. (The principle was established in **Hedley Byrne** *v* **Heller and Partners [1964] AC 465** and **Caparo Industries** *v* **Dickman [1990] 2 AC 605** (see p. 282).)

Excluding liability

Some professions are forbidden by statute to exclude or limit their liability for negligence, for example, auditors under the Companies Act 1985. Most professional advisers do not usually try to limit their liability. However, if they do, the Unfair Contract Terms Act 1977 as discussed earlier will apply and if the professional adviser is advising a client who is a consumer, the Unfair Terms in Consumer Contracts Regulations 1994 will apply. Note that any attempt to exclude liability for negligence caused to third parties can create problems, because a term in a contract will not be binding on that third party. However, a suitably-worded disclaimer might prevent a duty of care arising in the first place. Such disclaimers are now also subject to the provisions of the Unfair Contract Terms Act 1977 as amended by the Law Reform (Miscellaneous Provisions) (Scotland) Act 1990 s 68.

EMPLOYER'S LIABILITY FOR THE SAFETY OF HIS EMPLOYEES

The majority of claims for damages arise from injuries at work. If an employee is injured he has three possible forms of action:

1 If injured by another employee's negligence, he could sue the employee personally.
2 More likely, if he is injured by another employee, he can bring his action for damages against the employer of the employee, provided the negligent act was done 'during the course of employment'. The employer is vicariously liable.
3 A personal action for damages against his employer, either for breach of the employer's common law duty to take reasonable care for the safety of his employees or breach of statutory duty, for example the Factories Act.

This liability of the employer will be discussed fully in the section on employment law (see p. 347).

QUESTIONS

1 Harry was employed by Chemco Industries as a trainee in their factory. When he started work, Harry was told that he should always wear his protective gloves if he was working with chemicals. He was supplied with the gloves but he found them too big and after a while, he stopped wearing them, as he found them too uncomfortable. Harry has contracted dermatitis as a result of his hands being in contact with certain chemicals. A friend, who works for New Chem Ltd, has told him that in his firm everyone who works with chemicals is supplied with a special protective barrier cream. Harry would like your advice as to whether he can sue his employers for negligence.

2 Frank is a sales manager of a firm who are office suppliers. He has recently been left a substantial sum of money by his late uncle which he wants to invest. He is told by Harold, a stockbroker and a customer of his employers, that Scotia plc is currently enjoying considerable success and since Scotia plc's shares are under priced, Frank should buy them without delay. He offers to undertake the purchase for Frank if he wants him to. Frank met an old friend, Joe, for a drink in the pub. Joe is an under manager for Prudent Assurance and Frank asked him if he thought that Scotia plc would be a good investment. Joe said that although he does not have much experience in financial advising as yet, he always reads the business supplement in the Glasgow Herald. He said that the Herald had stated that Scotia plc is under valued since the company seems poised to declare record profits and so in Joe's opinion Frank should probably invest in Scotia plc.

After receiving this advice Frank invests heavily in the company. After three months the company goes into liquidation and it looks as if Frank has lost all his money. Advise him.

Part 8
EMPLOYMENT LAW

17 General introduction and the contract of employment

Employment law or labour law could be divided into two main areas. The first covers the law as it affects trade unions, their relationship with their members and also their relationship with employers. The second covers the law governing the relationship between the individual employee and his employer. This part of the book will be confined to explaining the law of employment as it affects the individual employee.

In the last few years three major consolidating acts have 'tidied up' the statutory sources of employment law. The Trade Union and Labour Relations (Consolidation) Act 1992 repealed the earlier trade union acts. The 1992 Act covers the main principles of industrial relations law. The Industrial Tribunals Act 1996 has consolidated the law relating to Industrial Tribunals and the Employment Appeal Tribunals. The Employment Rights Act 1996 has repealed and replaced most of the Employment Acts, the Trade Union Reform and Employment Rights Act 1993 and the Wages Act 1986 ss 1–11. The Act has also revoked the Employment Protection (Part-time Employees) Regulations 1995 and parts of the Collective Redundancies and Transfer of Undertaking (Protection of Employment) (Amendment) Regulations 1995. These Acts and Regulations are now incorporated in the Employment Rights Act 1996. The ERA 1996 applies in Scotland apart from the provisions relating to shop workers and betting shop workers working on a Sunday. The Act contains all the employee's employment protection rights.

SOURCES OF EMPLOYMENT LAW

Employment law is derived from two main sources, namely common law and statute. Until the 1960s the relationship between the employer and employee was regulated mainly by common law. Since then there has been a tremendous growth in statutory protection for individual employees accompanied by reform of more traditional areas of legal regulation such as the law concerned with health and safety. The importance of common law, as a source of law, must not be underestimated. It operates to provide a background set of rules to cover the many areas left unregulated by particular statutory provisions. For example, it is necessary to use common law to ascertain whether an individual worker is in fact an employee and not an independent contractor, and if he is an employee, what the terms of his contract of employment are. Common law also plays a part in the operation and interpretation of the statutory rules themselves. For example, the legislation on unfair dismissal gives a statutory definition of 'dismissal' but this cannot be properly understood without reference to the basic common law rules on breach of contract.

The main statutory sources of employment law are Acts of Parliament and statutory instruments. However, European Community law affects many aspects of employment law. The impact of the Treaty of Rome, its subordinate legislation (Regulations and Directives) and the case law from the European Court of Justice is likely to increase. Already European Community law has fundamentally affected the law in the United Kingdom covering sex discrimination, equal pay, redundancy, health and safety, and the transfer of undertakings. In the future there are bound to be more changes.

JURISDICTION OF THE COURTS AND INDUSTRIAL TRIBUNALS

At present, jurisdiction to hear and resolve disputes arising between employers and individual employees is divided between the ordinary civil courts (the Sheriff Court and the Court of Session in Scotland or the County and High Court and Court of Appeal in England) and industrial tribunals. The jurisdiction of the ordinary courts covers all disputes concerning the contract of employment as regulated by common law including claims by employees for damages for industrial injuries. The jurisdiction of the industrial tribunal is laid down and limited by the modern employment legislation. The vast majority of cases were brought under the **Employment Protection (Consolidation) Act 1978** (which has now been replaced by the Employment Rights Act 1996). In 1995, about 45 per cent of these cases dealt with unfair dismissal, 24 per cent dealt with unlawful deductions from wages and 17 per cent with common law breach of contract claims. The jurisdiction of industrial tribunals includes claims for damages for breach of contract which at present can still be heard in civil courts. However, claims for damages for personal injuries must still be brought in civil courts.

Composition and procedure of the industrial tribunal

Industrial tribunals were established under the Industrial Training Act 1964 and since then their jurisdiction has been gradually extended. They are independent judicial bodies that are intended to provide a quick, informal and inexpensive method of settling disputes and the rules of procedure are drafted simply with this aim in mind. Tribunals sit in most centres of population and in Scotland they are under the control of the Central Office of Industrial Tribunals (COIT) in Glasgow.

Three people sit on the industrial tribunal; a legally qualified chairman and two members, one from each side of industry. The chairmen are advocates or solicitors of at least seven years standing, appointed by the Lord President of the Court of Session. The other members are not required to be legally qualified and are chosen for their practical experience of industrial relations in industry, public service and commerce after consultation with a number of organisations representing employers and employees. Although the lay members represent the two sides of industry, they must act impartially and consider each case on its individual merits. In any proceedings where there is a chairman and two lay members, it is possible for the proceedings to continue with one lay member if both parties give their consent. The Industrial Tribunals Act 1996 provides that industrial tribunal proceedings can be heard by the chairman alone in certain circumstances. It is clear that the scope for chairman-alone tribunals has widened and includes hearings where the parties agree to have their case heard by the chairman or where one party withdraws or does not contest the case, or, in certain circumstances, claims for damages for breach of a contract of employment or for a sum due under such a contract. However, these new powers only potentially extend the scope for chairman-alone tribunals because the question of whether the case will be heard by a chairman alone is a matter for the chairman to decide having regard to the criteria set out in the ITA 1996 s 4. The criteria are: whether there is a likelihood of a dispute on the facts; whether there is a likelihood of an issue of law; any views of the parties as to whether the case should be heard by a full tribunal or by a chairman-alone; and whether there are other proceedings which could be heard concurrently but are not proceedings which can be heard by a chairman-alone. In all proceedings the applicant may conduct his own case before the tribunal or he may be represented by any other person. This person could be a solicitor, trade union official or a friend. The respondent employer may also represent himself, but often is represented by a solicitor or a member of his personnel or legal staff. There is no legal aid for the tribunal hearing, although an application may be made for legal aid for an appeal to the Employment Appeal Tribunal. Expenses are not usually awarded against the party who loses. However, if the tribunal thinks that a party, in bringing or conducting the proceedings, has acted 'frivolously, vexatiously, abusively, disruptively, or otherwise unreasonably' an order for expenses may be made.

Extension of tribunal's jurisdiction to hear contractual claims

Under the Industrial Tribunals Act s 3 and the Industrial Tribunals Extension of Jurisdiction (Scotland) Order 1994 an employee can bring a claim before an industrial tribunal where the claim arises on the termination of the contract of employment. The claim is for damages for breach of the contract of employment or other sum due under that contract on the termination of the employee's employment. There are certain exceptions to this kind of contractual claim: there can be no claim brought before an industrial tribunal for personal injuries and no claims for breach of a contractual term requiring the employer to provide living accommodation nor for breaches of terms relating to intellectual property nor for breaches of terms imposing an obligation of confidence nor for breach of a covenant in restraint of trade. Also employers are entitled to bring contractual claims in the industrial tribunal against employees with the same limitations which apply to employees claims. Note that any tribunal claim for damages is subject to a maximum of £25 000. This limit applies even when several claims are made relating to the same contract – the total amount cannot be more than £25 000.

The Industiral Tribunals Act 1996 and The Industrial Tribunals (Constitution and Rules of Procedure) (Scotland) Regulations 1993

An applicant commences proceedings by completing an originating application (an IT1 form) and sending it to the COIT which will then remit it to the relevant Regional Office of Industrial Tribunals (ROIT) for processing. The form is quite simple, requiring only a few particulars from the applicant and, if it is a claim for unfair dismissal, the reasons why he thinks he has been dismissed. A copy of the originating application is sent to the respondent employer along with a standard form, a notice of appearance (called an IT3 form), which asks whether the employer intends to contest the claim, whether he accepts that the employee was dismissed and on what grounds the employer intends to defend the case. Failure to reply within 14 days means the employer will not be allowed to take part in the hearing but he can apply to have the 14 days extended. In preparation for the hearing, either side may request of the other, further and better particulars of matters raised in the pleadings and the discovery or the production of relevant documents. When the IT3 form is returned to the ROIT a copy of the form is sent to the applicant. At this point, a copy of all application documentation will be sent on to the conciliation officers of ACAS (Advisory, Conciliation and Arbitration Service) which has a statutory duty to try to conciliate the parties. Many applications are settled or withdrawn at this point.

Pre-hearing reviews (PHRs)

A tribunal may at any time before the hearing, on the application of either of the parties or on its own motion, hold a preliminary review of the case based on the written and oral submissions of the parties but without witnesses. If, after the PHR the tribunal is of the opinion that one of the parties has no reasonable prospect of success, it may give a warning to that party, that costs may be awarded against him if he continues with the case and make an order against the party requiring him to pay a deposit of not more that £150 as a condition of being permitted to proceed. No order to pay a deposit shall be made unless the tribunal has taken reasonable steps to ascertain the ability of the party to pay the deposit and has taken account of any information received in deciding the amount of the deposit. The tribunal members who adjudicate at the PHR may not adjudicate later at the full hearing. If the warning is ignored and the party goes ahead with the full hearing, costs may be awarded against him if in the opinion of the tribunal, he has acted 'frivolously, vexatiously, abusively, disruptively or otherwise unreasonably'. Such orders are rare.

The deposit would be paid to the successful party in part settlement of the costs. The pre-hearing review may be carried out by a single person (the chairman) or by the full tribunal.

Review of tribunal decision

Under the regulations, provided an application is made within 14 days of the parties receiving the decision of the tribunal, the tribunal shall have the power to review and revoke or vary any decision on any of the following grounds:

1 the decision was wrong as a result of an error on the part of the tribunal staff;
2 a party did not receive notice of the proceedings;
3 the decision was made in the absence of a party entitled to be heard;
4 new evidence has become available since the conclusion of the hearing, the existence of which could not have been reasonably known or foreseen;
5 the interests of justice require such a review.

Appeal against tribunal decision

Provided an application is lodged within 42 days of the decision being registered, an appeal can be made to the Employment Appeal Tribunal (EAT) but only on a point of law. A further appeal may be made from the EAT decision to the Inner House of the Court of Session (or, in England, to the Appeal Court) and from there a final right to appeal to the House of Lords.

The composition of the Employment Appeal Tribunal is covered by the Industrial Tribunals Act 1996 and consists of a Court of Session judge as chairman, and two or four lay members from both sides of industry. The parties may be represented by whomsoever they please and legal aid is available. The ITA 1996 provides that, with the consent of the parties, appeals can be heard by a judge and either one or three lay members. An appeal from tribunal proceedings where the chairman sat alone can now be heard by the judge sitting alone.

The Advisory, Conciliation and Arbitration Service (ACAS)

ACAS was established by the Employment Protection Act 1975 s 1. Its work is directed by a council consisting of a chairman and nine members appointed by the Secretary of State. Three members are appointed after consultation with employers' organisations, three after consultation with trade unions and the remainder are independent. The service is divided into nine regions which perform most of the day-to-day work. ACAS is charged with 'the general duty of promoting the improvement of industrial relations'.

The particular duties of ACAS are:

1 **Advice**. ACAS may without charge, on request or on its own initiative, provide advice on any matter concerned with industrial relations or employment to employers, their associations, workers and trade unions.
2 **Conciliation** Where a trade dispute exists or is likely to arise, ACAS may by request or of its own volition, offer assistance with a view to bringing about a settlement. In doing so it may refer the parties to a third person for conciliation but first must encourage the parties to use any existing disputes procedures. In addition to collective matters, ACAS has the task of attempting the conciliation of the parties in tribunal cases. In 1995 ACAS received 91 568 individual

employment rights cases for conciliation.

3 **Arbitration**. At the request of one party and if all the parties consent, ACAS may appoint an arbiter or a panel from outside the service to resolve an actual or anticipated trade dispute. In performing this function, the service is obliged to consider whether the dispute could be resolved by conciliation and should not arrange arbitration until all existing procedures have been exhausted.

4 **Inquiries**. ACAS may inquire into any question relating to industrial relations generally, either in a particular industry or in a particular organisation. It may add its advice to its eventual findings and is empowered to publish both if it thinks publication desirable after the views of the parties have been taken into account.

5 **Codes of practice**. ACAS is also empowered to issue codes of practice containing practical guidance for the purpose of promoting the improvement of industrial relations. After considering representations from all the interested parties, ACAS submits a draft code to the Secretary of State for approval before it is laid before Parliament. If there are no objections, the Secretary of State may bring it into force by order. A code of practice is not law in itself and so a person is not liable for breach of it. However, a breach of a code of practice can be used as evidence against an employer in any tribunal proceedings.

The Central Arbitration Committee

The CAC, the successor to the Industrial Court, was established by the Employment Protection Act 1975. It is a permanent arbitration body, independent of ACAS and the Department of Employment, sitting in London or elsewhere as necessary. It consists of a chairman, a deputy-chairman and other members from both sides of industry appointed by the Secretary of State after consultation with ACAS. Apart from receiving requests to arbitrate directly from the parties to a dispute, the Committee also receives requests from ACAS. Additionally, under the 1975 Act, the CAC deals with complaints that employers have not disclosed bargaining information. No court can overturn a decision of the CAC unless it can be shown that the Committee has exceeded its jurisdiction or breached the rules of natural justice.

RELATIONSHIP BETWEEN THE EMPLOYER AND THE EMPLOYEE

Before examining the contract of employment, the reader must appreciate that there are two main ways in which an individual can perform work for an employer. First, the work can be done under a contract of service: a contract between an employer and his employee. Secondly, the work can be performed under a contract for services: a contract between the employer and an independent contractor or self-employed person. In many of the employment cases coming before the courts or the industrial tribunal, the first matter to be decided by the court is whether the contract of employment is a contract **of** service or **for** services. There are four main reasons why this might be necessary:

1 An employer is vicariously liable for the negligent acts of his employees if the act was done during the course of employment. The employer is not usually responsible for the negligence of independent contractors.
2 Under common law an employee owes a number of duties to his employer and the employer owes his employee a number of duties but the employer does not owe the same duties to an independent contractor.
3 Under the modern employment legislation, many new and important statutory rights (like the right not to be unfairly dismissed) have been conferred on employees but not on independent contractors.
4 If the employee is employed under a contract of service, the employer is under a statutory duty to deduct PAYE (pay as you earn) and national insurance contributions from the employee's wages or salary. An independent contractor is responsible for making his own income tax and national insurance returns.

The distinction in law between an employee and an independent contractor is therefore a crucial one. In some cases the courts have great difficulty in determining the borderline between the two different contracts. The statutory definition of 'an employee' is given in the Employment Rights Act 1996 s 230. An employee is defined as a person who has entered into or works or has worked under a contract of employment as opposed to a contract for services. A contract of employment means a contract of service or apprenticeship. Such a contract may be express or implied and where it is express it may be either oral or in writing.

The statutory definition is not particularly helpful so we will now look at the various tests which the courts have devised over the years to assist them in making the distinction.

The control test

This test has been used since the 19th century and reflects the difference in attitudes then towards employment relationships. Especially noticeable is the outdated concept of master and servant. The test is to decide whether the employer can control not only what work is done, but also when and how it is done. If the employer does exercise this kind of control over the individual then the contract will be one of service. Sometimes it will be unnecessary to use any other test. However, as technology has advanced and specialisation has become greater, the number of employers who can tell their employees how to do the job has declined. If one considers the job of a doctor or specialist engineer it is clear that this test has drawbacks so new tests were devised by the courts.

The integration or organisation test

This test was expounded by Lord Justice Denning in **Stevenson, Jordan and Harrison** *v* **Macdonald and Evans 1952 TLR 101**. The test is that under a contract of service, a person is employed as part of the business; whereas under a contract for services his work, although done for the business, is not integrated into it but is only accessory to it.

The multiple test

This test emerged after the decision in **Ready Mix Concrete (South East) Ltd** *v* **Minister of Pensions 1968 2QB 497**. The purpose of the case was to decide whether the drivers of the cement mixing lorries were independent contractors or employees of the company. One of the drivers, Latimer, had a written contract with the company that stated that he was an independent contractor. It also provided that mileage rates would be paid but Latimer, at his own expense, would carry concrete for the company in a lorry which would be bought by him through a hire purchase contract with a finance organisation associated with Ready Mix Concrete. Latimer was to maintain, repair and insure the vehicle, paint it in the company's colours and only work for the company. He was to wear the company uniform. However, he could with the company's consent hire a competent replacement driver if at any time he could not drive himself. Also, the company would be responsible for major repairs to the vehicle. The court decided, after considering all the terms of the contract, that the express term that Latimer was an independent contractor was not conclusive but they still found that Latimer was employed under a contract for services. They considered that the important factor was that the ownership of the assets, the chance of profit and the risk of loss in the business of carriage were Latimer's and not the company's.

The multiple test is that a contract of service exists if:

1 the employee agreed in return for remuneration to provide his own work and skill in the performance of some service for his master; *and*
2 the employee agreed expressly or impliedly that in the performance of the service he would be subject to the control of the other party sufficiently to make him master; *and*
3 the other terms of the contract are consistent with its being a contract of service.

This last condition allows the court a degree of discretion to balance those factors that are consistent with the contract being one of service against those that are consistent with the contract being one for services and after weighing up these factors, come to a conclusion.

Some of the factors that the court will consider when applying the test are:

(a) **Payment?** Is it by way of wages or salary, or is it by commission or fee? Also, who pays tax and national insurance? However, payment in some form is not absolutely necessary. In **Europanel Processing Co Ltd** *v* **Nimmo EAT 24.4.92 (732/91)** Nimmo, a manager, was paid a salary of £30 000 per annum and had a company car and a company pension scheme. In his second year of employment his salary was reduced to £20 000. Then for a period of ten months, until the company went into liquidation, he continued to work full time but drew no salary in order to obtain tax advantages, although he still had his car and was paid expenses. His company was bought by Europanel and he worked for them for three months in return for a salary of £30 000 until he was dismissed. He claimed unfair dismissal and to do so he had to show that he had been continuously employed for two years. The EAT decided that Nimmo still had the status of an employee during the ten-month period when he had not drawn his salary. In reaching this decision, a number of factors had been considered like the continuing control over him by the directors, the continued use of the company car, payment of expenses and pension contributions. Regarding the non-payment of his salary, that had been Nimmo's decision for tax reasons.

(b) **Who owns the equipment?** The employer or the employee? If the employer supplies the equipment and tools, then the contract is usually a contract of service but the converse is not always true.

(c) **Is there a personal obligation to work for just one employer?** If there is, this is consistent with the contract being one of service.

(d) **Are the hours of work fixed by the employer?** If they are, then the contract is usually one of service.

(e) **What label have the parties put on their relationship?** This will be considered by the courts but they will look behind the label at the economic reality of the relationship. In **Massey** *v* **Crown Life [1978] ICR 590** Massey had been an employee of Crown Life. For tax advantages, it was agreed with his employers that he could change his contract of employment and be treated as self-employed. He consulted his accountant and a written contract was drawn up. He was still doing the same work as he had done before. Then two years later, he was dismissed. In order to claim unfair dismissal, he had to establish that he was an employee of the company. The Court of Appeal held that he was an independent contractor working under a contract for services. The decision was reached because there was a written agreement from which it was clear that the intention of the parties was to change Massey's status to self-employed.

In **Young & Woods** *v* **West [1980] IRLR 201** Mr West, a skilled sheet metal worker, when joining the company, was offered the choice of either being paid as an employee or being treated as self-employed. West chose to be self-employed: no tax deductions were made from his pay and he was responsible for his own national insurance. He did not receive any holiday or sick pay from the company. He was eventually dismissed and brought a claim for unfair dismissal. The tribunal first had to decide whether he was eligible and that he was an employee. The Court of Appeal found that he was employed under a contract of service and stated that the employer and employee cannot, by a mere label, alter the realities of the employment relationship. The realities of this case were that West was in exactly the same situation as the other sheet metal workers who were doing the same job as him but under a contract of service.

(f) **Is there mutuality of obligation?** If the employer is under an obligation always to provide work for the individual and he in return is under an obligation to accept the work, then there will be an inference that the contract is one of service.

In **O'Kelly** *v* **Trust House Forte PLC [1983] IRLR 369** the Court of Appeal had to decide whether certain waiters employed by Trust House Forte as 'regular casuals' were employees and so qualified to claim unfair dismissal. The multiple test was used and the court found many factors consistent with the contract being one of service. For example, they worked more than 16 hours a week according to a weekly rota; clothing and equipment were supplied by the employers; they had to ask permission to take time off from the rota duties; they were paid weekly; tax and national insurance were deducted and they received holiday pay. A few factors were found not to be inconsistent with the contract being one of service (neutral factors). Finally, the following factors were found to be inconsistent with the contract being one of service: the appointment was terminable without notice by either party; the 'regular casual' could decide whether or not to accept work; Trust House Forte were under no obligation to provide work and also it was custom and practice in the hotel industry to regard 'regular casuals' as self-employed contractors. The court, although applying the multiple test, put particular stress on the factor of mutual obligations and found that O'Kelly and the others were employed under contracts for services.

(g) **Is the worker engaged in business on his own account?** In the case of **Lee *v* Chung [1990] IRLR 237(PC)** the Privy Council has made it clear that it considers the approach of the Court of Appeal in *O'Kelly*'s case with the stress on the mutual obligations factor to be wrong. The Privy Council stated that the fundamental test to be applied is, 'Is the person who has engaged himself to perform these services performing them as a person in business on his own account?' In other words, is the worker part of the employer's economic unit or is he operating as a separate economic unit? It can be seen that this decision will be very important to those employed as casual workers.

In this case Lee was a mason who was injured while working on a construction site and who wished to claim compensation for his injuries as an employee. His employer provided his tools and told him where to work but thereafter he worked without supervision. He was paid according to the amount of work done and was expected to be on site during regular working hours. He worked for others as well but always gave priority to Chung's work. The Privy Council held that he was clearly an employee, emphasising mostly economic factors. Lee did not price the job but was paid a fixed rate, had no responsibility for investment in or management of the site and the employer provided the equipment.

In **Lane *v* Shire Roofing Co (Oxford) Ltd [1995] IRLR 493,** the Court of Appeal said that the nature of the labour market was changing and employment relationships were more flexible, but there were good policy reasons in the safety at work field to ensure that the law properly categorises the status of the worker. The degree of control exercised over a worker was an important factor and the vital qusetion to be asked was 'Whose business was it?'

Homeworkers

In order to determine whether a homeworker is an employee or nor, the common law tests are applied to the circumstances of each case. The fact that the work is done at home and not on the employer's premises is only one factor to be considered. The problem for the homeworker might be to establish sufficient 'mutuality of obligations'. There are two important cases in which homeworkers were held to be employees. In **Airfix Footwear Ltd *v* Cope [1978] IRLR 386**, Mrs Cope assembled shoes at home for seven years. Mrs Cope had no other source of income, it was nearly full-time work and there was close supervision of her work. The EAT found evidence of a continuing and regular relationship over many years established by the conduct of the parties and held that Mrs Cope was an employee. Similarly in **Nethermere (St Neots) Ltd *v* Taverna and Gardiner [1984] IRLR 240** the two homeworkers worked for five to seven hours a day for three years at home sewing pockets on children's clothes. Some weeks there was no work for them. The homeworkers could specify how much work they wanted each day subject to a minimum imposed by the company. The Court of Appeal held that there was an employment relationship – that well-founded expectations of continuing homework consisting of the regular giving and taking of work over a period could crystallise into an enforceable contract of employment spanning weeks in which no work was done. There was an obligation on both sides to offer and accept work.

Specific cases

Company directors are not usually employees of the company but are 'officers' of the company and are paid fees. Some directors, usually managing directors, are employees employed under a contract of service. A partner in a firm is a self-employed person who is in business with others and who is entitled to a share of the profits of that business. In recent years, it has become quite common for people in business to be called partners or associate partners in order to give them status or prestige. If they do not have a share in the profits, they are in fact employees paid by salary.

A contract of apprenticeship for more than one year must be drawn up in writing. Apprentices are employees but trainees very often are not. Trainees under YTS and YOP have been held not to have a contract of service with the company which is training them and so are not protected by the employment protection legislation. However, protection is now given to such trainees under the Sex Discrimination Act 1975, the Race Relations Act 1976 and the Health and Safety at Work Act 1974.

THE CONTRACT OF EMPLOYMENT

Basically, the contract of employment is like any other contract and so subject to the principles of law discussed earlier in the book under the general principles of contract. The employment contract must have all the essential features of a contract. In the first place, *consensus in idem* or agreement on the important terms must be reached by the parties. In other words, the employer must make an offer which the employee unconditionally accepts in order to form a binding contract. From that point, neither party can unilaterally change the terms without the other party's agreement. The parties must also have contractual capacity; they must intend to be legally bound; there must be no error affecting their agreement; the contract must be possible to carry out and not be illegal.

Under common law, an illegal contract will not be enforced by the courts. In the context of the employment contract, an illegality may prevent the employee from exercising any of his employment protection rights under the Employment Rights Act 1996. A contract may be illegal at the time it is formed if it cannot be performed without being in breach of the law. Alternatively, it may be capable of being performed legally, but in fact it is performed in an illegal way. In the second case the courts might decide to enforce the contract. This will depend on whether public policy dictates that the contract should be enforceable. The main examples have been cases where it was clear that the employee knew that his wages were being paid in a way that defrauded the Inland Revenue. In these cases the courts would not enforce the contract of employment on the grounds of public policy, as to do otherwise would leave the court apparently condoning or encouraging a criminal act.

In **Hewcastle Catering Ltd** *v* **Ahmed and Elkamah [1991] IRLR 473** the Court of Appeal decided that the two employees could bring complaints of unfair dismissal. The employees were waiters who had been instructed by their employer's managers to issue a different type of bill to customers whom they knew were going to pay cash. These cash payments were not included in the employer's VAT returns. Criminal proceedings were brought against the employer's managers and the two waiters acted as prosecution witnesses at the trial. Subsequently, they were dismissed and the employer argued that they could not claim unfair dismissal because their contracts of employment were tainted with illegality. The Court of Appeal did not accept this argument. In this case the employment contracts were not entered into for the purpose of defrauding the VAT authorities; the employees had not benefited from the fraud; to deny these employees their statutory rights would discourage disclosure of frauds and would encourage employers to dismiss employees who assisted in fraud investigations.

Although the employer and employee are free (within the limits imposed by common law and particular statutory rules) to negotiate their own express terms, in practice many important terms of their contract are left undefined and are settled by the courts through the device of the implied term. Also, sometimes a term is incorporated into the contract from another source (for example, terms incorporated from collective agreements). Very often it is important to be able to ascertain what the terms of the contract of employment are because a dispute may arise later between the employer and the employee. Neither the employer nor the employee can change a term in the contract without the other's agreement. Many disputes arise because the employer unilaterally changes a term of the contract. In **MacRuary** *v* **Washington Irvine Ltd IDS Brief 518 (June 1994)** the EAT suggested a range of responses open to employees faced with a change to their contracts without their agreement:

1 They can do nothing thereby assenting to the change. Mere delay alone unaccompanied by any express or implied agreement does not constitute affirmation; though if it is prolonged it might indicate implied agreement.
2 The employees can resign and claim constructive dismissal (see page 395).
3 They can continue to work under protest and pursue other remedies. For example they could sue their employer for damages (see **Rigby** *v* **Ferodo [1987] IRLR 516**), or they might bring a complaint to the Industrial Tribunal under the ERA s 13 (see page 374).

Sources of the terms of the contract of employment can be usefully divided into the following categories: **express terms; terms incorporated from collective agreements; implied terms**.

Express terms

These are terms which have been specifically agreed either verbally or in writing by the parties. Apart from a few exceptions, there is no requirement that the contract of employment should be formed in writing. However, there is one statutory requirement that must be noted. Under the Employment Rights Act 1996 ss 1–6, within two months of starting work, the employee is entitled to a written statement of the main terms of his employment. This statement must be kept up to date and the employee notified in writing of any changes at the earliest opportunity or not later than one month after the change. The rules do not apply where there is in existence a written contract of employment which covers these matters.

The matters which the statement must cover are as follows:

1 It must identify the parties.
2 It must specify when the employment began and, if the contract is for a fixed term, the date when the contract expires.
3 It must specify whether any period of employment with a previous employer counts as part of the employee's continuous period of employment and if it does, the date on which it began.
4 The employee's job title.
5 The scale of remuneration or the method of calculating it, and the intervals at which it is paid.
6 Hours of work including any terms as to 'normal working hours'.
7 Any entitlement to holidays including public holidays and holiday pay.
8 Any terms dealing with incapacity due to sickness and sick pay.
9 Pensions and pension schemes.
10 The length of notice that the employee is obliged to give and entitled to receive.
11 Either the place of work or, where the employee is to work at various places, an indication of that and the address of the employer.
12 Any collective agreements which directly affect the terms and conditions of employment.
13 Where the employee is to work outside the UK for more than one month, he is to be informed as to the duration of the work, the currency in which he will be paid, any additional payments and benefits which he will be due and any terms and conditions relating to his return to the UK.
14 Rules and disciplinary procedures including rights of appeal or reference to a reasonably accessible document which specifies such rules.
15 Any grievance procedures or reference to a reasonably accessible document which explains them. But this does not apply to disciplinary and grievance procedures relating to health or safety at work.
16 A note stating whether a contracting-out certificate is in force for that employment.

If there are no particulars to be entered under holiday pay, sick pay or pensions, the written particulars may state that there are no particulars. Also, a written statement may for information on notice periods, sick pay, pensions and collective agreements given by the statement, refer the employee to some document (which could be a collective agreement) which the employee has a reasonable opportunity to read in the course of his employment or which is made reasonably accessible to him in some other way.

The status of the written statement

The duty to supply written particulars to the employee has caused some confusion as to whether the written statement is a written contract. In fact, it is not a contract. It is, however, evidence of the terms of the contract. This may seem a technical distinction but it has the important consequence that it is still open to an employee to argue in later proceedings that the statement was inaccurate. For example, the employee could produce evidence of what was said at the interview or in the letter of appointment and argue that his written particulars do not truly represent the terms of his contract. The basis for this is that in the 1996 Act there is no requirement that the terms of the statement should be agreed beforehand and it follows that the employer's duty is only to put down what he considers to be the main terms of the contract. If the employer fails to provide the written particulars or if the statement he gives does not comply with the statutory requirements the employee may apply to the Industrial Tribunal. The tribunal may confirm the particulars as included; amend those particulars or substitute other particulars for them. Very often, the employee is asked to sign the written particulars. The question can then arise as to whether there was an intention to turn the written particulars into a contract of employment. It has been held that the mere signing of the statement will not be regarded as anything more than the employee signifying his receipt of the statement. To transform a s 1 written statement into a contract would require clear words indicating that the employee was signing it as a contract.

Terms incorporated from collective agreements

A collective agreement is an agreement between the employers and the trade unions. The statutory definition of a collective agreement is found in s 178 of the Trade Union and Labour Relations (Consolidation) Act 1992 (TULR(C)A). It is any agreement or arrangement made by or on behalf of one or more trade unions on the one side and employers or employers' associations on the other side. It must also relate to one or more of the matters set out in s 244(1) of the same Act. These are briefly: the terms and conditions of employment; the hiring and dismissal of workers; allocation of work; disciplinary matters; membership of a trade union; facilities for union officials and the machinery for recognition of, or consultation with, the union.

Collective agreements are not legally enforceable between the parties to them – the parties being the trade union and the employer. TULR(C) Act s 179 states that any collective agreement shall be conclusively presumed to be not enforceable unless the agreement is in writing *and* contains a provision stating that the parties intend it to be legally enforceable.

Collective agreements and the individual contract of employment

Although collective agreements are not legally enforceable, that does not mean that the terms of the agreement cannot become part of the individual employee's contract. The mechanism for this lies in the process of incorporation. A term may be incorporated into a contract of employment either expressly or impliedly. Once incorporated, the employee and the employer will be bound by the relevant terms. This happens even if later the collective agreement is terminated. So if the employer has pulled out of a collective agreement, he can only vary an incorporated contractual term by agreeing the variation with the individual employee.

It must be noted that not all the clauses in the collective agreement will be suitable and appropriate for incorporation. The substantive terms will be appropriate – i.e., those terms which relate to pay, hours and conditions of service. The procedural clauses will not be appropriate – i.e., those dealing with collective matters like recognition or matters concerning industrial relations policy. Another point to note is that it is quite common for more than one collective agreement to be in force. For example, there could be a national agreement as supplemented by a local agreement. There is no rule as to which agreement takes priority but local agreements usually determine local pay and conditions. It will be a question of fact as to which collective agreement terms have been incorporated.

Express incorporation

This happens by the employer and the employee expressly agreeing that the relevant terms of a collective agreement will be binding on them. For example, the individual contract of employment could state that 'the employment hereunder is subject to the terms and conditions contained in the collective agreement for the time being in force between Union X and Company Y'.

Implied incorporation

It is possible for terms to be incorporated from a collective agreement by implication, although this is less desirable than express incorporation because of the uncertainties that can arise. If employees have specific knowledge of the collective agreement and there is conduct which demonstrates that they are willing to work under it, then the terms can be incorporated by implication. This is relatively straightforward in the case of employees who are members of the union but difficulties can arise with the position of non-union employees. If they have habitually accepted the terms negotiated by the union in the past, an implication arises that they will be bound by any terms incorporated from a new collective agreement. A problem can develop, if at any stage a non-union employee indicates that they are no longer willing to be bound by a new agreement.

In **Singh *v* British Steel Corporation [1974] IRLR 131** Singh and some others resigned from the union which subsequently negotiated a new shift system with the employer. Singh protested about the new system, refused to work it and was dismissed. One of the questions that arose in this case was whether the new shift system in the new collective agreement could be considered to have been incorporated into his contract. Thus his contract would have been changed and he would have been obliged to work the new shift. The tribunal held that it was not incorporated and so he remained subject to his original contract terms. The fact that he was no longer a member of the union was a factor that weighed heavily with the tribunal.

Final point

It is possible for terms to be incorporated into the contract of employment from the 'works rules' in the same way as terms are incorporated from collective agreements. Clearly, express incorporation is more advantageous as it leaves no room for doubt. The rules again would have to be suitable and appropriate and there would have to be no contradictory express terms in the contract. The essential difference between collective agreements and work rules lies in their subject matter. Most works rules are not appropriate as they are only instructions to the employees as to how to do their work or they cover minor matters like appearance or dress. The contents of the work rules book are unilaterally decided by the employer without necessarily consulting the employees or union and so have the advantage that they can be changed without the consent of the workforce.

Implied terms

Implied terms are those terms which become part of the contract without the parties expressly mentioning them. Apart from those implied by statute, they cannot override express terms which state the contrary. However, they can be used to qualify express terms (see p. 389).

There are three types of implied term:

1 those implied by statute;
2 those implied by custom and practice;
3 those implied by common law.

Terms implied by statute into the contract of employment

An example is the equality clause which, under the Equal Pay Act 1970 s 1, is inserted into all contracts under which men and women are employed in Great Britain and this clause, as we will see later, renders illegal discrimination regarding the terms of the contract.

Terms implied by custom and practice

Trade usage or custom may have a role to play in filling a gap in the terms of the contract. To be accepted a custom must be certain, well known in that particular trade or area and reasonable. The scope for custom establishing an implied term has decreased in modern times. This is mainly due to the compulsory statutory provisions.

Terms implied by common law

(a) **Terms inferred from the facts of any given employment**. Where there is a gap in the contract of employment, a court may have to find that a term is implied to make sense of the existing employment relationship. The courts can apply a subjective test or an objective test in these circumstances.

The subjective test: The courts can apply the '**officious bystander test**' which entails looking at what the parties themselves would probably have agreed, had they put their minds to it at the time they entered the contract. The basis being that if the officious bystander, when the contract was being formed, had suggested that the term should be in the contract, they would both have turned and said 'but of course that term is in the contract'.

The objective test: The courts imply a term into the contract on the ground that the term is reasonable in the circumstances. This test would be used where the intention of the parties is not clear but the court must still imply a term to make sense of the contract.

In **Mears *v* Safecar Security Ltd [1982] IRLR 183** the Court of Appeal were considering a case where there was a failure in the written particulars to give details as to the payment or non-payment of sick pay. They held that a court could declare what a term should be even where there is no evidence at all as to the intention of the parties and that the court should decide what the term is on the basis of what would be reasonable and sensible in all the circumstances. However, this decision must be questioned. In **Eagland *v* British Telecom [1992] IRLR 323**, the Court of Appeal said that this was incorrect and the court cannot invent terms which the parties have not agreed.

(b) **Terms implied by common law into all contracts of employment**. The fact remains that, despite the encouragement offered by the statutory duty imposed on employers to supply employees with written particulars, in most cases the parties do not fully define the content of their relationship. Such matters like pay, hours, holidays and place of work are usually expressly agreed but seldom do the parties agree on the extent to which the employee must obey orders or the level of skill expected from him. Over the years, the courts have recognised a number of duties arising from the employment relationship and which, in the absence of any express term to the contrary, are to be implied into the contract of employment. However, in certain circumstances implied terms can be used to qualify express terms or at least restrict the way in which the express terms are applied. In **Johnstone *v* Bloomsbury Health Authority [1991] IRLR 118** Dr Johnstone was employed as a senior house officer. Under the express terms in his contract of employment he was required to work 40 hours per week and to be 'on call' for up to a further 48 hours. He sought a declaration that the Health Authority's action breached their implied duty of care for his health and safety; that the express terms relating to working hours effectively operated to exclude the Health Authority's duty of care for his health and safety and were therefore void under the Unfair Contract Terms Act 1977. The case was settled out of court and Johnstone received £5600. The Court of Appeal stated that the employer's express contractual power to require J to work up to 88 hours a week on average had to be exercised in the light of the implied duty of care for its employee's safety. The Court unanimously agreed that UCTA potentially did apply to Johnstone's case.

These implied terms are referred to as the employee's common law duties and the employer's common law duties. Such terms will usually not have been discussed by the parties.

The employee's duties are: to render personal service; to obey the employer's orders; to take reasonable care in carrying out his job; loyalty; to act in good faith.

The employer's duties are: to pay his employee's wages; to a limited extent, to provide him with work; to co-operate with the employee and treat him with respect; to indemnify his employee for expenses reasonably incurred; to take reasonable care for his employee's safety at work.

THE EMPLOYEE'S COMMON LAW DUTIES

To render personal service

An employee cannot delegate his tasks to another person.

Obedience and co-operation

The employee must obey all lawful and reasonable orders given to him by his employer. Wilful refusal will amount to breach of contract. However, the employer should never insist on his employee doing anything unlawful like driving a company vehicle that is not taxed or insured. When considering what orders are reasonable, we have to decide what at common law is the extent of 'managerial prerogative'. If there is an express mobility clause in the contract of employment, then an employee would have to obey an order to move to a different location. If there is no express mobility clause, then such a clause will not be implied. It would be unreasonable to order the employee to move any great distance to a new place of work unless it was implied through custom, for example in the construction industry.

In **Aparau** *v* **Iceland Frozen Foods plc [1966] IRLR 119** Mrs Aparau was employed as a cashier. Her contract of employment contained no express terms as to her place of work nor to mobility. Iceland Foods took over her firm and issued new terms and conditions of employment to all employees. One provided that she 'may be required to work at a different location at any time'. Mrs A never signed or returned the form. Twelve months later a dispute arose with her store manager and she was ordered to transfer to another branch. She resigned and claimed constructive dismissal. If a tribunal were satisfied that her contract contained a mobility clause the employers would not be in breach by ordering her to move. The EAT held that Mrs A had not explicitly agreed to the new term and that her acceptance could not be implied from the fact that she continued to work for them for 12 months without objection. The EAT also held that in a contract of employment there must be a term as to the place of work but there was no necessity to have any clause about mobility.

Also it would be unreasonable to expect an employee to obey an order which would endanger his life.

In **Chakarion** *v* **The Ottoman Bank [1930] AC 277** a bank employee protested when he was asked to move to Constantinople, which was under Turkish control, as in the past he had narrowly escaped execution by the Turks. He went and again had to flee. It was held that he was not in breach of contract. Wilful disobedience of an order which will endanger the employee's life is justified.

An employee must obey an order which is covered by a term in his contract.

Refusal may be by words or conduct like 'a go slow' or a 'work to rule'.

In **Secretary of State** *v* **ASLEF [1972] 2 QB 455** during a dispute between British Rail and their employees, three trade unions representing the railway workers ordered their members to work strictly according to the rule book, and ban overtime, rest day and Sunday working. The instructions were obeyed and caused chaos and dislocation of services. The Court of Appeal held that although working strictly to rule did not amount to a breach of contract, the 'whole concerted course of conduct' had to be viewed together and did amount to a breach of an implied duty of co-operation. Lord Denning said, 'An employee must not wilfully obstruct his employer's business. It involves breaches by the employees of an implied term of the contract to serve the employer faithfully within the requirements of the contract' and 'An act which is lawful is rendered unlawful by the motive or object with which it is done ... wages are to be paid for services rendered, not for producing deliberate chaos'.

Competence and care

The employee must perform his job with reasonable care. If the employee is in breach of this duty of care, he could possibly be dismissed or sued for damages. The precise standard of care required will depend on his job and status. An employee who is a professional person or a tradesman will have to show the same skill and care that a reasonably careful and competent member of his profession or trade would show in the same circumstances.

If the negligence of the employee causes injury to another person (either a third party or a fellow employee), then the employer could be vicariously liable. The conditions for vicarious liability were discussed earlier in Chapter 13. If the employer is found liable, he could then sue the employee for an indemnity for the damages that he has had to pay to the injured party.

In **Lister** *v* **Romford Ice and Cold Storage Co Ltd [1957] AC 555** a lorry driver reversed and injured his mate, who happened to be his father. The employers paid damages to the father but then the insurance company, by virtue of the subrogation, successfully sued the son on the grounds that he was in breach of his implied duty to take reasonable care and skill.

In **Janata Bank** *v* **Ahmed [1981] ICR 791** a bank employee was successfully sued by his employers for losses caused by his negligence in authorising overdrafts for non-creditworthy customers.

Good faith

The employee is under a common law duty to do his work honestly and to avoid situations where his own interests might conflict with those of his employer. The duty to act in good faith can cover five areas: not to secretly benefit from working, to act honestly, not to harm his employer's interests, not to divulge confidential information and to give his employer the benefit of any invention:

1 An employee must look after customers' and clients' interests on his employer's behalf and not his own. If he uses his position to make secret profits for himself, he will be in breach of this duty and could be required to return the amount to

his employer. Also, he must not arrange to take over a client's business for his own purposes, even after he leaves employment. In **Industrial Developments Consultants *v* Cooley [1972] 2 All ER 162** while Cooley was working for IDC, the company tendered for a contract which they failed to get. Cooley left the company for health reasons and later set up a business of his own and he got the contract for the original work. It was held that this was a breach of his duty to act in good faith, even though in this situation he had not deprived IDC of the business.

2 An employee must always act honestly and with integrity. Even taking a few envelopes and pens from the place of work without permission would amount to a breach of this duty. In **Sinclair v Neighbour [1966] 3 All ER 988** a betting shop manager, knowing that he would not be permitted to do so, borrowed £15 from the till, leaving a signed IOU. He replaced the money the next day. The employer later discovered what had happened and was held entitled to dismiss the employee. The employee was in breach of his duty to act in good faith even though the money had been returned to the till.

3 An employee must not harm his employer's interests. The courts have always been reluctant to declare that what an employee does after work is any concern of the employer. However, the employer's interests could be affected by the employee working part-time for a competitor or another employer with the result that he is too tired to do his full-time job. This could possibly be a breach of the duty to act in good faith. To make the matter clear, the employer should put an express term in the contract of employment forbidding 'moonlighting'.

In **Hivac *v* The Park Royal Scientific Instruments [1946] 1 Ch 169** some of Hivac's employees worked for Park Royal in their spare time. The two companies both manufactured midget valves, a product which required highly skilled technical knowledge. There was no evidence that the employees had misused any confidential information which they might have acquired working for Hivac. The court held that in this case, even though there was no express term in the contract, the employees were in breach of their duty to act in good faith. The court also said that there is no 'hard-and-fast rule' and each case must be decided on its own facts. The employers, Hivac, did not want to dismiss their highly skilled employees. What they sought was an injunction (interdict in Scotland) ordering Park Royal to stop employing them.

Also, it is clearly harmful to the employer's interests to take part in, or support, industrial action. In **Ticehurst and Thompson *v* British Telecom [1992] IRLR 219**, an employee took part in industrial action, in spite of being warned that if she did she could be suspended without pay or notice. The dispute was still continuing when she went back to work and refused to sign a statement that she would thereafter work normally in accordance with her contract of employment. She was suspended without pay until the dispute was over. She brought a claim for her unpaid wages, saying she had been ready and willing and able to work. The Court of Appeal did not accept this and stated that by refusing to sign the statement she had indicated that she would continue to take part in the industrial action by withdrawing her goodwill, and this was in breach of the implied duty to act in good faith.

4 The employee is under a common law duty not to disclose confidential information which he has acquired through his work. He owes this duty both

during and to a lesser degree after he leaves his job. If an employer has trade secrets and secret processes, he would be wise to put an express restrictive term in the contract of employment. If there is no express term, then it is important to understand what amounts to confidential information.

The matter was discussed in **Faccenda Chicken Ltd *v* Fowler and Others [1986] IRLR 6**. Mr Fowler was employed as a sales manager of Faccenda Chicken, a company which breeds, rears, slaughters, prepares and sells chickens. Fowler established a van sales operation, whereby refrigerated vehicles offered fresh chickens to customers. In 1980, Fowler was arrested and charged with stealing 45 cases of chickens. On the day of the arrest, he offered his resignation and it was accepted. Subsequently, he was acquitted of the charges. In 1981, Fowler set up his own operation selling chickens from refrigerated vans and many of Faccenda's employees joined him. His new company was in direct competition to Faccenda which lost many of its customers to Fowler. Neither Fowler nor the other employees had an express term in their previous contracts, restricting their activities after leaving their employment with Faccenda. Faccenda brought an action for damages against Fowler and the others for breach of their implied duty to act in good faith in that they had used confidential sales information relating to the requirements of some of the customers and information on pricing. The Court of Appeal held that the implied duty to act in good faith, in particular the duty not to use or disclose confidential information, is more restricted once an employee leaves his employment. The duty does not extend to all information acquired while at work. The information would have to be classed as a highly confidential trade secret, sensitive, and easily isolated from other information which has become part of the employee's own skill and knowledge. In this case the sales information about the customers and pricing was well known by most of the employees at Faccenda and was not restricted to senior management. Fowler was not in breach of his duty to act in good faith.

5 Under common law, good faith would require an employee to disclose and give to his employer any rights to an invention which he had created either directly or indirectly during the course of his employment. **In British Syphon Co *v* Homewood [1956] 2 All ER 897** Homewood, a chief technician, as a result of his own interest in the task, invented an improved syphon. It was held that under common law he must give the patent rights to his employer. The employer benefited considerably from the invention.

The common law covering inventions has been reformed by the Patents Act 1977. Section 39 states that an employee's invention belongs to his employer, where it was made by the employee as part of his normal duties or if it was made outside his duties but it was the result of a specific assignment, or where the employee's duties impose on him a special obligation to further the employer's interests. In all other cases, the invention belongs to the employee and any express term to the contrary is invalid. An employee can assign the patent to the employer if he wishes, usually for money or a percentage of the profits. Even where the invention belongs to the employer and has proved to be of outstanding benefit, the court can award the employee compensation.

THE EMPLOYER'S COMMON LAW DUTIES

Many of the employer's duties are now purely statutory and we study these later. If an employer is in breach of one of his statutory duties, the employee's remedy is to apply to an industrial tribunal. If the employer is in breach of a common law duty, the employee's remedy has been to bring an action in the ordinary courts for damages for breach of contract. Alternatively, now that the tribunal's jurisdiction is extended under the Industrial Tribunals Act 1996 if the claim for breach of contract arises on the termination of the contract of employment, the claim can be brought before an industrial tribunal. However no claim can be brought in the industrial tribunal for damages for personal injuries.

In the absence of any express terms in the contract and in the absence of any specific statutory duty, the following duties will be implied into the contract.

Pay

The employer has a duty under common law to pay the employee's wages or salary. If the amount has not been agreed in advance, the employer must pay a reasonable sum. Payment of remuneration in exchange for services is fundamental to the contract of employment. This is often referred to as the 'work-wage bargain' – i.e., the employee who is ready and willing to work is entitled to be paid. Failure to pay will be a material breach of the contract (see the case **Rigby *v* Ferodo Ltd [1987] IRLR 516**). It follows that an employer, in the absence of an express term permitting it or a term implied by custom, cannot lay off workers without pay.

Work

The employer has **no** general common law duty to provide his employees with work although he must still pay wages. This means an employer can lawfully 'suspend an employee with pay' or, if dismissing an employee, the employer can give him wages in lieu of notice.

There are certain exceptions to this rule regarding the provision of work and in the following situations there is a duty to provide work:

1. Where the work provides the employee with an opportunity to enhance his reputation with the publicity. Actors are an example.
2. Where the employee is paid on a 'piece work' or 'commission only' basis. In these situations, the employee must have an opportunity to earn his commission.
3. Where the employer has, in effect, bound himself to provide work. An apprenticeship is an example.

Indemnify

The employer has a common law duty to indemnify the employee against all losses and liabilities which he incurs when properly carrying out his employer's instructions.

Respect

The employer is under a common law duty to treat his employee with trust and respect and to do nothing which might destroy the relationship which exists between them. This duty has only recently been developed by the courts. As we will see, it is a very important implied term in the context of constructive dismissal. The duty was discussed at length in **Woods *v* W M Car Services (Peterborough) Ltd [1982] IRLR 200**. The facts of the case were that Mrs Woods had been employed since 1952 at Todds Garage. In 1980 the business was sold to W M Car Services. The new company made an offer to Mrs Woods which she accepted to 'employ you on terms no less favourable to you in respect from those on which you were employed before'. Prior to the take-over Woods was described as 'chief secretary and accounts clerk'. She had another person working under her and spent most of her time as personal secretary and assistant to her boss. Gradually, the new company introduced new accountancy procedures. The woman who worked under her was made redundant and Woods was given a new job specification which meant that for 80 per cent of her time she would be doing accounts. Woods refused to accept the changes. She was told that she would be dismissed and so she resigned and claimed constructive dismissal.

The court had to decide whether there had been a repudiatory breach of the contract by the employer that would justify Woods resigning and claiming constructive dismissal. The question was whether the events taken together could be regarded as a breach of the implied term in the contract that the employers would not without reasonable and proper cause conduct themselves in a manner calculated or likely to destroy or damage the relationship of confidence and trust between the parties. The Court of Appeal upheld the tribunal's findings that there was no breach of this implied term. They held that the changes to Mrs Woods duties, proposed by her employer, did not justify her claiming constructive dismissal and these changes could not be regarded as perverse. The refusal of Mrs Woods to accept the changes was unreasonable in the sense that employers must not be put in the position where, through the wrongful refusal of an employee to accept change, they are prevented from introducing improved business methods in furtherance of seeking success for their enterprise.

References

One final point for the student to note is that the implied duties do not extend to writing a reference for an employee nor is there any such statutory obligation imposed on an employer. A refusal to provide a reference could make it very difficult for an employee to get another job. An employer could be reluctant to give a reference which might be critical of an employee because of the possibility of being sued by the employee for defamation. However, if he is sued for defamation, the law allows him two defences:

1 *Veritas*, which means that the reference was substantially truthful.
2 *Qualified privilege*. It is clear that employers should be encouraged to provide references and that they should be free to 'speak their minds', so this defence provides the employer with protection. The occasion is privileged provided the

person who receives the reference has a direct interest in its contents. This would cover a possible new employer but not a neighbour or friend. The privilege is destroyed if the defamed employee can show that the statement was made with malice and without belief in its truth.

However, the law in this respect has changed. Instead of suing for defamation a wronged employee could sue his employer for negligence. In the House of Lords decision in **Spring *v* Guardian Assurance Co [1994] ILRL 460 HL** it was held that an employer who provides a reference concerning an employee owes a duty of care to the employee regarding the content of the reference. It is reasonably foreseeable that the giving of a careless reference could cause economic loss to the subject of the reference. It was also held that there can in certain circumstances be an implied term in the contract of employment requiring an employer who provides a reference to exercise reasonable skill and care in its preparation and that the employer is under a duty to prepare such a reference. This would only apply where the contract relates to an engagement of a class of employment where the employee cannot be employed without a reference from his past employer. The LAUTRO rules, which were a feature of this case, require insurance companies to obtain references for potential employees prior to their employment and it would appear that in these circumstances insurance companies have a contractual duty to provide a reference. However, it should be noted that there is still no general duty on employers to provide a reference for employees (see p. 283).

Before leaving the law on references, the student should note that the employer could also be sued by the prospective employer on the grounds of fraudulent or negligent misstatement.

Safety

The employer is under a common law duty to provide for the safety of his employees at work. This duty arises not only as an implied term of the contract of employment but also, as was discussed in Chapter 16, under the law of delict. The distinction is not really important because both approaches give an injured employee the remedy of bringing an action for damages against the employer, who is in breach of his duty of care. In one situation, it is important to be able to regard the duty as an implied term of the contract and that is when an employee claims constructive dismissal. In order to succeed, the employee would have to show that the employer was in breach of this duty of care or that he did not listen to the employee's complaints about safety matters and this breach justifies him in resigning and claiming constructive dismissal.

The employer also has a statutory duty to provide for the safety of his employees under the Health and Safety at Work Act 1974. Breach by the employer of his duties under the Act provides no right of civil action for an injured employee but it amounts to a criminal offence and the employer could be prosecuted. The Health and Safety at Work Act will be examined in the next chapter.

THE EMPLOYER'S COMMON LAW DUTY TO TAKE REASONABLE CARE FOR THE SAFETY OF HIS INDIVIDUAL EMPLOYEES

There are a number of points to note regarding this duty to provide for the safety of employees at work:

1 The employer's duty is a personal one. He cannot avoid liability for the safety of his employees by delegating safety matters to, for example, a manager. This holds even if the employer is compelled by statute to delegate this duty to a technically qualified person. In **Wilsons and Clyde Coal Co Ltd** *v* **English [1938] AC 57** a miner was injured working in his employer's mine. The accident was caused because there was an unsafe system of working. The employers argued in their defence that they had delegated the duty of safety to a qualified manager. They referred to the Coal Mines Act 1911 which provided that only a qualified manager could control the technical management of the mine. It was held that the system was unsafe and the employers could not delegate their duty. It remained a personal duty, described by the court as three-fold, 'the provision of a competent staff of men, adequate material, and a proper system and effective supervision'.

2 The standard of the employer's common law duty is to take reasonable care for his employee's safety. He is required to take the same care a reasonable and prudent employer would take in the same circumstances. The degree of care depends on the circumstances. Where the risk of an accident happening is great, a prudent employer will take more care. He would have to balance on one hand the likelihood of injury and seriousness of the risk against how easy it would be to introduce safety measures on the other. In **Latimer** *v* **AEC Ltd [1953] 2 All ER 449** AEC Ltd had a large factory which was flooded by an unusually heavy rainstorm and the water mixed with an oily liquid which ran down channels in the floor. The floor was left very slippery. The employers had three tons of sawdust which they spread over most of the affected areas. Latimer slipped on part of the floor that had not been treated and injured his ankle. The employers were found not liable for his injuries. The employers had taken reasonable care to deal with the conditions. No-one else slipped that day on the floor, and it was not necessary – as the employee argued – to close the whole factory down in order to discharge the duty.

3 The employer's duty is owed to each individual employee, so he must take greater care of employees who, because of their youth, inexperience or any physical disability, are especially vulnerable. In **Paris** *v* **Stepney Borough Council [1951] 1 All ER 42** Paris worked as a garage-hand in the Council's cleansing department. He was blind in one eye. While working under a vehicle, in a freak accident, a piece of metal entered his good eye and rendered him blind. The question for the court to decide was whether the employers had taken reasonable care for his safety. It was not normal practice to supply goggles to employees working in the garage. Should goggles have been supplied to Paris? A similar accident happening to one of his fellow employees would not

have had such serious consequences. The court held that the duty to take reasonable care is owed to each employee. In this case the employers were held liable. They should have taken greater care for the safety of Paris, because, having only one eye, he ran a risk of greater injury.

4 The employees' safety may be considered under the following five headings:

The provision of a safe system of working

What constitutes a safe system will vary according to the circumstances and the nature of the work. The following factors will be relevant in deciding whether an employer has taken reasonable care to provide a safe system of working: the physical lay-out of the job; the sequence in which the work is to be done; the provision of warnings and notices; supervision and the issue of special instructions; general working conditions.

The employer has to devise a safe system of working which will eliminate, as far as reasonably possible, any danger. He must take reasonable care to ensure that the system is enforced, although if the employee departs from the system without the employer's knowledge and consent, the employer will not be liable. Each case will be decided on its own facts. In the following cases, the dangers were obvious but if the danger were not obvious, for example dangerous fumes, the duty would not only be to warn the employees of the danger but also to make sure that safety precautions are enforced. In **Woods *v* Durable Suites [1953] 1 WLR 857** Durable Suites made furniture and their employee, Woods, was a middle-aged, experienced glue-spreader. The employers were aware of the risk of contracting dermatitis from contact with glue and so provided adequate washing facilities and barrier cream for the use of employees. They also ran a poster campaign and had advised Woods personally to take precautions. They were unaware that Woods was not following their advice and eventually he contracted dermatitis and sued the company for failing to provide a safe system of working. The employers were held not liable; they had done all that was reasonably possible, short of having someone stand over Woods to make sure that he washed his hands. Woods had contributed to his own injury. The court did say that if Woods had been a new employee or a young trainee, then the duty to supervise personally would have been stricter.

In **Qualcast *v* Haynes [1959] 2 All ER 38** Haynes, an experienced metal moulder, burnt his foot when the ladle of molten metal he was holding slipped from his grasp. He was wearing ordinary boots at the time. His employers had a stock of protective spats which the employees only had to ask for and a supply of reinforced boots at a price. In deciding whether the employers had taken reasonable care in the circumstances, the House of Lords stated that these cases had each to be decided on their own facts. In this case the question to be decided was not whether the employers ought to provide protective footwear for the men – because they did. The question is, having done that, ought they to go further and urge the men to wear them? In this case, it was held that the employer had not failed to take reasonable care. The spats were there, this particular workman, Haynes, knew the danger without being told, but he chose to wear his own boots which he bought for work.

The risk was not obvious in the next case. In **Crookall *v* Vickers Armstrong [1955] 2 All ER 12** Crookall worked in a foundry. The foundry's sandy floor created a risk of silicosis, which was not an obvious risk. The employers provided the best available masks and the foundry manager went round from time to time explaining to the employees the need to wear the masks. Crookall did not wear his mask and developed silicosis. Vickers argued that they had done all they could, short of dismissal, to ensure that the employees wore their masks. The court held that their duty in the circumstances was an active one. They had failed to provide a safe system of working.

Employer's liability for work-related stress

The above cases all dealt with employees' claims for damages for physical injuries or damage to health. In the last few years the law has been developing and it would appear possible for an employee to claim damages for work-related stress. This arises from long term subjection of the body to mental stress in the form of overwork or worry which may result in mental illness like depression. In **Walker *v* Northumberland County Council [1995] IRLR 35** Walker was a social services officer. During the 1980s his work load increased dramatically and he suffered a mental breakdown which had been induced by stress at work. He returned to work having been promised assistance and support by his employers. This did not materialise, his workload was not reduced, and he suffered a second mental breakdown. He was dismissed on health grounds. Walker claimed damages on the grounds that his employer had breached their common law duty to take reasonable care for his safety and health in providing him with a safe system of work. The court did not accept the employer's defence that government-imposed financial constraints had made it unavoidable. The employers were not found liable for Walker's first breakdown because before it happened they could not have reasonably foreseen the risk. However, when he returned to work a reasonable employer should have foreseen the real risk of him suffering another breakdown and taken steps to reduce the risk by reducing the workload. The High Court held that the employers had unreasonably failed to provide a safe system of work. The Council decided not to appeal. Walker received £175 000 in an 'out of court' settlement. (See also **Johnstone *v* Bloomsbury Area Health Authority [1991] IRLR 118** on pp. 286 and 339.)

The provision of safe premises

The employer has a duty to take reasonable care to ensure that the place of work is safe and any dangers minimised. This point was discussed in **Latimer *v* AEC Ltd [1953] 2 All ER 449**.

The provision of safe plant and equipment

The employer has a duty to take reasonable care to provide proper and safe plant and equipment, to maintain it and remedy any known defects. In **Bradford *v* Robinson Rentals [1967] 1 WLR 337**, in severe winter conditions, an employer sent Bradford, a radio engineer, on a round trip of 400 miles in a van with a defective heater. He suffered from frost-bite and the employer was held liable.

Note that an employer cannot avoid liability for providing unsafe equipment by stating that, although he provided the equipment, the fault was latent and was the responsibility of a third party who supplied it to him. Since the **Employer's Liability (Defective Equipment) Act 1969**, if an employee is injured from using unsafe equipment and this is due to the fault of a third party, then the injury will be deemed due to the employer's negligence. The employer may then bring proceedings against the third party for an indemnity for the damages which he has paid his employee. For the purpose of the Act 'equipment' includes any plant, machinery, vehicle, aircraft and clothing. Two recent decisions have held that a ship and flagstone were also equipment and covered by the Act.

The provision of safe and competent fellow employees

The employer has a duty to take reasonable care in selecting safe and competent employees. If an employee is injured by another employee as a result of the latter's incompetence, lack of experience or lack of proper instruction, the injured employee can sue his employer for damages. The duty also extends to the continued employment of individuals who are potentially dangerous (for example, a bully or a dangerous practical joker). The employer would only be liable if he knew that the individual was a potential danger. His failure to take care of his other employees will only be shown if he does not reprimand, reform or threaten to dismiss the employee and allows the conduct to continue.

In **Hudson *v* Ridge Manufacturing Co [1957] 2 QB 348** Hudson fractured his wrist when he was tripped up at work by a fellow employee. For four years this employee had made a nuisance of himself by playing jokes on others. The employer was held liable as he had allowed this potentially dangerous conduct to continue for a long time and it was reasonably foreseeable that someone would be injured.

However in **Smith *v* Crossley Bros (1951) 95 SJ 655** an apprentice was injured when his fellow apprentices played a dreadful joke on him. The employer was not held personally liable as this kind of prank had never been done before. Also the employer was not vicariously liable for the actions of the apprentices as 'playing jokes' is outwith the scope of employment.

THE MAIN DEFENCES OF THE EMPLOYER

When an injured employee brings an action for damages against the employer on the grounds that the employer is in breach of his common law duty regarding the safety of his employees, the employer has certain defences:

1 That he did take reasonable care in the circumstances; that the injury was not reasonably foreseeable. Or he could argue that there was no connecting link between his breach and the actual injury.
2 The employer could argue *volenti non fit injuria*. This is a complete defence and basically means that the employee knew of the danger and voluntarily, in the fullest sense of the word, consented to accept the risk that he might be injured. This defence is rarely used successfully in employment cases because the fact that an employee continues working in dangerous circumstances will not be

sufficient to establish that the employee voluntarily consented to accept the risk and agreed to the employer doing nothing about the unsafe system of working.

In **Smith *v* Baker [1891] AC 325** Smith was working in an area where a crane was working above moving stones. Smith complained about this several times but continued working in that area. He was injured when stones fell on him and he claimed damages. The employer tried unsuccessfully to use the defence of *volenti non fit injuria.* It was held that there was no evidence that Smith had voluntarily undertaken the risk of injury.

However, if statute imposes a duty on an employee and he disregards that duty, the employer is more likely to be successful in using the defence. In **ICI *v* Shatwell [1965] AC 656** George Shatwell and his brother James were qualified shot-firers. One day they had prepared 50 shot holes, inserted electric detonators and connected them in a circuit. Before firing, it was necessary to test the circuit. The employers had told their employees to test the circuit from a shelter some distance from the site. This method of testing was also laid down in statutory regulations and the Shatwells were aware of them. They ignored the regulations and were injured when a detonator exploded. The employers successfully relied upon the defence of *volenti non fit injuria.*

3 The employer could use the defence of contributory negligence. While the duty to take reasonable care to provide safe working conditions remains with the employer, the employee still has a high degree of responsibility for his own safety and many employees have their damages reduced or defeated because of their own careless conduct. Since the **Law Reform (Contributory Negligence) Act 1945**, the courts can apportion liability according to the parties' fault and the employee's compensation is reduced accordingly. If a person has been found to have been 100 per cent contributory negligent, he will lose his claim altogether. In **Robinson *v* Pearce (1960) CA 267** a bricklayer, who was sent to repair a chimney with ladders but with no rope to secure them, was held 75 per cent to blame for his injuries after starting the job with an unsecured ladder.

VICARIOUS LIABILITY

Under common law an employer is vicariously liable for the wrongful and negligent acts of his employee, provided that the act was done within the scope or during course of his employment. Students are reminded that this topic was explained in detail in Chapter 13 and at this point, they should return to that section.

QUESTIONS

1 (a) Describe the structure and jurisdiction of the Industrial Tribunals.
(b) Describe the particular duties of the Advisory, Conciliation and Arbitration Service.

2 (a) Explain the difference between a contract of service and a contract for services. Explain the importance of this distinction.
(b) What tests have the courts devised to determine whether a contract of service exists or not?

3 Sandra has been employed by a large firm of stockbrokers for many years. She decided last year that it would be to her advantage to be classed as self-employed for tax purposes. After consulting an accountant, she asked her employers if she might change her status and they agreed. A new contract was drawn up in which Sandra was described as a consultant. The Inland Revenue were informed and they reclassified Sandra as self-employed. No other changes were made to Sandra's job. She still works the same hours, carries out the same duties and is on the same salary scale as before. She has now been given notice of redundancy. She wants to claim a redundancy payment but to qualify to do so, she must be an employee, working under a contract of service. She has asked your advice.

4 Explain in detail what written particulars must be given to an employee by his employer after he commences employment. Include in your answer an explanation of the legal status of these written particulars.

5 Describe the employee's common law duty, owed to his employer, to act in good faith. With reference to this duty and to decided cases, consider whether the following employees have been in breach of this duty:

(a) Susan borrowed £10 from the petty cash box without permission. She replaced the money two days later but one of her colleagues has told her employer.
(b) Jones, the company's best salesman, had no express restrictions as to his future employment in his contract of employment. He has resigned and taken the post of sales manager with the company's main rivals. The company are very worried because Jones knows all their sales and pricing techniques and was on good terms with the customers of the company. They realise that he will now call on these customers representing his new firm.

6 Satanic Mills Ltd have had a few problems at work.

Bill, who has worked in the warehouse, had complained to his supervisor several times that the wooden stairs which connected one part of the warehouse with another were unsafe. One day while carrying boxes up these stairs they collapsed and Bill has badly injured his back.

Fred, who works in the factory, has contracted dermatitis on his hands as a result of his hands being in contact with dangerous chemicals for a number of years. Satanic Mills have never advised him of the risk nor provided protective gloves.

Harold, who also works in the factory, was supplied with protective goggles. He never wears them and has now lost the sight of one eye after a sliver of wood flew out of a machine.

Sandra drives the delivery van. She was seriously injured when a wheel came off the van. The van had been serviced the previous day by Henry's Garage. A trainee mechanic, Dim, forgot to tighten the nuts on that wheel after replacing the tyre.

Bob was injured in the factory yard. He was waiting to unload wood from a lorry driven by Bert, a fellow employee of Satanic Mills. Bert's foot slipped on the accelerator and unfortunately Bob was run over by the lorry.

All these employees wish to sue their employer Satanic Mills. Advise them.

18 Health and safety and statutory employment protection rights

HEALTH AND SAFETY AT WORK ACT 1974

Introduction

At the end of the last chapter, we saw that employers have a common law duty to take reasonable care for the safety of their employees at work. Although such a duty constitutes an implied term in all contracts of employment, usually an injured employee will bring an action for damages based on negligence rather than contract. It is clear that the main function of common law is not to prevent accidents but to provide compensation where an employee has been injured. At this point, note that compensation payable to employees is covered by insurance. Under the Employer's Liability (Compulsory Insurance) Act 1969, every employer carrying on a business must maintain an approved policy with authorised insurers covering any bodily injury or disease of employees which might arise out of or in the course of their employment.

As early as 1833 when the first Factories Act was introduced, inspectors were appointed to investigate breaches of the safety legislation, and a breach of a statutory duty could result in the party in breach being prosecuted in a criminal court. It is not proposed in this book to explain the earlier safety legislation in detail. One point to note is that, although most of the legislation prior to the Health and Safety at Work Act 1974 (hereafter referred to as the HSAW Act) was intended to promote safety and prevent accidents, lawyers tended to approach it as if its primary purpose was to establish liability for damages after an employee had been injured. Since a statutory duty may be stricter or more precise than the common-law duty of care, it could be advantageous for an injured employee to bring an action for damages for his injuries under, for example, the Factories Act 1961. The statute upon which the action is based must be one that supports civil liability. The Factories Act 1961, the Mines and Quarries Act 1954 and the Offices, Shops and Railway Premises Act 1963 impose criminal sanctions and do not expressly confer the right to sue for damages on injured employees, but the courts have said that such rights are implicit. In this respect, this legislation differs from the HSAW Act. Under the HSAW Act s 47(1) a contravention of ss 2–8 does not confer a right of action in any civil proceedings. Nevertheless, breaches of duty imposed by previous legislation remain actionable under civil law.

REASONS FOR THE NECESSARY CHANGES IN THE SAFETY LEGISLATION

1 There were too many different acts and regulations covering different places of work. Much of the legislation was obscure, too detailed, out of date and some employees were not covered at all. Obviously, what *was needed* was a single piece of legislation covering all work activity, imposing general duties on all persons at work, and supported by regulations covering specific problems and flexible codes of practice.
2 It was recognised that there was one main cause for accidents at work and that was apathy – both by management and by the workforce. *What was needed* was a system whereby everyone at work (management, others and the workforce) became concerned with health and safety. For each individual it should be a matter of personal responsibility.
3 There were about nine different enforcement bodies – i.e., inspectorates – covering different areas of employment with overlapping jurisdictions and this was causing confusion. *What was needed* was one enforcement body to have overall responsibility for these inspectorates *and* a separate authority with the responsibility to promote the aims of the Act and issue regulations and codes of practice.
4 The existing legislation covered the health and safety and welfare of people at work. *What was needed* was protection for other persons against risks to their health and safety arising out of, or in connection with work activities.
5 *What was needed* was some control on the keeping and use of dangerous substances at work – many accidents happen through ignorance – and there should also be some control of the emission into the air of noxious or offensive substances from premises covered by the Act.
6 *What was needed* was legislation designed to prevent accidents happening at work in the first place and not legislation simply providing a punishment or a remedy for injured employees once an accident has happened. Warning notices should be given and safety representatives appointed.

THE HEALTH AND SAFETY AT WORK ACT

The HSAW Act is superimposed on the earlier existing safety legislation like the Factories Act. The earlier legislation was not repealed so the parties concerned must comply in some situations with the earlier legislation and the HSAW Act. The

HSAW Act is an 'enabling act' and the intention is to replace gradually the provisions of the earlier acts by a system of regulations and approved codes of practice, all operating together with the general duties and provisions laid down by the HSAW Act.

The HSAW Act is criminal legislation, is concerned with criminal sanctions and does not provide a remedy of damages for injuries suffered by employees. (As previously discussed, this is still available under common law and the existing legislation.) A prosecution can take place under the HSAW Act even though no accident has occurred as the aim of the Act is to tighten up safety in the workplace and prevent accidents happening at all. It would be preferable to avoid prosecution and enforce the law through persuasion. Accordingly, new enforcement powers have been given to inspectors.

The general statutory duties of the HSAW Act

The Act imposes general duties on a number of different persons or categories of person. Duties are imposed on: employers, manufacturers, designers, suppliers, the self-employed, controllers of premises and employees. Most of these duties are qualified in that the duty only extends to what is '**reasonably practicable**'. The effect of the qualification is to allow the person on whom the duty is placed to weigh up the seriousness of a risk and the likelihood of injury against the difficulty and expense of removing it. Where difficulty and cost are high and a careful assessment shows that the risk of injury is insignificant, then it may be that no action need be taken. However, if it is the case that the risk of injury or loss of life is high, then action must be taken whatever the cost and no allowance is made for the fact that it is a small organisation or that the business is struggling to survive.

Note: It is for the person alleging that he has done 'that which is reasonably practicable' to establish it (s 40). This is unusual, as normally in criminal prosecutions the procurator fiscal has to prove his case beyond reasonable doubt.

General duties of employers

Section 2(1) imposes a general duty on an employer to ensure so far as is reasonably practicable, the health, safety and welfare at work of all his employees.

Section 2(2) then continues by specifying five particular duties which spell out the general duty in detail:

(a) To provide and maintain plant and systems of work that are, so far as is reasonably practicable, safe and without risk to health.
(b) Arrangements must be made to ensure so far as is reasonably practicable the safety and absence of risk to health in the use, storage and transport of articles and substances.
(c) The provision of such information, instruction, training and supervision as is necessary to ensure, so far as is reasonably practicable, the health and safety at work of all his employees.
(d) So far as is reasonably practicable as regards any place of work under the employer's control, he must ensure its maintenance in a condition that is safe and without risk to health and provide a safe means of access and exit.

(e) The provision and maintenance of a working environment that is so far as is reasonably practicable, safe, without risks to health and adequate as regards facilities and arrangements for the welfare of employees at work.

Note: It can be seen that the above statutory duties are very similar to those owed by an employer to an employee under common law but they differ in that the duties under s 2 are enforced only by criminal sanctions.

Section 2(3) states that every employer (unless he has less than five employees) shall prepare, revise if necessary, and bring to the notice of his employees a written statement of his general policy with respect to the health and safety of his employees and the arrangements in force for the time being for carrying out that policy.

Section 2(6) states that it shall be the duty of every employer to consult any safety representatives appointed by recognised trade unions.

Section 2(7) states that if requested by the safety representatives, the employer has a duty to establish a safety committee.

Section 9 forbids employers to levy any charge on employees in respect of anything done or provided in pursuance of any specific requirement under the statutory provisions.

General duties owed by employers and the self-employed to non-employees

Section 3(1) states that every employer is under a duty to conduct his business in such a way so far as is reasonably practicable that non-employees are not exposed to risks to their health and safety. (This will include the general public, sub-contractors, visitors and even students on the college campus.)

Section 3(2) imposes a similar duty on self-employed persons in respect of themselves and other non-employees.

In **Regina** *v* **Swan Hunter Shipbuilders Ltd [1981] IRLR 403** the employers distributed a booklet to their employees giving practical safety rules for the use of oxygen equipment, in particular warning of the dangers of oxygen in confined spaces. The booklet was not given to the employees of their sub-contractor, except on request. A bad fire broke out on a ship because an employee of the sub-contractor left on an oxygen hose, resulting in the death of eight workmen. Swan Hunter were prosecuted and convicted of breach of ss 2(2)(a), 2(2)(c) and 3(1).

In **R** *v* **Associated Octel Ltd [1994] IRLR 546** a fire started when a chemical leak ignited, engulfing the plant in flames. Although no-one was injured the fire was classified by the HSE as a 'major accident' which endangered the safety of the employees, the neighbouring residents and the emergency services. The company admitted that they had failed to maintain plant and systems of work which were safe and without risk to health. The company was found guilty of breaches of ss 2 and 3 of the HSAW Act and fined £75 000 for each breach.

In **R** *v* **British Steel plc [1995] 1 WLR 1356** BS engaged subcontractors to reposition a platform. The subcontractors provided two men for the task and a BS engineer was to supervise the work. One of the men was fatally injured. BS had assigned an engineer to supervise but there was conflicting evidence as to whether he had done this properly. BS were found guilty of a breach of s 3(1) of the HSAW

Act. They tried to argue that if the engineer was at fault then they should not be liable for his fault and that they had taken such care as is reasonably practicable. The Court of Appeal dismissed this view and said corporate employers could not avoid criminal liability where the potential harmful event is committed by a person who is not 'directing the mind of the company'.

General duties of controllers of premises

Section 4 imposes a duty on people who have the control over non-domestic premises which are used by non-employees who work there or who use plant and the substances provided there. The duty is to take such measures so far as is reasonably practicable that the premises or any plant or substances on the premises are safe and without risk to health. Sections 3 and 4 could be regarded as the criminal counterpart of the Occupier's Liability (Scotland) Act 1960 and s 4 would apply to premises like a car wash, a coin-operated laundrette, a library or a school laboratory.

Section 5 imposed another duty on controllers of any premises of a class prescribed to use the best practicable means for preventing the emission into the atmosphere of noxious and offensive substances and for rendering them harmless. This section was repealed in April 1996, and is now covered by the Environmental Protection Act 1990.

General duties of designers, manufacturers, importers and suppliers

Section 6(1) states three duties for the above persons regarding articles for use at work:

(1) to ensure, so far as is reasonably practicable, that the article is so designed and constructed as to be safe and without risks to health when properly used;
(2) to carry out, or arrange for the carrying out, of tests and examinations of the articles;
(3) to ensure that there will be available, with articles for use at work, adequate information about their use and any tests that have been done on them.

Section 6(2) states that a designer or manufacturer of articles has a duty to carry out any research to discover and so far as is reasonably practicable eliminate any risks to health or safety.

Section 6(3) imposes a duty on erectors and installers of any article for use at work to ensure so far as is reasonably practicable that nothing about the way it is erected or installed will make it unsafe or a risk to health when properly used.

Section 6(4) places a similar qualified duty on persons who manufacture, import or supply any substance for use at work. So far as is reasonably practicable the substance has to be safe, tested and examined. Adequate information must be supplied with it, and necessary research carried out to eliminate any risks to health and safety.

General duties of employees

Section 7 imposes two main duties on the employee:

(1) He must take reasonable care for the health and safety of himself and of others

who may be affected by his acts or omissions at work. Thus, an employee who refuses to wear his safety harness or helmet, or who causes injury to another through his negligence or 'mucking about' is liable to prosecution under the Act.

(2) He must co-operate with his employer or any other person to enable them to carry out their statutory duty.

Section 8 states that no person (which includes employees) shall intentionally or recklessly misuse anything provided in the interests of health, safety or welfare in pursuance of the relevant statutory provisions.

THE ESTABLISHMENT OF THE COMMISSION AND THE EXECUTIVE

Sections 10–14 and s 18 of the Act provide for the constitution of two new corporate bodies: the Health and Safety Commission (HSC) and the Health and Safety Executive (HSE).

The Commission

This body has a chairman and not less than six, nor more than nine, other members, all appointed by the Secretary of State. Three are appointed after consultation with employers' organisations, a further three appointed after consultation with employees' organisations and the remainder after consultation with local authorities and professional bodies. The duties of the Commission are to promote the health and safety legislation; to carry out research; to publish information; and to prepare proposals for regulations and codes of practice to be introduced under the Act.

The HSE

This is the enforcement body. It is led by a director, appointed by the Commission with the approval of the Secretary of State and two other members, appointed by the Commission after consultation with the director. The HSE headquarters are in London with 21 area offices throughout the country. It has overall control of the various inspectorates. The duty of the Executive is to make adequate arrangements for the enforcement of the statutory provisions.

ENFORCEMENT OF THE ACT

A breach of any of the general duties under the Act or of any of the health and safety regulations can be dealt with in two ways:

1 new powers were given to inspectors which include the power to issue enforcement notices (see below);
2 a prosecution can take place as breach of any of the duties under the Act amounts to a criminal offence.

In Scotland, an inspector never brings a prosecution himself as happens in England. In Scotland, the inspector would collect the evidence and pass it to the Procurator Fiscal, who, after consulting the Crown Office, would decide whether to bring criminal proceedings. Apart from breach of the general duties, there are numerous other offences specified by the Act. For example, contravening any of the regulations made under the Act or obstructing an inspector. The maximum fine a sheriff can impose under summary procedure is £5000 (October 1992). In addition, under the Offshore Safety Act 1992 the maximum penalty for breaches of ss 2–6 of the HSAW Act, and for breaches of enforcement notices, under summary procedure, has increased to £20 000, and the sheriff can also impose a prison sentence of up to six months for breaches of enforcement notices. If a person is found guilty of an offence by a sheriff under solemn procedure, he could be fined an unlimited amount and/or imprisoned for up up to three years.

Improvement notice

If an inspector is of an opinion that a person (a) is contravening a relevant statutory provision, 2 or (b) has contravened one or more provisions in circumstances that make it likely that the contravention will continue or be repeated, then the inspector may serve an **improvement notice** stating that he is of that opinion, the relevant provisions which he thinks have been contravened, why he is of that opinion, and requiring that person to remedy the matter within a certain stated period (the period must not be less than 21 days). An appeal to an industrial tribunal can be made against such a notice within 21 days. The lodging of an appeal will suspend the notice until the appeal is heard. In February 1996 the HSC issued an enforcement policy statement that businesses have a right of representation before the formal issuing of an improvement notice. Before an improvement notice can be issued the business has a right to request a written explanation of the contravention, an outline of what needs to be done and the time scale for the work. The business has a two-week period from receiving the written notice during which it can make representations to change or cancel the notice. The proposed notice will then be reconsidered with regard to the representations. If no representations are received then the improvement notice will be issued.

Prohibition notice

If an inspector is of the opinion that an activity involves a risk of serious injury, then he may serve a **prohibition notice**. This notice will state: (a) that this is his opinion; (b) the matter which is giving rise to this risk of injury; (c) which statutory provision is being contravened; and will order (d) that certain activities should not be carried out until the matters specified in the notice have been remedied.

The notice can take immediate effect or it can be a deferred prohibition notice, taking effect at the end of a period specified in the notice. An appeal against a prohibition notice can be lodged within 21 days. Such an appeal does not automatically suspend the notice. The employer has to apply for this suspension and, if he fails, the notice will have effect, either immediately or within the period stated. Since this could seriously affect the employer's business, appeals are normally heard very quickly. There is no right to make representations before the issuing of a prohibition notice.

In **Associated Dairies *v* Hartley [1979] IRLR 171** the appellants, who used roller trucks, provided safety footwear for employees at cost price. One day, an employee's foot was injured. An inspector issued an improvement notice requiring the employers to provide suitable footwear free of charge. There was no statutory requirement to do this – and remember that an obligation under s 2 for providing for the safety of employees is qualified – so far as is reasonably practicable. In deciding whether the inspector's requirement was reasonably practicable, the tribunal had to balance the trouble, time and expense of providing free boots against the likelihood of such an accident happening again. In this case, it would cost £20 000 initially to provide the boots and £10 000 a year thereafter, and it was shown that the likelihood of such an accident happening again was remote. The tribunal allowed the appeal. They felt that the employer's arrangement of providing boots at cost price was satisfactory.

The Health and Safety (Enforcing Authority) Regulations 1977

These Regulations, amended in 1989, stated that certain premises were to be the responsibility of the HSE and some the responsibility of the local authorities (that is the local council through the Environmental Health Officers (EHO). EHOs have the same powers as HSE inspectors. However, the enforcement in a particular case can be transferred from one body to the other with the permission of the HSC. Most offices, shops, restaurants, warehouses and hotels are assigned to the local authorities, while most industrial business premises are the responsibility of the HSE inspectors who also inspect all premises occupied or controlled by the local authority and the Crown.

Apart from the use of enforcement notices, the local authority and HSE inspectors are given other wide ranging powers under the Act. These new powers relate to such matters as the right of entry to premises; the making of examinations and investigations; the taking of measurements, photographs and samples; insisting on the production of books and documents; questioning people; seizing articles and substances.

SAFETY REPRESENTATIVES

The Health and Safety at Work Act s 2, through the Safety Representatives and Safety Committees Regulations 1977, provides for the appointment by recognised independent trade unions of safety representatives from among the employees. It will then be the duty of the employer to consult with such representatives about health and safety matters at work.

The safety representatives' functions are:

1 To investigate potential hazards and dangerous occurrences at the workplace and to examine the causes of accidents there.
2 To investigate complaints by any employee they represent relating to that employee's health, safety and welfare at work.
3 To make representations to the employer on matters of health, safety and welfare.
4 To carry out inspections if they give the employer written notice. Inspections can only be made at three-month intervals, unless the employer agrees to more frequent inspections; or where there has been a substantial change in the working conditions; or if there has been a notifiable accident; or if there has been a notifiable illness contracted at the workplace.
5 To represent the employees in consultation with the various inspectors.
6 To receive information from inspectors.
7 To attend the meetings of safety committees.

The employer's duty to consult

The **Management of Health and Safety at Work Regulations 1992** clarifies the employer's duty to consult with safety representatives. Every employer shall consult safety representatives in good time with regard to the following:

1 The introduction of any measure at the workplace which may substantially affect the health and safety of the employees.
2 The employer's arrangements for appointing or, as the case may be, nominating competent persons to assist him in health and safety matters as required by the regulations.
3 Any health and safety information he is required to provide to the employees.
4 The planning and organisation of any health and safety training he is required to provide the employees.
5 The health and safety consequences for the employees of the introduction of new technologies into the workplace.

Appointment of safety representatives

Only recognised independent trade unions have the legal right to appoint safety representatives, although there is nothing to stop an employer allowing 'safety reps' in a non-unionised situation. Neither the regulations nor the code of practice specify how many should be appointed. However, the guidance notes suggest that the criteria to be adopted should take into account the following factors: the total number of employees and their occupations; the size of the workplace; the shift systems; the type of work done; and the degree and character of any inherent dangers.

A safety representative is entitled to have time off with pay during working hours to perform his functions and to undergo training in these functions.

Safety committees

The regulations state that an employer must establish a safety committee if requested to do so in writing by two safety representatives. He must consult with them and the trade union on this matter, but the actual composition of the committee can be decided by the employer. However, he must establish it within three months of the request.

The SRSC Regulations 1977 restricted the presence of statutory safety representatives and committees onshore to workplaces with a recognised inde-pendent trade union. This is not acceptable because of the decline in trade union membership and also because the UK has not fully implemented the EC Framework Directive's requirements that information, consultation and participation rights on health and safety be given to all workers regardless of whether they are covered by a recognised trade union. The HSC has drawn up proposals for new regulations and the rights granted to safety representatives will be extended to non-unionised workers. The employers have a choice of consulting their employees directly or with employee representatives. The new regulations (The Health and Safety Consultation with Employees Regulations) came into force on 1 October 1996 .

Protection against victimisation and dismissal

The Employment Rights Act 1996 s 44 gives rights to employees, regardless of their length of service, to protect them from being either victimised because of action they have taken or failed to take in connection with health and safety matters. In either case a complaint may be brought to an industrial tribunal within three months. If the tribunal finds that the employee has been victimised they may make an award of compensation, the amount being what the tribunal thinks is just and equitable in all the circumstances.

The protection is only given to an employee in the following circumstances:

1 When he has been designated by the employer to carry out activities in connection with preventing or reducing risks to the health and safety of employees at work and he carried out or proposed to carry out such activities.
2 When he is a safety representative or a member of a safety committee and he performed or proposed to perform any functions as such a representative or as a member of such a committee.
3 When he is an employee at a place where there is no safety representative or committee or if there is, when it was not reasonably practicable for the employee to raise the matter with them and he brought to the employer's attention by reasonable means the circumstances connected with his work which he believed were harmful to health and safety.
4 When he has left or proposes to leave his place of work in circumstances of serious and imminent danger which he could not reasonably have been expected to avert.
5 When, in circumstances of serious and imminent danger, he took or proposed to take appropriate steps to protect himself or other employees from the danger. Whether the steps in this case were appropriate shall be judged by taking into account all the circumstances, including in particular his knowledge and the facilities and advice available to him at the time. However, the employee is not protected if the employer shows that it was negligent for the employee to take these steps and that a reasonable employer might have treated him as the employer did.

In **Barton** *v* **Wandsworth Council COIT 11268/94** an industrial tribunal upheld the claim by an ambulance driver that he had been unlawfully disciplined in contravention of s 44. He had complained about the competence of some of his fellow workers who had been recruited as escorts, employed to assist patients with mental or physical disabilities.

The Employment Rights Act 1996 s 100 gives protection for employees who are dismissed in the same circumstances (see p. 409).

OFFENCES DUE TO THE FAULT OF ANOTHER

Section 36

When the commission of an offence is due to the act or default of another, that other person may be charged with the offence as well.

Section 37

Where an offence committed by a corporate body is proved to have been committed with the consent or connivance, or due to any neglect of any director, manager, secretary or other similar officer of the corporate body, then he, as well as the corporate body, shall be guilty of that offence.

Section 36, for example, applies to situations where an offence committed by one person is due to the act or default of another. Also note that ss 7 and 8 of the HSAW Act place general duties on all employees to take reasonable care for their own and other persons' safety. Junior managers might be prosecuted under s 36 along with possibly another employee. Senior officers who are considered to embody the corporate body itself may not be regarded as 'some other person' under s 36. That is why s 37 is there, to provide a means by which offences committed by a body corporate can be prosecuted. *Armour* v *Skeen* is one of the few successful prosecutions under this section. In a decision of the Court of Appeal in **R** *v* **Boal [1992] QB 59**, the manager of a bookshop, Mr Boal, was found not to be 'a manager or other similar officer of the body corporate'. Mr Boal, as manager of the bookshop, had only responsibility for the day-to-day running of the shop and did not enjoy any sort of governing role in respect of the affairs of the company. The word 'manager' in s 37 must be regarded as a person who is managing 'the whole affairs of the company and was entrusted with power to transact the whole of the affairs of the company'.

In **Armour** *v* **Skeen [1977] IRLR 310** Strathclyde Regional Council and its Director of Roads were both prosecuted for breach of safety regulations and lack of a safe system of working. As a result of these breaches, an employee of the Council was killed while painting a bridge over the river Clyde. The Director was found guilty of neglect in that he failed to have a good safety policy for his department and had not provided information to his subordinates, nor training, nor instruction in safe working practices. He was convicted – the offences were committed by the Council but, under s 37, were due to his neglect.

THE HSAW ACT IS AN ENABLING ACT – HEALTH AND SAFETY REGULATIONS

One of the main aims of the HSAW Act was gradually to modernise and replace the existing safety legislation with a system of regulations and flexible codes of practice. The HSAW Act is an enabling act which means that the Act confers power on, amongst others, the Secretary of State to make additional law by means of regulations. The Health and Safety Regulations are made by the Secretary of State on his own initiative or he bases them on proposals made by the HSC. Regulations, provided they are within the powers conferred by the parent Act, have the full force of law until amended or repealed. Many regulations have now been introduced under the HSAW Act. Some cover all employment situations, while others are more specific and are designed to apply to a particular hazard in a particular industry or industries. Here are some examples.

The **Reporting of Injuries, Diseases and Dangerous Occurrences Regulations 1995 (RIDDOR)** apply to employers, the self-employed and those in control of work premises. A record of any accidents, disease or dangerous occurrence must be kept. All injuries must be recorded in an accident book. The relevant authorities (Environmental Health Officer or the HSE) must be notified if there is a fatal or serious accident at work or if anyone is absent from work for more than three days as a result of an accident at work or because they are suffering from an occupational disease certified by a doctor. Also, any fatal injury of non-employees, major injury to non-employees or injuries to non-employee which require hospital treatment must be reported. The Regulations specify the information that must be given when an accident, disease or occurrence is reported and violent incidents are now reportable. The records must be kept for three years.

The Control of Substances Hazardous to Health Regulations 1994 (COSHH) revoke the 1988 COSHH Regulations and restate them with minor amendments. In particular the 1994 Regulations implement the Biological Agents Directives and the schedule contains special provisions relating to biological agents and extends the COSHH Regulations to offshore oil and gas installations. The Regulations also set new maximum exposure limits (MELs) for nine substance groups. (Note the HSC has issued a consultation document with proposed amendments to the 1994 Regulations. The amendments include the introduction of MELs for even more substances and are due to come into effect in January 1997.) The Regulations set out the essential requirements for controlling hazardous substances and the protection for people exposed to them. Substances include the following: those substances labelled as dangerous, agricultural pesticides and other chemicals used on a farm; harmful micro-organisms, quantities of dust and any material, mixture or compound used at work, or arising from work activities which can harm people's health. The Regulations impose the following requirements on employers:

1 They must assess the risk to health arising from work and any precautions needed.
2 They must introduce appropriate measures to prevent the exposure of employees to hazardous substances either by removing the substance or

replacing it with a safer form. If this is not reasonably practicable then they must adequately control the risk by enclosing the process or using ventilation equipment or by using safe systems of work and handling procedures. Personal protective equipment is only to be used as a 'last resort' where other measures cannot adequately control exposure.

3 They must ensure that the control measures are used and that the equipment is properly maintained and procedures observed.
4 They must, where necessary, monitor the exposure of workers and carry out appropriate health surveillance.
5 They must provide information, instruction and training for persons who may be exposed to substances hazardous to health.

The **Chemical (Hazard Information and Packaging) Regulations 1994 (CHIP2)** came into force on 31 January 1995 and replaced the 1993 Regulations. CHIP2 requires chemicals to be classified according to their physico-chemical properties such as its degree of flammability, explosibility and health effects such as toxicity, corrosivity and any harmful irritant, etc. There is an approved supply list of about 2000 substances classified by the HSE. Substances not listed must be self-classified by the supplier. Once classified the chemicals must be suitably packaged and labelled and accompanied by a safety data sheet except where the chemicals are supplied for retail sale, for example cosmetics or medicinal products, and there is sufficient information provided for the chemicals to be used safely. It is a criminal offence to supply any dangerous substance unless it has been classified under CHIP2. Also where a breach of a duty under CHIP2 causes injury there is a right to take civil action.

The **Construction (Design and Management) Regulations 1994 (CDM Regs)** apply to construction work which includes alteration, conversion, fitting out, renovation, repair, maintenance, demolition or dismantling a structure. The Regulations do not apply to construction work which is not notifiable in that it lasts less than 30 days or will involve less than 500 person days of work. The Regulations place wide ranging duties on the following specified persons involved in the various stages of a construction project:

The client must be satisified that each of the four parties below are competent and ensure the allocation of sufficient resources and that work does not begin until a satisfactory health and safety plan has been prepared.

The designer must ensure that structures are designed to avoid/minimise risks during construction and maintenance and provide adequate information where risks cannot be avoided, and alert clients as to their duties.

The planning supervisor has overall responsibility for coordinating the health and safety aspects of the design and planning phase. He is responsible for the early stages of the health and safety plan and must ensure that the health and safety file is prepared and given to the client at the end of the project.

The principal contractor must develop and implement the plan; take account of safety issues; coordinate the activities of contractors to ensure compliance with safety legislation; check on the provision of information and training for employees and ensure only authorised personnel are on site and notify the HSE.

Contractors must cooperate with the principal contractor and provide relevant information on the risks to safety arising from their work and on the means of control; must comply with any directions given to them by the principal contractor and with any rules in the health and safety plan.

A breach of any of the duties is a criminal offence. Such a breach does not confer a right in any civil proceedings. The only exceptions are the duties on the client to ensure work does not start before the safety plan has been prepared and on the principal contractor to ensure that only authorised personnel are allowed on site during construction.

At present most Regulations are introduced as a means of implementing Directives adopted by the EC Council of Ministers under Article 118A. We can only look at a few of these in detail but any employer or manager of a business should be aware of not only the general duties laid down by the HSAW Act but also of the more specific duties found in the Health and Safety Regulations, and, at the same time, anticipate any changes in law which will result from EC Directives. Failure to comply with the regulations is a criminal offence and could possibly incur civil liability if someone is injured, as most of the Regulations below, unlike the Act, do not expressly exclude the right of civil action.

In 1989 the Framework Directive was adopted by the Council of Ministers. The Directive proposed wide measures to encourage improvements in health and safety at work. The Framework Directive was accompanied by five individual Directives dealing with minimum health and safety requirements in connection with work equipment, personal protective equipment, display screen equipment, minimum workplace standards and for the manual handling of loads. The Directives have been implemented by new United Kingdom Regulations and codes of practice which came into force on 1 January 1993.

The **Management of Health and Safety at Work Regulations 1992** implements the EC Framework Directive and the Temporary Workers Directive. These regulations expressly state that they do not provide a civil remedy for an injured employee. Although in many ways the Regulations appear to be restating existing duties under the HSAW Act ss 2 and 3, the difference is the change of approach to safety at work and in most cases the employer's duties are absolute and not qualified by the term 'so far as is reasonably practicable'. The most important change is Regulation 3 which requires employers to make 'a suitable and sufficient assessment of the risks to the health and safety of employees and others affected by work activities'. Risk assessments have to be kept up to date and for employers with five or more employees the assessment has to be recorded. Guidance on assessment procedures is found in the Approved Code of Practice. Regulations 5 and 6 require employers to provide health surveillance and appoint one or more competent persons to assist him in health and safety matters. Employers must co-operate with these persons and ensure that they have adequate information and resources. Regulation 7 requires employers to establish procedures to be followed in the event of serious and imminent danger and anyone at work has a right to stop work and go to a place of safety. All employees must be given information on risks, preventive and protective measures, emergency procedures and the identity of the competent persons. The employer's duties extend to providing comprehensible information to other employers whose employees (usually for a short time) are carrying out work on his premises. These employees will either be contractor's men or employees temporarily hired to work under the first employer's control. The employer's risk assessment will also have to identify risks affecting these other employees. All employees have duties regarding their own health and safety and must use safety equipment safely and comply with their employers instructions and restrictions. Under Regulation 16 employers must consult safety representatives about health and safety matters. The **Management of Health and Safety at Work (Amendment) Regulations 1994** implemented the Pregnant Workers Directive – see p. 370. Note that in the HSE's *Stress at Work – a Guide for Employers*, the HSE makes it clear that stress at work should be treated like any other health hazard and that employers have a duty under the HSAW Act s 2 to ensure so far as is reasonably practicable 'a safe working environment'. Also, under the MHSAW Regs employers must assess risks to the health and safety of their employees. This includes workplace stress.

The **Manual Handling Operations Regulations 1992** implement the Directive on the manual handling of loads. This covers the transportation, support, moving, lifting, pushing, pulling, carrying, etc. of loads. The Regulations supplement the HSAW Act and the MHSW Regulations 1992 and apply to all manual handling tasks, ie by human effort as opposed to machines which involve risk, particularly of back injury. This would cover moving a patient who is receiving medical treatment. Regulation 4 requires employers, so far as is reasonably practicable, to avoid the need for his employees to undertake any manual handling operations at work which involve a risk of injury. If this is not reasonably practicable, then employers shall make a suitable and sufficient assessment of handling operations taking into account the task, the load, the working environment and individual capability and reduce the risk of injury so far as is reasonably practicable. The employer must decide what measures to introduce to reduce the risk of injury to the lowest level reasonably practicable and implement and review these measures and obviously train their workers as to how to handle heavy loads. Under Regulation 5 it is the duty of each employee to make full and proper use of any system of work provided by his employer in compliance with the Regulations.

The **Health and Safety (Display Screen Equipment) Regulations 1992** implement the Directive on minimum safety and health requirements for work with display screen equipment. The Regulations provide protection for display screen users, ie employees and self-employed persons who habitually use such equipment as part of their work. Thus secretaries, typists, data input operators, news sub-editors, journalists, tele-sales staff, customer complaints staff and accounts enquiries operators, air traffic controllers, librarians and financial dealers are all possible display screen users. Regulation 2 requires every employer to perform a suitable and sufficient analysis of the work stations of display screen users in order to assess the health and safety risks to which they are exposed. The principal risks will probably relate to physical problems, visual fatigue and mental stress. The assessment shall be reviewed as necessary and the employer shall reduce the risks identified by the assessment to the lowest extent reasonably practicable. This will probably involve repositioning equipment and under Regulation 4 introducing measures ensuring the users have regular breaks. Regulation 3 requires the employer to ensure that new work stations put into service after 1 January 1993 comply with the requirements laid down in Schedule to the Regulations and that other work stations already in use will comply by December 1996. Regulation 5 requires an employer to provide display screen users (who make such a request) with an appropriate eye and eyesight test to be carried out by a competent person and, if the test reveals that this is necessary, every employer shall ensure that each user is provided with special corrective spectacles appropriate for work if normal spectacles cannot be used. The eyesight tests and the special corrective appliances must be provided at the employer's expense. However, an employee cannot be forced to have an eye test if he does not want one. All users must be provided with adequate training and information in all aspects of health and safety relating to their work stations.

The **Provision and Use of Work Equipment Regulations 1992** are designed to tidy up the law relating to work equipment which at present covers particular kinds of equipment in different industries. The new Regulations place general duties on employers, persons in control of premises and the self-employed. Work equipment is defined to include everything from a hand tool like a hammer, bunsen burner, scalpel or ladder, machines of all kinds, including for example a power press or circular saw, up to a complete plant controlled to function as a whole, like a refinery or bottling plant. It also includes display screen equipment. The Regulations distinguish between existing work equipment and equipment provided for use after 1 January 1993. The Regulations apply to equipment, including second-hand equipment, provided after 1 January 1993. Existing work equipment is to be exempt from Regulations 11–24 until 1 January 1997 but will continue to be subject to existing legislation like the Factories Act during this period. The employer's general duties are to take into account the working conditions and risks in the workplace when selecting equipment, to ensure that equipment is suitable and that it is properly maintained, and to give employees and supervisors adequate information, instruction and training on its use. Suitable means suitable in any respect which it is reasonably foreseeable will affect the health and safety of any person. Specific and complex requirements are laid down to cover the protection of persons coming in contact with dangerous parts of machinery (thus replacing the current law covering the guarding of machinery in the Factories Act and accordingly in 1997 ss 12–17 of that Act will be repealed). Of course the Regulations extend those provisions of the Factories Act to all industries and include protection from other hazards like articles or substances being ejected from machines; maintenance operations will be restricted to persons who have been designated and trained to do the task. The Regulations require the provision of safe control systems or appropriate systems to start the machine, control its speed and stop it in an emergency. Work equipment must be provided with suitable means to isolate it from all its sources of energy quickly; employers must ensure that work equipment is stabilised by clamping or otherwise; and employers must provide suitable and sufficient lighting. Work equipment must be marked in a clearly visible manner for health and safety reasons and warning notices attached or incorporated into the equipment or close to it.

The **Workplace (Health, Safety and Welfare) Regulations 1992** replace much of the earlier legislation covering these matters, including parts of the Factories Act 1961 and the Offices, Shops and Railway Premises Act 1963, which covered many aspects of health, safety and welfare in specific places of work. The new Regulations lay down specific standards for all workplaces. These standards must apply to all new places of work starting after 1 January 1993. Old workplaces did not have to comply until 1 January 1996. Certain workplaces are not covered – means of transport, construction sites, quarries and fishing boats. The Regulations set general minimum standards to be met by the employer in four areas:

1 **The working environment** – standards to be achieved regarding temperature, ventilation, lighting including emergency lighting, room dimensions, suitability of work stations and seating and weather protection for outdoor work stations.
2 **Safety** – including safe passage of pedestrians and vehicles, windows and skylights regarding their safe opening and cleaning, glazed doors and partitions, doors, gates and escalators with safety devices, construction of floors.
3 **Facilities** – including separate toilets, washing, eating and changing facilities, clothing storage, seating, rest areas and rest facilities for pregnant women and nursing mothers.
4 **Housekeeping** – including maintenance of the workplace, equipment and facilities, cleanliness and the removal of waste materials.

The **Personal Protective Equipment at Work Regulations 1992** implement the Directive on the minimum health and safety requirements for the use by workers of personal protective equipment. The equipment includes the following when used for health and safety: aprons, clothing for adverse weather conditions, gloves, footwear, safety helmets, high visibility waistcoats, eye protectors, life jackets and safety harnesses, but not ear muffs, which are covered by the Noise at Work Regulations 1989. The 1992 Regulations require personal protective equipment (PPE) to be used when risks cannot be avoided or sufficiently limited by technical means or collective protection or by measures, methods or procedures of safe systems of work. PPE is equipment designed to be worn or held by the employees to protect them against one or more hazards likely to endanger their health and safety at work. Employers and the self-employed shall assess the risks posed and supply equipment which gives protection against these risks free of charge. The PPE provided must be suitable for the individual, must fit correctly and be compatible with the work for which it is provided. It must also comply with the relevant UK and European Community provisions on design and manufacture. It is the employer's responsibility to ensure that the equipment is clean and in good working order and he must provide appropriate accommodation for it when not in use. The assessment shall be reviewed when necessary. Information, instruction and training on using the equipment must be provided and employees or their representatives must be involved in the selection of PPE. It is the duty of the employees to use the PPE properly and to store it properly after use. Employees must not impede the employer in carrying out his duties and not intentionally damage the equipment. Any loss of or obvious defect in the PPE must be reported to the employer.

The EC Directive on the Improvements in the Safety and Health at Work of Pregnant Workers, Workers Who Have Recently Given Birth and Workers Who Are Breastfeeding. The Directive has now been implemented by the Employment Rights Act 1996 and the Management of Health and Safety at Work Regulations 1992 have implemented the proposals for risk assessments.

The Directive requires employers to consider the health and safety of pregnant workers and those who have recently given birth and to assess the nature, degree and duration of exposure for all their work activities which are likely to involve a specific risk of exposure to certain agents, processes or working conditions. There is a non-exhaustive list of agents which could affect the health and safety of these women. It includes physical agents like shocks, vibration or movement, the handling of heavy loads and also biological and chemical agents which are known to endanger the health of the woman or foetus. The EC Commission will be publishing guidelines on the assessment of these agents and also on which industrial processes are to be considered hazardous for the health and safety of these relevant workers. These will probably cover movements, posture, mental and physical fatigue and other kinds of physical stress connected with work.

If an assessment reveals a risk, the employer must decide on appropriate measures and communicate details of these and the assessment to the employees. The employers must try to avoid these women being exposed to any risk by either adjusting their working conditions or hours or moving them to another job. If this is not possible they should be granted leave in accordance with national legislation. Women who are pregnant or have recently given birth must not be obliged to perform night work if they submit a medical certificate stating that they must not do such work on health and safety grounds. The employer should then try to shift them to day work and if this is not possible give them leave. (See p. 381.)

Codes of practice

The HSC has the power to approve codes of practice which will offer practical guidance in understanding the general duties under the Act or the Regulations. Provided these codes have been drafted and published in accordance with the proper procedures under the HSAWA s 16 they will have the special status of Approved Codes of Practice. Failure by anyone to observe the provisions of an approved code of practice is not by itself unlawful, but failure to observe a code can be admissible as evidence that there has been a breach of one of the duties under the Act or a breach of the Regulations. Codes of practice are flexible in that they can be revised and amended as necessary and give good practical guidance on health and safety matters.

Special provisions regarding the use of approved codes of practice in criminal proceedings

The HSAWA s 17 provides that in criminal proceedings where a party is alleged to be in breach of ss 2–7 of the Act or of any of the relevant statutory provisions or regulations *and* there is an approved code of practice covering the provision *and* it is proved that there was a failure by the party to observe any provision of the relevant code of practice then the breach shall be taken as proved unless the court is satisfied that the requirement or provision had been complied with by some other means.

The above rule only applies to approved codes of practice issued by the HSC and not to guidance notes on how to comply with the legislation issued by the HSE.

QUESTIONS

1 Explain how the Health and Safety at Work Act 1974 is enforced and, in particular, what powers of enforcement are given to HSE inspectors under the legislation.

2 (a) Under the Health and Safety Act 1974 s 2, explain what general duties are owed by an employer to his employees.
(b) Compare the employer's statutory duty under the Health and Safety at Work Act 1974 with his common-law duty to take reasonable care for the safety of his employees at work.

3 Steven and Wendy work in the kitchen serving the works canteen of a large factory owned by Boxit Ltd. One day, when they arrived at work, they discovered that there had been a flood in the kitchen. The caretaker had been instructed to clean up the floor but he had not yet arrived. Steven and Wendy were told to start work but to 'be careful' of the floor. They had only been working for about ten minutes when Steven received a severe electric shock from the food mixer. (In the past, he and Wendy had frequently complained, in vain, to the management that it was faulty and urgently required replacing.) When Steven received the shock, Wendy ran across the floor to assist him. Unfortunately, she slipped on the treacherous surface and broke her leg. Steven and Wendy were both taken to hospital for treatment.

Have Boxit Ltd committed any offence under the Health and Safety at Work Act 1974? Consider whether, under common law, Steven and Wendy can sue Boxit Ltd for damages for their injuries.

4 Chemco Industries have five large tanks which are used in their production of noxious chemical compounds. Each week, one tank is taken out of use and is thoroughly cleaned. The task has been given to Harry, a 20-year-old trainee, who has been with Chemco for two months. To carry out this task, he was given cleaning materials, protective overalls, a protective mask and a short ladder, as he has to physically enter the tank and clean its sides, standing on this ladder. The ladder is fairly new and was supplied by a reputable company, Steptoe & Son. Last week, Harry was in the tank, standing on the ladder when it collapsed. When Harry fell, his mask was ripped from his face and he was immediately overcome by the noxious fumes. He was found unconscious, half an hour later, and rushed to hospital. His life is saved but his lungs are permanently damaged and he will never work again.

Advise Chemco Industries as to their possible liability under *civil* and *criminal* law.

STATUTORY EMPLOYMENT PROTECTION RIGHTS

There are a number of statutory rights given to employees. These rights are not to be regarded as terms of the contract but as rights that arise from the employment relationship. Most of these rights are to be found in the Employment Rights Act 1996. An employee who is denied his statutory rights may bring proceedings against his employer in an industrial tribunal.

Note the Employment Rights Act 1996 s 104 gives an employee, regardless of length of service, the right not to be unfairly dismissed if the reason for the dismissal was because either the employee brought proceedings against his employer to enforce a statutory right or the employee alleged, in good faith, that his employer had infringed a statutory right of the employee. The statutory rights covered by this section are those conferred by the Employment Rights Act which provides a remedy of a complaint to an industrial tribunal or those conferred by ss 68, 86, 146, 168, 169 and 170 of TUL(c) A 1992 (deductions from pay, union activities and time off). All provide a remedy of a complaint to an Industrial Tribunal.

WAGES

Under common law, we saw that an employer is under a contractual duty to pay his employees wages. We have also seen that, under Employment Rights Act 1996 s 1 (p. 335), the employer has a statutory duty to give each employee written particulars of the terms of his employment. These particulars must include information regarding the employee's pay, the scale of remuneration, when it is to be paid and whether there is any holiday or sick-pay entitlement and pension scheme.

Itemised pay statement

Under the ERA 1996 s 8, the employee is entitled to an itemised pay statement at, or before, the time at which any payment of wages or salary is made to him, containing the following information:

1 the gross amount of wages or salary;
2 the amount of any variable or fixed deduction taken from the gross amount and the purpose for which it was made;
3 the net amount of wages or salary;
4 the amount and method of each part-payment, if the net is paid in different ways.

Where an employer fails to issue an itemised pay statement, the matter may be referred to an industrial tribunal. An application can be made during employment or within three months of termination of employment. The tribunal may declare that there has been a failure to issue the statement or that the statement was incorrect. In addition, in respect of unnotified deductions made in the 13-week period prior to the application to the industrial tribunal, the tribunal has the power under the ERA s 12(4) to order the employer to pay the employee 'a sum not exceeding the aggregate of the unnotified deductions so made'. Thus, the Act imposes a penalty on the employer for failing to make proper notification of deductions.

Deductions from and reduction of wages

Under common law we saw that an employer is under a contractual duty to pay his employees wages. In **Rigby *v* Ferodo Ltd [1988] ICR 29** the employer cut wages by 5 per cent. This variation constituted a repudiatory and fundamental breach of contract. The employees refused to accept this change to their contracts and continued to protest. The House of Lords recognised that they could sue for damages, ie their lost wages. The disadvantage for the employee is that they would have to bring an action in the civil courts. They still have to do this even though industrial tribunals have jurisdiction for breach of contract actions because the action does not arise on the termination of the contract. As we shall see later, another remedy open to employees in this situation is to resign and claim constructive dismissal in an industrial tribunal. However, this also has the disadvantage that the employee has no job. Probably the best remedy is for the employee to complain to an industrial tribunal that the deduction or reduction in wages is unlawful under the Employment Rights Act 1996 ss 13–27 (formerly under the Wages Act 1986). Two recent decisions make this right clear.

In **Delaney *v* Staples [1991] IRLR 112** the Court of Appeal held that any shortfall in the payment of wages was to be treated as a deduction for the purposes of s 8 of the Wages Act (that section is now s 13 of the ERA). The fact that the tribunal had to make a decision as to the amount of wages properly payable before deciding whether there had been an unlawful deduction did not affect the jurisdiction of the tribunal to hear the complaint.

In **Bruce *v* Wiggins Teape (Stationery) Ltd [1994] IRLR 536** the employer decided to stop the enhanced overtime rates which were paid to the night shift and pay them normal rates. Both the workers and the union objected and when the new rates were introduced, the workers made it known that they were working under protest. They complained to an industrial tribunal that this reduction in their wages was an unauthorised deduction under the Wages Act (now the ERA). The industrial tribunal rejected their complaint on the grounds that the protection under the Wages Act was in relation to deduction from wages not reduction of wages. However, the decision was reversed by the EAT, who following *Delaney* said that any shortfall in the payment of the amount of wages properly payable to the worker is a deduction. The EAT said there was no distinction between a deduction and a reduction. In this case the workers had continued to work under protest and had not accepted the change. The employers had breached the Act as there was no prior authorisation for the deduction.

Protection of wages

Under the ERA 1996 s 13 an employer shall not make a deduction from the wages of a worker unless:

(a) the deduction is allowed by statute or authorised to be made by virtue of a statutory provision, or
(b) authorised by a relevant provision of the worker's contract, or
(c) the worker has previously signified in writing his agreement or consent to the making of the deduction

Under the ERA s 15 the worker has the right not to make payments to the employer unless the payment is authorised as under s 13.

Sums deducted because of overpayment of wages and sums due under a court order are not covered by the Act. The Act applies to all employees, manual and non-manual, but the main problem is that an employee may be forced, because he is desperate for a job, to consent to a far-reaching provision for the employer to make deductions from his wages. The Act does not state that the deductions have to be fair and reasonable, nor does it limit the amount of the deduction except in relation to retail workers.

Retail employees

Retail employment involves the sale or supply of goods or services, including financial services, to the public. Examples are employees in shops, petrol stations, bars and restaurants. Under the ERA 1996, provided the requirements of s 13 are satisfied, any deductions from their wages because of cash or stock deficiencies, on any one day, cannot exceed one-tenth of the gross amount of wages, payable on that day. This means that employers will often have to make a number of deductions over successive pay days to cover the one cash or stock deficiency. Even if there is an enormous stock deficiency, for which the employee might not even be responsible, there is nothing in the Act to stop the employer deducting one-tenth of the employee's wages every week until the loss is made up. An employer's demand for payment of such shortages must not only comply with s 13 of the Act but must be by prior written notification stating the employee's total liability and cannot be made more than 12 months after the shortage was, or ought reasonably to be, established.

Also, there is nothing in the Act limiting the deduction to one-tenth when the employment is ended, so the employer could deduct the full amount from the last payment of wages. Complaints of unauthorised deductions must be made to an industrial tribunal within three months of the deduction. If the tribunal finds that the deduction is unlawful, it makes a declaration to that effect and the employer can be ordered to pay the worker the amount of the deduction.

Guarantee payments

Unless an employer has in effect bound himself to provide work for his employee – for example, in a contract of apprenticeship – under common law, he cannot be liable for failing to provide work for his employee. The problem to consider is whether he can then say 'no work, no pay'. The answer depends on the facts. There are two basic rules:

1 employees are entitled to be paid their wages;

2 any attempt to reduce or suspend payment would be a breach of the contract of employment.

However, these rules could be subject to an express term in the contract which would permit the employer to suspend without pay. Alternatively, suspension without pay could be permitted under an implied term of the contract or by custom (e.g., in the construction industry, where work is often intermittent) and it could be found that there is an implied term that an employee can be laid off with no pay when there is no work. Usually, there will be a term in a collective agreement providing perhaps a guaranteed minimum working week.

Under the Employment Rights Act 1996 ss 28–35, a worker laid off for a whole day is entitled to a 'guarantee payment' of up to a statutory maximum of £14.50 per day. To qualify, he must have worked for at least four weeks before the lay-off and must have been taken on in the first place for more than three months. The amount he will receive is calculated by multiplying his normal daily hours by the guaranteed hourly rate – the hourly rate being found by dividing one week's pay by the normal weekly working hours. The guarantee payment is not intended to cover more than five days lay-off in any three-month period. An employee loses his right if:

(a) there is no work because of a strike, lock-out or industrial action;
(b) he refuses suitable alternative employment;
(c) he fails to comply with an attendance requirement.

If an employer fails to pay the whole or part of the guarantee payment, the employee may complain to an industrial tribunal. If the tribunal finds the complaint well-founded, they will order the employer to pay the amount due to the employee.

Working time

The Working Time Directive was adopted by all the member states of the European Union except the UK in 1993. The Directive was based on Article 118a of the Treaty of Rome which allowed the Directive to be adopted by a qualified majority. The UK challenged the validity of the Directive and maintained that it should have been adopted on the basis of Article 100 which requires unanimity. The Advocate General has given his opinion that the ECJ should dismiss the UK's application for annulment of the Directive. Assuming that the ECJ does so the UK government will have to implement the Directive. This will give employees the right to an average working week of not more than 48 hours including overtime and the right to be paid annual leave of 4 weeks.

Sick pay

Under the National Insurance Act 1948, employees are entitled to subsistence level payments when off-sick. For most employees, the question of sick pay will be covered by an express term in the contract of employment, usually a form of 'topping up' state sickness benefit and there will usually be a qualifying period for new employees, with the term stating how much it is and for how long it will be paid. In the past the question has arisen in cases where there is no express term as to whether there is an implied term or presumption in law that sick pay will be paid. The matter was settled in **Mears *v* Safecar Security Ltd [1982] 3 WLR 366** where it was held that there is no presumption. For such a term to be implied there would have to be clear evidence of, perhaps, past practice and custom.

Since April 1983 under the Social Security and Housing Benefits Act 1982 as amended, a new scheme of statutory sick pay (SSP) has been introduced and employers have to pay their workers SSP for the first 28 weeks of absence (originally eight weeks) after which the state scheme applies. There are various qualifications for payment. Some examples of those excluded from the scheme are: low earners not paying national insurance, employees taken on for less than three months and employees whose first day of sickness occurs during a trade dispute in which they are directly involved at their place of work. There is now one standard rate of SSP (£54.55 April 1996) which is payable to all employees who earn at least £61 per week. Employers can only reclaim the amount by which payments of SSP made in any tax month exceed 13 per cent of their gross National Insurance contributions.

Holiday pay

Employers are not generally obliged by law to give their employees holidays with or without pay. Holiday entitlement is a matter of negotiation and will usually be an express term of the contract or covered by a collective agreement.

Employees' rights in insolvency

When an employer becomes insolvent or bankrupt, certain debts are paid before, or in preference to, claims by other creditors. As a general rule, the wages due to an employee in respect of the period four months before insolvency are a preferential debt up to the maximum of £800.

The Employment Rights Act 1996 ss 182–190, gives additional protection and enables employees in this situation to claim from the Secretary of State the following: 8 weeks' wages (max. £210 a week); holiday pay due for previous 12 months (max. 6 weeks); amount due for period of notice (max. £210 a week); any guarantee payment; amount due for paid time off; payment due under a protective award; basic award of compensation for unfair dismissal; any statutory redundancy or maternity or sick pay; reimbursement of apprenticeship fee.

The payment is made from the National Insurance Fund. Once a payment is made, the Secretary of State may then seek to recover payment from the employer.

TIME OFF WORK

An employee, who is denied his statutory time off, or denied payment, if it is due, is entitled to bring a complaint to the industrial tribunal.

Time off work without pay

Employees who are **Justices of the Peace**, councillors, tribunal members or hold other public offices as specified in the **ERA 1996** s 50 must be given reasonable time off to perform their duties. What is reasonable must be considered by taking into account the amount of time off required and the size and requirements of the employer's business.

In **Ratcliffe** *v* **Dorset County Council [1978] IRLR 191** it was held that the entitlement is to actual time off work. In this case a college lecturer was a local authority councillor. He was given time off to attend council meetings but his teaching was not reduced. Instead his teaching hours were moved to suit the times of the meetings. The decision was that this was not good enough. The statutory entitlement was to time off work and not a reallocation of work.

Under the **TULR(C) Act 1992** s 170, **members of independent recognised trades unions** are entitled to reasonable time off during work to take part in the activities of the union. The ACAS Code of Practice No 3 – 'Time off for trade union duties and activities' – gives guidance on factors to be taken into account, when deciding what is reasonable time off. It makes it clear that 'activities' refer to attending meetings, voting at the workplace, etc, and excludes activities which amount to industrial action.

Time off with pay

The **TULR(C) Act 1992** s 168 allows **officials of independent recognised trades unions** to reasonable time off at their normal rate of pay for industrial relations duties which concern relations between the official's own employer and his employees, and time off for training programmes relevant to the official's duties or which may teach general industrial-relations skills. 'Officials' include union officers and shop stewards. This right to time off is limited to carrying out only those duties which are concerned with negotiations with the employer on matters related to, or connected with, those which fall within the definition of a 'trade dispute' under the TULR(C) Act 1992 s 178. Also included is paid time off for undertaking any duties on behalf of the employer which are related to, or connected with, the above and which the employer has agreed may be performed by the official.

Under the **ERA 1996** s 55 **pregnant employees** are entitled not to be unreasonably refused time off at their normal rates of pay to attend ante-natal care (see below).

Employees under notice of redundancy under the **ERA 1996** s 52 are entitled to time off with pay to find other work or make arrangements for training. This right applies only to those with two years continuous service. If an employee is refused paid time off he can complain to an industrial tribunal. The employee is allowed up to two-fifths of a week's pay.

The Pensions Act 1995 introduced safeguards for company pension schemes. Under the **Employment Rights Act 1996** s 58 employees who are **pension scheme trustees** are entitled to reasonable time off work to perform their duties or undergo training relevant to performing their duties. Failure to allow paid time off gives the employee the right to complain to an industrial tribunal within three months.

Under the **Health and Safety at Work Act 1974** and the Safety Representatives and Safety Committees Regulations 1977, recognised trade unions can appoint safety representatives who are entitled to paid time off work for their duties as safety representatives or to go for training. Employee representatives have similar duties (see p. 353).

Employee representatives

Under new provisions in TULR(c) Act 1992 and the **Transfer of Undertakings (Protection of Employment) Regulations 1981** there is no longer an automatic right of recognised trade unions to be solely consulted over collective redundancies and when a transfer of an undertaking is planned. In respect of redundancies and transfers after 1 March 1996, employers have the option of either consulting with a recognised independent trade union or elected employee representatives. Under the ERA 1996 ss 61–63 such an employee representative (or candidate in the election) has the right to reasonable time off with pay during working hours in order to perform his functions as such a representative. Failure to allow the employee paid time off gives him the right to complain to an industrial tribunal within three months of the time taken off.

THE EMPLOYEE'S RIGHT NOT TO BE DISCRIMINATED AGAINST FOR TRADE UNION REASONS

Under s 137 of the Trade Union and Labour Relations (Consolidation) Act 1992 it is unlawful to refuse a person employment because he is or is not a member of a union, or refuses to become or ceases to be a member or to make payments in that connection.

Under the Trade Union and Labour Relations (Consolidation) Act 1992 s 146, an employee has the right not to have action, short of dismissal, taken against him by his employer for the purpose of:

(a) preventing him from being a member of an independent trade union or penalising him for being a member; *or*
(b) preventing him from taking part in the activities of an independent trade union at the appropriate time or penalising him for doing so; *or*
(c) compelling him to become a member of a trade union.

The '**appropriate time**' is defined in s 146 as either outside working hours or during working hours with the agreement or consent of the employer. '**Working hours**' means times when the employee is actually performing his work. So, taking part in activities during a tea break or lunch break will be an 'appropriate time'.

If such action is taken against an employee, in contravention of s 146, he may complain to an industrial tribunal within three months of the action. The onus is on the employer to show the purpose for which he took such action and that it was not contrary to s 146. In considering the complaint, no account is to be taken of any pressure exerted upon the employer by industrial action or threats of action by a union (but the union could be cited as party to the claim). If the tribunal upholds the complaint, it may make an award of compensation as is just and equitable having regard to the employee's loss – for example, for stress and anxiety causing ill health, or the loss of the benefit of the trade union's advice.

In **Associated Newspapers Ltd *v* Wilson 1995 2 AC 454 HL** ANL derecognised the union (NUJ) and entered into new individual contracts. Those who entered into the new contracts received a pay increase while the others (including Wilson) did not. Then in **Associated British Parts *v* Palmer 1995 2 AC 454 HL** those employees who entered into personal contracts got increases which were substantially better than those increases given to employees who remained under the collective bargaining system (derecognition took place shortly after this). The two cases were heard together. The House of Lords held that the failure to give Wilson an increase or the payment of a lower increase to Palmer was not 'action' short of dismissal but an 'omission'. Also, there was insufficient evidence to establish that the employer's purpose had been to deter the applicants from being members of their trade unions or to penalise them for their membership and thus there was no infringement of s 146.

There is a new s 148 in TULR(c) A which permits differential treatment if the employer's intentions is to further a change in his relationship with all or any class of his employees. Thus an employer can offer increases to employees who accept individually negotiated terms and not to those who rely on collective bargaining.

At the time of writing (1996) the Public Interest Disclosure Bill is being considered by Parliament. If this Bill becomes an Act, employees and other individuals will be protected from dismissal or victimisation if they disclose significant misconduct or malpractice. To qualify for protection an employee must not act in bad faith; must believe on reasonable grounds that the information is accurate; must have taken reasonable steps to raise the matter internally and must inform the appropriate enforcement authority; while not acting for personal gain or benefit. The safety of the public and the safety of consumer products are covered by the Bill.

MATERNITY RIGHTS

Legislation provides the following essential rights to female employees associated with maternity.

Time off for ante-natal care

Under the Employment Right Act 1996 s 55, a pregnant woman is entitled to time off work for ante-natal care. The Act states that she is not to be 'unreasonably refused leave for this purpose' – which probably means that a part-time employee who could arrange an appointment outwith working hours might not be entitled to this right. The employer is entitled to require her to produce a certificate of pregnancy and an appointment card. She is entitled to be paid at her usual hourly rate. Failure to allow her paid time off gives her the right to complain to an industrial tribunal within three months of the appointment; the tribunal can order the employer to pay her what she was due.

The rights not to be unfairly dismissed because of pregnancy, childbirth and other maternity reasons

The Employment Rights Act 1996 s 99 applies to all employees, whatever their length of service. Now an employee shall be treated as automatically unfairly dismissed in the following circumstances:

1 If the reason or principal reason for her dismissal is that she is pregnant or is any reason connected with her pregnancy.
2 Her maternity leave is ended by dismissal and the reason is because she has given birth or is any other reason connected with her having given birth.
3 Her contract was terminated after the maternity leave and the reason for her dismissal is that she had taken maternity leave or had availed herself of the benefits of maternity leave.
4 The reason for dismissal is a requirement or recommendation referred to in s 66 (the new right to be suspended with pay on health and safety grounds).
5 The maternity leave period is ended by dismissal and the reason is that she is redundant, but the obligation to be offered a suitable available vacancy (if there is one) has not been complied with.

Section 99(4) states that an employee will also be regarded as unfairly dismissed if before the end of her maternity leave period, she gave her employer a medical certificate stating that she would be incapable of work at the end of her maternity leave and her contract of employment was terminated during the four-week period following the end of her maternity leave while she was still incapable of work and the reason is that she has given birth to a child or any other reason connected with having given birth to a child.

The right to be paid if suspended for maternity reasons

The ERA 1996 ss 66–70 confers rights on an employee if she is suspended from work because to continue working would be either:

1 in contravention of a statutory provision, *or*
2 contrary to a recommendation in a Health and Safety Code of Practice issued under the HSAW Act 1974 s 16,

and in both cases, if she is suspended on maternity grounds, i.e., because she is pregnant or has recently given birth or is breastfeeding, then she is to be paid her usual week's pay for each week of the period of suspension.

If the employer has available suitable alternative employment, the employee has the right to be offered that employment before being suspended on maternity grounds. If she is not offered this employment she has the right to bring a complaint to an industrial tribunal within three months. She also has the right to bring a complaint within three months if she is not paid during her suspension on maternity grounds. However, this right to be paid is lost if she was offered suitable alternative employment and she has unreasonably refused to do the job.

The right to statutory maternity pay

To qualify, the woman must pay national insurance and have been employed with the same employer for at least six months ending with the qualifying week which is the 15th week before the expected week of confinement. She must give her employer evidence of the date of confinement if required and, if possible, give him three weeks' notice before her intended absence. Alternatively, if she was pregnant and gave birth before the start of the eleventh week before the expected week of confinement, she is entitled to SMP.

The maternity pay period

Maternity pay is paid for 18 weeks. This does not fit neatly with the 14-week period of maternity leave and most women forfeit their right to the additional four weeks as they must return to work at the end of 14 weeks unless this is extended with a medical certificate.

The rate of payment

All women who have six months' service or more at the 15th week before the EWC are entitled to be paid at 90 per cent of normal weekly earnings for the first six weeks. The remaining eight weeks (or 12 as the case may be) are paid at the flat rate of SMP (which is the same as Statutory Sick Pay – £54.55 APR 1996). (Those women with less than six months' service are paid at the lower rate for the 14 or 18 weeks which again is in line with SSP. This is the Maternity Allowance paid by the Benefit Agency.)

All payments are subject to tax and national insurance. As with statutory sick pay, the employer will be responsible for making the payments but will be reimbursed 92 per cent of the amount of SMP through deductions from his national insurance returns. Small employers can reclaim 105.5 per cent.

The right to maternity leave with pay

The **Employment Rights Act 1996 ss 71–78** give all employees, irrespective of length of service, the right to 14 weeks' maternity leave subject to the usual conditions that she informs her employer in writing at least 21 days before her maternity leave starts (or if that is not possible as soon as is reasonably practicable) that she is pregnant and the date of the expected week of childbirth if the employer requests this. Failure to reply to this request will lose the employee her right to leave. The employee can choose when to start her maternity leave. However, women are prohibited from working during the two weeks following the birth. This prohibition will normally be encompassed within the 14-week maternity leave period. However, if the maternity leave period has already expired maternity leave will be extended to cover the two-week period. Section 71 states that all contractual rights except pay have to be maintained during this period of leave. The amount of statutory maternity pay is discussed above. If during the maternity leave period the employee is made redundant, then she will be entitled to be offered any suitable and appropriate alternative vacancy which is available. The new contract will have to take effect immediately and the terms and conditions must not be substantially less favourable than those she had under her original contract. During the 14-week maternity leave period a woman's contract of employment continues and to return to work she simply has to present herself at work as she would if she had been on annual leave.

Thus, *all* women, regardless of their length of service, are entitled to protection against dismissal for pregnancy reasons and *all* women are entitled to 14 weeks' maternity leave. All women can return to work after the 14 weeks' maternity leave unless they are still suspended on the grounds of health and safety. However, it still remains important to women to have two years' continuous service at the beginning of the eleventh week prior to confinement as these employees are entitled to the following right of a period of leave of absence of up to 29 weeks.

The right to extended leave of absence and to return to work

Under the ERA 1996 ss 79–85, an employee, who has been absent from work because of her pregnancy or confinement, has a right to return to work. She has the right to return to her original job on terms and conditions not less favourable than those which would have applied had she not been absent. 'Terms' will cover wage increases and pension rights.

To qualify for extended leave, she must remain in employment until immediately before the 11th week prior to confinement (unless dismissed earlier for pregnancy reasons) and have two years' continuous service. Three weeks prior to her absence she must inform her employer in writing:

1 that she will be absent to have a child;
2 that she intends to return to work;
3 the expected week of confinement.

Not earlier than 21 days before the end of her 14-week maternity leave period, the employer may send a written request asking her for written confirmation that she still intends to return to work. He must advise her that if she ignores this request she will lose her right to return. Within 14 days of receiving the employer's request she must give written confirmation that she is returning. From the employer's point of view, he has no statutory redress if the woman says that she is returning but does not.

The employee has the right to return at any time before the end of the period of 29 weeks (which begins with the week in which she has her baby). When she wishes to return, she must give the employer 21 days' notice in writing. The employer may postpone her return for four weeks beyond that date in order to make arrangements or to give notice to her replacement. She can also postpone her return beyond the date she has said (or on the expiry of the 29 weeks) for four weeks if she gives her employer a medical certificate saying that she is unfit for work (but she is allowed only one extension).

If the employee is not permitted to return and has fulfilled these conditions, she can claim unfair dismissal or redundancy and the tribunal will decide whether or not the employer has acted reasonably in treating the reason as justifying dismissal.

The ERA 1996 s 96 limits a woman's right to return in two ways:

(a) If she works for an employer of five or fewer employees and it is not reasonably practicable for the employer to permit her to return to work or to offer her suitable and appropriate work, then she loses her right to return completely. This also applies if the number of employees employed by her employer added to the number employed by an associated employer of his does not exceed five.

(b) If it is not reasonably practicable, for a reason other than redundancy, for the employer to permit her to return to her old job, he may offer her alternative suitable and appropriate work. If the terms and conditions are not substantially less favourable than her old position, she will lose her right to return if she unreasonably refuses the offer. Once she has accepted the new job, she cannot seek compensation for the loss of her previous position.

If a woman has a separate contractual right to maternity leave which is more favourable than the statutory right then she can exercise this right in preference to the statutory right and vice versa.

QUESTIONS

1 Explain clearly an employee's statutory rights when his employer repeatedly fails to give him an itemised pay statement with his pay cheque.

2 Derek Dim has been employed by Speedo's Garage to look after the cash desk, six nights a week, for a weekly wage of £130. During the first week of his employment, three cars drive off without paying for their petrol and this leaves the till short of £45 at the end of the week. When Dim receives the first payment of his wages, he discovers that Speedo has deducted the £45 from his pay. Advise him as to his legal rights.

3 John Black has been employed by Speedo's Garage as a mechanic. He has been paid £250 gross per week. Business has been poor and his employers have now decided to reduce his pay by £50 per week. John wants to keep his job and protested at this reduction in his wages. Advise him as to his legal rights.

4 It is generally accepted that there must be some form of legal protection for employees participating in trade union activities at their place of work. With reference to this statement and to the relevant legislation, describe the individual employee's rights in respect of:

(a) time off work for trade union activities;
(b) protection against action short of dismissal on the grounds of trade union membership or activities.
(c) protection against being denied an increase in salary because the employee insists on maintaining his membership of a trade union.

5 Janet and Lorna have both been employed by Buttercup Dairies for eight months. Janet works in the office as a receptionist and Lorna works in the dairy.

They are both about three months' pregnant. George, their employer, has grudgingly said that they can have time off to attend their ante-natal appointments but he has stated that they will definitely not be paid for those afternoons. He has now given the two employees four weeks' notice terminating their employment. Both girls are devastated as they were planning to come back to work after the birth of their babies. George told Janet that he could not have a pregnant receptionist dealing with the customers and she was bound to be off sick during her pregnancy anyway and he would have no-one to cover for her absence. He told Lorna that the reason for her dismissal was because her job entails lifting heavy crates of milk and that, in her condition, she would be better at home resting. Advise Janet and Lorna as to any statutory rights they might have in this situation.

19 Dismissal and redundancy

TERMINATION OF EMPLOYMENT AT COMMON LAW

Introduction

Before considering termination of a contract of employment, we must return to the general principles of contract and remind ourselves of the different ways a contract may be terminated and the remedies available for breach of contract.

A contract may come to an end in accordance with the wishes of the parties – ie through their mutual agreement. The contract could also end because one party is in breach of contract and this breach is a repudiatory breach (see below). The contract could also end through the operation of the law because one of the parties dies or becomes incapable of carrying out his duties for the other and the contract is frustrated.

Regarding breach of contract, there is a distinction between minor breaches (often referred to as 'non-repudiatory') and serious breaches (often described as 'repudiatory'). It is very difficult to explain clearly the difference between these two kinds of breach because, really, this decision as to the seriousness of the breach can often only be made after the breach has taken place. However, the distinction is important since the remedies available to the party not in breach are different:

1 A minor breach of the contract will entitle the innocent party to the contract to sue for damages in respect of the loss he has suffered but he will still be bound to carry out his part of the contract.
2 A repudiatory breach will also entitle the innocent party to sue for damages but because such a breach is taken by the courts as an indication that the party in breach no longer intends to be bound by the contract, the innocent party is also given the option, if he chooses, to terminate (rescind) the contract, and he is no longer bound to perform his obligations under the contract. He must therefore make up his mind as to which course of action will be more beneficial to him.

APPLICATION OF COMMON LAW PRINCIPLES TO THE CONTRACT OF EMPLOYMENT

Frustration of the contract of employment

Frustration terminates a contract when, through no fault of either party, circumstances change which make it impossible to perform the contract or, if performance is still possible, it is quite different from that which the parties originally intended it to be. If a contract is frustrated, it comes to an end and neither party can sue for damages. With the contract of employment, any supervening event which renders it impossible is capable of amounting to frustration. The outbreak of war or the destruction of the place of work have been held to be frustrating events. The question now to be considered is whether the long-term illness of the employee can terminate the contract through frustration. The matter was discussed in the cases below.

In **Marshall** *v* **Harland and Wolff Ltd [1972] IRLR 90** the employee was a manual worker who was absent from work for 18 months. While he was ill, the works closed down and his employers gave him notice of dismissal. He claimed a redundancy payment. The employers disputed his right, arguing that he had not been dismissed but that his contract had been terminated by frustration. It was held that, in considering whether a contract had been frustrated, a court would have to take account of a number of factors: the terms of the contract including the provisions as to sick pay; how long the employment was likely to last in the absence of sickness; the nature of the employment; the nature of the illness or injury; the prospects of recovery and the period of past employment. In this case it was expressly agreed in the contract that no pay, sick pay or pension contributions would be made during the period of the employee's illness. Furthermore, it was not the policy of the employers to terminate the contract on the grounds of sickness and, lastly, no medical evidence was produced that showed that the employee was permanently incapacitated. The decision of the court was that there were no grounds for holding that in future the employee would be incapable of performing his work.

In **Egg Stores (Stamford Hill) Ltd** *v* **Liebovici [1977] ICR 260** in this EAT case, Phillip J said that an important question to ask in such cases (but not the only question) is 'has the time arrived when the employer can no longer reasonably be expected to keep the absent employee's post open for him?'. The following factors were identified as relevant to considering whether the contract had been frustrated: the length of previous employment; the expected duration of employment were it not for the illness; the nature of the job; the nature, length and effect of the illness or disabling event; the employer's need for the job to be done and for a replacement to do it; the risk of a replacement acquiring employment protection rights; whether the employee continued to be paid; acts and statements of the employer including the dismissal or failure to dismiss the employee. In **Williams** *v* **Watsons Luxury Coaches 1990 ICR 536** the EAT added two more factors: the terms of the contract as to sick pay, if any and a consideration of the employee's prospects of recovery.

In **James** *v* **The Greytree Trust EAT (699/95)** James had worked as a cleaner for 18 years at a residential home for the elderly. She developed tennis elbow and had to take time off. She produced sick notes covering the period 1 March to 27 June. Her employers wrote to her on the 13 June stating that if she were unable to return on the 27 June they would treat the contract as frustrated due to ill health. James provided a further sick note covering the period 23 June to 23 December. On 30 June her employer terminated the contract on the grounds of frustration. James claimed unfair dismissal. The EAT applied the tests and considered the factors outlined in the **Marshall** and **Egg Stores** cases. They concluded that the employers had acted too quickly; they had not taken all factors into account and James' contract had not been frustrated. She had been dismissed.

Employer in breach of contract

When the common law principle is applied to the contract of employment, the first point to note is that, if the repudiatory breach by the employer is the dismissal of the employee, then the employee has no choice – he cannot continue working *but* if the repudiatory breach is a substantial change in the employee's job or a substantial reduction in wages, then the employee does have a choice (because from the employer's point of view the employment relationship is still continuing). He can either decide to accept the repudiation and leave *or* he can remain and sue for damages.

For example, in the House of Lords case of **Rigby** *v* **Ferodo Ltd [1987] IRLR 516** in 1982 the employers reduced Rigby's pay by £30 a week without his agreement and consent. This was a repudiatory breach of the contract which, if accepted by Rigby, would bring the contract to an end. Rigby did not accept the reduction as a repudiatory breach and chose to sue for damages. However, the employer argued that the damage suffered was the amount of the shortfall from the original contractual wage over the period of 12 weeks. What they were trying to argue was that their repudiatory breach was equivalent to the employee being given his notice – his statutory notice was 12 weeks, so after the 12 weeks, the contract could be lawfully terminated anyway. The House of Lords held that the employer's unilateral reduction of wages, although a repudiatory breach of contract, did not automatically bring the contract to an end if there was no acceptance by the employee (and there was not in this case as Rigby continued to work under protest). This being the case, Rigby's damages were not limited to the 12 weeks' notice period and covered the entire period over which he had been underpaid (see p. 374 for statutory remedy).

Employee in breach of contract

Where the employee commits an act which amounts to a repudiatory breach of the contract of employment, the employer can accept the repudiation and terminate the contract – i.e., dismiss the employee. If the employer does not wish to terminate the relationship, the question has arisen as to whether the employer will still be liable to pay the full amount of wages while the breach continues. In this situation the employer is opting for the remedy of damages. It will be difficult for an employer to bring an action against an employee for damages to compensate him for the loss which he has suffered so, as a practical alternative, can he refuse to pay the wages at all or make a deduction from the employee's wages?

In **Miles *v* Wakefield Metropolitan District Council [1987] AC 539** Miles was a Superintendent Registrar of births, deaths and marriages in Wakefield. He worked 37 hours per week and one important part of his job was conducting wedding ceremonies. The most popular time for these was Saturday morning when the office was open for three hours. He was a member of NALGO and, during an industrial dispute, his union told him not to conduct weddings on Saturday mornings. He attended the office on Saturday mornings but did other work. The Council, by letter, made it clear to him that if he did not conduct weddings on Saturday mornings he would not be paid. The Council deducted 3/37 of his salary from his wages until the dispute was over. The House of Lords held that they were entitled to do so.

Lord Templeman said, 'In a contract of employment wages and work go together. The employer pays for work and the worker works for his wages. If the employer declines to pay, the worker need not work. If the worker declines to work, the employer need not pay. In an action by a worker to recover his pay, he must allege and be ready to prove that he worked or was willing to work ... In the present case Miles disentitled himself to his salary for Saturday morning because he declined to work on Saturday in accordance with his duty. He offered to work inefficiently on Saturday but could not compel the Council to accept that offer, and upon their refusal, he ceased to be entitled to be paid for Saturday.'

Note the difference in the following case where the employer is seeking to make no payment at all. In **Wiluszynski *v* The Mayor and Burgesses of The London Borough of Tower Hamlets [1989] IRLR 259** W was an Estate Officer in the housing department, who, as part of a pay dispute again involving NALGO, refused to answer 'Members' Enquiries' as to estate matters (one or two might be asked in any given week). The dispute lasted for over a month, during which time W worked normally, apart from the boycott of Members' Enquiries. The Council knew he was working and took the benefit of that work. However, W was in breach of his contractual obligations and, as he was not willing to fully comply with his contract, he was not entitled to be paid. The staff were sent a letter saying that they would not be paid if they took such action. Each day at work the staff engaged on the dispute were reminded that they were working voluntarily and that they would not be paid. An important consideration was whether the Council were giving W directions as to the work he was doing and the evidence showed that no member of senior management made any requests or gave him any orders during this period. The Court of Appeal held that he was not entitled to be paid.

THE COMMON LAW RULES ON TERMINATION OF THE CONTRACT OF EMPLOYMENT: DISMISSAL UNDER COMMON LAW

First it must be noted that there is a considerable difference in the position of the employee at common law and his position under the modern employment legislation. Under common law, the employee has very few rights, and an employer is entitled to dismiss an employee for any reason or for no reason at all, provided the employer gives him proper notice. The length of the period of notice will be specified in the contract of employment. If there is no contractual period agreed, then the employee must receive reasonable notice. What amounts to reasonable notice under common law does not depend on length of service and in the past the period of notice was usually linked to how the employee was paid. For example, if he was paid monthly, he received a month's notice. Status of the employee was also important – a manager was entitled to longer notice than an unskilled worker. However, the importance of these rules as to notice has been dramatically reduced since 1963 and there are now statutory minimum periods of notice to be given on dismissal or resignation. Note that, although these are minimum periods of notice, they may be increased by an express term in the contract of employment. The statutory minimum period increases with the length of service of the employee.

Statutory minimum notice requirement

The law is now to be found in the Employment Rights Act 1996 s.86. Nothing in this section prevents the parties from waiving their rights to notice or an employee from accepting payment in lieu of notice. Also, the section still allows an employer under common law to summarily dismiss an employee for gross misconduct.

Section 86 provides that after one month's employment an employee will be entitled to one week's notice, and this will apply until he is employed for up to two years. Thereafter, he will be entitled to one week's notice for each year's employment (for example, six weeks' notice for six years' employment) up to a maximum of 12 weeks' notice (for example 12 weeks' notice for 15 years' employment). During the period of notice, the employee is entitled to be paid his average wages. The Act also provides that an employee must give a minimum of one week's notice (but remember that his contract may specify that a longer period of notice is required).

WRONGFUL DISMISSAL

Under common law, a breach in the form of a dismissal without any notice or without the full contractual amount of notice by the employer only gives the employee the remedy of claiming damages from the employer. This is a **claim for wrongful dismissal**. The amount of damages is limited to the sum due for unpaid salary plus any sum due for the period of notice plus any sum for the loss of any contractual entitlements. It is not possible to claim for hurt feelings or distress. It follows that if the employer gives the employee the correct amount of notice (either under the contract or under ERA s 86), no further damages or compensation will be payable as the employer is entitled to terminate the contract by notice under common law.

SUMMARY DISMISSAL

The general principle is that a repudiatory breach of contract by the employee will entitle the employer to dismiss summarily – i.e., without notice. (Statutory minimum notice is not required.) If the summary dismissal has been in response to a repudiatory breach by the employee, no damages or compensation will be payable. The employer has merely exercised his right to terminate the contract.

There are a number of well-recognised grounds on which an employee may be dismissed summarily, but a neat list cannot be given because it will depend on whether the employee's conduct amounts to a serious (repudiatory) breach of the contract of employment. For example, a wilful refusal to obey an order, gross neglect, dishonesty and gross misconduct. The employer must invoke the right to end the contract quickly because if he does not dismiss the employee within a reasonable period, he will be held to have waived his right to do so. What is reasonable will depend on the facts of the individual case. If an employee disputes the employer's right to dismiss him summarily, he may bring a claim for wrongful dismissal in the ordinary courts, or if he is eligible, a claim for unfair dismissal in the industrial tribunal.

THE DIFFERENCE BETWEEN WRONGFUL DISMISSAL AND UNFAIR DISMISSAL

A complaint of unfair dismissal is concerned with the statutory right of an employee not to be dismissed without a valid reason. It has been described as 'dismissal contrary to statute', for which claims are heard by an industrial tribunal.

Wrongful dismissal is dismissal in breach of the employee's contract of employment. It is based on the contractual relationship between the parties and is governed by common law. Tribunals now have jurisdiction over claims for wrongful dismissal and such claims may be pursued by bringing complaint to an industrial tribunal.

Most claims arising out of dismissals are unfair dismissal claims before an industrial tribunal. However, although this new right has largely overtaken the common law claims for wrongful dismissal, it has not superseded it. Both claims can be available to a dismissed employee. There can also be situations when the common law remedy is the only remedy available or indeed the more advantageous. In particular:

1 The maximum compensatory award for unfair dismissal is £11 300 + the maximum basic award £6300 (June 1996). So, a highly paid employee who is entitled to a long period of notice, which he has not been given, may be able to obtain substantially higher damages by bringing a claim for wrongful dismissal.
2 An employee who has not been employed for a continuous period of two years

might not qualify to bring a claim of unfair dismissal, however, he is still able to claim wrongful dismissal.

3 A claim for unfair dismissal may be time-barred after three months from the effective date of termination while a claim for wrongful dismissal may be brought in the ordinary courts within five years of the breach.

4 Some employees are unable to claim unfair dismissal because they are in an excluded category of employment, for example, share fishermen (i.e., those who share in the profits of the boat's 'catch').

Final point

Under common law, the employer was under no obligation to give the employee any reason for his dismissal. Under the ERA s 92, ex-employees with two years' continuous service are entitled to a written statement of the reason for their dismissal. The employee is only entitled to such a written statement if he / she requests one and the employer must provide the statement within 14 days. An employee who does not have two years' continuous service is entitled to a written statement if she is dismissed at any time while she is pregnant or after childbirth when her maternity leave period ends with dismissal.

TERMINATION OF EMPLOYMENT AS REGULATED BY STATUTE

Unfair dismissal

The law on unfair dismissal was introduced by the Industrial Relations Act 1971, following the recommendations of the Donovan Report. This Act has since been repealed and the law is now found in the Employment Rights Act 1996. In a dramatic departure from the common-law principles, the legislation proclaims in s 94 that every employee who qualifies has the right not to be unfairly dismissed.

AN OUTLINE OF THE STRUCTURE OF THE LAW ON UNFAIR DISMISSAL

Before looking at the legislation in detail, it is helpful to have an outline of the various steps in the Act that have to be taken in order to bring a claim for unfair dismissal:

1 The first hurdle for the employee is to establish that he qualifies and is eligible to bring a claim for unfair dismissal.

2 The next step is to show that he has been dismissed. There are three forms of dismissal defined by the Act in s 95.
3 The burden of proof switches to the employer who must show what was the reason or principal reason for the dismissal.
4 The reason must fall into one of two categories – i.e., potentially fair reasons or automatically unfair reasons. If the employee establishes that the reason is one of the automatically unfair reasons, then step 5 is not necessary.
5 If the reason is one of the potentially fair reasons listed in ERA s 98, the tribunal must then decide whether in the circumstances (including the size and administrative resources of the employer's undertaking) the employer acted reasonably or unreasonably in treating that reason as justifying the dismissal of the employee.
6 The last step in a successful claim is for the industrial tribunal to determine a proper remedy. The tribunal must first consider reinstatement, failing that, re-engagement or compensation.

We will now proceed to examine these six stages in turn.

Eligibility to claim

Only those employees, employed under a contract of service with at least two years' continuous service qualify. In the past, part-time workers had to have five years' continuous employment. The Employment Protection (Part-time Employees) Regulations 1995 changed this to two years' continuous service. The Regulations have been repealed and replaced by the Employment Rights Act 1996. Moreover, employees must not have reached the normal retirement age where they work, or where there is no normal retirement age, then age 65. This upper age limit applies equally to men and women. The only exception to these rules is where an employee is dismissed for trade union reasons or safety reasons, or unfair redundancy or enforcing a statutory right, then there is no qualifying period of two years or upper age limit.

A number of workers are specifically excluded from claiming unfair dismissal. They include: share fishermen who share in the profits of the catch; police officers; those whom the Minister has certified should be exempt from the protection for the purposes of safeguarding national security, like those employed at GCHQ; and those who work abroad.

Under ERA s 203 the general rule is that no-one can contract out of the provisions of the Act. One exception allowed by the Act (s 197) are employees who are employed under fixed-term contracts of one year or more, in which they have agreed in writing to forgo their unfair dismissal or redundancy rights, and the dismissal consists only of a failure to renew the contract.

To claim unfair dismissal, the complaint must be presented to the industrial tribunal within three months from the effective date of termination. The tribunals are very strict about this time limit and will only extend it if they are satisfied that it was not reasonably practicable for the complaint to be presented before the three months expired.

Continuity of employment

The concept of **continuous employment** is very important not only for the right to claim unfair dismissal but also because most of the employee's other statutory employment rights depend on it, either for qualification or for the purpose of calculating the benefits or compensation to be received.

There are a number of points to note:

1. Continuity of employment means generally with one employer. So, it does not matter if the employee has been promoted or has changed his job, department or even the terms of his employment. There is a statutory presumption of continuity unless the contrary is shown, and the burden of proof rests with the employer to show that an employee did not have the necessary continuity of employment.
2. The ERA ss 210–216 mentions 'weeks that do not count' in calculating the period of continuous employment. A week that 'does not count' will break the continuity of employment and so, if the employee returns to work, he must start again building up his period of continuous service. However, some weeks, particularly those spent on strike, do not count but at the same time do not break the continuity.
3. The following cover 'weeks that do count' and where continuity is preserved:

   (a) weeks when the employee is off-sick – the employee is entitled to add the first 26 weeks of his absence towards continuity;

   (b) weeks when the employee is absent from work on account of a temporary cessation of work. To assess whether or not the cessation is temporary, it is necessary to look back over the whole period of employment and the circumstances of each case. This provision was designed to cover those industries, like the construction industry, where there may be temporary lay-offs but it could also apply to many kinds of temporary job. In **Ford *v* Warwickshire County Council** [1983] IRLR 126 Mrs Ford was a teacher employed on a sessional basis. Each year she taught for three terms and in July her contract came to an end. This continued for eight years and then she was not re-engaged. She wanted to claim a redundancy payment but, in order to do so, she needed to establish continuity of service. Finally, the House of Lords held that she had been continuously employed for eight years;

   (c) weeks when the employee is absent from work by arrangement or custom. For continuity to be preserved, the arrangement must be in existence when the employee leaves. This would cover the situation where an employee works full time alternate weeks with another employee. In **Colley *v* Corkindale and Corker's Lounge Bar [1995] ICR 965** Miss Colley, from July 1988 until November 1992, worked two or more days as a bar person. Then from November 1992 until her dismissal in January 1994 she worked only every second Friday for 5½ hours. The problem rested on whether she had the necessary two years' continuous service in order to claim unfair dismissal. The EAT found no breaches in her employment during the course of her employment relationship. 'The fact that an employee works one week on and one week off does not have the effect of terminating the contract' at the end of her working week;

(d) weeks when the employee is absent because of pregnancy or confinement.

4 Continuity is preserved in some circumstances where there is a change of employer:

(a) continuity is preserved if the new employer agrees that the previous period of employment is to count;

(b) under the Transfer of Undertakings (Protection of Employment) Regulations 1981, if a trade or business or undertaking is transferred from one person to another, the period of employment of an employee at the time of the transfer shall count as a period of employment with the transferee and the transfer will not break the continuity of employment;

(c) the ERA 1996 s 218 expressly presumes continuity if: an Act of Parliament results in one corporate body replacing another as an employer; if there is a change in the partners or trustees who employ the individual; if the individual is taken into the employment of an associated employer; if the employer dies and the employee is re-employed by the personal representatives of the deceased.

The employee must have been dismissed before he can bring a claim of unfair dismissal

If the employee is eligible to claim unfair dismissal, his next step is to establish that he has been dismissed and that his dismissal is one of the three acceptable forms of dismissal allowed under ERA s 95. Section 95 states that there is a dismissal if and only if:

(a) the contract under which the employee is employed by the employer is terminated by the employer with or without notice; *or*

(b) where under the contract the employee is employed for a fixed term, that term expires without being renewed under the same contract; *or*

(c) the employee terminates that contract, with or without notice, in circumstances such that he is entitled to terminate it without notice by reason of the employer's conduct.

The first definition of dismissal appears quite straightforward. However, problems can arise as to whether the employer intended dismissal or not when he uses ambiguous words like 'get out' or 'that's it' or 'you are finished'. The court's answer would be to consider how a reasonable employee, in all the circumstances, would have understood the intention of the employer. Once notice to terminate a contract of employment has been given, it cannot be withdrawn unilaterally but only with the agreement of both parties.

There have been some difficulties with the third definition of dismissal, where the employee is entitled to terminate the contract by reason of the employer's conduct. This is called **constructive dismissal**. Initially, the courts were faced with the problem of deciding what kind of conduct by the employer would justify the employee in leaving. It appears that unreasonable conduct by the employer is not enough. The conduct by the employer would have to amount to a repudiatory breach of the contract of employment. The employee may leave, either giving notice or not, but he must make his mind up quickly for if he continues to work for any length of time, without protesting, he will lose his right to treat himself as discharged.

The matter was settled in the leading case of **Western Excavating Ltd *v* Sharp [1978] IRLR 27**. Sharp was dismissed for taking an afternoon off to play cards for his team. He appealed and his dismissal was reduced to five days' suspension without pay. As he had no money, he asked his employers for an advance on his holiday pay which was refused. He then asked for a loan of £40. The welfare officer refused the loan but told him to come back and see him. Sharp did not. Instead, he resigned in order to get his holiday pay and then claimed constructive dismissal. The Industrial Tribunal upheld his claim and awarded him compensation. On appeal, the EAT agreed with the tribunal's findings. The employer appealed to the Court of Appeal who allowed the appeal and said that there was no constructive dismissal as the employers were not in breach of the contract – they were entitled to discipline Sharp and they were under no contractual obligation to make the payment. Lord Denning clarified what was necessary for constructive dismissal and said, 'An employee is entitled to treat himself as dismissed if the employer is guilty of conduct which is a significant breach going to the root of the contract of employment; or which shows that the employer no longer intends to be bound by one or more of the essential terms of the contract ... the employee must make his mind up soon after the conduct of which he complains. If he continues for any length of time without leaving, he will be treated as having elected to affirm the contract and will lose his right to treat himself as discharged'.

Finally, accepting that the contractual test is the correct one to use in deciding whether an employee has been constructively dismissed, it must be noted that the repudiatory breach can be either of an express term or of an implied term of the contract of employment. If there is a breach of an express term – for example, the employer unilaterally reducing the employee's wages or not paying him at all – this will clearly entitle the employee to treat himself as dismissed.

In **Avery Label Systems Ltd *v* Toal EAT 4.11.91 (243/91)** Toal had worked his way up the company from apprentice to manager. As manager he was a salaried employee. The company employed business consultants who proposed a substantial restructuring of the organisation. Toal and some others would no longer be managers but would be called 'team leaders'. On the day that new system was to start, Toal resigned and claimed constructive dismissal. He had lost the status of being a manager and would in future have to report to another manager. He would be working alongside employees rather than managing them and instead of being on permanent day work, he would have to work shifts and he was not to be compensated for this by being given a shift allowance. The EAT did not accept the employer's arguments that the circumstances amounted to some other substantial reason for dismissal and were fair because the new terms and conditions were reasonable in the context of the reorganisation. The EAT decided that Toal's loss of status and the failure to compensate him for his forced return to shift work gave rise to circumstances which entitled him to claim unfair constructive dismissal.

There have been a wide range of examples of breaches of an implied term which have justified the employee's claim of constructive dismissal. For example, management's failure to investigate complaints about safety at work have been held to be a repudiatory breach of the employer's common-law duty to take reasonable care for the safety of his employees. Also, an employer could be in breach of his common-law duty to treat his employee with trust and respect. This has been demonstrated in past cases where the employer has used unjustified foul and abusive language and made unjustified complaints and statements which have seriously damaged the relationship between employer and employee.

In **Isle of Wight Tourist Board *v* Coombes [1976] IRLR 413** Mrs Coombes was the personal secretary of the Director of the Board. She resigned when, after a disagreement and in her hearing, the Director said to a fellow employee 'she is an intolerable bitch on a Monday morning'. The EAT held that she had been constructively dismissed as the relationship between someone in the position of the Director and his secretary must be one of complete confidence. They must trust each other and respect each other. By his remarks the Director had shattered the relationship.

A point to note is that the court will always take into account the individual circumstances of each case and the same decision would not have been reached if Coombes had been a labourer on a building site and the Director, his foreman.

In **Dryden *v* Greater Glasgow Health Board [1992] IRLR 469** Dryden had worked as a nurse for 12 years. Although the Health Board had a no smoking policy for many years, employees had been permitted to smoke in certain designated areas. In 1990, the board issued consultation papers to staff groups and the unions, proposing to ban smoking altogether. No representatives sought to discuss these proposals with the board. The Health Board went ahead with their plans and introduced the ban in July 1991. Staff who smoked were offered counselling and were warned that breach of the ban might result in dismissal. Dryden resigned after ten days and claimed the she had been constructively dismissed. The EAT held that there was no implied term to the effect that Dryden was entitled to smoke at work. When a rule is introduced for a legitimate purpose, the fact that one employee cannot comply with it does not mean that there has been a repudiatory breach by the employer and Dryden had not been constructively dimissed. The EAT went on to say that when policies are introduced which will cover the whole workforce for general purposes which are reasonable and which have been reasonably introduced this will be unlikely to give rise to a constructive dismissal of employees who as individuals cannot comply with the policy. However, this does not remove the need to look carefully at the position of individuals who are dismissed for contravening a general policy such as a smoking ban in order to decide whether the dismissal was fair.

Finally, it must be remembered that the breach has to be a repudiatory breach – i.e., a material breach going to the heart of the contract. In **Woods *v* W M Car Services (Peterborough) Ltd [1983] IRLR 386** which was discussed earlier in Chapter 17, although a number of changes were made to Mrs Woods' contract by her new employer, they were held by the court not to amount to a repudiatory breach of the contract.

The burden of proof shifts to the employer who must show the reason or principal reason for dismissal

Under ERA s 98(1), the employer has to state the reason for the dismissal and he must also show that the reason falls into one of the categories listed below or that it was some other substantial reason of a kind such as to justify the dismissal of an employee holding the position which that employee held.

It is clear that the employer must slot his reason under one of the listed 'potentially fair reasons'. Where no reason is given by the employer, a dismissal will be unfair as the employer has not discharged his statutory burden. Moreover, the dismissal might be unfair if the reason is one which is automatically unfair. These will be discussed later in this chapter.

The Employment Rights Act 1996 s 98 lists the 'potentially fair reasons', which are:

(a) the reason related to the capability or qualifications of the employee for performing work of the kind which he was employed to do;
(b) the reason related to the conduct of the employee;
(c) the reason was that the employee was redundant;
(d) the reason was that the employee could not continue to work in the position which he held without contravention (either on his part or on that of his employer) of a duty or restriction imposed by, or under, a statutory provision; *or*
(e) the reason was some other substantial reason of a kind to justify the dismissal of an employee holding that position.

These particular reasons will be discussed in detail but first it has to be noted that, at this stage, they are only 'potentially fair reasons'. This is because the next stage requires the tribunal to decide whether the employer's decision to dismiss was reasonable or not. This is often referred to as the 'reasonableness test'.

The reasonableness test

This is found in ERA s 98(4) which states that the tribunal's decision as to the fairness of that dismissal, having regard to the reason shown by the employer, shall depend on whether in the circumstances (including the size and administrative resources of the employer's undertaking) the employer acted reasonably or unreasonably in treating the reason as sufficient for dismissing the employee; and that question shall be determined in accordance with equity and the substantial merits of the case.

Reasonableness must be judged at the time of dismissal. So, in deciding whether a dismissal is fair, the tribunal 'must have regard to the reason shown by the employer' and not take into account subsequent misconduct discovered by the employer. In **W Devis & Sons *v* Atkins [1977] IRLR 314** the employee was dismissed for unsatisfactory work. After the dismissal, the employers discovered that he had been embezzling money from them. The House of Lords held that the dismissal was unfair on the grounds of unsatisfactory work and the employer could not rely on the new evidence to justify the dismissal. However, the new information can be taken into account in assessing the amount of compensation, and an employee could be found to have been unfairly dismissed but in the end be awarded no compensation.

The reasonableness test is an objective one and this is explained in **Iceland Frozen Foods Ltd** *v* **Jones [1982] IRLR 439** where the EAT gave guidelines for tribunals to use in applying the reasonableness test. First, the tribunal must consider the reasonableness of the employer's conduct and not simply whether they consider the dismissal to be fair; they must not substitute their view for the employer's view of what is reasonable. Second, in many (but not all) cases there is a band of reasonable responses to the employee's conduct within which one employer might reasonably take one view and another might quite reasonably take a different one. Third, the function of the tribunal is to determine whether, in the particular circumstances of each case, the decision to dismiss the employee fell within the band of reasonable responses which a reasonable employer might have adopted. If the dismissal falls within the band, the dismissal is fair and, if it falls outside the band, it is unfair.

It would appear that the tribunal must decide whether a reasonable employer in those circumstances, and in that kind of business, would have dismissed the employee and, provided the response is within the band of reasonable responses, it is not necessary that all reasonable employers would dismiss in those circumstances.

The 'reasonableness test' obviously will apply to dismissals for a wide range of reasons and the tribunal will have to examine (a) the factual circumstances and (b) the procedural circumstances of each case.

The factual circumstances

The factors commonly considered will include the size and administrative resources of the employer. For example, it could be fair to dismiss a driver in a small firm because he lost his driving licence, but unfair to dismiss him if the company is larger and he could be moved to another job. The employer should be consistent in his treatment of all his employees and should not dismiss, when in the past he has not done so in the same circumstances. The tribunal will also look at the employee's status and length of service and past record. In **Tiptools Ltd** *v* **Curtis [1973] IRLR 276** Curtis' dismissal for unsatisfactory workmanship after 19 years with the company was held to be unfair. He should have been given a chance to improve or alternatively been found work more suitable to his capabilities.

The procedural circumstances

A dismissal can be unfair because of procedural shortcomings even where the dismissal would have been justified if the employer had taken the proper disciplinary procedures. In the early days, there was some debate as to whether it was necessary to follow proper disciplinary procedures, if failing to do so would make no difference to the employer's decision to dismiss. The matter has now been settled by the leading case of: **Polkey** *v* **Dayton Services Ltd [1988] AC 344**. The employee was a driver. His employers decided that their drivers would in the future be salesmen as well as drivers. Some employees would have to be made redundant as they would not be capable of carrying out the new duties. The employers called Polkey into the office one morning and, completely ignoring the Industrial Relations Code of Practice (which has now been repealed), without prior consultation and warnings, informed him that he was redundant and then drove him home. The employers, admitting that they had not carried out the proper procedures for redundancies, argued that consultation would have made no difference to their decision to dismiss. The House of Lords held that the dismissal was unfair. EPCA s 57(3) (now ERA s 98(4)) does not ask whether an employee has been treated unjustly but whether an employer has acted reasonably. In most cases, an employer will not be acting reasonably if he omits certain procedural steps and only in exceptional circumstances would failure to observe the Code of Practice not render the dismissal unfair.

Procedural standards

There are two possible sources for procedural standards. The first is from the rules of natural justice, and the second is the guidelines laid down in the ACAS Code of Practice on Disciplinary Practice and Procedures. Recent decisions of the Court of Appeal indicate that while the rules of natural justice may be relevant to the devising of procedural standards, they cannot be relied upon as a source.

Disciplinary procedures

The employer should have disciplinary rules and procedures drawn up and brought to the attention of his employees. Rules set standards of conduct at work; procedure helps to ensure that the standards are adhered to and provides a fair method of dealing with alleged failures to observe them. There should be different procedures for different reasons for dismissal. For example, in cases of incompetence the procedures should provide the employee with an opportunity to improve his performance. In cases of dismissal for redundancy, the procedures should provide for warning the employees, and the employees should be given the opportunity through consultation to make suggestions as to how job losses could be avoided or why they should not be selected. In cases of misconduct, the rules should indicate what conduct will result in disciplinary action and who has the authority to take it.

Some guidance on disciplinary procedures is found in the 1977 ACAS Code of Practice on Disciplinary Practice and Procedures. Failure by an employer to observe the Code is not unlawful but such a failure can be admissible as evidence in tribunal proceedings. The ACAS handbook *Discipline at Work* 1987 does not have the status of the Code but complements it and gives guidance on other matters like absence and sub-standard work. The basic requirements of the Code of Practice are that when a disciplinary matter arises, it should be promptly investigated by the manager and careful records should be kept. When the facts call for action, the following procedure should be followed:

1 Warnings should be given. There is no 'hard-and-fast' rule about this but, for minor offences, the employee should receive a verbal warning, then a written

warning and then a final written warning stating that a recurrence of the offence may lead to dismissal.

2 Prior to any action leading to dismissal, an employer should carry out a proper investigation. He should discuss the matter with the employee and let him put forward his views. If there is a disciplinary hearing, the employee must be given notice of it, be allowed to attend and be entitled to representation by either a union official or a colleague.

3 An employee should always have the right to appeal to, if possible, a higher level of management.

PARTICULAR REASONS FOR DISMISSAL

Having considered the 'reasonableness test', we now take a detailed look at the potentially fair reasons listed in ERA s 98(2) (capability, misconduct, redundancy, statutory provision and any other substantial reason). We will then examine the automatically unfair reasons laid down in the TULR(C) Act ss152 and 153 (trade union reasons, selection for redundancy because of trade union reasons) and pregnancy and look briefly at dismissal on the transfer of an undertaking and the inadmissible reasons under s 100 ERA.

Capability or qualifications

Section 98(3) of the ERA explains that '**capability**' is to be assessed by reference to skill, aptitude, health or any other physical or mental quality; '**qualifications**' means any degree, diploma or other academic, technical or professional qualification relevant to the position which the employee holds.

The problem of lack of qualifications will usually arise early in the employment relationship. Possibly the employee, when he was being interviewed, said that he has a certain qualification and this turns out to be untrue. Lying at the interview could give grounds for dismissal, probably for misconduct. Failing to acquire a qualification which is a requirement of the job will give the employer a potentially fair reason to dismiss. In **Blackman *v* The Post Office [1974] ICR 151** the court found, as a matter of common sense, that for five years Blackman had proved his capability to do the job. However, he had failed three times to pass a special aptitude test, which was a requirement of the job, and the employer had a fair reason for dismissing him.

Examples of employees being incapable have included in the past: the slow employee; the new recruit whose performance has not matched his promises; the employee whose personality makes him unsuitable for the job; the inflexible and unadaptable worker; the worker who cannot do the job because of poor vision.

For dismissal on the grounds of lack of capability, it is sufficient that the employer believes, on reasonable grounds, that the employee is incapable or incompetent. The tribunal, also, has to be satisfied that the employer has acted reasonably in the circumstances and this will mean deciding whether proper training, supervision and encouragement were given to the employee. A reasonable employer would investigate the employee's weaknesses, warn him and give him a chance to improve, and then, if the employee cannot 'make the grade', decide whether he could be offered a less demanding job. However, it will always depend on the circumstances, and sometimes where there is gross incompetence with potentially disastrous consequences, warnings and a chance to improve will not be necessary. In **Taylor** *v* **Alidair [1978] IRLR 82** a pilot landed his plane so badly that it was damaged and the passengers were badly frightened. His dismissal was held fair even though the employers had omitted the usual procedures.

Ill-health problems

Lack of capability on the grounds of ill health could be applied to the employee who is off work for a long period of illness or it could apply to persistent short-term absences for a variety of ailments. In both cases, whether the dismissal is fair will depend on the circumstances of the individual case. We have seen, under common law, that an exceptionally incapacitating illness or accident could have the effect of frustrating the contract of employment. The statutory protection has mainly overtaken the common law and, if the employee has two years' continuous service, the courts will not readily decide that there has been frustration as this would deny the employee the possible remedy of compensation for unfair dismissal.

In these cases, the employer must reach a fair decision in all the circumstances, which will include the needs of the business, the nature of the illness, the likely period of absence, as to whether and when he can dismiss the employee and, since the *Polkey* case, he must be careful to follow a fair procedure. A number of cases have given guidelines and, taking into account this case law, advice is given in the ACAS handbook *Discipline at Work*. It must be remembered that the handbook is purely advisory and it does not have the legal status of a code of practice.

Long-term illness

Employers should treat the employee with consideration, keep in regular contact and advise him if his employment is at risk. With the employee's consent, a report should be obtained from his doctor. Where the employee refuses to cooperate in providing medical evidence or to undergo an independent medical examination, the employee should be warned in writing that a decision will be taken on the basis of the information available to the employer and that it could result in dismissal. If a report is supplied, then, on the basis of the report, the employer may consider whether there is alternative work for the employee. When the point is reached where the employee's job can no longer be kept open for him, and there is no suitable alternative employment, then the employer may dismiss the employee giving him the correct amount of notice and informing him of any right of appeal.

Persistent short-term absence

In these cases, a fair review by the employer should be made. Absences should be investigated promptly to discover if they are genuine and the employee asked for an explanation. Where there is no medical advice to support frequent self-certified absences, the employee should be asked to consult a doctor to establish whether medical treatment is necessary. If, after investigation, it appears that there were no good reasons for the absences, the matter should be dealt with under the disciplinary procedures. Where absences arise from domestic problems, employers should consider whether an improvement is likely. In all cases, employees should be told what improvement in attendance is expected and warned of the consequences if there is no improvement. If there is no improvement, then taking into account the usual factors – age, length of service, past performance and the effect of past and future absences on the business – the employer can decide whether to dismiss.

In **International Sports Co Ltd** *v* **Thompson [1980] IRLR 340** Thomson was absent for 25 per cent of her working days over a period of 18 months. Most of her absences were covered by medical certificates and covered a variety of different illnesses and complaints. Thompson was warned several times over a period of one year that her level of absenteeism was too high. The company doctor looked at her medical certificates and could see no link between her ailments and felt that no useful purpose would be served by examining her as she had recovered. Her dismissal was held to be fair.

Alcohol or drug abuse

Consideration should be given to introducing measures to help and identify employees suffering from alcohol and drug abuse and to encourage them to seek treatment. Where it is established that an employee is suffering from such dependency, a reasonable employer would probably consider it appropriate to treat the problem as a medical rather than a disciplinary one. In saying that, tribunals take a very strict view where safety is concerned and if the employee continues to drink while using machinery or driving, thus becoming a potential danger to his colleagues and the public, then dismissal will be potentially fair.

AIDS

Where an employee suffers from a medical condition which makes him unacceptable to colleagues, the employer might find himself faced with pressure to dismiss or threats of industrial action. The employer should bear in mind that he may have to justify to an industrial tribunal the reasonableness of any decision to dismiss. Before taking a decision, the employer should attempt to educate the workforce and explain that person-to-person transmission of the AIDS virus does not occur during normal work activities. He can also take into account disruption to working relationships and to the business, and the possibility of alternative work.

Misconduct

There are a number of forms of misconduct which will justify dismissal. Some examples could be absenteeism, bad language, disobedience, drinking at work, personal appearance, theft and violence. In all these cases, a reasonable employer will take all the circumstances into account – factual and procedural – before reaching a decision to dismiss.

In deciding whether the employer had a valid reason to dismiss an employee, the tribunal cannot require the employer to prove that the employee actually committed the act of misconduct complained of and the employer need only show that he had reasonable grounds for believing this to be so. A three-fold test was established in **British Home Stores** *v* **Burchell [1978] IRLR 379** where the EAT indicated that the test could be broken down into three elements. First, the employer must show that he genuinely believed that the employee committed the misconduct; secondly, that he had reasonable grounds on which to sustain that belief and, thirdly, that when he formed that belief, he had carried out a reasonable investigation. This means that, even if later it is quite clear that an employee did not commit the misconduct, or if later he is found not guilty by a criminal court, a tribunal could still find the employee's dismissal fair provided that the employer has satisfied the three-fold test in *Burchell.*

In **Boys and Girls Welfare Society** *v* **McDonald [1996] IRLR 129** McDonald was employed as a residential social worker in a children's home. During an altercation with a boy, M was alleged to have spat at the boy after being spat at himself and also hitting the boy in the face. An industrial tribunal found M's dismissal unfair because applying the threefold test in *British Home Stores* v *Burchell,* it was not satisfied that the employers had reasonable grounds for believing that the employee was guilty of the alleged misconduct or that they had conducted a reasonable investigation. The EAT reversed the tribunal's decision. The EAT held that as McDonald had admitted to the misconduct there was little scope for further investigation. In the *British Home Stores* case there was a suspicion or belief of the employee's misconduct. The EAT felt that the tribunal had been in error by placing emphasis on the *British Home Stores* guidelines. In the EAT's opinion, the threefold test was appropriate where the employer had to decide a factual contest but the test might not be necessary when the facts were not disputed. What the tribunal must decide is whether the decision to dismiss fell within the band of reasonable responses to an employer (see **Iceland Frozen Foods** *v* **Jones [1983] IRLR 439** on p. 398).

In the next case, the Court of Appeal acknowledged that the *Burchell* guidelines were helpful but that each case depended on its facts and, when there was more than one suspected person, the test ultimately to be used is the 'reasonableness test' as stated in what is now ERA s 98(4). This was said by Sir David Cairns in **Monie** *v* **Coral Racing Ltd [1980] IRLR 96**. In this case, there was suspected theft by an employee but it could have been done by one of two employees and the actual culprit was unidentifiable. The Court of Appeal held that where two employees are so suspected then, provided the employer carries out a reasonable investigation and if he still cannot discover which one is to blame, it may be fair to dismiss both on reasonable suspicion, short of actual belief. One can see that this decision offends the notions of natural justice, because it means that the innocent may be sacked along with the guilty. The reason a dismissal can be fair in these circumstances is because of the accepted interpretation of what is now ERA s 98(4) which concentrates on the fairness of the employer's decision rather than whether the employee has been treated fairly.

The same approach was taken by the EAT in a recent case, **Frames Snooker**

Centre *v* **Boyce [1992] IRLR 4721** . There had been three burglaries at the snooker centre. The police thought that they were 'inside jobs' and the suspects were the three managers who knew the safe combination. Two of the managers were dismissed, but the third, who was the daughter of the owner, was not dismissed because he had 'complete faith in her honesty'. The EAT said that in 'group dismissal' situations it is not necessary to dismiss everyone. The ERA s 98(4) states that the tribunal must decide whether the employer acted reasonably. The EAT said that the correct approach to group dismissals was to look at each individual employee who has been dismissed and ask the question, 'Has the employer acted reasonably?' If the employer is able to show sound and sensible grounds for differentiating between them then not dismissing one of them will not in itself render the dismissal of the rest of the group unfair.

A final point regarding misconduct concerns criminal conduct by the employee. Clearly, every employee who commits a crime at work, whether it be dishonesty or violence, runs the risk of being dismissed. However, if the criminal conduct takes place outside the place of work, and after working hours, it will not necessarily justify dismissal. Each case will depend on its facts but, as a guide, the following factors should be considered:

1 the nature of the employment;
2 the position held by the employee;
3 the nature of the criminal conduct;
4 the effect of the incident on customers and fellow employees;
5 the effect it will have on the employer's business.

Generally, if the conduct is going to affect the employer's business, and customers and other employees are not going to be happy dealing with the employee, then his dismissal will be fair. In **Richardson** *v* **City of Bradford Metropolitan Council [1975] IRLR 179** a Senior Meat Inspector was convicted of theft from his local rugby club. When his employers found out, he was suspended. Then, as there was no other suitable employment for him, he was dismissed. He was unsuccessful in his claim for unfair dismissal as the tribunal considered that the integrity of a public servant in a position of trust was of prime importance. However, in **Bradshaw** *v* **Rugby Portland Cement [1972] IRLR 46** Bradshaw was held to have been unfairly dismissed after being convicted of incest with his daughter. The tribunal considered that the conviction had not affected his work as a quarryman. He did not come into contact with the public and his fellow employees did not object to working with him.

Redundancy

As we will see later, redundancy can be automatically unfair under TULR(C) Act 1992 s 153, where the dismissal is for trade union reasons and other employees holding similar jobs were not dismissed. However, redundancy can be a potentially fair reason for dismissal under ERA s 98(2) provided that it is carried out reasonably. If the redundancy is fair, this, of course, does not affect the employee's right to claim a redundancy payment. It just means that he cannot claim unfair dismissal.

Unfair redundancy

An employee can still challenge the fairness of his dismissal by claiming that the employer has not acted reasonably in selecting him for redundancy or that fair procedures were not followed. In applying the 'reasonableness test' of s 98(4), the tribunals have developed three separate headings under which a dismissal for redundancy could be regarded as unfair in this context. They are:

1 where the employer's method of selection as between comparable employees has been unreasonable – i.e., there were not fair selection criteria;
2 where the employer failed to adopt proper procedures regarding warnings and consultation;
3 where the employer failed to try to make reasonable efforts to find alternative employment for the dismissed employee.

As a rule, therefore, the tribunal will be looking to see if the employee was selected for redundancy in accordance with fair, objective criteria and after due warnings and consultation have taken place. In **Williams *v* Compair Maxam Ltd [1982] IRLR 83** Williams was made redundant after many years of service and without prior consultation. The manager made the decision to dismiss him and in his view it would be in the best interests of the company. The employee was successful in claiming unfair dismissal. The EAT laid down five steps 'which a reasonable and fair employer at the present time would seek to take in dismissing unionised employees on the ground of redundancy'. They were that, whether or not the criteria to be adopted has been negotiated with the union:

(a) the employer will seek to establish criteria for the selection;
(b) the criteria, so far as possible, should not depend solely on the opinion of the person making the selection;
(c) the criteria can be objectively checked against aspects such as attendance record, efficiency at the job, experience or length of service;
(d) the employer should seek to ensure that the selection is made fairly in accordance with these established criteria;
(e) the employer should consider any representations the union has to make as to such a selection.

The guidelines in the *Williams* case are not rules of law and subsequent cases show that the courts sometimes accept that these rules must give way to more pressing considerations.

Breach of statutory duty

The fourth potentially fair reason for dismissal is that the employee could not continue working without contravention, either by him or by the employer, of a duty or restriction imposed by statute. For example, it could be potentially fair to dismiss an employee who is a driver and who loses his licence.

Some other substantial reason

An employer who cannot show that his employee's dismissal was for incapacity, misconduct, redundancy or breach of a statutory duty may, nevertheless, be able to show that his dismissal was for some other substantial reason. Obviously, the reason must not be trivial and could cover any type of conduct which makes it impossible or impractical for the relationship to continue. There are many cases, providing a variety of reasons which come under this heading. In **Foot *v* Eastern Counties Timber [1972] IRLR 83** a woman, employed as accounts clerk, often saw her employer's quotations and had contact with the firm's customers. Her husband started a similar business less than a quarter of a mile away. Although the firm had no complaint against her, she was inevitably one day going to be in a position where her domestic interests might conflict with her loyalties to her employer. Her dismissal was held to be fair.

In **Fair *v* Hoveringham Gravels Ltd [1972] IRLR 104** the company had a rule that employees must live within a reasonable travelling distance of the workplace, and they dismissed a manager who moved 44 miles away. A person in his position had to be prepared to turn out in an emergency and this would have been difficult because of the distance. His dismissal was held to be fair.

Business reorganisations

A business reorganisation often means that management, in the interests of greater efficiency, will make some employees redundant and insist that other employees agree to a change in their contractual terms and conditions. If the employees do not agree, they are informed that this could lead to their dismissal. A change in contractual terms without the employee's consent is unlawful under common law. Under the law of unfair dismissal, one would think that an employee in these circumstances would have the right to resign and claim constructive dismissal as in *Avery Label Systems Ltd* v *Toal* on p. 396. However, one finds that the consequent dismissal of dissenting employees has been held by the tribunal to be for some other substantial reason and fair. It is clear that the tribunals have been reluctant to interfere with the decisions of employers in managing their businesses, provided the changes are justified on economic grounds. Recent cases show that in applying the fair and reasonable test, tribunals must also carry out a balancing process, taking into account the disadvantages of the new contracts to the employees and the advantages to the employer.

In **Hollister *v* The National Farmers Union [1979] ICR 542** the London Headquarters of the NFU decided that the insurance business for Cornwall would be transferred from the Cornish Mutual to the NFU Mutual. This would mean a change of contractual terms and conditions for the Cornish group secretaries, one of whom was Hollister. He protested but was eventually told either to accept the change or be dismissed. He refused and was dismissed. The tribunal decided that his dismissal was for some other substantial reason and fair because there were 'sound good business reasons for the reorganisation' and the failure of the employer to consult the employee did not make the employer's decision unreasonable in the circumstances.

However, in **Catamaran Cruisers Ltd *v* Williams [1994] IRLR 386** the EAT held that in applying the reasonableness test what was required was a balancing process taking into account the disadvantages of the new contracts to the employees and the advantages to the employer in imposing them. Then in **McGibbon *v* Oil Ltd EAT 537/94** the EAT stated 'that it is not enough for an employer to say that it is convenient or helpful to him to carry out a reorganisation or that to do so would reduce his employment costs'. If the reason for dismissal is found to be a sound business reason, a tribunal must then carry out the balancing process mentioned in **Catamaran Cruisers Ltd *v* Willaims**.

Finally, under the ERA 1996 s 106, replacement employees who are dismissed will be regarded as having been dismissed for a substantial reason of a kind such as to justify the dismissal of an employee holding the position which the employee held. This section applies to employees who when they start work are informed in writing that this employment will terminate when the employee who is absent because of pregnancy or childbirth returns to work. Such a dismissal will be subject to the 'fair and reasonable test' in s 98(4).

AUTOMATICALLY UNFAIR REASONS FOR DISMISSAL

In ERA s 98, as we have just seen, Parliament stipulated that the major reasons for dismissal are listed as potentially fair reasons, subject to the 'reasonableness test'. Parliament also states that some reasons for dismissal are automatically unfair. In these cases, the tribunal must find the dismissal unfair no matter how the employer may seek to justify the dismissal. The tribunal has no jurisdiction to decide whether the employer acted reasonably or unreasonably, as the unfair reason overrides any mitigating circumstances. The employee does not need two years' continuous service to qualify for these rights. We will now examine these in turn.

Trustees of occupational pension schemes

The Pensions Act 1995 introduced new safeguards for company pension schemes. Under the ERA 1996 s 102 it is automatically unfair dismissal to dismiss an employee if the reason is that being a trustee of his occupational pension scheme he performed or proposed to perform his duties as a trustee.

Employee representatives

The Collective Redundancies and Transfer of Undertakings (Protection of Employment) (Amendment) Regulations 1995 require the employers who do not recognise trade unions to consult with appropriate employee representatives over collective redundancies and transfer of undertakings (see pp. 417, 431). Under the ERA 1996 s 103, it is automatically unfair dismissal to dismiss such an employee representative or candidate for the post for performing or proposing to perform any functions or activities as an employee representative.

Assertion of a statutory right

Under the ERA s 104 it is automatically unfair dismissal to dismiss an employee if the reason is that the employee brought proceedings against the employer to enforce a statutory employment right or because the employee alleged that the employer had infringed a relevant statutory right. There is no requirement that the employer has actually infringed the statutory right. (*Menell* v *Newell & Wright* (1996) IRLR 384.)

THE UNFAIR REASON FOR DISMISSAL – HEALTH AND SAFETY REASONS

The Employment Rights Act 1996 s 100 provides new unfair reasons for dismissal. The employee does not have to have two years' continuous service to claim that his dismissal was unfair under this section, which is in two parts. The first part, (a) and (b), provide safety representatives and others from being dismissed for carrying out their duties; the second part, (c), (d) and (e), provides protection against dismissal for employees where they leave their post or take other action like shouting that 'everyone should evacuate the premises' because there is danger.

In s 100(1) the dismissal of an employee shall be unfair if the reason for it was any of the following:

(a) The employee was designated by the employer to carry out activities in connection with preventing or reducing risks to the health or safety of employees at work and he carried out or proposed to carry out such activities.
(b) The employee was a health and safety representative or a member of a safety committee and he performed or proposed to perform any function as safety representative or as committee member.
(c) The employee was at a place where there was no such representative or safety committee or there was such a representative or safety committee but it was not reasonably practicable for the employee to raise the matter by those means and he brought to his employer's attention by reasonable means, circumstances connected with his work which he reasonably believed were harmful to health and safety.
(d) The employee (this could apply to any employee or to a safety representative) in circumstances of danger which was serious and imminent and which he could not reasonably have been expected to avert, left, or proposed to leave his place of work or while the danger persisted refused to return to his place of work.
(e) The employee, in circumstances of serious and imminent danger, took, or proposed to take, appropriate steps to protect himself, or other employees from the danger. Whether these steps were appropriate will be judged by taking into account all the circumstances of the case including the employee's knowledge and the facilities and advice available to him at the time. However, the dismissal

under (e) will not be unfair if the employer shows that it was negligent of the employee to take these steps and that a reasonable employer would have dimissed him from taking these steps.

An employee bringing a complaint of unfair dismissal on the grounds in (a) and (b) is entitled to a basic award of not less the £2770 and is also allowed to claim interim relief pending the outcome of the tribunal proceedings. This is the same right that an employee claiming unfair dismissal for trade union reasons has (see p. 410).

In **Kerr *v* Nathan's Wastesavers Ltd (EAT 91/95)** a van driver was dismissed after complaining that his van was overloaded and unsafe and he refused to drive it. The dismissal was found to be fair. The EAT stated that Kerr did not have reasonable grounds for his belief that there was a health and safety risk. He could have phoned for another vehicle to assist him or changed vehicles. The EAT said it was irrelevant whether or not the employers had acted unreasonably. The tribunal has to decide whether the employee had an honest belief that there were circumstances harmful to health and safety and should then decide whether this belief was based on reasonable grounds. The EAT did stress that they would not place too onerous a duty of enquiry on the employee.

Trade union membership or activities

Section 152 of the Trade Union and Labour Relations (Consolidation) Act 1992 states that a dismissal will be unfair if the principal reason for it was that the employee:

(a) was, or proposed to become a member of an independent trade union, *or*
(b) had taken part, or proposed to take part, in the activities of an independent trade union at an appropriate time, *or*
(c) was not a member of a trade union, or of a particular union, or had refused to become or remain a member.

In order to bring a claim under s 152, employees do not have to have two years' continuous service, nor is there any upper age limit. If the employee does not have two years' continuous service, the onus is on him to prove that his dismissal related to trade union reasons. If he has more than two years' service, the burden of proof rests with the employer to establish the reason for dismissal. If it is another reason, then the employee must try to show otherwise. To qualify for protection, the trade union activities must take place at the 'appropriate time'. The section indicates that this will either be outside working hours or within working hours, in accordance with arrangements agreed with the employer or with his consent.

Interim relief

An employee who thinks that he has been dismissed for trade union membership or activities or the activities of a safety representative (s 100) or an employee representative (s 103) or the trustee of an occupational pension scheme (s 102) is entitled to apply for a special speedy remedy to 'tide him over' until his case comes before the tribunal. He can apply for interim relief and, if he is successful, the tribunal can order that he is re-employed or at least paid his wages until the case is decided. However, in order to apply for interim relief, the employee must comply with a special procedure. He must ensure that his IT1 form and a written request for interim relief arrive at the Central Office of Industrial Tribunals office within seven days of his dismissal. The tribunal will grant the application provided it arrives in time and they are satisfied that the employee is likely to succeed at the full tribunal hearing and his dismissal was unfair under s 152 TULR(c) A 1992 or ss 100, 102 and 103 of the ERA 1996.

Pressure on the employer from the union

When it is claimed that the employer has been pressurised by the union to dismiss an employee because he was not a member of the union, the employer or his ex-employee can sist (ie join) a third party or the union to the unfair dismissal proceedings, with the result that the tribunal could order the third party to pay some or all of any compensation awarded. The sisted party has the right to attend the hearing, call evidence and cross-examine witnesses. If the claim is successful, the tribunal will apportion the amount to be paid by the employer and the union third party as it considers just and equitable in the circumstances.

Dismissal on the grounds of redundancy

Trades Union reasons

Section 153 TULR(C) Act states that where the reason for dismissal of an employee was that he was redundant, but it is shown that the circumstances constituting the redundancy applied equally to one or more other employees in the same undertaking who held positions similar to that held by the employee and the others have not been dismissed, and either:

(a) that the reason he was selected was for the trade union membership and activities reasons laid down in s 152, then the dismissal is unfair
(b) that he was selected for dismissal in contravention of a customary arrangement or agreed procedure relating to redundancy and there were no special reasons justifying a departure from that procedure or arrangement.

Inadmissable reasons

Under the ERA 1996 s 105 an employee will be regarded as automatically unfairly dismissed if:

(a) the reason or principal reason for the dismissal is that the employee was redundant, and
(b) it is shown that the circumstances constituting the redundancy applied equally to one or more other employees in the same undertaking who held positions similar to that held by the employee and who have not been dismissed, and
(c) the reason for which the employee was selected for redundancy was either:
    (i) the employee was pregnant or taking maternity leave as specified in s 99 ERA,
    (ii) the employee was carrying out health and safety duties as specified in s 100 ERA,

(iii) the employee was carrying out the duties of a trustee of an occupational pension scheme as specified in s 102 ERA,
(iv) the employee was carrying out the duties of an employee representative in consultation over impending redundancies or the transfer of the undertaking as specified in s 103 ERA,
(v) the employee had brought proceedings against his employer to enforce a statutory right as specified in s 104 ERA.

Pregnancy dismissals

Pregnancy-related dismissals and maternity leave were explained in detail on p. 381 The ERA 1996 s 99 applies to all employees, whatever their length of service. Now an employee shall be treated as automatically unfairly dismissed in the following circumstances:

1 If the reason or principal reason for her dismissal is that she is pregnant or is any reason connected with her pregnancy.
2 Her maternity leave is ended by dismissal and the reason is because she has given birth or is any other reason connected with her having given birth.
3 Her contract was terminated after the maternity leave and the reason for her dismissal is that she had taken maternity leave or had availed herself of the benefits of maternity leave.
4 The reason for dismissal is a requirement or recommendation referred to in ss 66–70 (the right to be suspended with pay on health and safety grounds).
5 The maternity leave period is ended by dismissal and the reason is that she is redundant, but the obligation to be offered a suitable available vacancy (if there is one) has not been complied with.

An employee who is dismissed during her pregnancy or during her maternity leave period will be entitled to written reasons for her dismissal under s 92 within 14 days of the dismissal. She does not have to request this.

TRANSFER OF UNDERTAKINGS (PROTECTION OF EMPLOYMENT) REGULATIONS 1981

These regulations represent the British attempt to implement the **EC Acquired Rights Directive 77/187** and deal with the rights and obligations of employees and employers when an undertaking is transferred to a new employer. The Regulations are in addition to the provisions of the Employment Rights Act 1996 s 218 which merely provides for the bridging of continuity of employment on the change of the employee's employer, while the 1981 Regulations transfer the contracts of employment of the workforce to the new employer of the business or undertaking so there is no dismissal. The new employer (the transferee) takes over **'all rights, powers, duties and liabilities under or in connection with such**

contracts'. As the TUPE Regulations were designed to implement the Acquired Rights Directive, the UK courts and tribunals must construe the TUPE Regulations in whatever manner is necessary to conform to requirements of the Directive as construed by the ECJ.

In the context of unfair dismissal the Regulations are important as transfer-connected dismissals are automatically unfair unless the dismissal was for an economic, technical or organisational reason entailing changes in the workforce.

Transfers covered by the Regulations

The 1981 Regulations only apply where there is a 'relevant transfer of an undertaking' in the UK.

A '**relevant transfer**' is defined as a transfer from one person to another of an undertaking which may be by a sale or through the operation of the law and may be effected by a series of two or more transactions. It does not matter whether property is transferred at the time or not. In **Charleton** *v* **Charleton Thermosystems and others [1995] IRLR 79** Mr and Mrs C were the directors and sole shareholders of a heating and ventilating company which was struck off the Register of Companies for failing to file accounts and was dissolved. Nevertheless, the Charletons carried on business for a few weeks before dismissing their employees. The EAT upheld the employees' claim for redundancy against the Charletons. Under the Transfer of Undertakings Regulations there had been a transfer of the undertaking of the company to the Charletons. After the company had been dissolved, the business retained its identity when run by the Charletons who operated it using the same assets and employees. That was held sufficient to protect the rights of the employees.

An '**undertaking**' includes any trade or business and may be part of an undertaking. The Regulations do not apply where there is a takeover of a company through the acquisition of a majority of the share capital of the company. The undertaking does not have to be a commercial venture. In **Dr Sophie Redmond Stichting** *v* **Bartol [1992] IRLR 366** the facts of the case are complicated but briefly they are as follows. The Sophie Redmond Foundation in Holland provided assistance to drug addicts, alcoholics and others and relied on local authority grants to do this. In January 1991 the local authority terminated its funding to the Foundation and switched the grants to the Sigma Foundation, which was to carry out similar tasks. Some patients were transferred to Sigma and some employees were offered new contracts of employment with Sigma while other employees, including Bartol, were not. The question to be decided was whether the Dutch law which implemented the Directive applied or not to such a transfer. A reference was sent to the ECJ for its opinion. The ECJ decided that the Directive applied. The term 'legal transfer' is wide enough to cover a situation like this in which a public body terminates a subsidy to one legal person and transfers the function in question to another legal person with similar aims and it did not matter that the decision to switch the subsidy was made without any consultation of the body being subsidised. Also, the fact that subsidies were granted to a charitable organisation whose services are not paid for did not mean that the transaction was excluded from the scope of the Directive. The ECJ stressed that the object of the Directive was to protect the rights of employees and it applies to all employees who are thus covered by protection against dismissal in the event of a transfer.

The ECJ stated that when deciding whether a 'transfer of an undertaking, business or part of a business' had actually taken place within the meaning of the Directive, the first matter to decide is whether the unit being transferred has retained its identity and, in deciding this, have all the factual circumstances been taken into account. The circumstances include the type of undertaking, whether the tangible assets are transferred, whether the majority of employees are taken over, whether the customers are taken over, the degree of similarity between the activities carried on before and after the transfer and the period if any for which the activities are suspended while the unit is being transferred. In **Watson-Rask & Christensen** *v* **ISS Kantineservice A/S ECJ 12.11.92 (C-209/91),** W and C were employees of a company called Philips, working in one of their canteens. Philips contracted out the running of this canteen to ISS who undertook to employ the canteen workers on the same terms and conditions. ISS made some changes to the terms and conditions, and dismissed W and C who had refused to continue working under the new conditions. The case was referred to the ECJ to decide whether this was a transfer covered by the Directive. The ECJ decided that the contracting-out of the running of the canteen to another company could be a transfer and potentially be covered by the Acquired Rights Directive. In deciding this, it was appropriate to look at the guidance given by the Court in the *Sophie Redmond Stichting* case and the factual circumstances which should be taken into account. If the Directive applies, then the transferee is bound to maintain the same terms and conditions agreed between the transferor and his employees. In **Schmidt** *v* **Spar etc [1994] IRLR 302 ECJ** Frau Schmidt had been employed by a bank to clean one of its branches. Then the bank decided to contract out its cleaning services for that branch. The contractor offered to employ Frau Schmidt but there was a disagreement as to the terms on which she would be employed and she rejected the offer and claimed that the Directive applied in her favour. Eventually ECJ made a ruling in her favour stating that the decisive criteria for deciding whether there has been a transfer is whether the business retained its identity. That identity is indicated by the actual continuation or resumption by the new employer of the same or similar activities and the Directive applied even though the cleaning services were performed by only one employee.

Compulsory Competitive Tendering (CCT) was introduced in 1980. Local Authorities were required to put out to tender building repair, maintenance highways and sewage works. In 1988 CCT was extended to other manual services – cleaning, refuse collection, catering, and ground and vehicle maintenance. In 1992 CCT was extended to a range of white collar services. The *Watson-Rask* and *Schmidt* cases covered the contracting-out of services in the private sector but there would appear to be no reason why the Directive could not in certain circumstances apply to the contracting-out of public services. The ECJ decisions make it clear that if a transfer of an undertaking is covered by the Directive then the terms and conditions of employment cannot be changed by the transferee without incurring liability. However, the Directive does not prohibit the changing of these terms by the transferee insofar as national law allows an employer to make such a change (provided of course the changes are not brought about as a result of the transfer).

It follows that if TUPE applies, contractors will not be able to change the terms and conditions of employees transferred to their employment. The Directive obliges the transferee to preserve the conditions entered into through a collective agreement until the date on which the agreement is cancelled, expires or is replaced by another. Currently this problem is facing the new 'trust hospitals' which have opted out of the NHS – the unions involved are arguing strongly that the TUPE Regulations apply to staff whose services are transferred.

The effect of a relevant transfer

Returning to the 1981 TUPE Regulations, **Regulation 5** provides that a relevant transfer shall not operate to terminate the contract of employment of an employee employed by the transferor (the first employer) immediately before the transfer. All the transferor's rights, powers, duties and liabilities under the contract of employment are transferred to the transferee. Because of Regulations 5 and 8, the transferee can be liable for the unfair dismissal of an employee. This potential liability would arise if the transferee refuses to engage any employee, but he can also be liable for the pre-transfer dismissal of the employee by the transferor. What has happened in practice is that the transferor and transferee have got together to try to ensure that the employees, who are surplus to the transferee's requirements, are not employed by the transferor immediately before the transfer. Why would they do this? If the first employer dismisses the 'surplus' employees well in advance of the date of the transfer, he will have to pay them a redundancy payment. If the second employer, the transferee, dismisses them he will have to pay compensation for unfair dismissal.

In **The Secretary of State for Employment *v* Spence [1986] ICR 651** it was held that the employees, who were dismissed three hours before a transfer, were not employed 'immediately before' the transfer and had no protection under the Regulations. The Court of Appeal stated that only employees employed in the undertaking up to the point of, or immediately before, the transfer will be transferred and covered by Regulation 5.

Tribunals were unhappy about colluding employers being able to avoid the effect of Regulations 5 and 8 by dismissing some of the workforce early, before the date of the transfer. There has been an important House of Lords decision which to some extent restores protection to a dismissed employee. In **Litster *v* Forth Dry Dock) Engineering Co Ltd [1989] IRLR 161** Forth Dry Dock went into receivership in September 1983. Forth Estuary Engineering Ltd was formed in order to acquire the business of Forth Dry Dock. The transfer of the business from Forth Dry Dock to Forth Estuary was to take effect at 4.30 pm on 6 February 1984. At 3.30 pm on that day Forth Dry Dock dismissed the entire workforce with immediate effect. Within 48 hours Forth Estuary began to recruit a new, but similarly sized, workforce at lower wages. Only three of the former workers successfully obtained employment with Forth Estuary. The Scottish Industrial Tribunal found that Litster had been unfairly dismissed and that the Regulations applied to his dismissal. Accordingly, the transferee, Forth Estuary, was liable to pay compensation to him. However, the Court of Session, following the decision in the *Spence* case, disagreed with the tribunal and stated that 'even one hour before the transfer' was enough to prevent an employee being employed 'immediately before' the transfer. Litster appealed to the House of Lords.

The House of Lords overturned the decision of the Court of Session. Their

Lordships held that the Transfer of Undertakings Regulations had to be construed to give effect to the UK's obligation under the EC Directive on Acquired Rights of workers on transfer of undertakings, as interpreted by a recent European Court of Justice decision. The Regulations had to be read to give effect to the European Directive. Accordingly, Regulation 5, which refers to 'a person being employed immediately before the transfer', should now read as if there were inserted immediately after these words the phrase 'or would have been so employed if he had not been unfairly dismissed in the circumstances described in Regulation 8'. As the principal reason for the dismissal of Litster and the others had been the transfer of the business to Forth Estuary, Litster had the benefit of the 1981 Regulations and could pursue a remedy against the transferee, Forth Estuary.

This means that the *Spence* case will not apply to pre-transfer dismissals unless it is a dismissal that is not automatically unfair under Regulation 8 (see below) or unless it was dismissal not connected with the transfer, like misconduct.

Note that pension rights are excluded from the TUPE Regulations. In **Adams and others *v* Lancashire County Council and BET Catering Services Ltd [1996] IRLR 154** the Council had it own catering service. Mrs Adams and her colleagues were employed as catering assistants. They were employed on low rates of pay but were entitled to join the local government pension scheme. In 1993 the Council put the school catering service out to tender. BET won the contract and Mrs Adams and the others were transferred to their employment. BET had a pension scheme but it only covered employees earning at least £15 000 and Mrs Adams was excluded from membership. The High Court held that the exclusion of pension rights from the TUPE Regulations is consistent with the provisions of the Acquired Rights Directive and Mrs Adams was not entitled to membership of BET's pension scheme. Furthermore, member states are only under a duty to provide protection in respect of pension rights which have accrued during the period of service with the transferor.

Regulation 8 provides that there is automatically unfair dismissal if an employee is dismissed, either before or after a relevant transfer, if the transfer is the principal reason for dismissal. Employees still need two years' continuous service to claim unfair dismissal There is an exception to this where the reason for dismissal is an 'economic, technical or organisational reason' entailing changes in the workforce of either the transferor or the transferee, either before or after the relevant transfer. Then the dismissal is to be regarded as being for some other substantial reason which could justify the dismissal subject to the 'reasonableness test'. The exception appears to take away the special protection (automatically unfair) that has been given by this Regulation because the new employer might very well want to cut down the number of staff – this would result in dismissals arising from the transfer – but he would argue that it was to cut costs and is therefore an economic reason. However, note that the employer can only rely on the exception if it entails changes in the workforce (ie dismissals) but not if it entails changing the terms and conditions of service which result in the employees claiming constructive dismissal. An employee's right to resign and claim constructive dismissal is preserved if there is a substantial change in his new working conditions which is to his detriment.

Regulation 10 states that 'long enough' before a relevant transfer to enable the employer of any affected employees to consult all the persons who are appropriate representatives of any of those affected employees, the employer must inform those representatives:

1 the fact that a relevant transfer is to take place;
2 when approximately this will happen and the reason for it;
3 the legal, economic and social implications of the transfer for the employees;
4 the measures which the employer envisages will be taken (or not taken) in connection with the transfer in connection with the employees;
5 if the employer is the transferor, the measures which the transferee envisages will be taken in relation to those of the transferor's employees who become employees of the transferee after the transfer or if no measures are to be taken, that fact.

Affected employees are any employees who may be affected by the transfer or measures taken because of it. Even if only one employee is affected, the employer's duty to consult will apply. Affected employees will usually be employees of the transferor but if the employees of the transferee are going to have, for example, changes to their contracts or working conditions then the transferee employer must consult and provide information for his employees. Regulation 10 also provides that the transferee must give the transferor such information at such time as will enable the transferor to perform its duty to inform his affected employees about the measures envisaged by the transferee.

The Collective Redundancies and Transfers of Undertakings (Protection of Emploment) Regulations 1995 amended Regulation 10 after 1 March 1996 so that all employers must consult appropriate representatives, that is either the representatives of recognised independent trade unions or elected employee representatives. Under Regulation 10(2A) of the TUPE Regulations, if there is a recognised trade union, the employer may choose whether to consult the elected representatives or representatives of the recognised union. Alternatively, the employer might consult a recognised trade union for one group of employees and elected representatives for another group who are not represented by a recognised trade union.

The information which is given to the appropriate representatives must be given to each of them by being delivered to them or sent by post. The duty to consult the appropriate representatives is 'with a view to seeking their agreement to measures to be taken'. The employer must consider any representations made by the appropriate employees and reply to them. If the employer rejects any representations he must state his reasons.

The only defence an employer might have is 'the special circumstances defence' which is the same for the statutory duty for consultation on impending redundancies (see p. 432). The remedies available for breach of the information and consultation requirements under Regulation 10 are the same as those available for non-compliance under s 188 of TULR(C)A 1992 (see p. 432), i.e., a complaint to an industrial tribunal and possibly appropriate compensation in the form of a protective award – maximum four weeks' pay. The new amendments to the TUPE Regulations give an employee the right to enforce a protective award against the transferor and this right does transfer under Regulation 5.

DISMISSAL IN CONNECTION WITH A STRIKE OR INDUSTRIAL ACTION

Before we look at the remedies for unfair dismissal, there is this final reason for dismissal to be mentioned. Under common law, striking is a material breach of the contract of employment by the employee which justifies the employer in dismissing him. Under statute, there is no right to strike or to take industrial action in the UK and a dismissed employee has only limited protection against selective dismissals.

Under the Trade Union and Labour Relations (Consolidation) Act 1992 s 238, an Industrial Tribunal has no jurisdiction to decide whether the dismissal was fair or unfair unless it is shown:

1 that one or more employees of the same employer have not been dismissed although they took part in the strike or industrial action; *or*
2 that any such employee who was dismissed was offered re-engagement within three months of the complainant's dismissal but the complainant was not offered re-engagement.

In short, provided the employer sacks all those who are on strike on the day of the dismissal, and does not offer to re-engage some of them within the next three months, the industrial tribunal has no jurisdiction to hear complaints of unfair dismissal. After the three months, the employer can safely re-engage whom he pleases.

Note that originally the restrictions on selective dismissals applied equally to official and unofficial strike or industrial action. The Trade Union and Labour Relations (Consolidation) Act 1992 s 237 provides that an employee who is selectively dismissed while participating in *unofficial* industrial action cannot claim unfair dismissal. Industrial action will be unofficial if it is not authorised or endorsed by a trade union.

REMEDIES

If the applicant is successful in claiming unfair dismissal, the final stage for the tribunal is to decide on the appropriate remedy.

There are three possible remedies. The primary remedy is re-employment. The tribunal must explain to the employee what orders for reinstatement or re-engagement can be made and ask him whether he wants such an order. There are three matters for the tribunal to consider:

1 Does the applicant want re-employment?
2 Is it practicable for the employer to comply with an order of re-employment?
3 Did the employee contribute to his own dismissal?

Having considered these matters, the tribunal either makes an order for reinstatement or re-engagement. If not, the tribunal will consider an award of compensation.

Reinstatement

The ERA s 114 defines reinstatement as 'an order that the employer shall treat the complainant in all respects as if he had not been dismissed'. The employee will get his job back without suffering any loss. The order will specify what arrears of pay are due to the employee and also any rights or privileges which include seniority and pension rights to be restored to him and any wage rises which he has missed because of his absence.

Re-engagement

The ERA s 115 describes re-engagement as an order that the employee is offered a job 'comparable to that from which he was dismissed, or other suitable employment'. With this kind of order, the tribunal has discretion as to whether to award arrears of pay or not, and so if the employee has contributed in any way to his own dismissal, he might not be awarded back pay.

Where the employer has appointed a permanent replacement for the dismissed employee, that fact will not be taken into account by the tribunal unless the employer can show that it was not practicable for him to have the dismissed employee's work done without engaging a permanent replacement.

Non-compliance with an order for reinstatement or re-engagement

Provided the employer cannot show that it was not practicable to comply with the order for reinstatement or re-engagement:

1 If such an order is made but is only partially complied with, the employee can return to the tribunal and seek compensation for any loss he has suffered as a result.
2 If an order is made but the employer does not comply with it at all to re-employ the complainant, then the tribunal will make an award of compensation calculated in the usual way (basic award + compensatory award) and will also make an additional award of compensation calculated in the following way:

   (a) Where the dismissal was an act of sex or racial discrimination, the additional award will be not less than 26 nor more than 52 weeks' pay (limit on a week's pay – £210).
   (b) Where the dismissal was for any other reason, the additional award will be not less than 13 nor more than 26 weeks' pay (unless the dismissal was for trade union reasons, when a special award will be made as we will see later).

Compensation

Compensation is the most common remedy and consists of a basic award and a compensatory award.

The basic award

This award effectively represents the employee's accrued redundancy rights. The amount takes into account the number of years an employee has been continuously employed, starting at the end of that period and working backwards (to a maximum of 20 years' service). Within that period the rates are:

1 One and a half week's pay for each year in which the employee was the age of 41 and above.
2 One week's pay for each year in which the employee was between the ages of 22 and 40.
3 Half a week's pay for each year in which the employee was 21 or under.

At present, the maximum weekly earnings taken into account are £210 and any amount over that figure is disregarded. The payment is reduced by 1/12 for every month of work after the employee's 64th birthday. Where the reason for dismissal was for trade union reasons under TULR(C) Act 1992 ss 152 and 153 or the reason for dismissal is one specified in the ERA ss 100, 102 or 103, the minimum basic award is £2770. The amount of the basic award may be reduced if the employee has unreasonably refused an offer of re-employment or if his conduct has contributed to his dismissal.

Compensatory award

This will be the amount that the tribunal considers just and equitable in all the circumstances, having regard to the loss sustained by the employee up to the present maximum of £11 300. The tribunal might take into account the following:

(a) The immediate loss of earnings up to the date of the hearing.
(b) The future loss of earnings. If the employee has found another job, then there will be no sum under this heading. If he has not, then the tribunal has to consider local employment conditions and how long the employee is likely to be out of work.
(c) The loss of benefits. This could include pension rights and other fringe benefits.
(d) The loss of his employment protection rights.
(e) The expenses to look for work.
(f) The manner of the dismissal. The tribunal will not consider the employee's hurt feelings but it will consider whether the dismissal was carried out in a way that makes the employee less attractive to other employers and consequently it will be harder for him to find another job.
(g) The tribunal may reduce the compensatory award if it considers that the employee's conduct has contributed to his dismissal.

The special award

This award is added to the basic and compensatory award where the dismissal is found to be unfair on the grounds of trade union membership or activities under TULR(C) Act ss 152 and 153 or where the employee was dismissed for health and safety activities under the ERA s 100 or carrying out his duties under the ERA s 102 (trustee of a pension scheme) or under the ERA s 103 (an employee representative):

(i) If the tribunal does not order re-employment, then the special award is one week's pay multiplied by 104 or £13 775 whichever is the larger sum but up to a maximum of £27 500.
(ii) If the tribunal orders re-employment and the employer does not comply with the order, then the special award is one week's pay multiplied by 156 or £20 600, whichever is the larger sum and this time there is no maximum figure.

When calculating the special award there is no maximum weekly pay.

QUESTIONS

1 Explain the difference between an action for wrongful dismissal and a claim for unfair dismissal.

2 If an employer can show that his reason for dismissing an employee is one of the potentially fair reasons listed in the Employment Rights Act 1996 s 98, explain what factors a tribunal would take into account in deciding whether the employer acted reasonably or unreasonably in treating his reason as justifying the dismissal of the employee.

3 Clarence has been a reporter with the newspaper *The Daily Blast* for the past four years. His employers have just discovered that, last week in court, Clarence was found guilty of gross indecency in a public place. His sentence was probation for one year. Everyone at work is talking about the matter. His employers are wondering if they have grounds for dismissal in these circumstances. Advise them.

4 Boxit Ltd have been having problems with absenteeism at work and they have asked your advice as to whether they can fairly dismiss three of their staff in the following circumstances:

(a) Jones is 52 and has worked as a warehouseman with the company for 15 years. He works in a very dusty warehouse. As a result of chronic bronchitis, he has been off work six times in the past three years. Each time he has been absent for about a month and his doctor has advised him that the conditions in the warehouse are aggravating his illness. He has now been off work for two months and this is causing staffing difficulties in the warehouse.
(b) Jane is 40 and has been with the company for 18 months as sales manager.

Recently she had a heart attack and the latest report from her doctor states that she is unlikely to be fit for work for another four months.

(c) Duncan, who is 25, has worked in the office for four years. He is frequently off sick, always for different ailments and he always has produced a sick line when required. The company are introducing a new computerised system in the office and Duncan's manager feels that he can no longer rely on him to be there to assist at this crucial time.

5 Joan has worked for Bloggs & Co for ten years. Last year Bloggs & Co introduced a no smoking policy after a period of consultation with the staff. Seventy per cent of staff were in favour of introducing such a policy – all staff were invited to comment on the proposed changes but none did. For a year, staff have only been permitted to smoke in certain designated areas. Now smoking is expressly forbidden anywhere in the building. The penalty for being found smoking is dismissal. Joan tried for a fortnight to get through her working day without smoking. She couldn't and has resigned claiming constructive dismissal. Advise Bloggs & Co.

6 As one response to the problem of minor theft from the company, the Managing Director had resolved in October that senior management and supervisors would spend one hour per week on duty at the staff exit checking that staff were not leaving the premises with unauthorised goods. Most managers co-operated with the system apart from two who said it was 'beneath their dignity to be asked to carry out such duties'. Two supervisors refused stating that 'such duties were not part of their job description'. The Managing Director was annoyed that not all managers and supervisors had obeyed his instructions and ordered that 'all staff not complying with his instructions would have their salary cut by 'one hours wages per week'. He never carried out this threat and the duties were suspended after Christmas but the Managing Director has stated that when they are reintroduced in October any manager or supervisor refusing to comply must realise that their work will be regarded as voluntary and no salary will be paid to them.

Advise the managers and supervisors as to the legal position.

REDUNDANCY

The right to a statutory redundancy payment was introduced by the Redundancy Payments Act 1965. This Act has now been repealed and the law is to be found in the Employment Rights Act 1996 and the Trade Union and Labour Relations (Consolidation) Act 1992. The policy behind the early legislation was to aid the elimination of restrictive practices and overmanning with the hope that this would help the movement of labour from declining to expanding areas of the economy.

The interaction of the law relating to redundancy and the law relating to unfair dismissal

The two concepts of unfair dismissal and redundancy often overlap and a dismissal for redundancy may also amount to unfair dismissal. It is quite common for an employer to maintain that the dismissal was for redundancy and be prepared to make a redundancy payment. Then he finds that the employee is arguing that it was an unfair redundancy or that the dismissal was for a different reason and unfair. This is because there is an advantage for the employee if the dismissal is found to be unfair, as the employee can seek the remedy of re-employment or compensation. The remedy of compensation is potentially and financially far greater than a redundancy payment.

It was explained that under the TULR(C) Act 1992 s 153 where other employees in similar posts have not been made redundant and the reason for selecting the employee for redundancy is for trade union membership or activities, the dismissal is automatically unfair.

Also, it was explained on p. 411 that under the ERA 1996 s 105, where other employees in similar posts have not been made redundant and the reason the employee has been selected for redundancy is either because the employee was carrying out the functions of a trustee of an occupational pension scheme or an employee representative or for health and safety reasons or the employee had asserted a statutory right – the dismissal is automatically unfair. Also if the employee has been selected because she is pregnant or on maternity leave, her dismissal will automatically be unfair (ERA s 99).

The other way a dismissal for redundancy can give rise to a claim for unfair dismissal is under ERA s 98(2). Redundancy is a potentially fair reason for dismissal but, whether or not there is an agreed procedure, the employee may still challenge the fairness of his dismissal for redundancy by claiming that the employer had not acted reasonably in carrying out the dismissal. While applying the 'reasonableness test' (s 98(4)), the tribunal could decide that the method of selection was unfair, or that the employer failed to adopt proper procedures and did not warn or consult, or that the employer failed to make reasonable efforts to look for alternative employment for the employee.

In this chapter we now examine the law relating to redundancy payments where the dismissal has not been unfair. When a redundancy situation arises, there are five areas which the employer must carefully consider:

1 Who qualifies to claim a redundancy payment?
2 Does the situation satisfy the definition of 'redundancy'?
3 Can the employer avoid making a redundancy payment by offering to renew the employee's contract or offering suitable alternative employment?
4 Has the employer fulfilled his statutory duties of notification and consultation under the Trade Union and Labour Relations (Consolidation) Act 1992 ss 188–198?
5 The calculation of a redundancy payment.

Before looking at these five areas, note that, in an industrial tribunal hearing, where the application is for a redundancy payment, the employee is assisted, in that the presumption is that the dismissal was for redundancy reasons and the onus of proving otherwise is on the employer. (For example, the employer might want to contest the redundancy claim by showing that he had a fair reason for dismissing the employee and so avoid having to make a redundancy payment.) However, if the employee is claiming unfair dismissal, there is no such presumption. The onus is on the employer to show that his reason for dismissal was one of the potentially fair reasons under the ERA s 98 and, if he states that the reason was redundancy, then he must show that the reason satisfies the definition of redundancy in ERA s 139.

Now to proceed to examine the main points of redundancy.

Who qualifies to bring a claim for a redundancy payment?

1 Only employees can claim a redundancy payment – not independent contractors.
2 The employee must have been continuously employed for two years ending with the relevant date, which is the date on which termination takes effect (if notice is given, it is the date on which that notice expires).
3 The employee must be at least 20 years or over. This is because the ERA states that the years prior to 18 are not taken into account for redundancy purposes, so the two years' continuous service must start at 18.
4 The employee cannot claim redundancy once he or she has reached retirement age for employees in that business. The Employment Rights Act 1966 s 156 makes the upper age of entitlement for redundancy pay for men and women as age 65 *or* the normal retirement age for the occupation concerned if that is less than 65.
5 Certain employees are excluded from claiming the statutory redundancy payment – share fishermen: certain Crown employees and office holders.
6 Also excluded are employees who are employed under a fixed term contract for more than two years and who have agreed in writing to exclude their right to a redundancy payment.
7 The claim for redundancy must be brought to the tribunal within six months beginning on the relevant date.

Note that in the past part-time employees had to have five years' continuous service before they could claim unfair dismissal or redundancy. The law was changed by the Employment Protection (Part-time Employees) Regulations 1995. These Regulations have been repealed and replaced by the Employment Rights Act 1996. Part-time employees only need two years' continuous service to qualify for a redundancy payment.

The employee must be dismissed

In order to bring a claim for a redundancy payment, the employee must establish that he has been dismissed and his dismissal is **one of the three forms of dismissal laid down in s 136 ERA**. These are the same definitions of dismissal that an employee had to satisfy in order to claim unfair dismissal. They are that either the employee's contract was terminated by his employer with or without notice, or his fixed-term contract expired without renewal, or that he was constructively dismissed.

A case on constructive dismissal and a redundancy situation is **Marriott *v* Oxford and District Co-op Society [1970] 1 QB 186**. Marriott was employed by the Society for seven years as a foreman. Then the Society found that they had insufficient work for him. His position of foreman was redundant and they offered him the position of supervisor at £3 less per week. He protested and tried to find work elsewhere. Later he was told that his wages would only be reduced by £1. Again, he protested but did not leave immediately. However, he eventually did three or four weeks after the reduction in wages.

The question was 'Had M been constructively dismissed?' as he had to be dismissed to be entitled to a redundancy payment. The court decided that the unilateral changes in his contract of employment were brought about by declining demand and that he had not agreed to these changes. The changes amounted to a repudiatory breach of the contract by the employer which justified Marriott in leaving and claiming constructive dismissal. The court also said that he should not lose his redundancy pay because he stayed on for four weeks as he protested all the time.

Note: It is very important that the employee is dismissed and his dismissal satisfies the definition in s 136 because, if he leaves on his own accord, knowing that redundancies are pending or having heard that he will be made redundant, then he will not be able to claim a redundancy payment.

However, under s 136(2) ERA, once an employee has been given notice by his employer, he can give his employer written counter-notice of his intention to leave earlier (for example, if he gets another job). If the employer accepts his counter-notice then the employee is still to be taken as dismissed and can claim a redundancy payment.

Being laid off or put on short-time working

If an employee always had to wait until he was actually dismissed, this could cause hardship in situations where work continues but at a reduced level. Accordingly, s 148 ERA provides that, even where there is no dismissal, an employee can claim a redundancy payment if he has been laid-off or kept on short-time for four consecutive weeks or for any six weeks in 13. In this context, 'laid off' means 'no work and no pay' and 'short-time' means that the employee is working fewer hours and receiving less than half a week's pay.

The employee must serve written notice on the employer that he intends to claim redundancy. An employer can resist such a claim if he produces a written counter-notice, within seven days of receiving the employee's notice, if he has reasonable grounds for thinking that full-time work is reasonably likely to resume within four weeks and that it will continue for at least three months. If the employer does not withdraw this counter-notice the employee is not entitled to a redundancy payment except in accordance with a decision of an industrial tribunal.

Note: Employers must remember that they cannot lay off staff or put them on short-time unless there is an express term in the contract of employment covering this, or unless such a term is implied by custom and practice (for example, in the construction industry). If there is no such term the employee could claim constructive dismissal.

Definition of redundancy

As explained at the beginning of this chapter, it is sometimes very important to establish (or to prove the contrary) that the situation is one of redundancy and that it satisfies the statutory definition. Section 139 ERA defines redundancy. There is redundancy under the Act (a) if the employee loses his job because his employer has ceased or intends to cease carrying out his business for the purposes for which the employee was employed by him, or he has ceased or intends to cease carrying on his business in the place where the employee was so employed; *or* (b) if the requirements of that business for the employee to carry out work of a particular kind, or for the employee to carry out work of a particular kind in the place where he was so employed, have ceased or diminished or are expected to cease or diminish.

What does the definition mean? Very simply it covers three situations:

1 the business is closing down;
2 the business is moving;
3 surplus labour.

Let us now examine each situation in turn.

The business is closing down

It could be completely closing down or perhaps just part of the organisation like a branch or a department is closing. The work 'ceasing' could mean either permanently or temporarily.

The business is moving

If the place of work is moving to a new location, very often the employees do not wish to move. Whether or not they can claim redundancy will depend on two factors. Firstly, does the contract of employment have a mobility clause and, secondly, if there is no mobility clause in the contract, how far away are the new premises?

If there is a mobility clause and the employee refuses to move, then the employee can be dismissed and he cannot claim redundancy. In fact, it is most unlikely that he could even claim unfair dismissal because the refusal will amount to a breach of contract by the employee and, provided the employer acts reasonably, this gives the employer grounds for dismissal for misconduct under s 98.

If there is no mobility clause and the employer moves the employee's place of work, whether the move is sufficient to constitute redundancy or not will be a question of fact and will depend on the distance between the old and the new premises and the resulting inconvenience for the employee.

In **O'Brien** *v* **Associated Fire Alarms [1969] 1 All ER 93** the employee was employed to supply and fit fire alarms in the Cheshire and Liverpool area. He was based in Liverpool, travelling daily to each assignment. When work declined in the Liverpool area, the company proposed that he should work in Barrow-in-Furness, some 120 miles away. O'Brien refused, as it would have meant working away from home and he was dismissed. The court held that there was no mobility clause in his contract of employment and nothing that implied a mobility clause of that nature. His refusal was justified and he was entitled to redundancy pay.

In **Jones *v* Associated Tunnelling [1981] IRLR 477** Jones was employed in 1964 to work at Chatterley Colliery some two miles from his home. In 1969 he was moved to Hem Heath Colliery some 12 miles from his home. He worked there until 1980 when he was offered work at another place easily accessible from his home. He refused and claimed redundancy. There was no mention in his contract as to the place of work. The court held that a contract could not be silent on such a matter and, if there was no express term, the court must imply a term which represents what it saw as an acceptable compromise. They held that the right term to imply in all the circumstances of this case was that Jones could be required to work at any place within reasonable daily commuting distance from his home. He was not entitled to a redundancy payment.

Surplus labour

In this situation, the employer requires fewer employees to do the existing work. This could be either because the business is declining or because the business is expanding but they have to reorganise the work to be more efficient or to introduce new technology. As we will see, it is easier to show that a redundancy situation exists when the business is declining. There are three possible situations:

1 **If an employee is dismissed and not replaced** and his work is done by the remaining workforce, then this will usually amount to redundancy.

   In **Hindle *v* Percival Boats [1969] 1 All ER 836** an elderly craftsman was employed to repair wooden boats. The amount of work declined because of the introduction of fibreglass. He could not adapt to the new work and, after a work study exercise was carried out, he was dismissed for being 'too good and too slow'. He was not replaced and the other employees did his work, working overtime. In spite of this, he was not entitled to redundancy. The court held in these circumstances that the reason for dismissal was due to a kind of incompetence. (This case was heard before unfair dismissal was introduced.)

2 **Redundancy and changed working obligations**. There is a distinction between a reorganisation which gives rise to a redundancy situation and a reorganisation to improve efficiency. Very often it depends on what the tribunal considered was the employer's motive for the changes. The former situation allows the dismissed employees to claim redundancy, whilst the latter protects the business. The idea is that a job may remain, in principle, the same despite the impact of the reorganisation upon the method of its performance. This does not give rise to a redundancy situation as long as the employer can show that he requires the work of the employees in question.

   In **Johnson *v* Nottinghamshire Combined Police Authority [1974] ICR 170** two female clerks worked at a police station from 9.30 to 5.30, Monday to Friday. The Authority proposed that they should work separate shifts: one from 8.00 to 3.00 and the other 1.00 to 8.00 six days a week, exchanging rotas each week. This involved working the same number of hours a week and there would be no change in the actual work. The women refused, were dismissed and claimed redundancy. The Court of Appeal said that the question to ask was, 'Is the change due to a redundancy situation or not?' If it is not, then the employee is not entitled to a redundancy payment. If, as in this case, the employer requires the same number of employees to do the same tasks and the reorganisation is in the interests of efficiency, then it does not give rise to redundancy (but possibly unfair dismissal if the employer is acting unreasonably).

In **Lesney Products & Co** *v* **Nolan [1977] ICR 235** because of falling sales the employer eliminated the night shift and reorganised the single day shift with overtime into a double day shift. All those who had been working the existing day shift were offered employment on the double day shift. Those who refused, including Mrs N, were dismissed. The issue is to decide whether the reorganisation was for efficiency or because there was less work. The employers proved that there was still the same amount of work for daytime workers and in fact they had replaced those employees who had left or had been dismissed. There was no work for the night shift. Accordingly, only night shift workers were entitled to redundancy. Day shift workers, including Mrs N, were not entitled to redundancy.

Note: It is clear that many decisions like these have allowed management to change unilaterally their employees' terms and conditions without satisfying the statutory meaning of dismissal. An employee might think that if he does not agree to the changes in his contract, he could resign and claim constructive dismissal. However, he might find that he is denied a redundancy payment because the reason for dismissal is not redundancy as narrowly construed by the judges. When an employer is reorganising his business for reasons of efficiency, he will dismiss the employees who do not agree to the changes and argue that this is a potentially fair reason for dismissal and that it is some other substantial reason justifying dismissal (s 98).

3 **If an employee is dismissed and replaced by a self-employed person**, then it is clear that the requirements of the business for employees to carry out work of a particular kind have ceased. Thus an employer could dismiss his joiner and immediately employ him to do the same work but as an independent contractor. In this situation he can claim redundancy. However, if an employee is dismissed and his job is done by a new employee, then it cannot be said that the requirements of the business have ceased. So there is no redundancy.

Thus in **Vaux's Brewery** *v* **Ward (1969) 7 KIR 309** the character of a pub was changed to attract a younger, trendier clientele. They dismissed a middle-aged barmaid and replaced her with a younger girl as they wanted a 'bunny girl' type of barmaid to fit their new image. The older barmaid was held not to have been dismissed for reasons of redundancy. (This case was heard before the unfair dismissal legislation was introduced – now she could claim unfair dismissal. The employer would have to give the reason as 'a substantial reason justifying dismissal', then the tribunal would have to decide if the employer acted reasonably, etc.)

The employer can avoid paying redundancy if he offers to renew the contract or re-engage the employee

If before the ending of a person's employment, an employer (or the new owner of the business) makes an offer either to renew the contract of employment or to re-engage the employee under a new contract and this contract is to take effect either immediately when the old contract ends or no more than four weeks after this date, **then an employee may lose any right to redundancy** (s 138 ERA) if he unreasonably refuses it.

The new contract must either contain the same terms as before or, if the offer is **alternative work**, it must be of **suitable** employment and, in either case, if the employee takes the work or **unreasonably refuses** the offer, he will not be entitled to a redundancy payment. The onus of proof is on the employer to prove both the suitability of the offer and the unreasonableness if the employee refuses it. So, what is 'suitable' and 'unreasonable'?

The suitability of the alternative employment must be assessed objectively, taking into account the following factors: the type of work; pay; status; overtime opportunities; shift work; fringe benefits; travelling time. (See *Marriott* v *Oxford & District Co-op Society* [1969].)

In **Taylor *v* Kent County Council [1969] 2 QB 560** a headmaster, who was made redundant, was offered a post at his previous salary, but as a supply teacher. The resulting loss of authority and status was held to be an important factor even though the pay was the same and so he could refuse the offer without losing his redundancy payment.

In **Nairn *v* Ayrshire and Arran Health Board 1990 Glasgow IT** Mrs Nairn was a 50-year-old, hospital hairdresser. When she was made redundant, she was offered the job as clerical officer in a hospital's medical records department for which she would receive training. Although the post had a higher wage and was eight hours a week less than her job as a hairdresser, Mrs Nairn turned it down as unsuitable because it was totally outwith any of her previous experience and it would have meant loss of freedom and status. She also felt that at her age she could not be retrained. The tribunal held that the alternative job offer was completely different from her previous job as hairdresser and that she was reasonably entitled to consider it unsuitable and should be awarded redundancy pay.

Acceptance – trial period

An employee who has been offered alternative work might worry that if he accepts it, then he will have lost his right to possibly claim his redundancy repayment.

Section 138 ERA allows the employee time to make a decision by giving him a trial period of four weeks (or longer if agreed in writing between the parties) to try out the new conditions of work to see if they are acceptable. If, during the trial period, the employee or the employer terminates the contract for any reason arising from the change, then the employee shall be treated for redundancy purposes as having been dismissed on the date the previous contract ended. It might still have to be decided if his refusal was unreasonable or the offer suitable.

Refusal must be reasonable. The factors that tribunals can take into account can be more personal than the factors for suitability of the job. The test is subjective and the tribunal can consider whether it was unreasonable for this particular employee to turn down a job which might be quite suitable for another employee. So, an employee might reasonably refuse an identical job to the one he had because the new job involved moving. He could argue either that he could not move because of his own ill health or because of matters concerning his dependent relatives or perhaps because he has just bought a house, or that his children's schooling might be seriously affected, or even because he has got another job.

In **Thomas Wragg & Sons** *v* **Wood [1976] IRLR 145** the employee was given notice on 24 October that he was dismissed for redundancy which was to take effect from 6 December. Wood looked for and obtained another job. On 5 December his employers offered him an alternative suitable job which was to start on the 9th. He refused their offer. The EAT held that Wood did not act unreasonably in refusing the offer and was still entitled to his redundancy payment.

In **Fuller** *v* **Stephanie Bowman (Sales) Ltd [1977] IRLR 87** Fuller rejected an offer of suitable alternative employment because the premises of the new job were upstairs from a sex shop in Soho. The tribunal, while recognising that a strong objection to any association with commercialised sex could be a valid reason for refusing otherwise suitable employment, concluded that her objection was not sufficient on the facts of the case. One of the facts relied on by the tribunal was that Fuller, a lady of 53, was unlikely to be mistaken for a prostitute while walking to work.

Redundancy, misconduct and industrial action

Section 140(1) ERA states that if an employee, who is aware that redundancies are probably pending (but notice of dismissal has not been given), commits an act of misconduct which entitles the employer to dismiss him without notice (ie the act justifies summary dismissal) and the employer does dismiss him with or without notice, the employee loses his right to a redundancy payment. This misconduct could be stealing or disobedience but it could also be going on strike.

Section 140(2) ERA is designed to protect an employee who goes on strike in protest against the redundancy notices. The subsection distinguishes strikes from other forms of misconduct. If he goes on strike after the notices are issued, then he can still claim his redundancy payment. The section operates only for a strike which takes place during the employee's period of statutory notice and not before.

Section 140(3) ERA states that if notice of redundancy is given and, during the period of notice, the employee commits an act of misconduct other than going on strike for which the employer is entitled to dismiss him, an industrial tribunal may, in so far as it is just and equitable to do so, award all or part of the redundancy payment.

Statutory procedures for handling collective redundancies (20 or more redundancies)

The Trade Union and Labour Relations (Consolidation) Act 1992 ss 188–198

These procedures were amended by the Trade Union Reform and Employment Rights Act 1993 in order to implement the Amendment to the Collective Redundancies Directive which was adopted by the EC Council of Ministers in June 1992 and which had to be implemented by June 1994 by the member states. In 1994 the European Commission brought infringement proceedings against the UK Government for its failure to implement fully the relevant Directives on Collective Redundancies. This was because the procedures for consultation at that time in the UK only applied where the employer had chosen to recognise a trade union.

As a consequence of the ECJ's ruling the government introduced the Collective Redundancies and Transfer of Undertakings (Protection of Employment) (Amendment) Regulations 1995. They apply to redundancies and transfers taking place after 1 March 1996. The Regulations amend the consultation provisions of the Trade Union and Labour Relations (Consultation) Act s 188 and the TUPE Regulations 1981 and provide **that employers must consult 'appropriate representatives' of the employees affected by redundancies or transfers.** 'Appropriate representatives' are either representatives of a recognised independent trade union or employee representatives elected by the employees affected. The employer has a choice as to whether to consult with union representatives or employee representatives and employers who recognise a trade union or unions can decide to by-pass the union and consult with elected employee representatives instead.

The Regulations do not require the elections of employee representatives when there is no redundancy or transfer situation. It is sufficient for an employer to invite employees to elect representatives when required and give enough time for elections before the consultation period. The Regulations do not specify how many employee representatives should be elected nor do they specify a procedure for the elections.

Note that the Trade Union and Labour Relations (Consolidation) Act 1992 s 195 states that for the purposes of this duty to consult, dismissal for redundancy means dismissal for a reason or reasons not related to the individual concerned. (This could cover dismissals in connection with a business reorganisation.)

Under the TULR(C) Act 1992 s 188 – as amended, where it is proposed that employees are to be dismissed for redundancy the employer has to consult appropriate representatives of the employees affected by the redundancies.

The duty to consult is restricted to cases where the employer proposes 20 or more redundancies within a period of 90 days at one establishment.

The Act as amended by the Regulations states that the consultation must take place in good time and in particular:

1 where at least 20 but fewer than 100 employees within a period of 90 days or less are to be made redundant, consultation must begin at least 30 days before the first dismissal takes effect; *or*
2 if more than 100 employees are to be dismissed within a period of 90 days or less, then consultation must begin at least 90 days before the first dismissal.

As well as the duty to consult the representatives, the employer also has a duty under s 193 to notify the Secretary of State in writing of his proposals for redundancies within the same periods as above. Failure to notify the Secretary of State is a criminal offence which could render the employer liable to pay a fine of up to £5000.

The employer's duty under s 188 is **to undertake consultation with a view to reaching agreement with the appropriate representatives.** The consultation has to include discussion on ways of:

(a) avoiding dismissals;
(b) reducing the numbers of employees to be dismissed;
(c) mitigating (reducing) the consequences of the dismissals.

The statutory duty is to disclose certain information to the appropriate representatives and receive, consider and reply to their representations. If the employer rejects any of these representations, he must state his reasons in writing.

Section 188 lists the information that the employer shall disclose in writing to the appropriate representatives:

(i) the reasons for his proposals;
(ii) the numbers and descriptions of employees it is proposed to dismiss for redundancy;
(iii) the total number of employees of any such description employed by the employer at the establishment in question;
(iv) the proposed method of selecting the employees to be dismissed;
(v) the proposed method of carrying out the dismissals, with due regard to any agreed procedure, including the period over which the dismissals are to take effect;
(vi) the proposed method of calculating the amount of any redundancy payments to be made if this differs from the statutory scheme.

The employer has only one defence as to why he did not consult and so he does not have to pay the protective award and that is that there were special circumstances which rendered it not reasonably practicable. This will have to be something drastic like an explosion at the place of work or their supplies being unexpectedly stopped. Certainly the circumstances will have to be out of the ordinary, so insolvency will not provide an excuse, as it is usually foreseen. Also, the employer cannot say that the decision to give notice of redundancies was made by a person controlling the employer and that person had not supplied the relevant information to the employer.

Failure by the employer to consult

Under s 189, if the employer fails to comply with s 188 and to consult then a complaint can be made to an industrial tribunal by any employee representative to whom the failure related or in the case of a failure to consult a trade union representative by the trade union. If there are neither employee representatives nor a recognised trade union the complaint can be brought by any of the individual employees who have been or may be dismissed as redundant. Unless the tribunal finds that there were 'special circumstances', it will make a declaration of non-compliance and in addition can make a **protective award**. This is an award of remuneration payable to employees specified in the award to cover a protected period. The protected period shall be the period the tribunal thinks is just and equitable considering the seriousness of the employer's default in not consulting. Where more than 100 employees are to go, it must not exceed 90 days; where at least 20 but less than 100 employees are to go within a 90 day period, it must not exceed 30 days.

The amount of the award is a week's pay for every week of the protected period. If the employer fails to pay the protective award, then the individual employee (not the union nor the employee representative this time) may complain to an industrial tribunal and the employer can be ordered to pay the amount due.

Calculating the redundancy payment

The redundancy payment is calculated in the same way as the basic award for unfair dismissal. This calculation was explained in the last chapter and takes into account the employee's age, length of service up to a maximum of 20 years and his gross weekly pay up to a maximum of £210. One point to note is that the employee's service prior to his 18th birthday does not count for the purpose of calculating length of service for redundancy payments. The employer must give the employee a written explanation as to how the redundancy award is calculated. Failure to do so is a criminal offence.

The National Insurance Fund

The Secretary of State controls and manages the National Insurance Fund. Where an employee claims that he is entitled to a redundancy payment from his employer but, after exhausting all reasonable steps, he has not been paid or the employer is insolvent, he can apply to the Secretary of State for payment. When a payment is made from the fund, then all rights and remedies of the employee transfer to the Secretary of State who may then take steps to recover the amount from the employer.

QUESTIONS

1 Explain the circumstances in which an employee, who has been dismissed for redundancy, might be able to bring a claim for unfair dismissal.

2 (a) Explain which employees qualify and are eligible to claim a redundancy payment.
(b) Are there any circumstances where an employee might be eligible to claim a redundancy payment but be precluded from making such a claim?

3 Tom, Dick, Harry and Ethel have all been served with redundancy notices by their employer, Computer Software Enterprises Ltd. They are all electronic engineers and have worked in the production department for many years. Tom has been offered a lower-paid job as a clerical officer in the legal department. Dick has been offered a similar job, at the same salary, at the firm's other factory, which is 100 miles away. Harry has been offered an alternative job as a salesman. He will be paid commission only on his sales but he will get a company car. Ethel has not been offered any alternative employment and maintains that she was selected for redundancy because she is a shop steward. Advise all four employees as to their legal rights.

4 Your company has a factory employing 2000 people. Demand for your product has declined and it is proposed to make 500 employees redundant. The Board of Directors has asked you whether it is possible to keep the news of the redundancies a secret until the last possible moment. They do not want their competitors or shareholders to hear of the company's problems. Advise the Board.

5 Makem Ltd are closing down their factory. Some of the staff have asked you whether they will be eligible for redundancy payments and, if so, how much they will be due. Neil is 19 and has been continuously employed for two years and earns £70 a week gross. George is 32, has been continuously employed for six years and earns £230 a week gross. Betty is 62 and has been continuously employed for 21 years and earns £130 a week gross. Lesley is 34 and has been employed part-time (8 hours a week) for three years and earns £24 a week.

20 Discrimination and equal pay

THE LAW RELATING TO DISCRIMINATION IN EMPLOYMENT

At common law, an employer is entitled to hire or refuse to hire whomsoever he pleases irrespective of the reasons for his recruitment decisions. However, in the UK statutory constraints are placed on an employer's freedom to hire so as to prevent certain forms of discrimination. While some groups enjoy protection, others do not; for example, it remains lawful to refuse to hire an individual because he is gay. In the case of **R *v* Ministry of Defence ex parte Smith and Ors [1955] IRLR 585** the English Court of Appeal rejected the argument that discrimination against homosexuals fell within the scope of the EC Equal Treatment Directive. The applicants, who were seeking judicial review of the policy preventing homosexuals serving in the armed forces, are to appeal to the House of Lords. However, in the case of **P *v* S and Cornwall County Council ECJ 30 March 1996 case C13/94** Advocate-General Tesauro was of the opinion that the Equal Treatment Directive gives protection to transsexuals who are dismissed because of a sex change. An employer may refuse to employ someone because of his political beliefs. Similarly, it is not unlawful to refuse to employ someone because of their age, unless the refusal also amounts to a form of sex or race discrimination. In mainland Britain, it is not unlawful to refuse to hire someone because of their religion, unless the refusal also amounts to discrimination on grounds of race. Accordingly, in Great Britain a person has no legal remedy if refused employment because he is Roman Catholic. The only part of the UK in which it is unlawful to discriminate on grounds of religion is Northern Ireland. In the UK a person has a legal remedy if discriminated against, only if he is a member of a group which enjoys statutory protection against discrimination.

Persons with criminal convictions

The Rehabilitation of Offenders Act 1974 prevents discrimination in employment against certain individuals who lead reformed lives after being convicted of criminal offences. Certain convictions are said to be 'spent' after a period of time has passed since the conviction, so long as there has been no further conviction in the meantime. The effect of a conviction being spent is that the individual is not required to disclose it to potential employers. However, if a potential employer refuses to employ an individual because of a spent conviction, the Act provides no remedy. Once an individual is in employment, it is automatically unfair to dismiss him because it is discovered that he has a spent conviction. Only certain convictions may be regarded as spent. The rehabilitation period which must elapse before a conviction is spent varies according to the severity of the sentence. Convictions which result in imprisonment for more than two-and-a-half years are never spent.

In addition, it should be noted that the Act does not apply to certain professions. Solicitors, doctors, dentists, accountants, nurses, opticians, dispensing chemists and teachers must disclose convictions to their professional bodies if asked. Applicants for employment in other occupations such as the police force or social work must not lie if asked about previous convictions.

Trade union members

Prior to the coming into force of the Employment Act 1990, a person had no remedy if refused employment because he was a trade union member. The law gave protection to union members only once they were in employment. In terms of provisions now found in the Trade Union and Labour Relations (Consolidation) Act 1992 it is automatically unfair to dismiss a person because of trade union membership or because of participation, at an appropriate time, in trade union activities. Section 146 of the 1992 s 152 Act provides that an employee has the right not to have action short of dismissal taken against him by his employer because of trade union membership or activities. Now, in terms of s 137 of the 1992 Act, a person may also complain to an industrial tribunal if he is refused employment either because he is, or because he is not, a trade union member.

Discrimination on grounds of sex, or race, or because a person is married or disabled

The major pieces of UK anti-discrimination legislation are the Equal Pay Act 1970 as amended, the Sex Discrimination Act 1975 as amended, the Race Relations Act 1976 and the Disability Discrimination Act 1995.

The Equal Pay Act 1970 makes it unlawful to discriminate between men and women in respect of pay and other contractual terms and conditions of employment.

The Sex Discrimination Act 1975 makes it unlawful to discriminate against either men or women, not only in relation to employment but also with regard to training, education, the provision of goods and services and in the disposal and management of premises. The 1975 Act also makes it unlawful to discriminate in relation to employment against married persons.

The Race Relations Act 1976 outlaws racial discrimination in employment, education, training, in the provision of goods and services and in the disposal of premises.

The Disability Discrimination Act 1995 aims to end discrimination against disabled people in employment, in relation to the provision of goods, facilities and services and in the disposal of premises.

It is intended to study the provisions of the legislation only in so far as they relate to employment.

THE SEX DISCRIMINATION ACT 1975

As previously stated, the Sex Discrimination Act 1975 makes it unlawful to discriminate against either men or women because of their sex, not only in relation to employment but also with regard to training, education, the provision of goods and services and in the disposal of premises. Accordingly, banks and building societies must not discriminate in the terms on which loans are offered. A pub cannot insist that women sit at tables if they allow men to be served at the bar. A landlord cannot discriminate when renting out accommodation. The Act also outlaws discrimination against married persons in the area of employment.

The European dimension cannot be ignored when considering the remedies available to people who believe they have been discriminated against because of their sex. The European Directive 76/207/EEC provides for equal treatment as regards access to employment and promotion; training; and working conditions including conditions governing dismissal. UK legislation passed both prior to and since 1976 should be interpreted so as to give effect to the provisions of the Directive.

What is discrimination?

In terms of the Sex Discrimination Act 1975, unlawful discrimination may take one of three forms: Direct Discrimination, Indirect Discrimination and Victimisation.

Direct discrimination – Section 1(1)(a)

There is direct discrimination if a person is treated less favourably than a person of the opposite sex is or would be treated. Direct discrimination may be summed up as *less favourable treatment* because of a person's sex. If a woman telephones a car showroom in response to an advert for a salesperson and is told that she will not be considered because 'selling cars is not a woman's job', that constitutes unlawful direct discrimination.

Where there is direct discrimination, the motive of the employer in treating a woman less favourably than a man is irrelevant. Absence of an intention to discriminate is not a defence. In **Grieg *v* Community Industry [1979] IRLR 158** two women were to join an all-male painting and decorating team as part of a YTS scheme. One of the women dropped out and the employer refused to allow the other woman to start work. He genuinely thought that it would not be in the woman's best interests to work with an all-male team. It was held that because the woman had been treated less favourably, there had been direct discrimination. It was irrelevant that the action had been taken with the best of motives.

Direct discrimination may occur as a consequence of applying generalised sex-based assumptions. It would be unlawful to apply a policy of never hiring young mothers because of the assumption that 'women with young children are always unreliable'. In **Hurley** *v* **Mustoe [1981] IRLR 208** Mrs H applied for a job as a waitress at 'Edward's Bistro'. The manager agreed to give her a one-night trial. Her work that evening was satisfactory but the owner instructed the manager not to employ Mrs H because she had four children. The owner had a policy of not employing women with children because he thought they were unreliable. Mrs H had previously worked for ten years as a waitress and had a good work record. However, the owner made no inquiries into Mrs H's personal work record and based his decision on his assumptions about the reliability of mothers in general. The owner tried to argue that there was no discrimination based on sex because he would have treated the father of young children in the same way. It was held that there was direct sex discrimination. There was no evidence that the owner's policy was aimed at both sexes but rather, the evidence indicated a policy not to employ **women** with children.

Similarly, in **Coleman** *v* **Skyrail Oceanic Ltd [1981] IRLR 398** the dismissal of Mrs C constituted direct sex discrimination. Mrs C was dismissed on the day after she married an employee of a rival travel firm. Both employers were afraid that there might be a breach of confidentiality. Accordingly, it was decided that of the two, Mrs C should be dismissed because 'the husband presumably was the breadwinner'. The English Court of Appeal found that the decision to dismiss Mrs C was based on a discriminatory assumption. Mrs C had been treated less favourably than a man in the same situation would have been treated and had been unlawfully discriminated against.

There has been recent case law in relation to employers' rules on dress codes. Traditionally, tribunals have held that so long as an employer has rules on clothing and appearance for both men and women, then even if the precise rules are different – e.g., women must not wear trousers, men must always wear a collar and tie – there would not be sex discrimination if a woman was dismissed for wearing trousers. This position was established in the case of **Schmidt** *v* **Austicks Bookshops Ltd [1977] IRLR 360** and found favour in the case of **Burrett** *v* **West Birmingham Health Authority [1994] IRLR 7**. In the *Burrett* case a nurse who was disciplined for refusing to wear a cap lost her sex discrimination claim because the requirement to wear a uniform applied equally to male and female nurses, albeit men did not have to wear a frilly cap. The fact that the nurse thought that wearing the cap was demeaning did not amount to less favourable treatment as required by the Act.

In **Smith** *v* **Safeway plc [1995] IRLR 132, [1995] ICR 472** a male employee who was dismissed for refusing to cut his hair was found by the EAT to have been unlawfully discriminated against. S was a delicatessen assistant whose pony tail became too long to keep under his hat. The employer's rule was that men should have tidy hair not below shirt-collar length while women with long hair could wear it clipped back. S lost his case before the industrial tribunal which held that there was no discrimination because there were rules governing the appearance of both women and men, although the rules in the two cases were not the same. However S won on appeal to the EAT which held that the employer could apply rules to both men and women requiring them to present a conventional appearance at work without placing the restriction on hair length for men only. The EAT thought it important to distinguish the situation in *Schmidt* where the restriction applied only whilst at work whereas in the present case the restriction on hair-length had effect at all times. Smith's victory was short lived because on 16 February 1996 the Court of Appeal allowed the Safeway's appeal. Lord Justice Phillips stated that '[i]f discrimination is to be established, it is necessary to show not merely that the sexes are treated differently, but that the treatment accorded to one is less favourable than the treatment accorded to the other.' The court also approved the approach of looking at the overall effect of an appearance code. The company was entitled to apply a dress code to require a conventional appearance and the terms of the code did not have to be identical for men and women. The court of appeal restored the decision of the industrial tribunal.

It has also been established that sexual harassment constitutes direct sex discrimination. In **Strathclyde Regional Council *v* Porcelli [1986] IRLR 134** Mrs P, a lab technician in a school, was driven to request a transfer to another school as a consequence of the behaviour of two male lab technicians. The two male technicians disliked Mrs P and set out to make life at school so unpleasant that she would leave. The men sabotaged her work, let doors slam in her face when she was carrying equipment and threw her personal possessions in the bin. However, some of their behaviour also had sexual overtones. The men used obscene language towards her. One of the men compared Mrs P's body with nude pictures in newspapers, made suggestive remarks and brushed himself against her. Mrs P brought a complaint to an Industrial Tribunal alleging that she had suffered a detriment as a consequence of direct sex discrimination. The industrial tribunal held that had the men disliked a male technician, they would have treated him equally badly. The tribunal dismissed Mrs P's case. However, on appeal, both the Employment Appeal Tribunal and the Inner House of the Court of Session found that there had been unlawful sex discrimination. A man might also have been treated badly but the nature of the unpleasantness would have been different; the sexual element would not have been present. The Regional Council had to pay Mrs P £3000 in compensation. The employer was held liable for the discriminatory acts of the men because no action had been taken when Mrs P complained to management. It should be noted that actual physical contact is not necessary to establish a complaint of sexual harassment.

It should also be noted that on 27 November 1991, the European Commission issued a Recommendation and Code of Practice on the protection of the dignity of women and men at work. It stated that conduct of a sexual nature, or other conduct based on sex affecting the dignity of women and men at work, including conduct of superiors and colleagues, is unacceptable if:

1 the conduct is unwanted, unreasonable and offensive to the recipient;
2 a person's rejection of or submission to such conduct is used as a basis for employment decisions affecting matters such as promotion, continued employment, salary, etc.; and/or
3 such conduct creates an intimidating, hostile or humiliating work environment for the recipient.

The Commission pointed out that such conduct may be in breach of the Equal Treatment Directive 1976. The Recommendation asked member states to implement the Code of Practice in the public sector and to encourage private sector employers to do likewise. The Code of Practice attached to the Recommendation contains policies and procedures which should be adopted by employers in order to ensure that sexual harassment does not occur, or, if it does occur, to ensure that measures are readily available to deal with the problem and prevent it happening again.

It appears that the Recommendation on sexual harassment has been taken into account by tribunals when interpreting the Sex Discrimination Act 1975. It has been established that a single incident can amount to sexual harassment; it is not necessary to establish a continuing course of conduct. In **Insitu Cleaning** *v* **Heads [1995] IRLR 4** the EAT held that a single remark of a sexual nature was sufficient to constitute sexual harassment. The EAT rejected out of hand the employer's argument that the remark could not regarded as 'unwanted conduct' because when it was made the man could not know what the woman's reaction would be. However in a surprising decision in **Stewart** *v* **Cleveland Guest (Engineering) Ltd [1994] IRLR 440** the EAT agreed that there had been no discrimination against a woman whose complaints about the display of nude pin-ups in the workplace had not been taken seriously by her employer. Their finding that she had not been subjected to less favourable treatment because a man could have been equally offended fails to take account of the fact that a woman is more likely to feel degraded or humiliated by such a display.

It should also be noted that tribunals can make a restricted reporting order in sexual misconduct cases. Anyone who then publishes or broadcasts a report which identifies the parties involved commits an offence.

It has now been established that to subject a woman to less favourable treatment because she is pregnant amounts to unlawful direct sex discrimination.

In terms of the Employment Rights Act 1996 s 99, it is automatically unfair to dismiss an employee because she is pregnant or for any reason connected with her pregnancy. However, prior to 19 October 1994, in order to bring an action of unfair dismissal because of pregnancy, a woman had to have two years' continuous service with her employer. A woman who was dismissed because of pregnancy and who did not have two years' service, had to attempt to establish a claim under the Sex Discrimination Act 1975. However, on 19 October 1992, the EC Council of Ministers adopted a Directive on the Protection of Pregnant Workers and the UK Government implemented the Directive by amending the Employment Protection (Consolidation) Act 1978. The relevant provisions are now contained in Employment Rights Act 1996. In so far as dismissal because of pregnancy is concerned, the main change was that pregnant women, irrespective of their length of service, may not be dismissed for reasons connected with their condition. Accordingly, an employee who is dismissed because she is pregnant is no longer required to have two years' continuous service in order to claim unfair dismissal and does not have to attempt to establish a sex discrimination claim.

However, dismissal is not the only 'less favourable treatment' a woman may be subjected to because of her pregnancy. A pregnant employee may be passed over for promotion or denied access to training. In addition a pregnant woman may not be recruited because of her condition. In such situations, a remedy must be sought under the Sex Discrimination Act 1975. Traditionally, sex discrimination claims by pregnant women failed because, since there is no such thing as a pregnant man, a pregnant woman could not show that she had been treated less favourably than a pregnant man would have been treated

More recently, pregnant women have been successful in establishing unlawful direct discrimination as a consequence of their pregnancy. In **Jennings** *v* **The Burton Group 1988** (unreported decision of Edinburgh I.T.) a pregnant employee, who worked in a Burton's store in Edinburgh, was dismissed when she was absent for five weeks because of a threatened miscarriage. She had less than two years' service and therefore could not bring an unfair dismissal claim. She brought a complaint of unlawful sex discrimination and won. Tribunals were now prepared to compare the treatment of a pregnant female employee with how the employer would treat a male employee who is sick or has to go into hospital for an operation. However, many people criticised the approach of comparing a pregnant woman with a sick man.

The matter was thought to have been put beyond doubt as a consequence of a decision of the European Court of Justice in the case of **Dekker** *v* **Stichting Vormingscentrum voor Jonge Volwassen Plus [1991] IRLR 27**. This case came before the European Court of Justice as a consequence of an Article 177 reference by the Dutch courts. Mrs Dekker, when applying for a job at a training centre for young persons, told the interviewing committee that she was pregnant. As she was the best candidate the interviewing committee recommended her appointment, but the centre management refused to appoint her. The reason given was that she would have to be given paid maternity leave. The centre normally reclaimed maternity payments from their insurers but their insurers had told them they could not do this in Mrs Dekker's case because she was already pregnant before taking up employment. The centre thought it would be too expensive to pay Mrs Dekker's maternity pay and the cost of a temporary replacement for her while she was on maternity leave. Accordingly, they decided not to appoint her. Mrs Dekker sought damages in the Dutch courts and the Dutch supreme court sought assistance from the European Court of Justice, in the interpretation of the Equal Treatment Directive 76/207. The European Court of Justice held that a refusal to employ a woman because she is pregnant is always direct sex discrimination; there is no need to seek to make a comparison between her treatment and that which would be afforded to a man. The employer's refusal cannot be justified by saying that it will cost too much to employ a pregnant woman. The court also held that there can be direct sex discrimination related to pregnancy even where there are no male candidates for a job. It should be noted that as the Equal Treatment Directive covers access to training and promotion as well as recruitment, an employer's failure to train or promote a woman because she is pregnant shall also amount to direct sex discrimination.

However, notwithstanding the *Dekker* decision, the English Court of Appeal subsequently upheld a decision of the Industrial Tribunal and the Employment Appeal Tribunal which proceeded on the basis of comparing the treatment of a pregnant woman with that which would have been accorded to a man in comparable circumstances. In the case of **Webb** *v* **EMO Air Cargo (UK) Ltd [1992] IRLR 116 (CA), [1993] IRLR 27 (HL), [1994] IRLR 482 (ECJ)** Carole Webb, who had been employed to provide cover during a Mrs Stewart's maternity leave, discovered within a few weeks of commencing work that she too was pregnant. Carole Webb had been recruited some months before Mrs Stewart was due to take maternity leave so that she could be trained to replace her. However, Carole Webb was recruited for an indefinite period as it was intended that she would continue to work for EMO after Mrs Stewart returned. On informing her employers that she was pregnant, Carole Webb was dismissed.

In dismissing Mrs Webb's appeal, the Court of Appeal stated that in determining whether dismissal by reason of pregnancy amounts to discrimination, 'it is necessary ... to decide whether a man with a condition as nearly as comparable as possible which has the same practical effect upon his ability to do the job would have been dismissed'. Mrs Webb had not been treated less favourably than the employers would have treated a man. It was plain the *Webb* decision did not sit easily with the reasoning in *Dekker*. Carole Webb appealed to the House of Lords, where the view was taken that the true reason for her dismissal was not her pregnancy as such, but the fact that she would be absent from work at a time when her presence was critical, the reason for her absence being largely irrelevant. However, recognising their obligation to interpret domestic legislation in compliance with EC law, the House of Lords decided to ask the European Court of Justice whether Mrs Webb's dismissal in these circumstances was contrary to the Equal Treatment Directive. The ECJ found in Carole Webb's favour, holding that dismissal of a pregnant woman who has been recruited for an indefinite period, could not be justified by the fact that she was prevented, on a purely temporary basis, from performing the work for which she has been engaged. The fact that initially she had been recruited to replace another employee during the latter's maternity leave was irrelevant. Further, it was stressed that there should be no question of comparing the situation of a woman in Carole Webb's position with that of a man similarly incapable for medical or other reasons.

On the return of the *Webb* case to the House of Lords as **Webb *v* EMO Air Cargo (UK) Ltd (No 2) [1995] IRLR 645**, the House of Lords tried to reconcile the ECJ decision with the provisions of the Sex Discrimination Act 1975. They did this by now regarding Carole Webb's pregnancy as a relevant circumstance which could not apply to a hypothetical man. In this way the court found that Mrs Webb's dismissal had in fact been contrary to the 1975 Act. However, great emphasis was placed on the fact that hers was an indefinite rather than a fixed term contract and those who are dismissed because their pregnancy prevents them fulfilling the whole period of a fixed term contract appear not to be protected. Meanwhile, back in Scotland, the 'sick man as comparator' appeared to be enjoying a comeback. In the case of **Brown *v* Rentokil 1995 IRLR 211**, which was decided prior to the House of Lords decision in *Webb (No 2)*, the Inner House held that the dismissal of a woman because she was off work for more than 26 weeks due to pregnancy-related illness did not amount to unlawful sex discrimination. The employer's rule that absence for a continuous period of more than 26 weeks would lead to dismissal applied to both sexes and a man had been dismissed under the rule in the past. The fact that the cause of Mrs Brown's illness was her pregnancy was thought to be irrelevant. The court distinguished between dismissal due to illness caused by pregnancy and dismissal due to the mere fact of being pregnant, citing as authority the European Court of Justice decision in **Hertz *v* Aldi Marked K/S [1991] IRLR 31**. In the *Hertz* case a woman was dismissed due to illness some 18 months after the end of her maternity leave albeit the illness was one which could be traced back to her pregnancy. It was decided that so long after her maternity leave, there should be no distinction drawn between illness which is pregnancy related and that which is not. The *Hertz* decision has been criticised but in any event is not comparable with the situation in *Brown* where the woman was actually pregnant when she was dismissed. The decision in *Brown* has been appealed to the House of Lords who have referred the matter to the European Court of Justice for a ruling.

As a final point it should be noted that the European Court of Justice in **Gillespie** *v* **Northern Health and Social Services Board [1996] IRLR 214** has held that women are not entitled to full pay while on maternity leave. The women had argued, post *Dekker*, that reducing their pay during maternity leave was directly discriminatory contrary to Article 119, the Equal Pay Directive or the Equal Treatment Directive. The European Court of Justice disagreed, but did hold that maternity pay should take account of any pay rises which are backdated to a date prior to the commencement of maternity leave. In Gillespie's case her maternity pay had not been increased to take account of backdated pay rises and it ought to have been.

Indirect discrimination – Section 1(1)(b)

There is indirect discrimination when a condition or requirement is applied equally to both sexes but the application of that condition has a **disproportionate adverse impact** on the members of one sex.

For example, an employer who is hiring labourers for a building site states that applicants must be over 510 tall. This requirement applies equally to both male and female applicants. However, it has a disproportionate adverse impact on women because a considerably smaller proportion of women than men are able to meet this height requirement. The requirement shall not constitute indirect discrimination if the employer can show that the condition is **justifiable** irrespective of the sex of the persons to whom it is applied.

Finally, there shall be no unlawful indirect discrimination unless a woman can show that it was to her **detriment** that she could not comply with the condition. Where a woman can establish that a considerably smaller proportion of women than men can comply with a requirement *and* that it is to her detriment that she cannot comply with it, it is then up to the employer to prove that the requirement is justifiable.

A condition or requirement imposed by an employer must be just that; failure to meet the condition must be an absolute bar to appointment or promotion etc. An applicant cannot complain of indirect discrimination if the employer lists characteristics which he would merely prefer candidates to have. When determining whether persons are able to comply with a condition or requirement the test is whether they are able to comply in *practice*. It is not enough to defeat a complaint of indirect discrimination that it is theoretically possible for women to comply with the requirement complained of.

One of the earliest cases on indirect discrimination was **Price** *v* **Civil Service Commission [1977] IRLR 291**. In this case the civil service required applicants for entry to the service on the executive officer grade to be no older than 28. Mrs P was 35 and was therefore barred from joining the civil service on that grade. The age requirement was one which applied equally to both sexes. Mrs P complained that the upper age limit amounted to indirect sex discrimination. She argued that the proportion of women who could comply with the age requirement was considerably smaller than the proportion of men who could comply. This was because many women in the required age bracket were out of the labour market because they were having and raising children. The Industrial Tribunal dismissed her complaint because they found that the numbers of men and women under 28 in the population were roughly equal. Accordingly, in theory, the same proportion of women as men could comply with the age requirement. The Employment Appeal Tribunal disagreed. The EAT found that the proper test was to look at the proportions of men and women who could comply *in practice* with the requirement. In practice, fewer women than men could comply. Mrs P's complaint of indirect discrimination on grounds of sex was upheld.

In **Clarke and Powell** *v* **Eley (IMI) Kynoch Ltd [1982] IRLR 131** a company made certain employees, including Mrs C and Miss P, redundant. The company decided to make part-time employees redundant first. Thereafter, full-time workers were to be selected for redundancy on a last-in-first-out basis. Forty-six full-time employees, 26 women and 20 men, were made redundant. The 60 part-timers who were made redundant were all women. Mrs C and Miss P, who had both worked part time, complained that this amounted to indirect sex discrimination. The EAT found that there had been indirect discrimination against both women. The company had imposed a requirement that employees work full time in order to be selected for redundancy on a last-in-first-out basis. A far smaller proportion of female employees than male employees could comply with this requirement. As a consequence of being unable to comply with the requirement, both women had suffered detriment; they had been made redundant.

There has been a great deal of debate recently about whether women who return to work after maternity leave are entitled to return to work either on a part-time basis or on a job-share basis. Does an employer's refusal to accommodate such arrangements amount to unlawful sex discrimination? In **The Home Office** *v* **Holmes [1984] IRLR 299** Ms H was due to return to work after maternity leave. She asked to be allowed to return to work on a part-time rather than full-time basis. This was refused. Ms H claimed that this amounted to unlawful indirect sex discrimination. Both the Industrial Tribunal and the EAT agreed that there had been indirect discrimination. The requirement that Ms H work full time had a disproportionate adverse impact on women, it was a requirement with which Ms H could not comply in practice and it caused Ms H to suffer detriment. It was found that the requirement to work full time was not justifiable in the circumstances of Ms H's case.

It must be stressed that the decision in the *Holmes* case is not authority for arguing that 3 all 1 women now have an automatic right to return to work part time or to job share. In many situations, the employer will be able to justify the requirement that a woman must work full time as in **Greater Glasgow Health Board** *v* **Carey [1987] IRLR 484**. Mrs C was a health visitor employed by the health board. After maternity leave she wished to return to work on either a part-time or on a job-share basis. The health board refused to allow job sharing. The health board agreed to allow Mrs C to work for fewer hours so long as she worked some hours every day of a five-day week. Mrs C complained that this amounted to indirect sex discrimination. Her complaint was upheld by the Industrial Tribunal but the health board appealed to the EAT and won. The EAT held that the requirement that health visitors work some hours every day was justifiable on grounds of administrative efficiency.

In the case of **Meade-Hill and National Union of Civil and Public Servants** *v* **The British Council [1995] IRLR 478** the Court of Appeal upheld Mrs M-H's claim that the inclusion of a mobility clause in her contract of employment could amount to indirect sex discrimination. A greater proportion of working wives earn less than their husbands. Accordingly, the court accepted that considerably fewer women than men, as the secondary earner within the household, could comply in practice with a requirement to relocate. This requirement would discriminate unless the employer could establish that the needs of the organisation required them to be able to order employees to transfer.

In a significant decision, **R** *v* **Secretary of State for Employment, Ex parte Equal Opportunities Commission and Another [1994] IRLR 176** the House of Lords held, on 3 March 1994, that statutory provisions requiring part-timers to complete five years' continuous service in order to have the right not to be unfairly dismissed, the right to compensation for unfair dismissal and the right to a redundancy payment, were unlawful. This was because these service thresholds were inconsistent with EC anti-discrimination law. Requiring part-time employees to have five years' continuous service in order to enjoy these rights as compared with only two years for full-timers amounted to unlawful indirect sex discrimination. This was because the great majority of full-time workers are men whereas the great majority of those working less than sixteen hours per week are women. Accordingly the service thresholds had a disproportionate adverse impact on women.

Even so, had the government been able to show that the discriminatory provisions had been based on objectively justified grounds there would have been no breach of EC law (**Rinner-Kuhn** *v* **FWW Spezial-Gebaudereinigung GmbH & Co KG [1989] IRLR 493**). The government sought to justify the difference in thresholds by arguing that more part-time work was available than would be the case if employers were liable for redundancy pay and unfair dismissal compensation. If thresholds were equalised it was alleged that fewer part-time workers would be employed. The court accepted that seeking to increase the availability of part-time work was a beneficial social policy aim. However, the court also had to be satisfied that the threshold provisions were suitable and requisite for achieving that aim. The court found that no objective justification for the thresholds had been established and declared that they were incompatible with Article 119 of the Treaty of Rome, the Equal Pay Directive 75/117/EEC and the Equal Treatment Directive 76/207/EEC.

In response to this decision the Government issued The Employment Protection (Part-time Employees) Regulations 1995 which came into force on 6 February 1995. The Regulations removed all hours-of-work thresholds and granted part-time employees the same statutory employment protection rights as full-time workers. The 1995 Regulations have been revoked as their provisions now form part of the Employment Rights Act 1996.

However, there is now the problem of whether part-time workers who were dismissed or made redundant, with less than five years service, either before the regulations came into force or even before the House of Lords decision, can now retrospectively seek compensation on the basis that their treatment had been unlawful under EC law all along. The problem lies in how to handle the fact that there are time limits for lodging claims with an industrial tribunal. For example, unfair dismissal claims must be presented to the tribunal within three months of the dismissal *unless* the tribunal is satisfied that it was not reasonably practicable for the three months time limit to be met.

In a decision of the EAT in Scotland, **Rankin** *v* **British Coal Corporation [1993] IRLR 69**, it had been held that where an applicant brings a case directly under Article 119, the application is to be regarded as a freestanding claim under EC law to which domestic time limits do not apply. In this case Mrs Rankin, who had not been entitled to a redundancy payment under UK law in 1987, was allowed to bring her claim to a tribunal in 1990 when it became apparent that under EC law she should have received redundancy pay. The EAT recognised that it is important that there should be legal certainty so that employers do not have to worry indefinitely about possible future claims. However, it was decided that allowing Mrs Rankin her rights prevailed over legal certainty, so long as her claim was brought within a reasonable time of the coming into force of legislation amending UK law to satisfy EC requirements. In another Scottish EAT case, **Methilhill Bowling Club** *v* **Hunter [1995] IRLR 232**, a similar approach was taken in respect of a woman whose earlier unfair dismissal claim had failed under UK legislation because, as a part-timer, she did not have five years' service. She was held entitled to bring a fresh claim under Article 119 of the Treaty of Rome as she had applied within a reasonable time of the House of Lords decision in the *EOC* case.

However, a contrary view has been taken in a number of cases in England, most significantly in the case of **Biggs** *v* **Somerset County Council [1996] IRLR 203** where the Court of Appeal held that an industrial tribunal did not have the jurisdiction to entertain a complaint of unfair dismissal brought, within three months of the House of Lords decision in the *EOC* case, by a woman dismissed from her post as a part-time science teacher in 1976. The court stated that it was 'reasonably practicable' for Mary Biggs to have presented her claim within three months of her dismissal. She should have been able to argue that the statutory restriction on claims by part-time workers which was then in force was indirectly discriminatory under EC law and should be disapplied. This view was taken despite the court conceding that in 1976 'the fact that ... UK legislation might have to yield [to EC law] was ... fully appreciated only by a comparatively small number of people'. The court also rejected the argument that Mrs Biggs could rely on her rights under Article 119. It is likely that *Biggs* will be appealed to the House of Lords. In the meantime it is worthy of note that the Court of Appeal decision has since been followed by the Scottish EAT in **Borders Regional Council** *v* **Cunningham** (EAT Decision 22 February 1996).

Another decision of major significance is that of the Court of Appeal in **R** *v* **Secretary of State for Employment ex parte Seymour-Smith and Perez [1995] IRLR 464**. The court upheld the claim of two women that the requirement of two years' continuous service in order to bring a claim of unfair dismissal constituted indirect sex discrimination. The qualifying period had been increased from one to two years by the Unfair Dismissal (Variation of Qualifying Period) Order 1985. It was found that the extension of the qualifying period had a disproportionate adverse impact in that the percentage of women who could satisfy the requirement was considerably smaller than the percentage of men. The government could not establish that the measure had promoted employment opportunities and accordingly failed to justify the requirement. The case is being appealed to the House of Lords.

Victimisation – Section 4

There is discrimination by way of victimisation where a person is treated less favourably because:

1 he has brought proceedings under the Sex Discrimination Act 1975 or the Equal Pay Act 1970; *or*
2 he has given evidence or information in connection with such proceedings; *or*
3 he has otherwise done anything under the Sex Discrimination Act 1975 or the Equal Pay Act 1970 in relation to the discriminator or any other person; *or*
4 he has alleged that the discriminator or any other person has acted so as to contravene either the Sex Discrimination Act 1975 or the Equal Pay Act 1970.

There is also discrimination where a person is victimised because he intends to do any of the above or it is suspected that he has done or intends to do any of the above. There is no discrimination by way of victimisation if a person is treated less favourably because of allegations made, *if* the allegations were false *and* not made in good faith.

In **Chadwick** *v* **Lancashire County Council Unreported Decision of Liverpool Industrial Tribunal Case Nos: 25130/84, 25133/84** Mrs C was a deputy headteacher who had alleged that appointing committees in Lancashire discriminated against women candidates when appointing headteachers. After making these allegations she had applied for two headteacher posts and had not been short-listed. She alleged that she had been discriminated against by way of victimisation. The Industrial Tribunal held that in each case Mrs C had been excluded from the short-list because of the allegations she had made and that she had been victimised contrary to s 4 of the 1975 Act.

Discrimination against married persons in relation to employment – Section 3

A married person is unlawfully discriminated against if he is treated less favourably than an unmarried person of the same sex is, or would be, treated – i.e., direct discrimination. A married person may also be the victim of indirect discrimination. There shall be indirect discrimination where a condition or requirement is such that a considerably smaller proportion of married persons than unmarried persons can comply with it. In order that a complaint of indirect discrimination may be upheld, the married person must also show that it is to his detriment that he cannot comply with the condition. There is no indirect discrimination if the employer can show that the condition is justifiable.

In **Hurley** *v* **Mustoe [1981] IRLR 208** which was discussed above, the refusal to employ Mrs H because she had young children was held to amount to direct sex discrimination. The refusal also constituted indirect discrimination on grounds of married status.

The scope of the Act in relation to employment – Section 6

It is unlawful for an employer to discriminate:

1 in the arrangements made for the purpose of determining who shall be offered employment. This provision covers the wording of job advertisements and job descriptions, the setting of qualifications required and the design of application forms. For example, terms such as 'waiter' or 'sales girl' should not be used. Employers must also ensure that interviews are conducted in a manner which does not discriminate;
2 in the terms on which employment is offered. For example, a woman may bring a complaint of unlawful discrimination if she is offered employment on terms less favourable than those offered to male candidates;
3 by refusing or deliberately omitting to offer employment because of a person's sex or because they are married;
4 in respect of access to opportunities for promotion, transfer or training, or to any other benefits, facilities or services;
5 by dismissing a person or subjecting them to any other detriment because of their sex or because they are married.

The Sex Discrimination Act 1975 as originally enacted, did not apply to any provisions relating to death or retirement so that it remained lawful to require women to retire at 60 but to allow men to continue to work until 65. As a consequence of the decision of the European Court of Justice in **Marshall** *v* **South West Hants Area Health Authority [1986] IRLR 40**, the Sex Discrimination Act 1986 was passed and since November 1987 employers have been unable to set different compulsory retiral ages for men and women. Mrs Marshall had been forced to retire at 62, although her male colleagues could continue to work until they were 65. The Industrial Tribunal and the EAT dismissed her sex discrimination claim because provisions relating to death or retirement were not covered by the 1975 Act. Mrs Marshall also argued that her treatment was in breach of the Equal Treatment Directive 76/207/EEC. The matter was referred to the European Court of Justice. It was held that to set different compulsory retiral ages for men and women was contrary to the Equal Treatment Directive. Mrs Marshall was also held to be able to rely on the Directive because she was a public sector employee, employed by a health board which was regarded as an organ of the state. This meant that after the European Court of Justice decision there was one rule for public sector employees and another for those in the private sector. This was because private sector employees could not rely on the Directive in actions against individual employers. Accordingly, the Government was forced to pass the Sex Discrimination Act 1986 which outlawed discrimination as between men and women in respect of compulsory ages.

Permissible discrimination where sex is a genuine occupational qualification – Section 7

It is not unlawful for an employer to discriminate in his recruitment arrangements or when selecting a person for promotion, transfer or training *if* being a man or a woman is a genuine occupational qualification for a job. Section 7 of the 1975 Act provides that being of a particular sex is a genuine occupational qualification only where:

1 for reasons of physiology (not physical strength or stamina) or authenticity a man or woman is required. A female actress is required to play Lady Macbeth or a male model is required for an advertisement; *or*
2 the job needs to be held by a person of a particular sex in order to preserve decency or privacy. This might involve a post as a lavatory or changing-room attendant. A person of a particular sex may be required for employment in a private home where the job involves a degree of physical or social contact with a member of the household or knowledge of intimate details of such a person's life. A job as a nurse or companion to an elderly person might come under this heading; *or*
3 the employee is required to 'live in', there is only single-sex sleeping accommodation and bathroom facilities and it is unreasonable to expect the employer to provide separate accommodation for members of the opposite sex; *or*
4 the job is in a single-sex hospital, prison or other establishment for persons requiring special care, attention or supervision and it is reasonable that the job is held by a person of that sex; *or*
5 the job involves providing individuals with personal services promoting their welfare or education and such services can be most effectively provided by a person of a particular sex. Such jobs might include certain social work posts or particular guidance posts in schools; *or*
6 the vacancy is for a post overseas where the law or customs are such that the duties could not be performed by a member of a particular sex; *or*
7 the job is one of two to be held by a married couple such as posts as house-parents in a children's home.

An employer cannot argue that being of a particular sex is a genuine occupational qualification, if he already has sufficient numbers of employees of that sex who could perform the duties covered by the s 7 provisions. For example in **Wylie *v* Dee & Co (Menswear) Ltd [1978] IRLR 103** Miss W was refused employment in a menswear shop because the job involved taking men's inside-leg measurements. The employers argued that being a man was a genuine occupational qualification in order to preserve privacy or decency. The employers argued that men might reasonably object to such measurements being taken by a woman. The Industrial Tribunal found in favour of Miss W. Being a man was not a genuine occupational qualification for the job for a number of reasons including the fact that the need to take such measurements did not arise that frequently and if it did, there were already seven male employees who could assist if required.

The same approach was taken in the more recent case of **Etam PLC *v* Rowan [1989] IRLR 150** where a man successfully claimed that the employer's refusal to employ him in a dress shop amounted to unlawful sex discrimination. The employer argued that being a woman was a genuine occupational qualification because female customers sometimes had to be measured. The EAT disgreed; if a woman needed to be measured, this particular task could be performed by one of the 16 existing female assistants.

The 1975 Act originally included an additional defence where the job needed to be held by a man because of legal restrictions regulating the employment of women in certain jobs, for example the employment of women underground in coal mines. As a consequence of the Employment Act 1989, this shall no longer be a defence to a sex discrimination claim. Lawful discriminatory acts in compliance with statutory provisions, whether passed before or after the 1975 Act, will be restricted to situations where such provisions protect women at work. Schedule 1 to the Employment Act 1989 specifies such provisions, which include regulations dealing with exposure to lead and ionising regulations.

Exceptions to the Sex Discrimination Act 1975

Employment overseas – persons working wholly or mainly outside Great Britain are not covered by the Act.

Police – male and female police officers may be treated differently in respect of requirements relating to height, uniform and equipment. Special treatment may be afforded to women police officers in connection with pregnancy and childbirth.

Prison officers – different height requirements may be applied to male and female prison officers.

Ministers of religion – particular faiths and denominations may require that their clergy be of one sex.

Provisions relating to death or retirement – section 6 as originally enacted provided that provisions relating to death and retirement were not covered by the 1975 Act. Section 6 has been amended by the Sex Discrimination Act 1986 so that it is now unlawful to discriminate in provisions relating to retirement in matters of promotion, transfer, training, demotion or dismissal.

Pregnancy or childbirth – special treatment may be afforded to women in connection with pregnancy or childbirth.

Positive action – Section 48

It is lawful to offer *training* to members of one sex only **if** it is found that in the previous 12 months, particular work has been done exclusively or mainly by persons of the other sex. It is unlawful to go so far as to positively discriminate in favour of these trainees when filling vacancies. If an employer finds that his workforce of ten is all male, he cannot lawfully advertise for women only to fill his next five vacancies in order to redress the balance of the sexes. Such action would unlawfully discriminate against men. Should an employer have 50 vacancies to fill he cannot lawfully advertise for 25 men and 25 women. The operation of such a quota system would amount to unlawful sex discrimination.

The European Court of Justice, in the case of **Kalanke** *v* **Freie Hansestadt Bremen [1995] IRLR 660**, considered a German law which provided that where women were underrepresented within a specified personnel group, women having the same qualifications as male applicants were to be given priority. The ECJ found that such positive discrimination was unlawful under EC law and did not fall within the limited exception provided by Article 2(4) of the Equal Treatment Directive 76/207 which allows the adoption of measures 'to promote equal opportunity for men and women'.

Liability of employers – Section 41

Employers are held liable for the discriminatory acts of their employees where the discrimination took place in the course of employment. The employer is liable whether or not the act was done with his knowledge or approval. However, it shall be a defence if the employer can prove that he took reasonable steps to prevent acts of discrimination by his workforce.

Enforcement action by individuals – Section 63

An individual who believes he has been the victim of unlawful sex discrimination must present a complaint to an industrial tribunal within three months of the act complained of. The burden of proving that unlawful discrimination has occurred is on the applicant. Legal aid is not available to applicants to Industrial Tribunals. However, if a case involves a complex point of law or where an important principle is at stake, the Equal Opportunities Commission is empowered by s 75 of the 1975 Act to give financial assistance to a complainant.

An applicant may be assisted in the preparation of his case by the use of a s 74 questionnaire which may be sent to the employer for completion. An employer may be asked why an applicant was treated in a particular way. If an employer fails to return the questionnaire or if any of his answers are evasive, the tribunal may draw the inference that there has been unlawful discrimination.

Where a complaint of discrimination has been presented to an industrial tribunal, a copy is sent to ACAS. An ACAS conciliation officer may attempt to have the matter settled without the need for a tribunal hearing. Should attempts at conciliation fail, the complaint is heard by the Industrial Tribunal consisting of a legally qualified chairman and two lay members.

Remedies – Section 65

Where the Industrial Tribunal finds that there has been unlawful discrimination on grounds of the applicant's sex or married status, the following remedies are available:

1 the tribunal may make an order declaring the rights of the parties.
2 the tribunal may order the payment of compensation. There is now no ceiling on the award of compensation. The sum awarded may include an amount to compensate for injury to feelings.
3 The tribunal may make a recommendation that the employer takes action within a specified period to remove or reduce the detriment suffered by the applicant. For example, if the complaint was in respect of a refusal to send a woman on a training course, the tribunal may recommend that the woman is sent on the next available course. The tribunal may only recommend such action, it cannot order it to be taken. However, should the employer fail to follow the tribunal's recommendation, the tribunal may increase the award of compensation.

It was the case of **Marshall *v* Southampton & South West Hampshire Area**

Health Authority (No 2) [1993] IRLR 445 which led to the removal of the ceiling on compensation for sex discrimination. Helen Marshall's first victory before the European Court of Justice was in 1986 when the court declared that her employer's decision to force her to retire at 62 while allowing her male colleagues to work until the age of 65 was contrary to the EEC Equal Treatment Directive 76/207.

However, that was not the end of Helen Marshall's story. Following her victory in Luxembourg, the case was sent back to an Industrial Tribunal to settle the matter of compensation. At that time the maximum award payable under UK legislation in respect of compensation for sex discrimination stood at only £6250. However the tribunal took the view that this amount did not provide an adequate remedy as required by Article 6 of the Equal Treatment Directive. Ignoring the statutory limit on compensation the tribunal proceeded to award Helen Marshall the sum of £19 405. This sum included £7710 by way of interest from the date of her dismissal to the date of the award. Her employers appealed to the EAT and won. Helen Marshall in turn appealed to the Court of Appeal where she lost. The Court of Appeal held that Miss Marshall could not rely on the Directive to override the limit on compensation in the Sex Discrimination Act. Helen Marshall appealed to the House of Lords. The House of Lords referred three questions to the European Court of Justice for a ruling in terms of Article 177 of the Treaty of Rome.

1 Did the setting of an upper limit of only £6250 as compensation for sex discrimination amount to a failure by the UK to implement properly Article 6 of the Equal Treatment Directive?
2 Was it essential for the proper implementation of the directive that the compensation awarded is no less than the full amount of the loss sustained by reason of the unlawful discrimination? Also, did this mean that interest was payable from the date of the discrimination until the date of the award?
3 If the European Court of Justice found that the answer to questions 1 and 2 was 'yes' – then did the Directive have vertical direct effect – i.e., could it be relied upon by an applicant when bringing an action against a public sector body which is an 'emanation of the state'? Basically, did the directive give Helen Marshall rights, as a public sector employee, which she could use to override the national legislation setting limits on the compensation payable?

On 2nd August 1993 the European Court of Justice answered these three questions in the affirmative. It is contrary to the Equal Treatment Directive to lay down an upper limit on the amount of compensation recoverable by a victim of sex discrimination where the result of this may be that the compensation is not adequate in relation to the damage actually sustained. Similarly, it is unlawful to exclude the award of interest. Finally, as a public sector employee, Miss Marshall was entitled to rely directly on Article 6 of the Equal Treatment Directive to challenge the UK legislation which placed a ceiling on compensation.

The practical consequences of the second Marshall decision were enormous. The government quickly issued the Sex Discrimination and Equal Pay (Remedies) Regulations 1993 which abolished the limit on compensation contained in s 65(2) of the 1975 Act (by then standing at £11 000) and allowed awards of interest with respect to injury to feelings from the date of the act complained of. In respect of other heads of compensation, interest will run from a date mid-way between the date of the act complained of and the date of the calculation being made. Power was also given to tribunals to award interest in equal pay cases but it remains the case that compensation in equal pay cases shall not exceed two years back-pay and the government do not intend to alter this provision. It is arguable that this may prevent adequate compensation of damage caused by pay discrimination.

In the case of **Harvey *v* Institute of the Motor Industry (No 2) 1995 IRLR 416** the EAT held that the regulations apply to all awards made after 22 November 1993, the date the regulations took effect, even if the act complained of occurred before that date. Also, prior to 25 March 1996, compensation could not be awarded in respect of *unintentional* indirect discrimination. However, The Sex Discrimination and Equal Pay (Miscellaneous Amendments) Regulations 1996 empower the tribunal to award compensation to a person who has suffered indirect discrimination, even where this was unintentional, if it would not be just and equitable only to make a declaration or recommendation.

The Equal Opportunities Commission

The Sex Discrimination Act 1975 established the Equal Opportunities Commission (EOC). The main duties of the EOC are to work towards the elimination of discrimination, to promote equality of opportunity between the sexes and to keep under review the working of the Sex Discrimination Act 1975 and the Equal Pay Act 1970.

In respect of certain types of unlawful discrimination, enforcement action may be taken only by the EOC. The EOC may issue a non-discrimination notice in respect of discriminatory practices, discriminatory advertisements, the giving of instructions to discriminate or the application of pressure to discriminate. Discriminatory practices arise where it is so well known that a particular employer will not employ women, no women bother to apply. This means that there is no individual victim available to bring a complaint to an industrial tribunal. If, following the issue of a non-discrimination notice, an employer persists in acts of unlawful discrimination, the EOC may seek an interdict from the Sheriff Court ordering that such acts cease. In respect of discriminatory advertisements and instructions or pressure to discriminate, the EOC may seek an immediate interdict if it appears that further discriminatory acts are likely to occur.

The EOC is also empowered to issue codes of practice to provide guidance for employers and employees. The EOC may also give advice to individuals and in certain cases, where an important point of law is at stake, may give financial assistance to complainants.

THE RACE RELATIONS ACT 1976

The Race Relations Act 1976 is modelled on the Sex Discrimination Act 1975 and the concepts of direct and indirect discrimination, victimisation and genuine occupational qualification are all reintroduced in the Race Relations Act.

In terms of the 1976 Act it is unlawful to discriminate against a person on grounds of race in terms of employment, union membership, education, the provision of goods and services, and in the disposal and management of housing and other premises.

Section 1(1)(a) defines discrimination as less favourable treatment on racial grounds – i.e., direct discrimination. Section 1(1)(b) outlaws indirect racial discrimination. Section 2 outlaws discrimination by way of victimisation.

Direct discrimination on racial grounds

This takes the form of less favourable treatment or equal but segregated treatment – e.g., the provision of separate toilet and washing facilities for Asian workers. Even if the facilities are of the same standard as those used by white workers such segregation still amounts to direct discrimination. However, it has been held in **Pel Ltd *v* Modgill [1980] IRLR 142** that where workers segregate themselves and this is the choice of the minority workers and is not enforced by the employer there is no discrimination.

In the case of **King *v* The Great Britain-China Centre [1991] IRLR 513** (CA) the Court of Appeal in England found that K had been subjected to direct discrimination on grounds of race. K had applied for the post of deputy director at the Centre but had not been interviewed. K had been born in China and spoke Chinese but had been educated in Britain. She had, however, spent three months travelling in China during the year prior to her application. It was found as matters of fact that the employer had made a misleading assertion that all those interviewed had worked in China for at least a year in the recent past; that no ethnic Chinese had been interviewed although five had applied; that K's formal qualifications met the requirements set out in the advertisement; and that the Centre had never employed an ethnic Chinese person. These facts were held to be sufficient to establish a finding of direct discrimination in the absence of a satisfactory explanation as to why K had not been called for interview.

There can be direct discrimination against someone who is not of the race discriminated against. In **Wilson *v* TB Steelworks IDS Brief 150** a white woman had a job offer withdrawn when it was discovered her husband was black. This was unlawful discrimination.

In **Showboat Entertainment Centre Ltd *v* Owens [1984] IRLR 7** the EAT held that it was unlawful discrimination on racial grounds to dismiss the white manager of an amusement centre for refusing to operate a colour bar against black youths.

Indirect discrimination on racial grounds

Indirect racial discrimination has four aspects:

1 a condition or requirement is applied to everybody;
2 the condition or requirement has a disproportionate adverse effect on some racial group – i.e., the proportion of persons of that racial group who can comply with the condition is considerably smaller than the proportion of persons not of that group who can comply with it;
3 the condition or requirement is not otherwise justifiable irrespective of race;
4 it is to the detriment of a member of the adversely affected racial group that he is unable to comply with the condition or requirement.

In the case of **J H Walker Ltd *v* Hussain & Ors EAT [1996] IRLR 11** the EAT upheld a tribunal's finding that there had been indirect discrimination on racial grounds against Asian employees who were disciplined for taking a day off work on the Muslim festival of Eid which marks the end of Ramadan. Muslim employees previously had been allowed to take time off for Eid, which is as important to Muslims as Christmas is to Christians. However, the employers had introduced a requirement that employees took no holidays during the company's busiest period, overlooking the fact that Eid fell within this period. When it was brought to their attention the employers refused to relax the requirement despite the employees undertaking to work extra hours to make up the lost time. The large number of Asian employees who took the holiday anyway were issued with a final written warning. There was no direct discrimination against the workers as Muslims because Muslims do not constitute a racial group (see discussion below). However there was indirect discrimination on grounds of race because a considerably smaller proportion of Asian employees than non-Asian employees could comply with the requirement to work during Eid.

The tribunal also had to consider whether the discrimination could be regarded as intentional. This was important because no compensation is payable in respect of *unintentional* indirect discrimination on grounds of race. The employers argued that their motive in imposing the requirement was to improve efficiency, not to commit an act of discrimination. However, the employers knew that the effect of their requirement would be that Asian employees would suffer a disproportionate adverse effect. In such a case the EAT held that the tribunal was entitled to infer that the employers wanted to produce such an effect. The employers' appeal was dismissed and the award of £1000 to each affected employee for injury to feelings was confirmed.

There shall be no unlawful discrimination on racial grounds if the employer can show that the condition or requirement was 'justifiable'. In **Panesar *v* Nestlé Co Ltd [1980] IRLR 64** a rule against long hair indirectly discriminated against Sikhs in that a smaller proportion of Sikhs could comply with it as compared with members of other racial groups. However, the rule was not unlawful because it was a condition which was justifiable in the interests of safety and hygiene.

Discrimination by way of victimisation

It is unlawful to treat someone less favourably because he has brought proceedings under the 1976 Act, or has given evidence or information in connection with such proceedings, or has made allegations of discrimination. It is not unlawful discrimination to treat a person less favourably where allegations have been made which were false *and* were not made in good faith.

What does 'on grounds of race' mean?

Section 3 of the Act defines 'racial grounds' as meaning any of the following: colour, race, nationality or ethnic or national origins. 'National origins' includes both race and citizenship. A 'racial group' means a group of persons defined by reference to colour, race, nationality or ethnic or national origins.

In a leading House of Lords decision, **Mandla *v* Dowell Lee [1983] IRLR 209**, it was decided that 'ethnic' was wider than race and that Sikhs did constitute an ethnic group and, accordingly, also a racial group for the purposes of the 1976 Act. This decision means that some religious groups, such as Sikhs, may come within the protection of the Act. This is not to say that *all* religious groups will constitute an ethnic group for the purposes of the Act.

For a group to be protected it should have shared characteristics which would include a common geographical origin; descent from common ancestors; common culture and social customs; a long shared history distinguishable from other groups; a common language, literature and religion; and being a minority group within a larger community.

It is probably the case that while Sikhs and Jews are protected, Catholics and Muslims are not; a common religion on its own is not enough, the other factors above must also be present. In **Commission for Racial Equality *v* Dutton [1989] 1 All ER 306** the English Court of Appeal held that gypsies constitute a racial group for the purposes of the 1976 Act.

The scope of the 1976 Act in relation to employment

In terms of s 4 it shall be unlawful, before a person is in employment, to discriminate against him on racial grounds in respect of the arrangements made for the purpose of determining who shall be employed. It is also unlawful discrimination to offer employment on terms less favourable than those offered to members of other racial groups. A person must not be refused employment because of his race.

Once a person is employed, it is unlawful to discriminate against him on racial grounds in his terms of employment. There must be no discrimination in respect of access to opportunities for promotion, transfer or training, or to any other benefits, facilities or services. It is also unlawful to dismiss someone or subject him to any other detriment because of his race.

Genuine occupational qualifications

In terms of s 5, an employer may insist on employing a member of a particular racial group where:

1 a member of a particular race is required for authenticity in the theatre or for modelling;
2 a member of a particular race is required for authenticity in an ethnic restaurant;
3 the holder of the job provides personal services which promote the welfare of persons of the same racial group, e.g., a community relations officer.

An employer cannot rely on the provisions of s 5 where he already employs members of a particular racial group in sufficient numbers to perform duties for which membership of that group is a genuine occupational qualification.

Exceptions to the Race Relations Act 1976

The provisions of the 1976 Act do not apply to employment in a private home nor do they apply to employment overseas. The 1976 Act does not apply to employment on board ships if a person applies from abroad.

The 1976 Act does not apply to immigration regulations or to rules placing limitations on the nationality of those applying for posts in the civil service. An employer may put forward as a defence to a claim of racial discrimination that he was acting in compliance with statutory requirements.

Positive action

In terms of the Race Relations Act 1976 s 38, training may be offered only to members of a particular racial group where an employer discovers that racial group has been under-represented in his workforce during the preceding 12 months. As with the similar provisions under the Sex Discrimination Act, the employer is not allowed to positively discriminate in favour of such trainees when filling vacancies.

Enforcement action by individuals

An individual who believes he has been the victim of unlawful racial discrimination may present a complaint to an industrial tribunal within three months of the act complained of. The burden of proving unlawful discrimination is on the applicant. The Commission for Racial Equality may give financial assistance to applicants in special cases and a questionnaire procedure similar to that which operates under the Sex Discrimination Act 1975 is also available. Again, an ACAS conciliation officer may attempt to effect a settlement prior to the tribunal hearing.

Remedies

If an individual is found to have been refused employment on racial grounds, or discriminated against while in employment or dismissed or chosen for redundancy because of his race, the Industrial Tribunal may make the following orders:

1 An order declaring the rights of the parties.
2 An order for the payment of compensation. The compensation may include a payment for injury to feelings. No compensation is payable in respect of *unintentional* indirect racial discrimination.
3 A recommendation that the employer take remedial action within a specified time to remove or reduce the detriment suffered by the complainant.

The Race Relations (Remedies) Act 1994 removed the ceiling on awards of compensation from 3 July 1994. The Race Relations (Interest on Awards) Regulations 1994 provide for the payment of interest on compensation. Research carried out by the *Equal Opportunities Review* (EOR 67 May/June 1996) disclosed that in comparison with awards in the year prior to the removal of the ceiling on compensation, in race discrimination cases, the average award made from July 1994 to the end of 1995 increased by 63 per cent and awards for injury to feelings increased by 55 per cent.

Although The Sex Discrimination and Equal Pay (Miscellaneous Amendments) Regulations 1996 empowered tribunals to award compensation for unintentional indirect discrimination on grounds of sex, there are no equivalent provisions as yet in respect of unintentional indirect discrimination on grounds of race.

The Commission for Racial Equality

The Commission for Racial Equality (CRE) was established by the Race Relations Act 1976 and its duties are to work towards the elimination of racial discrimination, to promote equality of opportunity and good relations between members of different racial groups and to keep under review the working of the Race Relations Act 1976.

Certain types of unlawful discrimination can be acted against only by the CRE. These include publishing discriminatory advertisements, instructing someone to discriminate or applying pressure on someone to discriminate and operating discriminatory practices. In respect of such matters, the CRE may conduct formal investigations and issue non-discrimination notices. In certain circumstances the CRE may seek an interdict from the Sheriff Court to prevent such unlawful activities continuing.

The CRE may offer advice to individuals and in certain circumstances may also offer financial assistance. The CRE is empowered to issue codes of practice to give guidance on race relations issues.

THE DISABILITY DISCRIMINATION ACT 1995

The Disability Discrimination Act 1995, which comes into force towards the end of 1996, aims to end discrimination against disabled people. It repeals the Disabled Persons (Employment) Act 1944 which required that where employers employed more than 20 employees, registered disabled persons had to make up 3 per cent of the workforce. Failure to comply with the Act's provisions was a criminal offence. However, in practice this quota system was ignored by employers and its provisions were not enforced. Moreover, the previous legislation did not afford a legal remedy to an individual who believed he had been refused employment because of his disability. The 1995 Act abolishes the quota system and individuals with a disability will be able to seek unlimited compensation if they can establish unjustified discrimination on the part of an employer. It should be noted that the provisions relating to discrimination in employment do not apply to employers who have fewer than 20 employees at the date of the discriminatory act.

Who is covered – what is the meaning of 'disability'?

Section 1 states that a person has a disability if he or she has a physical or mental impairment which has a substantial and long term adverse effect on his or her ability to carry out normal day to day activities. Protection against discrimination is afforded also to those who have had a disability in the past. Regulations will be made to clarify further what is and what is not to be treated as amounting to an impairment. However, in the meantime Schedule 1 gives some guidance.

Physical impairment includes sensory impairments, and severe disfigurements also are to be regarded as having a substantial effect on a person's ability to carry out normal day to day activities. Mental impairment must result from or consist of a mental illness which is 'clinically well recognised' by medical practitioners. It would include schizophrenia and manic depression but the government intends to exclude by regulations those with anti-social disorders, such as psychopaths, kleptomaniacs and paedophiles, and those with addictions to tobacco, alcohol and drugs. It is also intended to exclude those whose disfigurement is self-inflicted, for example by tattoos or body piercing.

In order to amount to a disability, an impairment must have a 'long term effect' which means it must last or be likely to last for at least 12 months. A condition is also 'long term' if it is likely to last for the rest of a person's life; this will cover those with a terminal illness who are unlikely to survive for 12 months. Conditions which recur, such as epilepsy, or which are progressive, such as cancer or multiple sclerosis, will be covered because, even though the 'substantial adverse effects' are not constant or current, such effects are likely to recur or result in the future.

An impairment is taken to affect a person's ability to carry out normal day to day activities **only** if it affects one or more of the following: mobility; manual dexterity; physical co-ordination; continence; ability to lift, carry or otherwise move everyday objects; speech, hearing or eyesight; memory or ability to concentrate, learn or understand; or perception of the risk of physical danger. The effect of the impairment must be 'substantial' and the Secretary of State for Employment will issue a Guidance Paper giving examples of the sorts of impairment which should be regarded as having a substantial adverse effect. Those whose visual impairment is corrected by wearing spectacles or contact lenses will not be regarded as having a disability. However, those whose condition is controlled by taking medication or who wear an artificial limb will enjoy the protection of the Act.

Discrimination in employment

Section 4 of the Act states that it is unlawful to discriminate against a disabled person in relation to recruitment; terms and conditions of employment; opportunities for promotion, transfer, training or receipt of other benefits; dismissal and any other detriment. It should be noted that the Act's provisions do not apply to those working overseas or to members of the armed forces, the police, prison officers or firefighters.

In terms of s 5(1), there is discrimination if, for a reason relating to his disability, a disabled person is treated less favourably than persons not suffering from such a disability are or would be treated and such treatment is *unjustified*. It must be noted therefore that in contrast to the provisions on sex and race discrimination, direct discrimination on grounds of disability can be justified by an employer – but only if he can show that the reason for it is both material to the circumstances of the particular case and substantial.

Duty to make adjustments

In terms of s 5(2), there is also discrimination if an employer unjustifiably fails to comply with his duty under s 6 of the Act. Section 6 imposes on an employer a duty to take *reasonable* steps to make adjustments to any arrangements or physical features of premises which place a disabled person at a substantial disadvantage. For example, employers could instal ramps for wheelchairs, acquire special equipment, allow the work to be carried out on the ground floor rather than on an upper floor or reallocate duties so that a task unable to be carried out by a disabled worker could be done by someone else. In determining what it is reasonable to expect an employer to do, regard can be had to the cost of making the adjustment and to the financial resources of the employer. The extent of any disruption which making an adjustment would cause to the employer's activities is also relevant. It is also relevant to consider whether the adjustment would in fact prevent the disabled person suffering a disadvantage. It should be noted that the Act does not impose a general duty on employers, for example, to upgrade their premises to make them accessible to persons in wheelchairs. The duty will arise only in respect of individual cases. A Code of Practice is to be issued to give guidance on the extent of the duty and examples of adjustments which would be appropriate in particular situations.

It will be seen therefore that an employer will be unable to justify a refusal to employ a person with a disability where it would be reasonable for him to make some adjustment to working arrangements or a physical alteration to his premises in order to overcome any obstacle to offering employment to that person. For example, a refusal to employ an otherwise suitable person only because there was no wheelchair access to the workplace, would amount to actionable discrimination if a ramp could be installed at a reasonable cost having regard to the financial resources of the employer.

It should be noted that, again unlike the provisions on sex and race discrimination, there is no express prohibition of indirect discrimination. However, the government took the view that the wording of the prohibition of discrimination for a reason 'relating' to a person's disability together with the duty to make adjustments, combined to outlaw all possible forms that discrimination against the disabled might take and rendered unnecessary any specific provision on indirect discrimination. The Act does give protection, against victimisation, of those who have brought proceedings under the Act or have given information or evidence in relation to such proceedings or have made allegations in good faith that the Act has been contravened. Such victimisation is to be regarded as a form of actionable discrimination.

Enforcement, remedies and procedure

Those who believe they have been subjected to discrimination contrary to the provisions of the Act must complain to an Industrial Tribunal within three months of the discriminatory act. This time limit may be waived if the tribunal considers it is just and equitable to do so. A questionnaire procedure similar to that available in sex and race discrimination cases is available so that the employer may be questioned on his reasons for acting in a particular way. Where the employer fails to respond or where his reply is evasive or equivocal, the tribunal is entitled to infer that there has been unlawful discrimination.

Where a person presents a complaint to an industrial tribunal, a copy is sent to ACAS to enable a conciliation officer to attempt to promote a settlement to avoid the need for a tribunal hearing. Where there is a hearing and the tribunal finds that there has been discrimination, it can:

1 make a declaration of the rights of the parties;

2 order payment of compensation;
3 recommend that the employer takes action within a specified period to reduce the adverse effect of the discrimination.

There is no maximum award of compensation and there can be an award of compensation for injury to feelings. The amount of compensation payable can be increased where the employer fails to comply with a recommendation. Regulations will be made to enable a tribunal to order interest to be paid on the award of compensation.

In addition to being liable for their own discriminatory acts, employers will be vicariously liable for discrimination by employees, whether or not it was done with the employer's knowledge or approval, if it was done in the course of their employment. The employer will have a defence, however, if he can show that he took such steps as were reasonably practicable to prevent employees from discriminating.

National Disability Council

The Act creates the National Disability Council to advise the Secretary of State on matters relevant to the elimination of discrimination against disabled persons and on measures likely to reduce or eliminate such discrimination. It will also give advice on the operation of the Act and regulations made under it. At the request of the Secretary of State, the Council shall prepare Codes of Practice. However, the powers of this new body are limited when compared to those of the Equal Opportunities Commission or the Commission for Racial Equality. It has no enforcement powers and cannot offer assistance to complainants bringing cases to tribunals. Financial assistance for those pursuing disability discrimination claims is likely to come from pressure groups and trade unions. In addition, advice to government on discrimination in employment will continue to remain the province of the National Advisory Council on Employment of People with Disabilities (NACEPD).

QUESTIONS

1 George has been employed as the manager of a betting shop for the last two years. He is dismissed when his employers discover that 15 years ago he spent six months in prison after being convicted of fraud. George had failed to disclose this conviction when he was interviewed for the manager's post. Advise George.

2 James applies for a post as a sales assistant in a unisex boutique. He is told that as there are already three male assistants and only two female assistants the owner wants to employ another woman. Advise James.

3 Jennifer works part time in a factory. There are 40 part-time workers of whom

35 are women. Due to a recession, management decides that 50 employees must be made redundant. It is decided to make the part-timers redundant first and Jennifer is told that she is to be dismissed by reason of redundancy. Advise Jennifer.

4 Stephen applies for a job as a sales representative. At his interview he is asked whether he is married. When he replies that he is, the managing director asks whether he would be prepared to travel away from home a lot. The managing director also comments that sales jobs are probably more suitable for persons without family ties. Stephen receives a letter stating that his application has been unsuccessful. He later discovers that all three successful applicants are single men. Advise Stephen.

5 Molly and Carol, who are employed by Bloggs Ltd, are delighted to discover that they are pregnant. When they tell the manager, Mr Smith, the good news he is less happy. Molly, who has worked for the company for only three months, is told that she is dismissed. Carol, who has worked for the company for three years, is told that she will not now be sent on a two-month training course as it would be a waste of time to send someone who will shortly be going on maternity leave. Advise Molly and Carol.

6 Linda sees an advertisement for machinists in her local newspaper. She telephones the factory and is told that there are still vacancies. She is told to pick up an application form from the factory. Later that morning when she goes to collect an application form she is told that all the posts have now been filled. Linda is black. A week later a white neighbour contacts the factory, is told that there are still vacancies, and is appointed after an interview. Advise Linda.

7 John, a white actor, is not allowed to audition for the part of Othello. He believes this is racial discrimination. Advise John.

8 Amanda has applied for the post of administrative assistant with Acme Ltd. She is the most suitable candidate for the post and Acme Ltd would have employed her but for the fact that she is a wheelchair user. They say that the three steps at the entrance to the building where she would be employed would prevent her gaining access. In addition, the office where she would work is situated on the first floor and there is no lift in the building. Advise Amanda as to her legal position.

EQUAL PAY

The concept of equal pay and the European dimension

The aim of the Equal Pay Act 1970 is to prevent discrimination as regards terms and conditions of employment between men and women. However, it should be noted that a significant gap remains between men's and women's pay. Although the pay gap between men and women is narrowing, the 1994 New Earnings Survey disclosed that women's average gross hourly earnings stand at approximately 80 per cent of men's average gross hourly earnings. The gap is even wider when average gross weekly earnings excluding overtime are compared; women earn on average only 72 per cent (£261.50) of men's earnings (£362.10). Another disturbing fact is that women remain concentrated in lower paid jobs at the bottom of the pay scale. In 1992 one-third of women but only 10 per cent of men earned less than £170 per week and while just under 25 per cent of men earned £420 per week or more, under 7 per cent of women achieved that level of pay.

The 1970 Act seeks to ensure that every term in a woman's contract is not less favourable than the equivalent term in a man's contract. A female employee may find that she is paid less than a male colleague doing the same job, or that she is entitled to fewer holidays. The Act also provides that where a beneficial term in a man's contract is missing altogether from a woman's contract, it shall be treated as being included in the woman's contract. A female employee may discover that a male colleague doing the same job is given luncheon vouchers or an interest-free loan to buy a season ticket whereas her contract contains no such provisions. All these differences in terms may be contrary to the Equal Pay Act 1970.

The Equal Pay Act 1970 also entitles men to bring an equal pay claim should they discover that any of their terms are less favourable than those enjoyed by a female colleague. However, whether or not a person is legally entitled to the same terms and conditions as a colleague of the opposite sex, depends on whether their claim satisfies the requirements of the 1970 Act.

In addition, there may be a remedy under European Community law. The Equal Pay Act 1970 as amended by the Equal Pay (Amendment) Regulations 1983 seeks to satisfy the requirements of Article 119 of the Treaty of Rome and the Equal Pay Directive 75/117/EEC. Article 119 requires member states of the European Community to ensure the application of the principle that men and women should receive equal pay for equal work. For the purposes of Article 119, 'pay' means the ordinary, basic or minimum wage or salary and any other consideration, whether in cash or in kind, which the worker receives, directly or indirectly, in respect of his employment from his employer. The European Court of Justice held in **Defrenne** *v* **Sabena No 2 [1976] ECR 445** that Article 119 is directly applicable within member states and that its provisions are enforceable in domestic courts against employers – i.e., it has *direct effect*.

The provisions of a Community measure which has direct effect can be relied upon by individuals in UK courts and tribunals without there having to be any UK legislation giving such rights. British employees have successfully relied upon the provisions of Article 119 where UK law failed to provide a remedy. In **McCarthys Ltd** *v* **Smith [1980] 2 CMLR 205** a woman discovered she was being paid less as manager than the man who held the post before her. The English Court of Appeal held that the wording of the Equal Pay Act 1970 allowed comparisons to be made only with men employed at the same time as the woman. However, the European Court of Justice held that comparisons under Article 119 were not restricted to comparisons with persons who are employed at the same time as the person seeking equal pay. The female applicant was entitled to compare herself with her male predecessor.

In **Garland** *v* **British Rail Engineering [1982] 2 ECR 359** the European Court of

Justice held that benefits such as the provision of concessionary travel for dependents of retired rail employees would fall within the definition of 'pay' for the purposes of Article 119.

In **Barber *v* Guardian Royal Exchange [1990] IRLR 240** the European Court of Justice was asked to consider whether benefits received by employees in connection with redundancy should be regarded as 'pay' for the purposes of Article 119 and the Equal Pay Directive. The court held that payments paid by an employer to a worker in connection with the latter's compulsory redundancy fall within the scope of Article 119, whether they are paid under a contract of employment, by virtue of statutory provisions or voluntarily. Having decided that redundancy payments came within the meaning of 'pay', the European Court then proceeded to address the question of whether Article 119 is infringed if a man and a woman, of the same age, are made compulsorily redundant in the same circumstances, and in connection with that redundancy, the woman receives an immediate private pension but the man's pension rights under the occupational pension scheme are deferred for another ten years. It also fell to be considered whether the principle of equal pay is infringed if the total value of the benefits received by the woman is greater than the total value of benefits received by the man. In summary, the *Barber* decision established that payments made by an employer in connection with redundancy must not discriminate on grounds of sex.

The Equal Pay Directive 75/117/EEC declared that the principle of equal pay for men and women outlined in Article 119 was to be taken as including the right to equal pay for work of equal value. This enables a woman to seek the same pay as a man doing an entirely different job where the woman believes her work is of equal value to his. The European Commission did not believe that the Equal Pay Act 1970, as originally enacted, adequately allowed for an equal pay claim to be brought upon the ground that a woman was doing work of equal value to that done by a man. Enforcement proceedings were brought against the UK and the Commission's complaint upheld, in **Commission of the European Communities *v* United Kingdom [1982] IRLR 333**. As a result, the UK government introduced the Equal Pay (Amendment) Regulations 1983 which introduced into British legislation the concept of the right to equal pay for work of equal value.

Decisions of the European Court of Justice relating to the interpretation of European Community law are binding on courts and tribunals within the UK. In addition, British courts and tribunals should interpret the Equal Pay Act 1970 so as to give effect to Article 119 and the Equal Pay Directive.

Article 119 and Pensions

The landmark decision of the European Court of Justice in *Barber* also declared that pensions paid under a contracted-out occupational pension scheme fall within the scope of Article 119 of the Treaty of Rome dealing with equal pay and therefore such schemes must not discriminate between men and women. However, the judgment gave rise to many issues which required clarification and there was doubt as to whether or not its effects were retrospective.

The question of the retrospective effect of *Barber* was answered in the **Ten Oever Case [1993] IRLR 601** in which the ECJ held that *Barber* was not retrospective and there could be enforcement of equalisation of pension benefits only in respect of service since 17 May 1990, the date of the *Barber* judgment. In *Ten Oever* the ECJ held that survivor's benefits are pay for the purposes of Article 119. However Mr Ten Oever's claim for a widower's pension following *Barber* failed because his wife had died before the date of the *Barber* decision.

On 28 September 1994 the ECJ issued decisions in six cases where clarification had been sought on the issue of equality in the area of occupational pensions. The issues raised were complex, but the key points to have emerged are given below.

Part time workers – access to pension schemes

To deny part-time employees access to an occupational pension scheme is actionable under Article 119 where the exclusion affects more women than men and the employer fails to justify their exclusion on grounds unrelated to their sex. Moreover, part-timers can make a retrospective claim dating as far back as 1976 – subject to the inevitable difficulties relating to time limits for raising actions (see the discussion above relating to the *Biggs* case). This aspect of the judgment is especially important to employees whose employers operate a non-contributory scheme. However where the scheme is contributory, the claimants would have to finance their own backdated contributions. (**Vroege *v* NCIV Instituut voor Volkshuisvesting BV [1994] IRLR 651; and Fisscher v Voorhuis Hengelo BV [1994] IRLR 662.**)

Equalisation of benefits

In terms of the equalisation of pension ages and benefits there are three distinct periods identified. Prior to *Barber* (17 May 1990) Article 119 could not be invoked to require equality of pension ages or entitlements. As regards periods of service between 17 May 1990 and the date on which a scheme provided equalised benefits, benefits payable to the disadvantaged sex had to be improved to equal those previously enjoyed by the advantaged sex. This means men would be able to retire at 60 and enjoy the same benefits as a woman retiring at 60. However, the ECJ held that as regards periods of service after steps are taken to eliminate discrimination in the operation of the scheme, equal treatment can be achieved 'by reducing the advantages which the advantaged employees used to enjoy'. What this means is that women can be forced to work until they are 65 – equality does not have to be achieved by improving the man's position, it can lawfully be achieved by worsening the woman's position. However, an employer cannot retrospectively raise the retirement age for women in relation to periods of service between 17 May 1990 and the date on which the scheme made provision for the equalised benefits. (**Smith and Others *v* Advel Systems Ltd [1994] IRLR 602; and Van den Akker & Others *v* Stichting Shell Pensioenfonds [1994] IRLR 616.**)

Transitional measures

In relation to the previous point it was also held that where the retirement age for women is raised, transitional measures cannot be introduced 'to limit the adverse consequences for women as regards benefits payable in respect of future periods of service'. (**Smith and Others *v* Advel Systems Ltd [1994] IRLR 602.**)

Transfer of pension

Should an employee change jobs and transfer pension rights from the former employer's scheme to the new employer's scheme then – in respect of service from 17 May 1990 – the new employer's scheme, the transferee scheme, must fund any increased benefits which it is necessary to pay in order to comply with the requirements of Article 119. Responsibility lies with the transferee scheme notwithstanding any shortfall in the monies transferred from the first scheme due to discrimination on the part of the former employer. (**Coloroll Pension Trustees Ltd** *v* **Russell & Others [1994] IRLR 586.**)

Pension scheme trustees

Article 119 may be relied on against the trustees of an occupational pension scheme as the trustees are bound to comply in their administration of the scheme with the principle of equal treatment. The trustees cannot argue that they are prevented by the rules of the trust from making the changes necessary to eliminate any discrimination. Should this be the case trustees would have to take all steps available under the law to seek to effect any changes. Such steps might include seeking the authorisation of the court to vary the provisions of the scheme. (**Coloroll Pension Trustees Ltd** *v* **Russell & Others [1994] IRLR 586.**)

Voluntary contributions

Article 119 applies the principle of equal treatment to all benefits paid by occupational pensions schemes irrespective of whether the scheme is contributory or non-contributory. However, benefits which accrue from the payment by an employee of additional voluntary contributions made to increase the size of his final pension are not covered by Article 119. (**Coloroll Pension Trustees Ltd** *v* **Russell & Others [1994] IRLR 586.**)

Survivor's benefits

Article 119 applies to survivor's benefits enjoyed by an employee's dependants. However equal treatment in respect of benefits payable to dependants – such as a widower's pension – can be enforced only in respect of service since 17 May 1990 – the date of the *Barber* judgement. In respect of survivor's benefits which are not linked to the employee's actual length of service – such as a death-in-service lump sum – equal treatment applies where the 'operative event', e.g., death, occurs after 17 May 1990. (**Coloroll Pension Trustees Ltd** *v* **Russell & Others [1994] IRLR 586.**)

Civil service pensions

Article 119 was held to apply to civil service pensions. (**Bestuur van het ABP** *v* **Beune [1995] IRLR 103.**)

Following the rulings in the European Court of Justice, the UK government introduced the Occupational Pension Schemes (Equal Access to Membership) Amendment Regulations 1995 (SI 1995/1215) which came into force on 31 May 1995 and outlaws both direct and indirect discrimination in relation to access to pension schemes. The regulations provide that ex-employees must raise actions under these regulations within six months of leaving employment. Moreover, any award can be backdated for only two years. However, in respect of any service after 31 May 1995, the full amount of any backdated contributions, including any employee's contributions, must be paid by the employer. In respect of any service before 31 May 1995, the employee will have to make retrospective contributions.

In addition, the Pensions Act 1995 s 62 implies into occupational pension schemes an equality clause so that where a woman is employed in like work, work rated as equivalent or work of equal value to that of a man (for a discussion of the meaning of these terms see below), any terms relating either to access to or benefits under the scheme that are less favourable than a man's are to be treated as modified so as to be no less favourable than the terms applicable to a man. However, any such difference in treatment may be able to be justified if it can be shown to be due to a genuine material factor which is unrelated to sex (see below for a discussion of the 'genuine material factor' defence in the context of the Equal Pay Act 1970).

The *Barber* decision did not apply to state pensions. The Pensions Act 1995 sets a common state pension age of 65 to be phased in between 2010 and 2020.

The relationship between the Equal Pay Act 1970 and the Sex Discrimination Act 1975

Although the Equal Pay Act was passed in 1970, it only came into force in December 1975 at the same time as the Sex Discrimination Act 1975. Employers were given five years in which to remove discrimination from their pay structures. It should be noted that there is no overlap between the 1970 and the 1975 Acts. A woman's complaint may fall under one or other of the two Acts but no single incident is covered by both.

The Sex Discrimination Act deals with discrimination before employment, for example, in relation to recruitment practices. The 1975 Act also deals with discrimination once the woman is in employment but only in relation to non-contractual matters such as promotion or dismissal.

The Equal Pay Act 1970 covers situations where an employee of one sex receives less favourable treatment than one of the opposite sex in respect of pay received or in respect of another contractual term, such as an entitlement to a company car.

The provisions of the Equal Pay Act 1970 as amended by the Equal Pay (Amendment) Regulations 1983

The 1970 Act operates by implying an equality clause into every contract of employment. The effect of the implied equality clause is that if a woman enjoys less favourable terms than a man, her contract shall be treated as modified so that her terms are no longer less favourable. If a beneficial term in a man's contract is missing altogether from a woman's contract, it shall be treated as being included in the woman's contract. However, before such modifications are made, the woman must show either:

1 that she is engaged in *like work* to that done by the man; *or*

2 that she is doing *work rated as equivalent* to that done by the man; *or*
3 that her *work is of equal value* to that done by the man.

Should an employer refuse to modify a woman's contract, she may present an equal pay claim to an industrial tribunal. Claims must be brought while in employment or within six months of leaving. If the tribunal is satisfied that the applicant has a valid claim, it can make an order declaring the rights of the parties and it can award the applicant up to two years arrears of pay.

A comparison must be made between the female applicant to the tribunal and a man employed by the same or an associated employer. It should be noted that unlike the Sex Discrimination Act 1975 where a woman can compare herself with a hypothetical man – for example, 'had I been a man I would have been hired' – under the Equal Pay Act 1970 a woman must find an actual comparator. The comparator must be a person of the opposite sex employed *in the same employment as the applicant*. This means that the comparator must be employed by the same or an associated employer. An associated employer will be a holding company or a subsidiary company of the company which employs the applicant, or a member of the same group of companies. The male comparator may work beside the woman applicant, or in a different part of the same workplace, or in a different workplace. A woman can compare herself to a man employed in a different workplace altogether only if the two workplaces share common terms and conditions.

The question of what is required to establish that a comparator is in 'the same employment' arose in **Leverton** *v* **Clywd County Council [1989] IRLR 29**. Mrs L, a nursery nurse, claimed equal pay under the equal value ground. She chose several male comparators employed by the Council in clerical posts at various workplaces. Mrs L and her comparators were all covered by the same collective agreement. The men were paid on a higher scale. However, Mrs L worked fewer hours and had longer holidays. Mrs L's employers argued that her claim failed to get off the ground because her comparators could not be said to be 'in the same employment' as Mrs L, as required by the Act. The employers argued that the different workplaces did not share common terms and conditions. The employers said this was so because of the marked differences between Mrs L's holidays and hours and those of the men. The Industrial Tribunal, the EAT and Court of Appeal agreed with the employers. However, the House of Lords disagreed. When the Act refers to two workplaces sharing common terms and conditions it does not mean that the personal terms and conditions of an applicant and her comparator have to be the same or similar. It is enough that the same collective agreement, applicable to a wide range of employees, covers workers at both workplaces. Although this point was cleared up in Mrs L's favour, her claim failed because it was held that there were genuine material factors which justified the difference in pay. The question of what is required to establish that a claimant and her comparator are 'in the same employment' although employed at different establishments was considered again more recently by the House of Lords in **British Coal Corporation** *v* **Smith and Others [1996] IRLR 404**. In this case 1286 female canteen workers and cleaners employed by British Coal claimed that their work was of equal value to that done by 150 male clerical workers and surface mineworkers. The women were employed at 47 different establishments, their comparators at 17. At issue was the requirement that where a claimant and her comparator are employed in different establishments, 'common terms and conditions of employment' are observed at each establishment. It was argued that the male surface mineworkers did not share common terms and conditions across the various establishments because of different local agreements on concessionary coal and incentive bonuses. The IT and the EAT took a broad comparison approach, taking the view that as these local agreements were derived from and based on national agreements, there were common terms and conditions observed as between the establishments. This was overturned by the Court of Appeal which held that the Act required that terms and conditions at different establishments are 'the same' rather than 'broadly similar'. However, the House of Lords disagreed and held that the tribunal had not erred in finding that there were common terms and conditions observed at the different establishments. Lord Slynn decided that the legislation did not require that comparators at various establishments share identical terms and conditions. What was required, he concluded, was that 'the terms and conditions of the [comparators] were sufficiently similar for a fair comparison to be made ... '. He further stated, '... the terms and conditions do not have to be identical, but on a broad basis to be substantially comparable ...'.

A woman who brings an equal pay claim must satisfy one of the following grounds.

'Like work'

The applicant must be doing the same or broadly similar work to that done by a member of the opposite sex. This is called **like work**. Any differences in the work done by the woman and her comparator should not be of practical importance and regard will be had to the frequency, nature and extent of any differences. When determining whether two jobs are 'broadly similar', a tribunal should take a wide view and minor differences in detail should not prevent a finding of 'like work'.

In **Capper Pass Ltd *v* Lawton [1976] IRLR 366** a female cook who worked in the directors' dining room sought equal pay with two male asistant chefs who worked in the main works canteen. She prepared ten to twenty lunches per day, whereas the men provided many more meals for workers over a number of shifts. The woman was held to be engaged in like work to the men. What was done was broadly the same and similar skills were required to be able to do the work. The applicant shall not be engaged in like work if the comparator's work involves more responsibility. For example, a woman may be working on components which are not particularly costly so that if she makes a mistake the loss to the employer would not be that great. The male comparator may be carrying out technically similar tasks but on very valuable components so that any error would be very costly to the employer. The greater responsibility borne by the man would prevent the applicant and her comparator being engaged on like work. The employer may try to prevent a finding of like work by pointing to contractual duties which a man may be called upon to perform. Different duties which a man may have to perform in theory will not prevent a finding of like work if it is found that, in practice, the man is never actually required to perform such tasks. This was so in the case of **Shields *v* E Coomes (Holdings) Ltd [1978] IRLR 263** where a female counterhand in a betting shop was paid 62p an hour whereas male counterhands received £1.06 an hour. The employers argued that the woman was not engaged in like work because the men were required by contract to deal with violent and difficult customers. It was found that the male comparator had never been called upon to deal with any violent customers and was not in any way trained or qualified to do so. In practice, the male and female counterhands were engaged in like work.

'Work rated as equivalent'

The applicant's job has been rated the same as that of a member of the opposite sex under a proper (analytical and not in itself discriminatory) job evaluation study. This is called **work rated as equivalent**. A job evaluation study attempts to give jobs a rating or score by breaking the job down into component parts and giving each a mark. Marks may be awarded for factors such as qualifications required to do the job or the amount of supervision required. Marks awarded for each factor are added together to give the job a total rating. An applicant will fail in an equal pay claim if the employer establishes that the comparator's job had a different value under a job evaluation study *unless* the applicant can show that the study itself was discriminatory. A job evaluation study only counts for the purposes of the Act if it is quantitative and objective rather than qualitative and subjective. In **Bromley & Others** *v* **H & J Quick Ltd [1988] IRLR 249** it was held that a study must be analytical and evaluate each of the jobs under various headings.

A job evaluation study might be discriminatory where it gives a high weighting to physical strength, which would favour men, and a low weighting to manual dexterity, where women would expect to score well.

'Work of equal value'

The above were the two original grounds contained in the 1970 Act as it stood prior to the 1983 Equal Pay (Amendment) Regulations. Since 1 January 1984 there has been a third ground which is that the applicant's work is of **equal value** to that of a member of the opposite sex in terms of effort, skill, decision making and the other demands it makes of the applicant. The applicant is entitled to compare her work to that of men doing entirely different jobs. The comparator must not be engaged in like work and the applicant's work must not already have been assessed under a job evaluation study. What the third ground really provides is the right to demand that a job evaluation study is carried out. Where the applicant's work is found to be of equal value to that of her comparator, she is entitled to the same terms and conditions of employment.

In respect of claims brought under the *equal value* ground, the Industrial Tribunal may proceed to determine the question or may appoint an independent expert to assess the relative worth of the jobs. The tribunal cannot proceed to commission an independent expert's report where it is satisfied that there are no reasonable grounds for determining that the work in question is of equal value. Both the employer and the applicant have the right to comment on any report, produce their own expert evidence and cross-examine the independent expert. Should it be decided that the two jobs are of equal value, the employer has an opportunity to persuade the tribunal that notwithstanding that fact, there is a genuine material factor which justifies the difference in pay.

An applicant is not barred from bringing an equal pay claim on the equal value ground just because there is a 'token man' employed on the same work as she is and who earns the same pay. In **Pickstone & Others** *v* **Freeman PLC [1988] IRLR 357** five female packers in a warehouse claimed that their work was of equal value to that of a male warehouse checker who was paid £4.22 per week more than them. There was a male warehouse packer doing the same work as the women and being paid the same as the women. The House of Lords decided that the only reason a woman would be barred from bringing an equal value claim is if her chosen comparator is doing like work or work rated as equivalent. She would not be barred by the fact that a man other than the comparator was doing such work and being paid the same as she. This prevents equal value claims being defeated by the employment of a token man on low paid work done by women. Once such women win on the equal value ground, the token man may then bring an equal pay claim based on the ground of like work with the women.

Another important equal value case is the House of Lords decision in **Hayward** *v* **Cammell Laird Shipbuilders Ltd [1988] 2 All ER 257**. Julie Hayward was a canteen cook in a shipyard. She brought an equal pay claim on the equal value ground, choosing as her comparators, a painter, a joiner and a thermal insulation engineer. She argued that as her work was of equal value to theirs, her basic pay and overtime rate should be the same. Although Ms Hayward's work was found to be of equal value to that done by the men, the English Court of Appeal took a 'whole package' approach and put a global value on all the provisions in the contract relating to pay. The Court of Appeal held that her basic pay and overtime rate need not be increased because her overall remuneration, taking into account sick pay and holiday pay entitlement, was worth as much as her comparators. The House of Lords overturned this decision. The House of Lords held that an applicant whose work is found to be of equal value to that of her comparators is entitled to have each distinct term of her contract of employment modified so that it is no less favourable than the corresponding term of her comparator's contract. Ms Hayward was entitled to an increase in her basic pay and overtime rates because each was a distinct contractual term in its own right. This decision means of course that the men could then bring an equal pay claim in order to have their sick pay and holiday pay entitlement improved to match Ms Hayward's.

It may be the case that should a woman bring an equal pay claim based on the equal value ground, the independent expert may find that although she is paid less, her work is of *greater* value than the work done by her male comparator. The European Court of Justice held in **Murphy** *v* **Bord Telecom Eiremann [1988] IRLR 267** that a woman can rely on Article 119 of the Treaty of Rome, which guarantees the principle of equal pay for work of equal value, where her work is of greater value. Such a woman should succeed in her equal pay claim.

Defences to an equal pay claim

Even if it is established that a woman is engaged in like work or work rated as equivalent or work which is of equal value to that done by her comparator, her contract shall not be varied if the employer can show that the difference in terms is justified because it is genuinely due to a **material factor** which is not the difference in sex. Where the claim is based on the ground of like work or work rated as equivalent, the factor *must* be a material difference between the cases. Where the claim is based on the equal value ground, the factor *may* be a material difference.

The practice of 'red circling' may amount to a material difference which justifies a difference in pay. In the event of a restructuring of the workforce, particular posts may be downgraded. All new entrants to the posts are paid at the new lower rate. However, the employers may agree to 'red circle' or maintain the higher rate of pay for those persons already employed before the posts were downgraded. This practice may be put forward as a defence to an equal pay claim. However, in **Snoxell & Davies *v* Vauxhall Motors Ltd [1977] IRLR 123** the defence of red circling failed because the reason why male machine inspectors had been paid more than women inspectors prior to downgrading was due to past sex discrimination.

At one time it was thought that in determining whether there was a material difference which justified the difference in pay, the difference had to be a personal difference between the applicant and the comparator. Differences which would justify a difference in pay might include the comparator having longer service or superior qualifications or the fact that the comparator is paid more because he works in London and receives a London 'weighting'.

In **Clay Cross (Quarry Services) Ltd *v* Fletcher [1979] 1 All ER 474** it was established that a female clerk was engaged in like work with a male clerk who was paid more than she. The employer argued that the difference in pay was due to a material difference other than sex, namely that when hired, the male clerk refused to take the job for less. The Court of Appeal said this did not amount to a defence. Genuine material differences should be limited to personal differences and could not include external factors such as market forces.

However, in **Rainey *v* Greater Glasgow Health Board Eastern District [1987] IRLR 26** the House of Lords upheld the decision of the EAT and the Inner House of the Court of Session that genuine material factors go beyond the personal equation where a difference in pay can be shown to be necessary to achieve a legitimate economic objective or for sound objectively justified administrative reasons. In this case, the fitting of artificial limbs was carried out in hospitals by prosthetists employed by outside contractors. In Scotland it was decided to set up a prosthetic service within the NHS. As there was no set pay scale for prosthetists, it was decided to pay them the same as medical physics technicians. Ms Rainey was a newly qualified prosthetist who had not worked in the private sector. The private sector paid more and so, in order to establish the NHS service, it was felt necessary to encourage some private sector prosthetists to transfer into the NHS by matching and thereafter maintaining their private sector rates of pay. The offer of transfer on these terms was made to 20 private sector prosthetists who 'all happened to be men'. The need to establish the new service was held to be a valid objective which justified the difference in pay. New entrants would be paid the NHS rates and the anomaly would disappear in time as the original 20 men retired or left. Ms Rainey's equal pay claim did not succeed.

Prior to the *Rainey* decision it had been supposed that the employer was given wider scope to establish a genuine material factor defence when defending an equal value claim than when defending an equal pay claim based on the other two grounds. However, since the *Rainey* decision, it is arguable that there is no real difference between the defences.

However, in the more recent case of **Ratcliffe and others *v* North Yorkshire County Council [1995] IRLR 439** the House of Lords has looked again at what is necessary to constitute a genuine material factor defence based on market forces. In this case three dinner ladies, whose work had previously been rated as equivalent to that done by male road sweepers and refuse collectors, had their wages cut when the council set up a direct service organisation (DSO) to compete with private firms bidding for school dinner contracts because of the requirements of compulsory competitive tendering. The DSO thought it could not compete with private firms which paid their workers less and so it had made the three women redundant and re-employed them on lower wages. The women brought equal pay claims to an industrial tribunal where they won; the tribunal held that the employers had not established a defence under s 1(3). The EAT and the Court of Appeal disagreed and decided that 'the need to compete with a rival bid was unconnected with the difference of sex between potential male and female employees'. However, the House of Lords upheld the dinner ladies' appeal. Basically this was a female-dominated workforce which was paid less precisely because it was a female-dominated workforce.

It is clear that an employer cannot use as a defence a factor which no longer applies. In **Benveniste *v* University of Southampton [1989] IRLR 122** a female maths lecturer was appointed at a salary far lower than a person of her age and qualifications might expect. She was paid less than four male colleagues already in post because the university was subject to severe financial constraints at the time of her appointment. A year after her appointment the financial situation improved but the university would not increase her salary. Dr Benveniste finally brought equal pay proceedings. She lost before the Industrial Tribunal and the EAT but the Court of Appeal allowed her appeal. The fact that there was once a material difference was held not to justify a difference in pay forever.

Indirect pay discrimination?

The Equal Pay Act 1970 does not offer a remedy in respect of indirect pay discrimination. Indirect pay discrimination occurs where apparently neutral criteria are applied equally to the sexes but the result is a disproportionate adverse impact on women's pay. However, there have been a series of European Court of Justice decisions which appear to recognise indirect pay discrimination as being actionable under Article 119 of the Treaty of Rome and the Equal Pay Directive 75/117/EEC. As these decisions are binding on British courts and tribunals, it would appear that employees in the UK have a directly enforceable right to take action in respect of indirect pay discrimination under European Community law.

In **Rinner-Kuhn *v* FWW Spezial-Gebaudereinigung GmbH [1989] IRLR 493** Mrs R-K who worked only ten hours per week was refused sick pay by her employers in reliance upon West German legislation which entitled only employees working more than ten hours per week to six weeks' wages while unfit to work because of illness. The German Labour Court asked the European Court of Justice whether the statutory entitlement to sick pay came within the meaning of 'pay' for the purposes of Article 119. The court was also asked whether statutory provisions excluding part-time workers contravened Article 119 if they had a disproportionate adverse impact upon women. The European Court held that Article 119 must be interpreted as forbidding national legislation which permits employers to exclude certain part-time employees from entitlement to sick pay where that legislation affects a considerably greater number of women than men *unless* the member state can show that the legislation is justified by objective factors unrelated to any discrimination on grounds of sex. Accordingly, statutory rights which have a discriminatory effect may be challenged under Article 119.

In **Handels-OG Kontorfunktionaerernes Forbund I Danmark** *v* **Dansk Arbejdsgiverforening – The 'Danfoss' case – [1989] IRLR 532** the employers paid the same basic pay to workers in the same pay grade. A collective agreement allowed the employer to pay to individuals additional payments depending on a number of factors including flexibility, quality of work, vocational training undertaken and seniority. A survey of employees' pay revealed a 6.85 per cent difference between the average pay of male and female workers within the same grade. It was argued that this amounted to a prima-facie case of discrimination. The Danish tribunal asked the European Court of Justice to rule on the legitimacy of taking into account particular factors when determining pay increases. The European Court held that the employer does not need to justify paying employees more if they have longer service (but see *Nimz* decision below). However, in respect of extra pay for flexibility and training, the court held that the employer had to be able to show that such flexibility and training were important in practice in the employee's actual performance of his duties. The employer cannot justify paying extra for things which are not actually required for the job *if* such payments operate to the disadvantage of women doing the same work. 'Merit' pay cannot be legally justified where the result is a significant difference between the earnings of men and women doing equal work. The court refused to accept that male workers could always deserve merit pay more than female workers.

As we have seen, in the *Danfoss* decision the European Court of Justice took the view that employers did not have to justify making long service payments 'since seniority goes hand in hand with experience which generally places a worker in a better position to carry out his duties'. However, in certain jobs longer service will not of itself mean that one worker is better at his job than another worker with less service. This aspect of the *Danfoss* decision has been overruled by the more recent European Court of Justice decision in **Nimz** *v* **Freie und Hansestadt Hamburg [1991] IRLR 222**. Mrs N worked for the City of Hamburg and her terms and conditions were governed by the collective agreement for public sector employees known as the BAT. Under the BAT, full-time employees on the Category 1 pay scale automatically moved up to the Category 2 pay scale on completion of six years' service. However, part-timers, who worked less than three-quarters of full-time hours, had to have 12 years' service in order to receive the upgrade in pay. Mrs N worked for only 20 hours per week and her employers refused to move her on to the higher salary scale after six years' service. As 90 per cent of part-time staff were women while only 55 per cent of the full-time staff were women, Mrs N argued that this amounted to indirect discrimination. She further argued that there were no objectively justified reasons for doubling the period of service required by part-time employees in order to move up to the higher salary scale. The court held that such a provision as was contained in the BAT would discriminate against women when a considerably smaller percentage of men than women are employed part-time *unless* the difference in pay can be objectively justified by factors unrelated to any discrimination on grounds of sex. The employers attempted to argue that an employee acquires greater competence over time and full-time employees acquire such competence more quickly. However, the court held that such arguments were generalisations which could not amount to objective criteria. In order to justify long service payments, the employer must be in a position to provide evidence of the advantages which long service actually brings to his business.

In **Kowalska *v* Freie und Hanestadt Hamburg [1990] IRLR 447 ECJ** the European Court of Justice found that the terms of a collective agreement were contrary to Article 119. Mrs Kowalska's terms of employment were governed by a collective agreement which provided that full-time employees were entitled to a severance grant on retirement. When Mrs Kowalska retired her employers refused to pay the grant because she worked only part time. Mrs Kowalska complained to the Hamburg Labour Court that this amounted to unlawful indirect discrimination. The Hamburg Labour Court referred the matter to the European Court of Justice for consideration. Firstly, the court considered whether Article 119 prohibited a collective agreement from providing that only full-timers would be eligible for a severance grant, where a significantly higher proportion of women than men were part-timers. The court's decision was that severance pay could constitute 'pay' for the purposes of Article 119. Moreover, a collective agreement would be contrary to Article 119 if, in enabling employers to exclude part-timers from the benefit of a grant, it appeared in practice that a considerably lower number of men than women worked part time.

To escape a finding of discrimination an employer must establish that the provision was justified on objective grounds other than sex. In cases such as *Mrs Kowalska*'s, a finding of discrimination should lead to the payment of a severance grant *pro rata* with the grant payable to full-time employees.

Another significant decision of the European Court of Justice is that of **Arbeiterwohlfahrt der Stadt Berlin eV *v* Botel [1992] IRLR 423**. In this case Mrs B worked part-time as a nurse in Berlin. As a member of the Staff Committee, she was entitled under German legislation to time off without reduction in salary to attend training courses relevant to the work of the committee. Mrs B attended six courses and was paid for her normal working hours but because the courses lasted longer than her normal working hours she spent 50.3 hours of her own time at the courses. Mrs B sought either overtime pay or paid time off to compensate for this. The Berlin Labour Court upheld her claim and her employers appealed. On appeal the matter was referred to the European Court of Justice. The first important point to note is that the Court decided that compensation in the form of paid time off to participate in training in accordance with statutory provisions is to be regarded as 'pay' for the purposes of Article 119 and the Equal Pay Directive. It was held that 'although such compensation does not arise from the contract of employment, it is nevertheless paid by the employer by virtue of legislative provisions and by reason of the existence of an employment relationship with an employee'. The second point is that, since the effect of the legislation was that full-time employees would receive more by way of compensation for attending courses than part-time employees, this would amount to indirect discrimination contrary to both Article 119 and the Equal Pay Directive unless the legislation could be justified by objective factors unrelated to any discrimination on grounds of sex. This decision may have an impact on the rights of British trade union officials to paid time off for trade union duties. First, under UK law, part-time employees working between 8 and 16 hours per week have no right to paid time off for trade union duties until they have five years' service.

Secondly, in the case of **Hairsine** *v* **Kingston-upon-Hull City Council [1992] IRLR 211**, the EAT held that the entitlement to time off with pay relates only to hours when the employee would otherwise have been at work; there is no entitlement to be paid for training which takes place outwith normal working hours. Both these aspects of UK law are likely to be challenged in the light of the decision in the *Botel* case.

British employees have a directly enforceable right to take action in respect of indirect pay discrimination. Although no such right is available under the Equal Pay Act 1970, the employee's claim can rest on a breach of Article 119 of the Treaty of Rome.

QUESTIONS

1 There are three grounds upon which a woman may bring an equal pay claim; what are they?

2 Sandra has been employed as a lab technician in a school for three months. She discovers that a male technician, Fred, is paid more than she is. Sandra thinks this is unfair as she works much harder than Fred. Sandra is told that Fred is paid at a higher rate on the Technician Grade Pay Scale because he has five years' service. If Sandra had five years' service she would be paid the same as Fred. Sandra is considering bringing an equal pay claim. Advise Sandra.

3 Mary is employed as a supervisor in a garment factory. She supervises the work of 50 female machinists. Mary discovers that she is paid £20 per week less than Jim, the Dispatch Supervisor. He supervises the work of ten warehousemen who make up orders and load cartons of finished garments on to trucks for delivery to customers. Mary believes that her job is every bit as demanding as Jim's and does not think that the difference in pay is justified. Advise Mary.

4 Sonia is employed by a building society as a part-time clerical assistant. She discovers that full-time employees are given preferential interest rates on mortgages taken out with the society. Sonia is told that she is not entitled to the preferential rate because she works part time. Seventy per cent of full-time staff are male, while 95 per cent of part-time staff are female. Advise Sonia.

5 Jean is employed as an accountant with a large engineering company. She and another accountant, Bill, were employed three years ago during a period of recession in the engineering industry. Both Jean and Bill were appointed at the bottom point on the salary scale because at that time, the company could not afford to pay any more. The company is now doing very well and Jean has asked for her salary to be increased to match that of other accountants who have similar experience but are paid more. Bill would like his salary increased as well. The company refuse to increase their salaries. Jean is the only female accountant employed by the company. Advise Jean and Bill.

Index